Human Rights: Chinese & Canadian Perspectives

Editors:

Errol P. Mendes and Anne-Marie Traeholt

The Human Rights Research &
Education Centre, University of Ottawa

1997

The Human Rights Research & Education Centre

The Human Rights Research and Education Centre (HRREC), the first university-based human rights centre in Canada, was established at the University of Ottawa in 1981. Since then, it has been delivering an active and extensive research and education program, both domestically and internationally. The HRREC's mandate is:

-Furthering the discussion of the linkages between human rights, governance, legal reform and development.
-Supporting national human rights institutions in Canada and abroad.
-Evaluating and working to improve domestic social justice institutions and programs.
-Engaging in multi-disciplinary research and education in the above areas.

The viewpoints expressed in this collection are those of the individual authors of each paper and do not necessarily represent those of the HRREC.

Additional copies may be ordered from:

The Human Rights Research & Education Centre
University of Ottawa
Fauteux Hall
57 Louis Pasteur, 5th Floor
Ottawa, Ontario K1N 6N5, CANADA

Tel: (613) 562-5775
Fax: (613) 562-5125
E-mail:hrrec@human-rights.cdp.uottawa.ca

ISBN 0-9695848-7-3

Contents

TABLE OF CONTENTS

Acknowledgments

The research for this publication was conducted under the auspices of the Human Rights, International Organizations and the Rights to Development (HRIOD) project. This project, which was approved bilaterally by the Canadian International Development Agency (CIDA) and the Chinese Ministry of Foreign Trade and Economic Cooperation (MOFTEC), was jointly implemented by the Human Rights Research and Education Centre (HRREC) of the University of Ottawa and the International Law Institute (ILI) of Beijing University. Funding by CIDA is gratefully acknowledged.

The HRIOD project could not have been accomplished without the hard work, friendly cooperation and commitment of our Chinese colleagues at the ILI, especially Professors Wang Tieya, Rao Geping, Bai Guimei, Li Zhaojie and Gong Renren. We are also grateful to all the Canadian and Chinese researchers and participants who shared their time, knowledge and expertise for the benefit of promoting a deeper level of cross-cultural understanding in the area of international human rights.

The editors would like to thank Karen L. Rudner for her invaluable assistance in formatting and proof-reading the final manuscript; Jiang Shengtao and Wang Xuemei for their help in translating the Chinese texts into English; the Chinese graduate students of Beijing University who contributed to making the Beijing Symposium a truly worthwhile experience; and, our co-workers at the HRREC who have all, in some way or other, contributed to the successful completion of the project.

Notes on Contributors

(The notes on contributors have been arranged in alphabetical order according to family name)

BAI GUIMEI is an Associate Professor in the Law Faculty, Peking University. Her expertise is in international law with a special focus on international human rights law and the jurisprudence of international law. Professor Bai's publications include: *Human Rights in International Law*, co-author (Peking University Press, 1997); "On the Human Rights of the New Generation" (*Studies in the Science of Law*, No. 5, 1991); "On the People's Right of Self-Determination" (*Chinese Yearbook of International Law*, 1993).

DOUGLAS M. BROWN is currently engaged in doctoral studies at the University of Melbourne, Australia. He is the former Executive Director of the Institute of Intergovernmental Relations, Queen's University, Canada, and worked for several years for the Intergovernmental Affairs Secretariat, Government of Newfoundland. Mr. Brown is the author and editor of several publications related to Canadian federalism, intergovernmental policy and regional politics, including co-editor of the annual series *Canada: The State of the Federation* (1989-96) and co-editor of *Options for a New Canada?* and *Canadian Federalism: Meeting Global Challenges?*

LINDA CARDINAL, Ph. D. in Sociology, is an Associate Professor of the Dept. of Political Science at the University of Ottawa who also teaches in the Women Studies Programme. She does research on women and linguistic minorities in Canada and is experienced in preparing and conducting surveys. Has worked with various women's groups/networks in Canada, including CRIAW, MATCH and the Table féministe francophone de concertation provinciale in Ontario, and is a founder of the Réseau des chercheures féministes de l'Ontario français. Closely associated with the Human Rights Research and Education Centre, University of Ottawa, Professor Cardinal has represented the Centre at the Coalition of Human Rights Groups interested in promoting women's rights and human rights in La Francophonie.

CHEN ZHISHANG is a Professor in the Department of Philosophy, Peking University. He teaches and conducts research on the works, theories and history of Marxism. One of his most important achievements has been to systematize and promote theoretical studies on human beings. He is the editor of the *Dictionary of Humanology* (China International Broadcasting Press, 1990), the first dictionary of its kind in China and worldwide. He also edited the book

Marxism and Human Beings (Peking University Press, 1990) and is the author of "Humanology - Significant Science in the 21st Century" (*Journal of Peking University, No. 3, 1995)*, among others.

GONG RENREN, Professor of Law in the Law Faculty, Peking University, holds a Doctor of Law Degree from Hokkaido University, Japan. His main research interests are in international law. Professor Gong's publications include: *Some Perspectives on the Japanese Judicial System* (Beijing: World Affairs Press, 1993); *A Comparative Study of State Immunity* (Beijing: Peking University Press, 1993); "The Historical Evolution of the Principle of State Immunity in International Law" (*Hokkaido Law Review*, Vol. 40, No. 1-2); and "The Historical Evolution of Human Rights Protection in International Law" (*Chinese Yearbook of International Law*, 1990).

JAMES GROEN completed his Ph.D. at Queen's University and is an instructor in Political Science and Public Administration at the Univerity of Gdansk, Poland. From 1995-97, he served in a similar capacity at the University of Wroclaw, Poland. His teaching and research interests include comparative local government, subnational international activity and organizational theory.

JIA JUNLING is an Associate Professor in the Law Faculty, Peking University. Her expertise is in labour law, and she participated in the drafting of the *Labour Law of the People's Republic of China*. She has published numerous articles in leading Chinese law journals and is the author of *Labour Law* (Peking University Press, 1995) and *The Legal Practice of Modern Enterprises* (Chinese Procuratorate Press, 1996).

JIANG WENRAN is Coordinator for East Asian Studies and Assistant Professor of Political Science at the University of Alberta where he teaches courses on development and East Asia. He is currently conducting an extensive study of labour protection practices by foreign invested enterprises in the PRC. Professor Jiang has published articles on the impact of income distribution on Japan's social and political changes, and on Japan's foreign relations. He has also translated from Japanese to English: *China's Economic Development: A Comparison with the Japanese Experience* (Japanese edition by Ryoshin Minami, 1990, Tokyo), London: MacMillan Press, 1994; *Japan: The Governing of a Great Economic Power*, (Japanese edition by Takashi Inoguchi, 1993, Tokyo). London: Routledge, 1998.

RYSZARD KOMENDA is a human rights consultant. Since 1993, he has been a Research Associate with the Human Rights Research and Education Centre of the University of Ottawa. In his capacity he was responsible for formulating policy on the promotion and protection of the rights of racial, ethnic and linguistic minorities within federal states. Mr. Komenda has worked as an Advisor to the Human Rights Commissioner of the Council of the Baltic Sea States, where he advised on the rights of minorities in the Baltic Sea Region. He has also served as a Legal Research Officer at the Bureau of Research and Analysis of the Cancellery of Sejm in Poland. Mr. Komenda received his LL.M. from Ottawa University and his Magister Juris Degree from the University of Gdansk.

LI ZHAOJIE, an Associate Professor with the International Law Institute, Peking University, received his LL.B. from Peking University, his LL.M. from the University of California at Berkeley, and his SJD from the University of Toronto. His expertise is in legal effects of international law in domestic legal orders, and international air law. Professor Li's major publications include: "The Effect of Treaties in the Municipal Law of the People's Republic of China: Practice and Problems" *Asian Yearbook of International Law*, Vol. 4, 1995; "Teaching, Research, and the Dissemination of International Law in China: the Contribution of Wang Tieya" (*Canadian Yearbook of International Law*, 1993); and "Intertemporal Law in International Law" (*Chinese Yearbook of International Law*, 1989).

LIU XINSHENG is a specially invited researcher with the Institute of International Law, Peking University. He has a Masters of Public International Law from Peking University and has served as a member of the Chinese Permanent Mission to the UN in New York from 1988-1992. His main areas of research are in international law and international human rights law. He is the co-author of the *Chinese Dictionary of Law, Volume on International Law* and co-author of *International Law* (Law Press, 1995), and he has published numerous articles in the *Chinese Yearbook of International Law*.

LUO YANHUA is an Associate Professor of the Institute of International Relations, Peking University. Her main areas of research are human rights, cultural factors in international relations, American foreign policy and Southeast Asian studies. Professor Luo has published widely on these topics, and her publications include: "The Relationship between Human Rights and Development - Focus on the North-South Human Rights Debate in the Post-Cold War Era" (*World Economics and Politics*, Vol. 8, 1996); "The Impact of

Traditional Culture on the Asian Human Rights Perspective" (*Contemporary Asia-Pacific Studies*, Vol. 6, 1996).

MA YINAN is an Associate Professor in the Law Faculty, Peking University, and the Director of the Legal Office of Peking University Women's Studies Centre. She specializes in issues related to marriage, the family and women's rights. Professor Ma's publications include: *Chinese Law and Women's Human Rights* (1993); *A guide to the Law to Protect the Rights and Interests of Women* (1992); *Ideas about Perfecting the Law to Protect the Rights and Interests of Women* (1994); and *A Course in Marriage and Family Law* (1996).

KATHLEEN MAHONEY, Professor of Law at the University of Calgary, is an expert in human rights law and constitutional law. Professor Mahoney pioneered the concept of judicial education on gender, race and class issues in order to improve the administration of justice and to avoid discrimination in the courts. She has also participated and organised judicial education projects in South Africa, Australia and Canada and is a consultant to the Family Court of Australia and the Chief Justice of Western Australia on gender bias issues. She has sucessfully litigated sex equality issues in the Supreme Court of Canada, most notably the leading cases in Canada on pornography and hate propaganda.

ERROL P. MENDES is the Director of the Human Rights Research and Education Centre at the University of Ottawa where he also teaches in the Faculty of Law. He received his Bachelor of Law Degree from the University of Exeter, England, and obtained his Master of Laws Degree from the University of Illinois in the United States. Professor Mendes has taught, researched, consulted and published extensively in the area of constitutional law and human rights law. He is Editor-in-Chief of *The National Journal of Constitutional Law*, and a member of the Canadian Human Rights Tribunal Panel.

JEREMY T. PALTIEL is Associate Professor of Political Science at Carleton University in Ottawa, Canada where he specializes in East Asian politics with a special focus on China. He holds a B.A in East Asian Studies from the University of Toronto (1974), a diploma in Philosophy from Beijing University (1976), and an M.A. (1979) and Ph.D. (1984) in political Science from the University of California, Berkeley. He has published widely on China, including articles on constitutionalism, civil-military relations, tradition and human rights and human rights in Sino-Canadian relations.

PITMAN B. POTTER is Professor of Law and Director of the Centre for Asian Legal Studies at the University of British Columbia, Faculty of Law. Professor Potter received his B.A. in Chinese Studies (History) from George Washington University in 1978. He pursued graduate studies at the University of Washington, where he received his M.A. (1980) and Ph.D. (Political Science, 1986), as well as his law degree (JD, 1985). Dr.Potter practised law full time beginning in 1985, including a three-year posting in Beijing as resident attorney for the firm of Graham and James. In addition to his current research and teaching activities, Professor Potter continues to advise governments and private companies on Chinese affairs. He is Consultant to the Vancouver Law firm of Ladner Downs. Dr. Potter's publications include "Legitimation and Contract Autonomy in the PRC: The Contract Law of China" (1992), "Domestic Law Reforms in Post-Mao China" (1994), and "Foreign Business Law in China: Past Progress Future Challenges" (1995), as well as numerous articles on Chinese law and politics. Dr. Potter is currently working on a major research and programming project on infrastructure finance in the APEC region.

RAO GEPING is a Professor of Law and the Executive Director of the International Law Institute, Peking University. Professor Rao focuses his research on issues related to the United Nations and international organizations. He is the editor-in-chief of the publication *Law of International Organizations* (Peking University Press, 1996) and co-author of *International Law* (Law Press, 1995). His articles include: "The UN as a Guardian for Future Generations" (*Future Generation Journal*, Vol. 1, 1995) and "Implied Powers of International Organizations" (*Chinese Science of Law*, No. 4, 1993.)

WANG DEYI, a former Associate Professor of Family Law in the Law Faculty, Peking University, is currently the top official in the Marriage Management Section of the Department of Civil Administration in China. Her main area of expertise is problems of society and the family. Her publications include: *A Course on Marriage Management*, chief editor (Chinese Society Press, 1990); *Studies in Divorce in the 1980s*, co-chief editor (Peking University Press, 1994); and *Encyclopedia of China's Social Work* (Chinese Society Press, 1995).

XU WEIHUA is the Director of the Department of Rights and Benefits of the All China Women's Federation. Her main responsibilities relate to legislation, supervision of law enforcement and research into the rights of women and children. She also handles significant cases of infringements of the rights of women and children. She is co-author of the publications *Textbook of Law for*

Women Cadres (1988) and *Basic Knowledge about the Law to Protect the Rights and Interests of Women* (1992).

YANG YIWEN is Director of the Center for the Protection of Minors in Beijing, Director of Legal and Psychological Consultative Service Center for Youth in Beijing, and Director of the Beijing Donation Center of the "Project of Hope" (a nationwide project which supports poor children's enrolment in school). Her expertise is in the rights and interests of youth. Her publications include: *The Law is Just Next to You--Legal Awareness and Self-Protection of Middle School Students* (Education Press, 1991); "The Practice and Effect of the Regional Laws of Beijing" (*Learning and Studies*, Vol. 5, No. 5, 1987).

Introduction

Chinese and Canadian Perspectives on Human Rights -- a Clash of Civilizations or Normal Dialectics on the Road to Modernity?

In his 1987 book, *China's Second Revolution*, Harry Harding wrote of the relationship between China and the United States that,

> Ameliorating the tensions that will inevitably accompany China's emergence as an important force in world affairs will require constant dialogue and coordination between China and the United States,.... The United States, with its open society and wealth of foreign affairs institutions, is ideally qualified to sponsor much of this dialogue.[1]

Ten years later, it has become clear that one of the major tensions accompanying China's increasing role in world affairs relates to human rights and the various cultural perspectives on human rights. This tension exists not only between China and the United States but also between China and many other nations and cultures, including Canada.

In his widely read 1993 article, "The Clash of Civilizations", Professor Samuel P. Huntington articulated a post-Cold War world which focused on a global emphasis and persistence of cultural and civilizational divisions. In this vision, Confucian civilization, centered in China, and Islamic civilizations, would pose the greatest conflictual problems with the West and hence be a major source of global instability.[2]

Professor Huntington's and other similar theories make Harding's call for constant dialogue with China even more pressing, not in the least when it comes to the issue of human rights, this most contested of civilizational values. It has become questionable, however, whether the United States is indeed "ideally qualified" to spearhead this dialogue. The high profile which characterizes the United States' relationship with the rest of the world is perhaps not the ideal backdrop for a productive human rights dialogue with China.

Canada, on the other hand, with its longstanding friendly relationship with China (which at least dates back to the days of Dr. Norman Bethune), and its experience in implementing international legal obligations in a vast multi-governmental setting, is well equipped to engage China in a meaningful human rights dialogue. With this in mind, leading Chinese and Canadian human rights scholars entered into a dialogue in 1993. Although it was only four years after the June 4, 1989 Tiananmen incident, the Chinese government nevertheless agreed to the Canadian International Development Agency funding a low profile human rights dialogue project, jointly managed by the International Law Institute of Beijing University (Beida), and the Human Rights Research and Education Centre at the University of Ottawa (HRREC). This became one of the first Canada-China bilaterally approved projects with a specific focus on human rights.

The stated aim of the project leaders, namely the leading International Law scholar of China, Professor Wang Tieya of Beida, and Professor Mendes, Director of the HRREC, was to find the common ground, if any, between Chinese and western conceptions of human rights and thereby enhance mutual understanding between China and Canada, and internationally, of the different cultural approaches to human rights.

The project was given the title "Human Rights, International Organizations and The Right to Development". The two universities each assembled a team of leading scholars within their respective countries and the papers collected in this volume represent the combined scholarly contribution to the dialogue. These papers were presented and discussed in detail at one of the first unofficial human rights symposiums held in China at Beida in the summer of 1996, (hereafter the Beida Symposium). This symposium was also attended by some of China's top policy makers in the human rights field, including two of the authors of the Human Rights in China White Paper.[3]

The dialogue and research exchange on human rights between the Chinese and Canadian scholars centered around the following themes:

- The philosophical and legal foundations of human rights in China and Canada with a particular focus on **different cultural values and traditions, the nature of rights, and human dignity.**

- International organizations and the question of **state sovereignty, international law** and human rights.

- Economic and sociological foundations of human rights and, in particular, the meaning and hierarchy of **the right to development.**

- **Women's rights as human rights** in Canada and China.

Underlying all these issues, however, was the question of cultural relativism versus universal and indivisible norms of human rights and who gets to determine how human rights must be respected and promoted.

The Philosophical and Legal Foundations of Human Rights in China and in Canada

On Asian Values

Confucian ideology has in the past few years played a definite role in the context of the human rights approach adopted by China and other East Asian societies, such as Singapore and Malaysia. This approach centers around the notion that there exists a core of "Asian Values" which are fundamentally different from those of "Western" societies and, therefore, these countries also take a different approach to the issue of human rights. Professor Potter notes in his paper that, whereas the Western born natural rights theories view rights as intrinsic to the human condition, the so-called Asian approach suggests that social organizations, such as families, communities, and governments, confer rights upon citizens. The PRC Constitution, for example, speaks of rights being granted by the state. (Potter, p. 104) The most fervent promoters of this approach are the former Prime Minister of Singapore, Lee Kuan Yew, the present Prime Minister of Malaysia, Dr. Mahathir Mohamed and more recently President Jiang Zemin of China.[4] Although there exists, as of yet, no East Asian human rights instrument, other East Asian countries' governments have tended to rally behind China in defending an Asian approach to human rights or, at the very least, a different approach which emphasizes collective rights before individual rights and thus differs from the approach usually associated with the Western developed countries. This emphasis on collective rights is particularly apparent in the promotion of the right to development.

The Human Rights in China White Paper, published by the Chinese government in 1991[5] in response to the international outcry over the 1989 Tiananmen Square massacre, sets out the official Chinese approach to human rights. The document attempted to show that China was incorporating human rights perspectives in its laws and policies, but that such perspectives would be informed by China's painful history and its present social and economic needs. Therefore, the government stated that its fundamental approach to human rights would place the greatest priority on the right to subsistence and economic development as a precondition to the full enjoyment of all other human rights. The underlying message of the White Paper was that stability of the system, which was providing the right to subsistence and development, was China's highest priority. Anyone's individual human rights could be legitimately sacrificed to further the right to subsistence and development.

Even before the publication of the White Paper, China had begun to assert an Asia-wide role to champion the right to development. Through active participation in every session of the governmental experts group organised by the U.N. Commission on Human Rights to draft the *Declaration on the Right to Development*, China was instrumental in getting the Declaration passed by the 41st session of the General Assembly in 1986.

In December of 1991, China also achieved a major coup for Asian Values when it engineered regional preparatory conferences before the 1993 Vienna Conference on Human Rights. Many Western countries opposed the regional conferences, arguing that since human rights were universal there was no need for the regional conferences. An alliance forged by China achieved an expression of Asian Values at the March 1993 Asia Preparatory Conference in the *Bangkok Declaration* signed by 49 governments. The "aspirations and commitments of the Asian region" were emphasized in the document while the concept of the universality of human rights was downplayed.[6] Japan and South Korea, while reluctant to do so, finally signed on to the priority of Asian Values over universal conceptions of human rights, unwilling to resist China's desire to show Asian solidarity against Western hegemony on human rights.[7]

The final declaration of the actual World Conference on Human Rights in Vienna in the summer of 1993 affirmed the universality and indivisibility of human rights. The force of Asian Values from the *Bangkok Declaration*, however, found its way into the final Declaration with several expressions of cultural relativism, including the affirmation that the right to development was as universal and inalienable a right as other fundamental human rights.[8]

Perhaps the seemingly manufactured clash between Chinese traditions and universal human rights can be regarded as normal dialectics in the evolution of a cultural modernity in China.

Masakazu Yamazaki, in his essay in the journal *Foreign Affairs*, defines modernity as "the spirit of living in constant contrast to the past."[9] The manufactured clash by authoritarian Asian rulers between Asian Values and human rights may be an attempt to seek an Asian modernity where one has never existed. Given the immense territory of Asia and the multiplicity of cultures, traditions, histories and even civilizations, the fact that there is an attempt to manufacture something called Asian Values is highly significant. The irony of Asian Values, as Yamazaki has stated, is that the force behind the convergence observable in the region today is modernity, which was born in the West but radically transformed both East and West in this century.[10]

Yamazaki describes the emergence of a "global cultural modernity" in Asia in the following terms:

> ...the peoples of East Asia...can be said to partake of modern Western
> civilization at the topmost stratum of their world, to retain their national

civilizations and nation-states in the middle stratum, and to preserve their traditional cultures in their day-to-day lives. In political affairs, human rights and democratic principles belong to the first stratum, distinct bodies of law and political institutions to the second, and the political wheeling and dealing to the third.[11]

In fact, the author appears to be describing perfectly the global cultural modernity that characterises modern Japan. Indeed, some argue that Japan should take a stronger role in promoting democratic reforms and human rights across Asia, given its economic power and prestige.[12] The newer democracies in Thailand, South Korea, Taiwan and the Philippines can also be similarly characterised. President Fidel Ramos of the Philippines has consistently rejected the position of other Asian leaders that Asian priorities to economic development or Asian Values should ride roughshod over human rights and constitutional guarantees.

Key intellectual and civil society leaders in Singapore and Malaysia are urging full membership in the community of democratic states.[13] The Deputy Prime Minister of Malaysia, Mr. Anwar Ibrahim, although intensely disliking what he calls the sermonising and hectoring tone of the West on human rights[14], acknowledges the possibility of a global cultural modernity in these words:

> If we in Asia want to speak credibly of Asian Values, we too must be prepared to champion these ideals which are universal and which belong to humanity as a whole. It is altogether shameful, if ingenious, to cite Asian Values as an excuse for autocratic practices and denial of basic rights and civil liberties. To say that freedom is western or unAsian is to offend our traditions as well as our forefathers who gave their lives in the struggle against tyranny and injustices. It is true that Asians lay great emphasis on order and social stability. But it is certainly wrong to regard society as a kind of false god upon altar [sic] the individual must constantly be sacrificed. No Asian tradition can be cited to support the proposition that in Asia the individual must melt into the faceless community.[15]

Professor Luo Yanhua's paper provides a detailed account of several East Asian governments' position on these issues. As Professor Luo notes, however, these are only the voices of governments, and one must be aware that Asian NGOs have refuted their governments' claim that human rights are incompatible with Asian Values. Many representatives of Asian civil society have asserted that this emphasis on Asian Values as being in conflict with human rights is an attempt by governments to legitimise their authoritarian regimes.[16]

More recently, in the struggle for confirmation of his leadership succession in the post Deng Xiaoping era, President Jiang Zemin and his politburo and military allies have attempted to revive the "spiritual civilization" and promote the "socialist ethical and cultural progress" of the Chinese people.[17] One Asian review predicts that the use of these Chinese Values is an attempt by Communist Party Chief Jiang Zemin to consolidate his power by dominating political discourse. In practice, this will mean more media censorship, patriotic exhortations and an emphasis on traditional virtues such as Confucianism and respect for authority.[18] Ironically, Confucianism had been vilified and eradicated from mainstream culture by Mao. Now his successors, seeing a largely cynical populace in the face of the failings of the Communist Party's record, including rampant corruption, are attempting to rehabilitate themselves through a rehabilitation of selective Confucianism.[19]

On Confucianism

Despite the Chinese leadership's manipulation of the ancient Chinese moral system, and recognizing that many conflicting views exist on the impact of Confucianism on modern Chinese society, an examination of Confucianism is still valuable from a theoretical point of view. It is also useful as a point of reference for making comparisons against Canadian and other Western value systems and approaches to rights to determine if indeed there is necessarily a clash of cultural civilizations.

In his paper, Professor Paltiel of Carleton University denies that Confucianism and Western liberal values are so conflictual as to be mutually exclusive. Professor Paltiel stresses that differences between the two civilizational values are exaggerated and that both share common attributes of humanity. While he acknowledges that these attributes may not share the same terminology relating to Western legal definitions of rights, they can and do share common values of humanity. "The traditional Chinese culture cherishes many of the same values as those in the post-enlightenment West, but does not express these in rights language." (Paltiel, p. 42)

Demonstrating that the so-called clashing civilizations do share common ground, Professor Gong of Beijing University also concluded in his paper that, although ancient China had highly developed humanistic notions, human rights never appeared as a distinct concept, in large part due to the lack of a legal concept of rights (Gong, p. 88). Professor Gong, however, also firmly roots modern day notions of human rights in the concept of human dignity, even if the definition of this concept varies between China and the West.

Such observations on traditional schools of thought, however, should not necessarily guide the discourse on current approaches to human rights because times have changed and people's aspirations and ideologies have changed accordingly. Moreover, this century alone has seen many so-called Western ideas "leaking" into China and taking shape according to the Chinese reality. Marxism, imported from the Soviet Union, is just one very obvious example. Today, modern communications technology, the growing number of Internet users in China, and the ongoing educational exchanges between China and other countries will introduce even more outside ideas into China. Furthermore, the impact of the one-child policy and modern city lifestyles are causing the demise of the extended family, one of the main pillars of traditional Confucian ideology. All of these factors work together to create a new cultural modernity in the country. However, elements of Confucian ideology can still be found in contemporary China--evident, for example, in the treatment of women in family relationships and in society in general (see papers by Bai Guimei and Wang Deyi, among others).

In the end, one has to recognize, in the words of Professor Paltiel, that "'Chinese culture' today is a hybrid which is capable of adapting and absorbing new values and ideas. ... Rights are part of the contemporary Chinese vocabulary, which is as different from the classical Chinese lexicon as a Long March rocket is from a sedan chair." (Paltiel, p. 25)

On the Nature of Rights

Thus, while China along with other Asian nations and the West may be moving toward a modernity that accepts the rights language of the United Nations and the vocabulary of international human rights norms, in many instances, however, there remains significant discord about the nature of rights and how rights should be balanced when they conflict with each other.

Professor Mendes has observed that the philosophical differences between Chinese and Canadian approaches to human rights are rooted in the "conflict between the collectivist nature of social and economic rights encompassed in the notion of the right to development and most of the civil and political rights which are rooted in classical liberal notions of individual autonomy" (Mendes, p. 130). This observation corresponds with Beijing University Professor Li Zhaojie's analysis of the Chinese notion of dignity (see section "On Human Dignity" below).

Seeking to identify common ground between the Chinese emphasis on collective rights and the Canadian approach to rights, Professor Mendes illustrates how Canadian courts have, in fact, attempted to balance individual rights with fundamental societal interests by applying the "fundamental justice and law of proportionality". This notion of proportionality is based on a recognition that individual rights may, within fundamental parameters of justice, be subject to limitations if in conflict with pressing and substantial state interests and vice versa. Noting some similarities between article 51 of the Chinese Constitution and the first section of the *Canadian Charter of Rights and Freedoms*, on which the principle of proportionality is based, Professor Mendes proposes that the Chinese legal system might be able to apply some of the same principles as have been applied by Canadian courts in determining the outcome of specific cases, as described in his paper.

This proposed meeting ground between Chinese and Canadian implementation of rights encourages respect for the Rule of Law and transparency by governments in their treatment of the rights of their people. It also vitiates the need to use collective rights, such as the right to development, to crush other types of human rights, especially civil and political rights.

Professor Mendes' paper received positive feedback from Chinese participants at the Beida Symposium. However, fundamental differences still exist between Canada's and China's legal systems, such as the fact that China's judiciary is not independent of the state. Furthermore, respect for concepts fundamental to the proportionality principles, such as the Rule of Law, has yet to be entrenched in the Chinese legal system. Perhaps in time, the fundamental concepts necessary to the application of the proportionality principles will evolve in the Chinese legal and political system.

The Chinese approach to rights places much emphasis on history and the "evolutionary nature" of human rights. The human rights concept has always been and is still evolving with other changes in society. In this context, the Chinese are still going through a process of questioning and criticizing the origins of the human rights concept and debating the applicability of many facets of the human rights concept to contemporary Chinese conditions. As Professor Li Zhaojie argues, "the major international human rights documents were drafted predominantly by Western men who had little direct interest in, or experience with, the compelling challenges and pressures confronting many of the non-Western nations." (Li, p. 187)

In addition, as Professor Gong rightfully lays out in his paper, the so-called western approach to rights underwent various stages of "refinement" (such as the abolition of slavery, granting women the vote, growing recognition of indigenous and minority rights, etc.) before arriving at what exists today in terms of constitutional and legal protections of rights. In the Chinese view, this evolutionary process continues, and the concept of human rights will alter its shape according to changing values in the global community. The growing support for the right to development is just one example of how the voice of the developing world is influencing the international human rights agenda.

On Human Dignity

What seems to bring Chinese and western liberal traditions together is a recognition that the concept of human rights is rooted in a belief that human dignity is a prerequisite for maintaining a civilized community. But what constitutes human dignity? Professor Li Zhaojie concludes that,

> ...compared to Western liberalism and individualism, the prevailing Chinese definition of human dignity places more emphasis on collective welfare and social harmony and order, since both the traditional notions as well as sinicized Marxist precepts perceive the meaning of the human person from his/her social being in an intricate web of social relationships rather than from his atomized autonomy. Thereby, values such as liberty and autonomy are not prized as the ends in themselves in the same way that they are in contemporary Western democracies. (Li, p. 188)

At the Beida Symposium, such philosophical differences were discussed quite extensively. It became clear that to the Chinese, the concept of dignity goes far beyond concern for individual human dignity to a strong concern for national dignity, and such national dignity can only be preserved by a completely sovereign and independent state, as described below.

International Organizations, the Question of State Sovereignty, International Law and Human Rights

In the Chinese view, there is a direct link between state sovereignty and the protection of human rights. One Symposium participant stated: "Without state sovereignty, there can be no human rights." The root of this argument lies in the historical fact that China as a nation was exploited and semi-colonized by foreign powers for long periods of time leading up to the revolution. The effects of such colonization were visible in the lack of respect afforded to the Chinese people in their own country, a fact which is often illustrated by the example of the sign board in Shanghai parks which forbade Chinese and dogs to enter the parks. Clearly, the Chinese of those days did not have many rights to speak of. Thus, the equation appears logical: Without state sovereignty and independence (freedom from all kinds of foreign colonization, aggression and interference), national dignity cannot be guaranteed. Without national dignity, how can one even think of individual dignity if the concept is based on a notion of collective welfare? And without individual human dignity, there is no basis for human rights.

This is essentially the same argument which the Chinese government uses to fend off foreign criticism of its human rights record today, and this is where the dialogue between China and western countries falters. The polemic in this year's (1997) and previous years' sessions of the UN Human Rights Commission is evidence of the very complex factors, both cultural and political, which complicate multilateral cooperation in the area of human rights. While the UN Human Rights Commission ought to be **the** place in which human rights issues of all kinds can be debated freely in a multilateral setting, China has repeatedly managed to block a resolution condemning its human rights record. There is a strong element of pride involved in the Chinese approach which necessitates viewing human rights in a historical perspective and which does not allow other nations to disregard past foreign aggressions against China and the resulting Chinese "national humiliation", as Professor Jiang of the University of Alberta, calls it in his paper. Such events of the past cause China to be even more aware of any interference in what it sees as its internal affairs today, including human rights. Sovereignty and independence are the ultimate prerequisites for human rights.

But does the equation work the other way? Does state sovereignty automatically lead to effective protection of international human rights standards?

Professor Li Zhaojie offers a compelling argument for maintaining state sovereignty **and** enforcing international human rights standards by relying on and improving the enforcement mechanisms of domestic legal instruments. While he supports the idea that gross violations of human rights, such as genocide and apartheid, should still be addressed on the international level, he questions the efficacy of a potentially very bureaucratic international legal order in addressing rights violations which are rooted in specific social and cultural contexts. Instead, he proposes a "soft landing of international human rights standards on local circumstances with international principles and rules serving as binding norms of reference..." (Li, p. 191) Where an international system might not turn out to be accessible to individuals for various reasons, Professor Li suggests that,

...if the notion of state sovereignty is understood in its modern sense as a relative concept subject to restrictions necessitated by the international system, sovereign states, which constitute the major actors of the international community and which can effectively wield power to enforce the law, may not necessarily stand in the way of the effective enforcement of international human rights. (Li, p. 191)

This surprising position by a leading Chinese legal scholar may not satisfy some of the more radical human rights activists in the West, but it is nonetheless a practical meeting ground between the West and China in the evolutionary promotion of human rights in the Middle Kingdom.

Professor Li's thesis, however, requires much negotiation and discussion to improve international standards, to convince sovereign states to subscribe to these standards and, subsequently, to bring domestic legal standards into line with international standards. As Professor Gong has noted in his paper, large gaps still exist between international human rights law and Chinese law and practice:

[T]he Chinese constitution does not provide for the following important rights and freedoms listed in the Universal Declaration of Human Rights: the right to life, the right to be free of torture or other inhuman treatment or punishment, the right to a fair and open trial, the right to non-interference with private life, the presumption of innocence, the right to free movement of place or residence, and the right to freedom of thought and conscience. Nor has the Chinese constitution accepted the concept of natural rights that "persons are born equal", as expressed in the *Universal Declaration of Human Rights*. (Gong, p. 91)

The quiet determination of some of China's emerging scholars, such as Professor Gong, could lead to some of the gaps being filled. A recent advance has occurred in the area of criminal law. On March 17, 1996, China's National Peoples Congress (NPC) passed reforms to the *Criminal Procedure Law* which promotes international human rights standards in the areas of pre-trial detention, the right to counsel, prosecutorial determination of guilt and trial proceedings. The changes came into effect on January 1, 1997. Subsequently, the *Criminal Code* has also been revised, but the verdict is still out, however, as to whether these major criminal justice reforms will actually be implemented.[20] Perhaps the apparent increasing influence of the NPC and the push by NPC leader Qiao Shi towards separation of Party and government[21] will lead to stronger rule of law and, eventually, to independence of the judiciary.

These reforms fit well into the theoretical framework for Chinese notions of sovereignty and international human rights norms espoused by Professor Li.

In the context of sovereignty, it should also be mentioned here that two of the Canadian research papers (MacKay and Komenda) deal quite extensively with the issues of sovereignty and the right of self-determination as they relate to the rights of national minorities and indigenous peoples. It was the aim of the project to include a broad range of topics into the Canada-China dialogue and the Canadian delegation to the Beijing Symposium included Mr. Clem Chartier of Saskatchewan, who spoke of the experience of the Metis community in Canada. However, only limited discussion took place at the Beijing Symposium on these particular issues, as they are still too politically sensitive in China--particularly with the plight of the Tibetan and the Uygur minorities making headlines in the world's media.

China's minority populations are not considered to be indigenous peoples but national minorities. There are at least 56 officially recognized national minorities in China, of which very few might technically be considered indigenous peoples in the sense that their existence in their present location preceded the Han Chinese.[22] Thus, the Chinese Constitution (1982) states in the preamble that "China is a unitary multinational state built up jointly by the people of all nationalities."[23] Furthermore, article 4 of the Constitution states of China's nationalities that "acts which undermine the unity between them are prohibited".[24] In other words, sovereignty and the right of self-determination are not options for the various minority populations in China. China belongs among those states "who view rights claims by groups, such as indigenous peoples and minorities, as competing claims to sovereignty and disruptive of national unity." (MacKay, p. 240)

Curiously, however, when the talk shifted to Canada, some of the Chinese participants were very intrigued by the issue of Québec and the relatively peaceful process of the 1995 referendum.

The Meaning and Hierarchy of the Right to Development

Professor Potter's paper forcefully and succinctly outlines the international discourse on the right to development and how such discourse incorporates many dimensions and is conditioned by various institutional interests, such as the interests of state governments, aid agencies, non-governmental organizations and the scholarly community.

At the Beida Symposium, a lively discussion took place on the nature and the content of the right to development. At the theoretical level, the Symposium discussion included questions regarding the source of the right to development; the beneficiaries of the right to development; the role of the state in protecting the right to development; whether the right to development is an individual or a collective right; the relationship between the right to development and other human rights; and more. While it was not possible to agree on a definite answer to each question, there was a general consensus at the Beida Symposium that the right to development should be equal to other rights. The Canadian participants were generally adamant that there was no need for the right to development always to take priority to other forms of rights, civil and political rights in particular.

At the level of daily life in China, however, the official Chinese human rights policy still prioritizes the right to development and the right to subsistence before other rights. The 1991 Human Rights in China White Paper states: "It is a simple truth that, for any country or nation, the right to subsistence is the most important of all human rights, without which the other rights are out of the question."[25]

What western human rights activists should not ignore is that this statement is not completely without substance in the context of the huge developmental challenges that face China. As Professor Rao Geping states so aptly in his paper, China is a country in development and will probably remain so for quite a few years. He points out that while the large cities and coastal regions have experienced massive economic growth and improvements in living standards in the past 12-15 years, problems of extreme poverty, illiteracy, shortage of basic facilities, endemic diseases, etc., persist in some remote, inland regions. In such areas, it is indeed questionable if political rights, for example, would be of much concern to the local population before their basic needs for food, shelter and clothing were satisfied.

Canada has its own issues to address in the context of regional disparities. Although widespread poverty and endemic diseases can no longer be said to be part of the Canadian situation, problems persist with respect to employment and educational opportunities in the less wealthy provinces. (See Brown's & Groen's paper for an outline of Canada's efforts at providing regional equity.)

In this sense of development, the role of the state is of extreme importance. As Professor Rao discusses in his paper, the UN *Declaration on the Right to Development* requires states to

> undertake, at the national level, all necessary measures for the realization of the right to development and shall ensure, *inter alia*, equality of opportunity for all in their access to basic resources,

education, health services, food, housing, employment and the fair distribution of income.(quoted in Rao, p. 364)

This brings into question the issue of "trade-offs". If development and the right to development and subsistence take such prominent positions in official government policy, does it necessarily follow that other societal interests must be traded-off or sacrificed temporarily? If this is the case, how long is the temporary period? Could the law of unintended consequences also be applicable here? The unquestioning drive for economic growth as an indicator of development may actually undermine central development goals.

Jiang Wenran's paper analyses three different development models in China's recent history: the Soviet model (1949-58), the self-reliance model (1960-78), and the socialist market model (1978-present). According to Jiang's analysis, the first two periods of the People's Republic saw some trade-offs of needs (essentially a lowering of living standards) and liberty (restrictions on political and civil rights), but less equality trade-offs as there was a heavy emphasis on equal distribution of resources and gender equity. The third period, however, has seen a considerable rise in the trade-off of equality. This, according to Jiang, is directly attributable to the government's development objectives which allow some people to get rich first and which emphasize heavily the development of a (socialist) market economy. Such development objectives have caused an increase in regional disparities and gaps between rich and poor, and the introduction of market forces in the economy have brought along a host of social and environmental problems, including unemployment, corruption, crime, and an escalation of discrimination against women.

In a sense, then, a paradox has been created whereby the government, in an effort to protect the right to development--which is usually associated more with economic, social and cultural rights--has implemented development policies which have ended up affecting negatively the same economic, social and cultural rights that they should be promoting. The law of unintended consequences should always be borne in mind in the context of the right to development.

Professor Potter identifies the crux of the problem to be China's focus on economic growth as the main indicator of development, an approach fostered by the *Bangkok Declaration* and also typical of other countries in the East Asian region. He concludes that

[t]he problems besetting China's development effort would appear to stem, to a large degree, from the combination of an over-emphasis on economic growth aspects of development and a corresponding lack of attention to social, cultural, and political elements. ... In the absence of

meaningful channels for public participation in the political process and the articulation of popular views critical of corrupt officials, popular disquiet simply festers until a crisis erupts--such as occurred in April to June 1989. (Potter, p. 108)

Thus, in answer to the question of how long other rights can temporarily be sacrificed in order to promote development, clearly it would not be desirable to do so for a long time because it necessarily leads to a variety of severe problems, as described above. Instead, a balance must be sought between the promotion of the right to development as a collective right and the protection of the rights of the individual.

One could say that the Chinese government is seeking to establish such a balance by, on the one hand, initiating various programs to alleviate poverty and reduce regional disparities by pouring resources into developing impoverished regions (see Professor Rao's paper for details on such programs) and, on the other hand, setting up a comprehensive social security system to safeguard the interests of individuals affected by the various social changes (see Professor Jia Junling's paper for a description of the Chinese approach to social security vis-a-vis human rights). And to complement these measures, a number of new laws have been introduced in recent years, such as the *Labour Law*, the *Social Security Law*, and the *Law to Protect the Rights and Interests of Women*, among others.

Such measures are certainly a step toward better protection of social and economic rights. From a Canadian perspective, however, the lack of parallel attention by the Chinese government to political reforms that ease the plethora of restrictions on the Chinese people is a cause for concern.

This brings us back to the fundamental difference between Canada and China in interpreting the nature of rights, a difference underscored by the fact that, at the time of writing, China still has not signed and ratified either of the two important human rights conventions of the United Nations, namely the *International Covenant on Civil and Political Rights* (ICCPR) or the *International Covenant on Economic, Social and Cultural Rights* (ICESCR). (It should be noted, however, that during this year's (1997) session of the UN Human Rights Commission, China made a promise to sign the ICESCR before the end of the year.)

Women's Rights as Human Rights

The 1992 *Law to Protect the Rights and Interests of Women* represents the Chinese state's "will" to promote equality between the sexes.

While gender equality has been a Communist Party ideal at least since the 1949 Revolution, and the situation of women in China has certainly improved since then, the ideal has far from been attained. On the contrary, it appears that many of the traditional attitudes toward women have resurfaced along with other social problems, including unemployment and discrimination against women in the job-market.

This observation is confirmed by the existence of explicit stipulations in the relevant laws and legislation to protect women against such ills as arranged marriages, interference with divorce, discrimination against women who give birth to baby girls, domestic violence, etc.

But while such social problems remained hidden within the family or simply were not recognized as problems in traditional China, today, Chinese women are slowly becoming more attuned to the global women's rights movement. Where human rights is generally a politically sensitive issue in China, women's rights have become almost mainstream, in part due to the promulgation of laws such as the *Law to Protect the Rights and Interests of Women* and, in part, due to such events as the United Nations Fourth World Conference on Women (held in Beijing, September 1995).

Chinese women's exposure to international standards and increased international exposure to the plight of Chinese women have helped focus attention on specific issues of common concern to women across the globe, such as domestic violence. As Professor Bai notes in her paper, the term "domestic violence" was

> ...a novel, rarely heard term to ordinary Chinese people. Until 1994, the international year of the family, Chinese academics had only just begun to touch upon the issue of "domestic violence", a topic which had already been widely debated abroad. (Bai, p. 589)

The phenomenon of domestic violence certainly was not new to China, but it was hidden in the private sphere, as has been the case in many countries. When domestic violence was raised at the Beida Symposium, the discussion quickly centered on the problem of private versus public, and everyone agreed on the importance of bringing such problems into the open, a prerequisite for protecting any rights under the law.

The process of addressing this very serious human rights problem, however, remains very slow. Not only do local customs and attitudes often stand in the way, but international laws are also lacking in various respects, for example when it comes to precise definitions of standards and enforceability of these, as articulated by Professor Bai in her paper. In addition, there are those who argue that international laws to protect women's rights are inherently flawed because they were "built on the male experience and have not responded to women's needs or realities". (Mahoney, p. 543)

The Chinese *Law to Protect the Rights and Interests of Women*--in part a result of China's effort to fulfil its obligations under the UN *Convention on the Elimination of All Kinds of Discrimination Against Women* (CEDAW)--has its limitations as well, in particular with respect to enforceability, as Professor Ma demonstrates in her paper. The challenge facing Chinese women is how to make the women's law enforceable through political and social strategies, if the legal avenues are not yet available to them under the same law. At the Beida Symposium, Professor Mahoney offered the experience of Canadian feminists who utilised both the existing laws and political and social strategies to fight for substantive equality in their own country.

In this context, the work of the All China Women's Federation (ACWF) is crucial (see Xu Weihua's paper for a description of the ACWF). Currently, no other women's rights NGOs exist in China who could undertake the immense task it is to disseminate knowledge of the laws to women at all levels of Chinese society. In the long run, however, it is questionable if this one organization, in spite of its mass character, will be able to respond to the various needs of all the women in China. As Professor Cardinal demonstrates, some Canadian women's NGOs have had to repeatedly reinvent themselves and restate their raison d'être, both in the Canadian and the global context, to ensure that they remain attuned to the specific needs of the community that they purport to serve. Given the distinctness of China's many regions and provinces, it would seem that single issue women's NGOs could play a major role--in addition to the work done by the ACWF--in advancing women's rights and interests in China.

At the international level, the CEDAW remains probably the most important instrument for the protection of women's rights. However, as Professor Mahoney points out, even the CEDAW has come under criticism as some argue that it marginalizes women's rights. As a result, since the Vienna World Conference on Human Rights (1993), many feminists have turned to the approach of "women's rights as human rights", an approach which, according to Professor Mahoney, consists of at least three conceptual steps: 1) human rights must be defined from women's perceptions of what is central to their basic integrity as human beings; 2) rights violations must be made visible; 3) the breaches of women's rights must be analyzed through the existing human rights regimes, but in a way that takes account of women's lives. (Mahoney, p. 547)

Whichever theory or approach is utilized, one challenge facing both Chinese, Canadian and women from other countries in the world is how to keep up the momentum of such events as the Vienna World Conference on Human Rights and the UN Fourth World Conference on Women in their quest to further women's rights as the world moves toward a global modernity. The linkage between women's rights as human rights and development, such as practiced by the two Canadian groups analyzed in Professor Cardinal's paper, has created a common platform for women's groups in both developed and developing countries. It is still necessary, however, that "feminists ... investigate more fully the relationship between global feminism, national contexts and the global politics of modernization" (Cardinal, p. 495), so as to enable women to deal with issues of cultural relativity in the context of human rights, to respond to the ongoing changes in the global community, and to overcome cultural and civilizational clashes as those portrayed by Professor Huntington.

Conclusion

It is trite to observe that present day human rights dialectics between the West and Asia, in particular China, have replaced the ideological battles of the Cold War. It is therefore a little astonishing and encouraging that leading Chinese intellectuals and their Canadian counterparts have begun to find common ground in this very contested area. Yet, as discussed above, there are huge differences in background that remain a source of conflict.

Overall, this unique dialogue between China and Canada has found critical common ground in at least three major areas as evidenced by the papers in this text and also by the discussion at the Beida Symposium.

First, despite different origins of the establishment of human rights in the West (primarily through the philosophy of Natural Law) and in China (primarily through international treaties and Confucian notions of a ruler's virtue and duties to citizens), the primordial source of human rights obligations are the same. That source is the concept of human dignity, even if its definition has different parameters in China and the West.

Second, the right to development, which many regard as a collective right, and civil and political rights need not be placed in a conflictual hierarchy to each other.

Canadian constitutional jurisprudence and traditions have shown that collective and individual rights can be balanced in a fashion that promotes universal concepts of justice and proportionality. Two of these concepts involve acceptance of the Rule of Law and the principle that the ends never justify the means. Many of the Chinese participants in this dialogue project came to accept this position.

Finally, the Chinese and Canadian participants reached a consensus on the need for both nations and the international community to implement women's rights as human rights domestically and internationally. The reality of domestic violence, female infanticide and denial of substantive equality in the areas of education, health and employment for most women across the globe, make a mockery of the myriad of laws, domestic and international, that supposedly protect women's rights.

These three areas of common ground can and have become a foundation for Canada and China to create a new global and non-adversarial dialogue on how to effectively cultivate fundamental human values even in countries that do not share the historical, political and legal traditions of the West.

There will and should be major differences between China and Canada over human rights positions adopted by China and the West. This publication, and the dialogue that created it, calls for building upon the common ground, even in this most contested area of human values between two civilizations.

E.P. Mendes and A-M. Traeholt
April 1997

Notes:

1. Harry Harding. *China's Second Revolution*. (Washington, D.C.: The Brookings Institution, 1987) 270.

2. Samuel P. Huntington. "The Clash of Civilizations". *Foreign Affairs*, Vol. 72, No. 3, Summer 1993.

3. Information Office of the State Council, *Human Rights in China*. November 1991, Beijing, China.

4. See also the writing of such promoters of Asian values, e.g. Lee Kuan Yew, "Culture is Destiny" *Foreign Affairs*, 73, no. 2, (March/April 1994), 114; Koh, "Does East Asia Stand for Any Positive Values?" *International Herald Tribune*, December 11-12, 1993; Goh Chok Tong, "Social Values, Singapore Style," *Current History* (December 1994) 417.

5. Supra, note 3.

6. Report of the Regional Meeting for Asia of the World Conference on Human Rights (Bangkok, March 29 - April 2, 1993), UN Doc. A/Conf.157/ASRM/ paragraph 8.

7. Sophia Woodman, "Asian Views: Defining Human Rights for a Region?", *Human Rights in China* (Winter 1994), 14.

8. U.N. Doc. A/Conf.157/23 (July 12, 1993).

9. Masakazu Yamazaki, "Asia, a Civilisation in the Making," *Foreign Affairs* 75, no. 4, (July/August 1996), 118.

10. Ibid., 107.

11. Ibid., 116.

12. See, for example, David Arase, "Japanese Policy Toward Democracy and Human Rights in Asia," *Asian Survey* XXXIII, no. 10, (October 1993).

13. See, for example, Melanie Chew, "Human Rights in Singapore: Perceptions and Problems," *Asian Survey* XXXIV, no. 11, (November 1994).

14. See *The Far Eastern Economic Review*, June 2, 1994, 20.

15. Address entitled "Media and Society in Asia," keynote speech at the Asian Press Forum, Hong Kong (Dec. 2, 1994), 3-4. Cited in Hoong-Phun Lee, "Constitutional Values in Turbulent Asia", 17.

16. For Asian NGOs' reaction to the governmental Bangkok Declaration, see *Our Voice: Bangkok NGO Declaration on Human Rights.* Reports of the Asia Pacific NGO Conference on Human Rights and NGOs' Statements to the Asia Regional Meeting (Bangkok: Asian Cultural Forum on Development, 1993.)

17. See *The Far Eastern Economic Review*, October 24, 1996, 28.

18. Ibid.

19. Alan Dupont, "Is There An 'Asian Way'?" *Survival*, Vol. 38, No. 2, Summer 1996, 22-23.

20. For an analysis of these reforms, see "Opening to Reform? An Analysis of China's Revised Criminal Procedure Law", Lawyers Committee for Human Rights, October 1996. The report was written by Jonathan Hecht.

21. See Willy Wo-Lap Lam, "Qiao ahead in battle to state case for place as Deng's heir", *South China Morning Post* for the weekend beginning April 12, 1997, 8.

22. Nicholas Tapp, "Minority Nationality in China: Policy and Practice", in R.H. Barnes, A. Gray and B. Kingsbury, *Indigenous Peoples of Asia*. (Ann Arbor, Michigan: Association for Asian Studies, 1995), 203.

23. Hurst Hannum, ed., *Documents on Autonomy and Minority Rights*. (Dordrecht/Boston/London: Martinus Nijhoff Publishers, 1993), 192.

24. Ibid.

25. Supra, note 3, 1.

1 Philosophical, Political and Legal Foundations of Human Rights, Collective Rights and the Right to Development

Cultural and Political Determinants of the Chinese Approach to Human Rights

JEREMY T. PALTIEL

Introduction

"Chinese Culture" is contested and political rather than static or immutable. As Barrett McCormick and David Kelly argue, culture is "an open-ended repertoire of symbolic forms and practices."[1] A discussion of "Chinese culture" today cannot ignore the fact that some notion of "western culture" is never outside the frame of reference. In 1995, there is not, nor can there be a pristine Chinese culture "uncontaminated" by western values, concepts and theories.[2]

The profound impact of Marxism-Leninism, however ultimately judged in the long sweep of Chinese history, positively demonstrates that western ideas can find hospitable soil on the banks of the yellow river. There was some resonance or affinity between the revolutionary ideology of Marxism-Leninism and some aspects of indigenous Chinese thought[3], but it is equally certain that the revolution created a genuine hiatus in the official ideology and major social institutions. Mao Zedong himself claimed to "sinify" Marxism -- "integrating" its theory with "Chinese practice". The resulting synthesis is one aspect of contemporary "Chinese culture." However, just as China's official ideology has been transformed dramatically less than two decades after the death of its founding father, "Chinese culture" today is a hybrid which is capable of adapting and absorbing new values and ideas. Alongside other Western ideas, Chinese have responded to the language of rights. There is a substantive body of Chinese academic discussion; constitutional texts; as well as a history of political action explicitly founded on the language of rights. Rights are part of the contemporary Chinese vocabulary, which is as different from the classical Chinese lexicon as a Long March rocket is from a sedan chair.

Unlike imported technology, rights language achieves utility within a social and historical context, and is itself capable of transforming that context. Rights in the West pertain to the domain of the rightful/lawful/morally acceptable exercise of (state) authority. So long as rights claims gain legitimacy in social practice, it may be irrelevant that certain practices and values have indigenous roots and others are imported. It remains to be seen whether there is any practical distinction to be made between imported and indigenous elements in the culture and under what circumstances this distinction becomes operative or contested.

In China's traditional political vocabulary rights language is wholly absent. Nevertheless, traditional Chinese thought provides a very rich vocabulary for making claims on the state, and the basis of these claims can be compared against Western rights discourse.

The Chinese Tradition and Moral-Political Claims

The moral dimensions of power

The Chinese tradition has a rich repository of debates and discussions over the moral dimensions of political power. This cultural vocabulary is normally traced back to Confucius, but it is also possible to trace it back into high antiquity through the religious practices of the Shang (1766-1122 BC). Early in Chinese history an outlook emerged which conveyed a sacral quality to rulership and a central role for the state in the cosmology linking Heaven and human.[4]

In Chinese political theory, the emperor (Son of Heaven) is the link between Heaven and Earth. As the Book of Documents states, the Emperor Yao "reached to the heavens above and the earth below." The imperial system forms the nexus in the axis between Heaven and Man (Tian ren zhi Ji). "Heaven gives charges to those who have virtue. There is a correspondence between the upper and lower world."[5]

The relationship between governance and the divine is quite familiar in western thought.[6] The psycho-social dimensions of power everywhere engender deliberate or spontaneous associations with the supernatural. However, the form this association takes is not incidental; rather it lies at the basis of legitimacy. Hence, this relationship structures both the claims **of** the power holders and the claims which may legitimately be made **on** the power holders. The insistence on moral quality of rulership, namely *de*, (moral power; also translated as "virtue"), makes it possible that a power-holder might attempt to govern without the necessary *de* or moral requisites of rule.[7] This grants a non-ruler an entry point to make judgments or claims on power. Lucian Pye has pointed to the distinctive capacity of Asians, including Chinese, to view power in non-utilitarian terms.[8] Power is not merely a function or an attribute of status. The two are nearly coterminous. Since *de* is the basic attribute of the power holder, it would be inadmissible to judge the exercise of power on any grounds other than "virtue." No other values or goods are intended to be satisfied through the exercise of power.

In Confucian writing, it is assumed that all good follows from the manifestation of virtue. Thus, a virtuous ruler is not merely the prerequisite of community good, nor does a virtuous character imply the potential for good. It is that good achieved. One of the oldest texts in the Confucian canon, *The Book of Documents* links the personal virtue of the ruler with the achievement of order in society:

> He was able to make bright his lofty virtue and so he made affectionate the nine branches of the family. When the nine branches of the family had become harmonious, he distinguished and honoured the hundred clans. When the hundred clans had become illustrious, he harmonized the myriad states. The numerous people were amply nourished and prosperous and became concordant.[9]

Throughout the Chinese tradition, the state is closely identified with the moral qualities of the individual ruler or power holder.

Western political theory, at least as far back as Plato, has viewed justice as one of the principal values underlying governance and the ordering of society. In China, by contrast, justice is conspicuous by its absence as a universal principal. The modern equivalent for "justice" in Chinese, *gongzheng*, is made up of two characters, *gong* - "public" and *zheng* - "rectitude". This is an odd juxtaposition. *Zheng*, "regulation" referred first of all to the self. It occurs in two of the cardinal texts of Confucianism. Confucius (551-479 BC) calls on the king to first regulate himself, then his family in order that the country be well regulated.

> To govern is to set things right (*zheng*). If you begin by setting yourself right, then who will deviate from the right?[10]

Note that unlike the objective stance operative in the Western approach to distributive justice, the Chinese take a subjective stance. One gives others their due by beginning with an appreciation of one's own relative position.

> He cultivates himself so as to be able to bring comfort to other people...He cultivates himself so as to bring comfort to the entire populace....even the sage kings were dissatisfied with themselves on this point.[11]

Thus justice is not, as in the western tradition, a function of the relation of rulers to subjects and a means of judging the quality of the rulers and the rules which they apply, but rather, an attribute of persons in relation.

Therefore, if "rights" are one form of claim about the power of the state, then in China, the moral basis and the vocabulary for making analogous claims is established very early on. Moreover, there is a long tradition of making political claims, both individually and collectively. Did an individual have to have a particular status in order to make such a claim, or, could one, in a direct analogy with "human rights", establish a claim purely on the basis of being human?

There is no simple answer to this question. Confucianism is very particular about status distinctions, but insists on the potential of every person to <u>achieve</u> a status of moral worth. "One's nature is inborn (heaven born), virtue (*de*) is brought to completion by the self." The entire corpus of Confucian thought, and the reason for dominance of Chinese ethical discourse over two millennia, rests on the universal potential for human beings to achieve moral personhood.[12] However, Confucius makes a sharp distinction between taking a moral stance and making a claim for power:

> In serving his mother and father a man may gently remonstrate with them. But if he sees he has failed to change their opinion, he should resume an attitude of deference and not thwart them; he may feel discouraged, but not resentful.[13]

This statement about making moral claims within the invidious status relations of the family has a direct counterpart in the state. "How can he be said to be truly loyal who refrains from admonishing the object of his loyalty?"[14] Mencius (c. 372-289 BC) makes it clear that there is a moral obligation to speak back to those in authority, but that a moral claim does not erase status distinctions: "When the prince is in grave error [the ministers'] duty is to warn him, and if this should happen repeatedly and he disregards them, they should resign."[15]

The state had moral obligations to every one of its subjects and was ultimately accountable for this. Like western social contract theory, traditional Chinese political discourse assumes reciprocity between rulers and subjects. The notion of reciprocity, in fact, underlines all social relations.[16] Human beings participate in the creation of a celestial order through the admonition to "assist Heaven" (*peitian*). A coeval relationship between Heaven, Earth and Man defines the context for moral-political action. The very ancient text asserts: "Heaven hears as my people hear; heaven sees as my people see."[17] The sympathy of the people becomes a symbol of the will of Heaven.

> Mencius said: Jie and Zhou lost the empire because they lost the people. By losing the people, I mean lost their sympathy. There is a way to win the empire: gain the people and win the empire. There is a way to gain the people: win their hearts and you will gain them. There is a way to

win their hearts: share with them the abundance of what you wish for and do not impose what you dislike on them. The people turn in allegiance to Humanity as surely as water runs down.[18]

The "Mandate of Heaven"(*tianming* -- also translated as "the command" of heaven) provides a mechanism for evil regimes to be replaced:

Properly speaking, may a subject slay his prince? Mencius replied: "A man who despoils Humanity I call a robber; a man who despoils Justice, a ruffian. Robbers and ruffians are mere commoners. I was aware that the commoner Zhou was slain, but unaware that a prince was slain.[19]

Only ex-post facto does one know with certainty that the mandate of heaven has been lost. Mencius' formula illustrates the gap between this and the nexus of rights and legitimacy which developed in the West from the *Magna Carta* through the *Petition of Right* and the *American Declaration of Independence*. The Confucian moral requirement to observe one's station in life[20] and to act in a disinterested manner, serves as a "catch 22" which preempts a strict nexus between "rights" and obligations. There are mutual obligations but no strictly defined "rights." The obligations of rulers to their subjects are very clear, as are the obligations of a subject to behave with loyalty. However, there is no formula which releases a subject from his obligations. Indeed, the entire corpus of the Confucian moral-political nexus enjoins a person to remain engaged in his social-political context.

Individualism and egotism

Confucianism consistently and resolutely eschews individualistic utilitarian calculus. Nothing could be more alien to Confucian thought than the rationalistic self-interested individual. One of the fundamental problems addressed by Chinese philosophers was human nature, and whether its source was good or evil. Mencius claimed that human nature was good; Xun Zi (c. 312-238 BC) that it was evil. The Neo-Confucian orthodoxy established by Zhu Xi (1130-1220 AD) followed Mencius. However, the two schools were not in conflict over what constituted "good" or "evil". For Xun Zi,

The nature of man is evil; his goodness is only acquired through training. The original nature of man today is to seek for gain. If these tendencies are followed, injury and destruction follows; loyalty and faithfulness are destroyed.[21]

At first glance this looks remarkable similar to Hobbes.

To give rein to man's original nature, to follow man's feelings, inevitably results in strife and rapacity, together with violations of etiquette and confusion in the way of doing things, and reverts to a state of violence. Therefore the civilizing influence of teachers and laws, the guidance of rules of proper conduct and justice are absolutely necessary. Thereupon courtesy results; public and private etiquette is observed; and good government is the result.[22]

Mencius and Xun Zi agree that education is the antidote to evil. Mencius, however, claims that the capacity for empathy is innate, and hence the capacity for goodness. This capacity for empathy, or "human heartedness" is the positive aspect of human nature to be cultivated in social relations. Unmistakably however, both thinkers equate evil with selfishness and good with proper behaviour and altruism. "Ego claims" (*si li*) are specifically denied moral value. This is fundamentally at odds with the western notion of rights which recognizes ego claims as valid moral entitlements:

> A right-holder <u>exercises</u> his right; he claims it and thus brings it into play. This activates the duty-bearer's obligation to <u>respect</u> that right. If it is respected, the right-holder will <u>enjoy</u> the right. The result of this process, as well as its ultimate aim, is to secure the right-holder's enjoyment of the <u>object</u> of the right.[23]

As Jack Donnelly points out, the exercise of rights involves 1) a right holder, 2) an object of the right and 3) a duty-bearer. Rights involve positive claims against duty bearers, claims that may "trump" (to use Ronald Dworkin's language)[24] other forms of moral claim. The sense of rights as moral trumps is difficult to reconcile with the Chinese tradition. The language of rights appears egocentric, and hence impermissible to Chinese eyes. Confucianism enjoins another sort of discourse with respect to the moral obligations of superiors-- remonstrance--to remind superiors of their obligations. Rights language, Donnelly points out, asserts the moral priority of the claimant:

> "having" a right is therefore of most value precisely when one does not "have" the object of the right--that is, when one is denied direct or objective enjoyment of the right. I call this "the possession paradox" of rights: "having" and "not having" a right at the same time, the "having" being particularly important precisely when one <u>does not</u> "have" it.[25]

It is therefore easy to see the contrast between rights thinking and the moral calculus cultivated in the Chinese tradition:

Confucianism would consider it a failure for society to aim at securing a minimum level of basic rights for alienated individuals unable or unwilling to participate cooperatively in collective living. If one accepts that there is no way to escape the self-interested passions and desires of the animal world, then there is no hope for a humane society. Confucius realized that laws cannot force people to be humane. For society to achieve collective humanity, the people that constitute it must be willing to put aside narrow self-interest and see their interests as inextricably tied to societal interests.[26]

The essence of the political and social thought of Confucius and Mencius is found in the concept of ren.[27] Ren may be regarded as the moral attribute of acting consciously to do right in relation to others. Hence, Hall and Ames choose to translate the term as "authoritative personhood", a translation also supported by the social psychologist Francis L.K. Hsu, who translates the term as "personage".[28] "The Chinese concept of man," states Hsu, "is based on the individual's transactions with his fellow human beings."[29] The ethical imperative contained in the idea of ren means to become an ethical social personality -- to "be" a man (zuo ren). This imperative, while always contextual, is not limited by any specific context. In "socializing" the individual, **society** rather than the birth of the individual, imparts to each person the qualities of moral personhood. Human beings develop into moral persons through their interaction with others and do not acquire the qualities of moral personhood apart from others. The notion of individual autonomy, wrapped up in Western myths of an individual "born free" is antithetical to classical Chinese thought:

> After you are born you can not be independent, you still need parental nurturing and care. Your conscience must reciprocate your parents' nurturing care, and there must therefore be filial piety. When Chinese speak of parental love and filial piety, they are just aspects of what we call ren. This term, ren can be said to be the heart/mind of the human species, which at the same time is human nature.[30]

Western individualism may be contrasted with the Chinese or Confucian concept of person in terms of the way each looks at the distinguishing marks of personhood: "difference is prized in western society as a mark of creativity and originality, while in China the goal of personality development involves the achievement of interdependence through the actualization as integrative emotions held in common among individuals."[31]

To be a man among men is Confucius's fundamental aim. Reciprocity, then becomes the basis of self cultivation. Man defines his "self" in relation to others in a way which unites them. Thus is constituted the web of reciprocal obligations or moral relations in which a man finds himself, defines himself. Apart from these he can have no real identity. And yet, these relations alone, it is equally important to recognize, do not define man totally. His interior self exists at the center of this web and there enjoys his own freedom.[32]

The contextualized nature of individual moral self-assertion should not be misunderstood as a distinction between Chinese "collectivism" versus western "individualism".[33]

If we were to attempt a comparison of Confucius' understanding of ren with European theories, then we would have to note that this concept is on the one hand different from that on an emphasis on groups and the de-emphasis of the individual as encountered in collectivism and simultaneously is dissimilar to the aggrandizing of the self and the restraining of the state in individualism. For both of these acknowledge the antithesis of the individual and society, whereas Confucians obliterated such boundaries and effected a unity of mankind with the self.[34]

Here, therefore, stands a cardinal difference which defines the perspectives which will inform conceptions of rights. In Locke's theory, rights form a set of boundaries which delimit the extent of the public sphere and protect a sphere of private endeavour beyond the reach of the state. Rights as "boundaries"[35] become the definitive characteristic of what later becomes classified by Isaiah Berlin as "negative rights."[36] However, it is precisely these "negative rights" which undergird the entire tradition of western rights discourse.

Human personality and political claims

"To associate oneself with others" is a fundamental premise of Confucius' thought. There can be no fulfilment for the individual in isolation from his fellows. To think of oneself as an island apart, or as an individual abstracted from humanity as a whole is impossible. Nor is it just a matter of human beings as social animals; what distinguishes them from the birds and the beasts is their moral sense, the inborn, Heaven endowed sense of mission to make the Way prevail in the world, which compels Confucius to associate his own fulfilment with the fulfilment of others. "The humane man if he seeks to establish himself will help others to succeed. To be able to judge others by what one knows of oneself is the method of achieving humanity" [6:28].[37]

"Humane rule" (*renzheng*) includes such attributes as restraint from harsh punishment and the death penalty; avoidance of aggressive warfare, and the promotion of public welfare by refraining from heavy taxation. These however, are achieved by self-restraint on the part of a ruler, not by restrictions placed on government.[38] Ethical rule and the limits of formal authority are inseparable from the dimensions of ethical personhood rooted in a concept of humanity and personhood which is fundamentally contextual. "It is the cultivation of rightness through the dynamics of interpersonal conduct and its realization in the social and political orders which enables people to integrate themselves in the cosmic order and to participate in an essentially moral universe -- this is the 'way' of human beings."[39] Thomas Metzger has characterized the tension between *neisheng* (inner sagehood) and *waiwang* (external kingship) as the fundamental problem of neo-Confucianism.[40] Each person possesses the same moral faculties as the sage-kings Yao and Xun but may lack the opportunity to lead or to serve the state (as Confucius did).[41]

Zhu Xi, the great synthesizer of Neo-Confucian thought in the twelfth century saw selfish desire as a kind of fog which intervened between the self and one's moral faculty or "nature". Morality consisted of penetrating heavenly principles while banishing selfish desires. These "heavenly principles", however, are near at hand. The neo-Confucian achieves moral personhood while remaining in context. The neo-Confucian personality aims at achieving a transcendence of self, while remaining fully engaged in his (this was a male discourse) social context. Therefore, the achievement of inner harmony and tranquillity is associated with the exercise of moral duties and emotions of interconnectedness.

Should you cause human beings in groups to interact with fellow feeling, with rightness, with order and with faithfulness, then the way of man will spontaneously be clarified. These five qualities of fellow feeling, of rightness, of difference, of order and faithfulness all are external actions mainly the behaviours of man to man, and are controlled by each person. If you behave with utmost filial piety towards your parents, whether they accept this or are disgusted by it does not matter. So long as you yourself practice 'the way' and are achieving virtue you are actually becoming a filial son and the main person being influenced is your self. If you behave with faithfulness to your friend, there is still no certainty that your friend will trust you but there is no doubt that you will be influenced yourself, becoming in turn a trustworthy person. Therefore while the actions are directed externally, the influence necessarily extends to the self.[42]

"Self-cultivation" is both a social practice and a psychological exercise aimed at raising an individuals's moral self-awareness. Prof. William Theodore de Bary has attempted to distill a Chinese "liberal tradition" by analogizing and extending the moral self of neo-Confucianism to the individual conscience of Western liberalism and by comparing neo-Confucian dedication to public affairs with Western notions of republican virtue.[43] I believe, however, that the neo-Confucian moral self and western liberal individualism may be more accurately contrasted, without inviting invidious opposition. This may broaden cross-cultural understanding of the self by distinguishing between a concept of individuation through the promotion of self-interest and a concept of personhood rooted in ethical action.

Chinese thought has its own tradition of "public" (*gong*) and "private" (*si*). There the distinction is not between a private sphere of independence or autonomy and a public sphere of political authority. Rather, it is a distinction between egocentrism and other-directed, public-spirited moral action. It is the distinction between ethical action and selfishness. That is one reason why the Chinese legal tradition consists almost entirely of criminal law, and is relatively silent in the domain of private law.

Law and the regulation of interest

Confucians objected to impartial and impersonal law, and saw legal sanctions as undermining the claims of morality by substituting external standards for the internalized behaviour prescribed by ritual, or li.

Lead the people by laws and regulate them by penalties, and the people will try to keep out of jail, but will have no sense of shame. Lead the people by virtue and restrain them by the rules of decorum, and the people will have a sense of shame and moreover will become good.[44]

Hall and Ames see the contrast between law xing (as used above by Confucius) and rites or ritual li in the "meaningfulness of ritual performed with personal significance (*yi*) and the mainly coercive functioning of non-personal law (*xing*) which originates in expediency."[45] The ultimate source of ritual action is not a universal ethical norm but "a human being striving to achieve appropriateness in his ethical and natural context."[46] Ultimately, in the Chinese tradition, the need to invoke law or fa represents the failure "to achieve the harmony possible by ritual action."[47] Law is confined to the realm of punishing the transgression of ethical norms. It is a supplement to an order based on "rite" or decorum. All law in dynastic China was criminal law, and had to do with the punishment of transgression, rather than the establishment of norms. As such, it is a second-best instrument inferior to ritual or rite. Chinese culture has had a very different outlook on the relationship between law and morality than its western counterpart.

The Confucian approach to law developed in the context of a competing political philosophy of "legalism" (fa jia). The Legalists, exemplified by the thinkers Shang Yang and Han Fei, saw law as a bureaucratic tool of statecraft, seeking to aggrandize the power of the state by establishing an administration which would strictly enforce a legal code of rewards and punishments.[48] The tyrannical state of Qin, which followed the philosophy of Han Fei and Shang Yang, eventually unified China in 221 BC. The persecution of Confucian scholars under the First Emperor, Qin Shihuangdi, earned the enduring hatred of Confucians, and reinforced the notion of law as a strictly punitive instrument. Nevertheless, the demands of bureaucratic administration and universal empire bequeathed a highly developed legal culture.

> [I]n China the initial stimulus for law was no more economic than it was religious. Economic growth, to be sure, no doubt played a role in transforming the society of feudal China to a point where it could no longer get along without a written law. When this law appeared however, it was used neither to uphold traditional religious values nor to protect private property. Rather, its primary purpose was political: that of imposing tight political controls upon a society which was then losing its old cultural values and being drawn by inexorable new forces along the road leading eventually to universal empire.[49]

Legal practice was reconciled with Confucian norms and values. Penal law represented a failure of norms rather than a manifestation of a transcendent order. Whereas the codes of laws and the need for law may have originated in Legalist notions of statecraft, the practice of adjudication was infused with the ethos of the Confucian ideal of harmony. There is a distinction between the way in which order is brought about, according to Chinese principles, and the principles of justice underlying Western legal systems:

The difference between the two contrasting states of order and harmony is reflected in the means adopted to sustain them. In western society, where concepts of order prevail, disputes are resolved and breeches of order are corrected by measuring them against rigid, universal codes of imperatives external to the parties in adjudication. In the society of traditional China, where concepts of harmony prevail, disputes are resolved and disturbances of harmony corrected (ideally within the immediate group where they arose) by relating them to the personalities, the exigencies and the surrounding circumstances of the particular case with a view to instructing the parties in the conduct expected of them and the punishment of those disturbing harmony.[50]

The crucial difference between rights discourse as it has developed in the west, and the language of moral-political claims as it evolved in China, is that Western rights discourse is egocentric in form as well as in content. Chinese moral discourse disapproves of egocentric moral discourse, and devalues claims posed in the language of interest.

[T]he Confucian concept of li [rites] becomes linked to the Confucian attitude toward the whole realm of what we would call "individual rights." Individuals have legitimate interests, to be sure, and in the good society these interests will be taken care of... To surround these interests with an aura of sanctity and to call them "rights," to elevate the defence of these individual interests to the plane of moral virtue, to "insist on one's rights"-- is to run entirely counter to the spirit of li [rite].The proper disposition with regard to one's interests is the predisposition to yield rather than the disposition to insist.[51]

Therefore, the ethical connotations of law in the Chinese and Western traditions are fundamentally dissimilar. Since the concept of "human rights" is imbedded in a thick rule of law tradition, it may be useful to look back at the contrasting tradition in China.

Law and nature in the Chinese tradition

The genealogy of western rights discourse can be traced to the idea of natural law.[52] Human rights are ,in general, a modern transformation of the theory of Natural Rights. While the adoption of the *Universal Declaration* and the *International Bill of Rights* have, in important respects, removed the discussion of human rights from the realm of the discussion of the political theory of Natural Rights to the legal domain, the robust sense in which "human rights" are seen to be "inalienable" cannot easily be separated from their parentage in the theory of Natural Rights. It is here also that a fundamental divergence opens between Western liberal discourse and Chinese discursive traditions concerning the political order.

The historian of Chinese science, Joseph Needham, finds that the European idea of laws of nature was itself rooted in a notion of a "reign over the world" which

> originated from a hypostatization into the divine realm of men's conceptions of earthly rulers and their reigns and should look at concomitant social developments to reach an understanding of the change which took place... If then, we may relate the rise of the stoic doctrine of Universal Law to the period of the rise of the great monarchies after Alexander the Great, we may find it equally reasonable to relate the rise of the concept of Laws of Nature at the Renaissance to the appearance of Royal Absolutism at the end of feudalism and the beginning of capitalism. It is not mere chance, say Hegel, that the Cartesian idea of God as the Legislator of the universe developed only forty years after Jean Bodin's theory of sovereignty.[53]

The Chinese tradition rests on a fundamental notion of immanence rather than transcendence. There is therefore no divine legislator, nor is it reasonable to assume any kind of legal order (such as natural rights) which transcends the phenomenal order.

> The ubiquity of the concept of transcendence in the Western tradition has introduced into our conceptual inventory a host of disjunctive concepts -- God and the world, being and not being, subject and object, mind and body, reality and appearance, good and evil, knowledge and ignorance. ... The mutual immanence of the primary elements of the Confucian cosmos -- heaven earth and man-- precludes the use of the language of transcendence and therefore renders any sort of dualistic contrast pernicious.[54]

The only form of law recognized in the Chinese tradition is positive law. Without a tradition of natural law or divine law to sustain the idea of law as the origin of order, positive law takes on a purely instrumental meaning, with a very much contested moral force.

In western thought, the antithesis of chaos is order, and order is thought of, both cosmologically and philosophically as an artificial objective deliberately brought about, managed, and controlled on predetermined forms according to the conscious will of a transcendent power exterior to the flux, by enforcement of codes of rigid, universal, specific imperatives constraining conduct. In Chinese thought and cultural tradition, the antithesis of chaos is harmony which is brought about simply as a natural characteristic of a state of affairs that arises and persists so long as all the individual parts of the universe, even the smallest, and all persons in it, perform the duties and offices faithfully "according to the internal necessities of their own natures" in whatever station or function of life they find themselves born to or assigned by superior authority.[55]

Joseph Needham connects the Chinese aversion to positive law to the absence of any notion of "laws of nature".[56] There can be no divine law without a divine lawgiver. Moreover, it is precisely the connection of positive law with particular rulers which makes Chinese suspicious of it as an instrument of rule. To be applied properly to the particular context still requires a moral and just ruler. If applied bluntly, and impartially, as was suggested by the rivals of the Confucians, the legalists, then the law is no better than arbitrariness and is at best amoral, if not immoral. Confucians preferred to cultivate inward virtue, and to find justice in virtuous rulers. These would take as their standards the rites, rituals or decorum required in every particular situation. The moral faculty links all persons and the cosmos and all things. Instead of a transcendent God, Confucianism sees the cosmos as a seamless web of relations, the jigang where each node may not be disturbed without affecting the shape of the web as a whole.[57] The cosmos is fundamentally a moral cosmos and nature is the same as human nature (xing ji tian).

Personhood, morality and legitimacy

The intriguing discussion of nature in relation to law and morality in the Chinese philosophical tradition thus, parallels but does not mirror Western discussion of "natural law".[58] Chinese discussions of the proper place of human relations of "rite" (li) and "rightness"(yi) in the Confucian tradition place a heavy emphasis on a natural order rooted in "heaven" or tian. However, the Confucian tradition adopts a perspective based on the moral cultivation of the self or subject in relation to others, eschewing an "objective" standard of the hypostatized "other" or an abstract standard of justice. Moral calculus tends towards "equity" rather than "right."[59]

> The coextensive relationship existing among the dimensions of personal, social and political order has the effect of precluding the employment of categories familiar from Western philosophical theory. Confucius, given his distinctly social perspective with regard to the project of person making does not perceive a corresponding degree of difference between public and private, between ethical and political concerns, between social and political structures.[60]

If, "in the course of human events", western enlightenment intellectuals engaged in political action in defence of certain "inalienable rights", their Chinese counterparts are drawn into public activity by the need to "achieve rightness" in human relations. An uprising is qiyi, literally a "rising up for rightness, which is not egocentric, but public spirited.

A simplistic generalization would be that both the Chinese and the Western traditions arrive at an ethical position which gives limited moral sanction to authority, and recognize the legitimacy of moral claims established on the basis of inappropriate application of power. Both traditions sanction the "questioning of authority". Broadly stated, however, the Chinese tradition does so from the perspective of the moral obligations[61] of those already in authority, whereas the Western tradition evolves a concept of ego-regarding rights. In sum, therefore, the two traditions are neither contradictory, nor strictly speaking, complementary.

In the Chinese tradition, since rulership can be claimed from Heaven only on the basis of "virtue," it is then incumbent on power holders at all times to proclaim their virtue and to monopolize its definition. Conversely, claims may be made on government only in terms of culturally acceptable notions of virtue. Fortunately or unfortunately, Confucian notions of order also placed paramount value on loyalty to one's superior, making both loyalty (*zhong*) and its familistic equivalent, filial piety (*xiao*) standard components of any culturally acceptable definition of virtue. The Confucian equivalent of "loyal opposition" therefore takes the form of "remonstrance" or, more particularly, attempts to teach the ruler virtue. The precise value in Confucianism placed on strict maintenance of one's status in the social hierarchy means that no-one can legitimately claim to displace the ruler. The best hope of the morally cultivated individual is to become "tutor to the king," and to realize the blessings of the "kingly way" in service to the government.

The cosmological significance of political rule entails a symbiosis between the ruler and the educated officials. He depends on them not only to carry out his will in administering the state, but also, to proclaim his virtue and thus assure his legitimacy. The scholar-officials, for their part, depend on the monarch not just for their offices and salaries, but because only through the exercise of public functions can they participate in the cosmological order realized through the emperor. This symbiosis of the civil elites with the structures of political power was one obvious inhibitory factor on the formation of some sort of autonomous "civil society" which could give rise to rights discourse by combining the protection of its own material interests with an ideological preference for autonomy.

While the emperor monopolized the function of uniting heaven and earth, he did not, however, have a monopoly on virtue. Virtue may be cultivated by all, but given the cosmological significance of political rule, the highest exercise of virtue by a non-ruler would be to imitate Confucius and attempt to persuade the ruler to become virtuous. The identification of authority with morality may serve as a weapon for the weak and the subject. This, however, can only be exercised under the specific condition that the legitimacy of authority be recognized. Dependency is the price of remonstrance. The remonstrant must appeal to the moral obligations of the powerholder in order to advance his claim of virtue unfulfilled. This exercise, implying that the current ruler lacks virtue, is dangerously fraught. Consequently, martyrdom is an acceptable manner to demonstrate the virtue of one's cause while remaining loyal to the ruler.

Opposition can certainly be morally justified, but it is also hazardous. Thus, unlike the claims of citizenship, which can be advanced without simultaneously recognizing the legitimacy of the ruler, the Chinese remonstrator must first proclaim his loyalty as a subject before advancing a claim. In effect, by recognizing a claim, the ruler reinforces his own legitimacy. The claims of subjects are made valid only because of the obligations of authority -- not because of any inherent rights of the subject. The obligations of rulers are not specific and contractual but are diffuse and moral. An upright person may refuse to serve a corrupt state, but is left with no outlet to serve society.

Specific claims may then become entangled in the politics of "face" which is none other than the social "face" of an individuals de or"moral power." Therefore the substance of a specific claim may be denied in order to protect the generality of the ruler's claim to legitimacy, a factor which may also provoke harsh retaliation.[62] In the Western tradition these problems have been finessed by recourse to an independent judiciary. They can also be avoided by making distinctions between the institutions and rulers, offices and incumbents. These abstract distinctions may be rooted in the West in the conflict between Church and state, and perhaps traced to western beliefs in a single, transcendent and impartial God -- a principle without exact equivalence in the Chinese tradition.

Herein lies the resistance of Chinese power holders to rights language. To press one's claim, one in effect proves that one's rights were denied, establishing in fact that the power holder, or duty-bearer failed in his or her duty. In a situation where power and authority are viewed in peculiarly moral terms, this admission is both dangerous and corrosive since it shifts the discourse away from what Donnelly calls the object of the right, towards the moral status of the duty-bearer. In questioning his moral status, one simultaneously calls into question his power status -- or legitimacy.

Chinese political theory, from Confucius through Mao and his slogan of "fight self," (*dousi*) was never able to deal adequately with self-interest. This quality of Chinese morality, where other-directedness becomes self-discipline, cannot easily be reconciled with rights, which are necessarily claims for the self against others. Chinese political thought makes no distinction between public and private virtue. The effect of this, throughout history, is to give political criticism a particularly ad-hominem flavour and to allow critics to disguise their own self-interest in the guise of pointing out the personal foibles, and hence, the unworthiness of their opponents. The excesses of critics during the Cultural Revolution of the 1960s are paralleled by the vicious slanders heaped on the reformer Wang Anshi of the Song Dynasty in the 1060s, or during the final years of the Ming Dynasty when the Donglin Faction of officials went on a moralistic crusade.[63] Comments made about political criticism under the Song are equally valid today:

> The criticism soon degenerated into vicious slander. At the top appeared such allegations as high treason, disloyalty, disrespect to the emperor, and the like; at the bottom levels came accusations with respect to private conduct and domestic relations.[64]

The practical effect of blurring the distinction between public and private morality is to blur the distinction between personal ethics and professional conduct; or between the technical efficiency and effectiveness of an organization, on the one hand, and the personal qualities of incumbent office holders, on the other.

Political authority is placed in a double bind by its insistence on legitimacy according to virtue and its refusal to recognize self-interest. The state must motivate officials while denying any necessity to bow to the interests of subordinates. The cosmological importance of centralized authority also breeds hypocrisy in the refusal to legitimate separate or subordinate centres of power.

In the world's largest unitary state, central laws were honoured as often in the breech as by strict obedience. The traditional state pretended to defer to administration by "non-action" (*wuwei*) as an ideal. The state often accommodated plural interests, tolerating these by ignoring them, rather than by recognizing and incorporating them. Indeed, officials and rulers derived smug self-satisfaction from such tolerance as a measure of their "benevolence," or susceptibility to "reason". Explicit insistence on difference would however entail severe loss of face and would likely solicit swift retaliation. Toleration of anomalies can be accommodated under the Confucian "doctrine of the mean". Yet this political rhetoric masked enduring suspicion about the consequences of recognizing competing centres of power. Any derogation from the principle of power deriving from a single source was regarded as invited chaos -- *luan*, a situation akin to the Hobbesian state of nature.[65] The traditional Chinese state left no legitimate space for political opposition, nor did it recognize competing centres of power consistent with "civil society". Instead, the universal moral claims of the state adjusted to the overlapping claims of kinship (through filial piety) to form "zones of indifference, personal spaces beyond the reach of the state and the grass-roots community."[66]

Confucian Chinese values and western liberal values are not mutually exclusive, but they are different. To view cultures in dichotomous terms exaggerates these differences and destroys points of tangency. Intercultural encounters can recognize common attributes of humanity. These attributes need not form the same categorical list, nor be easily reconciled with the rights and values enumerated in the *International Bill of Rights* of the United Nations. Therefore, common values of humanity need not be coterminous with human rights. The theory of "human rights" may be looked upon as a practical legal tool to limit the power of modern states, distinguishing between "human rights" and those humane values which human rights discourse serves to protect. The traditional Chinese culture cherishes many of the same values as those in the post-enlightenment West, but does not express these in rights language. Furthermore, the significance of rights discourse in the Western tradition appears in the context of a legal discourse which privileges legal texts and constrains the exercise of authority by strict reference to them. China does not share the same traditional reverence for legality, nor, has it been argued, does the Chinese tradition approach "sacred texts" in quite the same way.[67] It is important not to identify "difference" with rejection or absence. The extent to which Chinese discourse adapts or adopt rights discourse today has much less to do with primordial factors in the Chinese tradition, than with the circumstances which have forced Chinese to turn their attention to Western modes of political discourse.

Rights and the Chinese Tradition in the Contemporary Period

Beginning with the Opium War in 1839, Western imperial powers asserted the superiority of their own civilization by force of arms, combining economic and military penetration with missionary activity aimed at spreading the virtues of their own triumphant ideology. The humiliation inflicted on dynastic China rendered traditional China obsolete and, at least in some respects, bankrupt. In the first response to the challenge of the West during the Self-Strengthening Movement of the 1860s,[68] the ti and yong ("substance" and "utility") formula[69] emerged as a way of insulating "Chinese values" from the reluctant necessity to adopt western technology. Since the 1860s, the effort to reconcile the absorption of foreign teaching with the reassertion of Chinese value has taken different forms, most recently in Deng Xiaoping's formula of "socialism with Chinese characteristics." The logic of "substance" and "utility" was rationalized in the 1860s as in the 1990s, as a problem of means and ends, but the distinction ultimately gets consumed in an irresolvable debate over identity. How far can the Chinese identity be redefined in the pursuit of national power?

Since the humiliation inflicted in the 19th century, Chinese intellectuals (and Chinese broadly) have come to near unanimity on the idea of progress or evolution. Intellectuals came to see their own tradition as genetically defective and to grant some sort of "competitive advantage" to the modern west.[70] There may be disagreement about the exact location and nature of this genetic defect, but no disagreement as to its presence. For Chinese intellectuals, therefore, any search for value in the Chinese tradition has become an exercise akin to sifting through the ashes in search of the few objects of value left behind by the great conflagration which consumed dynastic China. The effort to come to terms with national humiliation left a hiatus in the Chinese culture, whereby the tradition lost the aura of "sanctity" which once clung to it.[71] Most prefer to turn their attention outwards, towards the shining towers and gleaming machinery of the West, rather than expend their effort to pour moribund ashes through a sieve to discover the rough nuggets left behind. For those that do, the "sieve" is almost always constructed according to "Western" principles.

In a process, which Joseph R. Levenson called the search for equivalence[72] between China and the West, Chinese intellectuals have attempted to find ways of incorporating in their own views of China, the things that they valued in the West, and at times to look back at the Chinese tradition for answers to the problems which they see as arising from the development of the West.

The collapse of the traditional dynastic system in 1911 ended the role of orthodox Confucianism as a ruling ideology. In the aftermath, traditional culture was blamed for allowing China to fall behind the West. Contemporary China continues to be shaped by the iconoclastic tradition born during this period. It is therefore inappropriate to identify the contemporary Chinese approach to human rights with "the Chinese tradition". The cultural revaluations and self-reflection of Chinese intellectuals have raised a new problem concerning the way in which rights discourse fits into contemporary political debates, rather than the degree of fit between rights discourse and the Chinese tradition.

In the context of professing allegiance to the ideal of progress and acknowledging the advance of the West, Chinese disagree over the traditional values they might wish to reaffirm. The quest for "national salvation" has involved several generations in a shopping spree of imported ideas as well as Western technology. Alongside support for "Mr. Science" and "Mr. Democracy", the resounding slogan of the May Fourth Movement (1919) was "Down with Confucius & Co." Some have viewed the hiatus of the Chinese tradition as a historical process analogous to the European renaissance. Chou Tse-tsung, the foremost historian of the May Fourth movement, disagrees. Instead, he insists that it marks a true hiatus -- a reevaluation of the Chinese tradition and a turn towards the West.[73] The central problem which arose at this time was how to revive China as a symbol of pride, while systematically rejecting all of its moribund traditions. This debate forms part of the problem of history and value.[74] The intellectual history of modern China is a narrative of contested authority and contested legitimacy. For a while, Communist ideology, particularly in its Leninist form, provided an answer. China could join the vanguard of history, overtaking the "moribund" capitalist West, even as it rejected its own tradition.

Scholars both inside and outside China disagree vigorously over the extent and depth of Confucianism in the contemporary Chinese political culture. Only in the process of trying to establish some value in the maintenance of a distinctive Chinese identity, pressured by the overwhelming weight of invidious comparison, do Chinese scholars turn towards the treasury of cultural tradition. To be full participants in the modernization project and not mere objects of modern utility, Chinese must reaffirm something in their own identity. At the same time, to explain why it is that China seemed for so long to fall by the wayside, it is important to critique it. Scholars therefore approach the traditional culture from these two directions, as tropes of debate and engagement. The Chinese tradition is almost always an object to be evaluated and used rather than a continuous fountainhead of values.

Unanimous acceptance of evolution and progress, and constant international comparison and attention to relative international position has not yielded a unified world view, except when in the throes of enforced ideological conformity. The ideal of progress may be adopted from two different and potentially conflicting value premises. One view is cosmopolitan, and sees progress as participation and involvement in a universal project which distributes value according to the relative contribution to this universal goal. A different approach to progress is utilitarian and particularistic. Here progress is a means or a tool to reestablish the innate glory and greatness of China. The latter approach begs the question of why the glory of China -- which in turn leads reflexively back to a definitional problem rooted in the Chinese tradition -- results in formulas such as "Socialism with Chinese Characteristics" and a concomitant search for the value premises of China's greatness. Scholars of the former type may be called modernists of a cosmopolitan universalist persuasion and scholars of the latter type may be termed nativist and utilitarian modernists. The place of human rights in the mix of universal values (which join China to the mainstream of world-historical development) depends on the kind of political claim one wishes to advance and the target audience against whom that claim is to be asserted.

Liberal ideas have been one ideological weapon with which to attack the failures of the Chinese state. However, the liberal impetus of the Chinese revolution was undermined by the need to create a new state which would be capable of protecting the Chinese culture and society from foreign invasion and occupation as well as internal turmoil. In the first half of the twentieth century, there was widespread acceptance of the notion that the central political problem was not to limit the power of the Chinese state, but to increase it.[75]

Despite the fact that China's entry into rights discourse came as a result of coercive intervention, constitutional documents dating back to the early part of this century have attempted to address human rights, and all major constitutional documents, including the four constitutions of the People's Republic of China, have had bills of rights modelled on Western norms.[76]

One peculiarity of the approach to rights in Chinese constitutional theory and practice, which could, in theory be regarded as rooted in Chinese cultural tradition, is that rights were seen as something granted by the state or society to the individual rather than as something inherent in the human personality. As Andrew J. Nathan notes:

> A tradition of rights thinking emerged in a series of texts. Its six identifying characteristics were that it derived rights from citizenship of membership in the people rather than from human personhood as such; that it permitted considerable variability in the context of rights from constitution to constitution in light of the changing needs of the state; that it treated some rights as programmatic goals rather than as immediate claims on government; that it gave the government the power to limit rights by acts of legislation; that it did not establish effective

means of independent review of the constitutionality of laws; and that it did not provide for the effective exercise of popular sovereignty.[77]

Mao Zedong and tradition

China's political leaders have been active participants in debates concerning culture. Mao Zedong, whose judgments on the traditional culture were the official orthodoxy for more than a quarter century, viewed the traditional culture in starkly invidious terms:

> There is in China an imperialist culture which is a reflection of imperialist rule, or partial rule in the political and economic field...China also has a semi-feudal culture which reflects her semi-feudal politics and economy, and whose exponents include all those who advocate the worship of Confucius, the study of the Confucian canon the old ethical code and the old ideas in opposition to the new culture and new ideas. Imperialist culture and semi-feudal culture are devoted brothers and have formed a reactionary cultural alliance against China's new culture. This kind of reactionary culture serves the imperialists and the feudal class and must be swept away. Unless it is swept away, no new culture of any kind can be built up. There is no construction without destruction, no flowing without damming and no motion without rest; the two are locked in a life and death struggle.[78]

And yet, the same article reveals unresolved tensions, and a deep ambivalence as the following quotations show:

> To nourish her own culture China needs to assimilate a great deal of foreign progressive culture, not only from present-day socialist and new democratic cultures but also from the earlier cultures of other nations. For example, the culture of the various capitalist countries in the Age of Enlightenment. However we should not gulp any of this foreign material down uncritically, but treat it as we do our food -- [first chew it, then digest it to absorb its nutrients].[79]

> A splendid old culture was created during the long period of Chinese feudal society. To study the development of this culture, to reject its feudal dross and assimilate its democratic essence is a necessary condition for developing our new national culture and increasing our

self-confidence but we should not swallow anything and everything uncritically.[80]

The ambivalence revealed here was reflected in Mao's own life. He sent Red Guards rampaging against China's cultural monuments, but was himself absorbed in reading dynastic history and classical poetry.[81] The violent dichotomies -- progressive/reactionary; national/imperialist; socialist/capitalist-- employed by Mao, exemplify the revolutionary impulse in the modern Chinese political culture. Any approach to human rights would be conditioned by such sharp juxtapositions throughout the period of Mao's rule and beyond.[82] The term "human rights" almost never appeared without the modifier "bourgeois" and, hence, to claim such rights was an automatic ideological error, if not an outright crime. As late as 1982 (the same year the current Chinese constitution was promulgated), a standard dictionary of the social sciences defined "human rights" as "a class concept" raised by the bourgeoisie in the Enlightenment "against feudalism."[83] The standard approach to human rights was one which was conditioned by ideological discourse rooted in Marxism. Confucianism was all but embalmed and placed in the museum prior to the Cultural Revolution.[84] Prior to the end of the 1980s, "culture" was never raised as a significant reason to reject human rights standards of the West.

The mobilizational regime created by Mao Zedong and the Chinese Communists, subordinated the individual to the group in a manner never seen before in Chinese history. It would be as wrong to view the Maoism of the Cultural Revolution (1966-76) as the quintessence of Chinese culture as it would be to look upon Fascism and Nazism as the exemplars of the West. During the radical totalitarian iconoclasm of the Cultural Revolution, there was direct, officially sanctioned, anti-traditionalism. This culminated in the vandalism of "smash the four olds" (old habits, old thinking, old culture, old tradition) at the outset of the Cultural Revolution (1966-76). Later on, in 1973-75 another campaign directly targeted Confucianism (the anti-Confucius, anti Lin Biao campaign). During these periods, positive expressions towards Confucianism or traditional culture became serious crimes which were severely and harshly punished, not excluding the threat of death. While this enforced conformity did not reflect the views of large numbers of intellectuals, it was, nevertheless, the outgrowth of one strong segment of iconoclastic political opinion concerning the relationship of traditional thought to the modern state. However, the fact that this period of Chinese history represents an aberration, both from Chinese culture and from Western liberalism, has since become the basis from which to propose a radical rupture with the Chinese tradition (with which some may identify) and, by contrast, to propose a partial return to the more pristine Chinese culture.[85]

Cultural self-reflection in the post-Mao period

The reaction to the frightening and tragic extremism of the Cultural Revolution opened up a space for the reassessment of traditional thought, which might now be judged relatively benign in comparison with the excesses of the immediate past.[86] Confucianism regained some respect as a martyred object of persecution in the Cultural Revolution. However, the overwhelming desire to turn towards the mainstream of world history, to return to the project of "modernization" and back out of the cul-de-sac of radical ideology, also opened up a new set of invidious comparisons between the developed West and "backward" China during the period of the "open door." It was as if to turn one's back in search of things of value left from the past might distract China from the great project of catching up and overtaking the developed West. In certain respects, the contrasting views about the origins and implications of the Cultural Revolution underline the contemporary Chinese debate over human rights and liberalism.[87] Throughout the 1980s, there was a broad-ranging movement of cultural reflection, known as *wenhua fansi.*[88]

Perhaps the best example of this is the TV series *River Elegy* (*He Shang*) which aired in China in the year prior to Tiananmen and which so angered the authorities as to force its author into exile. The program draws an explicit contrast between the silted up flow of the Yellow River representing Chinese traditional culture and the deep blue sea representing modernity, openness and the West. The Yellow River culture is explicitly tied to authoritarianism and backwardness, explicitly illustrated by the person of Mao Zedong in the guise of Emperor. The program's message is that China must dredge up its culture in order to reach the sea. Chinese dissidents reach outside of China, and implicitly continue the iconoclastic revolutionary culture to tap sources of authority to critique the Chinese state.[89] The Tiananmen demonstrators explicitly tied themselves to the iconoclastic traditions of the May Fourth Movement and its slogans of "democracy and science" in the campaign against the contemporary policies of the Chinese state. It should therefore come as no surprise that those who see themselves in conflict with the Chinese state adopt international standards. The example of liberal thinkers who have become dissidents, such as Yan Jiaqi and Fang Lizhi, is well known.[90] Fang Lizhi in particular, was explicitly accused of "wholesale westernization" for his advocacy of universal standards of democracy and freedom of speech.[91]

The vast majority of dissident critics are, for the very same reason, highly critical of the traditional culture and tend to tar the regime and the traditional culture with the same brush.[92] The "progressive" orientation of dissidents tends to look at China's lagging position with respect to individual rights as a example and consequence of Chinese "backwardness." Dissidents, such as the long-term human rights activist Ren Wanding who was arrested after the "Democracy Wall" period of 1978-79 and again in 1989, tend to blame the absence of rights on the "Chinese tradition."

> [T]he long-term goal of China's democratic movement is a peaceful transformation of the monistic political and social structure of the Communist Party, replacing it with a pluralistic socio-political structure, a pluralist structure of democracy, a pluralist culture and a pluralist ethnic structure.... The monistic socio-political structure of China is an outcome of protracted feudalism and backward productivity. It will inevitably disappear in the wake of economic development, an increase in production, and an open society.[93]

Not only do dissident liberal intellectuals tend to an anti-traditional stance, so do supporters of "neo-authoritarianism" who oppose them. The latter adopt authoritarianism as a pragmatic utilitarian tool for the rapid transformation of Chinese society, loosely basing their arguments on the experience of the "Four Dragons" of South Korea, Taiwan, Singapore and Hong Kong, as well as the ideas of the American political scientist Samuel Huntington.[94]

Those who uphold "neo-authoritarianism", such as the social scientist He Xin, do not favour it on value grounds, and do not base their arguments on the Chinese traditional culture. Instead, they see authoritarianism as a means to development. As He Xin argues, if China were to pursue the political system recommended by the United States, "China would only become a 'soft state' fragmented and lacking in national cohesion." Such a state, he argues, "would lose its last opportunity and hope to catch up to the developed countries."[95]

Barrett McCormick and David Kelly have argued that the decline of Marxism in China has weakened opposition to liberalism, and has increased the likelihood that both state elites and anti-state elites will adopt liberal discourse as a means of furthering their interests.[96] Even the most foremost exponent of "neo-Confucianism" outside China, the Harvard Professor Tu Weiming, concedes that his project to pursue a "third wave" of Confucianism involves grafting the western liberal sense of "the dignity, independence and autonomy of the person into [the Confucian] concept of selfhood as a centre of relationships and as a broadening process of self-realization."[97]

"Modernization" and human rights

Following the death of Mao Zedong, Deng Xiaoping consciously promoted a policy of international comparison in an effort to speed up China's modernization. The repudiation of the Cultural Revolution and the open door have stimulated broad-based value changes. In the first place, the effort to repudiate the Cultural Revolution and the "Gang of Four" reawakened interests in the liberal elements of the Marxist tradition and, in particular, "socialist legality" and "socialist democracy".[98] In the second place, the marketizing elements of economic reform, legitimated profits, private property, and individual interests. Legal reform increasingly looked to Western jurisprudence and legislation to accommodate political and economic change.

The near unanimous acceptance of the idea of progress means that in particular disciplines which are of utilitarian or applied practical value to the processes involved in progress -- economic growth, technological innovation, industrialization etc. -- there is unquestioning acceptance of Western models and at least rhetorical rejection of traditional influence. In these fields, the Chinese philosophical tradition may even be repressed into the subconscious and receive no conscious or explicit recognition. In recent years, law has also developed within this framework. While there are certainly "Chinese characteristics" to the practice of law in China, professional discourse within the discipline is overwhelmingly Western in orientation, and traditional references are marginal at best. The vast majority of contemporary Chinese legal scholarship investigates the inadequacies of the contemporary Chinese legal system and seeks to improve it by explicit reference to Western models. There is almost an implicit recognition of something shameful in the Chinese legal tradition, as well as a somewhat uncritical acceptance that the radical excesses of the revolutionary period, and the Cultural Revolution in particular, can somehow be attributed to the deficiencies of the Chinese legal tradition. In some ways, the Chinese tradition is a convenient whipping boy for current political and social ills which it is less risky to blame than Communist ideology or the leadership of the Communist Party.

Here is an example of this tendency to view the tradition in contrast to the West and in somewhat invidious terms:

> The humanist spirit of Chinese traditional political culture is completely different from the humanism of the contemporary West. Traditional Chinese humanist thought took the recognition of basic human nature as its starting point, ancient thinkers used morality as their standard, to distinguish qualities that is, whether human nature was good or bad.

However, regardless of whether human nature was seen as good or bad, the point of return was always about how to establish the control of the group and society over the individual. Therefore the traditional theory of human nature always emphasized obligations rather than the value of the individual. The value of the individual could only be realized in a social setting.[99]

Here, the substance of the analysis, is not different from the comments cited earlier from Hall and Ames. However, more interesting is the invidious and negative tone of the discussion.

Because the Chinese tradition exemplified by Confucianism restricted the desire of people to seek the truth, this resulted in the inability of natural science to develop for a long time, and caused social development to lack a theoretical basis; in resolving the relationship between the individual and the collectivity it did not pay attention to the individual and the value of the self; in formulating personality it emphasized a modal personality of 'superficial moral power', without stressing the stratum of human needs and for this reason right up to the modern era China never achieved a rennaissance equivalent to that of Italy, or an intellectual current equivalent to the humanism of France during the period of the bourgeois revolution. All this was determined by the inner specificities of the humanistic spirit of the traditional Chinese culture. The incompleteness of modern opposition to feudalism by the bourgeoisie has a profound ideological-cultural basis, which is because of the absence or incapacity of an important ideological weapon.[100]

There is an acute consciousness of "difference" which may be used either in a radical direction to build up "obstacles" to China's "modernization" which must be removed, or in a conservative direction, to construct "national characteristics" (*guoqing*), which limit the applicability of "Western" principles to China.[101]

The distinctions between Chinese and western cultures are sharply defined over attitudes towards what is a human being and what are human rights. This distinction does not seem to some as outstanding as [differences in social system or the status as a developing country] and some do not think it crucial to the discussion of human rights. Precisely the opposite is true.... In contrast to the Western tradition which considers the humanity of human beings entirely in the concept of human freedom, the Chinese tradition views what makes people human totally in terms of their relationships. Although freedom and "humanization" are not necessarily mutually exclusive in essence, they obviously emphasize quite contrasting things. For this reason the two types of culture and philosophical anthropologies deeply influenced history down to this very day.[102]

There is some justification for the widespread Chinese position in the 1950s up to the 1980s which saw the law of international human rights largely as a pretext of imperialism to interfere in the internal affairs of other states.[103] Given the fact that China had suffered the coercive impact of Western institutions, it is understandable why China, alongside other countries subjected to imperialist domination, would be reluctant to embrace the values of the erstwhile imperial powers. Instead of universal values, international human rights are scrutinized and accepted as a set of political claims. Reluctance to accept international (read foreign) human rights standards is asserted as a defense of Chinese state sovereignty.

> [S]overeignty had always been and still was the most basic principle of international law and the most valuable characteristic of the state. There could not be any power superior to the sovereign state. Any attempts to subvert, dilute or transform sovereignty through such devices as "world law" or "transnational law" were contrary to international law. The problem of modern states was how to maintain, not how to relinquish or diminish, sovereignty.[104]

Contemporary Chinese authorities, that is, official spokespersons for the Chinese regime, have adopted the theory of the coincidence of rights and duties adapted from the constitutional theory of the former Soviet regime, in particular the theoretical framework of the 1977 ("Brezhnev") Soviet Constitution. As Jack Donnely points out, this constitutional theory of rights can be made logically consistent and coherent:

> If the logic of rights does not render rights and duties coincident, the only way I can see to accomplish this is to treat all rights as social grants. If A (society), transfers $\underline{x}$ (e.g., jobs) to B (citizens), conditional on B accepting certain parallel or reciprocal duties (e.g., work), B's right to $\underline{x}$ would be simultaneously a duty... Such an analysis is particularly attractive because it reflects basic philosophical and ideological precepts of the Soviet system. The focus is unambiguously

social, and the state is given a prominent place, with the individual conceptualized largely in terms of his social capacity. Furthermore, the emphasis is on objective and concrete rights, which the individual enjoys only through state agency, rather than subjective, abstract or formal rights inhering in the individual per se. A full system of such rights would involve the organic unity of rights and duties, and such a system would be full of rights. Human rights, however, would be entirely absent, for these rights are not grants, either conditional or unconditional, of state or society but are inherent to all human beings.[105]

Such a schema is doubly attractive to the ideologists in Beijing. Not only can they justify a schema of rights and make the state the linchpin of the system, but also, by making rights a grant of society and the state, satisfy the general discomfort of the Chinese tradition with the isolated individual. In effect, the individual becomes the object of rights rather than the subject of rights. The subject of rights is society as a whole or the state. Such a scheme can be reconciled with the Confucian desire to substitute moral duties for interests and to subsume the satisfaction of interests in the performance of moral duties.

We need only quote one of the architects of the current Chinese constitution, the veteran Communist Peng Zhen, one of the early victims of the Cultural Revolution. Here, the Chair of the National Peoples's Congress discusses the rights granted under the Chinese constitution:

Our constitution proclaims "All power in the People's Republic of China belongs to the people." In our country the people enjoy broad democratic rights impossible under any system of man exploiting man. There is only one restriction, namely, "When citizens of the People's Republic of China exercise their rights and freedoms they must not harm the interests of the State, the society, and the collective nor infringe on the legitimate rights and freedoms of other citizens." Without this restriction, the democratic rights and basic interests of the mass of people would not be guaranteed, the individual rights of the citizen would also not be truly guaranteed.[106]

In the aftermath of Tiananmen, and China's growing participation in the international arena and in particular United Nations diplomacy, the Beijing authorities belatedly recognized in 1989 that they required a domestic body of specialists in human rights law to answer China's foreign critics. This is a significant change. The post-Tiananmen world coincided with the collapse of the old Soviet bloc and the 1993 U.N. Conference on Human Rights in Vienna. This context invited the first effective Chinese recognition to demonstrate that rights exist. Accordingly, China issued its first White Paper on human rights. The Chinese authorities once again stressed the importance of national independence as the first principle. "Without national independence, there would be no guarantee for the people's lives."[107] Nevertheless, by the early 1990s, Chinese observers were ready to concede:

> The recognition of human rights, respect for human rights, and the protection of human rights has already become a common faith of humankind. Nevertheless, based on differences in political economic or cultural background, there are major differences existing between different human rights concepts; however, after the second World War, the contemporary world has at least achieved this kind of cultural ambience: public professions of behaviour which does not recognize, does not respect and does not protect human rights no longer has any market.[108]

However, in the context of sharp exchanges over human rights, Chinese observers argued: "Some western personages raise their own human rights notions to be the common standard based on considerations of political privilege and cultural self-centeredness, and moreover use this to judge and to make demands on peoples and states with different cultural traditions and different actual circumstances who have chosen different social systems and different developmental paths."[109]

The post-Tiananmen period witnessed concerted efforts to draw distinctions between Chinese human rights standards and Western demands. These distinctions may be drawn either from ideological considerations, or, as has been more evident in the 1990s, by reference to "cultural specificity". Joining other Asian states, the Chinese claim a purported tradition that "rights" pertain to states and society as well as, or prior to, the individual.[110] However, the language of difference also continues to be ideological, as the following example shows:

> Internationally, capitalist countries are always using "human rights" spokespersons as part of their design for "peaceful evolution." They always use "human rights" spokespersons to attack the principles and standpoint of Marxism and socialism on questions of human rights, slander socialist countries for suppressing, disregarding and showing contempt for human rights, and raise their voices to proclaim that through "human rights offensives" they will force socialist countries to enter into a human rights dialogue with "the free world". They take on

the identity of the international police and saviours of "the protection of human rights" to foment, instigate and support a tiny number of liberalizing elements in the socialist countries to take part in anti-communist and anti-socialist activities, to the extent of ignoring the most basic principles of international law to interfere in the internal affairs of socialist states. This time the anti-Chinese and anti-communist "human rights" clamour raised by the western states led by the United States over the just actions of our country to pacify a violent riot is just a typical example.[111]

It is impossible to emphasize strongly enough the degree to which authority and legitimacy are contested in China. Underlining most objections to individual rights there is a concern for the fragility of the state. To a very great extent, the Chinese tradition is today even more remote than Western liberal discourse, and aspects of Marxist discourse continue to legitimate this trend.

Unanimous belief in "modernization" and progress, means on the one hand, that official spokespersons for the Chinese government insist on the significance of the "right to development" as a basic human right proclaimed by the General Assembly of the United Nations in 1979 and 1986.[112] This position tends to relativize the importance of individual rights, and also to view rights as programmatic and evolutionary rather than as absolute claims.[113]

Liberal economics and the new legalism

Given the rise of a market ideology and the impact of the open door,[114] there is a natural affinity growing between the development of the Chinese economy and the legal and ideological concepts of the liberal West. The old dichotomy of "bourgeois" and "proletarian" or "socialist" and "capitalist" has broken down.[115] Not surprisingly therefore, legal scholars can find points of contact between rights thinking and the progressive elements of Marxism, as can be seen in the following:

To regard human rights as those rights which a person should enjoy depending solely on his/her natural belonging and social essence and to deny that human rights are a gratuitous grant from any sort of external agency provides the most powerful ideological weapon of any oppressed people, any oppressed nation and all weaker members of society in order to struggle for gain and protect human rights. Interests lie at the basis of rights. The relationship between the rights and duties of people is essentially a relationship of interest.[116]

There has been a sea change in intellectual life generally. An ongoing debate on the value basis of the law, and in particular the rule of law couched in the language of ben wei ("standard" or benchmark), illustrates how far the discourse has changed.[117] Significantly, the debate over the standard of rights did not end in June 1989 and expanded to more legal journals. The debate continues in legal journals based in Beijing and Shanghai up to June of 1992, with no sign of the advocates of rights yielding any ground.

1. We require a common understanding, and could we not say this for people living in the contemporary period: an ideal legal system, or at least one worthy of respect, should cause people to equally enjoy various basic rights and be equally bound by obligations. It [the legal system] should justly protect all rightful interests. If we could come to a common understanding on this basic value, then a discussion over "the standard of rights" (quanli benwei) is possible because both sides would have common value objectives, both sides would be limited to discussion of means (modalities) and technical questions.

2. Conceptual boundaries. The standard of rights arises from this underlying belief: only by making each and every person equally enjoy sacred and inviolate basic rights (human rights) then, and only then, could a just society be built; binding obligations will become necessary if and only if these are required to guarantee and realize these equal rights. In relation to obligations, rights are the goal, they stand in the dominant position, while in relation to rights, obligations are a means.

3. Rights are the legal guarantee that the people may freely arrange their activities and exercise their interests.

4. The basic place of rights is the demonstration of multiple interests [in society][118]

In another more recent article responding to the one above, the author refers to the work of John Rawls. He sums up the position in the following language:

Put simply, the standard of rights has two major components: equal rights as the basic principle of social justice and the legislative principle that obligations (duties) are subordinate to rights. This is not just a certain recognition of the relationship of rights to duties, but is first and foremost an ideal concept of social justice.[119]

To give a sense of how far things have moved in China, the following is an excerpt from an author who disagrees with the former two and whose article is salted with quotations from Marx and Engels and reflects the prevailing official view:

> The author holds that the crux of whether contemporary China will fully realize the value objective of social order [the author's position on the question of the impetus behind law] depends on whether the state can legislate the following aspects of the allocation of rights and duties. First, by the allocation of rights and duties ensure that state power is firmly in the hands of the people (that is 99.95% of the citizens) and that the people are endowed with broad and effective powers to participate in decision making and to avoid the situation in some socialist states where mistakes by some leaders have led to nationwide chaos. Second, to carry through the principle of the unity of rights and duties so as to build a structure whereby citizens rights check state power and to guarantee citizens rights in order that state corruption may be stopped. Third, to adjust rights and duties in step with the requirements of social and economic development, in order to ensure that rights are consistent with the social value contributed by different classes and interest groups and to the greatest extent possible to alleviate social discontent, to stimulate the enthusiasm of the whole citizenry and to strengthen social solidarity and legal authority.[120]

Naturally, the point of view expressed above was opposed by those with a more traditional -- that is both Marxist and Confucian -- position arguing that "obligations" are central to law.

> The formulation that "obligations are central to law" indicates, that insofar as law is a means to organize social order, it achieves the realization of goals mainly through categories of obligation. That is to say, that after the value objective of a law has been specified, or in a class society, the will of the ruling class has been clarified, the legislature takes this as its priority and directs its attention to the duties to be specified in law as well as the negative consequences of the duties thus specified are flouted, so that it is carefully crafted to enable the law to be effective.[121]

The reference to **class will** is instructive here, yet an early participant who does not agree that rights are primary in law, curtly dismisses the relevance of Marxist discourse.

> We believe that "the will of the ruling class" is far from able to delimit the basic qualities of law, and rather that to understand the law from the perspective of the self-regulation of society is much more in accordance with objective reality.[122]

The former author, however, bases his discussion of duty on a very different conception of society than do the proponents of rights:

> The formulation that obligations are central is based on an uncomplicated understanding that society is made up of persons capable of wilful action (without consideration of any binding conditions). Society has spontaneous tendencies both to order and to disorder and the main goal of self-organization is social stability and development... Human society is a mechanism with tendencies both towards conscious control and against control. The main role of law is to stabilize a certain order in order to have society display a certain order and stability.[123]

This debate arises in the context of changes in the Chinese political economy. As the first article puts it:

> With the reforms and opening up, along with which have come the development and construction of democratic politics and a commodity economy, a situation of pluralized interests has begun to appear. Independent individual and group economic interests as well as independent political interests have become the dominant subjects of the commodity economy and democratic politics. Our legal system is faced with an inevitable choice between a system based on obligations and one based on rights. Otherwise our laws will not be able to effectively protect various legitimate interests and there will be no basis for the development of democratic politics and a commodity economy.[124]

The sentiments reflected in the above quotations are, I believe, generally representative of the trained legal community. Over the past years, the legal profession has arrived at a position which recognizes the universality of human rights and, moreover, the applicability of international conventions. While national sovereignty is still perceived as the premise of any human rights regime, it is now recognized that "sovereignty is not higher than rights".[125]

Conclusion

Rights discourse has begun to penetrate society, at least among urban intellectuals, but not simply as an ideological construct. Among articulate members of Chinese society, there is an awareness and a responsiveness to rights discourse which belies assertions that Chinese culture is hermetically sealed off. Granted, this paper has focussed mainly on the views of educated elites and intellectuals, and for reasons of methodology and subject matter has not made a systematic evaluation of public opinion.[126] We should bear in mind, however, that those outside positions of power will tend to employ the language which is most effective in pressing their claims -- language which is capable of gaining recognition and which is made available by those in power. Intellectuals and other articulate elites have a broader lexicon available, as well as a wider audience to appeal to. From this perspective also, we should be cognizant of the trends which have expanded the language of rights. The rule of law is no longer just seen as a counterpart or juxtaposition to "rule by men", it is seen as involving the exercise of rights by an engaged citizenry.

Notes

1. Barrett L. McCormick and David Kelly, "The limits of anti-liberalism," *The Journal of Asian Studies* Vol. 53 , no. 3 (August 1994) p. 804.

2. "We live in an era in which a critique of west has become not only possible, but mandatory. Where does this critique leave those ethnic peoples whose entry into culture is precisely because of the history of western imperialism, already "westernized"?... The task facing us is not the advocacy of a return to pure ethnic origins. Rather it is to articulate the specific ways in which ethnicity, as a site both of an inevitable cultural predicament and of possible formation of collective identities-in-resistance, functions." Rey Chow, *Woman in Chinese Modernity: the Politics of Reading Between East and West* (Minneapolis: University of Minnesota Press, 1991) p. xi.

3. For a comparative discussion of the cultural dimensions of the Great Revolutions of modernity, see, S.N. Eisenstadt, "The Civilizational Dimension of Politics: Some Indications for Comparative Analysis," in Dankwart A. Rustow and Kenneth Paul Erickson eds. *Comparative Political Dynamics: Global Research Perspectives* (New York: HarperCollins, 1991), pp. 54-71.

4. See Benjamin I. Schwartz, "The Primacy of the Political Order in East Asian Societies: Some Preliminary Generalizations," in Stuart R. Schram, ed., *Foundations and Limits of State Power in China* (Hong Kong: The Chinese University Press, 1987) pp. 1-10.

5. *Shu Jing, Gao Yao* [The Book of Documents] in Sebastian de Grazia, ed., *Masters of Chinese Political Thought* (New York: Viking, 1973) p. 17.

6. Examples include not only Pharaonic god-kings and the Divine Right of Kings in early modern Europe, but also the more contemporary, the tortured biblical arguments utilized by Hobbes to justify his political theory in *The Leviathan* as well as the religious dimensions of the controversy between Locke and Fillmore.

7. For a discussion of the origins and development of this term see Donald J. Munro, *The Concept of Man in Early China* (Stanford, CA: Stanford University Press, 1969), pp. 185-197.

8. Lucian W. Pye, *Asian Power and Politics: the Cultural Dimensions of Authority* (Cambridge, Mass.: The Belknap Press, 1985) pp.31-54.

9. *Shu Jing, Gao Yao*, supra, note 5, p. 12.

10. Confucius, *Analects* XII:17.

11. Confucius, *Analects* XIV:45.

12. Donald Munro argues on this basis that Chinese political philosophy is founded on the notion that human beings were naturally equal. See, *The Concept of Man in Early China*, supra, note 7.

13. Confucius, *Analects* IV, 18.

14. Confucius, *Analects* XIV, 8.

15. *Mencius* V.B9.

16. Lien-sheng Yang, "The Concept of 'Pao' as a Basis for Social Relations in China," in John F. Fairbank, ed. *Chinese Thought and Institutions* (Chicago: University of Chicago Press, 1957) pp. 291-309.

17. *Shu Jing Gao Yao*, supra, note 5.

18. *Mencius* IV.A.10.

19. *Mencius* IB.8.

20. "Duke Jing of Qi asked master Kong about government. Master Kong replied saying, Let the prince be a prince, the minister a minister, the father a father and the son a son." Confucius, *Analects* XII:11.

21. From Homer H. Dubs, tr., *The Works of Hsun Tzu*, as excerpted in De Grazia, ed., supra, note 5, p. 176.

22. Ibid.

23. Jack Donnelly, *Universal Human Rights in Theory and Practice*. (Ithaca, N.Y.: Cornell University Press, 1989) p. 10.

24. See, Ronald Dworkin, *Taking Rights Seriously* (Cambridge, MA: Harvard University Press, 1977).

25. Supra, note 23 at p. 11.

26. R. P. Peerenboom, "What's Wrong with Chinese Rights?: Toward a Theory of Rights with Chinese Characteristics," *Harvard Human Rights Journal* Vol. 6, 1993, p. 42.

27. Transliterated in Wade-Giles as jen and variously translated "humanity"; "benevolence"; "human heartedness" or "Goodness".

28. See, F.L.K. Hsu, "Psychological Homeostasis and Jen: Conceptual Tools for Advancing Psychological Anthropology," *The American Anthropologist* no. 73 (1971) 23-44; see also Michael Harris Bond and Kwang-kuo Hwang, "The Social Psychology of Chinese People, " in Michael Haris Bond, ed., *The Psychology of the Chinese People*, (New York: Oxford University Press, 1986) p. 220.

29. Ibid., p. 29, Emphasis in original.

30. Qian Mu, *Zhonghua Wenhua Shi'er Jiang*, (Taibei: DongDa Tushu Gongsi, 1985) pp. 20-21.

31. David L. Hall and Roger T. Ames, *Thinking Through Confucius* (Albany: SUNY Press, 1987) p. 23.

32. William Theodore De Bary, "Individualism and Humanism in Ming Thought" in De Bary, ed., *Self and Society in Ming Thought* (New York: Columbia University Press, 1970) p. 149.

33. See Thomas A. Metzger, *Escape From Predicament: Neo-Confucianism in China's Evolving Political Culture* (New York: Columbia University Press, 1977), p. 42.

34. Hsiao Kung-chuan, *A History of Chinese Political Thought* (Princeton: Princeton University Press, 1979) p. 103.

35. For a critique of the conception of rights as boundaries, see, Jennifer Nedelsky, "Reconceiving Autonomy: Sources, Thoughts and Possibilities," *Yale Journal of Law and Feminism* Vol. 1, no. 1 (Spring 1989), p. 7.

36. Isaiah Berlin,"Two Types of Liberty," *Concepts and Categories* (New York: Vintage, 1987).

37. William Theodore De Bary, *Learning For One's Self: Essays on the Individual in Neo-Confucian Thought* (New York: Columbia University Press, 1991) pp. 2-3.

38. For a description of humane government turn to the *Mencius*, Books I, II, and IV.

39. Roger T. Ames, *The Art of Rulership* (Honolulu: University of Hawaii Press, 1983) p. 2.

40."For Confucians man in his ordinary condition has available to him a power which the Judeo-Christian tradition reserves for God. Because man draws on the sources of moral power 'given' to him by 'heaven' man is not god. But man is godlike because he is the sole existing vehicle of that moral assertion needed to put the world right." Supra, note 33 at p. 38.

41. See William Theodore De Bary, *The Trouble With Confucianism* (Cambridge: Harvard University Press, 1992).

42. Supra, note 30, p. 27.

43. See, William Theodore De Bary, *The Liberal Tradition in China* (New York: Columbia University Press, 1983).

44. Confucius, *Analects* II:3.

45. *Thinking Through Confucius*, Supra note 31 at p. 170.

46. Ibid, at p. 172.

47. Ibid, at p. 173.

48. For the writings of Shang Yang see, J.L.L. Duyvendak, tr., *The Book of Lord Shang* (Chicago: University of Chicago Press, 1963); for Han Fei's writings see, Burton Watson, tr., *Han Fei Tzu* (New York: Columbia University Press, 1967).

49. Derk Bodde and Clarence Norris, *Law in Imperial China* (Philadelphia: University of Pennsylvania Press, 1967) p. 11.

50. Thomas B. Stephens, *Order and Discipline in China: The Shanghai Mixed Court 1911-27* (Seattle: University of Washington, 1991) pp. 4-5.

51. Benjamin Schwartz, "On Attitudes toward Law in China," in Milton Katz, *Government under Law and the Individual* (Washington, D.C., 1957) p. 31.

52. See, Ernest Barker, *Social Contract* (New York: Oxford University Press, 1962) xvi "We are generally prone to think of Locke as the exponent of the Social Contract. It would be more just to think of him as the exponent of the sovereignty of Natural Law. He put into plain English, and he dressed in an English dress of sober grey cloth, doctrines which ultimately go back to the Porch and the Stoic teachers of antiquity. There is, he taught, a Natural Law rooted and grounded in the reasonable nature of man; there are Natural Rights, existing in virtue of such law, among which the right of property, in things with which men have mixed their labour, is cardinal; and finally there is a natural system of government, under which all political power is a trust for the benefit of the people (to ensure their living by natural law, and in the enjoyment of natural rights), and the people themselves are at once the creators and

beneficiaries of that trust."

53. See Joseph Needham, *Human Laws and Laws of Nature in China and the West* (London: Oxford University Press, 1951) p. 22.

54. Supra, note 31, at p. 17.

55. Supra, note 50, p. 4.

56. Supra, note 53.

57. Ibid, at p. 22.

58. See, for example, Luo Guang, *Zhongxi falü zhexue zhi bijiao yanjiu* (A comparative study of Chinese and Western legal philosophy) (Taipei: Zhongyang wenwu gongyingshe, 1970) pp. 41-57.

59. Ibid.

60. Supra, note 31 at p. 160.

61. Even the Chinese approach to "obligations" is not exactly equivalent to its Western counterpart. As has already been seen, the Chinese approach eschews strictly defined "rules." By contrast, the legal positivist H.L.A. Hart argues, "the statement that someone has or is under an obligation does indeed imply the existence of a rule." H.L.A. Hart, *The Concept of Law* (New York: Oxford University Press, 1961) p. 83.

62. Lucian W. Pye has attempted to explain the entire drama of the events of April May and June 1989 in Beijing in terms of the values scripted by traditional culture. "Indeed the story points to a host of well-established conclusions about Chinese political culture. These include such themes as the sensitivity of authority to matters of "face," the need for authority to pretend omnipotence, the legitimacy of bewailing grievances, the urge to monopolize virtue and to claim the high ground of morality, the drive to shame others, an obsession with revenge, the inability to compromise publicly, and so on. All of which seems to come down to a basic problem in the Chinese political culture, the management of aggression." See, "Tiananmen and Chinese Political Culture: the Escalation of Confrontation from Moralizing to Revenge," *Asian Survey* Vol XXX, No. 4 (April 1990) pp. 331-347 at. 331-2.

63. For a discussion of what he calls the "moral crusade" of the Donglin faction of officials, see, Charles O. Hucker, "The Tung-lin Movement of the Late Ming Period," in John K. Fairbank, ed., *Chinese Thought and Institutions* (Chicago: University of Chicago Press, 1957), pp. 132-162.

64. James T.C. Liu, *Political Institutions in Traditional China* (New York: Wiley, 1974) p. 130

65. See Richard Solomon, *Mao's Revolution and the Chinese Political Culture* (Berkeley, CA: University of California Press, 1971).

66. Ann Kent, *Between Freedom and Subsistence: China and Human Rights* (Hong Kong: Oxford University Press, 1993) p. 31.

67. See Janet E. Ainsworth, "Interpreting Sacred Texts: Preliminary Reflections on Constitutional Discourse in China," *Hastings Law Journal* No. 43 (1992) pp. 273-300.

68. For a full discussion of this period see, Mary C. Wright *The Last Stand of Chinese Conservatism: The T'ung-chih Restoration 1862-1874* (New York: Columbia University Press, 1966).

69. The formula comes from the Chinese reformer Zhang Zhidong, who advocated "Chinese learning as the substance (or essence -- *ti*) and western learning for use (or utility -- *yong*). For a fuller discussion of the formula see Min Tu-ki, "Chinese 'Principle' and Western 'Utility': A Reassessment" in Philip A. Kuhn and Timothy Brook, eds. *National Polity and Local Power* (Cambridge, MA: Harvard Yenching Institute, 1989) pp. 52-88.

70. For a recent example of such negative views about Chinese tradition see the open letter sent by 45 leading scientist and academics and written by Xu Lianying and Lin Mu, in an accompanying letter, which focused on the UN designation of 1995 as the Year of Tolerance the authors write "China's traditional culture... is accustomed to enforcing a unified way of thinking... The lack of a spirit of tolerance is the major obstacle in achieving China's modernization." See "Chinese scholars demand freedoms" *The Globe and Mail* May 17, 1995 p. A7.

71. This is the thesis of Joseph Levenson's seminal work, *Confucian China and Its Modern Fate* (Berkeley: University of California Press, 1968).

72. See Joseph R. Levenson, *Liang Ch'i-ch'ao and the Mind of Modern China* (Berkeley: University of California Press, 1967) pp. 1-8.

73. "The assumption that the study of China's cultural heritage by modern methods resembled a feature of the European Renaissance is not even half true. The early critical study of Chinese antiquity and the classics was really an attack upon them aimed at replacing the old by new findings. "Down with Confucius and Sons" was the spirit of the times. The main current in the May Fourth Movement was never the restoration of the ancient spirit. If there was any restoration, it was a rediscovery of the real nature of antiquity as a result of the New learning from the West. The new learning of the modern world constituted a driving force of the movement, while the study of the heritage was only one of the fruits of this new learning....Chinese antiquity and classics differed in essence from those of ancient Greece. Science and democracy were not features of ancient China." Chou Tse-tsung, *The May Fourth Movement: Intellectual Revolution in Modern China* (Stanford, CA: Stanford University Press, 1967), p. 340.

74. J.R. Levenson, "'History and 'Value': the Tensions of Intellectual Choice in Modern China," in Arthur F. Wright, ed. *Studies in Chinese Thought* (Chicago: University of Chicago Press, 1953) pp. 146-194. For further discussion of Levenson's views on the problem of history and value see the foreword by Frederick E. Wakeman to Joseph R. Levenson, *Revolution and Cosmopolitanism: The Western Stage and the Chinese Stage* (Berkeley: University of California Press, 1971) pp. ix-xxix.

75. "It is hardly surprising that the Chinese bourgeoisie and part of the May Fourth intelligentsia arrived at the conclusion that it was necessary to restore government authority and that despite the fact that it meant giving up the autonomy they had acquired thanks to the economic expansion and the decline of the bureaucratic apparatus over the preceding years they worked toward that end" Tu Weiming, "Intellectual Effervescence in China" *Daedalus* Vol. 121 No. 2 (Spring 1992) p. 279.

76. For an extensive discussion of the evolution of bills of rights in Chinese constitutions, see, R. Randle Edwards, Louis Henkin and Andrew J. Nathan, *Human Rights in Contemporary China* (New York: Columbia University Press, 1986).

77. Andrew J. Nathan, "Sources of Chinese Rights Thinking" in ibid., pp. 125-126.

78. Mao Tsetung, "On New Democracy," *Selected Works II* (Peking: Foreign Languages Press, 1965) p. 369.

79. Ibid at p. 380.

80. Ibid., at p. 381.

81. Some flavour of Mao's private reading can be gleaned from photographs of his study -- all of which feature traditional volumes placed in horizontal pigeonholes rather than modern hardcover books placed spine upright. A devastating portrait of Mao's private life confirms his preference for classical reading. See, Li Zhisui, *The Private Life of Chairman Mao* (New York, Random House, 1994).

82. For example, even though the Chinese Communists and the PRC has always proclaimed the principle of popular sovereignty, "the people" too, is a dichotomous concept. The "people"is defined in relation to those defined as "the enemy". See Mao Tse-tung, "On the People's Democratic Dictatorship" *Selected Works* Vol. IV (Beijing: Foreign Languages Press, 1975) pp. 411-424.

83. "Human rights: generally refers to rights of the person and democratic rights, a class concept which has its historical developmental process. Initially, the bourgeoisie raised "human rights" in opposition to feudal privilege and clericalism....the fundamental purpose and core of the bourgeois slogan of human rights is the protection and development of the bourgeois ownership system. The proletariat does not human rights in general and on the contrary may in some circumstances also insist on the protection of fundamental human rights. For the proletariat to achieve its own human rights, and truly gain emancipation it must first destroy the system of private property and establish public property. For this reason the proletariat never makes human rights its basic program but instead subsumes its own task and slogan in the destruction of the system of private property." *Jianming Shehuikexue Cidian* [A Concise Dictionary of the Social Sciences] (Shanghai: Shanghai Cidian Chubanshe, 1982) pp. 16-17.

84. See, Joseph R. Levenson, *Confucian China and Its Modern Fate* (Berkeley: University of California Press, 1968) Vol. III *The Problem of Historical Significance* p. 114.

85. "The national effort of introspection, painful though it is, is actually one of the most helpful indicators that we have for the prospect of democratic political reform in China. As many Chinese tell me, if it were not for the cultural revolution, China's chances for democracy would not be as good as today they are. In a sense, precisely because they are so pessimistic about China, that I am relatively optimistic." Andrew J. Nathan, *China's Crisis* (New York: Columbia, 1990) p. 125.

86. One article concerning the development of the study of Confucius and Confucianism in the post-Mao period (referred to as the "period following the smashing of the Gang of Four) lamented the fact that "politics had swallowed up academic discussion" Interest had overtaken the pursuit of truth. "Once the only standard of true and false was that which was articulated by leaders, then the masses had no right to judge what was right and wrong, without the standard of right and wrong contributed by the masses, the leaders standard of right and wrong lost its value, and there was no standard of truth. Since everyone had no sense of right and wrong, academic discussion was just chaos." Long Bu "Ping Sannian lai de Kongzi Pingjia" [an evaluation of evaluations of Confucius over the past three years] *Renmin Ribao* January 29, 1980.

87. For a fascinating debate concerning the origins of the Cultural Revolution according to whether it was seen as "anarchic" or a manifestation of "traditional despotism," see, "Liang dai zhishifenzi duihualu"; Zhang Zuoyi, "He laoshimen tantan xin"; Ran Jie, "Women bu pa jianku, zhi pa pinyong" *Zhongguo Qingnian Bao* October 9, 1986; Gao Jie, "Guannian gengxin--liangdai zhishifenzi de jichu" *Zhongguo Qingnian Bao* October 29, 1986.

88. See, Leo Ou-fan Lee, "The Crisis of Culture", *China Briefing 1990* (Boulder, CO: Westview, 1990) p. 83-105; a more critical view of this movement from the perspective of the idiosyncratic dissident critic Liu Xiaobo, see, Geremie Barmé, "Confession, Redemption, and Death: Liu Xiaobo and the Protest Movement of 1989," in George Hicks ed., *The Broken Mirror: China After Tiananmen* (Harlow, Essex U.K.: Longman, 1990) pp. 52-99.

89. Andrew Nathan has exposed the fallacious argument of *River Elegy*, "its assumption that Chinese civilization today is still traditional Civilization. This ignores the very facts that make *River Elegy* and works like it possible -- the historic experience of Maoism, the ability of Chinese to draw lessons from that experience and the force of the new attitudes that *River Elegy* and works like it embody." Supra, note 85 at p. 125.

90. Both Yan and Fang, political scientist and astrophysicist respectively, began as members of the intellectual establishment. Yan Jiaqi is the former director of the Political Science Institute of the Chinese Academy of Social Sciences (CASS); Fang Lizhi was President of the China University of Science and Technology in Hefei until January 1987. For a compendium of Yan's liberal ideas, se, David Bachman and Dali L. Yang eds. *Yan Jiaqi and China's Struggle for Democracy* (Armonk, N.Y.: M.E. Sharpe, 1991); for Fang's ideas, see, "On Patriotism and Global Citizenship" xxi-xxv; Perry Link, "The Thought and Spirit of Fang Lizhi," in *Hicks*, Supra note 88 at pp. 100-114.

91. Deng Xiaoping alludes to his authorship of this epithet in "Paichu ganrao, jiandingde shixing kaifang zhengce" [Overcome the trable, resolutely carry out the policy of reform and opening up," in *Shiyizhong Sanquanhui yilai zhongyao wenxian xuandu* [Selected Readings of Important documents since the Third Plenum of the Eleventh Central Committee] (Beijing: Renmin Chubanshe 1987) p. 1193.

92. Despite this, Peter Moody believes they still betray the elitism of the traditional literati rather than modern democrats, see, Peter R. Moody Jr., "The Political Culture of Chinese Students and Intellectuals: A historical Examination," *Asian Survey* XXVIII, No. 11 (November 1988) pp. 1140-1160.

93. Ren Wanding, "On the Historical Tasks and Goal of the Fighting People's Democratic Movement," in James Tong, ed. *Death at the Gate of Heavenly Peace: the Democracy Movement in Beijing April-June 1989 (1) Chinese Law and Government* Vol. 23, No. 1. (Spring 1990) p. 38.

94. For a discussion of "neo-authoritarianism" see, Barry Sautman, "Sirens of the Strongman: Neo-Authoritarianism in Recent Chinese Political Theory," *The China Quarterly* no. 129 (March 1992) pp. 79-102.

95. "Guanyu Zhongguo de Minzhu yü Weilai" [On China's Democracy and Future] *Beijing Ribao* June 22, 1990.

96. "The Limits of Anti-Liberalism in China", supra, note 1.

97. Tu Weiming "Intellectual Effervescence in China" *Daedalus* Vol. 127, no. 2. (Spring 1992), p. 288.

98. The opening salvo in this came in a an long article on "Democracy and the Rule of Law" by a "Special Commentator" published in the *People's Daily Renmin Ribao* July 13, 1978. The article reads in part, "Our socialist society, was born out of a semi-feudal semi-colonial Old China with no democratic tradition. Feudal ideas, feudal ethics, and feudal habits are quite deep, and seep into the corners of social life. The old society has been destroyed, but the old ideology cannot be destroyed all at once. We can clearly see the feudal specter hovering over the 'Gang of Four'. Therefore to clean out the poisonous influence of the Gang of Four also means to clean out the poisonous influence of feudal autocracy."

99. Zhu Riyao, Cao Deben, Sun Xiaochun, *Zhongguo chuantong zhengzhi wenhua de xiandai sikao* [A modern consideration of the traditional Chinese political culture] (Changchun: Jilin Daxue chubanshe, 1990) p. 28.

100. Zhang Huibin, "Zhongguo Chuantong Wenhua Renwen Jingshen de tedian" [The special character of the humanistic spirit of the Traditional Chinese Culture] *Xuexi yü Tansuo* No. 52 (October 1987) pp. 57-65 p. 62.

101. For a broad-ranging survey of the political contestation in contemporary Chinese historiography see, Jonathan Unger ed., *Using the Past to Serve the Present: Historiography and Politics in Contemporary China* (Armonk, N.Y.: M.E. Sharpe, 1993).

102. Yang She, "Renquan lilun yanjiu: renquanguan he Zhongxi wenhua chuantong chayi" *Beijing Daxue Xuebao* (Zhexue Shehuikexue ban) No. 3, 1992 pp. 41-42. [Studies on Human Rights: Views on human rights and differences between Chinese and Western culture]

103. See Hungdah Chiu, "Chinese Attitudes Toward International Law of Human Rights in the Post-Mao Era.," in Victor Falkenheim, ed., *Chinese Politics From Mao to Deng* (New York; Paragon House, 1989) pp. 237-270.

104. Samuel S. Kim, *China, the United Nations and World Order* (Princeton, N.J.: Princeton University Press, 1979) p. 410.

105. Supra, note 23 at p. 56.

106. Peng Zhen, "Guanyü Shehuizhuyi jingshen wenming jianshe zhidao xixiang de jige wenti" [On some problems of the Guiding Ideology behind the building

of Socialist Spiritual Civilization] *Shiyizhong Sanquanhui yilai zhongyao wenxian xuandu* [Selected Readings of Important documents since the Third Plenum of the Eleventh Central Committee] (Beijing: Renmin Chubanshe 1987) p. 1176.

107. Information Office of the State Council "Human Rights in China" (White Paper on Human Rights) *Beijing Review* Nov. 4-10, 1991 p. 9.

108. Xu Weidong, Shen Zhengwu, Zheng Chengliang, "Lun Renquan de Yishixingtai biaozhun yü Falü biaozhun" [On Ideological and Legal Standards of Human Rights] *Zhongguo Faxue* No. 1 (1992) p. 3.

109. Ibid.

110. This was the position enunciated by the Chinese delegation to the Bangkok Conference of February 1993: "In the long process of history, the hard-working, brave and intelligent Asian people have created the splendid cultural tradition of respecting the rights of the state, society, family and individuals. This particular culture had played an important role in promoting the stability of the state and promoting the steady development of economy and society." See, Sidney Jones, "Culture Clash: Asian Activists Counter their Government's Restrictive View of Human Rights," *China Rights Forum*, Summer 1993, p. 9.

111. "Makesizhuyi Renquanguan" [The Marxist View of Human Rights] in Dong Yunhu, Liu Wuping, eds., *Shijie renquan yuefa zonglan* [A Compendium of World Human Rights Documents] (Chengdu: Sichuan Renmin Chubanshe, 1991) p. 3.

112. Ibid., p. 182; pp. 209-210. See also, "Human Rights in China", supra note 107, pp. 43-45.

113. In what is in effect an extended response to the Chinese White Paper, Ann Kent has written a wide-ranging evaluation of Chinese human rights in thought and practice. See, Ann Kent, *Between Freedom and Subsistence: China and Human Rights* (Hong Kong: Oxford University Press, 1993).

114. The former editor of the *People's Daily* and a prominent "liberal" forced out of the Chinese Communist Party argues that "Basing ourselves on the knowledge that the traditional notions are now changing as well as an analysis of the current situation we can put forward the following recognition -- the

development of the market will become the basis and the motive force for Chinese democracy." He distinguishes the traditional system where political power was bases on the direct control of one person by another, to a system where more and more people are able to pursue their own values and realize their own interests. See, Hu Jiwei, "Shichang Jingji: Shixian Zhongguo Minzhu de Jichu he Dongli," [The Market Economy: the basis and motive force of Chinese Democracy] *Ming Bao Yuekan* (June 1994) pp. 83-87.

115. During his "southern tour" of February 1992, Deng Xiaoping in effect called for a moratorium on the employment of these dichotomous concepts, with his call to end debate over whether phenomena are called "socialist" or "capitalist" (*xingze; xingshe*). See, Deng Xiaoping *Wenxuan* III.

116. Li Buyun, "Shehuizhuyi Renquan de Jiben Lilun yü Shijian," [The Basic Theory and Practice of Socialist Human Rights] *Faxue Yanjiu* No. 4 (1992) p. 3.

117. Historians may remember the brief assault by intellectuals close to the KMT in the thirties on "Chinese Culture as benwei".

118. Zheng Chengliang, "Quanli Benwei Shuo" [Talking of the basic position of rights] *Zhengzhi yü Falü* [Political Science and Law] no. 4, 1989, pp. 2-5.

119. Bei Yue "'Yiwu Zhongxin' yu 'quanlibenwei' bianxi" (Debating and analyzing the centrality of obligations and the basic place of rights) *Zhongwai Faxue* (Peking University Law Journal) no. 3, 1992, pp. 17-23.

120. Xie Pengchen, "Quanli Yiwu Silun" (Four Doctrines about rights and duties) *Faxue Yanjiu* no. 3, 1992 1-7.

121. Zhang Hengshan, "On Obligations as the Centre of Law", *Zhongguo Faxue* no. 5, 1990, pp. 29-35 at 30.

122. Zhang Hengshan, "Faxue Bujieshou 'quanli benwei'"[Jurisprudence will not accept the standard of rights] *Zhengzhi yu Falu*. 4, 1989, pp. 6-9.

123. Zhang Hengshan, supra note 121, p. 31.

124. Zheng Chengliang, supra note 118.

125. "With respect [to the relationship of human rights and sovereignty] there are three points of view: human rights are higher than sovereignty; sovereignty is higher than human rights; human rights and sovereignty are closely linked, in line with one another. With respect to any particular country, without sovereignty, there can be no human rights, and sovereignty is a precondition for human rights. However, in some countries, having sovereignty does not necessarily imply that human rights are present. Therefore, to surmise that sovereignty is higher than human rights would not be favourable to the self-conscious and diligent improvement of the human rights situation in some countries according to international conventions, social morality and public opinion. Therefore, the majority of scholars believe that the third point of view is relatively scientific." "Zhongguo Faxuehui Faxue jichulilun yanjiuhui" [The Chinese Legal Association Conference on Fundamental jurisprudential theory] *Zhongguo Faxue* No. 4, 1992, pp. 113-114.

126. Some preliminary efforts in that direction were made by Andrew Nathan and Tianjian Shi, "Cultural Requisites for Democracy in China: Findings from a Survey," *Daedalus* Vol. 122 No. 2 (Spring 1993) pp. 95-123. The findings do indeed demonstrate some significant differences between educated and less educated Chinese. Surprisingly, on a comparative basis, less educated Chinese showed relatively high expectations of equal treatment from government officials, despite the fact they also showed low awareness of the impact of government in their lives. By contrast the better educated, particularly those with tertiary education, were much more skeptical.

International Human Rights, Comparative Constitutionalism and Features of China's Constitution

GONG RENREN

The Historical Linkage Between International and Domestic Human Rights Law

Modern international law was linked to the idea of human rights from the start. As is well known, H. Grotius, the "father" of international law, was also the founder of the notion of natural law which forms the basis of human rights theory. It was Grotius who freed political philosophy from its link to theology and established a humanistic basis for the modern theory of natural law.

From the 19th century onwards, however, international law did not advance at the same speed as domestic law with respect to individual human rights protection, and a gap opened between the two. This was due, on the one hand, to the expansion of imperialism and European colonialism and, on the other hand, to the rise of dualism and positivism in the jurisprudence of international law.

By the end of World War II, the atrocities of fascist countries had shocked the conscience of all of humanity, which resulted in a revival of natural law thinking in the fields of philosophy and legal theory. This led to a close linkage between international law and domestic human rights law.[1]

Although not everyone today embraces the "state of nature" hypothesis as the supra-experiential basis for the notion of human rights, most legal scholars in both the international and the domestic law fields, as well as philosophers and theorists, agree at least theoretically and morally that each individual is entitled to certain basic rights.

The Metamorphosis of Human Rights in Modern Times: New Privileges in the Name of "Human Rights"

The end of the 18th century was a flourishing period with respect to human rights thinking. The United States *Declaration of Independence* of 1776, the French *Declaration of the Rights of Man and the Citizen* of 1789, and the United States Constitution's Amendments (the *Bill of Rights*) of 1789, have been regarded as the most important human rights declarations in modern history.

Although these documents stated that "everyone is born equal", history, at least prior to World War II, reveals a merciless truth: the human rights proclaimed in these documents were not available to every human being. It reveals a history of privileges for the minority and a lack of rights for the majority of the people.

The privileges of males

Both the United States *Declaration of Independence* and the French *Declaration of the Rights of Man* use language which clearly excludes females (referring to "man" or "homme" or "citoyen"). The human rights they provide are in fact male privileges. In the 1791 French Constitution, the masculinization of rights became even stronger. That was why Ms. Olympe de Gouges published her *Declaration of the Rights of Women and Female Citizens* in 1791.

The privileges of the wealthy

For a long period of time, most capitalist countries used property ownership and indirect elections to limit the civil rights (political participation) of the poor, and to protect the interests of the propertied class. Furthermore, in the period of liberal capitalism, the focus of constitutional protection was on property rights, freedom of contract, and freedom of economic activity, leaving the working class in a tragic socio-economic position.

The privileges of a minority of whites

Because of the system of slavery, the Constitution of the United States did not include a clear provision on the principle of equality. Although the Constitution did not openly employ the term "slave", it nevertheless acknowledged the legitimacy of the system (Article 1, Chapter 9 and Article 4, Chapter 2). The 1857 *Dred Scott* v. *Sandford* decision of the Supreme Court of the United States gave further constitutional protection to the system of slavery.[2]

As early as 1835, the French thinker, Tocqueville, contended that the abolition of slavery and the establishment of equality under the law would only increase racial discrimination and daily inequalities against the Blacks because the decision to abolish slavery was founded on the interests of whites, not Blacks.[3]

Unfortunately, history proved Tocqueville correct. After the Civil War, although the system of slavery was abolished by the 13th constitutional amendment, America's Blacks were still faced with a long future of discrimination and segregation. In the 1896 case of *Plessey* v. *Ferguson*[4], the Supreme Court affirmed the principle of "separate but equal" by maintaining that, as long as the provision of public facilities was equal, the system of racial segregation did not violate the law. Thus, constitutional protection was provided for the system of racial segregation.

The status of American Indians

In the years from 1778 to 1868, the American federal government and the Indians concluded 367 treaties[5], which forced the Indians to yield tens of millions of acres of land and move to the barren lands west of the Mississippi River. In fact, the American federal government was simultaneously employing the tactics of assimilating and exterminating the Indians.

The Chinese Exclusion Acts

In 1882, the United States Congress passed the first *Chinese Exclusion Act* which prohibited both skilled and unskilled Chinese workers from entering the United States for a period of ten years, and which also prohibited Chinese who were already living in the United States from applying for naturalization. In 1888, the United States Congress passed an additional provision to the *Exclusion Act* which prohibited Chinese people from re-entering the United States, even if they had just left the country temporarily. In 1892, the *Chinese Exclusion Act* was extended for another ten years, and in 1904, all Chinese Exclusion Acts were extended indefinitely and applied universally to all American islands.[6]

The privileges of colonialism

In fact, the privilege of colonialism is the extension and expansion of the above mentioned race-based privileges of white men beyond the borders of their own countries. This was mainly reflected by the various privileges that the European colonialists had obtained by infringing upon the human rights of the local people in Asian and African regions. For example, the British used the Opium War to turn China into a semi-colonial country. Other western countries took advantage of the occasion to conclude many unequal treaties with the Chinese Qing government. By these treaties, Western countries established the system of consular jurisdiction and foreign concessions, a system which violated the local judicial powers and infringed upon the rights of the Chinese people.

If human rights mean inherent rights that every human being, regardless of sex, race, property and religious belief, should enjoy, there were no real human rights in the major western countries prior to World War II, only privileges--the privileges of rich white men. Therefore, Swiss scholar Senger suggests referring to the human rights of this era as "European rights".[7]

The Historical Patterns of Human Rights Protection in International Law

Until World War II, human rights protection was seen exclusively as a matter of domestic law. However, there were some exceptions, treaties or practices in the international sphere which touched upon the protection of human rights.[8]

Protection of minorities

Protection of minorities refers to the protection by treaty of racial, linguistic or religious minorities within the borders of a state. All such early treaties had a common shortcoming, that is, the lack of a supervisory organ that could determine whether a treaty had in fact been violated or not. If a violation of treaty-protected minority rights occurred, international society relied mainly on the following two measures of action: First, if the minorities whose rights had been violated were citizens of a foreign state, that state could exercise diplomatic protection. This kind of diplomatic protection, however, has always been regarded as a right of the affected state.[9] Second, if the affected minorities were citizens of the state that violated their rights, other states might intervene citing humanitarian grounds. In practice, this usually meant unilateral intervention by European and American powers in pursuit of some other interest of theirs, and there was hardly ever a case of true humanitarian intervention.[10]

The establishment of the League of Nations after World War I created the possibility that minority rights would be protected by an international organization. In addition, a series of treaties was established to protect minority groups in Eastern and Central Europe in order to prevent a recurrence of local tensions and conflicts involving different minorities.

Even though the *League of Nations Covenant* did not include any specific provisions on the protection of minorities, in practice the League of Nations system gave rise to a set of programmes and procedures, such as the creation of a petitioning system and the establishment of a minorities commission in the League Council. Generally speaking, however, the League of Nations' performance in the field of minority rights protection was a failure. A major reason for this failure was a lack of universality of the system to protect minorities. In other words, the duty to protect minorities had not yet become a universal duty of all states, but was limited to a minority of states.[11]

Prohibition of slave traffic

In modern history, the large scale, international slave trade was mainly comprised of slaves from Africa. Slave mongers from Portugal, Spain, England, Holland, France, the United States and other countries, were all engaged in the African slave trade. Over the course of four hundred years, tens of millions of persons were traded, and more than 70 million Africans died in the slave trade.[12]

In the 19th century, pressure from the anti-slavery movement and the unfolding of the capitalist revolution led some countries to abolish the slave system. In some western countries, however, the objective for abolishing the slave system was not based entirely upon humanitarian considerations. Rather, the industrial revolution made slavery out-of-date as the advancement of technology needed overseas markets, not cheap labour. At this point, colonial exploitation and domination was an even more profitable and "legitimate" kind of exchange.

Before World War I, a series of treaties prohibiting the slave trade were concluded. Among the most important treaties were: the 1815 *Vienna Declaration*, the 1841 *London Treaty*, and the 1885 *Berlin General Act*. All of these treaties, however, were confined by historical circumstances. First of all, these treaties only prohibited the slave trade, but not the slave system, as such. Second, they did not offer a clear definition of slave trade or slavery, and they lacked effective supervisory mechanisms.

On September 25, 1926, the *International Treaty on the Prohibition of Slavery* was signed under the direction of the League of Nations. This treaty offered, for the first time, a clear definition of slavery as well as specific practical measures to prevent, and eventually eliminate, the trade in slaves. Yet, there were no provisions for enforcement and implementation of the treaty.

The International Labour Organization and human rights protection

The establishment of the International Labour Organization (ILO) after World War I was the combined result of the various forms of labour movements and struggles, the efforts by certain capitalist countries to maintain social order, and economic competition and compromise between the major capitalist countries.

Before World War II, the ILO adopted 67 conventions which dealt with various labour rights, such as labour conditions, protection of women workers,

prohibition of child labour, etc. But very few conventions offered protection of
workers' basic rights.

The Internationalization and Universalization of Human Rights

The reasons for including human rights in the field of international law

Although prior to World War II, there were some treaties and systems which
touched upon human rights issues, these were rather limited in scope and content
and were often closely linked to the political powers of some of the major
countries. As Professor L. Henkin said, although the end result was
humanitarian, the motivation for concluding these treaties was political, not
humanitarian.[13]

During World War II, the barbaric human rights violations and the ruthless
expansionism of the fascist and militarist regimes, especially Nazi Germany's
extermination of the Jews, not only outraged the world community but also
proved that, if there is a close link between a government's barbarous treatment
of its citizens and its aggression against other states, there is, likewise, a close
link between respect for human rights and preservation of world peace. The
world community's deep reflections on the experiences of World War II led to
universal international concern for human rights issues.

The *United Nations Charter* and human rights

The current *United Nations Charter* provisions on human rights emerged out
of a process of development and change. In the original draft, there was only one
reference, at Chapter IX Sec.(A)(1), to the organization's task of "promoting
respect for human rights and fundamental freedoms".[14] The principle of respect
for human rights had not yet been elevated to its current status as one of the
guiding principles of the United Nations organization, and there was no
provision for a human rights commission under the Economic and Social
Council. Clearly, at that time, some of the major states took a fairly passive
attitude with regard to placing promotion of human rights prominently in the
Charter.

Due to pressure from various states and some civil organizations from the
United States, the San Francisco version of the *Charter* preamble was enriched
with references to human rights in articles 1, 13, 55, 56, 62, 68 and 76.

However, the provisions were abstract, there were no clear definitions of the concept of human rights and no concrete provisions for the protection of human rights.

Although international legal scholars from different countries hold different views on the legal force of the *Charter's* human rights provisions, four widely recognized principles have taken shape, as pointed out by the former Judge of the ICJ and the British scholars Jennings and Watts.[15] These four principles are: (1) In certain circumstances, the domestic human rights practices of a state are no longer purely the concern of that state; (2) a state's obligation to respect human rights applies not only to its treatment of aliens, but also to the treatment of its own citizens; (3) although some concrete aspects are still being disputed, several human rights obligations of states have become part of international customary law; (4) human rights obligations could become the obligations of all states.

The formation of international human rights law

The *Universal Declaration of Human Rights* adopted by the United Nations General Assembly in 1948, does not have the legal force of a treaty, but as "a common standard to be striven for by all peoples and states", it became the basis for later international human rights documents emerging from the United Nations system.

The two 1966 international conventions on human rights, that is, the *International Covenant on Economic, Social and Cultural Rights* and the *International Covenant on Civil and Political Rights* and the *Optional Protocol* of the latter covenant were of epochal significance in marking the first formation of international human rights law, constituting, along with the *Universal Declaration of Human Rights*, the *International Bill of Rights*.

So far, the United Nations system alone has adopted over 70 human rights documents, including declarations, suggestions, treaties, and decisions, of which over 20 are treaties touching on various aspects of human rights.

A broad and multi-level implementation system of international human rights has taken shape. In the United Nations system alone there are over 40 human rights mechanisms. In 1993, at the 48th session of the General Assembly, a high commission for human rights was established. Other implementation systems include the reporting and investigation system, the system for dealing with communications that come from within states, the individual complaints system by which a complaint can be made under an optional clause of a treaty, the United Nations "1503 procedure", and so on.

There are also some regional human rights mechanisms, such as the *European Convention for the Protection of Human Rights and Fundamental*

Freedoms, the *Americas Convention on Human Rights*, and the *African Charter on Human and People's Rights*. So far, only Asia has not institutionalized a regional human rights protection system. This is due to major differences in political, economic and social systems among states in the region. Yet, the *Bangkok Declaration* of 1993 acknowledged the need to explore the possibility of establishing a regional Asian human rights protection scheme.

In addition, some non-governmental organizations (NGOs), like Amnesty International, the International League for Human Rights, and the International Commission of Jurists, have played an active role.

The features of international human rights are: (1) making the basic worth and dignity of human beings the basis for respecting human rights; (2) prohibiting discrimination and protecting the weak; (3) defining human rights in a multi-level, multi-dimensional way that includes not only political and civil rights but also social, economic and cultural rights, and not only individual but also collective or group rights.

Human rights and constitutionalism

Constitutionalism originated in the West. The American scholar Carl J. Friedrich pointed out that constitutionalism has three ideological roots: liberalism, rationalism, and individualism.[16] In the early days, narrow constitutionalism involved only the limitations and separation of government power. Thus, a form of government could be constitutional without being democratic, or democratic and not constitutional. Similarly, a constitutional system could be a monarchy or a republic. However, the constitutionalism that we are speaking of here is modern constitutionalism in the broad sense. This includes power, popular sovereignty, separation and the balance of powers, protection for individual human rights, and the principle of the rule of law.

The implications of constitutionalism have developed since World War II. Today, protection of human rights should be the foremost goal of modern constitutionalism, and other principles of constitutionalism should serve this goal. For example, the purpose of limiting state power is, first of all, to protect the individual from being violated at will by the state; the purpose of the separation of powers is to protect people's right to political freedom and to oppose dictatorship; the purpose of the rule of law is, likewise, to protect human rights through the constitution and the laws. Thus, the core function of modern constitutionalism is to pursue the goal of individual human rights protection by the method of political rule. This core function of constitutionalism ,in the broad sense, could also be termed "constitutional democracy", or "human rights constitutionalism".[17]

Constitutionalism is no longer limited to the West. It has taken on a certain international and universal significance. For example, Paragraph 9 of the preface of the *Vienna Declaration and Program of Action* adopted June 25, 1993, declares:

> We take into consideration the major changes which are taking place on the international stage and the hopes of all peoples for international order; the United Nations Charter principles, including promoting and encouraging respect for all persons' human rights and basic freedoms and respect for the principles of equal rights and self-determination of peoples; and the need to base ourselves in peace, democracy, justice, equality, rule of law, pluralism, development, higher living standards, and unity.[18]

The evolution of human rights protection in post-war constitutions

Since the end of World War II, protection of human rights has become an important part of post-war constitutions which share the following features:

a. Universal recognition of human rights;
b. Widespread acknowledgment of economic and social rights;
c. Widespread establishment of system of judicial review;
d. Evolution of some new human rights concepts such as the right to respect, the right to personal dignity, the right to freely move one's place of residence, environmental rights, the right to privacy, the right to information, the right to access, the right to demand compensation from the state. In criminal procedure, the trend has been towards even more comprehensive rights (such as fair trials, protection of the indigents' right to a defense, prohibition of torture, etc.). Federal German Basic Law provides the right of conscientious objection;
e. Constitutions that undertake to respect international law recognize international law as part of domestic law. Some constitutions even provide that the state may make necessary limitations or concessions of sovereignty for purposes of peaceful cooperation. In some constitutions, the state gives up the right to use war to resolve international conflicts or promises not to engage in wars of aggression.

Negative Factors Impeding the Protection of Human Rights in International Society

The influence of the east-west Cold War

The Cold War manifested itself mainly in the arms race between the United States and the Soviet Union. The two countries spent much money engaging in an arms race which sacrificed the economic interests and welfare of the two countries' peoples. The arms race contributed to the collapse of the Soviet system, and also led to mounting deficits in the United States.

Another consequence of the Cold War was that countries in both the East and the West violated their own people's human rights. Take for example the United States and China:

United States society is afflicted by the "fear-of-communism and anti-communism syndrome". Thus, from Loyalty Oaths to MacCarthyism, the basic spirit of the *Declaration of Independence*, the freedoms of speech and belief provided by the Constitution's Amendments, and the democratic system in the United States were badly ravaged. Essentially, MacCarthyism was a kind of United States style fascism.

In addition, during the Cold War, the Supreme Court of the United States, in carrying forward the legacy of the *Chinese Exclusion Acts*[19], ruled that on immigration issues the legislative and executive branches could, in an anti-communist spirit, do whatever they wished to foreign immigrants. This was in contravention of international law and of due process in domestic law relating to criminal procedure.

In the United States society, it was better to be "right" than "left". The opposite was true for Chinese society where, for a long time, it has been better to be "left" than "right". For various reasons, after the establishment of the People's Republic of China, the Chinese Communist Party continuously increased the pressure of the anti-capitalist "class struggle" by conducting several "political movements". This culminated in the "Cultural Revolution" which did unprecedented damage to the Chinese people's human rights. Such human rights violations have been called Chinese-style fascism or "feudal fascism".[20]

Politicization of international human rights

The politicization of international human rights was, in some sense, a reflection of some countries' foreign policies during the Cold War. The phenomenon had a negative influence on the development of post-war international human rights. Professor O. Schachter states: "The general impression is that governments by and large react to such infringements of rights largely on the basis of political rather than legal considerations."[21]

The politicization of human rights is demonstrated by the use of a double standard. For example, the standards that the U.S. government has used to evaluate itself are different standards from those they have used to evaluate other countries in order to achieve its anti-communist purposes. As Professor L. Henkin states:

> To the world, the United States has not been a pillar of human rights, but a "fly buttress" -- supporting from the outside. For the United States, it has been charged, human rights have been a kind of "white man's burden"; international human rights have been "for export only". Congress has invoked international human rights standards only as a basis for sanctions against other countries. President Carter invoked human rights agreements in criticism of others. In a word, it is charged, Americans have not accepted international human rights for themselves, only for others.[22]

In the main organs of the United Nations, one also sees many countries using double standards to serve various interests. For example, the developing countries criticized Israel and South Africa but had nothing to say about Uganda under the Amin dictatorship or the Central African Empire under the Bokassa dictatorship. A minority of developed countries like England and the United States were unwilling to impose sanctions on the South African apartheid regime because of their own economic and military interests.[23]

Limitations of International Human Rights Law

Limitations of international treaties

At present, international human rights, especially individual rights, are mainly expressed in treaties and agreements. Treaties are binding only upon countries party to the treaties. Few countries recognize international treaties as having priority over their own constitutions. On the contrary, many countries consider domestic law to be equal to or to have priority over treaties.[24]

Definition of international customary law

In international human rights law there is no unified standard as to which parts belong under international customary law, the latter of which is generally binding upon all states.

The human rights content of international customary law, as referred to by international authoritative organs like the International Court of Justice, is mostly linked to collective rights, such as the prohibition of genocide[25], prohibition of slavery, prohibition of apartheid and racial discrimination.[26] This reveals one special feature of international human rights law.

The articles of the draft *Code of Crimes Against the Peace and Security of Mankind*, drafted by the International Law Commission of the United Nations, provide, in the second section, a definition of "Crimes Against Peace and Security of Mankind." This category of crimes include colonial rule in violation of people's right to self-determination, genocide, apartheid, and planned and large-scale violations of human rights.[27]

International legal scholars tend to expand the content of international human rights customary law, but sometimes this is rather idealistic. Section 702 of the third *Restatement of the Law* of the Foreign Relations Law of the United States listed such elements of customary law as: (a) genocide; (b) slavery or slave trade; (c) murder or causing the disappearance of individuals; (d) torture or other cruel, inhuman or degrading treatment or punishment; (e) prolonged arbitrary detention; (f) systemic racial discrimination; and (g) consistent pattern of gross violations of internationally recognized human rights.[28]

Professor T. Meron adds other customary norms, such as self-determination, humane treatment of detainees, and legitimate legal procedures in criminal cases.[29] However, Professor O. Schachter raises the question of whether some of these actually belong to customary law.[30]

Limitations of international customary law

Although in theory, customary law should have priority over the laws of each state[31], in reality many states lack specific regulations on the effect of customary law upon domestic law. For example, the United States Supreme Court has placed international customary law at the same level as treaties and federal law. In the United States adjudication experience, a subsequent federal law will have priority even over an international treaty and international customary law.[32] In addition, international law accepts that a state that has objected to a rule of customary law from the beginning is not bound by that rule.[33]

From this we can conclude that in an international society composed of sovereign states, international human rights law remains at an immature stage. Its ethical and idealistic authority is greater than its purely legal authority.

The Chinese Constitution and Human Rights Issues in International Society

Understanding two key factors in modern chinese politics

The historical legacies of China's system of feudal Autocracy

China is different from Western European societies. The latter not only had ancient democracy but also a medieval dualistic structure of church and secular rule[34]. China, from the Qin Dynasty of 221 B.C. to 1911, was a centralized, monolithic, monarchical despotism. Unlike the pre-modern European monarchies, the Chinese monarchical system had no transitional character.

After the establishment of the Chinese system of centralized monarchical despotism, the central concept of Chinese political thought was to maintain the supreme position of the emperor. The cruelty and persistence of the authoritarian strain in Chinese thought and culture has been illustrated from Qin Shi Huang's "burn the books and bury the scholars" to Han Wu Di's "abolish the hundred schools and establish Confucianism" to the "Prison of Letters" of the Ming and Qing dynasties.

The fact that the Chinese feudal-autocratic society never developed the legal concepts of equality and rights is also different from the European experience. In Europe, the mutual rights and duties of lord and vassal were primarily established by contract. The movement "from status to contract" as identified by Maine, occurred relatively early.[35] At the same time, because of the legacy of ancient Roman Law and the development of contract, the concept of rights in private law was relatively clear. With the subsequent development of public law, and the Renaissance, Reformation, and Enlightenment, the traditional rights concept became linked with humanism to form the basic theory of human rights.

In China, however, the pre-Qin feudal (enfeoffment) system was established on the basis of a patriarchal clan law relationship. After Qin Shi Huang unified China and abolished the fief system, he established a system of central totalitarianism, monarchical despotism, and agricultural bureaucracy. Thus, there was no Maineian transition from status to contract in ancient or modern Chinese society. From the Han Dynasty on, it was chiefly Confucianism, a philosophy which justified the clan (or lineage) system, which was established as the official ideology.[36] Such a philosophy, rooted in the clan system and patriarchal law, became the theoretical basis of Chinese law. The resulting social structure and ideology stressed obedience, harmony, collectivism, and order. The character for "state" in Chinese combines the elements for "country" plus "family", thus the monarch was the highest family patriarch. The most important social relationships were the "three bonds and five constants" (kin and kin-like loyalties).

The concept of "right" in the Western countries refers to a morally just or lawful claim. However, in Chinese history, the term used to translate "right" means power and property.[37] Hence, as a Chinese scholar said, although ancient China had highly developed humanistic notions, the concept of human rights never appeared, largely because of the lack of a legal concept of rights.[38]

The deep influence of the soviet model

People easily overlook the Soviet influence on China's modern political history. In fact, the Soviet influence is no less significant than that of the feudal past.

The formation of the Soviet model underwent a distinct process. During Lenin's time, internal unification of the Communist Party of the Soviet Union, strict discipline, and a one-party leadership over the state had taken shape. After his death, Stalin assimilated Lenin's ideas about the leadership of the Party and of a centralized system and discipline, but abandoned the democratic elements of Leninism along with Lenin's idea of setting up supervisory mechanisms. He then took the centralist strain of Leninism to the extreme in the form of a one-man centralized leadership.

The 1936 Soviet Constitution acknowledges the principle of Party leadership. According to article 126, the Communist Party of the Soviet Union was regarded as the core leadership of all social groups and state organs. The Japanese constitutional scholar, Professor Sugihara, stated, "This provision violates constitutionalism by placing the Party above the constitution such that, in case of conflict, the constitution would bow to the party leadership. Also, it violates the principle of popular sovereignty under which the power-holders should be selected and supervised by the people. If the Communist Party of the Soviet Union can rule without going through such a procedure, then popular sovereignty becomes Party sovereignty. This could lead to the formation of an anti-people bureaucratic state and society, and to the easy misuse of power."[39]

Marxism, as it was transmitted to the first generation of Chinese communist leaders, came almost exclusively from Russia. The Soviet-led Comintern played an important role in convening the First Party Congress which established the

Chinese Communist Party in 1921. This Congress resolved that the Chinese Communist Party should accept the leadership of the Comintern, and become a branch of it.[40]

After 1935, the Chinese Communist Party under Mao Zedong's leadership changed its early tradition of blind worship of the Comintern and placed more emphasis upon the special features of the Chinese revolution and the independence of the Chinese Communist Party. When the Chinese Communist Party came to power in 1949, however, it still adopted the "lean to one side" policy, and basically implemented the Soviet model. Historically, a major external reason for the Chinese Communist Party's adoption of this policy was the United States' support of Chiang Kai-shek in the 1940s.[41]

After the establishment of the People's Republic of China, the country essentially followed the Soviet model except for certain special policies. In particular, China followed the Stalinist intra-party system and the state system set down in the 1936 Soviet Constitution. Key points were: Party-led political structure; a constitutional structure with a Soviet-type National People's Congress as the highest organ of state power; a highly centralized, centrally planned economy; and a political-legal system in which the police, procuratorates and courts were combined three-in-one. China had a lengthy Stalinist-style experience of the Party replacing the state, total concentration of power in an individual, and the cult of the individual.

To summarize, feudal despotism and the Soviet Stalinist leadership model both played important roles in modern Chinese politics. In the 1981 "Resolution on Some Questions in Our Party's History", the Party Central Committee summarized the lessons of the Cultural Revolution and its social causes as follows:

China is a country with a long feudal history...... Several historical factors caused us to be unable to systematize and legalize democracy in our Party's internal functions and in the political and social life of the state; even when certain laws were established, they lacked the appropriate authority. This created the conditions under which the Party's power was excessively concentrated in an individual, and intra-party individual despotism and the cult of the individual flourished, so that the Party and the state were unable to prevent or control the outbreak and development of the Cultural Revolution.[42]

Human rights processes and issues in China

Since the establishment of the People's Republic of China, four constitutions have been written one after another.

The 1954 Constitution established a fairly broad scope of citizens' rights and duties. There were 14 articles on rights alone.

The 1975 Constitution was a product of the Cultural Revolution. A striking feature of this Constitution was that it greatly reduced the number of items pertaining to citizens' rights to only three articles. In contrast to the custom in most constitutions, the 1975 Constitution listed citizens' duties before citizens' rights. The provision of the 1954 Constitution stating that everyone was equal before the law was abolished. As Professor Nathan pointed out, this was the first constitution since the end of the Qing Dynasty not to include this provision.[43]

The 1978 Constitution was adopted after the end of the Cultural Revolution. In part, it restored the normal state of affairs. It also showed the residual influence of the Cultural Revolution, as it failed to restore the provision of equality before the law, of the citizens' right to petition state organs for compensation, and the provision for secrecy of correspondence.

The 1982 Constitution, which is currently in effect, was better than the several previous constitutions in regard to both form and content of citizens' basic rights. With respect to form, the 1982 Constitution placed the section on citizens' rights and duties in the second chapter, before state organs, thereby reversing the order of the previous three constitutions. The number of articles on citizens' rights was increased to 18. New items were added, such as Article 38 (protection of citizens' right to dignity and to protection against insult, slander and libel), and article 41 (citizens' right to criticize or make suggestions to any state organ or employee). Such norms are doubtless the product of reflection upon the experience of past political movements and, especially, the invasion of rights during the Cultural Revolution. The 1982 Constitution also restored some rights that were present in the 1954 text but had been left out of the subsequent two constitutions, such as the right to equality before the law (Article 33), the right to compensation from state organs or personnel if they have violated a citizen's rights (Article 41), and the right to secrecy of correspondence (Article 40). At the same time, the 1982 Constitution abolished the right to strike, which had been included in the previous two constitutions, and affirmed the amendment that had been passed in 1980 which abolished the right to "speak out freely, air views fully, hold great debates and write big-character posters".

Objectively speaking, after the end of the Cultural Revolution, especially after the implementation of the reform and open door policies, the Chinese human rights situation underwent many improvements. The constitutional provisions are not only better than those of the past, but the National People's Congress also adopted a series of laws in recent years to protect citizens' rights, such as the *State Compensation Law*, the *Labour Law*, the *Administrative Litigation Law*, the *Law to Protect the Disabled*, the *Law to Protect Women's Rights and Interests*, and the *Law to Protect Minors*. Furthermore, the *Law on Education*, the *Law on Associations*, the *Law on Information*, the *Social Security Law* and others are currently being finalized. This is undoubtedly a historical advance compared to the past few decades when there were no laws to rely on or the laws that existed were without substance.

However, there are still gaps between international human rights law and Chinese law and practice. For example, the Chinese Constitution does not provide for the following important rights and freedoms listed in the *Universal Declaration of Human Rights*: the right to life, the right to be free from torture or other inhuman treatment or punishment, the right to a fair and open trial, the right to non-interference with private life, the presumption of innocence, the right to free movement of place or residence, and the right to freedom of thought and conscience. Nor has the Chinese Constitution accepted the natural rights concept that "persons are born equal", as expressed in the *Universal Declaration of Human Rights*. China remains the only large country that has not acceded to either of the two important 1966 international covenants on human rights.

In addition, China lacks a system of judicial review, which means that it is difficult to enforce the rights provided in the Constitution directly against legislative and administrative organs. In China, human rights cannot be used in opposition to the legislature. Gaps in Chinese human rights legislation are large, such as the lack of a news law, a publications law, a law of associations, a law on education, a supervision law, and a civil law of appeal. In reality, situations still occur where the Party supersedes the government, the word (of a person in authority) supersedes the law, power trumps law, and even where persons bend the law for private reasons.[44]

In conclusion, respect for human rights has already entered the common consciousness of the international community. However, realizing the protection of human rights is a long and arduous historical process which, in the end, depends on the protection offered by the constitutional system of each nation. In its project of realizing the "high goal of enabling people to enjoy the fullest human rights", China still needs to study in depth and widely absorb the experiences and lessons of other countries' constitutional systems.

This paper was first presented to a seminar on "China and Constitutionalism" at the Law School of Columbia University in April of 1995. This english version of the paper is based on the summary translation by Professor Andrew J. Nathan.

Notes

1. H. Lauterpacht, *International Law and Human Rights*, Garland Publishing, Inc., New York & London, 1973, pp. 112-114.

2. 60 U.S. (19 How) 393.

3. D'Alexis de Tocqueville, *De La Démocratie en Amérique*, (1835), Chinese Translation (1988), Commercial Affairs Press, Beijing, p. 401.

4. 163 U.S. 537.

5. F. P. Prucha, *American Indian Treaties: The History of a Political Anomaly*, University of California Press, Berkeley, 1994; Deng Shusheng, *The United States and Immigrants*, Chong Qing Press, Chong Qing, 1990, p. 76.

6. Chen Hansheng, *The Collection of Materials of Chinese Workers Abroad*, Vol. 7, China Shu Ju Press, Beijing, 1984, pp. 5-7.

7. H. von Senger, "From the limited concept of human rights to the universal concept of human rights", *The New Tendency of Comparative Law*, edited by Shen Zhongling and Wang Chenguang, Peking University Press, Beijing, 1993, p. 140, p. 150.

8. Gong Renren, "The Historical Patterns of Protection of Human Rights in Traditional International Law", *1990 Yearbook of Chinese International Law*, pp. 225-246.

9. E. B. Borchard, *The Diplomatic Protection of Citizens Abroad*, The Banks Law Publishing Co., New York, 1916, p. 357.

10. I. Brownlie, *International Law and the Use of Force by States*, Oxford University Press, Oxford, 1963, p. 340.

11. Gong Renren, "International Law and Protection of Human Rights Between the Two World Wars", *Peking University Law Review*, 1992, No. 1, p.55.

12. J. Walvin: *Slavery and Slave Trade: A Short Illustrated History*, London: Macmillan, 1983, p. 40.

13. L. Henkin, ed., *The International Bill of Rights*, Columbia University Press, New York, 1981, p. 4.

14. *U.N.C.I.O. Docs*, 1945, Vol. 3, p. 19.

15. *Oppenheim's International Law*, Ninth Edition, Vol. 1, edited by Robert Jennings and Arthur Watts, Longman Group UK Limited, 1992, p. 1000.

16. C. J. Friedrich, *Constitutional Government and Democracy*, Blaisdell Publishing Co., 1967, pp. 6-7.

17. L. W. Beer, ed., *Constitutional Systems in Late Twentieth Century Asia*, University of Washington Press, Seattle and London, 1992, p. 8.

18. U.N. Doc., A/CONF.157/23, p. 3.

19. L. Henkin, "The Constitution and United States Sovereignty: A Century of Chinese Exclusion and Its Progeny", *Harvard Law Review*, Vol. 100, 1987, pp. 859-860.

20. "The Historical Judgement", *People's Daily*, Jan. 26, 1981.

21. O. Schachter, *International Law in Theory and Practice*, Martinus Nijhoff Publisher, Dordrecht, 1991, pp. 346-347.

22. L. Henkin, *The Age of Rights*, Columbia University Press, New York, 1990, p. 76.

23. A. Cassese, *Human Rights in a Changing World*, Polity Press, Cambridge, 1990, p. 144.

24. Li Haopei, *Law of Treaty*, Law Press, Beijing, 1987, pp. 393-400.

25. Advisory Opinion in the Reservations to the Genocide Convention Case, *ICJ Report* (1951), p. 23.

26. Barcelona Traction Case (Second Phase), *ICJ Report* (1970), p. 32.

27. *ILC Report*, 46th Session, Supplement No.10 (A/46/10) 1991, pp. 243-250.

28. *Restatement of the Law, Third, Foreign Relations Law of United States*, Vol. 2, American Law Institute Publishers, 1987, p. 161.

29. T. Meron, *Human Rights and Humanitarian Norms as Customary Law*, Clarendon Press, Oxford, 1989, pp. 96-97.

30. O. Schachter, *International Law in Theory and Practice*, Martinus Nijhoff Publishers, Dordrecht, 1991, p. 339.

31. L. Henkin: "The Constitution and United States Sovereignty: A Century of Chinese Exclusion and Its Progeny", *Harvard Law Review*, Vol. 100, 1987, p. 869.

32. Ibid, pp. 872-874. R.B. Lillich, "The Role of Domestic Courts in Enforcing International Human Rights Law", *Guide to International Human Rights Practice*, second edition, edited by H. Hannum, University of Pennsylvania Press, Philadelphia, 1992, p. 229.

33. In the Fisheries Case, *ICJ Reports* (1951), pp. 183 ff.; I. Brownlie, *Principles of Public International Law*, Fourth Edition, Clarendon Press, Oxford, 1990, p. 10.

34. H.J. Berman, *Law and Revolution*, Harvard University Press, 1983, p. 520, p. 554.

35. H.S. Maine, *Ancient Law*, John Murray, London, 1874, p. 170.

36. Feng Youlan, *History of Chinese Philosophy*, Peking University Press, Beijing, 1985, p. 24.

37. *Etymology*, Commercial Affairs Press, Beijing, 1993, p. 892.

38. Xia Yong, *The Origin of Human Rights Concept*, Chinese Political and Law University Press, Beijing, 1992, p. 27.

39. Y. Sugihara, *The Thought of People's State*, Japan Comment Press, 1992, pp. 152-153.

40. Xiang Qing, Shi Zhifu and Liu Dexi, eds., *Soviet and Chinese Revolution*, Centre of Translation and Editing Press, Beijing, 1994, p. 47.

41. He Di, "The Evolution of the Chinese Communist Party's Foreign Policy during 1944-1949", in Yuan Ming and H. Harding, eds., *The Troublesome Period in the Historical Relationship between China and the United States*, Peking University Press, 1989, p. 93.

42. *The Historical Resolution of the Chinese Communist Party Central Committee on Some Questions Since the Establishment of the PRC*, People's Press, Beijing, 1981, p. 33.

43. A.J. Nathan, "Political Rights in Chinese Constitutions", *Human Rights in Contemporary China*, co-written by R.R. Edwards, L. Henkin and A. Nathan, Columbia University Press, New York, 1986, p. 111.

44. Pu Zhengyuan, "The Chinese Constitution and Protection of Human Rights", *Constitution and Democratic Politics*, edited by Xu Chongde, Chinese Procuratorate Press, Beijing, 1994, p. 212.

The Right to Development: Philosophical Differences and Political Implications[*]

PITMAN B. POTTER

Introduction

The right to development has been the focus of much debate and discussion, particularly in the context of its relationship to other human rights and in light of the economic development achievements and aspirations of states in the East Asian Region. A comparison of two major human rights documents of 1993 - the *Bangkok Declaration* and the *Vienna Declaration* - reveals significant differences of view concerning the right to development and its place in international human rights law.

The *Bangkok Declaration* suggested that state governments should be free to give development goals priority over other human rights policies, which themselves could be limited by local cultural and historical conditions.[1] This approach was viewed with some trepidation by outside observers, in part because the *Bangkok Declaration* also suggested that the recognition and enforcement of human rights generally should be controlled by local governments free from outside scrutiny.[2]

The *Vienna Declaration*, by contrast, stressed that the lack of development may not be used to justify abridgement of internationally recognized human rights, thus underscoring the principles accepted elsewhere that all human rights (including the right to development) are universal, indivisible, and interrelated.[3]

The contradiction over the relationship of the right to development and its attendant circumstances and other human rights reveals significant philosophical differences concerning the nature of development and the nature of rights. While these contradictions are unlikely to be resolved in the short term, the approach to development embodied in the *Bangkok Declaration* may have less than positive political implications for authoritarian development regimes.

[*] I would like to thank Doris Buss, a graduate student at UBC Law Faculty for her invaluable research assistance during the course of preparing this article. I would also like to thank Doris Buss, Ivan Head and Karin Michelson at UBC Law Faculty for their helpful comments.

This paper will examine these issues with specific reference to the case of China, which was a key architect of the *Bangkok Declaration* and has been a dramatic example of economic growth policies in the East Asian region.

Summary of the Discourse of the Right to Development

While it would be superfluous in the extreme to retrace in detail the geneology of the right to development, a brief summary may be useful as background. It is useful, as well, to note the institutional context within which these debates take place.

Recognition of the right to development as a human right

International recognition of the right to development as a human right has often been traced to a speech by Mr. Justice Keba M'Baye, First President of the Senegal Supreme Court, presented to the International Institute for Human Rights in 1972.[4] However, the idea has long-standing roots in the United Nations *Charter*, the *Universal Declaration of Human Rights*, the *International Covenant on Economic, Social and Cultural Rights*, the *International Covenant on Civil and Political Rights* and other international instruments.[5] The politics of North-South relations and particularly, the call for a "New International Economic Order" have contributed as well to assertions about the existence of a right to development.[6] Support for the right to development has been found in scholarly studies,[7] and gradually a series of international instruments has emerged recognizing and expanding on the right to development.[8] Ideas about the right to development have undergone further revision in the context of the dynamic growth of economies in the East Asian region, and suggestions that these economic successes vindicate an "Asian" cultural approach to development that stands as an alternative to much of Western human rights thinking.[9]

There have, however, been dissenting voices. Some suggest that the right to development is little more than an attempt by authoritarian governments to insulate their regimes from outside scrutiny.[10] Skeptical observers also suggest that the right to development has little if any legal support and is, in effect, an attempt to enshrine the laudable goal of development as a right, rather than recognizing that development may be the end-product of the enforcement of various civil, political, economic, social and/or cultural rights, but is not (and should not be) a right in itself.[11] Other critics have suggested that the emerging doctrine of the right to development gives undue attention to economic growth, which not only entrenches a flawed view of development generally, but also works to further the subjugation of disadvantaged groups for whom the right to development ought to operate most strongly.[12]

A middle ground of sorts is occupied by observers who accept the notion of a right to development, but who insist that it operate only as a complement to and not a substitute for other human rights.[13] The interaction of development with other human rights has been seen to require that the local peoples affected by economic development projects have meaningful opportunities for participation and consultation.[14] The right to participation has been expanded yet further in an effort to suggest that it might be a basis for protection of cultural rights against oppression from authoritarian states.[15]

Institutional contexts

Debates over the right to development operate against a background of political structures that affect and often pre-determine the content of the debate. Of particular importance are the views of national governments, international aid agencies, non-governmental organizations and the scholarly community. Although there are, of course, significant interdependencies among these institutions, their identity, power, and goals each play a significant role in determining the content of views expressed by their representative interlocutors.

State Governments

As international law is the creation of states, it is not surprising that state governments have played a critical role in discussions of the right to development. Governments in developing states have been particularly eager to have a right to development recognized at the international level, and for institutional mechanisms for enforcement to be put in place. Thus, for example, the UNESCO Secretary General's Report on the right to development emphasized the moral duty of industrialized states to repair the economic disparities that characterize their relations with developing countries, an NIEO theme that has been taken up repeatedly in subsequent instruments on the right to development.[16] Obviously, such an approach to international rights and duties suits the economic interests of developing states, particularly where implementation mechanisms and policies are established. On the other hand, international instruments on the right to development also reflect the views of industrialized states in noting the importance of domestic development efforts.[17]

International aid agencies

Much of the discussion over the right to development has concerned efforts by international aid agencies to explain and justify their activities. As with most formal institutions, international aid agencies have organizational interests and a parochial commitment to continuing their work and maintaining control over it.[18] Thus, aid agencies have been quick to respond to human rights criticisms of their work. Employees of aid agencies, while careful to note that they speak in their personal capacity, more often than not reflect the views of their employers. Thus, in response to claims that international aid should be tied to the human rights records of recipient counties, the General Counsel of the World Bank has argued that the Bank's charter mandates an effort to promote economic development and the raising of living standards, without direct attention to political questions.[19] As well, the point is made that the right to development gives the Bank's activities a direct human rights element. In response to claims that they play insufficient attention to local participation, international aid agencies often resort to examples of linkages with local elite organizations without much reflection as to whether these linkages contribute to meaningful local participation.

Non-governmental organizations

The role of NGOs in the debates over the right to development has become increasingly important.[20] While they often are subject to repression from local governments - either through direct repression or through the establishment of government organized competitors (GO-NGOs),[21] non-government organizations have often embarked on courageous efforts to articulate views on development matters that stand in contrast to those of state governments and international development agencies.[22] And while they are often accused of being dominated by local elites rather than broadly participatory, NGOs have shown a capacity for expanding the discourse of the right to development beyond the confines often imposed by state governments.

The scholarly community

While academic scholars are usually employed by universities, their loyalties are often to schools of thought rather than to the organizations with which they are associated. These loyalties play a significant role in setting the parameters for academic discussion. Thus, for example, scholars who criticize the right to development adopt liberal paradigms which focus on the individual as the primary beneficiary of political rights.[23] Other critics have challenged the right to development through allegiance to and application of the principles of feminist theory.[24] By contrast, those who have argued in support of the right to development have done so by reference to ideas about the importance of collective rights as at least equal to (and often with priority over) individual rights.[25] In each of these lines of argument, the views expressed owe as much to the authors' underlying conceptual paradigms as they do to their immediate research and analysis. Thus, along with the political perspectives of national governments and the institutional perspectives of aid agencies and their employees, the views of academics on the right to development reveal structural determinants which are not less real for their basis in ideas rather than organizations.

The Nature of Development and the Nature of Rights

A discussion about the right to development reflects different ideas about the nature of development and the nature of rights. An examination of these underlying paradigms is useful in understanding the broader debates about the right to development.

Dimensions of development

Among the many points of conflict in approaches to development are the questions about the international dimensions of development and underdevelopment; the goals of development; and the implications of development for social, economic and political relations.

International dimensions of development: the issue of dependency

Between supporters and opponents of the right to development, the basic issues revolve around the international political economy. Proponents of the right to development are heavily influenced by the conclusions of dependency theory.[26] Critics, on the other hand, suggest that dependency theory explains very little and that local conditions offer more powerful explanations for development and under-development.

The cadre of scholars broadly labelled dependency theorists hold, in general, that underdevelopment in all its forms is due in large part to the exploitation and oppression of the industrialized West - first through colonialism and later through domination of the international finance, technology, and commodity systems.[27] Early proponents of dependency portrayed local elites rather crudely as corporatist allies of foreign capital, serving as conduits for investment and also as the primary local beneficiaries.[28] Their commercial and consumption activities are seen to support the objectives of foreign investment by substituting short-term parochial goals for priorities of building the technological and infrastructural foundations for long-term development.[29]

Critics have suggested that proponents of dependency theory have indulged in whollistic ideological viewpoints that are not amenable to falsification or testing, even to the point of descending into what one observer has called a "fusion of scholarship, politics, and theatre".[30] Rather than explain conditions and causes of underdevelopment, dependency theorists are accused of overlooking local political and policy causes for underdevelopment.[31] Pointing to the successes of the East Asian NICs, critics of dependency theory have suggested that local conditions can overcome the effects of external oppression, even to the point of rendering it irrelevant to the question of development.[32]

While arguments continue to proliferate as to the strengths and weaknesses of dependency theory, it remains influential in the discourses of the right to development and of human rights generally. Indeed, many East Asian political leaders have suggested that the human rights agenda of the West is aimed at perpetuating the dependency of the developing world.[33]

The goals of development

Among proponents of the right to development, there is substantial disagreement over the goals of development. While most scholars and international instruments agree that development means more than simply economic growth, some national governments have suggested that economic growth is the primary feature of development.

The primary documents articulating a right to development are fairly clear that development entails more than simply economic growth. Thus, the UNESCO Secretary General's Report indicates that development includes both material and non-material elements.[34] The UN General Assembly Resolution on the Right to Development contains similar provisions - indicating that development is a comprehensive phenomenon entailing economic, social, cultural, and political elements.[35] These views are supported and reiterated by a substantial body of scholarly literature. In the wake of perceived failures of development policies that gave primacy to economic growth,[36] the field of development studies has moved steadily toward a multi-dimensional view of development.[37] This theme appears throughout the literature on the right to development, which asserts consistently that development means more than simply economic growth.[38]

Despite this apparent uniformity, a number of national governments in the East Asian region suggest that development means primarily, if not exclusively, economic growth. Thus, the *Bangkok Declaration* draws an explicit link between development and the international macroeconomic system.[39] In its 1991 Human Rights White Paper, the government of the PRC explicitly adopted a position supporting the primacy of economic growth by stressing the right to subsistance as a primary right from which all other rights derive.[40] Similarly, the yearly reports issued by the PRC government on economic and social development give clear priority to economic achievement.[41] Singaporean representatives have consistently made clear their conclusions about the primacy of economic growth as a precursor to other aspects of development.[42] These views stand in marked contrast to the conclusions of international instruments and development scholars that development must mean more than economic growth. More importantly, they have implications for the ways in which state governments address the relationship between economic development and other social, cultural and political relationships.

Development and social, economic and political relations

Tied closely to notions about the goals of development are questions about the relationship of development to social, economic and political relations. Thus, as might be expected, international instruments and scholarly analyses that assert development to mean more than simply economic growth also argue that the pursuit of development cannot operate to the detriment of other human rights. The UNESCO Secretary General's Report asserts that the right to development operates in tandem with other civil, political, social, cultural, and economic rights.[43] The UN General Assembly Resolution on the Right to Development asserts that, as a human right, the right to development is indivisible and interdependent on other human rights.[44] Similarly, the scholarly literature is nearly uniform in its insistence that the right to development cannot be used to justify denial of other human rights.[45]

However, these views are contradicted by policies and behavior of various governments in the East Asian Region. Reflecting their conclusions about the economic bases for development, some states have subordinated the enforcement of human rights norms in social, economic, and political relations to policy goals of economic development. Relying partly on a critique of liberal paradigms that limit state involvement in economic life through to the establishment of free market systems supported by private law rules and institutions,[46] the right to development has been used to justify continued restriction of effective judicial systems that might lay a foundation for meaningful civil and political rights.[47] By asserting that countries have the right to determine their own political systems through which to pursue economic, social, and cultural development, the *Bangkok Declaration* clearly subordinated the pursuit of civil and political rights.[48] The emphasis of China's 1991 Human Rights White Paper on the right to subsistence implies that civil and political relations must continually be subordinated to the pursuit of economic development.[49] Indeed, in explaining the PRC's White Paper on Human Rights, the Director of the State Council Information Office explained the primacy of economic conditions as the basis for development: "we enable our people to have the economic foundation upon which they can enjoy political rights."[50]

The nature of rights

Debates over the right to development also reflect fundamental differences about the nature of rights. These differences include divergent views on the sources and beneficiaries of rights.

Sources of rights

Much of what might be termed the conventional human rights discourse derives from European ideas about the nature of rights. The inalienable character of human rights and the claim that they are enjoyed by virtue of being human is entrenched in the *Universal Declaration of Human Rights* as well as the *International Covenants on Civil and Political and on Economic, Social, and Cultural Rights*. These ideas about the inherency of rights reflect European natural law theories about the equality of human beings,[51] which in turn derived from a range of political and economic interests.[52] Despite recent efforts to reconceptualize rights as claims set in a context of diverse social, political and economic interests,[53] the notion of inherency retains its appeal and distinguishes the European ideal of rights from that which is emerging in the East Asian region.[54]

In contrast to natural rights theories that view rights as inalienable and intrinsic to the human condition, proponents of the so-called Asian approach to rights suggest that rights are conferred by social organizations - families, communities, and governments. The PRC Constitution, for example, speaks of rights being granted by the state rather than as inherent to the human conditions. [55] Article 33 of the 1982 PRC Constitution goes farther, and conditions the extension of legal and civil rights on performance of the "duties prescribed by the Constitution and the law". Under this approach rights are not inherent, to be enjoyed by virtue of being human, but rather are specific benefits conferred and enforced at the discretion of the state. Such an approach permits governments to silence their critics under the guise of legal process.

Beneficiaries of rights

Divergent views on the sources of rights have led, in turn, to significant differences concerning the beneficiaries of rights. In keeping with natural law theories that treat rights as inherent to human beings, the European liberal tradition has long held that human individuals are the primary beneficiaries of rights.[56] Reflecting this tradition, international human rights instruments provide that human rights are enjoyed by individuals, while the bulk of scholarly literature on human rights suggests, as well, that the primary beneficiary is the individual.[57] While there is currently a growing body of literature that challenges this view,[58] or at least suggests that individual rights can be meaningfully enforced only in the context of community,[59] the primacy of the individual in the dynamic of legal rights and obligations remains a dominant feature of European and North American rights doctrine.

In the course of the human rights discourse, many East Asian governments have claimed that groups and communities should be the primary beneficiaries of rights and, by implication at least, that the rights of individuals should be subordinated.[60] This approach is supported by arguments about social and historical traditions, and references to an East Asian familial tradition that derives from Confucianism and its assumptions about authority and hierarchy in social organization.[61] In this regard, it is useful to note that while the tradition of collective rights in the Asian tradition is much discussed, there is also significant evidence to suggest that the role of the individual was once highly prized.[62] The importance of the individual in traditional Chinese philosophy came gradually to be suppressed as a result of the political and ideological imperatives of the Chinese state.[63] Moreover, it should be noted that Confucianism and the collectivist norms it has engendered have been severely criticized by many contemporary Chinese thinkers as overly authoritarian and repressive.[64] Nonetheless, the Confucian tradition remains important in the views of some governments in East Asia regarding the beneficiaries of rights.

These basic differences over nature of development and the nature of rights pose significant obstacles to attempts to reconcile differing approaches on the human right to development - differences which are entrenched further by the institutional contexts within which the various views are articulated. In this regard, it is of particular interest to note the emphasis placed by the 1993 *Bangkok Human Rights Declaration* on a "dynamic and evolving process of international norm-setting" as a context for human rights ideals.[65] This suggests a hope on the part of some East Asian governments that the human right to development as a multi-faceted, inherent and inalienable right might ultimately yield to a different vision. A vision that holds the right to development as a priority that permits economic growth to take precedence over such other human rights as may be conferred by state governments on their subjects.

Implications of the Bangkok Approach: The Case of China

The Bangkok approach to development, which focuses primarily, if not exclusively, on economic growth and which subordinates other human rights to the pursuit of this goal, has the potential to obstruct the pursuit of develoment generally. In the shadowlands between liberal free-market economies and the kinds of state-directed bureaucratic economies that have become common in the East Asian region, there is the potential that development will suffer the worst of both worlds - an inattention to social, cultural and poltical development brought on by a myopic pre-occupation with economic growth, and limited potential for long term economic growth due to the inefficiencies attendant to state-directed markets. One example of this dilemma is China, where the pursuit of economic growth has led to corruption, environmental degradation, decline of working conditions, and other ills that may well undermine China's long-term development prospects.

China's economic growth strategy has been aimed, in part at least, at achieving rather vaguely conceived goals of popular welfare. As the Communique of the 1978 Third Plenum indicated, a major impetus for economic reform was the need to improve living standards.[66] The legal and regulatory foundations for economic reform made constant reference to the need to protect the state and public interest.[67] Laws on local and foreign investment paid substantial attention to labor conditions and benefits.[68] Environmental regulations also began to receive attention.[69] Thus, the ideals of popular welfare were evident in the policy and institutional foundations for China's development effort.

However, realizing such ideals depends on Beijing's ability to control behaviour at the local level. This has severely constrained the interrelated phenomena of local corporatism and corruption. As studies of village and township enterprises have shown, local businesses are often controlled by local political figures - themselves encouraged by the policy of xiahai (jumping into the sea of commerce).[70] The alliance of local political and economic interests has benefitted from the decline in central authority, and increases the potential for abuse of political power in pursuit of local commercial interests. Despite central government attempts to control the problem, the decline of the central state would appear to be contributing to the merging of local government and business interests, heralding the emergence of local corporatism.

China's crisis of corruption is widely recognized. The 101,000 cases of corruption reportedly handled by the courts in 1992 were merely emblematic of a much deeper problem.[71] By the admission of the Chinese government, corruption has penetrated to virtually every level of the Chinese society. The Great Wall financial scandal of 1993 and the mammoth corruption charges that led to the dismissal of former Beijing Mayor Chen Xitong in early 1995, while revealing the politics of China's anti-corruption efforts, indicate the heights to which corruption has penetrated. At more mundane levels, a county near Beijing was deprived of over one million Chinese yuan (approximately C$200,000) in tax revenue by one company's ability to "pursuade" the county secretary to waive the taxes due on a single land transaction.[72] Corruption has gone so far as to subvert the state's own information gathering processes, thus undermining the ability to manage policy effectively.[73] Rampant corruption adds to the structural aspects of Beijing's weakening power over the localities, a behavioural element that undermines the authority of state institutions wherever they operate.[74] The dire warnings against corruption sounded by Premier Li Peng at various NPC meetings indicates both the seriousness of the problem and the continued inability of the central government to deal with it thus far.

Under these conditions, it is not surprising to observe economic development pursued at a significant cost to local living and working conditions. The decline in China's environmental conditions has been noted by virtually all serious observers.[75] While environmental protection ideals are continually reiterated in regulatory and legislative language,[76] actual enforcement remains virtually nonexistent. Yet popular efforts to remonstrate with the government over declining environmental conditions have met with vigorous repression.[77]

As well, workers in China have seen their conditions deteriorate steadily during recent years.[78] Many of the regulatory measures enacted to protect workers have been ignored or distorted to suit the interests of local officials, with little direct benefit to local workers. Recently, and particularly after the Tiananmen uprising which saw multitudes of state enterprise workers demonstrate their dissatisfaction with the government,[79] the state's solicitude for workers has begun to give way to calls for stability and discipline. On the one hand, the central state appears unable to control labor conditions at the local level.[80] On the other hand, the state opposes local efforts at labor organization. Just as China's 1991 "White Paper on Human Rights" makes the point explicitly that stability and production are fundamental goals taking precedence over other matters,[81] the state's response to the activities of Han Dongfang and other activists signal its reluctance to permit the emergence of independent labor unions.[82]

The problems besetting China's development effort would appear to stem, to a large degree, from the combination of an over-emphasis on economic growth aspects of development and a corresponding lack of attention to social, cultural, and political elements. Economic growth policies have tended to overlook issues of environmental protection and working conditions in the quest for efficiency and production. Moreover, the continued role of the state in market activities often restricts access to economic opportunities to those with political connections - in effect excluding the vast majority of the populace from direct benefits of China's economic growth while still saddling them with many if not most of the costs. Local citizens are increasingly disenchanted with the government's inability or unwillingness to confront these problems, as escalating unrest among the peasantry and urban workers suggests the extent of dissatisfaction. In the absence of meaningful channels for public participation in the political process and the articulation of popular views critical of corrupt officials, popular disquiet simply festers until a crisis erupts - such as occurred in April to June 1989. As indicated by the experience of the Republican government in the 1930s,[83] such an approach to development is not likely to succeed in either its social, cultural and political elements or ultimately in its economic aspirations.

To its credit, the Chinese government has recognized these difficulties, and has begun to try to address them. The December 1995 White Paper devotes considerable attention to problems of disparities in income and the challenge of alleviating poverty.[84] Still, there remain the challenges of implementation. Realizing the ideals discussed in the most recent White Paper depends on Beijing's willingness to impose policy priorities that favour the human dimension of development. Unfortunately, the government sets conflicting tasks for local officials. For example, directives on improving living and working conditions are contradicted by insistence on continued economic growth and employment. Moreover, the central government virtually ensures the supremacy of economic growth policies over human development concerns by providing detailed economic performance targets and incorporating these into the local cadre rating system, while at the same time issuing ambiguous policy directives on human development issues without providing for meaningful enforcement. While the 1995 White Paper demonstrates the beginning of a commitment to a more balanced approach to development, it remains largely silent on specific mechanisms for enforcement.

Conclusion

The discourse of the right to development is characterized by fundamental differences over the nature of development and the nature of rights. While there is significant consistency among the international instruments and scholarly studies concerning the multi-faceted nature of development and the imperative that the right to development not be used to suppress other human rights, state practices in many areas of East Asia seem at variance with these doctrinal norms. Justifying these disparities as little more that the product of diversity in cultural and historical circumstances, and characterizing the doctrine itself as a temporary condition in a "dynamic process of norm-setting", some East Asian states continue to cling to notions that economic growth is the primary goal of development and that a vast array of internationally recognized civil, political, social, economic, and cultural human rights may be sub-ordinated to this goal. While these views might be comforting as the basis for short-term political expediency, the growing socio-economic problems in China suggest that, in the long run, uni-dimensional views of development may be counter-productive.

The affirmation of the human right to development has put fundamental questions about development and rights on the public agenda of international law and politics. The discourse may yield increasingly effective calls for a multi-dimensional approach that validates social, cultural, and political development as essential counterparts to economic growth. While it remains to be seen whether authoritarian regimes in the East Asian region will come to adopt such an approach in the near term, the liberalization policies of Taiwan and South Korea suggest that political self-preservation may mandate the adoption of comprehensive development strategies. The development aspirations of the people in the region generally would seem to depend on similar transitions from state-controlled uni-dimensional economic development to a more comprehensive approach. This, in turn, will depend on how the philosophical differences and political implications of the right to development are resolved.

Notes

1. See, "Final Declaration of the regional meeting for Asia of the World Conference on Human Rights" (Bangkok Declaration) (April 2, 1993), Art. 8, 14 *Hum. Rts. L. J.* 370 (1993).

2. Article 24 of the Bangkok Declaration ("Final Declaration of the regional meeting for Asia of the World Conference on Human Rights", *supra*) provides that the conceptualization and eventual establishment of national human rights institutions should be left to the States to decide.

3. See, United Nations World Conference on Human Rights: Vienna Declaration and Programme of Action, Arts. I (5) and I (10), in 32 *I.L.M.* 1661 (1993) at 1665 and 1666. While the Bangkok Declaration repeated some of the standard doctrinal language of human rights law on universality and indivisibility, its emphasis on the prerogatives of state governments and the contextualization of rights marked a significant departure.

4. See, M'Baye, "Le Droit au developpement commen un droit de l'Homme", 5 *Revue des Droits de l'Homme* 503 (1972). Also see, Hector Gros Espiell, "The Right to Development as a Human Right", 16 *Texas Int'l L. J.* 189, 192 (1981); Russel Lawrence Barsh, "The Right to Development as a Human Right: Results of the Global Consultation", 12 *Hum. Rts. Q.* 322 (1991).

5. See, e.g., Roland Y. Rich, "The Right to Development as an Emerging Human Right", 23 *Vir. J. Int'l L.* 287 (1983); Ved P. Nanda, "The Right to Development: An Appraisal", in Nanda, George W. Shepherd Jr., and Eileen McCarthy-Arnolds, eds., *World Debt and the Human Condition* (Westport Conn.: Greenwood Press, 1992) pp. 41-61.

6. For a useful collection of articles presented at a 1991 seminar convened in Calcutta by the Committee on Legal Aspects of the New International Economic Order of the International Law Association, see, Subrata Roy Chowdhury, Erik M.G. Denters, & Paul J.I.M. de Waart, eds., *The Right to Development in International Law* (Dordrecht: Martinus Nijhoff, 1992). Also see, Mohammed Bedjaoui, "Some Unorthodox Reflections on the 'Right to Development'", in Francis Snyder & Peter Slinn, ed., *International Law of Development: Comparative Perspectives* (London: Professional Books, 1987), pp. 87-116.

7. Among the earliest and most articulate proponents of the right to development have been Roland Rich and Philip Alston. See, e.g. Roland Rich, "The Right to Development as an Emerging Human Right", 23 *Vir. J. Int'l L.* 287 (1983) and "The Right to Development: A Right of Peoples?" in James Crawford, ed., *The Rights of Peoples* (Oxford: Clarendon, 1988) at pp. 39-54; Philip Alston, "Development and the Rule of Law: Prevention versus Cure as a Human Rights Strategy", in Int'l Comm. of Jurists, *Development, Human Rights and the Rule*

of Law (1981); "Making Space for New Human Rights: The Case of the Right to Development", 1 *Hum. Rts. Yrbk.* 3 (1988) and "Revitalizing United Nations Work on Human Rights and Development", in 18 *Melbourne Univ. L. Rev.* 216 (1991). For a critical review of Alston, see, Jack Donnelly, "In Search of the Unicorn: The Jurisprudence and Politics of the Right to Development", 15 *Cal. W. Int'l L. J.* 473 (1985).

8. Of particular importance have been the UNESCO Secretary General's *Report on the Right to Development* (E/CN.4/1334) (1979); the United Nations General Assembly's *Declaration on the Right to Development* (Res 41/128 (1986); and the UNESCO Commission on Human Rights' *Report on the Global Consultation on the Right to Development as a Human Right* E/CN.4/1990/9/Rev.1 (1990).

9. Perhaps the most comprehensive articulation of the right to development in the context of the East Asian experience was the 1993 *Bangkok Declaration*, in which the emphasis was placed on local historical, cultural and religious conditions as context for human rights conditions. See, "Final Declaration of the Regional Meeting for Asia of the World Conference on Human Rights" (Bangkok Declaration), *supra.* Also see, "Human Rights: Vienna Showdown", in *Far Eastern Economic Review*, June 17, 1993 at p. 16.

10. See, Michael Vatikiotis and Robert Delfs, "Cultural Divide: East Asia claims the right to make its own rules", in *Far Eastern Economic Review* June 17, 1993, p. 20.

11. See, e.g. Jack Donnelly, "In Search of the Unicorn: The Jurisprudence and Politics of the Right to Development", *supra.* Cf. John O'Manique, "Human Rights and Development", 14 *Hum. Rts. Q.* 78 (1992); John O'Manique, "Development, Human Rights and Law", 14 *Hum. Rts. Q.* 383 (1992).

12. See, e.g., Hilary Charlesworth, "The Public/Private Distinction and the Right to Development in International Law", in 12 *Australian Yearbook of International Law* 190 (1992); Jonathan L. Mannina, "The Human Rights Implications of Economic Development: A Case Study of the Huaorani People of Ecuador", 5 *G'town Int'l Envtl. L. Rev.* 91 (1992).

13. The text of the 1994 *Vienna Declaration* stands as a forceful articulation of this view,

"While development facilitates the enjoyment of all human rights, the lack of development may not be invoked to justify the abridgement of internationally recognized human rights"

See, United National World Conference on Human Rights, "Vienna Declaration and Programme of Action", Art. I (10), in 32 I.L.M. 1661 (1993) at 1666. For scholarly expressions of this perspective, see e.g., Rhoda Howard, "Law and Economic Rights in Commonwealth Africa", 15 *Cal. W. Int'l L.J.* 607 (1985); Kivutha Kibwana, "Human Rights And/Or Economic Development: Which Way Africa?", (1993) *Third World Legal Studies* 43; Wade Mansell and Joanne Scott, "Why Bother About a Right to Development", 21 *J. of L. and Soc.* 171 (1994); Yemi Osinbajo and Olukonyisola Ajayi, "Human Rights and Economic Development" 28 *The Int'l Lawyer* 727 (1994).

14. See, e.g., Konrad Ginther, "Participation and Accountability: Two Aspects of the Internal and International Dimension of the Right to Development", in (1992) *Third World Legal Studies* 55; James C.N. Paul, "Law and Development in the 1990s: Using International law to Impose Accountability to People on International Development Actors", in (1992) *Third World Legal Studies* 1 and; "The Human Right to Development: Its Meaning and Importance", 25 *John Marshall L. Rev.* 235 (1992); and Daniel D. Broadlow, "Human Rights,Public Finance and the Development Process: A Critical Introduction", in 8 *Am. Univ. J. Int'l L. & Pol'y* 1 (1992).

15. See, e.g., Michele L. Radin, "The Right to Development as a Mechanism for Group Autonomy: Protection of Tibetan Cultural Rights", in 68 *Wash. L. Rev.* 695 (1993).

16. See, UNESCO Secretary General, *Report on the Right to Development* (E/CN.4/1334) (1979) at p. 20; United Nations General Assembly, *Declaration on the Right to Development* (Res 41/128 (1986) at Preamble; and UNESCO Commission on Human Rights' *Report on the Global Consultation on the Right to Development as a Human Right* E/CN.4/1990/9/Rev.1 (1990) at Art. V (F).

17. See, United Nations General Assembly, *Declaration on the Right to Development* (Res 41/128 (1986) at Art. 3 and UNESCO Commission on Human Rights' *Report on the Global Consultation on the Right to Development as a Human Right* E/CN.4/1990/9/Rev.1 (1990) at Art. V (A).

18. See, generally, Robert A. Packenham, *Liberal America and the Third World* (Princeton: Princeton University Press, 1973).

19. See, Ibrahim F.I. Shihata, "The World Bank and Human Rights: An Analysis of the Legal Issues and the Record of Achievements", 17 *Den. J. Int'l L. & Pol'y* 39 (1988) and "Human Rights, Development, and International Financial Institutions", in 8 *Am. Univ. J. of Int'l L. & Pol'y* 19 (1992). Also see, Mr. Shihata's comments on a panel entitled "Environment, Economic Development and Human Rights: A Triangular Relationship?", in *Proceedings of the Eighty-Second Annual Meeting of the American Society of International Law* (1988) at pp. 41-45.

20. See, Sidney Jones, "The Organic Growth: Asian NGOs have come into their own", in *Far Eastern Economic Review* June 17, 1993, p. 23. For discussion of the potential role of NGOs in human rights monitoring, see, Ann Kent, "China and the International human Rights Regime: A Case Study of Multilateral Monitoring, 1989-1994", 17 *Hum. Rts. Q.* 1 (1995).

21. See, Geoffrey Crothall, "Outlawed Dissent: The stranglehold on unofficial groups", in *China Rights Forum Winter*, 1993, pp. 8-9; Sharon Hom, "Listening for Diversity", *China Rights Forum* Winter, 1993, pp. 12-15.

22. For discussion of the role of NGOs at the Bangkok Conference, see, Sidney Jones, "Culture Clash: Asian Activitsts Cpounter Their Governments' RestriveView of Human Rights", in *China Rights Forum* Summer 1993, pp. 8-9, 22. Also see, "Mangu fei zhengfu zuzhi xuanyan (zhaiyao)" (Bangkok NGO communique - excerpts), in *China Rights Forum* Summer 1993, pp. 35-36.

23. See, Jack Donnelly, "In Search of the Unicorn: The Jurisprudence and Politics of the Right to Development", *supra*.

24. See, e.g., Hilary Charlesworth, "The Public/Private Distinction and the Right to Development in International Law", supra; Marilyn Waring, "Gender and International Law: Women and the Right to Development", in 12 *Australian Yearbook of International Law* 177 (1992).

25. See, e.g. Roland Rich, "The Right to Development as an Emerging Human Right", *supra* and "The Right to Development: A Right of Peoples?" *supra*; Philip Alston, "Development and the Rule of Law: Prevention versus Cure as a Human Rights Strategy", *supra*; "Making Space for New Human Rights: The

Case of the Right to Development", *supra* and "Revitalizing United Nations Work on Human Rights and Development", *supra*.

26. For example, the Human Rights White Paper issued by the People's Republic of China in 1991 makes much of the century of colonial oppression suffered by China during the 19th and early 20th centuries. See, "Text of Human Rights White Paper", in *FBIS Daily Report - Supplement*, Nov. 21, 1991.

27. There is a rich and wide-ranging literature on the problems of dependency. Among the most useful works are Paul A. Baran, *The Political Economy of Growth* (New York: Monthly Review Press, 1968); Andre Gundar Frank, *Capitalism and Underdevelopment in Latin America* (New York: Monthly Review Press, 1967); Celso Furtado, *Development and Underdevelopment: A Structural View of the Problems of Developed and Underdeveloped Countries* (Berkeley: University of California Press, 1964); Johann Galtung, "An Economic Theory of Imperialism", in *Journal of Peace Research* Vol. 2, 1971, pp. 81-117; Alexandro Portes, "The Sociology of National Development: in *American Journal of Sociology*, Vol. 82, No. 1 (1976), pp. 55-85; Immanuel Wallerstein, "The Rise and Future Demise of the World Capitalist System: Concepts for Comparative Analysis", in *Comparative Studies in Society and History*, Vol. 14, No. 4 (1974), pp. 1-26; and Charles K. Wilber, ed., *The Political Economy of Development and Underdevelopment* (2d ed.) (New York: Random House, 1979). For a survey, and no uncritical, survey of the dependency literature, see, Robert A. Packenham, *The Dependency Movement: Scholarship and Politics in Development Studies* (Cambridge, Ma and London: Harvard University Press, 1992).

28. See, generally, Fernando H. Cardoso and Enzo Faletto, *Dependency and Development in Latin America* (Barkeley: University of California Press, 1979); Paul Baran, "On the Political Economy of Backwardness", in Charles K. Wilber, ed., *The Political Economy of Development and Underdevelopment* (2d ed.) (New York: Random House, 1979), pp. 91-113. Also see, Charles K. Wilber and James H. Weaver, "Patterns of Dependency: Income distribution and the History of Underdevelopment", in Wilber, *The Political Economy of Development and Underdevelopment*, pp. 114-129. For a critique, see, Packenham, *The Dependency Movement, supra*, p. 93-94.

29. See, generally, Mark Singer, *Weak States in a World of Power: The Dynamics of International Relationships* (New York: Free Press, 1972) and Ronald Muller, "The Multinational Corporation and the Underdevelopment of

the Third World", in Wilber, *The Political Economy of Development and Underdevelopment*, pp. 151-178.

30. See, Packenham, *The Dependency Movement, supra*, esp. p. 315.

31. See, Stephen Haggard, *Pathways From the Periphery: The Politics of Growth in the Newly Industrialized Countries* (Ithaca and London: Cornell University Press, 1990), at pp. 19-22.

32. See, e.g., Yemi Osinbajo and Olukunyisola, "Human rights and Economic Development in Developing Countries", 28 *The Int'l Lawyer* 727 (1994).

33. See, comments of Malaysian Prime Minister Datuk Seri Mahathir Mohammad in Michael Vatikiotis and Robert Delfs, "Cultural Divide: East Asia claims the right to make its own rules", in *Far Eastern Economic Review* June 17, 1993, p. 20.

34. UNESCO Secretary General, *Report on the Right to Development* (E/CN.4/1334) (1979), p. 13. Most recently, see, the UNESCO Secretary General's Position Paper delivered to the 1995 Copenhagen Summit, in which the point is made that development is first and foremost social, rather than economic.

35. See, United Nations General Assembly *Declaration on the Right to Development* (Res 41/128 (1986), Preamble and Art. 1.

36. See, e.g., Walt Whitman Rostow, "The Take-Off to Self-Sustained Economic Growth", in Rostow, ed., *Stages of Economic Growth: A Non-communist Manifesto* (Cambridge: Cambridge University Press, 1960).

37. A seminal work in pointing to the failures of uni-dimensional development policies was Robert A. Packenham, *Liberal America and the Third World: Political Development Ideas in Foreign Aid and Social Science* (Princeton: Princeton University Press, 1973). Other influential early works were Mahbub Ul-Haq, *The Poverty Curtain: Choices for the Third World* (New York: Columbia University Press, 1976).

38. See, e.g, Theo C. van Boven, "The Right to Development and Human Rights" (1980); Hector Gross Espiell, "The Right to Development as a Human Right", 16 *Texas Int'l L. J.* 189 (1981); Roland Y. Rich, "The Right to Development as an Emerging Human Right", 23 *Virginia J. In'l L.* 287 (1983); Ved P. Nanda. "The Right to Development Under International Law -

Challenges Ahead", 15 *Cal. W. Int'l L. J.* 431 (1985); Rhona E. Howard, "Law and Economic Rights in Commonwealth Africa", 15 *Cal. W. Int'l L. J.* 607 (1985); Daniel D. Bradlow, "Human Rights, Public Finance and the Development Process: A Critical Introduction", 8 *Am. Univ. J. Int'l L. & Pol'y* 1 (1992); James C.N. Paul, "Law and Development in the 90s: Using International Law to Impose Accountability to People on International Development Actors", (1992) *Third World Legal Studies* 17; Kivutha Kibwana, "Human Rights And/Or Economic Development: Which Way Africa?", (1993) *Third World Legal Studies* 43; Wade Mansell and Joanne Scott, "Why Bother About a Right to Development?", 21 *J. L. & Soc.* 171 (1994); Hilary Charlesworth, "The Public/Private Distinction and the Right to Development in International Law", in 12 *Australian Yearbook of International Law* 190 (1992).

39. See, *Bangkok Declaration, supra*, Preamble and Art. 18.

40. See, "Text of Human Rights White Paper", in *FBIS Daily Report - Supplement*, Nov. 21, 1991.

41. See, e.g., "Statistical Communique of the State Statistical Bureau of the People's Republic of China on the 1993 National Economic and Social Development" (Feb. 28, 1994), in *China Economic News* Supp. No. 3, Mar. 14, 1994, in which nearly six pages of the seven page report are devoted to economic growth statistics. This pattern was repeated in the 1994 Communque. See, "Statistical Communique of the State Statistical Bureau of the People's Republic of China on the 1994 National Economic and Social Development", in *China Economic News* Supp. No. 1, Mar. 27, 1995.

42. Speaking "in his personal capacity", Kishore Mahbubani, a deputy secretary of Singapore's Ministry of Foreign Affairs, suggested that "[e]conomic development is the only force that can liberate the Third World". See, Kishore Mahbubani, "Live and Let Live: Allow Asians to choose their own course", in *Far Eastern Economic Review* June 17, 1993, p. 26. Also see, Chong Li Choy, Tan Chwee Huat, Wong Kwei Cheong, and Caroline Yeoh, ed., *Business, Society and Development in Singapore* (Singapore: Times Academic Press, 1990, which emphasizes economic and business growth as the touchstone of Singapore's development. Similar sentiments are evident in Linda Low and Toh Mun Heng, ed., *Public Policies in Singapore: Changes in the 1980s and Future Signposts* (Singapore: Times Academic Press, 1992). Also see, comments of Chen Heng Chee, Executive Director of the Singapore International Foundation in Hans De Jonge, "Democracy and Economic Development in the Asia-Pacific

Region: The Role of Parliamentary Institutions", 14 *Hum. Rts L. J.* 301 (1993).

43. See, UNESCO Secretary General, *Report on the Right to Development* (E/CN.4/1334) (1979), p. 13.

44. See, United Nations General Assembly *Declaration on the Right to Development* (Res 41/128 (1986), Art. 6.

45. See, sources cited in note 14, *supra*.

46. Liberal economic policies are seen to undermine local capacity to control foreign capital, as the transnational character of foreign business inhibits control by local governments through traditional legal mechanisms. See, generally, Robert O. Keohane and Van Doorn Ooms, "The Multinational Firm and International Regulation", in *International Organization*, Vol. 29, No. 1 (1975), pp. 186-206. Also see, Yash Ghai, Robin Luckham, and Francis Snyder, eds., *The Political Economy of Law: A Third World Reader* (New Delhi: Oxford University Press, 1987); Francisco Orrego Vicun, "The Control of Multinational Enterprises" and Franklin B. Weinstein, "Underdevelopment and Efforts to Control Multinational Corporations", both in George Modelski, ed., *Transnational Corporations and World Order: Readings in International Political Economy* (San Francisco: W.H. Freeman & Co., 1979), at pp. 296-308 and pp. 338-346; Ronald Muller, "Poverty is the Product", in *Foreign Policy* Vol. 13 (Winter 1973-74), pp. 71-102; United Nations, *Multinational Corporations in World Development* (New York: United Nations, 1973); and Stephen Hymer, "The Multinational Corporation and the Law of Uneven Development", in Jadwish N. Bhagwati, ed., *Economics and World Order* (New York: MacMillan, 1972), pp. 113-135. In the international trade context, see, David Kennedy, "Turning to Market Democracy: A Tale of Two Architectures", in *Harvard International Law Journal*, Vol. 32, No. 2 (1991), pp. 373-396.

47. Perhaps the most direct expression of this sentiment has been attributed to Malaysian Prime Minister Mahathir Mohamad: "developing nations cannot always afford luxuries such as human rights . . . liberty must take a back seat to the exigency of economic expansion ... you must eat before you vote." See, Boo Tion Kwa, "Righteous Talk", in *Far Eastern Economic Review*, June 17, 1993, p. 28.

48. See, *Bangkok Declaration, supra*, Art. 6.

49. See, "Text of Human Rights White Paper", in *FBIS Daily Report - Supplement*, Nov. 21, 1991.

50. See, "Interview with Zhu Muzhi, Director of the State Council Information Office" (*Xinhua*, Nov. 2, 1991), in *FBIS Daily Report-China*, Nov. 4, 1991, pp. 15-16 at p. 16.

51. See, generally J. Murphy and J.L.Coleman, *Philosophy of Law: An Introduction to Jurisprudence* (Revised ed., 1990). among the primary sources for this view are Aristotle's *Ethics and Politics*; Cicero's, *The Republic*, and Aquinas' *Treatise on Law*. Also see, generally, Stephen Lukes, *Individualism* (1973) and Joseph Raz, "Rights and Individualism", in *The Morality of Freedom* (1986).

52. Michael Tigar and Marion Levy, *Law and the Rise of Capitalism* (1977) and Harold Berman, *Law and Revolution*.

53. See, generally, J. Waldron, *Theories of Rights* (1984) and Joseph Raz, "On the Nature of Rights", 93 *Mind* 194 (1984).

54. See, Ronald Dworkin, *Taking Rights Seriously* (1978)

55. See, *Constitution of the People's Republic of China* (1982), Articles 33-34.

56. See, generally, Stephen Lukes, *Individualism* (1973) and Joseph Raz, "Rights and Individualism", in *The Morality of Freedom* (1986).

57. See, generally, Hugh M. Kindred, et al., ed., *International Law: Chiefly as Interpreted and Applied in Canada* (Toronto: Emond Montgomery, 1993), Chapter Ten.

58. See, generally, Bryan Schwartz, "Individuals, Groups and Canadian Statecraft" in Richard F. Devlin, ed., *Canadian Approaches to Legal Theory* (Toronto: Emond Montgomery, 1991), pp. 39-56.

59. See, e.g. Jeremy Waldron, "Can Communal Rights by Human Rights?", 27 *Arch. Europ. Sociol.* 296 (1987) and Gillian Triggs, "The Rights of Peoples and Individual Rights: Conflict or Harmony?", in James Crawford, *The Rights of Peoples* (Oxford: Clarendon, 1988), pp. 141-157.

60. For indicators of the Chinese view, see, references to the primacy of national political stability and the livelihood of people throughout the country, in *PRC Human Rights White Paper, supra*, p. 4 and referenes to human rights conditions of the Chinese people as whole in "Interview with Zhu Muzhi, Director of the State Council Information Office" (*Xinhua*, Nov. 2, 1991), in *FBIS Daily Report-China*, Nov. 4, 1991, pp. 15-16. See, e.g. Hans De Jonge, "Democracy and Economic Development in the Asia-Pacific Region: The Role of Parliamentary Institutions", *supra*. Also see, Boo Tion Kwa, "Righteous Talk", in *Far Eastern Economic Review*, June 17, 1993, p. 28.

61. See, generally, Ann Kent, *Between Freedom and Subsistence* (Hong Kong: Oxford University Press, 1993), pp. 30-32; David E. Christensen, "Breaking the Deadlock: Toward a Socialist Confucianist Concept of Human Rights in China", 13 *Mich. J. Int'l L.* 469 (1992). The importance of Confucianism as a basis for a collectivist legal order is the focus of many officially sanctioned studies of Chinese legal culture. See, e.g., Chinese Society for the Study of Confucianism and Legal Culture, ed., *Confucianism and Legal Culture* (Shanghai: Fudan University Press, 1992.)

62. See, Donald J. Munro, *The Concept of Man in Early China* (Stanford: Stanford University Press, 1969), p. 17: "all people are equally deserving; all should be tolerated, none singled out for favor". While the Taoists did espouse a primitive solidarity within society, this was derived from a fundamental respect for the identity of the individual. See, generally, Joseph Needham, *Science and Civilization in China* Vol. II (Cambridge: Cambridge University Press), pp. 99, et seq. and pp. 139, et seq.

63. For discussion of individualism and its suppression by early Confucian orthodoxy, see, Etienne Balazs, *Chinese Civilization and Bureaucracy* (A.F. Wright, ed., H. M. Wright tr.) New Haven: Yale University Press, 1964), pp. 21-22, 177. The emergence of activism and reformism in the "new text Confucianism" of the 19th century raised the possibility of increased tolerance for individualistic scholarship and research within the literati elite - a significant departure from the staid intellectual collectivism of prior years, although this too was ultimately unsuccessful. See, Benjamin A. Elman, *From Philosophy to Philology: Intellectual and Social Aspects of Change in Late Imperial China* (Cambridge, Mass.: Harvard University Press, 1984), pp. 26-36 and *Classicism, Politics, and Kinship: The Ch'ang-chou School of New Text Confucianism in Late Imperial China* (Berkeley. Los Angeles and London: University of California Press, 1990) Chapter Nine.

64. See, e.g., Bo Yang, *The Ugly Chinaman and the Crisis of Chinese Culture* (Don J. Cohn and Jing Qing, tr.) (St. Leonards NSW: Allen and Unwin, 1992); Wang Ruoshui, "Wei rendao zhuyi bianhu" (In defense of humanism), in Wang Ruoshui, ed., *Wei rendao zhuyi bianhu* (Beijing: United Press, 1986), pp. 217-233. Also see Ann Kent, *Between Freedom and Subsistence: China and Human Rights* (Hong Kong: Oxford University Press, 1993), pp. 136-153.

65. See, "Final Declaration of the Regional Meeting for Asia of the World Conference on Human Rights" (1993), *supra*, Art. 8. Also see, "Human Rights and Economic Development" 28 *The Int'l Lawyer* 727 (1994).

66. See, Third Plenum Communique, *supra*, p. 21.

67. See, e.g., Economic Contract Law of the PRC (1981), Art. 4; General Principles of Civil Law (1986), Art. 7; Foreign Economic Contract Law of the PRC, Arts 4 and 9.

68. Shortly after the reform program was initially approved, existing laws and regulations on workers were supplemented by new measures addressing worker training, safety conditions in factories, and labour insurance and other issues of workers' rights. See, e.g., "Guowuyuan guanyu laodong jiaoyang de buchong guiding" (State Council supplemental regulations on the training of workers) (Nov. 29, 1979); "Guanyu jiaqiang guang kuang qiye fang chen fang du gongzuo de baogao" (Directive on strengthening the prevention of dust and gas in factories and mines) (March 10, 1979); and "Guanyu zhengdun yu jiaqiang laodong baoxian gongzuo de tongzhi" (Circular on rectifying and strengthening labour insurance work) (March 14, 1980), in State Economic Committee Economic Laws and Regulations Bureau, Beijing Political Legal Institute Economic and Civil Law Teaching and Research Office, ed., *Zhonghua renmin gongheguo gongye qiye fagui xuanbian* (Compilation of laws and regulations on industrial enterprises) (Beijing: Law Publishers, 1981), at p. 462, pp. 532-538, and pp. 545-546. More extensive measures were enacted to govern foreign-invested enterprises. See, e.g. Implementing Regulations for the Joint Venture Law of the PRC, Art. 87 (concerning pre-profit payments to worker bonus and welfare funds) and Arts. 91, et seq. (concerning maintenance of labor conditions and benefits), in CCH *China Laws for Foreign Business*, para. 6-550. Also see, "Regulations of the PRC on Labour Management in Joint Ventures Using Chinese and Foreign Investment" (1980) (JV Labor Regulations), in CCH Australia, *China Laws for Foreign Business*, para. 6-520; and "Provisions for the Implementation of the Regulations on Labour Management in Joint Ventures

Using Chinese and Foreign Investment" (1984) (JV Labor Implementing Rules), in CCH Australia, *China Laws for Foreign Business*, para. 6-522.

69. See, e.g., Lester Ross and Mitchell A. Silk, "Environmental Law and Policy in China," *Chinese Law and Government* Spring, 1986.

70. See, generally, Kristen Parris, "Local Initiative and National Reform: The Wenzhou Model of Development", 134 *The China Quarterly* 242 (1993).

71. See, *Xinhua* reporting on PRC Supreme People's Court President Ren Jianxin's reports to the First Session of the Eighth National People's Congress March 22, 1993, in "Curt President Ren Jianxin Reports to Session", *FBIS Daily Report-China* Mar. 23, 1993, pp. 40-42.

72. Interviews conducted by the author during April-May 1995.

73. See, generally, Chen Feng, "Dalu [Wu gua feng] meng gua bu zhi" (The wind of corrupt reporting in the Mainland is blowing unceasingly), in *Zhengming* (HK), No. 198, Apr. 1994, p. 19.

74. See, generally, John Kohut, "Going to War on Corruption", in *South China Morning Post*, Apr. 17, 1994, p. 5.

75. See, e.g, Vaclav Smil, "China's Environmental Morass," in *Current History*, September, 1989.

76. See, "Environmental Protection Law of the PRC" (1990), "State Council Decision on Further Stengthening Environmental Protection Work" (1990).

77. See, e.g., "Damming Debate", in *China Rights Forum* Spring 1993, pp. 14-16.

78. See, Liu Ping, "Dying for Development", in *China Rights Forum* Fall, 1994, pp. 14-15, 27.

79. See, generally, Elizabeth J. Perry, "Casting a Chinee "Democracy Moverment: The Roles of Students, Workers, and Entrepreneurs", in Jeffrey N. Wasserstrom and Elizabeth J. Perry, eds., *Popular Protect & Political Culture in Modern China: Learning From 1989* (Boulder: Westview, 1992), pp. 146-164, at pp. 154,
et seq.

80. See, Mobo C.F. Gao, "On the sharp end of China's economic boom - migrant workers", in *China Rights Forum*, Spring 1994, pp. 12-13, 27.

81. See, "Text of Human Rights White Paper", *FBIS Daily Report-China*, Supplement, Nov. 21, 1991, at p. 2-4.

82. See, generally, see, Ann Kent, *Between Freedom and Subsistence: China and Human Rights* (Hong Kong: Oxford University Press, 1993), p. 204. Also see, "China: New Arrests Linked to Worker Rights", in *Human Rights Watch/Asia*, Mar. 11, 1994.

83. See, generally Lloyd E. Eastman, "Nationalist China During the Nanjing Decade (1927-1937)", in John K. Fairbank and Albert Feuerwerker, ed., *The Cambridge History of China: Volume 13 - Republican China* (Cambridge: Cambridge University Press, 1986), pp. 547-608.

84. See, "The Progress of Human Rights in China", Xinhua Domestic Service Dec. 27, 1995, in *FBIS Daily Report* Dec. 28, 1995, pp. 8-26.

The Legal and Constitutional Basis of Human Rights, the Right to Development and the Law of Proportionality

ERROL P. MENDES[*]

Historical Introduction

Human Rights in Western Europe and North America arose as a consequence of the end of the shackles of the Middle Age feudal society.[1] Throughout human history, feudal societies have been characterised by isolated, intolerant rulers who transformed even noble ideologies into prisons for the economic and political bondage of the governed. This was true of the natural law foundations of medieval Europe when rulers focused on the duties of God's children to justify massive human rights abuses. With the ascent of the Rennaisance and the decline of European feudalism, the long transition from duties of the citizen to the rights of the citizen under natural law began.[2]

The first major legal and constitutional entrenchment of human rights in western civilisation began with the *Magna Carta* of 1215, the *Petition of Right* of 1628 and the English *Bill of Rights* in 1689. The fundamental principle upon which all these documents rested was that no ruler could be above the law or, to put it another way, that no governing power could be absolute, arbitrary or irresponsible.[3]

The transition from duties to rights was assisted by the new natural law theories postulated by the great philosophers of the seventeenth and eighteenth centuries, in particular John Locke, Montesquieu and Jean-Jacques Rousseau.[4] The influence of these philosophers continue to the present day.

In the 17th Century, John Locke asserted that the Sovereign State did not create the rights of its citizens. Rather its citizens created the state to preserve their inalienable fundamental rights, including the rights to life, liberty and to private property. It can justifiably be said that the acceptance of these rights laid the foundations for the legitimacy of the free market economy.[5] The right to liberty was interpreted to include the freedom from arbitary rule. Similar

---

[*] The author wishes to thank Karen L. Rudner for her invaluable research assistance on this article.

philosophical theories which advocated that fundamental individual rights pre-existed the Sovereign State were also accepted in France and other European countries. This included Jean-Jacques Rousseau's social contract thesis in the eighteenth century which laid the philosophical foundations for the French Revolution, which in turn established the French *Declaration of the Rights of Man and of the Citizen* of August 26, 1789.

The American Revolutionary leaders, including Thomas Jefferson, learning from the French and English philosophers, translated their deeply-held beliefs that fundamental civil and political rights pre-existed the State into the famous words of the U.S. Declaration of Independence which was promulgated on July 4, 1776:

> We hold these truths to be self-evident, that all men are created equal,
> that they are endowed by their Creator with certain unalienable Rights,
> that among these are Life, Liberty and the Pursuit of Happiness.

These philosophical earthquakes that profoundly affected the development of human history arose out of the rejection of unfettered political power and the "Divine Rule of Kings". The lessons learned even today from this history is that the Rule of Law is a force that no power on earth can resist forever.

Eventually these beliefs were constitutionally entrenched in the *U.S. Bill of Rights*. However, while the theory that fundamental civil and political rights pre-existed States became the most entrenched ideology of Western Europe and America, it soon drew its critics. In particular, because natural rights were couched in absolutist terms such as "inalienable", "unalterable" or "eternal", there was a fear that such rights could undermine the State's attempt to advance the general welfare of the whole community.

In particular, the founders of the Utilitarianism philosophical movement grappled with the State's duty to provide for the general welfare of the people - which is in essence "the right to development".

Jeremy Bentham in the 19th century argued that the major purpose of law should be to provide for the greatest happiness of the "greatest number of people" which could again be the essence of the right to development. This concept of general average welfare encompasses what has come to be known as economic, social and cultural rights which the State creates. According to accepted Western liberal philosophy, these rights do not pre-exist the State as opposed to civil and political rights.

With the passing of the *Universal Declaration of Human Rights* by the U.N. General Assembly, and the promulgation of the Covenants on Civil and Political Rights, and Economic, Social and Cultural Rights, many developing countries around the world, including the People's Republic of China, have asserted that despite the teachings of Western political and legal philosophy, civil and political rights cannot take primacy over economic, social and cultural rights, including the right to development.

In the 1982 *Constitution of the People's Republic of China*, there seems to be guarantees of a range of rights that are similar to those of Western Democracies founded on the liberal philosophy discussed above. Among these rights are freedom of speech, press, association, religious belief and practice, inviolability of the person and protection from unlawful arrest and search of the person. In addition, there are some social and economic rights in the Chinese constitution which are not found in many western constitutions, including that of America. These include the right to employment and security and free access to medical care.[6]

However, Article 51 of the Chinese Constitution then places a substantial caveat on the guarantee of these rights by stating: "The exercise of citizens of the PRC of their freedoms and rights may not infringe upon the interests of the state, of society and of the collective or upon the lawful freedoms and rights of other citizens."[7]

It is, in this context, that China has insisted that the rights of the individual must be balanced against the "foremost" right of the Chinese people, namely the right to subsistence. The White Paper on Human Rights in China put it this way:[8]

It is a simple truth that, for any country or nation, the right to subsistence is the most important of all human rights, without which the other rights are out of question. The Universal Declaration of Human Rights affirms that everyone has the right to life, liberty and the security of the person. In old China, aggression by imperialism and oppression by feudalism and bureaucrat-capitalism deprived the people of all guarantee for their lives, and an uncountable number of them perished in war and famine. To solve their human rights problems, the first thing for the Chinese people to do is, for historical reasons, to secure the right to subsistence.

Jeremy Bentham could have been commissioned by China to write such sentiments.[9] However, as we shall see, legal and constitutional development in western countries, like Canada, have attempted to find a middle path between the seeming absolutism of natural rights and the dictates of societal utility.

Many developing countries, including the People's Republic of China, have supported the view that the right to development or subsistence should be regarded as primordial as civil and political rights. The concern by many Asian leaders is that fundamental civil and political rights are rooted in western philosophical, legal and constitutional traditions of individualism, as described above. In contrast, the primary political and legal agendas of many Asian countries are to secure the collective rights of their people to economic and social development. Therefore, the main efforts of many Asian countries, including China, in the area of legal and constitutional guarantees of human rights is to ensure that the collective rights of their peoples are not undermined by the primacy of civil and political rights of individuals originating from western liberal traditions.

Western governments and non-governmental organisations fear that this approach would ultimately result in the gross abuse of individual civil and political rights in the pursuit of the right to development.

The different perspectives of the Western legal and constitutional traditions and Asian perspectives on fundamental human rights was the major focus of a heated debate in Vienna during the 1993 World Conference on Human Rights which discussed progress in the area of human rights since the Teheran declaration on Human Rights twenty-five years previously. The following are samples of the statements made by some of the major western governments at the Plenary Sessions: World Conference held in Vienna in June, 1993.

1) By Warren Christopher, U.S. Secretary of State: "That each of us comes from different cultures absolves none of us from our obligation to comply with the Universal Declaration [of Human Rights]. Torture, rape, racism, anti-Semitism, arbitrary detention, ethnic cleansing, and politically motivated disappearances -- none of these is tolerated by any faith, creed, or culture that respects humanity. Nor can they be justified by the demands of economic development or political expediency."[10]

2) By Martin Morland, U.K. Permanent Representative to the U.N. at Geneva: "Some here will say that respect for human rights must take second place to development. I believe that this is wrong, a serious political and social heresy. I do of course recognize that human rights and prosperity are inter-related. But that means they support one another and grow together. Respect for human rights is no more an optional luxury than is development itself. Indeed lack of respect for human rights will blight economic advance faster than almost anything."[11]

3) By Dr. Klaus Kinkel, Minister for Foreign Affairs for Germany: "It must be stated clearly that neither a lack in social and economic

development nor an ideology solely aimed at achieving affluence can serve to justify the denial of fundamental freedoms and political rights."[12]

In contrast, at the fourth session of the preparatory committee meeting to the Vienna Conference, held at Geneva in April and May of 1993, China emphasized the fundamental importance of the right to development through the statements by Ambassador Jin Yongjian, the Chinese Head of Delegation to the meeting:

> The Bangkok Declaration adopted at the [Asian Regional] meeting showed the willingness of Asian countries to respect the principles and purposes of the UN Charter to safeguard and promote human rights and fundamental freedoms as well as their ideals and determinations to adopt practical measures to raise the level of human rights enjoyment by the Asian people. The basic spirit and contents of the Bangkok Declaration should be fully reflected in the final document of the World Conference.
>
> In our view the final document of the World Conference should:
>
> 1) Emphasize the respect of principles of national sovereignty, territorial integrity, non-interference in the internal affairs of state and the non-use of human rights as an instrument of political pressures, [including right to a) determine own political system; b) freely pursue economic and social development; c) discourage use of human rights as a conditionality for extending development assistance; d) elimination of practice of selectivity and double-standards];
>
> 2) Underline the essential need to create favourable conditions at both national and international levels for the effective enjoyment of human rights, bearing in mind the significance of national and regional particularities and various historical, cultural and religious backgrounds;
>
> 3) Reiterate the interdependence and indivisibility of economic, social, cultural, civil, and political rights, and the need to give equal emphasis to all categories of human rights;

4) Strongly oppose the manifestations of mass and flagrant violations of human rights caused by racial discrimination, racism...colonialism, foreign aggression and occupation... neo-nazism, xenophobia and ethnic cleansing;

5) Reiterate that the right to development...is a universal and inalienable right and an integral part of fundamental human rights, which must be realized through international cooperation, and recognize that the main obstacle to the realization of the right to development lies at the international macro-economic level;

6) Emphasize the necessity of guaranteeing the human rights and fundamental freedoms of vulnerable groups...;

7) Emphasize the necessity to rationalize the United Nations human rights mechanism[s]...and call for increased representation of the developing countries in the Centre for Human Rights.

So far as the UN is concerned, there are organs like the General Assembly, the Security Council, ECOSOC and so on. They have their respective mandates in political, economic, social and other fields. The mandates and spheres of activities of these organs differ from one another. Only by fulfilling its own mandates by each organ, can the United Nations perform its duty well. Therefore, we should adopt a practical and realistic attitude, neither neglecting the protection of human rights nor putting these issues in an appropriate scale, thus affecting or even replacing the normal activities of other organs.[13]

Prior to the Vienna World Conference, China had been very active in promoting the right to development as a fundamental human right. In the official Government White Paper, it is noted that China participated in every session of the governmental experts group organised by the U.N. Commission on Human Rights to draft the *Declaration on the Right to Development* and made positive suggestions until the Declaration was passed by the 41st session of the UN General Assembly in 1986. The White Paper goes on to note that China energetically supported the Commission on Human Rights in conducting worldwide consultation on the implementation of the right to development.[14]

The final declaration of the 1993 Vienna World Conference on Human Rights attempted to mask the substantial differences by emphasising both

Western and Chinese perspectives on the right to development. Paragraph 10 of the *Vienna Declaration* states:

> The World Conference on Human Right reaffirms the right to development, as established in the Declaration on the Right to Development, as a universal and inalienable right and an integral part of fundamental human rights.
>
> As stated in the Declaration on the Right to Development, the human person is the central subject of development.
>
> While development facilitates the enjoyment of all human rights, the lack of development may not be invoked to justify the abridgment of internationally recognized human rights.
>
> States should cooperate with each other in ensuring development and eliminating obstacles to development. The international community should promote an effective international cooperation for the realization of the right to development and the elimination of the obstacles to development.
>
> Lasting progress towards the implementation of the right to development requires effective development policies at the national level, as well as at the international level.[15]

One annotated commentary of the *Vienna Declaration* noted that the reference to the right to development as an inalienable right led some states to voice concern that other rights would not enjoy the same degree of absoluteness.[16] The philosophical basis of fundamental human rights have turned full circle. Now we see Bentham's principles of utility and the general average welfare given the same status as the natural rights of citizens which he so derided.

The reality that a deeper philosophical, legal and constitutional basis is required to balance civil and political rights with the right to development is illustrated by other comments by states at the Vienna Conference, such as the view that protection of a free press means nothing if the people are illiterate. The final declaration of the Vienna Conference has only papered over a fundamental conflict between the West and some Asian countries, including China, as to the relationship between social and economic rights embodied in the right to development and civil and political rights.

But must civil and political rights and economic, social and cultural rights encompassed in the right to development be placed in a hierarchy in a cold confrontational manner which pits North and some Asian countries as perpetual adversaries? At the fundamental root of the conflict is the so-called conflict between the collectivist nature of social and economic rights encompassed in the notion of the right to development and most of the civil and political rights which are rooted in classical liberal notions of individual autonomy.

The Constitutional Basis of Human Rights in Canada and the Canadian Reconciliation of the Conflict Between Individual and Collective Rights

Canada is the western country that can argue that individual and collective rights need not be perpetually in conflict but rather can be reconciled in a practical and pragmatic fashion.

Canada is both a very new country, less than 200 years old and also a very old country since its first inhabitants, the Aboriginal people of Canada, have lived here from time immemorial. We have, in comparison to many European nations, a very diverse population. Over one-third of Canadians can trace their origins from France and are concentrated in the province of Quebec, where they form a powerful majority. Increasingly, Canadian society is becoming a mirror of the global society as we welcome immigration from all over the world. Very soon our major cities - Toronto, Montreal and Vancouver - could become majority non-European in origin, creating calls by racial and ethnic minorities for collective rights to equality.

The collective rights of all these diverse parts of Canadian society have been guaranteed in the *Canadian Charter of Rights and Freedoms* entrenched in our Constitution in 1982.[17] In the Constitution, we recognize the collective rights of our Aboriginal people, and our multicultural and multiracial communities. Through court decisions and provisions of the original Constitution and the Charter of Rights, we recognize the collective rights of our French-speaking population.

The wording of some of the provisions in the Canadian *Charter*, which recognize collective rights, pose some interesting dilemmas for those who are steeped in the natural rights philosophy of western classical liberalism. To give some examples:

• Section 23(3) which entrenches minority linguistic rights in Canada states:

The right of citizens of Canada under subsections (1) and (2) to have their children receive primary and secondary school instruction in the language of the English or French linguistic minority population of a province

> (a) applies wherever in the province the number of children of citizens who have such a right is sufficient to warrant the provision of them out of public funds of minority language instruction; and

> (b) includes, where the number of those children so warrants the right to have them receive that instruction in minority language educational facilities provided out of public funds.

This is a curious type of right to be found in a constitutional document in a western liberal democracy where the exercise of the right is contingent on the number of people who wish to exercise it! Imagine a similar contingent right related to the freedom of speech. This entrenchment of linguistic rights in Canada points to the fact that collective rights require an examination of the sociological, economic and cultural backgrounds from which they arise.[18]

• Section 35(1) which entrenches the rights of the aboriginal peoples of Canada states:

The existing aboriginal and treaty rights of the aboriginal peoples of Canada are hereby recognized and affirmed.

The case law on this Section has clearly indicated that included in this right is the right of the Aboriginal peoples of Canada to their traditional means of subsistence and development, including their inherent right to self-government.[19]

• Finally in Section 27 of the Charter, one finds an interpretive Section which reinforces the view that racial and ethnic minorities in Canada have socio-cultural collective rights. It states:

This Charter shall be interpreted in a manner consistent with the preservation and enhancement of the multicultural heritage of Canadians.

This Section requires that all rights and freedoms in the *Charter* be interpreted in a manner that, not only ensures the survival of the collectivist principle of cultural pluralism, but also promotes its actual enhancement. Does it not seem paradoxical that individual rights found in other sections of the *Charter* must be interpreted in a way that not only preserves but enhances the collectivist principle of cultural pluralism?

Let us examine what this collectivist principle of multicultural heritage of Canadians consists of as set out in Section 27. For the purpose of the ensuing discussion, I am assuming that the concept of multiculturalism is equivalent to the concept of multicultural heritage of Canadians. It is imperative to define multiculturalism first. Attempts to define multiculturalism have usually set out an historical evolution of Canadian nationhood accompanied by what the concept means or should mean today. The 1987 House of Commons Report entitled *Multiculturalism*[20] arrives at the following essential features of multiculturalism:

• Multiculturalism is a principle applicable to all Canadians and it seeks to preserve and promote a heterogeneous society in Canada. The principle refutes the idea that all citizens should assimilate to one standard paradigm over time.

• Multiculturalism is today most fundamentally concerned with ensuring substantial equality for all Canadians regardless of what cultural groups they belong to.

If this is correct, then the interpretive rule in Section 27 is a mandate for Canadian courts and governments to interpret all rights and freedoms in the *Charter*, even those focused on individual rights, in a manner that preserves cultural pluralism and substantive equality among all citizens in Canada. This is a fundamental principle of distributive justice.

As others have expounded, distributive justice encapsulates every aspect of all human societies because all human societies are also institutions of distribution. Different political and legal systems promote different distributions of society's most valued assets such as power, knowledge, wealth, security of the person, health and education. In human history, some societies have either expressly (e.g. the former apartheid regime in South Africa) or de facto (including many so-called western liberal democracies) allowed full and equal access to the above-mentioned societal goods only to those who conform to a singular and dominant racial, ethnic, linguistic or cultural paradigm. This has been the root cause of much of the racial and ethnic strife that we see around the world today. The multicultural principle denies that such societal distributional criteria can ever be just. Such a collectivist principle regards that all manifestations of race, language, ethnicity or national origins are equally worthy. The multicultural principle aims at the establishment of a society where no one segment of society can claim that they have the singular and dominant racial, cultural, ethnic or linguistic paradigm and on that basis have the predominant access to society's most valued goods. This is also the predominant value behind the equality guarantee in Section 15 of the *Canadian Charter of Rights and Freedoms* as confirmed by the jurisprudence of the Supreme Court of Canada.[21]

The most relevant and controversial conclusion from this analysis of Section 27 is that there will be situations when the exercise of individual rights will, in some circumstances, have to give way to the collectivist principle of cultural pluralism, where the exercise of such rights impedes the equal access by minority groups to the most important goods in our society. This has been illustrated in the area of hate propaganda, as will be discussed below.

But the *Canadian Charter of Rights and Freedoms* and Canadian society also recognize the equal value of civil and political rights based on the dignity of the individual human being. Many of the civil and political rights are stated in absolute terms that seems to allow little room for abridgement. For example, Section 2 of the *Canadian Charter of Rights and Freedoms* states:

> Everyone has the following fundamental freedoms:
> (a) freedom of conscience and religion;
> (b) freedom of thought, belief, opinion and expression, including freedom of the press and other means of communication;
> (c) freedom of peaceful assembly; and
> (d) freedom of association".

The jurisprudence of the Canadian Supreme Court has imposed a two-step approach to interpreting rights such as these in any litigation process. First, the complainant who is alleging that his or her rights have been infringed must establish a *prima facie* case that the government has violated the guaranteed right. This first step is almost a process in natural law thinking. No governmental justification for abridgement of the right is permitted at this stage. For example, even the curtailment by government action or legislation of the vilest forms of hate propaganda has been ruled a violation of Section 2. The Supreme Court has held that any form of communication has expressive content and government restriction of any such form of expression is a violation of Section 2(b).[22]

However, despite this seemingly initial natural law approach to civil and political rights, we do not put collective rights and interests of groups and society always in a subordinate position to individual liberty and freedom. Rather we attempt to balance the categories of rights by what I call "the fundamental justice and law of proportionality".

This concept of proportionality is introduced in the first Section of our *Charter*, which I suggest has some striking similarities to Article 51 of the Chinese Constitution. This section states:

> The rights set out in the Charter are subject to reasonable limits demonstrably justified in a free and democratic society.

The section comes into operation after the plaintiff has proven that there is a *prima facie* violation of his or her rights, as described above. The burden of proof then switches to the government to show that it can justify such a violation on the basis of the criteria set out in Section 1. If it can, its actions will be deemed constitutional and valid. In effect, the Canadian Supreme Court will allow governments to override rights to promote the "general average welfare" of the people, where the fundamental justice and law of proportionality is satisfied. Perhaps this is the ideal fashion in which to exercise the foremost right of the Chinese people, namely the right to subsistence and development.

The law of proportionality entrenched in Section 1 of the Canadian *Charter* has been interpreted by the Canadian Supreme Court to contain fundamental principles of justice. The rest of this chapter will:

- discuss the birth and evolution of Section 1;

- examine each of the requirements embodied in the distinct phrases in Section 1, namely "reasonable and demonstrably justified", "prescribed by law" and, "free and democratic society";

- analyse the four branches of the *Oakes* test which set out the requirements that must be fulfilled for a limit to be "reasonable and demonstrably justified in a free and democratic society"; and

- discuss how the Supreme Court of Canada seems to be rejecting a strict and rigid interpretation of the *Oakes* test in favour of an analysis which searches for a background theory of social justice.

Origins of Section 1

Section 1 was included in the *Charter of Rights and Freedoms* as a reaction to the fact that the American *Bill of Rights* guaranteed individual rights absolutely, without any limitations.[23] Fearful of creating a society that may guarantee its liberty, but lose its values of community and representative democracy, the constitutional drafters sought to wrap the guaranteed rights and freedoms with an extremely flexible limitation clause. Such a clause would offer society, through its legislative and executive representatives, a recourse to avoid liberty and freedom, undermining the very community whose rights and freedoms the *Charter* was supposed to protect.

Section 1 was amended to its present form, as set out above, in April of 1981. The original 1980 version provided that Charter rights were "subject only to such reasonable limits as are generally accepted in a free and democratic society with a parliamentary system of government."[24] This original draft came under severe criticism by among others, the Canadian Human Rights Commission. The Commission issued a statement to the Hays-Joyal Committee submitting that the original version offered "unacceptably broad excuses for the limitation of rights and freedoms...any general limitation clause in the Charter should accord with the accepted clauses in the International Bill of Rights (i.e. the Universal Declaration of Human Rights, the International Covenant on Economic Social and Cultural Rights, the International Covenant on Civil and Political Rights, and the Optional Protocol to that Covenant)..."[25]

In the face of such opposition to the original version of Section 1, amendments were made to harmonize the wording with Canada's obligations under international human rights instruments and customary international law.

However, opinion was still divided as to the efficacy of including a limitation clause since some feared that it might water down the *Charter*.[26]

Distinct phrases in Section 1

The reasonable and demonstrably justified standard: two requirements articulated as one standard

While Section 52 seemingly grants Courts the wide latitude to deem legislation to be of no force or effect, Section 1 limits this power of judicial review, stating that legislation that contravenes a right can still be preserved if it is reasonable and demonstrably justified in a free and democratic society. Thus, the Court will not proceed to a Section 1 analysis unless the legislation in question is deemed to have violated one of the rights or freedoms guaranteed by the *Charter*.

Although the rights and freedoms guaranteed by the *Charter* are not absolute, in order for a Court to uphold a law that limits a right, it must balance the value of that individual freedom against the value of the collective goal. A

Court must be satisfied that a limit on such a right is <u>both</u> reasonable and demonstrably justified. These two requirements, however, have not been dealt with separately by the courts but rather have been treated as a single standard. This may be explained by the fact that logic dictates that in order for a limit to be demonstrably justified it must also be reasonable, therefore making a double inquiry redundant.[27]

Prescribed by law

The addition of this phrase in the April 1981 amendment meant that a law that violates a *Charter* right cannot be upheld as a "reasonable limit" if it has not been "prescribed by law." The Supreme Court first elaborated upon this term in *R v. Therens,*[28] when Mr. Justice Le Dain stated:

> The requirement that the limit be prescribed by law is chiefly concerned with the distinction between a limit imposed by law and one that is arbitrary. The limit will be prescribed by law within the meaning of s.1 if it is expressly provided for by statute or regulation, or results by necessary implication from the terms of a statute or regulation or from its operating requirements. The limit may also result from the application of a common law rule.[29]

The Supreme Court in *R. v. Therens* held that the failure of a police officer to inform the accused of his right to retain and instruct counsel, when demanding a breathalyzer test pursuant to s. 235 of the Criminal Code, was a violation of s. 10(b) of the *Charter*. Furthermore, this violation resulted from the officer's own failure to pay attention to the guarantees expressed in the *Charter* rather than from any limit prescribed by Parliament.[30]

Sopinka J. in *R. v. Butler*[31] adopted the test set out in *Osborne v. Canada (Treasury Board)*[32], namely "whether the law is so obscure as to be incapable of interpretation with any degree of precision using the ordinary tools...".[33] The legislation at issue was s.163(8) of the Criminal Code which provided that "any publication a dominant characteristic of which is the <u>undue</u> exploitation of sex, or of sex and any one or more of...crime, horror, cruelty and violence, shall be deemed to be obscene" [emphasis added].[34] Sopinka J. cited *R. v. Morgentaler*[35] in which Beetz J. found that a provision can still be prescribed by law even though terms contained therein may be subject to different legal interpretations by the courts. Since the term "undue" had been given meaning in prior judgments, it was considered to be "prescribed by law" despite the lack of a precise technical definition.[36]

It should be noted that the idea of the paramountcy of "law" ie. formal executive and legislative action over the arbitrary acts of private individuals and government officials is not a new concept unique to Section 1, but is rather a fundamental principle articulated as "the rule of law".[37]

Put another way, the phrase "prescribed by law" requires that "the legislature [provide] an intelligible standard according to which the judiciary must do its work."[38]

In recent years, however, the Courts have ascribed less and less importance to this requirement to the extent that in *Canada (Human Rights Commission) v. Taylor*, McLaughlin J. did not consider "prescribed by law" as part of the Section 1 inquiry. She first concluded that Section 13(1) of the *Canadian Human Rights Act*, S.C. 1976-77, c. 33 constituted a limit prescribed by law and then proceeded to a Section 1 analysis.[39]

Free and democratic society

Chief Justice Dickson, in *R. v. Oakes* focused upon the final words of Section 1 as they were seen as "the ultimate standard against which a limit on a right or freedom must be shown, despite its effect...".[40] Because Canada is a free and democratic society, the courts must be guided by the values inherent in these concepts such as:

> ...respect for the inherent dignity of the human person, commitment to social justice and equality, accommodation of a wide variety of beliefs, respect for cultural and group identity, and faith in social and political institutions which enhance the participation of individuals and groups in society.[41]

Lamer J. gave further meaning to these principles in *Reference re ss. 193 & 195.1(1)(c) of the Criminal Code (Man.)*[42] when he stated that citizens living in a free and democratic society should be "able, as far as possible, to foresee the consequences of their conduct, in order that persons be given fair notice of what to avoid, and that the discretion of those entrusted with law enforcement is limited by clear and explicit legislative standards."[43]

In addition, McIntyre J. in *Irwin Toy* stated that freedom of expression is "a principle of vital importance in a free and democratic society."[44]

These interpretations of a free and democratic society, are open-ended and may possibly conflict with each other.[45] However, inherent in the discussion about the meaning of the phrase is a struggle to find a background theory of social justice that would form the basis of the interpretative task set by Section

1. Yet these pronouncements seem to have fallen into the dark recesses of *Charter* precedent, while formalistic tests that form the basis of the rest of the interpretation of Section 1 have taken overwhelming prominence. These formalistic tests were to be subsumed under the name of the first case in which the Supreme Court undertook to wrap the open-texture of Section 1, *R. v. Oakes.*[46]

The Oakes Test

The four requirements

Dickson C.J.C., speaking for a unanimous Court in *Oakes* adopted a formalistic approach to the interpretation and application of Section 1. He articulated the following four requirements that must be satisfied to prove that a law limiting a right is reasonable and demonstrably justified in a free and democratic society:

1) Sufficiently Important Objective:
Dickson C.J.C. stated: "...the objective, which the measures responsible for a limit on a Charter right or freedom are designed to serve, must be 'of sufficient importance' to warrant overriding a constitutionally protected right or freedom".[47]

The remaining three requirements set out "a form of proportionality test" which evaluates the means adopted to achieve the objective. Defined by Dickson C.J.C. in *Oakes*, they are as follows:

2) Rational Connection to the Objective:
"...the measures adopted must be carefully designed to achieve the objective in question. They must not be arbitrary, unfair or based on irrational considerations. In short, they must be rationally connected to the objective."[48]

3) Least Drastic Means:
The law in question "should impair "as little as possible" the right or freedom in question."[49]

4) Proportionality Between Effects and Objective:
"...there must be a proportionality between the effects of the measures which are responsible for limiting the Charter right or freedom, and the objective which has been identified as of `sufficient importance.'"[50]

Analysis of the Four Requirements

1) Sufficiently Important Objective:

Dickson C.J.C. in *Oakes* outlined the criteria necessary to demonstrate that the objective of the impugned law is of sufficient importance to justify limiting a *Charter* right:

> The objective must be consistent with the "principles integral to a free and democratic society... at a minimum...an objective [must] relate to concerns which are pressing and substantial in a free and democratic society..."[51]

These requirements appear at first sight to place a rather onerous burden on the party wishing to have the limitation upheld since, for example, the term "pressing" denotes only those goals which are immediate in nature. Thus, an objective designed to combat unfairness or injustice over the long term could be rejected,[52] because they impact on rights and freedoms in the present. Such was the case in *National Citizen's Coalition Inc. et al. v. Attorney General for Canada* [53] where the Court held that Sections 70.1(1) and 72 of the *Canada Elections Act* which prohibited third party campaign spending during elections violated Section 2(b) and could not be saved by Section 1. The Court reasoned that:

> Fears or concerns of mischief that may occur are not adequate reasons for imposing a limitation. There should be actual demonstration of harm or a real likelihood of harm to a society value before a limitation can be said to be justified.[54]

However, in *Andrews*, McIntyre J. of the Supreme Court of Canada[55] recognized the difficulties inherent in requiring that the objective be "pressing and substantial." He stated that such a test may deny Canadian society the benefits of "sound social and economic legislation."[56] In its place, he would apply a less stringent test:

In my opinion, in approaching a case such as the one before us, the first question the Court should ask must relate to the nature and the purpose of the enactment, with a view to deciding whether the limitation represents a legitimate exercise of the legislative power for the attainment of a desirable social objective which would warrant overriding constitutionally protected rights.[57]

In general, the courts have often been reluctant to second guess the legislature's choice of objective, if the legislation can be championed as having a social justice agenda.

There is one notable exception in the jurisprudence to such deference to the legislature, namely the landmark decision in *R. v. Big M Drug Mart Ltd.*[58] In that case, the Supreme Court held that the objective of the *Lord's Day Act*[59], the federal Sunday closing law, was to "compel the observance of the Christian Sabbath."[60] Given the fact that the purpose of the impugned legislation was clearly religious (thereby contravening the *Charter* right of freedom of religion) rather than the secular objective of providing a common day of rest for employees, it could not be said to justify limiting that constitutionally guaranteed freedom.

Perhaps the anomaly that this case represents could be explained on the basis that where the Supreme Court finds no secular social justice agenda involved in the impugned legislation, they will apply a more formalistic interpretation of the "pressing and substantial" test.

In order to discover the true objective of the Act, the Supreme Court in *Big M.* focused on its legislative history and noted that an objective cannot evolve with the passing of time or change with the social climate. In the words of Dickson C.J.C.: "Purpose is a function of the intent of those who drafted and enacted the legislation at the time, and not of any shifting variable."[61]

However, in *R. v. Butler,*[62] Sopinka J. writing for the majority failed to give credence to the shifting purpose rule as argued by the challengers to the obscenity provisions of the Criminal Code. They argued that the original purpose was to safeguard society from the corrupting influence of obscene materials but the government was now characterizing the objective as preventing violence against women and children. Sopinka J. deferred to the legislature by framing the objective in general terms as preventing harm to society. Thus, it did not matter whether the harm was immorality or violence.

Conversely, if the Court wishes to take an activist stance to strike down legislation that does not have a defendable social agenda and find the impugned legislation invalid it will define the objective very narrowly. For example, in *Andrews*, the majority defined the purpose of s.42 of the *Barrister and Solicitors*

Act [63] which limited membership to the bar to Canadian citizens as restricting entry to the legal profession. However, as we have seen in the *Butler* decision, the Court seems to have shied away from this activist position and has, more often than not, interpreted the impugned legislation as having a defendable social agenda. *Rodriguez v. British Columbia (A.G.)* is yet another example of this trend away from the activist position. In that case, the objective of the Criminal Code provisions against assisted suicide were construed very broadly as preventing human life from being devalued. [64]

McLachlin J. in *R.J.R- MacDonald Inc. v. Canada (A.G.)*, however, cautioned against stating the objective too broadly when she concluded that the objective should be phrased in terms of the impugned measure rather than the whole legislative and policy scheme. [65]

It is interesting to note that the courts have frowned upon the legislature citing administrative convenience as a justification for limiting a *Charter* right. For example, Lamer J. stated in *Reference re s.94(2) of Motor Vehicle Act (British Columbia)* [66] that "administrative expediency [should only be considered a legitimate objective] in cases arising out of exceptional conditions, such as natural disasters, the outbreak of war, epidemics and the like." [67] This opinion was reiterated by Wilson J. in *Singh v. Minister of Employment & Immigration* [68], by Lamer C.J.C. again in *Schacter v. Canada (Employment and Immigration Commission)* [69] and by Dickson C.J.C. in *R. v. Schwartz* who stated that "administrative convenience...is rarely if ever an objective of sufficient importance." [70] The legislation in *R. v. Edward Books and Arts Limited* fell within this exception for the Chief Justice because "alternate forms of business regulation do not generally impinge on the values and provisions of the Charter of Rights and the resultant legislation need not be tuned with great precision in order to withstand judicial scrutiny". [71] In addition, in *R. v. Lee* [72] the majority upheld a section of the Criminal Code which provided that an accused lost his/her right to be tried by a jury if he/she did not appear for trial and had no legitimate excuse. Thus, in that case the majority considered cost efficiency and the reduction of administrative inconvenience to be a legitimate objective. [73]

2) Rational Connection to the Objective:

This second step can only be reached when the objective of the law has been deemed to be of sufficient importance to justify limiting a *Charter* right.

The requirement that the means by which the law is implemented be rationally connected to the objective "calls for an assessment of how well the legislative garment has been tailored to suit its purpose." [74] To illustrate, at issue in *Oakes* was the validity of s.8 of the *Narcotic Control Act* [75] which placed the onus on the accused to prove that he/she was not in possession of an illegal substance for the purpose of trafficking when it had been proven that he/she was in possession. Although the objective (to curtail drug trafficking) was held to be legitimate, no "rational connection between the basic fact of possession and the presumed fact of possession for the purpose of trafficking"[76] could be found. Put another way, the means used were too heavy-handed or too extreme given the objective since a person could be charged with the serious offence of trafficking even though he/she was in possession of a very small quantity of drugs.

It is rare that the courts will find that a law is not rationally connected to the objective. However, McLachlin J., speaking for the majority in *Miron v. Trudel,* found that excluding unmarried partners from receiving accident benefits available to married couples was not rationally connected to the legislative goal of reducing the economic hardship on families when one member is injured in a motor vehicle accident.[77] L'Heureux-Dubé J. and Iacobucci J., in their respective dissents in *Egan v. Canada*, found that the exclusion of same-sex couples in the *Old Age Security Act* was not rationally connected to the objective of ensuring that when one partner retires, the couple will continue to receive income equivalent to the amount that would be earned if both were retired.[78]

Generally, however, the Court seems to apply a standard of "minimal rationality"[79] requiring the government to only demonstrate that the means chosen will further the objective. This standard is reflected in cases such as *Rocket v. Royal College of Dental Surgeons of Ontario*[80] where McLachlin J., writing for the majority, found that legislation which limited the ability of dentists to advertize was rationally connected to the objective because the "objectives of promoting professionalism and avoiding irresponsible and misleading advertising will clearly be furthered by s.37(39)".[81] Another example of this relaxed standard used in the civil context can be found in *Edmonton Journal v. Alberta (A.G.)*[82] in which Wilson J. found it sufficient to state, without further explanation. that legislation which limited media coverage of matrimonial proceedings was rationally connected to the objective of protecting privacy.[83] Furthermore, in *RJR-MacDonald*, McLachlin J. stated that scientific evidence was not required to establish a rational connection between the impugned measure and its objective where the legislation in question is aimed at changing human behavior.[84] In the recent cases of *Ross v. New Brunswick School District* and *Butler*, the Supreme Court further developed the relaxed standard. For example in *Ross*, LaForest J. accepted that it was "reasonable to presume" a causal relationship between a teacher's public discriminatory statements and the harm to students, thus, the Board of Inquiry order removing him from his teaching position was found to be rationally connected to the objective of ensuring discrimination-free educational services.[85]

It should be noted that this more flexible approach has not been limited to the civil context. For example, the Supreme Court held in the *Prostitution Reference*[86] that Criminal Code provisions which prohibited communication for the purpose of solicitation in places open to public view were rationally connected to the objective of preventing "the public display of the sale of sex and any harmful consequences that flow from it."[87] Lamer J. had no difficulty justifying this finding on the basis that the legislation "reduce[s] or limit[s] the mischief"[88] by criminalizing the conduct that produces it. In addition, Dickson C.J.C. writing for the majority in *R. v. Keegstra*[89] found that the hate propaganda sections of the Criminal Code would satisfy the rational connection test unless the party challenging the provisions could demonstrate that they had either an adverse or no impact on the objective.[90]

3) Least Drastic Means:

Once the legitimate objective and rational connection requirements are satisfied, only then can the legislation in question proceed to the third step of least drastic means which was adopted from American jurisprudence dealing with the First Amendment.[91]

While the courts have been quick to conclude that a legislative objective is sufficiently important and that a law is rationally connected to the objective, the same `rubber stamp' has not been applied to the requirement of least drastic means.[92] Indeed this requirement has been the focus of the Section 1 inquiry. For example, Lamer J. speaking for the majority in *R. v. Généreux*[93] focused his decision upon the least drastic means requirement and effectively ignored the other branches of the test.[94]

Dickson C.J.C. in *Oakes* described this branch of the test as requiring that the impugned legislation impair the right or freedom "as little as possible."[95] This definition placed an unreasonable burden on those seeking to uphold the legislation because it was easy to imagine an alternative that may have been less effective but which impaired the right to a lesser extent.[96] For example, requiring the exclusive use of French in commercial signs was deemed to be far too drastic a means of promoting and maintaining the French language.[97] Prohibiting the media from covering matrimonial proceedings was held to be too drastic a means of protecting privacy.[98] The rape shield provisions of the Criminal Code restricting the defence's right to cross examine and lead evidence of a complainant's sexual conduct during a sexual assault trial was held to be too drastic a means of preventing false inferences that the complainant may have consented or is lying.[99]

In *Edward Books*, Dickson C.J.C. seemed to recognize that too high a standard was demanded of the legislature since he reformulated the test to require that the law impair the freedom in question "as little as is reasonably possible."[100] The inquiry focused on "whether there is some reasonable alternative scheme which would allow the province to achieve its objective with fewer detrimental effects...".[101] A certain amount of deference to the legislature was implied when he further stated that the court was "not called upon to substitute judicial opinions for legislative ones as to the place at which to draw a precise line."[102] LaForest J. also observed that "a legislature must be given reasonable room to manoeuvre."[103] In a later case, he reiterated that this branch of the *Oakes* test must be characterized by flexibility.[104] In so doing, he criticized Dickson C.J.C.'s statement in *Oakes* that the means should impair "as little as possible": "The difficulty I have with this approach is that it seeks to apply the Oakes test in too rigid a fashion, without regard to the context in which it is to be applied."[105]

In *Irwin Toy*, the majority held that the courts should practice judicial restraint only in cases where the government is "mediating between the claims of competing groups" or safeguarding the interests of vulnerable groups.[106] In those cases, the government need only demonstrate a reasonable basis for believing that the means employed were the least drastic means possible. In contrast, the courts must adopt a hard line approach in those cases in which "the government is best characterized as the singular antagonist of the individual whose right has been infringed."[107] In other words, in criminal cases, the Court recommends a rigid application of the *Oakes* test. As the legislation in question in *Irwin Toy* banned commercial advertising aimed at children under the age of thirteen, it could be seen as protecting a group vulnerable to media manipulation and thus merited a more relaxed application of the *Oakes* test. This analysis was applied by Lamer C.J.C. in his dissent in *Rodriguez v. B.C.(A.G.)*.[108] While the impugned legislation was a criminal code provision, the state could not be seen as the "singular antagonist of the individual" because the case had not been generated by a criminal prosecution.[109]

The trend towards deference to legislative decisions was taken a step further in *R. v. Chaulk*,[110] in which Lamer C.J.C. formulated the test as "whether Parliament could reasonably have chosen an alternative means which would have achieved the identified objective as effectively."[111] In formulating this question, Lamer looked to *Irwin Toy* and *The Prostitution Reference* as the basis for the conclusion that Parliament has no obligation to chose the "absolutely least intrusive means" of meeting its objective.[112] It is sufficient that Parliament has chosen from a "range of means" which infringe the *Charter* right "as little as is reasonably possible."[113] While he listed several hypothetical provisions which might infringe upon the *Charter* to a lesser extent, he acknowledged that these may or may not achieve the desired objective as effectively as the legislation already in place.[114]

This much less demanding test of efficacy is also reflected in the majority decision of Dickson C.J.C. in the *Prostitution Reference* in which he phrased the question as "can effective yet less intrusive legislation be imagined?"[115] Thus, the government is not obligated to devise "...the perfect scheme that could be imagined by this Court or any other Court"[116] to satisfy this branch of the test.

Yet another variation of this more deferential approach to *Oakes* can be found in *Tétreault-Gadoury v. Canada (Employment and Immigration Commission)* where the Court asked whether the government could "show that it had a reasonable basis for concluding that it has complied with the requirement of minimal impairment."[117]

4) Proportionality Between Effects and Objective:

Even if the impugned legislation satisfies all three previous steps, "it is still possible that, because of the severity of the deleterious effects of a measure on individuals or groups, the measure will not be justified by the purposes it is intended to serve."[118] Thus in theory, even if the least drastic means are employed, they may still be too severe to maintain. Indeed, the more severe the deleterious effects, the more important the government objective must be in order to satisfy this branch of the *Oakes* test. As Dickson C.J.C. stated in *Edward Books*, the "effects [of the legislation] must not so severely trench on individual or group rights that the legislative objective, albeit important, is nevertheless outweighed by the abridgement of rights."[119]

It is often the case that once the court finds that the least drastic means requirement is satisfied, it will deem there to be proportionality between effects and objective as well. Indeed, in certain cases such as *RWDSU v. Saskatchewan* and *McKinney v. University of Guelph*[120] and *Rodriguez,*[121] this latter requirement was not analysed as a component separate and apart from the least drastic means test.

However, in *R. v. Morgentaler,*[122] Madam Justice Wilson began her Section 1 analysis by focusing on this last branch of the *Oakes* test and virtually ignored the least drastic means requirement. The pivotal question for her was: "at what point in the pregnancy does the protection of the foetus become such a pressing and substantial concern as to outweigh the fundamental right of the woman to decide whether or not to carry the foetus to term?"[123]

Professor Peter Hogg has described this fourth step as a test of the objective of the law rather than of the means since it weighs the benefit of the objective against the cost of the violation of the Charter right.[124] As such, it is seen as merely reiterating the "sufficiently important objective" test. In fact, Professor Hogg surmises that if an objective is held to be sufficiently important, the effects of the legislation will not be deemed to be too severe.[125]

Other authors, such as Pierre Blache and The Honourable Mr. Justice Roger P. Kerans have commented on how ineffectual this last branch of the *Oakes* test seems: The former advanced the view that"...the third step has no real weakening impact on the first two steps. It comes too late in the process...it seems that it is a step that should almost never be reached."[126] The latter that the last two branches of the *Oakes* test are really in fact one: "One requires that the limit `impair the right as little as possible'; the other that it not `so severely trench' that its legislative objective is outweighed by the abridgment of rights."[127]

Burden and standard of proof

The burden of proof in a Section 1 defence "rests upon the party seeking to uphold the limitation"[128] and the civil standard of "proof by a preponderance of probability"[129] is to be applied "rigorously". However, in *Edward Books*, Dickson C.J.C. advocated a more relaxed approach when he stated that "[b]oth in articulating the standard of proof and in describing the criteria comprising the proportionality requirement the Court has been careful to avoid rigid and inflexible standards."[130]

Conclusion

While the Supreme Court continues to cite *Oakes* in an almost ritualistic fashion, various judges have expressed a discomfort with the rigid and inflexible test which originated from one criminal case involving legal rights. Thus, as we have seen, the test had to be reshaped and moulded carefully to adapt to changing needs, the nature of the interests in question and the particular circumstances of the case. Indeed, Dickson C.J.C., the creator of the test, recognized this and wished to make it "clear that a rigid and formalistic approach to the application of Section 1 must be avoided".[131]

LaForest J. offered an alternative to *Oakes*: "I prefer to think in terms of a single test for s. 1, but one that is to be applied to vastly differing situations with the flexibility and realism inherent in the word 'reasonable' mandated by the Constitution."[132]

From the analysis of the Canadian Constitutional principles on the justice and law of proportionality, we see that there is a possible universal approach to reconciling individual freedoms with the collective rights and goals of groups and societies. Such an approach respects all societies' right to development and fundamental social and economic rights, but insists on minimal safeguards when the pursuit of such collective rights and goals infringe on fundamental individual rights and freedoms. These minimal safeguards that comprise the justice and law of proportionality can be summarized as follows:

- Any limitation on rights must be prescribed by law. This essentially means the Rule of Law. Limits on rights must be clear, precise and not based on administrative discretion or government policy. Citizens must have certainty and predictability in how their governments behave towards them.

- The limit on rights (whether individual or collective) must invoke an urgent and substantive societal interest, not just a desire to keep a particular government or party in power.

- The limit on rights (whether individual or collective) must be done in the least intrusive way. In other words, the government's action to promote the welfare of the people must be proportionate not excessive.

- If the government's actions to promote the people's welfare has excessively damaging consequences (whether intended or not), such action may become disproportionate to the government's objectives and so violate the law of proportionality.

The Supreme Court of Canada has applied this law of proportionality on many occasions to show that civil and political rights can be balanced with economic, social and cultural rights.

In conclusion, I would urge the North and the South to cease an expensive and ultimately empty conflict over human rights and the right to development and examine the Canadian solution, namely the law of proportionality.

I would urge the examination of the law of proportionality in all areas of the legal system and institutions for a more fundamental reason. The justice of proportionality makes law and governments the servants of the people. This is the true meaning of democracy. It is when the people become the servants of the law and governments that tyranny and injustice begin.

Notes

1. See Burns H. Weston, "Human Rights" in R.P. Claude and B.H. Weston (eds) *Human Rights in the World Community: Issues and Actions* (Philadelphia: University of Pennsylvania Press, 1989) at 13.

2. Ibid.

3. J. Bartlet Brebner, "Magna Carta" in R.M. MacIver (ed.) *Great Expressions of Human Rights; A Series of Addresses and Discussions* (Port Washington, N.Y.: Kennikat Press, 1969)

4. Supra note 1 at 13-14.

5. Id. at 14.

6. R.P. Peerenboom "What's wrong with Chinese Rights: Toward a Theory of Rights with Chinese Characteristics" (1993) 6 *Harvard Human Rights Journal* 29.

7. *Zhongguo Renmin Gongheguo Xianfa* [Constitution of the People's Republic of China] as cited in Ibid. at footnote 1.

8. Information Office of the State Council, *Human Rights in China* (Beijing, China: Information Office of the State Council, 1991).

9. Bentham in work entitled "An Introduction to the Principles of Morals and Legislation" in J.C. Smith and D.N. Weisstub (eds), *The Western Idea of Law* (Toronto : Butterworths 1983) 506, states at page 506:

> Nature has placed mankind under the governance of two sovereign masters, *pain* and *pleasure.* It is for them alone to point out what we ought to do, as well as to determine what we shall do. On the one hand the standard of right and wrong, on the other the chain of causes and effects, are fastened to their throne. They govern us in all we do, in all we say, in all we think: every effort we can make to throw off our subjection, will serve but to demonstrate and confirm it. In words a man may pretend to abjure their empire: but in reality he will remain subject to it all the while. The *principle of utility* recognizes this

subjection, and assumes if for the foundation of that system, the object of which is to rear the fabric of felicity by the hands of reason and of law. Systems which attempt to question it, deal in sounds instead of sense, in caprice instead of reason, in darkness instead of light..."

10. *Plenary Sessions: World Conference* (Vienna, 1993) as cited in Jan Bauer, *Report on United Nations World Conference on Human Rights* June 14-25, 1993, Vienna, Austria (Ottawa: Human Rights Research and Education Centre, 1993) at 144. (N.B. the excerpts and summaries of government statements were derived from written texts, which bore the caveat "check against delivery")

11. Ibid.

12. Id. at 129.

13. Id. at 121-122.

14. Supra note 10 at 81-82.

15. Vienna Declaration and Programme of Action, World Conference on Human Rights, Vienna, 14-25 June, 1993, in U.N. Doc. A/Conf.157/23 (12 July 1993)

16. Jan Bauer, *Report on United Nations World Conference on Human Rights*, June 14-25, 1993, Vienna, Austria (Ottawa: Human Rights Research and Education Centre, 1993) at 69.

17. *Canadian Charter of Rights and Freedoms*, Part 1 of the *Constitution Act, 1982*, being Schedule B of the *Canada Act 1982* (U.K.), c. 11 [hereinafter the *Charter*].

18. For example, in *Mahe v. Alberta*, [1990] 1 S.C.R. 342, it was held that the number of francophone students in the Edmonton area justified the establishment of a separate francophone school and the representation by francophone parents on the school board, with a measure of management and control of the school. However, there were not enough francophone students to justify an independent francophone school board. Where the numbers warrant, Section 23 confers upon minority language parents a right to management and control over the educational facilities in which their children are taught, to ensure their language and culture flourish.

19. In *R. v. Sparrow*, [1990] 1 S.C.R. 1075, the Court had to determine the status of aboriginal or treaty rights that had been extinguished or regulated before 1982. The Court held that the word "existing" in Section 35 meant "unextinguished". Therefore, a right which had been validly extinguished before 1982 was not now protected by Section 35. However, in *Sparrow*, the Court refused to imply an extinguishment of the aboriginal right to fish by the *Fisheries Act*, despite its extensive regulatory scheme because it did not demonstrate "a clear and plain intention to extinguish the Indian aboriginal right to fish" (at page 1099). An unextinguished aboriginal right should be treated as existing in its unregulated form. An existing aboriginal right cannot be read so as to incorporate the specific manner in which it was regulated before 1982. The phrase "existing aboriginal rights" must be interpreted flexibly so as to permit their evolution over time. The Court further held that Section 35(1) is to be construed in a purposive way. A generous liberal interpretation is demanded given that the provision is to affirm aboriginal rights. However, although Section 35 is not part of the *Charter* and therefore not subject to a Section 1 analysis, *infra*, the Court held that these Section 35 rights were not absolute, but were subject to regulation, provided that any impairment must be a justified impairment, pursuing an object that was "compelling and substantial" (at 1113).

20. House of Commons Standing Committee report on *Multiculturalism; Building the Canadian Mosaic*, 2nd. Sess. 33rd Parl., 1987, pp. 22-23.

21. Section 15 of the *Charter* provides:

15.(1) Every individual is equal before and under the law and has the right to the equal protection and equal benefit of the law without discrimination and, in particular, without discrimination based on race, national or ethnic origin, colour, religion, sex, age or mental or physical disability.

(2) Subsection (1) does not preclude any law, program or activity that has as its object the amelioration of conditions of disadvantaged groups including those that are disadvantaged because of race, national or ethnic origin, colour, religion, sex, age or mental or physical disability.

For example, in *Andrews v. Law Society of British Columbia*, [1989] 1 S.C.R. 143, Andrews, a British subject permanently resident in Canada, met all the requirements for admission to the British Columbia bar, except that of

Canadian citizenship. He sought a declaration that this statutory requirement violated Section 15(1) of the *Charter*. The Supreme Court of Canada found that a rule which barred an entire class of persons from certain forms of employment, solely on the grounds of citizenship status and without consideration of educational and professional qualifications or the other attributes or merits of the individuals in the group, infringed Section 15 equality rights. The Court found that the impugned Section 42 of the *Barristers and Solicitors Act* was such a rule.

22. *Irwin Toy Ltd. v. Quebec (Attorney General)*, [1989] 1 S.C.R. 927 (hereinafter *Irwin Toy*); *R. v. Keegstra*, [1990] 3 S.C.R 697 (hereinafter *Keegstra*).

23. See J. Cameron, "The Original Conception of Section 1 and its Demise: A Comment on *Irwin Toy Ltd v. Attorney General of Quebec*" (1989), 35 *McGill Law Journal* 253 at 254,257; and H. Marx, "Entrenchment, Limitations and Non-Obstante" in W.S. Tarnopolsky & G.-A. Beaudoin, eds, *The Canadian Charter of Rights and Freedoms: Commentary* (Toronto: Carswell, 1982) at 63-66.

24. *Proposed Resolution for Joint Address to Her Majesty the Queen Respecting the Constitution of Canada*, Tabled in the House of Commons and the Senate, October 6, 1980 as cited in A.F. Bayefsky, *International Human Rights Law: Use in Canadian Charter of Rights and Freedoms Litigation* (Toronto: Butterworths, 1992) at 39.

25. Ibid. Indeed, Dickson stated in *Reference Re Public Service Employee Relations Act (Alberta)*, [1987] 1 S.C.R. 313 at 349: "I believe that the Charter should generally be presumed to provide protection at least as great as that afforded by similar provisions in international human rights documents which Canada has ratified."

26. P.W. Hogg and R. Penner, "The Contribution of Chief Justice Dickson to an Interpretive Framework and Value System for Section 1 of the Charter of Rights" (1991), 20:2 *Manitoba Law Journal* 428 at 431.

27. P.W. Hogg, "Section 1 Revisited" (1991), 1 *N.J.C.L.* 1-24 at 2.

28. [1985] 1 S.C.R. 613. Le Dain's definition was approved by the Court in *R. v. Thomsen*, [1988] 1 S.C.R. 640 at 650-651.

29. *R v.Therens, id.* at 645.

It should be noted that previous lower court decisions articulated the meaning behind "prescribed by law." For example, the Divisional Court in *Re Ontario Film & Video Appreciation Society and Ontario Board of Censors* (1983), 41 O.R. (2d) 583 at 592,(affirmed by C.A. (1984) 5 D.L.R. (4th) 766) held that the censorship provisions of the *Theatres Act* violated the applicant's freedom of expression and were not "prescribed by law." Although the board had been granted the power by the legislature to prohibit the exhibition of any film to which it disapproved, these limits were not prescribed by law due to their discretionary character. "...[L]aw cannot be vague, undefined, and totally discretionary; it must be ascertainable and understandable. Any limits placed on the freedom of expression cannot be left to the whim of an official; such limits must be articulated with some precision or they cannot be considered to be law."

In addition, the Federal Court of Appeal in *Re Luscher* (1985) 17 D.L.R. (4th) 503 held that a law that prohibits the importation of obscene and immoral material is too vague and imprecise to constitute a reasonable limit prescribed by law.

Serge Gaudet sees these judgments as "formalistic" rather than "legalistic" interpretations. Whereas the former focuses on the form/content of the law or regulation, etc. and requires that it be reasonably accessible and sufficiently precise, the latter simply gives a rubber stamp to any legislation that has come into effect in conformity with the judicial system in place. (in S. Gaudet, "La regle de droit au sens de l'article premier de la Charte Canadienne des droits et libertes: Commentaires sur l'affaire Slaight Communications Inc. c. Davidson, [1989] 1 *R.C.S.* 1038" (1990), 20 *R.D.U.S.* 448 at 456,458-461,463.)

30. Supra, note 28 at 662.

31. [1992] 1 S.C.R. 452.

32. [1991] 2 S.C.R. 69 at 94.

33. Supra, note 31 at 490.

34. *Criminal Code*, R.S.C. 1985, c. C-46.

35. [1988] 1 S.C.R. 30 at 107. *Butler, supra* note 31 at 491.

36. Ibid.

37. For example, in *Re Resolution to Amend the Canadian Constitution*, [1981] 1 S.C.R. 753 at 805-806, the Court referred to the rule of law as "a highly textured expression...conveying, for example, a sense of orderliness, of subjection to known legal rules and of executive accountability to legal authority."

In addition, the majority in *Reference re Manitoba Language Rights*, [1985] 1 S.C.R. 721 at 748-749 described the rule of law as a "fundamental principle of our Constitution" and defined it as meaning that "the law is supreme over officials of the government as well as private individuals, and thereby preclusive of the influence of arbitrary power." Further, "the rule of law expresses a preference for law and order within a community rather than anarchy, warfare and constant strife..."

Also see: L.E. Weinrib, "The Supreme Court of Canada and Section One of the Charter" (1988), 10 *Supreme Court Review* 469 at 475-477.

38. *Irwin Toy*, supra, note 22 at 983.

39. [1990] 3 S.C.R. 892 at 954. See also Dickson C.J.'s comments agreeing with McLachlin J. at 915-916.

40. [1986] 1 S.C.R. 103 at 136 [hereinafter *Oakes*].

41. Ibid.

42. [1990] 1 S.C.R. 1123 (hereinafter *Prostitution Reference*).

43. Id. at 1152. Lamer J. indicated that in the criminal law context, this takes on an added importance.

44. Supra, note 22 at 1008.

45. The Supreme Court seems to have valued the "commitment to social justice and equality" over the other principles as this can be reconciled with the inherent dignity of the human person. See E.P. Mendes,"In Search of a Theory of Social Justice; The Supreme Court Reconceives the Oakes Test" (1990), 24:1 *La revue juridique thémis* 1 at 6, footnote 15.

46. Supra, note 40.

47. Id. at 138, quoting *R. v. Big M Drug Mart*, [1985] 1 S.C.R. 295 at 352 (hereinafter *Big M*).

48. Id. at 139.

49. Ibid, quoting *Big M*, supra, note 47 at 352.

50. Ibid.

51. Id. at 138-139.

52. Mendes, supra, note 45 at 7.

53. (1985), 11 D.L.R. (4th) 481 (Alta. Q.B.).

54. Id. at 496.

55. *Andrews v. Law Society of British Columbia*, [1989] 1 S.C.R. 143.

56. Id. at 184.

57. Ibid.

58. [1985] 1 S.C.R. 295 (hereinafter *Big M*).

59. R.S.C. 1970, c.L-13.

60. Supra, note 58 at 351.

61. Id., at 335. Also see The Honourable Mr. Justice Roger P. Kerans, "The Future of Section One of the Charter" (1989), 23:3 *University of British Columbia Law Review* 567 at 573.

62. Supra, note 31.

63. R.S.B.C. c.1979, c.26.

64. [1993] 3 S.C.R. 519 at 613.

65. [1995] 3 S.C.R. 199 at 335. McLachlin J. stated that the objective of the impugned provisions of the *Tobacco Products Control Act* (which prohibited advertising and promotion of tobacco products unless the package included prescribed health warnings and a list of the toxic contents) was to prevent Canadians from being persuaded by advertisements to use tobacco products.

However, the objective of the general legislative and policy scheme was to safeguard Canadians from the risks of tobacco use.

66. [1985] 2 S.C.R. 486.

67. Id. at 518.

68. [1985] 1 S.C.R. 177.
This case revolved around the question whether every refugee arriving to Canada had to be given a full hearing. The Attorney General of Canada justified limiting rights under section 7 as this would save the government time and money. Wilson J. rejected these utilitarian considerations when she wrote:
> Certainly the guarantees of the Charter would be illusory if they could be ignored because it was administratively convenient to do so...The principles of natural justice and procedural fairness which have long been espoused by our courts, and the constitutional entrenchment of the principles of fundamental justice in s.7, implicitly recognize that a balance of administrative convenience does not override the need to adhere to these principles... (at 218-219).

69. [1992] 2 S.C.R. 679 at 709. Lamer J. emphasized that budgetary considerations are not a legitimate objective and thus cannot justify an infringement under section 1.

70. [1988] 2 S.C.R. 443 at 472.

71. [1986] 2 S.C.R. 713 at 772. (hereinafter *Edward Books*). Dickson C.J.C. stated that "simplicity and administrative convenience are legitimate concerns for the drafters of such legislation." (ibid.).

72. [1989] 2 S.C.R. 1384.

73. Wilson J., in her dissent, remained true to form when she held that the objective of reducing administrative inconvenience and expense was not a sufficiently important objective that could justify limiting section 11(f), ie., the *Charter* right to a trial by a jury. (*Id*, at 1420).

74. *Edward Books*, supra note 71 at 770.

75. R.S.C. 1970 c. N-1.

76. Supra, note 40 at 141.

77. [1995] 2 S.C.R. 418 at 503.

78. (1995), 124 D.L.R. (4th) 609 (S.C.C) at 680.

79. R. Elliot, "Developments in Constitutional Law: The 1989-90 Term" (1991), 2 *Sup. Ct. L. Rev.* (2d) 83 at 142.

80. [1990] 2 S.C.R. 232.

81. Id. at 250.

82. [1989] 2 S.C.R. 1326.

83. Id. at 1367.

84. Supra, note 65 at 339.

85. [1996] S.C.J. No. 40 at 49.

86. Supra, note 42.

87. Id. at 1212.

88. Id. at 1195-6.

89. Supra, note 22.

90. Id. at 768.

91. P.A. Chapman, "The Politics of Judging: Section 1 of the Charter of Rights and Freedoms" (1986), 24:4 *Osgoode Hall L.J.* 867 at 883.

92. Supra, note 27 at 17.

93. [1992] 1 S.C.R. 259.

94. Id. at 313-314.

95. Supra, note 40 at 139.

96. Chapman, supra, note 87 at 883.

David Beatty is quoted as stating: "All of its [the Supreme Court's] most famous decisions in which it rules that laws...were unconstitutional can be explained as instances in which the Court, or at least a majority of its members, were satisfied that there were alternate policies available to the Governments involved in those cases which would have interfered with important aspects of human freedom less." (David Beatty, "The end of law: At least as we have known it" (University of Toronto, 1990 [unpublished]) cited in H. Stewart, "What is a Social Critic? Or The End of Beatty (At Least as We Have Known Him)" (1991), 49:1 *University of Toronto Faculty of Law Review* 186 at 189.

97. *Ford v. Quebec (Attorney General)*, [1988] 2 S.C.R. 712 (hereinafter *Ford*). The Court held that the *Charter of the French Language*, R.S.Q., c.C-11, did not impair freedom of expression as little as possible:

> "whereas requiring the predominate display of the French language, even its marked predominance, would be proportionate to the goal of maintaining a French "visage linguistique" in Quebec, and therefore justified under the Quebec Charter and the Canadian Charter, requiring the exclusive use of French has not been so justified. French could be required in addition to any other language or it could be required to have greater visibility than that accorded to other languages" (at 780).

See also *Irwin Toy*, supra note 22, where the Court commented on *Ford*, stating that the government failed to introduce any evidence "to show that the exclusion of all languages other than French was necessary to achieve the objective of protecting the French language..."(at 999).

98. *Edmonton Journal*, supra note 80.

99. *R. v. Seaboyer*, [1991] 2 S.C.R. 577 at 626. (McLachlin J.)

100. Supra, note 70 at 772.

101. Id. at 772-3.

102. Id. at 782.

103. Id. at 795.

104. *United States of America v. Cotroni*, [1989] 1 S.C.R. 1469 at 1489 (hereinafter *Cotroni*). In support of this view, he cited *R. v. Jones*, [1986] 2 S.C.R. 284 at 300; *Edward Books*, supra note 70 at 768-69, 772.
   LaForest J., speaking for the majority in *Cotroni* held that section 6 (mobility right) was infringed as little as possible by the extradition of a Canadian citizen to the United States.

105. *Cotroni*, ibid.

106. Supra, note 22 at 993-4.

107. Id. at 994. Also see Elliot, supra, note 77 at 146-147.

108. [1993] 3 S.C.R. 519.

109. Id. at 563.

110. (1991), 2 S.C.R. (4th) 1. The impugned legislation was s.16(4) of the *Criminal Code*, the presumption of sanity, which the challengers argued was contrary to s.11(d) of the *Charter* (the presumption of innocence).

111. Id. at 31.

112. Id. at 33.

113. Ibid. McLachlin J., in *RJR-MacDonald*, affirmed this principle. Supra, note 65 at 342-343.

114. *Chaulk*, supra note 110 at 32-33.

115. Supra, note 42 at 1137. Dickson C.J.C. emphasized that the Fraser Committee and the Justice and Legal Affairs Committee had presented many alternatives that were considered less effective than the legislation in question (at 1137-8). Lamer J. reiterated this view and further stated that because prostitution is "an especially contentious and at times morally laden issue", the Court has an obligation to defer to the choice Parliament made after it weighed the "competing political pressures" (at 1199).
   Lamer C.J.C. reiterated this position in *Rodriguez* and cited the *Prostitution Reference,* when he stated that assisted suicide may also be seen as "contentious" and "morally laden" requiring a certain amount of deference towards the state's choice of policy options (at 564; Sopinka J. concurring at

614). However, Lamer C.J.C. still found that s. 241(b) of the *Criminal Code* which prohibited aiding a person to commit suicide, failed the least drastic means test as it "encompass[ed] not only people who may be vulnerable to the pressure of others but also persons with no evidence of vulnerability" (at 567).

116. *Prostitution Reference*, *Id.* at 1138. Madam Justice Wilson, in her dissent, adopted a hard-line approach to the "least drastic means test" when she asserted that prohibiting any and all means of communication with a person in a public place for the purpose of prostitution was broad and over-inclusive, as it could criminalize even communication for a lawful purpose (at 1210-1211)

See also: D. Stuart, "Will Section 1 Now Save any *Charter* Violation? The Chaulk Effectiveness Test is Improper" (1991), 2 *C.R.* (4th) 107 at 111.

117. [1991] 2 S.C.R. 22 at 44.

118. Supra, note 40 at 140.

119. Supra, note 71 at 768.

120. [1987] 1 S.C.R. 460 and [1990] 3 S.C.R. 229, respectively. Laforest J. for the majority in *McKinney*, concluded that it was "evident" from his analysis of the minimal impairment test that the effects of the university's mandatory retirement policy did not outweigh the objective and that "...the same factors have to be balanced in dealing with deleterious effects and I need not repeat them" (at 289).

121. Supra, note 108 at 615. Sopinka J. speaking for the majority, felt that no analysis was necessary as "[i]t follows from the above [analysis of the least drastic means test] that I am satisfied that the final aspect of the proportionality test, balance between the restriction and the government objective is also met."

122. Supra, note 35.

123. Id. at 181.

124. Supra, note 27 at 23.

125. Id. at 24.

126. P. Blache, "The Criteria of Justification Under Oakes: Too Much Severity Generated Through Formalism" (1991), 20 *Manitoba Law Journal* 437 at 443.

127. *Kerans*. Supra, note 61 at 570.

128. *Oakes* supra, note 40 at 137.   Dickson C.J.C. points to the word "demonstrably" as indicating that the burden of proof will be shouldered by those wishing to limit the *Charter* right.

129. Ibid. The Court did not adopt the more onerous criminal standard of 'proof beyond a reasonable doubt' because "concepts, such as `reasonableness', `justifiability' and `free and democratic society' are simply not amenable to such a standard." However, section 1 demands a very high degree of probability considering that the party is attempting to justify an infringement of a right guaranteed by the *Charter* (at 138).

It is interesting to note that in *Andrews,* supra, note 12, Wilson J. for the majority seemed to indicate that the weight of the burden of proof would vary according to which section of the *Charter* has been infringed: "Given Section 15 is designed to protect those groups who suffer social, political and legal disadvantage in our society, the burden resting on government to justify the type of discrimination against such groups is appropriately an onerous one." (at 154).

130. Supra, note 71 at 768-9.

131. *Keegstra* supra, note 22 at 737. Dickson C.J.C. writing for the majority.

132. *Andrews* supra, note 21 at 198.

Philosophical Foundations of Human Rights in China: A Marxist Perspective

CHEN ZHISHANG

Human rights is an important subject in humanology research. This essay strives to expound ten theoretical issues related to the philosophical foundation of human rights from a marxist perspective.

The Method of "Seeking the Truth from Facts" Should be Applied to the Study of Human Rights

When researching an issue, one must first acquire the proper research method. The method of "seeking the truth from facts" was Mao Zedong's way of using a Chinese idiom to express the Marxist way of thinking and working. Deng Xiaoping believed that it was the quintessence of Marxism and the principle of building socialism with Chinese characteristics. In fact, it means to apply the world outlook and methodology of dialectical materialism and historical materialism to understand and to deal with all issues. To be more specific, when researching an issue, one's point of departure should not be *a priori* hypotheses, abstract doctrines or subjective aspirations. The point of departure should be the realities of objectively existing targets and subjects, and from there discovering and mastering the essence and laws of the issue. Therefore, the foundation of understanding should be formed on the basis of practical activities of observing and changing the targets. Theories should spring from practice and then become guidance for the correct practice. Failure of the practice becomes a standard against which to examine the accuracy of understanding (theory, plan, design, goal, etc.). As reality is constantly changing, people's social practice is constantly developing as well. Therefore, people's ideas and theories must not remain at a standstill, they must not be conservative to the point of becoming ossified, and they must not be restricted by already out-dated traditional ideas and principles. People's ideas and theories should follow the development of the practice of humanity and the progress of the times. People should consciously change their own ideas and theories, bravely explore and create new theories which are suitable to reality and capable of correctly guiding their practice. This is called liberating ways of thinking, destroying old ideas and establishing new ones. Human rights research should be like this.

For the theory of human rights to become science, the correct premise and starting point based on argumentation must be in place first. Research should commence with the objective facts of reality, i.e. people's social lives, and not with *a priori* doctrines or abstract principles. The theory must be based on humanity's entire practice of human rights. It must not be restricted to a specific era or a partial experience. Human rights is a kind of social phenomenon. Therefore, in order to establish a correct human rights conception it is necessary to be guided by a correct world outlook and social concept of history, to inherit the cultural heritage of humanity's human rights thinking and to refer to the results of other humanistic and social sciences. All of the above are beneficial to enlightening one's thinking, and to explore and to create a scientific human rights theory. However, the theoretical research of human rights must not be limited to simply repeating certain traditional ideas, and it definitely should not idolize certain old theories or practical models (such as the human rights theory and practical model of the 18th century capitalist countries) as the absolute truth and universal standard and thus restrain people's thinking. As times have changed, humanity's experience with human rights practice has already developed significantly. Therefore, in researching human rights it is necessary to eliminate superstitions and to liberate one's thinking. Only then will it be possible to "seek the truth from facts".

Human rights is a hot topic in contemporary politics, but it is still a weak spot in the academic world. This is evidenced by the fact that the theoretical achievements in human rights are still backward compared to the achievements in other academic fields. New ideas often are not widely accepted among scholars. This shows that these theories are not fully developed. There are many reasons why this is so. From the point of view of understanding, it may be related to the difference in research methods. For example, some research tends towards a Euro-centric approach similar to that of studies in history, and it is only based on the human rights materials and experiences of a minority of developed countries, but neglects the human rights materials and experiences of the developing countries in which the majority of the world's population lives. Some academic research is clearly obstructed by politics. For example, as some governments implement the so-called "human rights diplomacy", interfere with the domestic affairs of other countries, and practice hegemonism and power politics, some scholars raise the arguments that "human rights have no borders" and "human rights are superior to sovereignty". These arguments are in fact tailored to the needs of and provide the necessary theoretical validation for carrying out the above kind of politics. The results of this kind of research often deviate from and even distort the real situation in the human rights domain. They run counter to the principle of objectivism and their scientific value is questionable. From this point of view it can also be said that, whether or not it is possible to change the relative backward *status quo* of human rights research so as to maintain an environment for attaining high-level results, depends on whether or not one consciously applies the method of "seeking the truth from facts".

Human Rights is a Product of Social History

According to the traditional western human rights theories, human rights are either given by the Creator or they spring from the nature of human beings and therefore they penetrate human society from beginning to end and as such will never change. This opinion has been accepted by many people, but it has not been scientifically proven. It is merely a kind of *a priory* hypothesis. The Marxist point of view is directly contrary to this way of thinking. On the basis of materialism, it draws upon Hegel's rational ideas, and human rights are regarded as a social phenomenon and a product of history.

Historical facts prove that human rights did not exist from the very beginning of history. During the many years of primitive societies, there was no social phenomenon of human rights in the modern sense, and people did not have a concept of human rights. The foundation of the primitive societies was the clan system. The precondition for its existence was extremely undeveloped production and a very sparse population and, therefore, people had to depend upon each other. The primitive community was made up of blood ties. Its economic structure consisted of simple joint production and equal distribution, therefore, the primitive peoples were only concerned with the interests of the whole clan, not of the individual. No conflicts of interest existed between the individual and the clan or between individuals. People were only conscious of the whole, and not of the individual. Some rules to govern daily affairs existed within the clan, which have been termed by modern scholars as primitive rights and obligations. In fact, they were just an expression of the primitive community's need for survival. Through the accumulation of production and life experiences over a long period of time, behavioral norms were defined by local customs and commonly approved by the members of the clan. These were rules which governed the relationships of the primitive society, they were not "human rights" in the modern sense of the term. Engels said:

The greatness of the clan system was at the same time its limitation, namely that there was no room for domination or slavery. Within the clan system there was no difference between rights and obligations; the question of whether or not it was a right or an obligation to take part in public affairs, to carry out blood revenge or to accept atonement for such actions never existed for the Indians; to the Indians, such a question would have been as absurd as the question of whether or not it was a right or an obligation to eat, sleep or hunt.[1]

Along with the evolution to a civilized society, and with the development of production forces, the increase of society's wealth, the development of labour division and exchange, the privatization of the means of production and the emergence of classes, conflicts of interest arose between different groups of people. Relying on their ownership of the means of production and their material wealth, as well as their control of state power, one group of people had gained political, economical and social privileges, and they had then been able to exploit and suppress another group of people. As a result, the lives of the working people, who made up a majority of the population, were threatened. They not only lost the opportunity to pursue happiness and to develop freely, they also lost the most basic powers of a human being. It is exactly because of such inequality and lack of freedom in real life that the issue of human rights has turned into a struggle against the privileges of the exploiting class, to enable the exploited and suppressed class and all members of society to attain the same conditions and opportunities for survival and development. People then began to develop a consciousness of the social issues, i.e. so-called freedom and equal rights, which were raised for the first time by the emerging social forces (through their political representatives).

However, since the primitive, simplistic concept of equality and freedom of ancient times, human rights thinking underwent a long and tortuous development period from the middle ages through the Renaissance period, and only then did the "human rights" theory, the core of which was to oppose the feudalist autocracy and class privileges and to emphasize capitalist notions of freedom and equality, start to take shape. Until the 18th century, human rights was promoted as the guiding political principle of the countries of Europe and America during their capitalist democratic revolutions. It then underwent another long historical process. This process was closely linked to social, economic and cultural development, mainly centering on the development of modernized large scale production, commodity economy and world trade in western Europe and North America, and it was also linked to the development of the parallel mass revolutionary struggle, which includes capitalism, against feudalism. The victory of the capitalist revolution resulted in a replacement of the feudal society's class privileges by the concept of human rights which governed capitalist social relations.

With the establishment of capitalism in a dominant position in the world, the inherent conflicts within the capitalist system as well as unavoidable and insurmountable social evils created by the exploitative nature of capitalism gradually began to erupt and intensify. The reality of the inequality between the different classes of the new society ruthlessly deemed the theory that "human rights are God given" as false preaching. More people became aware of the historical limitations of human rights under the capitalist system.

The proletariat's and the working people's struggle against class exploitation and social repression gave rise to a new human rights approach, the core content of which was to eliminate exploitation, to eliminate classes and to attain a new level of social freedom and equality. This is precisely the human rights theory of scientific socialism. In countries where the socialist revolution was successful and where socialist systems were consequently established, this kind of theory is turning into reality. However, as Marx pointed out: "Rights must never exceed the social economic structure or the cultural development of society which is conditioned by the economic structure."[2] In a country like China, which is still at the initial stage of socialism, it is unavoidable that numerous inequalities exist between people due to the currently rather undeveloped economy and culture as well as the uneven development of the different regions. Regulation, realization and social guarantee of human rights will progress along with the socialist cause, from incompletion to gradual perfection.

With respect to the future of human rights, Marx formulated the following hypothesis based on historical dialectics: with the establishment of a socialist society and the elimination of classes, all members of society will enjoy a new level of equality and rights. Not only will they, on the political side, become masters of the state, they will also, on the economic side, own all the means of production and be allocated means of subsistence according to amount of labour. This is a historical step forward. However, there still exists for each person a "natural privilege" to receive different levels of remuneration based on one's ability to work. This means that real inequality among members of society in terms of satisfying their needs will persist. "In order to eliminate such social evils, rights should not be equal, they should be unequal."[3] Only after the forces of production in society have been greatly developed, after the economy and culture have reached a high level of development, and after wealth is continously forthcoming, only then will all members of society gradually begin to see beyond the narrow horizon of simply pursuing individual interests and to realize that the value of the individual is, according to human nature, equal to the value of all individuals in society. Society must provide equal conditions and opportunities for everyone to develop freely. Once such recognition becomes a reality of life, i.e. once society starts to allocate means of subsistence according to needs and not according to amount of labour, the notion of human rights will loose its meaning in terms of adjusting the people-to-people relationships based on profit. It will change and develop into a new custom almost as if returning to the primitive society, and it will finally complete its historical mission and wither away.

Human Rights is the Regulator of Existing Social Relations

Western human rights theories, whether they talk about "human rights are God given", "social contract", "legal rights" or "welfare rights", are all based on abstract theories of human nature, and with various subjective and lop-sided hypotheses on human beings, human character or the nature of human beings. They all emphasize the individual. Thus, in reality their philosophical foundations are all historical idealism. The Marxist human rights theory differs from the above in that its philosophical foundation is historical materialism.

First, the Marxist human rights theory is consistent with the natural sciences. According to Marxism, human beings are not created by a God but are the result of a long-term natural evolution. The needs of human beings have long exceeded the physiological needs of animals and have developed into advanced social needs. The methods of satisfying the needs have also long exceeded the animal's passive, inactive, instinctive way of relying on its own organs to adapt to its surroundings. Human beings can take initiative and actively create and use tools to change their surroundings and to engage in creative activities. Therefore, in order to survive and develop, human beings must not "resign themselves to fate" but they must "challenge fate", learn to correctly recognize and apply the rules of nature, to utilize natural resources in a rational manner and to manage well the relationship between people and nature. In other words, they must seek subsistence and freedom from the natural world. This special character of human beings, which is so different from that of all other beings, is the reason why humans can create wealth, make themselves more valuable than all other creatures, i.e. create the inherent foundation of value. This is also the reason why humans, as a matter of course, are able to achieve the inherent foundation of the right to life, enjoyment and development, etc. Therefore, human beings can proudly say that their rights are not given by God, neither are they bestowed by Nature. They have been fought for and achieved by human beings themselves through hard work and experience. In fact, the real conditions of humanity's existence is, in the final analysis, dependent on the depth and expansiveness of human beings' transformation of Nature. The emergence, change and final resolution of the human rights issue are also related to the specific historical stages of the development of society and production.

More important is the fact that Marxism is consistent with anthropology and other social sciences in its conviction that human beings are not only natural beings, they are also social beings. The truth is, the lone individual who has distanced himself from the unity of the group cannot survive. And the group is not simply a gathering of individuals, it is an organic social system with a most complex activity structure. The modern human being is a kind of advanced living matter which can only survive and continue to develop under definite social material conditions by forming definite social relations, and by continuously engaging in material production and other practical activities so as to satisfy its own constantly growing material and cultural needs, and to gain more freedom. The nature of human beings is to engage in production and other practical activities within the realm of social relations. Therefore, the actions of human beings are not only conditioned by the law of nature, they are also, more importantly, conditioned by the social regulations of their own activities. The human rights issue, from a social point of view, deals mainly with the relationship between people, rather than the relationship between people and Nature, i.e. it is an issue of social relations. Thus, the points of departure must be the existence of human beings in society, the conditions for material life in society, the changes and developments of the methods of production in society, or in summary, the foundation of all of humanity. In other words, people's material practices and their material social relations must be the points of departure for investigating the actual historical processes that human rights give rise to and develop. Then, by linking them up with the series of intimately related issues such as being human, human character, human nature, as well as the needs, interests, values, freedom, equality, etc. of human beings, and by researching them further, only then will it be possible to draw up scientific norms on human rights.

Human rights is not a product of some "God", "reason" or "free will". It is not some abstract, inherent and never changing "innate quality". People's rights and their corresponding obligations together form a kind of social phenomenon which is linked to the specific historical stages of social development, and they constitute the kind of social relations which people form through practice. The notion of human rights is then a reflection of people's consciousness of these kind of social relations. Ideally, human rights are people's demands for future social relations. In reality, human rights are a way of regulating existing social relations. The implication is that, based on the contemporary economic structure and level of cultural development, society must (through laws and ethics) acknowledge and guarantee that its members are able to attain normal subsistence, development and enjoyment of necessary social conditions and conduct. In a narrow sense, human rights are those most basic rights which directly relate to surviving, living a normal life, and independently controlling one's own destiny in a modern society. In a broad sense, human rights are the common form of rights expression, i.e. the common denominator for all the political, economic, cultural and social welfare rights which people enjoy in society.

Human Rights is a Systemic Concept Which Must Be Understood in its Entirety

People's social lives and experiences are multifarious, their social relations are multi-layered, and therefore, people's rights (and corresponding obligations) are complex. The human rights system consists of many kinds of rights. Each kind of human right is based on certain needs of people's social lives, and each right is a certain kind of regulation of people's social relations. The position of each human right within the entire system of human rights, and the implication of each right for the individual, the nation, the state and even for all of humanity, however, varies. Thus, the category of human rights is a systemic concept of many layers and varied contents, and one should apply the method of dialectic materialism when carrying out scientific analysis and developing syntheses on human rights.

Human rights can be divided into many categories. For example, the two major categories of material life and spiritual life. It can also be divided into political, economic, cultural, social welfare and other categories. Some scholars in the West itemize human rights as freedom, equality, property, security, opposition to oppression, etc. When analyzed from the point of view of a systemic structure, we believe that human rights can be divided into three levels. The first level comprises people's basic rights which include: 1) the right to life and fundamental freedoms (it means for the individual security of person, personal freedom, acknowledgment and guarantee of personal dignity, enough food and clothing, no infringement on dwelling, freedom of thought and belief, etc. For the collective, it means the right to state independence and sovereignty, the right to national self-determination and autonomy); 2) the right to employment and the right to control and use the income (i.e. personal property) earned from such employment; 3) the right to equality; 4) the right to development.

Every human being living in modern civilization is, from the time of birth, bestowed all of these rights by society. They are the minimum conditions due a person and must not be taken away.

The second level of rights includes civil rights, the rights to which a citizen of a country is entitled. Apart from the above-mentioned basic rights, civil rights refer mainly to political freedom and democratic rights. This means that, on the basis of the country's Constitution and laws, its citizens have the right to participate in the community and in political activities. These are rights which adults can only realize together with others. For example, the right to elect and to be elected. When citizens violate the law, this kind of right can be restricted or taken away.

The third level of rights includes all the rights that human beings have or ought to have. Apart from the above-mentioned basic human rights and civil rights, the third level of rights comprise concrete political, economic, cultural and social welfare rights. For example, intellectual property rights, employment and unemployment protection, the right to rest and leisure, the right to peace, environmental rights, etc. Also included are special individual and group rights and regulations, such as those which apply to the elderly, women, children, the disabled, the sick, prisoners of war, criminals, ethnic minorities, people without nationality, immigrants, etc. Such special rights and regulations do not provide these individuals or groups with more rights than ordinary people. Such rights exist in order to guarantee the weak and disadvantaged equal enjoyment of basic human rights. In fact, such rights are supplementary human rights which must not be omitted in the overall realization of human rights.

When researching human rights, one must analyze the background and content of every level and every aspect of human rights as they are being realized in contemporary society. One must clarify the relationship between each human right and then combine it with the historical examination of the source and development of human rights, as presented in the second section of this essay. Only then will it be possible to develop an in depth comprehension of the essence and norms of human rights from an overall perspective.

The Right to Subsistence is the Most Basic Human Right

This is an important inference drawn by the Chinese government in analyzing the contemporary human rights situation in China and abroad on the basis of the basic theories of Marxism.

According to historical accounts, during the capitalist revolution of western Europe, some philosophers and politicians had already raised the theory that the right to subsistence is the foremost human right. However, their understanding of the right to subsistence was comparatively narrow. They frequently equated it with the right to life, and they used the ideas that rights are given by God or have emerged from the nature of human beings (self-preservation, desire, reason) to substantiate their theory. Today, unfortunately, only very few western scholars are paying any attention to and carrying forward this cultural legacy of humanity.

The right to subsistence, as it is upheld by China today, sums up the practice and experience of the Chinese people and of people all over the world in their struggle for survival. In content it has evolved far beyond the level reached by western philosophers of two hundred years ago. The right to subsistence means that society acknowledges and guarantees for every member of society personal safety, freedom, dignity, as well as the necessary basic material and spiritual living conditions and facilities to function, to survive and to lead a normal social life. Human beings are living things. In order for them to subsist, they must first be able to survive, to eat their fill, to dress warmly and to have a roof over their heads. In order words, they must be provided with the very basics of material life. This alone, however, is not enough. They also need definite guarantees in terms of politics and other social conditions. Were human beings to live in an environment in which their lives were constantly being threatened and violated by outside forces and in which their personal freedom and dignity was not being recognized and respected, and they could be arbitrarily exploited, oppressed, mistreated, traded, insulted, or even killed like domestic animals, they would have lost their basic rights as human beings. Therefore, the right to subsistence is not only limited to the right to life. Its foundation is economic rights, and it also includes basic political and cultural rights and many other categories under the comprehensive heading of social rights. We say that the right to subsistence is the most important right because it is the prerequisite for the realization of other human rights. If the right to subsistence cannot be guaranteed, we simply cannot begin to talk about other human rights. We must also recognize that the right to subsistence is not only a matter of the individual's right to freedom, it is also the collective right of the people, the nation and the state. Experience has proven that, it will only be possible to recognize and guarantee the right to subsistence of each individual member of the group and society when the following conditions have been met: the state has become independent, the nation has been liberated and has achieved equality; the people have escaped oppression, exploitation and slavery and become masters of the country; production has developed in the entire society; it has become possible to produce enough goods to satisfy the needs of all members of society and rational distribution of these goods had been ensured. In other words, the right to subsistence of each individual will be guaranteed when the right to subsistence of the state and the nation have been recognized and guaranteed.

Regarding the right to subsistence as the foremost basic human right is of great significance to setting the direction for the practice of contemporary human rights. First, the right to subsistence is the most pressing and real human rights issue to the developing countries which are home to the majority of the world's population. Due to the histories and social systems of these countries, various social conflicts exist between different classes, nationalities and religions. Such conflicts often lead to social instability, confrontations or even war, and thousands of people have lost their jobs, gone bankrupt, are starving or have lost their lives. Because some developed countries are practising hegemonism and power politics and making huge economic profits by taking advantage of the unbalanced development between the South and the North, the total debt of the developing countries reached 1,350 billion US dollars in 1990 and is increasing annually. The majority of the developing countries still have not been able to solve the problem of feeding and clothing their people, thus many people are living in poverty and struggling to survive. A 1993 report of the United Nations Centre for Human Rights stated: "1.4 billion people in the world are still living in abject poverty, and another 1 billion people are struggling below the poverty line, they have been deprived of all their economic rights." The report recognized that "at least half of the world's population has been deprived of basic human rights." Second, even to the small number of developed countries, the right to subsistence remains the human rights issue of most significance. In these countries, because of the polarization between rich and poor, growing unemployment, racial discrimination, unchecked social corruption and the constant increase in the crime rate, the safety of people's lives and property is often threatened, their fundamental freedoms and personal dignity often are not being respected, and there are always a number of people living in misery below the poverty line. To these people, whose right to subsistence has in fact not been recognized and guaranteed, other human rights exist only on paper. Those who believe that the right to subsistence is no longer an issue in the developed countries are thoroughly mistaken.

China sometimes juxtaposes the right to development and the right to subsistence as the two most important basic human rights. This is because both rights not only complement each other in content, they also promote each other in practice. Realization of the right to subsistence is the prerequisite for the right to development, and the right to development is an extension of the right to subsistence. Only by realizing the right to development can the quality of subsistence be continually improved, and thereby sustained, and reliable guarantees for realizing the right to subsistence would be ensured. This, in turn, would become the driving force behind promoting and realizing the right to development.

Political Rights and Social and Economic Rights are Mutually Dependent and They Promote Each Other

Some people argue that, in examining the issue of human rights, marxism and socialism only address economic and cultural rights while neglecting political rights. We think such arguments indicate a misunderstanding, to say the least.

According to marxism, politics, economics and culture are necessary elements of social life. Of these, the economy forms the foundation; politics represent a concentrated expression of the economy; culture reflects the politics and the economy and its development is conditioned by them. At the same time, culture also plays a major role in influencing the politics and the economy. Therefore, these three elements are mutually dependent, mutually conditioning and they cannot be separated. By examining the human rights issue from this point of view, it becomes apparent that human rights are comprehensive, and people need both political rights and economic and cultural rights in their social practice and social relations. Therefore, be it in theory or in practice, the one kind of right should not be over-emphasized at the expense of the other kind of right. Of course, this is not to say that, in struggling to achieve human rights or in the process of establishing human rights, all kinds of human rights must advance at the same pace all the time. According to the specific circumstances surrounding the practice of human rights in various countries, certain rights could be developed ahead of others according to importance within a limited time frame. But in terms of the strategy and the guiding principle, equal consideration should be given to political, economic, cultural and other rights, so that they can advance together and develop in a comprehensive fashion. China's experience is a good example of this approach.

When the Chinese Communist Party led the Chinese people in the struggle for their rights, it consistently linked together the people's demands for freedom and human rights with the political struggle to overthrow the rule of imperialism, feudalism and bureaucrat-capitalism. This experience proved that, only after the Chinese people had won the revolution, had gone from being oppressed to becoming the masters of the country, and had for the first time achieved democracy and political rights, only then were they able to create the right conditions and provide guarantees for advancing economic, cultural and social rights. This experience also proved that the realization of economic and cultural rights cannot be achieved by the same method used to attain political rights, i.e.

by changing the political system. Apart from depending upon administrative forces to change the economic system, realization of economic and cultural rights depend even more on the level of development of the economy and culture in society. The old China, however, left behind rather backward forces of production. To properly feed and clothe 1.2 billion people, and to satisfy them in terms of subsistence, development, enjoyment, and economic, cultural and social needs, might require several decades or even close to a hundred years of hard work. For this reason, the state must make it a priority to develop the forces of production, and promote the overall progress of society by focussing on economic and cultural development. With regards to human rights, apart from protecting the political rights and freedoms which people have already achieved, the government should, over a relatively long period of time, focus on widespread realization of people's rights to subsistence and development, and highlight the establishment, realization and guarantee of economic, cultural and social rights. Realization of these rights will then, in turn, further consolidate and accelerate the advancement and expansion of people's political rights. Along with the overall development of the socialist cause, each and every right as gained by the people will be continuously substantiated and developed. Therefore, in socialist China where Marxism is the guiding philosophy, people's political rights and their economic and cultural rights are developing in a mutually dependent and mutually enhancing way.

In fact, when studying the history of human rights in the world, it becomes apparent that some western countries have had similar experiences with human rights practice. The real disparity between Eastern and Western approaches to human rights lies in the difference in understanding and the variance in the standards of appraisal. From our point of view, apart from the fact that, in the realization of human rights, differences exist due to uneven levels of cultural and economic development, the socialist approach to human rights is superior to the capitalist approach in that it is far-reaching, genuine and relatively fair. The capitalist approach to human rights is rather narrow, hypocritical and unfair.

The Notion of Human Rights is a Combination of Universality and Particularity

This is an important principle to adhere to in the study of human rights.

According to the theory of materialist dialectics, everything is both universal and particular, that is, a combination of the common and the unusual. This means that any category or system is a dual-sided amalgamation of universality and particularity, and all component parts (phase, realm, molecule) of such an amalgamation are, on the one hand, inter-connected and unanimous and of common attributes and characteristics, and that is what constitutes universality. On the other hand, they are also distinct from each other with separate, special attributes and characteristics, and that is what constitutes particularity. The universal exists within the particular and is expressed through the particular. Therefore, when researching an issue, one must analyze the research target in detail to uncover the concrete situation, get a grasp of the universal and the particular and the relationship between the two, and by all means avoid separating the two. To only acknowledge the universal while denying the particular, or to emphasize the particular while denying the universal, are both expressions of the one-sided approach of metaphysics. When dealing with human rights, one must consider both the universal and the particular.

Human rights are, at the same time, universal and particular. The subjects of human rights are real human beings and the contents of human rights are the regulations which govern the social practice and social relations of human beings. The movements and developments of human society are ruled by common regulations. The social practice and interaction of modern people have long gone beyond the scope of one country to comprise world scale mass production and political, economic and cultural interaction of global universality. In other words, both domestic and international relations exist among modern people. Thus, based on the common needs and common interests for the survival and development of humanity, a specific, shared conception of human rights might naturally emerge and become further regulated and affirmed through international documents such as the *Universal Declaration of Human Rights*, which then becomes the human rights standard acknowledged and protected by each country party to the *Declaration*. This is the universality of human rights. It is only one side of the issue, however. On the other side, until today (and into the foreseeable future), domestic social practice and social relations are still very basic. Because the level of economic and cultural development varies from country to country, and because of the difference between each country's social system, historical traditions, national mentality, religious beliefs, etc., disparities would naturally exist between people from different countries with respect to collective and individual social needs and interests. For this reason, there are different value systems. There are bound to be different ways of understanding, regulating and realizing human rights, and this results in the existence of different human rights models. This is the particularity of human rights. To admit to this point of view is to respect the objective facts of history, and to show real respect for the rights of people in all countries. Therefore, Marxism emphasizes the importance of combining the universality and particularity of human rights and recognizes that every country has a right to select its own human rights model. Because every human rights model is an expression of the particularity of human rights, it adds to the experience of substantiating, correcting and developing the universality of human rights. Whether in theory or in politics, the universality and the particularity of human rights should not be separated and set against each other. To affirm the universality of human rights while denying the particularity, or vice versa, is wrong. It is even more wrong to magnify one kind of particularity (such as the human rights model of North America and Europe), to pass it on as the universal and international standard of human rights and to force it upon other people.

The Notion of Human Rights Has Both a Common Nature and a Class Nature

To study the relationship between the common nature and the class nature of human rights is to deepen the study of the relationship between the universality and the particularity of human rights. This involves applying the Marxist method of analyzing classes to human rights research.

Whether or not there is a class nature to human rights has long been debated within the field of human rights research. We believe that when conducting a comprehensive analysis of the historical realities of the origin and development of human rights, one must acknowledge both the common nature and the class nature of human rights. The key is to correctly comprehend the relationship between the form and the class nature of human rights.

History shows that human rights are different from privileges. The slave and feudal societies clearly dictated that only slave owners, landlords, aristocrats, clergymen and other members of the ruling classes were entitled to certain privileges to which slaves, peasants and ordinary citizens had no right. And the notion of human rights has emerged to negate these privileges. The first Constitution (of 1791) after the French Revolution, proclaimed very clearly:

From now on, there will be no more aristocracy, nobility, hereditary titles, class differences, feudal systems, hereditary jurisdiction, and no more titles or privileges arising from the above-mentioned system, and no one group of citizens or individuals will be entitled to any privileges.

The *Universal Declaration of Human Rights* of 1948 clearly stated:

Everyone is entitled to all the rights and freedoms set forth in this Declaration, without distinction of any kind, such as race, colour, sex, language, religion, political or other opinion, national or social origin, property, birth or other status.

This means that human rights are different from privileges. The subject of human rights is not merely a minority of people, it is the entire society.

The replacement of privileges by human rights was a great step forward in human civilization. As a result of the anti-feudalist democratic revolution, it was bound to happen in the course of society's development. At the same time, it was also an expression of the common interests and demands of the masses, which included capitalists, workers and farmers, for the elimination of feudalism and the establishment of a democratic system. At that time, to be able to enjoy human rights on an equal basis was the minimum social condition required for people to lead normal lives in a modern society of advanced production and living, and it was also the basic condition required for the survival of society. Because the notion of human rights constitutes a set of common values which exceed class privileges and accord with the needs and interests of all people, and because it embodies the shared wealth of human civilization, the socialist revolution is able to carry forward the rational factors of the capitalist human rights concept and to link them up with the proletarian struggle against capitalism and exploitation. By improving and developing them they will eventually form a socialist human rights concept.

However, to talk about the existing capitalist human rights concept is only one aspect of the fact. It is mainly the aspect which deals with the form. A more important aspect relates to the essence of the fact, i.e. the actual implementation of human rights under a capitalist system carries with it strong capitalist characteristics. This is demonstrated by the fact that the dominant human rights ideas and theories are based on a capitalist world view, and conceptions of social history and value systems mainly reflect capitalist goals and aspirations. They belong to a system of capitalist ideas. Although countries have adopted a common form of "everyone is equal" in human rights laws and implementation, under conditions where the system of private ownership holds a dominant position, they are, after all, only able to protect capitalist social relations and to safeguard capitalist "patent rights". All the improvements and progress in the area of human rights will not be able to exceed the limited scope of fundamental capitalist interests. Thus, already 150 years ago, Marx sharply criticized the hypocrisy of the capitalist human rights concept and pointed out that capitalist human rights constitute rights for selfish egotists. "The notion of human rights is in itself a privilege, and the system of private ownership is a monopoly". "To exploit workers equally is the foremost human right of the capital."[4]

The reason why the notion of human rights has both a common nature and a class nature lies in the complex character of people's social practice and social relationships. There are two sets of facts: on the one hand, in a society where people are divided by class, their social relationships are mainly expressed in class relationships. The class oppression and exploitation which create the disparities in people's social status, the conflicts between interests as well as various other social inequalities, are the reason why human rights have become the objective basis for critical social issues. Therefore, people of different class backgrounds cannot possibly have the exact same understanding, demands and practice with respect to human rights. On the contrary, divergence and even confrontations are unavoidable. Even more significant is the fact that the implementation and guarantee of human rights depend on a country's laws and administrative measures and the country is always controlled by the ruling class, so the laws also mainly reflect the aspirations of the ruling class and serve to protect existing social relationships and social order. Therefore, although the current legal form of human rights goes beyond class privileges, is universal and everyone enjoys them, in terms of practical implementation it cannot avoid having a class nature. The real distinction lies in whether different social systems and different countries implement human rights which reflect the interests and aspirations of a minority of people of the exploiting class or the majority of the people. On the other hand, even in a class society there is more than the class struggle and class relationships. As mentioned above, people's social practice and social relationships are multi-layered and complex. Class relationship are also intricate. People from different class backgrounds or even from classes with conflicting fundamental interests, cannot avoid a certain amount of mutual dependency and infiltration as they co-exist in one society. Sometimes, as each class seeks to survive and develop, there might be some form of compromise, rapprochement, or even consensus between classes in terms of interests, and as such there might also be joint efforts in practice. It is precisely these common characteristics, expressed in the practice, interests and needs of all the people coexisting in one society, that form the objective basis of the common nature of human rights. Some people are of the opinion that to emphasize that the notion of human rights has both a common nature and a class nature is a contradiction in terms. In fact, this is not a problem of logical contradiction, it is simply a reflection and an expression of the current contradictions in society.

The form of human rights under which everyone enjoys freedom, equality, property, safety and other rights veils its nature of protecting and guaranteeing capitalist "privileges". This is an inherent contradiction which cannot be overcome within a capitalist human rights system, and it is also the root of the hypocritical nature of the capitalist human rights concept. To deal with such a two-sided concept of contradictions between the form and the nature and to turn the human rights concept into a genuine concept of a comprehensive nature, i.e. to enable all members of society to enjoy human rights on a truly equal basis, classes must be eliminated. The regulation and realization of human rights must be built upon the foundation of a society that owns all the means of production, and upon an economic foundation where labour is allocated as a product. This is the reason why the socialist human rights concept may be fundamentally superior to the capitalist human rights concept.

Human Rights is a Combination of Individual Rights and Collective Rights

In Western human rights theory there is a popular point of view according to which human rights are simply individual rights, and so-called collective rights are rejected. The Marxist point of view differs in this regard. From a Marxist perspective, human rights is a combination of individual rights and collective rights.

Historical materialism views contemporary society as an organic whole made up of individuals and groups according to a set formula. On the one hand, individuals are the cells of society. Without each and every individual there would be no society. After all, the existence and development of society depend on the quality, initiative and creativity of every individual member of society. On the other hand, the cell cannot be separated from the organic whole. The subsistence and development of each individual depends on the group and on society which form the precondition and the formula for the survival and development of the individual. This kind of inter-dependent relationship between the individual and the group as determined by the social nature of human beings, is the objective basis for combining individual rights and collective rights. Thus, the socialist principle of human rights mandates a proper combination of individual rights and collective rights. We must strive to protect and guarantee collective rights and we must also fully respect and guarantee individual rights. The individual must protect the rights of the country and of the people. Society must develop the rights of the country and of the people, and eventually, this will afford even more rights for the individual.

In fact, it is not that the capitalist human rights practice does not deal with collective rights at all. One characteristic of the capitalist democratic revolution was the emphasis on establishing a modern nation state. The constitutions of many countries emphasize, first of all, the rights of the people and the interests of the state, and they provide that the realization of individual freedoms and rights may not jeopardize other people and society. This is, in reality, a recognition of collective rights and a demand for proper handling of the relationship between individual rights and collective rights. After the Second World War, international human rights practice was characterized by an emphasis on protecting and guaranteeing collective rights, e.g. the right to national independence, the right to national self-determination, the right to development, the right to peace, environmental rights and the right to racial equality. Therefore, to negate the collective rights position is to completely negate the history and reality of human rights.

Some people say that socialism negates individual rights. This is also a distortion of the facts. The real distinction between capitalism and socialism on the human rights issue is that:

1) The concept is different. The capitalist human rights concept is established on an economic foundation, the mainstay of which is the capitalist private ownership system. Its ideological core and value systems are all individualistic, with the individual as the touchstone and the interests of the individual as the ultimate goal. Therefore, there is a requirement to put the rights and fundamental freedoms of the individual before any other rights. The socialist human rights concept is established on an economic foundation, the mainstay of which is the socialist public ownership system. Its ideological core and value systems are all collectivist (or for the people), with the people as the touchstone and the interests of the people as the ultimate goal. Therefore, there is a requirement to put the rights and fundamental freedoms of the people before anything else. In realizing the collective rights of the people, the rights of the individual will be realized too. This is possible because many individuals constitute the people, the individual is a part of the people, and the fundamental interests of the individual and of the people are the same.

2) The collective character of socialism is real, but the collective character of capitalism is hypocritical towards the working people. In socialism, the collective refers to the masses of people comprising mainly workers, farmers and intellectuals. Because the power is controlled by a representative of the people, the interests of the state becomes a concentration and representation of the interests of the people, and the state power must, first of all, guarantee and develop the common interests of this largest collective (the people). This kind of collective, and at least the majority of individuals, have the same basic interests. This is the objective basis for a proper combination of individual rights and collective rights. This is exactly what is lacking in some societies and countries, including capitalist ones, that are built on the basis of class conflicts.

3) With regards to individual rights, the socialist concept is even broader in scope, more fair and more genuine than the capitalist concept.

Protecting Human Rights, Respecting Sovereignty, and Opposing Hegemonism

There is currently a theory in the West which upholds the claims that "human rights are borderless" and "human rights come before sovereignty". From a marxist perspective, such a theory is complete erroneous in that it distorts the relationship between sovereignty and human rights, and between human rights under domestic jurisdiction and human rights under international protection.

The concept of sovereignty has two separate meanings: It refers to the relationship between the people and the state power. This is called "sovereignty in the hands of the people". The emphasis is on the notion that state power is conferred by the people, and the people are the masters of the state. This reflects the unanimity between the people and the state. In this sense of the concept, sovereignty is a consolidated expression of the rights of the people and, as such, it is a kind of collective human right. To say that the government may not abuse its power to violate the rights of citizens and that the government must protect and guarantee the rights of citizens is, of course, correct. But there is another side to this issue. The rights of the individual are not absolute. The realization of individual rights may not put other people or collective rights in jeopardy, and protection of state interests as well as compliance with law and morality are imperative.

Sovereignty also refers to the relationship between states. The concept of sovereignty implies the right to state independence and equality. No country may violate another country's right to sovereignty as this would constitute a violation of the human rights of all the people in that country. In this sense of the concept, sovereignty is consistent with human rights and it is also a kind of collective right.

Therefore, irrespective of the different meanings of the concept of sovereignty, it is incorrect to summarize the relationship between human rights and sovereignty in terms of "human rights coming before sovereignty", as this would put the two up against each other and separate them. In fact, sovereignty is the foundation and the guarantee for human rights. In a certain sense it could be argued that sovereignty is more important than human rights. If a state looses its sovereignty, its people might suffer under the oppression of colonial imperialism and hegemonism, and then there would be no more human rights to speak of. Meanwhile, improvements to a country's human rights situation can only be realized by the efforts of the people itself under the guidance of a sovereign state power.

Because of the internationalization of people's social practice and social relationships, there is indeed an aspect of human rights which has already gone beyond the scope of one country so as to deal with the social relationships within the international community. So far, however, the social practice and social relationships of individuals are still, for the most part, limited to the domestic realm. Therefore, the issue of individual rights still belongs under the domestic jurisdiction of a country. The main targets of international human rights protection and intervention involve mainly collective human rights issues such as violating a country's right to sovereignty, equality, etc. In this respect, two points need to be raised:

First, the subject of international law is the sovereign country. The United Nations organization is not above the individual country. The international society's aim to promote human rights and certain international human rights issues, such as environmental rights, the right to peace and the right to development, can only be realized through standard international cooperation and through the domestic legislation of individual sovereign countries.

Second, there are conditions and limitations for international protection and intervention with respect to human rights. Countries must abide by, and not violate, the principles and regulations of the United Nations *Charter*. Respect for national sovereignty and domestic jurisdiction over human rights is imperative because the sovereignty of a country is a shared, fundamental interest of all the people of a country, and from it comes the strength of human rights. There is no difference between protecting human rights and respecting sovereignty.

The theory that "human rights are borderless" argues that human rights issues should not be restricted to a country's domestic jurisdiction and that any country may interfere with another country's internal affairs if there is believed to be a human rights problem. This theory actually distorts the conditions for international human rights protection and intervention, and it further creates a bias for hegemonism and for power politics with its "human rights diplomacy" and interference with other countries' internal politics. On the surface, arguments such as "human rights are above sovereignty" and "human rights are borderless" seem to convey the message that "human rights are above everything". However, such arguments take the value systems and human rights standards and models of a small ruling clique from certain developed countries in the West and force them onto the people of the world under the pretence that these are the common value systems and sole human rights standards and models of all of humanity. This runs counter to the internationally recognized principles that "all countries are equal" and that "sovereignty must not be violated". It also shows contempt for the freedom of thought and personal dignity of the majority of people in the world and, as such, it is an anti-human rights fallacy. Therefore, in order to protect and develop the human rights of all the people in the world and to eliminate the disruptions caused by erroneous ideas, human rights scholars have the obligation to correctly propagate the relationships between human rights and sovereignty and between the domestic and the international protection of human rights.

Translated by Shengtao Jiang and Anne-Marie Traeholt

Notes

1. *Selected Works of Marx and Engels*, Chinese edition, vol. 4, p. 155.

2. Ibid., at p. 12.

3. Ibid.

4. *The Collected Works of Marx and Engels*, Chinese edition, vol. 1, pp. 437-439; vol. 3, p. 229; vol. 23, p. 324.

2 International Organizations, Human Rights, Collective Rights and the Right to Development

Cultural Relativity and the Role of Domestic Courts in the Enforcement of International Human Rights: A Survey of the Practice and Problems in China

LI ZHAOJIE[*]

Introduction

In reviewing the past and projecting forward to the future, the idea of using domestic courts to safeguard and enhance the credibility of international human rights standards has become a more intelligent and practical, if challenging, approach to achieving greater efficacy for the promotion and the protection of human rights at the international level. This approach adds weight to the current debate on another equally topical, but much broader, issue, namely, the effect of international law on municipal legal systems. This is a subject which has gained salience in the study of international law in recent years.

Indeed, to address the role of domestic courts in enforcing international human rights, one must try to understand the manner in which the international law of human rights is applied in municipal legal orders. This involves several political and legal questions: First, is there a need for using domestic courts in enforcing the international law of human rights? If such a need can be established, one must also ask whether domestic courts are suitable and able to enforce the international law of human rights and how such enforcement is carried out. These questions also raise a more fundamental issue, namely, the attitudes of governments towards the interaction of international and municipal laws in regard to the protection of international human rights standards.[1]

This essay focuses on questions which are related to the People's Republic of China. It maintains that the use of domestic courts in the enforcement of international human rights constitutes a more practical and intelligent approach to the strategy for the realization of a genuine global commitment to the universality of human rights. The essay also deals with the practice and problems

---

[*] This author extends his heartfelt thanks to Professor Ronald St. J. Macdonald for his enthusiastic encouragement and valuable advice and comments.

inherent in using domestic courts for the enforcement of international human rights in the People's Republic of China. In doing so, the essay proceeds against the background of the effect of international law in China's domestic legal system. Inevitably, it touches upon some of the underlying issues which have shaped China's practice and problems in this respect, and the explanations provided are based solely on my personal opinions.

The Relative Character of International Human Rights and its Impact on Enforcement Mechanisms

If, until the end of World War II, the manner in which a State treated its own nationals was a question with which other states had no right to concern themselves, the current unprecedented burgeoning of human rights as a major area of international legal concern represents one of the most striking breakthroughs in the development of the international law of our times. This development is a reflection of the unremitting aspirations and commitment of mankind to build and promote universally-based social justice for all human beings.[2] It is also the result of a profound change in governmental attitudes towards the respect for and the protection of human rights as a legitimate global issue.[3]

One achievement in this respect is unquestionable: Today, in trying to deflect international concerns and criticisms about the violation of universally accepted norms of human rights in any country, the argument that the issue falls exclusively within a country's domestic jurisdiction--a typical argument based on the Westphalian concept of state sovereignty--has proven unwarranted in contemporary international law, both in theory and in practice.[4] As international human rights are increasingly serving as a standard for measuring national legal behaviour on the international plane, more states are eager to be perceived as playing a positive role in promoting and protecting international human rights.[5] Moreover, the very fact that at least nominal recognition of the notion of rights has been written into constitutions of almost all states in the world is itself an important sign of universal assent. This bears testimony to a belief that, despite their apparent particularities and diversity, human beings share a core of fundamental interests, concerns, qualities, traits and values which can be identified and articulated as the framework for a common culture of universal human rights.[6] These core human rights belong to an individual simply because this individual is a human being.[7]

On the other hand, however, the landscape of the international law of human rights is by no means a rose garden. Many years after the adoption of a body of general principles and rules on international human rights, violations of international human rights continue to occur in most of the world. Establishing an international framework, with binding principles and rules and with adequate mechanisms for their enforcement, remains more of a promise than an achievement. In order to reaffirm genuine global commitment to the ideal of the universality of human rights and to transform this ideal to substantial progress in practice, it is incumbent upon human rights lawyers of various nations to seek a deep understanding of the underlying causes for the continuing discrepancy between the theory and practice and, on that basis, work out viable solutions.[8]

It is generally accepted that the idea of human rights has been brought to life through a process of historical and social evolution. In other words, the development of the idea of human rights in a society is always circumscribed by that society's historical, social, political and economic conditions. Very often, these conditions as a whole are seen by many commentators as the culture of a society which, in turn, forms the source of both the individual and communal values and interests of that society, and of the legitimate means to pursue them.[9] This is not the place to elaborate on how culture as such contributes to the development of the idea of human rights. Nevertheless, it is clear that human rights, in a legal institutional setting, reflects the normative proposition of these values, interests and means. As a result, an element of cultural relativity is inevitably, introduced into the legal norms of human rights, though such an element often goes unnoticed "precisely because it is so powerful and deeply embedded in our own identity and consciousness.[10]

This observation is also valid as far as the legal regime of international human rights is concerned. What is more important and significant is that the international norms of human rights are conceived and intended to work within the framework of the international community. However, the members who have created and developed these norms are independent nations with tremendous cultural diversity. In addition, the major international human rights documents were drafted predominantly by Western men who had little direct interest in, or experience with, the challenges and pressures confronting many of the non-Western nations. This generates an inherent tension within the framework of the international law of human rights. Moreover, the generally recognized concept of international human rights as a whole encompasses a wide spectrum of rights, ranging from political and civil to social, economic and cultural rights. These rights not only address the individual dimension of self-fulfilment of the individual but are also concerned with the collective dimension of a decent human existence.[11] In a broad sense, therefore, cultural diversity has a more far-reaching impact upon the development and operation of the international regime of human rights. Within this context, it is not surprising that states hold diverse and often contradictory views on international human rights. Nor is it inconceivable that some nations place more emphasis on a certain category of rights than other nations, or that even for the same category of rights, different standards of protection may be applied.

It should be stressed that, to point out this culturally relative character of the international standards of human rights does not mean a repudiation of the integrity of the concept of human rights, nor should it be charged with "neutralizing moral judgment and thereby impairing action against injustice."[12] It simply gives a candid recognition of the fact that perception of the international standards of human rights bears cultural imprints which are deeply ingrained and widely dispersed in each nation.

One glowing example of this is demonstrated in the Western and Chinese definitions of human dignity. As argued earlier, the universally accepted precept underlying the international standards of human rights is that of fundamental human dignity.[13] While it is true that both the Western liberal tradition and the Chinese schools of thought are concerned with promoting human dignity, as W.P. Alford has noticed, "their respective ways of fostering it and their sense of its purpose are different in important regards."[14] As compared to Western liberalism and individualism, however, the prevailing Chinese definition of human dignity places more emphasis on collective welfare and social harmony and order, since both the traditional notions as well as sinicized Marxist precepts perceive the meaning of the human person from his/her social being in an intricate web of social relationships rather than from his atomized autonomy. Thereby, values such as liberty and autonomy are not prized as the ends in themselves in the same way that they are in contemporary Western democracies. With this in mind, I am not saying that there is no respect for human dignity in the Chinese cultural context, but rather that its basis is different. Respect for human dignity in the Chinese cultural context lies in the integrity of harmonious and orderly social bonds and is meant to be exercised for the purpose of fostering collective welfare through moral exhortation internalized in the individual, rather than the legal formality of government power vis-à-vis the individual.[15]

To note the difference between the Western and Chinese concept of human dignity should not entail an "all-or-nothing" view of the cultural relevance to international human rights standards. Actually, culture itself is by no means ossified and static, but susceptible to reinterpretation and development through internal and external discourses.[16] However, the above-mentioned example serves to inform us that the lack of cultural homogeneity amongst universal human rights advocates often generates conflict between the uniform international standards of human rights and various cultural particularities. Therefore, like a seed which cannot blossom and bear fruit if it fails to adapt itself to the soil in which it is planted, international standards can only provide faint, if any, guidance for the efforts to advocate international human rights, and will be unlikely to succeed if cultural circumstances in a society are not taken into account.[17] In this sense, as A.A. An-Na'im has correctly advised us, as normative propositions, human rights are much more credible and thereby stand a better chance of implementation if they are perceived to be legitimate within the various cultural traditions of the world.[18]

Therefore, the universalization of the practice of human rights would require a dynamic process of constantly redefining the concepts of recognized human rights standards within multi-cultural or cross-cultural settings, thereby reflecting the most urgent needs of the world today.[19] Given the diversity and plurality of the world community today, this process will continue to prove very arduous and complex. So far, except for establishing the core principles and rules based on a minimum consensus, progress made by the international community in this respect is marginal.

These underlying causes of the existing discrepancy in the field of human rights underscore the complexity of the question of enforcing and implementing the established principles and rules of international human rights. The efficacy of the protection of human rights depends on the existence of adequate mechanisms by which to ensure adherence to human rights standards established under existing law, such as receiving complaints from victims and ordering sanctions against violators. This is what protection means.[20] In striking contrast to the progress by which a body of general principles and rules providing for the protection of human rights has gained universal recognition, however, the progress in building mechanisms for the enforcement and implementation of human rights on the international plane is lagging. Except for some regional conventions which have established fairly sophisticated institutional frameworks to ensure the protection of human rights, most states are reluctant or refuse to participate in creating significant comprehensive international mechanisms. The existing international organs enjoy very limited powers in this domain.

Some scholars blame the prevailing organizational structure of the international community, particularly the persistant concern about the preservation of state sovereignty, for the inadequacy of and obstacles to effective protection of international human rights. According to them, there is inherent tension between the structure of the international community and the effective enforcement and implementation of international human rights standards. Thus, it seems that, without the emergence of a new legal order based on the notion of a world government, the protection of international human rights is doomed to be weak and marginal.[21] It is submitted that the lack of central legislative, administrative and judicial authorities, inherent in the contemporary international legal order, is a factor responsible for the present state of affairs regarding the enforcement of international human rights standards. However, the question remains how and when such a new legal order can possibly be brought about. If effective mechanisms for enforcement cannot be achieved in relatively small communities, how could a new legal order guarantee the creation of a better situation under a world government? And what about the dangers of such a government?[22] The danger lies in that, if our diagnosis of the problem deviates from the existing reality, the prescription may be reduced to an undue formalism or naive idealism.

Of course, the paucity of comprehensive international mechanisms for the enforcement of human rights should not be used as an excuse to repudiate the desirability and importance of such mechanisms. On the contrary, in case of any substantial infringement of international human rights standards, particularly in cases where such infringement constitutes persistent and gross violations or involves a class of persons or a pattern of activity, experience has shown that international mechanisms are better situated to undertake appropriate actions to deal with such infringements. This has been amply illustrated by the anti-apartheid campaigns. In such cases, international mechanisms are not only desirable but indispensable.[23] Remarkable, albeit slow and insufficient, progress has been made in this area in recent years.

However, when a case of infringement of human rights does not involve gross violations such as apartheid, genocide, officially condoned racial or gender discrimination, but value judgments of which the criteria can be measured only in light of the cultural circumstances pertinent to the particular society,[24] questions arise as to whether the international enforcement mechanisms can be politically acceptable, socially and culturally desirable, economically viable, administratively manageable, and legally effective.

In seeking answers to these questions, we should always be reminded that the rights to be enforced must be those that are consistent with the prevailing values and their development within a society. In other words, the rights to be enforced must be perceived by the general populace to be legitimate within the nation's cultural context. In addition, enforcement of these rights must be possible under the existing social and economic conditions. Empty remedies which create unrealistic expectations would easily backfire and eventually jeopardize the validity of the entire enterprise of international human rights. In this regard, A.F. Bayefsky warns that, even when better international enforcement agencies are created, in reality they often turn out to be inaccessible to individual victims. Lack of resources, local officials' ignorance of international remedies, bureaucratic international organs, as well as unfamiliarity and misconceptions of problems particularly pertinent to local situations, may cripple the function of the conceived international organs.[25] In this regard, it is submitted that, if the notion of state sovereignty is understood in its modern sense as a relative concept subject to restrictions necessitated by the international system, sovereign states, which constitute the major actors of the international community and which can effectively wield power to enforce the law, may not necessarily stand in the way of the effective enforcement of international human rights.

In view of the foregoing reflections, it follows that resort to domestic apparati for the enforcement of international human rights offers a logical, less complex, less threatening, but more effective, alternative. This approach does not lead to a deviation from the existing principles and rules of international human rights. Instead, there are compelling reasons to work within the framework of these principles and rules. Notwithstanding the existing problems, if we discard these basic principles and rules, we would regress to the dark ages. What this approach seeks is a "soft landing" of international human rights standards on local circumstances, with international principles and rules serving as the binding norms of reference and points of departure. The enforcement of international norms by national agencies can make application of international standards more pertinent to local situations, thereby diminishing the gap between victims and remedies. In return, the feedback can also improve the work of international institutions. International organs can benefit from informed interpretation of international standards by a variety of national apparati.[26]

Noticeably, even in the very sophisticated European system for the protection of human rights, established under the *European Convention for the Protection of Human Rights and Fundamental Freedoms*, the European Court of Human Rights still often faces the dilemma of how to remain true to its responsibility of developing an effective and reasonably uniform standard of protection under the entire Convention while, at the same time, recognizing the diversity of political, economic, cultural, and social situations in the societies of the contracting parties. To meet this challenge, the Court created and developed the doctrine of national margin of appreciation.[27] In order to shed light on our present discussion, it is worth mentioning some of the Court's decisions which give expression to this doctrine.

The Court's judgment in *Handyside* (1976) remains the basis of the doctrine. In this case, the applicant, Mr. Handyside, had challenged the British government's censorship of a controversial alternative lifestyle handbook. The Court was requested to decide whether such censorship was "necessary in a democratic society", "for the protection of morals". The Court pointed out that "the machinery of protection established by the Convention is subsidiary to the national systems safeguarding human rights."[28] The Court placed particular emphasis on the absence of a uniform European conception of morals and on the fact that the requirements of morals vary from time to time and from place to place. The Court found that,

> By reason of their direct and continuous contact with the vital forces of their countries, *State authorities are in principle in a better position than the international judge* to give an opinion on the exact content of these requirements as well as on the 'necessity' of 'restriction' or 'penalty' intended to meet them. (Italics added by the author).[29]

In *Ireland v. U.K.*, in determining whether public emergency threatened the life of the nation so as to justify derogations from the obligations under the Convention, the Court relied heavily on *Handyside* to rule that,

> By reason of their direct and continuous contact with the pressing needs of the moment, the national authorities are in principle in a *better position than the international judge* to decide both on the presence of such an emergency and on the nature and scope of derogations necessary to avert it. (Italics added by the author).[30]

In *Lithgow and Others v. U.K.*, which concerned the nationalization of interests in the United Kingdom, the Court declared that,

> A decision to enact nationalization legislation will commonly involve consideration of various issues on which opinions within a democratic society may reasonably differ widely. *Because of their direct knowledge of their society and its needs and resources, the national authorities are in principle better placed than the international judge to appreciate what measures are appropriate in this area and consequently the margin of appreciation available to them should be a wide one.* (Italics added by the author)[31]

In *Weeks v. U.K.*, which dealt with the lawfulness of detention, the doctrine was again reaffirmed by the Court. As to whether deprivation of an indeterminate life sentence conviction by a competent court is lawful, the Court ruled that "the national authorities are to be recognized as having a certain discretion since they are better placed than the international judge to evaluate the evidence in a particular case."[32]

As indicated by the italicized words, even under the European Convention, of which the contracting parties possess more common cultural kinship to the concept of human rights as understood in the West, certain evaluations and value judgments about human rights standards are still left to the competence of state authorities and cannot be substituted by evaluations and judgments of the European Commission or the Court.[33] Therefore, according to R. St. J. Macdonald, the doctrine of national margin of appreciation illustrates the Court's general approach to the delicate task of balancing the sovereignty of contracting parties with their obligations under the Convention.[34]

It is also noted that an overwhelming number of existing international human rights treaties and documents address the state parties' obligation for the protection and enforcement of human rights. With few exceptions, the language contained in these instruments is all that guides state parties to respect certain rights, to enforce them, to enact domestic laws for safeguarding them, and to prevent any violation of them by virtue of its judicial apparatus. Rarely are there any provisions for an individual's possession of a specific right that could be enforced directly by international mechanisms.[35] Nevertheless, a closer look into those exceptional cases reveals that it is still concerned states which are obliged to enforce any decision made by an international tribunal in favour of an individual complaint.[36] Whereas the present international law of human rights primarily focuses on sovereign states, each government is the key law enforcement authority which undertakes primary responsibility for protection and enforcement of human rights within its jurisdiction. It follows therefore, that it would be a corollary of the states' obligations under international instruments of human rights to endeavour to find incentives to encourage domestic judicial bodies to enforce international human rights standards.[37]

The Development of Judicial Culture and its Impact on the Enforcement of International Human Rights

In discussing the role of domestic courts in enforcing the international law of human rights, the development of a country's judicial culture should in particular be noted. The term "judicial culture" refers to how aware judges and prosecutors in charge of the enforcement are of the valid principles and rules of international human rights and how ready and able they are to apply them. It can also refer to how informed the public is of these valid international principles and rules and how willing the public is to resort to them in cases of infringement of international human rights. While an adequate account of these conditions in China is beyond the scope of this presentation, it is important to give a brief account of the current state of the Chinese "judicial culture" and its specific relevance to our discussion.

The current legal system in China is virtually the result of the campaign for the reconstruction of China's legal system which started roughly after the "Cultural Revolution" (1966-1976).[38] Although great achievements have been made since then,[39] much more remains to be done before a full-fledged legal system, which corresponds to the needs of society's political, social and economic development, can actually take root in China. The challenge to the effective administration of the existing legal system and to its future development comes primarily from the inadequacy of qualified legal professionals and the still strong antipathy of the general populace towards law which has existed in China for many centuries.

In regard to the former, China's population has now reached over 1.14 billion, whereas its licensed lawyers merely total 34,000, according to the official statistics of 1991.[40] Experts have estimated that, in the light of the current scale of social and economic development, the actual need amounts to at least one million professionally trained lawyers. However, if China relies on the capacity of the existing legal educational institutions in China, it will take forty to fifty years to meet this target.[41] The great shortage of qualified lawyers in China has led to serious underrepresentation in civil and criminal litigation. In 1990, of the 3.21 million law suits tried in the courts of China, the parties involved were represented by lawyers in only 580,000 (18%) of the cases.[42] To compound that, as of 1990, of the 190,000 judges and 160,000 public prosecutors in China, only 70,000 (34%) and 70,500 (44%), respectively, had undergone qualified college-level professional training. The inadequate training of the majority of China's "judicial workers" has jeopardized their ability to correctly understand and apply the laws enacted by China's own legislature, let alone the relatively sophisticated international rules.

As to the latter case, unlike in Western nations, law in China was traditionally equated with coercion and was regarded as an inferior means of affecting behaviour. Under the precepts of Confucianism, society depended on virtues and rites, rather than on rules which were seen as exterior to each individual. In other words, through a painstaking process of socialization, education and suasion, people were expected to, first and foremost, learn and then internalize the rules of proper behaviour. Only when a person was an extreme recalcitrant, or when the educational system failed, would it be necessary to use severe legal punishment. When society was functioning harmoniously, law was something to be avoided. Thus, resort to law was regarded as an admission of the loss of virtue and failure in human and communal relations. More laws did not make for a better or more harmonious society. On the contrary, the emphasis on law made people more litigious and "loophole-happy", and also diverted attention away from the more important work of moral education.[43]

Although, since the beginning of the 1980s, nationwide educational campaigns have been introduced to eradicate the nation's inherited "legal illiteracy" and to teach the public to comply with the law and apply the law for the protection of their own interests and benefits,[44] the deeply-rooted traditional inertia of loathing the law remains. In contrast to the continuing efforts to expand the role of law in Chinese society, such antipathy towards the law constitutes a great obstacle towards resorting to law to protect one's lawful rights and interests.

Within the context of the Chinese judicial culture, another relevant and noteworthy factor is China's attitude towards the usefulness of international law in protecting human rights. Modern international law originated in Europe and used to be applied exclusively to relations between states of European background. It was introduced to China in a systemic manner after the expanding Western powers forced open China's door in the mid-nineteenth century.[45] Although China, in its participation in international relations, eventually accepted Western international law, such acceptance was, at the outset, a by-product of Western expansion and domination. Thus, as Western powers were not sincere in applying international law to their relations with China, China also did not completely trust the usefulness of this exotic legal institution for defending its interests.[46]

The history of the full application of international law in China is very short. International law did not gain ground in China until China was transformed from a semi-colonial and semi-feudal society into an independent republic and a major world power. Given this historical background, international law has been regarded by China as more relevant to protecting itself against foreign interference in its internal affairs and ensuring its normal relations with other nations than to enhancing individuals' human rights at the international level.[47]

The culturally relative character of international human rights and the risk that human rights may be used by large and powerful states to impose their own values and political systems upon small and weak states makes China sceptical about the value of international law in defining and enforcing such human rights standards as can be meaningfully measured only in the light of the cultural circumstances pertinent to a specific nation. This partly explains why China has persistently maintained that human rights are essentially matters within the domestic jurisdiction of a state.

This short account illustrates that, although great progress has been made compared to the situation ten or fifteen years ago, the judicial culture in China still cannot fully sustain the use of China's courts for enforcing international human rights. The Chinese people and government are faced with a great and long-term challenge to better the quality and quantity of its legal professionals and to change the public's attitude towards the value and function of law. While this state of affairs obviously limits the use of China's courts for the enforcement of international human rights, it does not follow that China's courts have no role in this respect. Since 1980, the Chinese government has ratified and acceded to several international conventions on human rights. Under international law, China must perform its obligations under these conventions in good faith. Thus, the question concerning the role of China's courts in enforcing international human rights arises in connection with how these international human rights conventions are accorded legal effect in China's domestic legal system.

The Relationship Between International Human Rights Law and Domestic Law

Using domestic courts in adjudicating international human rights presupposes that the international law of human rights is given legal validity in domestic jurisdictions. International law generally imposes upon states the obligation of carrying out in good faith their international legal obligations. The manner in which international law is given effect in domestic jurisdictions is usually left up to states themselves, provided they do not invoke their domestic laws as justification for derogations from their international legal obligations. The practice of states in this area varies, depending on their attitude towards the relationship between international law and domestic law. The attitudes of states in this regard are often, if not always, determined by the desirability of seeking protection from the rules of international law or, reversely, of remaining free within their domestic legal orders vis-à-vis the requirement of their international obligations.

The traditional approach to this question was always predominated by the antithetical debate between monism and dualism. While the debate has generated wisdom, its scholastic nature oversimplified the complex reality which gave rise to the question, thus leading to few practical solutions.[48]

In China, the approach to the question of the relationship between the two legal systems generally follows a dialectical line of thinking.[49] Noting that domestic law is enacted by states and international law is formulated through the participation of states, the Chinese approach is more concerned with the interrelations, rather than the conflicts, between the two. The prevailing Chinese theory maintains that, in principle, the two legal systems infiltrate and supplement each other. Without the necessary domestic rules, many international obligations cannot be performed. On the other hand, if domestic rules are enacted contrary to international obligations, thereby infringing upon the rights and interests of other states, it incurs state responsibility for international illegal acts. Therefore, when states enact municipal laws, they should take into account their obligations under international law. Similarly, before states enter into international obligations, they should bring domestic laws into line with such obligations.

In the final analysis, the question of the relationship between international human rights law and domestic law deals with how a state enforces and implements international law in its domestic sphere, and how it performs its obligations under international law. To the Chinese, the importance lies in maintaining the integrity of, and harmony between, the two legal systems, so as to ensure faithful performance of all obligations under international law. This approach emphasizes the practical coordination and reconciliation between the two legal systems.[50] Under this approach, the presumption is that domestic law does not conflict with general international law, i.e. customary international law. In regard to treaties, efforts should be made to avoid conflicts between the two systems both in treaty-making and legislative processes in China.[51] If doubt arises or when conflicts between the two systems become unavoidable, the balance is tipped in favour of international law.[52]

Treaties

Today, treaties are playing a dominant role in the development of international law. For this reason, in China, the discussion on the relationship between international law and domestic law is primarily focused on the relationship between treaties and domestic statutes. The effect of international treaties in China's domestic legal order has a special bearing on our discussion, given that multilateral conventions constitute the principal source of the international law of human rights.[53]

Along the line of its approach to the relationship between international law and domestic law, China has put into effect a system under which international treaties are generally accepted as part of its domestic legal order. Although the *Constitution of the People's Republic of China* (PRC) is silent on this specific issue, such a point of view can be deduced from the relevant statutory provisions enacted by the Chinese legislature. A typical statutory provision to substantiate this speculation is found in article 238 of the PRC *Civil Procedure Law*, which provides:

If any international treaty concluded or acceded to by the People's Republic of China contains provisions differing from those found in this Law, the provisions of the international treaty shall prevail, except for those provisions to which China has declared its reservations.[54]

While this provision lays down the principle that international treaties can be applied in civil proceedings in China, it also implies that the application of treaties by the Chinese courts does not require transformation of the treaty into a domestic statute. Instead, a valid treaty on the international plane becomes part of China's domestic law. Under this provision, what the court shall apply is the treaty provision which is in conflict with the relevant provisions of the domestic law. Therefore, in China, acceptance of treaties into its domestic legal order takes the form of adoption. Treaties derive their validity in the Chinese domestic legal order as soon as they enter into force under international law.[55]

It is significant that, under the Chinese system, all valid international treaties on human rights which China has ratified or to which China has acceded, automatically become valid in the Chinese legal order. In an official statement delivered by a PRC representative at the session of the UN General Assembly's Third Committee (Social, Humanitarian and Cultural Committee) on November 14, 1991, concerning China's position on the prohibition of torture and other cruel treatment and inhuman punishment against prisoners, the Chinese representative spoke on record that, as a contracting party to the *UN Convention against Torture and Other Cruel, Inhuman or Degrading Treatment or Punishment*, China will perform in good faith her international obligations based on this Convention.[56] He continued that, under the Chinese legal system, once a relevant international treaty is ratified or acceded to by the Chinese government and subsequently enters into force, and is thus binding upon China, the Chinese government will perform these treaty-based international obligations without the need to transform the treaty into domestic law. In other words, this Convention automatically becomes valid in China, and it is unnecessary to draft special laws to ensure its conformity. Thus, all acts of torture and other cruel, inhuman or degrading treatment or punishment, as defined by this Convention, have been and will be sternly prohibited. The statement went on to say that China shall exercise the jurisdiction, within the scope of its obligations under this Convention, over all crimes as defined by it, whether or not they occur within China.[57] It is submitted that this is a statement which demonstrates the Chinese government's attitude towards its policy to prohibit torture and other cruel treatment of criminals. Incidentally, it also deals with the domestic legal effect of treaties to which China is a party. Therefore, it should be regarded as a valid expression of

China's general position on the issue of the validity of treaties on human rights within the Chinese legal system.[58]

At the time of writing, the Chinese government had signed, ratified and acceded to the following treaties on human rights: The *Convention on the Prevention and Punishment of the Crime of Genocide*; the *International Convention on the Suppression and Punishment of the Crimes of Apartheid*; the *Convention on the Elimination of all Forms of Discrimination against Women*; the *International Convention on the Elimination of All Forms of Racial Discrimination*; the *Convention Relating to the Status of Refugees*; the *Protocol Relating to the Status of Refugees*; the *Convention on the Rights of the Child*; four 1949 Geneva conventions on combatants, prisoners and civilian persons in time of armed conflict, and protocols additional to these conventions; *ILO Convention (No. 100) Concerning Equal Remuneration for Men and Women Workers for Work of Equal Value*; and the *Convention against Torture and Other Cruel, Inhuman or Degrading Treatment or Punishment*.[59] In view of the foregoing reflections, it follows that all these treaties are valid as part of the Chinese domestic legal order. Moreover, the Chinese government has always submitted reports on the implementation of the related conventions.[60]

To date, however, China has not yet signed the two most universal international conventions on human rights, namely, the *International Covenant on Civil and Political Rights* (114 ratifications) and the *International Covenant on Economic, Social, and Cultural Rights* (117 ratifications).[61] Apart from other complicating factors,[62] a difficult technical obstacle to Chinese participation in these two universal conventions lies in the inconsistency between some of the provisions of the Covenants and the existing statutes, regulations and practice in China.

For instance, due to the huge disparities in economic development and living standards between urban and rural areas, and under the pressure of the continuing paucity of housing resources, public facilities and job opportunities, individual citizens' freedom to move, to choose one's place of residence and to choose work cannot be guaranteed. Thus, the 1982 *Constitution of the People's Republic of China* does not recognize, as constitutional rights, the freedom of movement and residence from one place to another, and the freedom to choose one's work. However, Article 12, paragraph 1 of the *International Covenant on Civil and Political Rights* provides that "[e]veryone lawfully within the territory of a state shall, within that territory, have the right to liberty of movement and freedom to choose his residence."[63]

Another apparent discrepancy lies in the right to strike. Article 8, paragraph 1 (d) of the *International Covenant on Economic, Social, and Cultural Rights* provides that the contracting parties to the Covenant undertake to ensure the right to strike, provided that it is exercised in conformity with the laws of the particular country. While the right to strike was written into China's previous constitutions, the current constitution has ruled it out.

A more difficult problem exists in criminal justice. Under Article 14, paragraph 2 of the *Covenant on Civil and Political Rights*, "[e]veryone charged with a criminal offence shall have the right to be presumed innocent until proven guilty according to the law." In this regard, however, Chinese criminal justice follows a different line of jurisprudence. As a counterpart of the principle of the presumption of innocence, the guiding principle for criminal proceedings in China is "taking facts as the basis and the law as the criterion." Under the current *Criminal Procedure Law* of the People's Republic of China, a defendant is presumed neither guilty nor innocent during the trial until he or she is convicted on the basis of evidence. To ensure the fairness and lawfulness of a criminal trial, judges undertake the primary responsibility to investigate the facts and evaluate the evidence with an open mind and from many perspectives. Thus, the accused's guilt or innocence can be rightfully proven and a correct verdict can be rendered. On the other hand, a defendant is entitled to a defence, public trial and other procedural rights. Also, all evidence must be verified, and obtaining confessions by intimidation and torture is forbidden. Moreover, a criminal defendant shall not be found guilty if he/she confesses in the absence of corroborative evidence.

The result of applying the Chinese criminal procedural rule may substantially vary from applying the principle of presumption of innocence. According to the latter, for instance, the burden of proof is placed solely on the shoulders of the prosecutor, any evidence against a defendant must be beyond any reasonable doubt, illegally collected evidence is not accessible to the court, and a defendant has the right to remain silent. Under the Chinese principle, however, the law does not specifically provide that the burden of proof is on the state, although one can make an argument to that effect.[64] As the law itself is unclear in this regard, questions like "If you are innocent, why have you been detained or arrested?" are often raised by the police, prosecutors and even judges during criminal proceedings. Any evidence, however collected, is accessible to the court to the extent that it can prove a relevant fact. Moreover, confessing to a crime is encouraged as it will mitigate the penalty, while remaining silent is taken as an expression of resistance to the law, and often leads to more severe punishment. In addition, the Chinese system results in extra-legal detention. Often, prior to being formally arrested, the accused is subjected to a lengthy period of detention before any criminal charge is filed.

Some Chinese scholars argue that the fundamental spirit of the two covenants are, in general, consistent with the principles of the law and the basic policy of China.[65] Given that China's attitude and approach towards the question of the relationship between international law and domestic law underscores the performance in good faith of its international obligations, it is technically difficult for China to ratify the two covenants. It would require incorporation of the particular treaty obligations into China's domestic legal norms, which are, in part, inconsistent with the former. Under the Chinese domestic legal system, treaties to which China is a party are given priority over its domestic statutes. Before China ratifies a treaty, its relevant governmental organs are required to conduct a comprehensive examination of the obligations incurred by the treaty, particularly to check out whether any conflict exists between the treaty provisions and the domestic statutes.[66] If such conflict exists but can be eliminated by interpreting the domestic law in a manner which is consistent with the treaty obligation, the conflict can be avoided by means of interpretation. If the conflict cannot be removed, the treaty in question will prevail over the conflicting domestic norms.[67] However, this only happens when the ratification of the treaty becomes a matter of paramount importance. Otherwise, ratification of such treaties has to be shelved until the conflict between the treaty provisions and domestic statutes is eliminated.

Before these inconsistencies are removed from China's domestic law, or before reservation or some interpretative declaration is allowed to be made relating to these conflicting international provisions, ratification of the two covenants would cause a very embarrassing situation which contravenes China's basic position on the relationship between international law and domestic law. The elimination of these ostensible discrepancies from its domestic law is a high-level policy matter for China. Such a matter is determined by China's own desire to depend on these two covenants for the promotion of human rights standards, by the value which China places on its domestic law as assessed against that of the two covenants, and by China's perception of the importance of accepting these two covenants into its legal order.[68]

At present, China maintains that human rights are essentially matters within the domestic jurisdiction of a state. Respect for each country's sovereignty and non-interference in internal affairs are universally recognized principles of paramount importance in the international legal order. A human rights system must be established and safeguarded by each sovereign state through its domestic legislation. The international system should be aimed at promoting normal cooperation in the international field of human rights and international harmony and peace, and thus concentrate on such gross human rights violations as colonialism, racism, foreign aggression and occupation, as well as apartheid, racial discrimination, genocide, slave trade and serious violations of human rights by international terrorist organizations.[69] Based on these policy concerns, it does not appear that the elimination of these discrepancies from its domestic law can be a high priority issue on the agenda of the Chinese government in the years to come.

Customs

The prominence and importance of treaties in forming a principal source of international human rights law does not, and cannot, preclude international customary rules from continuing to be another major source of the law. It is generally agreed that, when a provision of a convention proves to be a general international customary rule, it can be invoked as a source of rights and obligations to bind a state which is not a contracting party to that convention. In this case, the binding rule is not conventional but customary. This observation has a special bearing on our discussion, given that China is among those countries whose participation in the human rights conventions is minimal. Therefore, in regard to international human rights treaties to which China is not a contracting party, provisions of these treaties may still be invoked to bind China if they can be proven to constitute generally established international customary rules. However, two sets of problems have complicated this approach.

The first of these arises from the fact that it is always the lawyers' work to argue that a certain rule has become a general rule of international customary law, thus having binding effect upon all states. Given the complexity involved in defining international human rights standards, extraordinary scrutiny needs to be exercised for such an argument to succeed. To date, except for the general principles of international human rights which have been enshrined in the UN Charter and repeatedly affirmed by both the UN resolutions and ICJ decisions, it is very controversial whether a particular right has been crystallized as a customary rule. China has always held that the generally established international rules for the protection of human rights only encompass those which prohibit colonialism, racism, foreign aggression and occupation, as well as apartheid, racial discrimination, genocide, slave trade and serious violations committed by international terrorist organizations. These acts warrant interference by the international community.[70] In regards to rules concerning rights other than the foregoing categories, they do not bind states in general, unless they constitute the legal obligations which have arisen from an international treaty to which these states are contracting parties.[71] Within this context, it follows that, although both the Chinese government and scholars have given high praise for the Human Rights Declaration and the two Covenants in particular,[72] it is difficult to substantiate that such praise has resulted in the formation of China's *opinion juris* relating to all the contents of these international instruments.

The second set of problems arises from the fact that China did not participate in the creation and development of most of the so-alleged customary rules of international law. As a result, the Chinese government feels very reluctant to apply them, particularly when these rules are considered volatile, and subject to the interpreter's own perception. This is believed to be one of the important factors which has resulted in the Chinese government's ambivalent position on the validity of international customary law in its domestic legal order. Not only China's Constitution remains silent on this issue, but other subordinate and subsequent statutes enacted by the Chinese legislature also seem shy to articulate it.[73] The *General Principles on Civil Laws of the People's Republic of China* chooses a rather equivocal term, namely, "international practice (guoji guanli) to be seemingly the substitute for the term "international customs" (guoji xiguan). In Article 142, it provides that,

> Where no (applicable) provisions can be found either in the laws of the People's Republic of China or in the treaties concluded or acceded to thereby, international practice can be applied.

The term, "international practice" itself is a myth. It may include both international customary rules and international usage, or either of the two. Assuming it encompasses established customary rules, then customary rules can also be applied as "the law of the land" by the Chinese domestic courts without transformation. The status of the ranking of customary law, however, is lower than the treaties and the domestic statutes. Thus, even if one can successfully argue that there exists a customary rule which is binding on China, the possibility of applying this rule will be excluded when a domestic statute or an international treaty, to which China is a party, can be invoked to govern the subject matter. Furthermore, correct as it may be, such speculation is based on a specific provision of China's civil code, which is obviously short of general significance and, thus, can hardly be invoked to apply to a situation concerning human rights.

Question Concerning Direct Application of International Human Rights Law

Using domestic courts to enforce the international law of human rights also requires that the courts are accorded with judicial competence to apply the law in their jurisdictions. As mentioned above, given that the dominant part of international human rights law consists of multilateral treaties, my discussion in this section will concentrate on the application of treaties by domestic courts.

If a treaty is given legal validity in a domestic jurisdiction by becoming the law of the land, it seems a logical consequence that this treaty should be directly applicable in the domestic legal system in the same way that the domestic law is. In other words, the courts should be able to apply this treaty in the same manner as they would a domestic statute. In reality, however, direct application of treaties in domestic jurisdictions is a far more complex issue. Noticeably, almost every state where treaties are automatically adopted into the domestic legal order, imposes certain limitations on the scope of their direct application by its domestic courts. The reason for doing so is that treaties which can be directly applied in domestic courts must possess certain qualifications. These qualifications are usually embodied in the contents and purposes of the treaties. In many countries, for instance, the concept of self-executing treaties is developed as the criterion against which to measure the direct applicability of treaties in the domestic courts.

In China, direct application of international treaties in its domestic courts is also subject to certain restrictions. Although China's Constitution is silent on this issue, such restrictions can be discerned from some of the statutes enacted by China's legislative body and certain regulations formulated by China's State Council (the cabinet or executive body of the government). Similar provisions can also be found in the PRC *General Principles of Civil Law*, PRC *Administrative Procedure Law*, PRC *Law on Economic Contract Involving Foreign Interests*, the *Rules for the Implementation of the PRC Water Pollution Control Law*, PRC *Environmental Protection Law*, PRC *Regulations Concerning Diplomatic Privileges and Immunities* as well as the PRC *Regulations on Consular Privileges and Immunities*. These statutes each have a special chapter which addresses the application of the law in legal proceedings involving foreign interests. Pursuant to the relevant provisions of these special chapters, if any international treaty concluded or acceded to by China contains provisions which are different from those of these statutes, the provisions of the treaty in question shall prevail. Therefore, under these statutes, China's domestic courts should be able to directly apply the treaties governing the same subject matter as regulated by the statutes.

In some cases where the assumed discrepancy between treaties and domestic statutes does not exist, a treaty can still be directly applied, if such direct application is required by the provisions of the treaty. In such a case, the domestic statutes will require that the relevant transactions are directly governed by treaties. Parties concerned are entitled to directly apply the treaty in the same way as they apply a domestic statute. For example, Article 9 of the PRC Trademark Law provides that,

> Where a foreigner or foreign enterprise applies for trade mark registration in China, the matter shall be handled in accordance with agreements its country has concluded with the People's Republic of China or international treaties to which both are parties,...[74]

Under this article, when the "matter", as defined by this article, arises, parties concerned can directly invoke relevant treaties to which China is a party, as the governing law. A more prominent area of direct application of treaties by the Chinese domestic courts is judicial assistance in China.[75] In this case, the direct application of treaties is generally required by the treaty-based obligations. In recent years, as China's treaty relations with other nations and international organizations are steadily growing, cases involving direct application of international treaties are increasing. In practice, the Chinese courts have, on several occasions, directly applied treaty provisions as the governing law for the transactions in question.[76]

Although direct application of treaties by the Chinese domestic courts cover a considerably wide spectrum of activities, it must be noted that the domestic statutes which allow direct application of treaties in China's domestic legal system, are only those which govern such specific subject matters as have been identified earlier. The want of a general rule on this issue, in the light of the maxim, *affirmatio unius est exclusio alterius*, suggests that international treaties which can be directly applied in the Chinese domestic legal order should be limited only to those which deal with these specific subject matters. As a result, even though some treaties are regarded as self-executing in other states, it cannot be directly applied in China if there is no domestic enabling law. The same is true of the case where the treaty-based obligation itself requires direct application. If the necessary enabling law does not exist and the treaty-based obligation requires that the treaty is directly applied in China's domestic courts, a decision made by the Chinese legislative body--in this case the Standing Committee of the PRC National People's Congress--to sanction the required direct application becomes indispensable. Such a decision is, in effect, tantamount to a supplement to the existing statutes.[77]

Thus, it is submitted that, within the Chinese domestic legal order, direct application of international treaties on human rights to which China is a party, must satisfy all the conditions as identified above. First, in all cases which call for direct application of treaties on human rights, there must be a domestic enabling law which allows the Chinese domestic courts to directly apply the treaty provisions as the governing law. On this basis, except for the situation where direct application is required as the treaty-based obligation itself, the issue of direct application of treaties of human rights will not arise, unless discrepancies or differences are found between treaty provisions and the domestic statutes. As the foregoing reflections have demonstrated, of the existing statutes which carry the enabling clauses upon which the Chinese domestic courts are given the competence to directly apply treaties in their jurisdictions, few, if any, address the issue of human rights. Thus, there is only a small chance that a Chinese court could directly apply the treaties on human rights to which China is a contracting party.

If the field of international human rights can be broadened to embrace prevention and punishment of terrorism, as argued by some Chinese scholars,[78] then it is possible to find a legislative document issued by the Standing Committee of China's National People's Congress which enables the Chinese courts to directly apply relevant treaties. On June 23, 1987, the Standing Committee adopted a decision which declares that the People's Republic of China will, "within its treaty obligations, exercise criminal jurisdiction over the crimes prescribed by international treaties concluded or acceded to by the People's Republic of China."[79] Attached to this decision are the relevant articles of the international treaties in question.[80] This decision is intended to allow the Chinese courts to directly apply the provisions of these treaties which oblige a contracting state to take the necessary measures to establish its jurisdiction over the crimes, if the alleged offender is present in its territory and it does not extradite him or her to other parties. The reason for making this decision, it is submitted, is that the PRC *Criminal Procedure Law*, which was enacted in 1979, contains no provision for the direct application of international treaties in so far as the question of jurisdiction is concerned. Therefore, in order to directly apply the treaty obligations which, in this case, are to exercise jurisdiction over the crimes prescribed by the international treaties to which China is a party, it is necessary to have such a decision as a supplement to the PRC *Criminal Procedure Law*.[81]

While most human rights treaties to which China is a contracting party are unlikely to reach China's domestic legal proceedings due to the lack of a statutory enabling law, the non-directly applicable nature of these treaties does not necessarily lead to non-performance of the treaty obligations.

Non-direct applicability in this case merely means that the court in question cannot apply a treaty in the same way as it does a domestic statute. Many other nations, where valid international treaties are automatically accorded legal effect in their domestic legal orders, face similar problems. In a sense, direct application of the international treaties on human rights is but one road, albeit an important one, leading to the strengthening of the role of domestic courts in adjudicating international human rights. In addition to this, there are alternative mechanisms to enforce these treaties. One way for China to enforce its legal obligations, as established by the international human rights treaties to which China is a party, within its domestic legal order, would be to make the relevant domestic laws comply with the corresponding international legal obligations.

At this point, it should be mentioned that what is prohibited by international human rights law is also prohibited by Chinese domestic law. Within this context, enforcement of China's international legal obligations for the promotion and protection of human rights is transformed into an effort to strengthen the country's legal system, to ensure the rule of law and, in particular, to safeguard the rights enjoyed by Chinese citizens under the present Constitution. In this regard, China can better its performance in carrying out its international legal obligations for the promotion and protection of human rights, by making the best use of the relevant international instruments to inform the interpretation and application of the rights guaranteed by China's Constitution as well as the scope of their limitations.

One example is the implementation of China's legal obligations under the *UN Convention against Torture and Other Cruel, Inhuman or Degrading Treatment or Punishment*. Under Article 32 of the PRC *Criminal Procedure Law*, the extortion of confessions by means of torture, and the collection of evidence by threat, enticement, deceit or other illegal means are strictly prohibited. Article 136 of the PRC *Criminal Law (Penal Code)* provides that:

> It is strictly prohibited to extort a confession by torture. A state official who extorts a confession by torture shall be sentenced to either fixed-term imprisonment for not more than three years or detention. A person who disable another by use of corporal punishment shall be charged with the crime of personal injury and shall be severely punished.

By ratifying the *UN Convention against Torture*, it has become part of China's domestic law. While the provisions of the Convention are found consistent with China's domestic rules, the Convention gives a relatively explicit definition of the term 'torture', and detailed provisions concerning jurisdiction over the offence. Now, it has become China's international legal obligation to bring the application of its relevant domestic rules into compliance with the Convention and to ensure that the Chinese domestic courts exercise criminal jurisdiction over the offence ,as required by the Convention.[82]   Thus, the Canadian Supreme Court reasoned that, the fact that a value has the status of an international human right, either in customary international law or under a treaty to which Canada is a contracting party, should generally be indicative of a high degree of importance attached to that objective.[83] Such reasoning is equally valid in China, given its tradition of always attaching high importance to its international undertakings.

Thus, it is assumed that, if the Chinese judicial world were better informed about the requirements for cracking down on torture and other cruel, inhuman or degrading treatment, not only in the Chinese criminal code, but also in its international legal obligations under the *UN Convention against Torture*, its legal and administrative actions in this respect would become more effective. In 1990, China's procuratorial organs filed 472 cases for investigation which involved extorting confessions by torture.[84] Last year, in his Work Report submitted to the first session of the Eighth National People's Congress of the People's Republic of China, the President of the PRC Supreme People's Procuratorate intentionally linked actions against torture and other related illegal activities with the issue of human rights. This linkage, while partly serving propaganda purposes, was also intended to draw more attention from the Chinese judicial circles to the seriousness of the issue.

The domestic implementation of the *Convention on the Elimination of all Forms of Discrimination against Women* is another example. On April 3, 1992, the PRC National People's Congress adopted the PRC *Law on the Protection of the Rights and Interests of Women*, which came into effect six months later. This statute contains 54 articles which specify rights to participation in political activities, education, work, property, marriage and family, and other personal interests which women enjoy in China. While this statute is aimed at bringing into full play women's role in China's political, social, economic and cultural life and meeting the pressing challenge for the protection of women's special rights and interests in China, the statute's draft committee particularly noticed the performance of China's international legal obligation under the *Convention on the Elimination of all Forms of Discrimination against Women*.[85] The Convention not only lays down substantive provisions concerning women's rights but also requires each contracting party to enact the law according to its domestic circumstances, so as to ensure the full development and progress of women. Therefore, China's domestic statute has become the embodiment of its international obligations under the Convention. The application of this statute by China's domestic courts is tantamount to its enforcement in the Chinese domestic legal system.

Conclusion

Although most of the international treaties on human rights to which China is a party can hardly be applied directly by the Chinese courts in the Chinese domestic legal system, the courts can still play an active role in enforcing the domestic statutes which embody its international legal obligations. In late 1986, this author had the opportunity to attend a lecture in Beijing which was presented by the then principal legal officer of the UN Office of Legal Counsel on International Human Rights. When he was asked how the promotion and protection of human rights could be achieved in China, a country where the prevailing concept of human rights was not based on the natural law theory, his answer was simply that, if China could ensure the faithful application of the Chinese constitutional provisions concerning citizens' rights, and safeguard their enjoyment by the public, China would have no serious problem in the field of international human rights. Although he said these words seven years ago, his points are still valid. The challenge presently confronting the Chinese people and government is still how to safeguard the enjoyment of the individuals' rights as provided by China's Constitution. However, tremendous progress has been made in this respect compared to the situation ten or fifteen years ago. Given China's historical, social, cultural, political and economic development pertinent to human rights, it is a long-term historical commitment of the Chinese people and government to meet that challenge.

Notes

1. Very often the role of the judiciary in enforcing international law is determined by the trust which a state gives to the international system, the weight of the value of the domestic law as perceived against that of international law, the extent of the leeway which a state cares to remain in its legal system vis-à-vis the requirement of its international obligations. In regard to the Chinese practice in this respect, see Li Zhaojie, "The Effect of Treaties in Domestic Law, Practice of the People's Republic of China", 16 *Dalhousie Law Journal*, No. 1 (Spring 1993), at 96-97.

2. Sir H. Lauterpacht, *International Law and Human Rights*, (New York: Garland Publishing, 1973).

3. Ibid., at 981-983. Also, Burns R. Weston, "Human Rights" in *Human Rights in the World Community--Issues and Action*, ed. by Richard Pierre Claude and Burns H. Weston, 2nd ed. (1992), at 14-31.

4. Ian Brownlie, *Principles of Public International Law*, 4th ed., (Oxford: Clarendon Press, 1990) 553-554. J.G. Starke, *Introduction to International Law*, 9th ed., (London: Butterworths, 1984) at 349-350. Rudolf Bernhardt, "Domestic Jurisdiction of States and International Human Rights Organs", 7 *Human Rights Law Journal* (1986) No. 2-4, at 205. According to K. M. Davidse, in recent years, there are not many countries left solely relying on the argument of non-intervention in reacting to criticism from abroad on their human rights record. K. M. Davidse, "The 48th Session of the UN Commission on Human Rights and UN Monitoring of Violations of Civil and Political Rights", 10 *Netherlands Quarterly of Human Rights* (1992), No. 3, at 283-302.

5. Anne F. Bayefsky, *International Human Rights Law--Use in Canadian Charter of Rights and Freedom Litigation*, (Toronto: Butterworths, 1992) at 1.

6. Abdullah Ahmed An-Na'im, "Towards a cross-cultural approach to defining international Standards of Human Rights", in *Human Rights in Cross-Cultural Perspectives--a Quest for Consensus*, University of Pennsylvania Press, ed. by Abdullah A. An-Na'im (1992), at 21.

7. Noticeably, an increasing number of Chinese scholars tend to agree that, despite substantial differences in the concept of human rights which are generated by the diversity of political, economic and cultural backgrounds, certain universal standards of human rights must and do exist as a mirror of human dignity and conscience. See Xu Weidong, et al., "Lun Renquan De Yishixingtai Biaozhun Yu Falu Biaozhun" (On the Ideological and Legal Standards of Human Rights), 1 *Zhongguo Faxue* (Journal of Chinese Law), 1992; "Study on the Theories of Human Rights", *Beijing Daxue Xuebao* (Journal of Peking University--Philosophy and Social Sciences Edition), 1992, No. 2, at 5-13, No. 3, at 41-59. The Chinese Government's White Paper on Human Rights in China states at the outset that "[i]t has been a long-cherished ideal of mankind to enjoy human rights in the full sense of the term", *Human Rights in China*, Information Office of the State Council, PRC, November 1991, at 1.

8. Abdullah Ahmed An-Na'im, supra, note 6, at 1.

9. Ibid., at 23.

10. Ibid.

11. The last two decades have witnessed the rise of the so-called "third generation" of human rights which are sometimes referred to as "collective rights". This third category contains the right to national self-determination, to development, to peace, to utilization of the natural wealth and resources of one's native country, to co-ownership of the common heritage of mankind, to a clean and healthy environment. "Human Rights as Individual and as Collective Rights", in Jan Berting et al., eds., *Human Rights in a Pluralist World: Individuals and Collectivities*, (Westport, Connecticut: Meckler, 1990) at 33-108.

12. Abdullah Ahmed An-Na'im, supra, note 6, at 24.

13. The *Charter* of the United Nations solemnly declares: "WE THE PEOPLE OF THE UNITED NATIONS DETERMINED...to reaffirm faith in fundamental human rights, in the dignity and worth of the human person,..." Also, see Article 1 of the UN *Universal Declaration of Human Rights*.

14. William P. Alford, "Making a Goddess of Democracy from Loose Sand: Thoughts on Human Rights in the People's Republic of China", in A.A. An-Na'im ed., supra, note 6, at 73.

15. J.C. Hsiung, ed., *Human Rights in East Asia: A Cultural Perspective*, (New York: Paragon House Publishers, 1985) at 11.

16. R. Falk, "Cultural Foundations for Protection of Human Rights", in A. A. An-Na'im, ed., supra, note 6, at 45, 57.

17. In this context, if one criticizes China's strict "one-child" policy and its rigid nationwide campaign for the control of population growth as a violation of the right of people who have reached the age of majority to found a family, the antithesis could equally be that, given the compelling population challenge to China's economic and social development, China has only two alternatives in tackling its population problem: either to exert strict control of its family planning policy or to allow unlimited birth growth. The former helps enhance the social welfare thus enabling the majority of the people to improve their living conditions, while the latter will undoubtedly lead to mass malnutrition and even

starvation and concomitant loss of human dignity by large. Alford, supra, note 14, at 74-75.

18. Abdullah Ahmed An-Na'im, supra, note 6, at 1-6.

19. Ibid. Also, see I. Brownlie, supra, note 4, at 601-602.

20. K. Vasak, "Distinguishing Criteria of Institutions", in K. Vasak (ed.) *The International Dimensions of Human Rights* (Westport, Connecticut: Greenwood Press, 1982), at 215-216.

21. Richard Falk, supra, note 16, at 55.

22. Richard Falk, "Responding to Severe Violations", in Jorge I. Dominguez, et al. (eds.), *Enhancing Global Human Rights*, (New York: McGraw-Hill, 1979) at 253.

23. B.G. Ramcharan, *The Concept and Present Status of the International Protection of Human Right: Forty Years after the Universal Declaration*, (Dordrecht: Martinus Nijhoff, 1989) at 10-11.

24. A prominent example of this is the prohibition and prevention of cruel, inhuman, or degrading treatment or punishment. While some international human rights instruments provide that no one shall be subjected to cruel, inhuman, or degrading treatment or punishment, they do not give a detailed definition of what constitutes the prohibited acts as they do in regards to torture. The UN 1984 *Convention against Torture and other Cruel, Inhuman or Degrading Treatment or Punishment* makes a distinction between "torture" and "cruel, inhuman or degrading treatment or punishment". Under the *Convention*, "pain or suffering arising only from, inherent in or incidental to lawful sanctions" has been excluded from the definition of torture. However, the "lawful sanctions" can be held to violate the prohibition of cruel, inhuman, or degrading treatment or punishment. According to R. St. J. Macdonald, it is not entirely clear whether it is a question of degree of physical or mental violence that differentiates the two, or whether it is the requisite state of mind that determines the issue, or whether it is both considerations that decide whether the act falls within the category of "torture", on the one hand, or "cruel, inhuman or degrading treatment or punishment", on the other. Moreover, criteria of "cruel", "inhuman" and "degrading" are different in various cultural contexts. R. St. J. Macdonald, "International Prohibitions Against Torture and Other Forms of Similar

Treatment or Punishment", in *International Law at a Time of Perplexity (Essays in Honor of Shabtai Rosenne)*, ed. by Y. Dinstein, 1988, at 385-406.

25. A.F. Bayefsky, supra, note 5, at 1-2.

26. Ibid.

27. Ronald St. J. Macdonald, the "Margin of Appreciation in the Jurisprudence of the European Court of Human Rights", *Collected Courses of the Academy of European Law*, Volume I, Book 2, at 95-161.

28. Ibid., vol. 1, para. 48, at 753.

29. Ibid., at 753-754.

30. *European Human Rights Reports* (ed. by Graham Zellick), (London: European Law Centre Ltd., 1979-80), vol. 2, para. 207, at 91.

31. Ibid., vol. 8, para. 122, at 373.

32. Ibid., vol. 10, para. 50, at 312.

33. There are also cases in which the Court drew the line beyond which the doctrine of national margin of appreciation cannot go. It should be noted that even in cases where the application of the national margin of appreciation was justified, it was done so on the basis of treaty obligations and as a result of interpretation and application of treaty provisions. R. Macdonald, supra, note 27.

34. Ibid., at 109.

35. Bin Cheng notes that although Article 6 of the 1948 *Universal Declaration of Human Rights* and Article 16 of the 1966 *International Covenant on Civil and Political Rights* have stated that everyone has the right to recognition everywhere as a person before the law, it would be erroneous to conclude therefrom that individuals are subjects of international law. The *Covenant* is, in fact, explicit on what its provisions intend to achieve by providing that "Each State Party to the present Covenant undertakes to respect and to ensure to all individuals within its territory and subject to its jurisdiction the rights recognized in the present Covenant". So, according to Bin Cheng, the Covenant has set out to enumerate the rights, the respect of which States Parties to the Covenant undertake to ensure in their municipal laws. Bin Chen, "Introduction to Subjects

of International Law", in *International Law: Achievements and Prospects*, ed. by Mohammed Bedjaoui (1991), 28.

36. For instance, Article 5 of the 1966 *Convention on the Elimination of All Forms of Racial Discrimination* which accords every individual, without discrimination of any kind, the right to have access to any place or service is intended for use by the general public. Article 25 of the *European Convention* is another prominent exception at regional levels.

37. Jost Delbrueck, "International Protection of Human Rights and State Sovereignty", in *Third World Attitudes towards International Law: an Introduction*, ed. by Frederick E. Snyder, et al., at 269.

38. Wu Jianfan, "Building New China's Legal System", in *China's Legal Development*, ed. by John R. Oldham, 1986, at 1-40; Victor H. Li, "Reflections on the Current Drive toward Greater Legalization in China", 10, *Georgia Journal of International and Comparative Law*, 1980 (Issue 2), at 221-232.

39. To name a few: beginning in 1979, nationwide legal education was restored in China's universities and colleges which had trained, as of 1990, more than 50,000 law graduates. A series of the most important legislation has been made, including the *Constitution* (1982), *Penal Code* (1979), *Criminal Procedure Law* (1979), *General Principles of Civil Law* (1986), *Civil Procedure Law* (1982 for interim implementation, and 1991 for final revision), *Administrative Procedure Law* (1989). In addition to this, from 1979 to 1989, more than 150 statutes were enacted by the PRC legislature, and more than 1,000 administrative regulations were promulgated by the PRC State Council (the executive body of the PRC Government). As of 1990, the number of judges had increased from 60,000 in 1978 to 190,000. *Yearbook of China Law*, 1991.

40. Yearbook of China Law, ibid., at 939.

41. The largest yield of law graduates happened in 1990. In that year, over 20,000 people graduated from China's law schools. Ibid., at 955.

42. Ibid., at 104.

43. Victor H. Li, supra, note 38, at 223.

44. Yearbook of China Law, supra, note 39, at 947-962.

45. Wang Tieya, "International Law in China: Historical and Contemporary Perspectives", *II Recueil Des Cours 1990* (Collected Courses of the Hague Academy of International Law), (Paris: Hachette) at 226-264.

46. Ibid., 354.

47. See, Samuel S. Kim, "The Development of International Law in Post-Mao China: Change and Continuity", 1 *Journal of Chinese Law*, No. 2 (Fall 1987), at 117-160.

48. Francis G. Jacobs, et al. (eds.), *The Effect of Treaties in Domestic Law*, United Kingdom National Committee of Comparative Law, (London: Sweet & Maxwell, 1987).

49. It should be pointed out that the current PRC Constitution concentrates more conspicuously on the general principles which govern China's international behaviour while remaining silent on specific issues of dealing with the relationship between international law and domestic law, e.g. the question of the domestic validity of international law.

50. Wang Tieya and Wei Min, *Guoji Fa (International Law), Falu Chubanshe (Law Press) 1982*, 42-47. Zhou Gengsheng, *Guoji Fa* (International Law), Shangwu Chubanshe (Commercial Press), 1976, at 16-20.

51. Li Zhaojie, supra, note 1.

52. Ibid.

53. According to Human Rights Law Journal, some 72 treaties are identified as international legal instruments on human rights. 14 *Human Rights Law Journal* (February 26, 1993, No. 1-2), 59-61.

54. With mutatis mutandis, the current PRC *Civil Procedure Law* which was promulgated by the PRC President on, and effective from, April 9, 1991 has replaced the PRC *Civil Procedural Law* for Trial Implementation promulgated in 1982. For the Chinese text, see *Zhonghua Renmin Gongheguo Quanguo Renmin Daibiao Dahui Changwu Weiyuanhui Gongbao* (Gazette of the Standing Committee of the PRC National People's Congress), 1991, No. 3, at 41.

55. Li Haopei, *Tiaoyue Fa Gailun* (Law of Treaties), Falu Chubanshe (Law Press) 1987, 384.

56. According to the official statistics, during the last five years, 1,687 cases of torture committed by police and other judicial officials were prosecuted and tried. Various criminal penalties were imposed on the perpetrators.

57. *Renmin Ribao* (People's Daily, overseas edition), November 16, 1991, at page 4. Similar statement was also made in April 1990. U.N. Committee against Torture, Fourth Session, Summary Record of the 51st Meeting, Geneva, April 27, 1990, CAT/C/SR.51 (May 4, 1990), 2.

58. The PCIJ, in its advisory opinion in the case of Legal Status of Eastern Greenland, declared that communication of an official character on a matter within the [Foreign] Minister's province, was regarded as "beyond all dispute... binding upon the country to which the Minister belongs."

59. Supra, note 53, at 71.

60. Ibid., 62-70.

61. Supra, note 51, at 62.

62. To the knowledge of this author, until the abrupt outbreak of the June 4th tragedy in Beijing, 1989, serious consideration of ratifying the two *Covenants* was given by both the Chinese governmental authorities and academicians. The outbreak of the June 4th tragedy, and the events which developed prior and subsequent to it in China and the world, has obviously led to the delay of the Chinese participation in these two Universal Covenants.

63. In recent years, with the rapid economic development, this right has in fact been exercised in China. Statistics compiled in 1989 suggest that rural migrants in search of jobs were among the 50 million Chinese "on the move", outside the family program and subject to no one's jurisdiction--i.e. one in twenty of China's people. However, the concomitant problems have also become increasing prominent. Each year, after China's spring festival, major cities in China are plagued with hundreds of thousands of rural migrants looking for jobs.

64. However, this argument cannot prevail in a case of embezzlement, in which a defendant is presumed guilty if he or she cannot prove the legal source of his or her property.

65. Xu Hong, "Respect Human Rights and Demand Social Progress-- Commemorating the 20th Anniversary of the Adoption of the International

Covenant on Economic, Social, and Cultural Rights and the International Covenant on Civil and Political Rights", *Journal of Chinese Legal Affairs*, December 15, 1986, p. 4.

66. Li Zhaojie, supra, note 1, 73.

67. Ibid., 88-93.

68. Supra, note 1.

69. *Human Rights in China* (White Paper on Human Rights in China), issued by the Information Office of the State Council, Nov. 1991, 79-86.

70. Ibid., 85-86.

71. "The Principle of Non-Interference in Internal Affairs in International Relations", *Renmin Ribao* (People's Daily), August 25, 1989.

72. During the debate of the 41st Session of the General Assembly of the United Nations, the PRC Foreign Minister in his speech praised the two *Covenants* highly. According to him, "these two instruments have played a positive role in realizing the purposes and principles of the UN Charter concerning the respect for human rights. The Chinese government has consistently supported these purposes and principles." In September 1988, the Chinese foreign minister pointed out in his speech at the 43rd session of the UN General Assembly that the "Universal Declaration of Human Rights" is "the first international instrument which systematically sets forth the specific contents regarding respect for and protection of fundamental human rights. Despite its historical limitations, the Declaration has exerted a far-reaching influence on the development of the post-war international human rights activities and played a positive role in this regard." Ibid., 80.

73. According to this author's interview with some officials who work as international lawyers in the PRC Ministry of Foreign Affairs, China's ambivalent attitude towards customary international law arises from the following concerns: China did not participate in the formation of most of the alleged customary rules. Thus, it feels uncertain about the utility of these rules in practice. This concern is reinforced by the fact that interpretation of customary rules is often volatile and subject to the interpreter's own perception.

74. *Laws of the People's Republic of China*, (1979-1982) Foreign Languages Press, Beijing, at 306. Without such treaties, the matter will be handled in accordance with the principle of reciprocity.

75. Similar provisions can also be found in the PRC Law of Succession. Li Zhaojie, supra, note 1.

76. *Zhongguo Jinianlai Shewai Shegangao Anjian* (Cases Before China's Courts in Recent Years Which Involve Foreign, Hong Kong and Macao Interests) ed. by Ma Shouren, 1990.

77. Li Zhaojie, supra, note 1, 83-84.

78. Wang Tieya and Wei Min, supra, note 50, 265-266.

79. Wang Tieya, supra, note 45, at 329.

80. They are: the *Convention on the Prevention and Punishment of Crimes against Internationally Protected Persons including Diplomatic Agents* of 1973, the *Convention for the Suppression of Unlawful Seizure of Aircraft* of 1970, the *Convention for the Suppression of Unlawful Acts against Safety of Civil Aviation* of 1971, the *Convention on the Physical Protection of Nuclear Materials* of 1980 and the *Conventions against the Taking of Hostages* of 1979. By the decision of the Standing Committee to ratify the *Convention on Suppression of Unlawful Acts against the Safety of Maritime Navigation* of 1988 and the *Protocol for the Suppression of Unlawful Acts against the Safety of Fixed Platforms Located on the Continental Shelf* of 1988, these two treaties should also be added to this list.

81. Article 67 (3) of the Constitution empowers the Standing Committee to make supplements as well as amendments to the laws enacted by the National People's Congress.

82. Since the provisions of the Convention concerning the jurisdiction over the offence are identical with the provisions in the Chinese penal code, it is thus not necessary to enact an enabling law to enforce it.

83. Anne F. Bayefsky, supra, note 5, at 76.

84. Supra, note 69, at 31.

85. <u>Fazhi Bao</u> (Legal Daily), April 10, 1992.

The People's Republic of China and the United Nations Commission on Human Rights

LIU XINSHENG

The year 1995 marks the 50th anniversary of the founding of the United Nations (UN). As the most universal, international intergovernmental organization, the UN has made an important contribution to preserving world peace and security during the 50 years after World War II. According to the "UN Charter", the main purpose of the UN is to:

> achieve international cooperation in solving international problems of an economic, social, cultural, or humanitarian character, and in promoting and encouraging respect for human rights and for fundamental freedoms for all without distinction as to race, sex, language, or religion.

The UN has organized many activities in order to promote respect and protection of human rights.

As a founding member of the UN and a permanent member of the UN Security Council, the People's Republic of China has always respected and supported the "UN Charter" principle of promoting and protecting human rights. China appreciates the effort made by the UN to promote human rights universally and takes active part in the activities organized by the UN in the human rights field in order to contribute towards realizing this key principle.

1

The *UN Charter* clearly expresses the international community's deep concern about the promotion and protection of human rights. In the Charter, the United Nations expresses its determination "to reaffirm faith in fundamental human rights, in the dignity and worth of the human person, in the equal rights of men and women and of nations large and small"; to attain the goal "to practice tolerance and live together in peace with one another as good neighbours"; and "to employ international machinery for the promotion of the economic and social advancement of all peoples."

According to the UN's principle of promoting and protecting human rights, Article 55 of the *UN Charter* stipulates:

> With a view to creating conditions of stability and well-being which are necessary for peaceful and friendly relations among nations based on respect for the principle of equal rights and self-determination of peoples, the United Nations shall promote [...] universal respect for, and observance of, human rights and fundamental freedoms for all without distinction as to race, sex, language or religion.

According to Article 56, Members of the UN "...pledge themselves to take joint and separate action in cooperation with the Organization for the achievement of the purposes set forth in Article 55."

China has always taken the *UN Charter* principles of respecting and protecting human rights as its own obligations. Even when China was unjustifiably deprived of its lawful seat in the UN because of certain Western countries' attempts to isolate the new China, the Chinese government and people still recognized and respected the *UN Charter* goal and principle of protecting and promoting human rights and fundamental freedoms. In April 1955, China's Premier Zhou Enlai attended the Asian-African Bandung Conference in Indonesia and signed the *Final Communiqué of the Asian-African Conference* ("Bandung Declaration"). This Communiqué announced that the Asian-African Conference fully supports the basic principle of human rights as stated in the *UN Charter*, and the sentence "Respect basic human rights, respect the goal and principle of the *UN Charter*" was entered as the first of ten principles for peaceful co-existence. In his speech, Zhou Enlai announced: "The people of all dependent states should enjoy the right to national self-determination [...], people of every nationality should enjoy basic human rights without distinction as to race and skin colour"; and "Respect for basic human rights and respect for the goal and principle of the *UN Charter*, [...] have always been a main concern of the Chinese people, and they have always been principles that the Chinese people respect."

In participating in the activities of the UN human rights bodies, China, like other developing countries, actively protects and develops the concept of human rights in step with the development of the history of humanity and international convention. China has contributed much to the international community's effort to promote and protect human rights. China plays a unique role in the protection and development of the human rights concept, and it has received favourable responses from the international community.

Respect and support for the basic UN principle of promoting and protecting human rights

In December 1988, at the UN commemorative meeting to celebrate the 40th anniversary of the *Universal Declaration of Human Rights*, the Chinese representative made a speech in which he evaluated the historical significance of the *Declaration*, promised that the Chinese government and people would continue to respect human rights and fundamental freedoms, support and carry out the human rights related principles of the *UN Charter*, and take active part in UN activities. The Chinese representative pointed out that the *Universal Declaration on Human Rights* was the first international document which systematically raised the issue of protection and respect for human rights. It stresses freedom, equality, opposition to discrimination, and it includes both civil and political rights and economic, social and cultural rights. Many important principles of the *Declaration* have become the theoretical foundation for drawing up international human rights instruments and organizing human rights activities in the UN. The significance of the *Declaration* lies in the fact that it reflects the aspirations of people from all over the world to achieve equality and freedom, and its influence has been continuously strengthened with the renewal and enrichment of the original content.

On April 6, 1994, when Chinese Vice-Premier and Foreign Minister Qian Qichen met the former UN Secretary-General Waldheim, he said that the Chinese government has always supported the efforts made by the UN to promote and protect human rights and fundamental freedoms according to the goals and principles of the *UN Charter*. China believes that the *Universal Declaration of Human Rights*, passed by the UN in 1948, is the first international document which systematically encourages the respect and protection of basic human rights in concrete terms. The *Declaration* has had long-lasting influence on and played an active role in the development of post-war international human rights activities. The Chinese government has announced many times that it would respect the stipulations of the *Universal Declaration on Human Rights* as well as the various international human rights instruments, and make its own contribution to protecting human rights and fundamental freedoms. China is willing to cooperate with other countries on human rights issues, and it believes that such cooperation should be based on equality and mutual respect. China, as always, will work hard with the international community to strengthen international cooperation in the human rights field.

Maintaining a comprehensive, indivisible human rights concept

It has already been 50 years since the establishment of the UN, and the concept of human rights has undergone much development. At present, the international community speaks of human rights issues which include civil and political rights, economic, social and cultural rights, the rights of the individual, the right to self-determination and the right to development. Human rights has become a synthesis of individual rights and group rights. Some countries place undue emphasis on civil and political rights and thereby neglect economic, social and cultural rights. China emphasizes the evolutionary and comprehensive nature of human rights and has consistently opposed splitting the human rights concept. To place undue emphasis on the individual's civil and political rights is of no benefit to the universal realization of all human rights and fundamental freedoms. China stresses that these two kinds of basic human rights should be paid the same amount of attention and that, in the case of developing countries, the realization of the right to independence, the right to subsistence and the right to development is most important. The Chinese position and its advocacy of these issues has met with wide-spread understanding and support from developing countries.

China also believes that the concept of human rights is a product of historical development, and that it is closely related to specific social, political and economic conditions, as well as to a country's unique history, culture and ideas. Countries with different historical traditions and cultural backgrounds and at different stages of development differ in their perception and practice of human rights. Every country should have the right to choose its own political system, path to development and value system, and other countries have no right to interfere.

With respect to the relationship between development, democracy and human rights, China is of the opinion that comprehensive and balanced development of the economy and society is the basis for people to fully enjoy all human rights. Whichever form of democracy a country adopts should be chosen by the people of that country. The democratic form of a country is closely related to its history, culture, religion, national characteristics and level of economic development, and it cannot be separated from the overall conditions of the country. At the same time, it is difficult to find one model that will suit all countries. Regarding the relationship between democracy and human rights, putting undue emphasis on one kind of democratic model should be avoided. Every country should be encouraged to develop and perfect a democratic system and democratic form which suits the national characteristics of the country. In promoting democracy, people should respect each country's right to self-determination. At the international level, the democratisation of international relations should be promoted, and the principle of equality between nations should be upheld regardless of whether they are big or small, poor or rich, strong or weak. A single country or a group of countries should be prevented from forcing their wills upon others.

Upholding the right to national self-determination

Since China began taking part in UN human rights activities, it has consistently protected and upheld the right to national self-determination. The right to national self-determination, as defined in the *Declaration on the Granting of Independence to Colonial Countries and Peoples* passed by the UN General Assembly in 1960, was a summary of the achievement of national independence and liberation gained by the people of certain countries who suffered oppression and colonialism over a long period of time. It also encouraged and motivated many Third World countries in their struggles against foreign military invasion, occupation and interference, to defend their sovereignty and independence. Recognizing the right to national self-determination means respecting the sovereignty, independence and territorial integrity of all countries. It also means letting the people of each country choose their own political and economic system and path to development, and determine their own destiny in accordance with the realities of the country. Protection of the right to self-determination, and opposition to foreign invasion, interference and control, is the foundation for a country's existence and the basis for the people to fully enjoy all other human rights and fundamental freedoms.

China actively supports the people of all countries who suffered under colonial rule, foreign invasion and occupation, and their struggle to achieve the right to self-determination. China supports the people of all countries in defence of their sovereignty, independence and territorial integrity, and their right to determine their own political and economic system and path to development, in accordance with the realities of the country and without pressure from the outside. China also emphasizes that any actions, under the banner of the right to self-determination, which create national contradictions and conflicts to the point of splitting a sovereign country, are against the principles of the *UN Charter*, and should be opposed by the international community. The right to national self-determination applies to the people who are under foreign rule, colonial rule or foreign occupation, and should not become an excuse for supporting actions which jeopardize a country's territorial integrity, sovereignty and political independence. It is of immediate importance to strictly follow these principles in today's international relations. The events that have occurred in certain regions of the world have proven that to unilaterally explain and apply the principle of self-determination and, in the name of the right to self-determination, to jeopardize the independence and integrity of a country, would only cause or intensify national conflict and social instability, or even result in civil war or regional conflict. This would, in turn, lead to serious threats to world peace and security.

China is of the opinion that many national conflicts which had been over-shadowed by ideology and the Cold War are now re-emerging and creating new crises, conflicts and even wars. Under such circumstances, upholding the principle of the right to national self-determination remains an important topic facing the people of the world. At the UN human rights conference, Chinese representatives strongly refuted the fallacies that "self-determination is out-of-date" and "self-determination applies within a nation". They firmly fought against the theory of distorting the principle of self-determination and opposed the erroneous practice of inciting separation and hatred between nationalities within a country.

Establishing and realizing the right to development

At the end of 1979, when developing countries for the first time put forward the idea of the right to development in the General Assembly, China immediately showed strong support. In order to encourage the establishment of the right to development, China has, since 1981, sent delegates to attend all the meetings of the Government Expert Working Groups of the Commission on Human Rights to draft the *Declaration of The Right to Development*. With the combined efforts of China and other developing countries, the *Declaration* was finally approved by the 41st Session of the UN General Assembly in 1986.

China stresses the issue of the right to development, and believes that it is a human right of which a country should not be deprived. Promoting the realization of the right to development is a long-term task facing the international community. Confronted with the argument that the right to development is not a human right but an economic goal, Chinese representatives pointed out, at the 48th Session of the UN Human Rights Commission, that simply viewing the right to development as an economic goal and separating economic rights from other rights is really to misinterpret the right to development. Even though the concept of the right to development includes economic factors, its implications are much more numerous. The emphasis is on the inter-dependent and indivisible character of human rights and fundamental freedoms. Development, democracy and human rights re-enforce each other. To put undue emphasis on one set of factors and disregard others, and to mechanically copy development strategies and political models which are unsuitable to a country's domestic situation, will result in conditions unfavourable to the realization of the right to development and to people's enjoyment of all human rights and fundamental freedoms.

The Chinese government believes that the right to development is the most basic and most important human right to many developing countries, including China. Realization of the right to development is still a most urgent task for the international community. In the nine years since the approval of the *Declaration of the Right to Development*, a majority of countries already recognize the right to development as a human right of which a country should not be deprived. Until recently, however, the right to development has not received enough attention. For many years, the tendency within the UN human rights fields has been towards only emphasizing civil and political rights and neglecting economic, social and cultural rights and the right to development. Some countries do not accept the difference of approach to human rights which is based on different national situations, and they neglect economic, social and cultural rights and the right to development. Certain countries are even of the opinion that economic, social and cultural rights and the right to development do not belong in the human rights category. They obstruct and oppose the demand of developing countries to establish the right to independence and the right to development as the most basic and foremost of the human rights. The Chinese government believes that the basic pre-condition for realizing the right to development is to recognize that the it is a universal and fundamental human right, and that economic, social and cultural rights are as important as political and civil rights. The international community should pay more attention to the right to development, strengthen international cooperation, and ensure implementation of active, balanced and non-confrontational measures in order to realize the right to development, eliminate selectiveness and double standards and establish efficient monitoring and deliberation mechanisms to promote the right to development.

In order to achieve full realization of the right to development, it is necessary to eliminate the obstacles within the international community which stand in the way of the smooth development of a country, and it is necessary to create conditions favourable to its realization. It cannot be denied that, in today's world, incidents of colonialism, racism, foreign invasion and occupation, deprivation of state sovereignty, independence and self-determination still occur. All these problems hinder the full realization of the right to development. Elimination of these hindrances requires a joint effort from the international community, the creation of a favourable international environment, and especially the establishment of a new international political order in which countries respect each other's differences, do not interfere with each other's internal affairs, treat each other equally and work together for mutual benefit. Only through the establishment of such a new international political order can realization of the right to development be fulfilled on a large scale.

In order to fully realize the right to development, it is also necessary to establish a new international economic order. In the international economic sphere, an economic environment which is both unfair and unequitable to developing countries causes the gap between rich and poor in the North and the South to widen, and poverty has become a major obstacle to the full enjoyment of human rights. Currently, there are 41 countries in the world that belong to the category of least developed countries. The economies of most developing countries are becoming increasingly troubled, the average income has decreased and a third of the population is living below the poverty line. Although developing countries have put much effort into solving their problems and although they have achieved a certain measure of success, they cannot possibly bring about fundamental changes to their unfavourable position, because their backward economic situation is caused by long-term effects of an unfair international economic order. The economy of a few developed countries still depend on sacrificing the interests of many developing countries. To change such an extremely unfair situation while establishing a new international political order, it is also necessary to change the current international economic order, to eliminate unfair and unjust practices in the international economic structure, to improve the international economic conditions, and to resolve and slowly eliminate the unfavourable factors which restrict development in developing countries. Developed countries have a special obligation to actively help developing countries in the areas of debt, capital, trade assistance, technology transfer, etc., and to help developing countries overcome economic difficulties and diminish the gap between North and South, in order that both sides can reach the goal of shared development and shared prosperity.

It should be pointed out, in particular, that some countries are linking the provision of international economic aid to the recipient country's "human rights situation" and thus turning aid into a political tool. Such a theory and practice is of no benefit to developing countries in their pursuit of economic, social and cultural rights and the right to development. It places the recipient country in an unequal position vis-à-vis the donor country, and it also deprives the developing countries of their right to choose their own political, economic and social systems. This constitutes interference in the domestic political, economic and social development of the recipient countries, and this is unacceptable.

Realization of the right to development is a lengthy and arduous task. It would be difficult to achieve the desired results by relying only on the efforts of international human rights organizations. Therefore, it is necessary to coordinate the efforts of governments of all countries, UN agencies and other relevant organizations. It is well known that the world economy is an indivisible entity. The development of a country is closely connected to that of other countries. The prosperity of a minority of countries cannot be sustained on the basis of long-term under-development and poverty in the majority of countries. Development of the developing countries will help achieve shared prosperity in both developed countries and developing countries. Therefore, realization of the right to development is not only essential for developing countries, but also of great significance to developed countries. China is willing to cooperate with the international community in an effort to eliminate the obstacles to the realization of the right to development and to fulfil the lofty goal of the UN *Declaration of the Right to Development.*

On the right to subsistence

On November 1, 1991, the Information Office of the Chinese State Council published the White Book, "Human Rights in China". This book gives a systematic and objective introduction to the human rights situation in China, and it elaborates on Chinese human rights theory and practice. For the first time, the White Book puts forward the new human rights concept of the right to subsistence. It states: "To a country or a people, human rights first of all means people's right to subsistence. Without the right to subsistence, other rights cannot be realized." In order to realize the right to subsistence, a country must first fight for and defend its right to independence and then, on this foundation, develop the economy in order to be able to guarantee the basics of life for its people.

The right to subsistence combines the right to self-determination with the right to development to form an organic whole. The concept of the right to subsistence is of a widely representative character and has struck a sympathetic chord with a number of developing countries.

On the relationship between human rights and sovereignty

The Chinese government believes that there is an important relationship between state sovereignty and human rights. The two can be integrated, they do not contradict each other. State sovereignty is the basis and precondition for people to enjoy human rights. Without state sovereignty, there can be no human rights, whether it is individual rights or group rights, political and civil rights or economic, social and cultural rights. The Chinese government indicates that there are human rights issues which are of an international character, but there are also issues which fall within the scope of state sovereignty. All issues related to large-scale human rights violations caused by colonialism, imperialism, hegemonism, racism, foreign invasion and occupation are human rights issues of an international character. All issues concerning a country's methods of implementing civil rights belong to that country's internal affairs. Respect for state sovereignty is a commonly recognized principle of international law which applies to all areas of international relations, and should also apply to human rights issues.

China recognizes and supports the *UN Charter* goal and principle of protecting and promoting human rights and fundamental freedoms, and China takes active part in the human rights activities of the UN. China has never been opposed to the UN's concerns over human rights, especially not the concerns over large-scale human rights violations caused by racial discrimination, racial segregation, colonialism, foreign invasion and occupation. However, China does not agree with the practice of using human rights as an excuse for promoting a country's own value system, ideology, political standards and development models, and making unwarranted accusations and attacks against other countries. In fact, such practice is no longer a human rights issue. It is a manifestation of power politics and interference with others' internal affairs.

2

Since regaining its lawful seat in the UN in 1971, China has proceeded step by step in joining the UN's human rights activities. Since 1971, the Chinese government has sent delegates to take part in all the meetings of the UN Economic and Social Council and the UN General Assembly. At those meetings, the Chinese representatives participated actively in the discussions on human rights topics, they expressed their own opinions on human rights issues, and they made their own contributions to the enrichment of the human rights concept. Beginning in 1979, China attended the Annual Sessions of the UN Commission on Human Rights as an observer, for three consecutive years. In 1981, at the UN Economic and Social Council session, China was elected as a member country to the Commission on Human Rights, and has, since then, sent official delegations to all the annual sessions of the Commission on Human Rights. Since 1984, human rights experts recommended by the Chinese government have repeatedly been selected as members and alternate members of the "Sub-Commission on the Prevention of Discrimination and Protection of Minorities". These specialists have since become members of the "Working Group on Indigenous Populations" and the "Working Group on Communications."

China mainly takes part in the UN human rights activities in the following areas:

China takes part in drawing up international human rights documents and has acceded to eight important international human rights conventions

Since 1981, China has sent delegates to participate in most of the working groups to draft international human rights documents. These include the working groups involved in the drafting of the *Declaration of the Right to Development*, the *Convention on the Rights of the Child*, the *International Convention on the Rights of Migrant Workers and the Members of Their Families*, the *Convention against Torture and Other Cruel, Inhuman or Degrading Treatment or Punishment*, the *Declaration on the Right and Responsibilities of Individuals, Groups and Organs of Society to Promote and Protect Universally-Recognized Human Rights and Fundamental Freedoms*, the *Declaration on the Protection of National, Linguistic or Religious Minorities*, the *Declaration on Enforced or Involuntary Disappearances*.

To date, China has acceded to eight international human rights conventions, including: the *Convention on the Prevention and Punishment of the Crime of Genocide*, the *Convention Relating to the Status of Refugees*, the *Protocol Relating to the Status of Refugees*, the *International Convention on the Elimination of All Forms of Racial Discrimination*, the *International Convention on the Suppression and Punishment of the Crime of Apartheid*, the *Convention on the Elimination of All Forms of Discrimination against Women*, the *Convention against Torture and other Cruel, Inhuman or Degrading Treatment or Punishment*, the *Convention on the Rights of the Child*.

With respect to these conventions, China has always carried out its obligations diligently, submitted reports according to regulations, and cooperated with the monitoring bodies of the conventions. Experts recommended by China have repeatedly been selected as members of the committees on the Elimination of Racial Discrimination and the Elimination of Discrimination against Women. Chinese human rights experts have made their own contribution to encourage countries party to a convention to carry out their obligations.

Prohibition of actions of large-scale human rights violations

According to UN General Assembly resolution no. 32/130, the UN human rights system should give priority to investigating the phenomenon of large-scale human rights violations caused by colonialism, racism, racial discrimination, racial segregation, foreign invasion and occupation.

China has always taken a stand against racism, racial discrimination and racial segregation. During the Human Rights Commission discussions on racial discrimination in South Africa, China criticized the criminal system of apartheid and its discrimination against and persecution of black people and supported the fight for justice of the people of South Africa against racism. China was also party to the joint draft resolution and donated money each year to the UN Trust Fund for South Africa. China highly praised and supported the UN organized activities of the "First Decade of the Fight Against Racism and Racial Discrimination" and the "Second Decade of the Fight Against Racism and Racial Discrimination". China believes that all these activities have had a significant impact on the realization of the goal to eliminate all kinds of racial discrimination.

At the 3rd Committee of the 49th Session of the UN General Assembly, the Chinese government representative Feng Cui asserted that racial segregation has already become history. Yet, in today's world, prejudice, xenophobia and other forms of racism based on race, skin colour, blood lineage or different ethnic backgrounds have spread in some developed countries. Anti-foreign and ultra-rightist activities have attracted concern and attention within the international community. Under these new circumstances, the task of fighting against racism and racial discrimination remains rather difficult. The international community should be inspired by the success of South Africa, seize the momentum and continue the struggle against racism.

The Chinese government has formulated concrete suggestions concerning the UN organized "Third Decade of Fighting Against Racism and Racial Discrimination". These suggestions include:

- "Elimination of racism and racial discrimination" should remain an important item on the agenda at the UN General Assembly meetings;

- Establishment of a Special Rapporteur to deal with new forms of racism is necessary for the fight against racism. In order for the Special Rapporteur to be able to play a fully functional role, the international community must create the right conditions and the secretariat must be responsible for the necessary personnel and resources;

- As an important organ for the fight against racism and racial discrimination, the Committee on the Elimination of Racial Discrimination must continue its functions. Apart from the routine examination of the reports from countries party to the agreement, the Committee should also give its opinion and make suggestions on issues concerning the struggle against racism and racial discrimination;

• The UN and all its relevant agencies should act quickly to collect information on "the criminal history of South African apartheid, the history of the South African people's struggle and the support from the international community" to serve as references or teaching materials so that people may learn from history;

• With regards to the Programme of Action for the Third Decade, it should support African countries' suggestions for revisions in accordance with the changing circumstances. It should also be guaranteed the necessary personnel and resources in the UN budget and avoid making the same mistakes as were made during the implementation of the Second Decade.

The Chinese government supports resolution no. 1993/20 of the Commission on Human Rights which authorized a special rapporteur to research contemporary forms of racism, racial discrimination, xenophobia and incidents of intolerance of dissent. China believes that, in order to eliminate the above-mentioned problems, full equality must be guaranteed between all member countries of the international community. No country or group of countries should be allowed to take a superior position to others or to criticize another country's internal affairs. We must eliminate all intolerant attitudes, practices and expressions. Based on an attitude of equality, good-will and cooperation, we must carry on dialogues and discussions on all topics, including how to promote and protect human rights, in order to attain our common goal.

China has always supported the struggles against foreign invasion, occupation of and interference with the people of all countries. In 1982, when China for the first time took part in a Commission on Human Rights session, the Chinese representatives spoke in support of the Palestinian people's fight for the right to be able to return home, establish a country, and the Arab countries' demand that Israel return the occupied territory. China supported the UN Human Rights Commission's attention to the human rights issue of the occupation of Palestinian and the Arab territory, and China took part in the joint draft resolution on related issues. Recently, supported by China and many other developing countries, the Commission passed a resolution, by an overwhelming majority, to criticize Israel's acts of aggression and its human rights violations.

With respect to the Afghan and Cambodian people's fight for justice against foreign invasion and interference, China offered its firm support and favoured

UN discussions on the large-scale human rights abuses created by foreign invasion of and interference in these countries. China called for foreign troops to pull out of these countries, and to let the people decide their own destiny. China then voted in support of the relevant resolutions.

China's efforts to maintain justice and to prevent human rights violations caused by racial discrimination, racial segregation, foreign occupation, invasion and interference have been praised by many developing countries.

Focus on reform and rationalization of the Commission on Human Rights

In recent years, the issue of reform and rationalization of the Commission on Human Rights has become an important topic in the UN human rights field. China believes that, with the post-war developments in the international community, the Commission must undergo reform. Since the *Universal Declaration on Human Rights* was passed, the UN system, especially the Commission on Human Rights, with help from the UN member countries, have made beneficial contributions to the promotion and protection of human rights. These include: fighting against large-scale human rights violations caused by racism, racial segregation, colonialism, foreign invasion and occupation; protecting small countries' right to self-determination and recognizing that the right to development is an inalienable human right; drafting many human rights documents; continuously developing and enriching the concept and scope of human rights, and breaking through the traditional confines of individual human rights; protecting the basic rights and interests of women, children, the disabled, refugees and migrant workers; and, establishing human rights monitoring bodies.

However, many irregular phenomena, dating back from the time of the Cold War between east and west, still have not been eliminated. Ideological inclinations persist. The erroneous practice of dividing the concept of human rights and applying double standards have not been properly corrected. Certain countries do not respect the sovereignty of other countries, but use human rights issues for political purposes or interfere in other countries' internal affairs. Such behaviour constitutes a serious obstruction to normal international cooperation in the human rights field.

China believes that the reform of the work of the Commission on Human Rights should include reform of the overall system, not only a realignment of the topics for discussion. The purpose of the reform is to make the work of the Commission adhere more strictly to the principles of the *UN Charter*, and to eliminate the problems of politicization of human rights, double standards and other irregular phenomena, in order to genuinely promote the realization of human rights and fundamental freedoms. On the basis of mutual respect and equality, the Commission should encourage dialogue and cooperation among countries, increase understanding, and try to eliminate conflicts and criticism. The Commission should simplify the administrative structure, reduce overlap, increase cooperation and cut back on expenses. The concrete set-up of the Commission should be based on the principle of fair regional representation. The agenda of the Commission should maintain a balance between the different groups of rights so that enough time can be guaranteed to discuss the issues of concern to developing countries.

With regards to the work of the Sub-Commission of the Commission on Human Rights, Chinese representative Liu Xinsheng pointed out at the 50th session of the Commission on Human Rights that, according to relevant regulations, as a subsidiary body to the Commission on Human Rights, the Sub-Commission's function is very clear. Its function is to undertake studies in the light of the *Universal Declaration on Human Rights* and other international human rights documents, to make recommendations regarding concrete problems in the Commission's work, and to carry out any other task entrusted to it by the Economic and Social Council or the Commission on Human Rights. Generally speaking, the Sub-Commission is fulfilling its functions. Most of its members have contributed positively to the human rights activities of the Economic and Social Council and the Commission on Human Rights. However, we must point out that the work of the Sub-Commission is still haunted by some irregular practices which affect its ability to function efficiently and which has damaged its reputation. For example, some members are politicising human rights, applying double standards and selectiveness. They often replace serious human rights discussions with their own political opinions, inclinations or sentiments, thus violating the basic principle of fairness and objectivity which should be pursued by the Sub-Commission. There is an excess of overlapping topics between the Sub-Commission and the Commission on Human Rights, which not only creates duplications of UN activities and wastes resources, but also complicates coordination between the two bodies. Too many research projects and special reports are produced by the Sub-Commission, and it is necessary to readjust the work of the Sub-Commission according to the principle of reform and simplification of the administrative structure.

Resisting hegemonism in the human rights field and promoting normal international cooperation

For a long time, the UN human rights system has been an arena for carrying out a "Cold War" between different political groups and ideologies. It has been commonplace for countries to use double standards, selectiveness, pragmatism, as well as human rights, as an excuse to interfere with other countries' internal policies. This has resulted in a serious confrontational atmosphere within these organizations. After the end of the Cold War, some countries still have not completely given up such erroneous practices. On the contrary, they have further intensified the use of human rights to force their own political and value systems onto others. They wantonly attack other countries with different social systems and developing countries who do not follow their orders, and they even interfere with these countries' internal affairs. This has not diminished the confrontational atmosphere within the human rights field.

China has always called upon every country that participates in UN human rights activities to make the principles of the *UN Charter* and the principle of "promoting international cooperation, solving international problems in the areas of economy, society, culture and the welfare of humanity, furthering and encouraging respect for human rights and fundamental freedoms without distinction as to race, sex, language or religion" a basis for carrying out fair exchange and cooperation in promoting and protecting human rights. China has stood together with other developing countries in firmly resisting the hegemonical and power-political ways of using human rights as an excuse to criticize other countries and force a country's own political system and value system onto other countries. At all the past sessions of the Commission on Human Rights, Chinese representatives have spoken out from a sense of justice and stood up for those developing countries who were being criticized. China voted against the proposals which were clearly using human rights to criticize developing countries.

In November 1994, the Chinese government invited the Special Rapporteur on Religious Intolerance of the UN Commission on Human Rights to visit China. This was the first time that China had invited a UN human rights rapporteur to visit China, and it was also the first time the Special Rapporteur on Religious Intolerance was invited to visit a country. During the trip, the Rapporteur met with leading cadres of the Chinese Foreign Ministry, the State Council Bureau of Religious Affairs, the Public Security Ministry, and the Justice Ministry, among others. They also visited many places of religious activity in Beijing, Lhasa, Chengdu and Shanghai, and talked to representatives and clergy of local religious communities and temples. Through this visit, both sides strengthened cooperation and developed a deeper sense of understanding. The Rapporteur saw that the Chinese government was making a sincere effort to protect and promote human rights, especially respect for and protection of religious freedom.

In recent years, some Western countries have increased their pressure on China, and five consecutive times they have put forth proposals accusing China of violating human rights. Faced with this challenge, the Chinese government and conference representatives are upholding their principles and waging a tit-for-tat struggle against the West. With the support of countries who uphold justice, the Chinese government and conference representatives have repeatedly defeated the West's anti-China conspiracy and defended their national sovereignty and honour.

Translated by Shengtao Jiang and Anne-Marie Traeholt

The Rights of Indigenous Peoples Under International Law: Selected Issues

FERGUS MACKAY

Until this moment, we have had our place in world civilization determined by the so-called modern industrial nations and ranked according to their values - values which have placed indigenous peoples at the very bottom of the human family. Today the United Nations begins the process of knowing us, not thorough the distorted history of the colonizers, but by hearing own voices, looking into our own hearts, and coming to understand our humanity. Today, you begin the process of seeing indigenous peoples of the world not as primitive and backward, but rather as human beings with our own dreams and aspirations, our own value systems, our own yearning for international recognition of our human rights, including the right of self-determination.[1]

Introduction

The past fifteen years, and particularly the last ten, have seen a remarkable amount of interest in indigenous peoples and their human rights concerns. This interest has been translated into policy and action by intergovernmental organizations, international development actors and, to a lesser extent, by states. International instruments incorporating the rights of indigenous peoples have been promulgated, or are in the process of development, by the International Labour Organization ("ILO"),[2] the United Nations ("UN")[3] and the Organization of American States ("OAS").[4] Multilateral development banks and organizations, such as the World Bank,[5] the Inter-American and Asian Development Banks[6] and the UN Development Programme[7] have also contributed by issuing policy guidelines and directives that attempt to account for the needs and concerns of indigenous peoples. We have also seen numerous conferences, workshops and speeches;[8] calls for the establishment of a permanent UN forum for indigenous peoples;[9] not to mention an International Year come and go, the start of an International Decade and the proclamation of an International Day of the World's Indigenous People.[10] However, with a few notable exceptions, international organizations, and especially international law have yet to adequately accommodate the demands and aspirations of indigenous peoples.

There are a number of reasons for the recent attention accorded to indigenous peoples. Of particular note are: the global environmental movement, which has highlighted, albeit somewhat romantically, indigenous peoples' holistic approach to the environment; a change in the conceptualization of development from an economics-centered approach to one that, in theory at least, focuses on human needs and well being and environmental sustainability; a rejection of assimilation and integration and a valuation of cultural diversity, and; most importantly, a concerted and vocal campaign by indigenous peoples, which began with a few North American organizations and now encompasses indigenous peoples and organizations from most regions of the world. This campaign is using, as one of its primary tools, the discourse of human rights to put pressure on the state and international power structures to recognize indigenous peoples' inherent rights as peoples and to put an end to the pervasive abuses perpetrated against them.

While progress has been made, especially in the recognition that indigenous peoples' rights are qualitatively distinct from the rights of minorities, a number of obstacles and limitations inherent to international law and relations continue to hamper the effective recognition of the rights of indigenous peoples. First, intergovernmental organizations and international law are dominated by what has been termed "the club of states."[11] This club is exclusive and in most respects goes to great lengths to remain so. It does this by limiting the access of other, often logical beneficiaries, including indigenous peoples, to international law's protections, decision-making processes and enforcement mechanisms - in short, to international legal personality. While the excluded have been making in-roads recently, international law remains fundamentally the domain of states, which determine its scope and direction. Consequently, this process is essentially political rather than one primarily based upon principle or law, and international law, as the formalization and codification of this process, has been slow and reluctant to accommodate the voice of the powerless.

Second, while international human rights law does recognize certain collective rights, its focus remains almost exclusively on the individual. Furthermore, collective rights, which have been described as "an inherent and essential element of indigenous rights,"[12] are a controversial subject, resisted by many states who view rights claims by groups, such as indigenous peoples and minorities, as competing claims to sovereignty and disruptive of national unity. This does not mean that states are unwilling to recognize some measure of rights for these groups, to the contrary, many have detailed and extensive provisions in their domestic legislation. However, states have historically formulated policies to integrate and assimilate minorities and indigenous peoples into mainstream society. Their goal was, and in most cases still is, to have a homogeneous population whose primary allegiance is to the state, not to national or ethnic identity. The problem, from the position of states, is that ethnic identity has not disappeared, indeed, in most cases it has endured, if not remained as strong as, or stronger than it was before. This is illustrated by the fact that today, wars are far more likely to be state-ethnic (nation) or inter-ethnic conflicts - the Zapatistas in Mexico and the Karen in Myanmar (Burma), for instance - than direct state-state, international conflicts.

That ethnic or national identity has not disappeared has compelled the conclusion, by some at least, that assimilation and integration are not viable solutions to ethnic strife. This is coupled with the realization that individual rights alone do not adequately protect the rights of minorities and indigenous peoples, who require the simultaneous protection of the people or collectivity as a whole.[13] This is especially true of cultural, religious and linguistic rights, and in the case of indigenous peoples, rights to lands, territories, resources and self-determination. Consequently, one of the main tenants of the indigenous rights movement has been to stress the necessity of protecting indigenous peoples' collective rights as peoples as opposed to individual rights or those rights that attach to "persons belonging to ... minorities."[14]

A full discussion of the subject of indigenous peoples, international organizations and human rights law is beyond the scope of this paper.[15] Consequently, it will selectively focus on a few developments that are of particular significance including: the UN Working Group on Indigenous Populations ("Working Group") and the proposed permanent UN forum for indigenous peoples; the UN draft *Declaration on the Rights of Indigenous Peoples* ("Draft Declaration") and the right to self-determination; the International Labour Organization and; the protection of indigenous peoples' rights under intergovernmental human rights procedures.

The Working Group on Indigenous Populations and the Proposed Permanent UN Forum for Indigenous Peoples

The Working Group, established in 1982, is a subsidiary body of the Sub-commission on the Prevention of Discrimination and the Protection of Minorities ("Sub-commission"). Its mandate is two-fold: "a) to review developments pertaining to the promotion and protection of human rights and fundamental freedoms of indigenous populations . . . and; b) to give special attention to the evolution of standards concerning the rights of indigenous populations . . . ."[16] This body has been instrumental in promoting indigenous peoples' rights under international law and has been a focal point for indigenous peoples pressing to have their voices heard and their rights recognized.

Since 1985, the Working Group has been engaged in setting standards on the rights of indigenous peoples to be included in an UN Declaration. Also, a binding Convention open for signature by UN member-states based on the Draft Declaration is assumed to follow.[17] Although the Working Group essentially concluded its standard-setting activities at its eleventh session in 1993, work continues on a number of other important areas of concern to indigenous peoples. These include studies on treaties, agreements and other constructive arrangements concluded between states and indigenous peoples[18] and intellectual and cultural property rights;[19] the International Decade of the World's Indigenous People and; defining the institutional and operational parameters of a permanent UN forum for indigenous peoples.[20]

Indigenous peoples' access to the Working Group has been facilitated by a policy of unrestricted attendance and participation that is unique within the UN system. Some remarkable successes have been achieved therein, in particular in conveying an understanding of indigenous cultures and aspirations. However, the Working Group is the lowest of a succession of increasingly, political UN organs. Therefore, if indigenous peoples are to continue to have an impact on the UN system, additional participation and access will be required at all, and, especially at higher levels.[21] Recognizing this fact, indigenous peoples have been pushing for the establishment of a permanent UN forum in which they can represent and speak for themselves.

Indigenous peoples have proposed a number of different models for a forum in the UN system.[22] However, irrespective of the precise form and place of the forum in the UN system, the common theme and concern among indigenous peoples is that the forum must be effective, participatory and imbued with more than token powers. Consequently, indigenous peoples have suggested a number of specific powers that they believe the forum should have, including: the authority to hear and resolve disputes, a complaints or petitions procedure, authorization to monitor the implementation of international instruments, the provision of advisory and technical services and the power to initiate and conduct situation or thematic reports.

While some governments have publicly been supportive of the idea of establishing a forum, they have been cautious in their approach to the subject and restrictive with regard to its focus and prospective powers.[23] Undoubtedly, there is some reluctance on the part of states to see the creation of a permanent forum for indigenous peoples, particularly if that body has the power to publicly question and criticize their actions.

The Chairperson of the Working group, Professor E-I. Daes, has drafted a set of recommended guidelines to be used in defining the forum.[24] These guidelines define the forum's powers as: monitoring and reporting on the implementation of the Draft Declaration; gathering and publishing annually, in cooperation with other UN organs and specialized agencies, information on the "conditions and needs" of Indigenous Peoples and; the promotion, evaluation and coordination of international action, including development-related activities of concern to indigenous peoples.[25]

Although silent as to the relative decision-making power of indigenous and state representatives, the guidelines state that the forum should be open to "equal participation" by indigenous peoples and that observers from governments, non-governmental organizations and UN bodies and specialized agencies should also be included. Therefore, regardless of the precise membership structure of the forum, indigenous peoples would be accorded at least equal representation. Also, the guidelines do not explicitly define the precise form and location of the forum in the UN hierarchy. However, guideline 8 states that the forum should report to the Economic and Social Council, therefore, it should be located somewhere under that body. Perhaps, the creation of a Commission on Indigenous Peoples is contemplated, on par with the Commission on Human Rights and the Commission on Sustainable Development. If so, this would at least recognize that indigenous peoples' concerns are not limited to solely human rights, but also encompass a myriad of other issues.

The establishment of a permanent UN forum for indigenous peoples, should it be approved by the Commission on Human Rights ("CHR") and its parent bodies, would certainly go far in recognizing indigenous peoples as legitimate international actors and in educating the UN and its member-states about their concerns, cultures and needs. However, if the forum's mandate is weak and limited and it is not respected by the UN and its members, it may only contribute to indigenous peoples' growing sense of frustration and disillusionment with the UN system, particularly in light of the shortcomings of the International Year.[26]

UN Draft Universal Declaration on the Rights of Indigenous Peoples[27] and the Right to Self-Determination

The Draft Declaration represents the culmination of almost ten years work by the Working Group, indigenous peoples and states.[28] It is, without a doubt, the most important and significant development to date in the movement for the recognition of indigenous peoples' inherent rights under international law. This is true, first and foremost, because it recognizes indigenous peoples' collective rights as distinct peoples, including the right to self-determination as that right applies to other peoples.[29] These measures can only be described as giant leaps forward, both legally and psychologically.

In connection with the right to self-determination, the Draft Declaration also recognizes that indigenous peoples have rights to self-government and autonomy;[30] a substantial measure of control over their lands, territories and natural resources,[31] including environmental safeguards;[32] rights to political participation;[33] guarantees against genocide and ethnocide;[34] respect for and enforcement of treaties concluded with states[35] and; self-control over their economic, social and cultural development.[36]

However, the Draft Declaration has yet to be approved and its language is subject to modification and amendment, in particular by the CHR, as it progresses through the political organs of the UN hierarchy to the General Assembly. The CHR has recently decided to establish an open-ended Working Group ("CHRWG"), which will focus exclusively on the Draft Declaration.[37] This Working Group is authorized to review the document and its specific language and to modify its content and the scope of its application. It has also been directed to complete its evaluation of the Draft Declaration and submit it to the General Assembly for approval therein within the International Decade of the World's Indigenous People (before 2004).[38]

The creation of a Working Group by the CHR is widely perceived by indigenous peoples to be an attempt by states to water down the Draft Declaration or, at the very least, to delay its transmission to the General Assembly. It will certainly face its most substantial challenge to date therein, as its members are direct, political appointees rather than independent experts as they are in the Working Group and the Sub-commission. However, should the Draft Declaration reach the General Assembly in its present form and be approved therein, it will mark a significant turning point in the historical context of indigenous peoples' rights. It will be the first time that a contemporary international instrument has recognized indigenous peoples as distinct peoples, entitled to all the attendant rights, and the first time that the artificial constraints placed upon the right to self-determination have been rejected. It will also be the next step in taking the necessity of decolonization and the right of *all* peoples to live in freedom and dignity to its logical conclusion.

Self-determination[39]

As indicated by the quote that begins this paper, a primary concern for indigenous peoples is the recognition of their right to self-determination. This is by no means an exclusive preoccupation as indigenous peoples' concerns are multi-sectoral, however, the right to self-determination is viewed as the framework within which they can exercise and enjoy all human rights and ensure their cultural integrity and survival.

The application of the right to self-determination to indigenous peoples challenges a number of assumptions fundamental to international law and relations, which are founded upon state sovereignty and territorial integrity. Consequently, some states have registered objections and even outright rejections. Other states are willing to recognize that indigenous peoples have a right to autonomy and self-government, or internal, as opposed to external, self-determination which may include a right to secession and independence.[40] Most other states fall somewhere in between the two poles and few are willing to recognize an unqualified right to self-determination as demanded by indigenous peoples, who state that creating a legal distinction between indigenous peoples and other peoples is racist, relegates their rights to a second class status and perpetuates a convenient legal fiction that has justified their domination by other peoples.

The preceding is, in large part, due to conflicting expectations and aspirations on the part of states and indigenous peoples or, as one commentator conceptualizes it, a failure to accommodate conflicting rights.[41] States continue to consider their sovereignty paramount, viewing indigenous rights claims as threats thereto, whereas, indigenous peoples are demanding that their rights to self-determination, to their lands and territories and to maintain their distinct identities and cultures be recognized, and that they be accorded the status of full partners in the democratic and legal order of the state from which they have been historically excluded.

Another major problem is that the right to self-determination has yet to be applied to peoples other than those living under alien or colonial domination by an overseas power.[42] This so-called 'salt-water test' restricts the application of the right to self-determination to clear cut, colonial situations involving an overseas or geographically distinct power. Furthermore, the application of the right of self-determination, and the extent to which it applies beyond the context of decolonization, especially with regard to indigenous peoples, has been problematic and remains unclear. The reasons for this are many: of particular relevance are, the failure, some would say the conscious failure, to define what constitutes a 'people' for the purposes of self-determination and; states' fear of secession and territorial dismemberment.

The use of the term indigenous peoples, as opposed to indigenous populations or people, has been a contentious issue in many international fora because of its implications for the applicability of the right to self-determination, in that "all peoples" have the right to self-determination.[43] It is for this reason that what may at first appear to be a quibble over semantics has assumed a prominent place in the indigenous rights movement - the "s" has become a symbol for indigenous aspirations to self-determination and its inclusion in various instruments and official statements is consistently opposed or qualified by certain states.[44]

However, the Chairperson of the Working Group has said that, "[i]ndigenous groups are unquestionably "peoples" in every political, social, cultural and ethnological meaning of this term" and that "it is neither logical nor scientific to treat them as the same "peoples" as their neighbours, who obviously have different languages, histories and cultures."[45] She goes on to say that, "[t]he United Nations should not pretend, for the sake of a convenient legal fiction, that those differences do not exist."[46]

The fear of secession and territorial dismemberment has led to the coupling of self-determination provisions with statements declaring the invalidity of secession as an exercise of self-determination. For instance, the *Declaration on Granting Independence to Colonial Countries and Peoples* states that: "[a]ny attempt aimed at the partial or total disruption of the national unity or territorial integrity of a country is incompatible with the purposes and principles of the Charter of the United Nations."[47] However, a major UN study on self-determination concludes that: "if the national unity claimed and the territorial integrity invoked are merely legal fictions which cloak real colonial and alien domination resulting from the actual disregard of the principle of self-determination, the subject people or peoples are entitled to exercise, with all the consequences thereof [presumably including secession], their right to self-determination... ."[48] This sentiment is echoed by the Chairperson of the Working Group in her explanatory note on the Draft Declaration.[49] In conclusion, a standard has evolved, at least with regard to external self-determination (secession and independence), that cannot, or has yet to be applied beyond the context of peoples under alien and colonial domination in territories not conforming to the legal construct of a state.

With regard to indigenous peoples, the conflict between self-determination and territorial integrity does not necessarily arise. This is the case because indigenous peoples, with few exceptions, deny aspirations to independence or secession, and instead, stress the need for autonomy and control over the direction of their lives and affairs through constitutional and democratic reform. The recognition that the exercise of self-determination is dependent upon the circumstances in which it is invoked and includes a range of options in addition to independence, is of particular importance in this context. The *Declaration on Principles of International Law Concerning Friendly Relations and Co-operation Among States in Accordance with the Charter of the United*

Nations,[50] for instance, states that: "[t]he establishment of a sovereign and independent State, the free association or integration with an independent State or the emergence into any other political status freely determined by a people constitute modes of implementing the right of self-determination by a people."[51] Therefore, it would appear that the core of the peoples' right to self-determination in international law is the right to freely determine the nature and extent, if any, of their relationship with other peoples and need not necessarily involve secession or territorial dismemberment.

Given the preceding, how is the right to self-determination for indigenous peoples defined in the Draft Declaration? Basically, the self-determination, autonomy and self-government provisions, when read in conjunction with the political participation rights, comprise the essence of the right to self-determination contained in the Draft Declaration, although most of the provisions are in some way related to the overall framework of self-determination. Articles 3 and 31, the Draft Declaration's primary self-determination and autonomy provisions, state that:

> Indigenous peoples have the right to self-determination. By virtue of that right they freely determine their political status and freely pursue their economic, social and cultural development (art. 3).

> Indigenous peoples, **as a specific form of exercising their right to self-determination**, have the right to autonomy or self-government in matters relating to their internal and local affairs, including culture, religion, education, information, media, health, housing, employment, social welfare, economic activities, land and resources management, environment and entry by non-members, as well as ways and means for financing these autonomous functions (emphasis added) (art. 31).

Article 3, using the same language found in other UN instruments, states the general principle that indigenous peoples have the unqualified right to self-determination, as that right applies to other peoples. However, when read together with article 31, the right to self-determination for indigenous peoples could be interpreted as: indigenous peoples have the right to self-determination, which shall be exercised as, and limited to autonomy and self-government. This apparent ambiguity has led many indigenous observers to the conclusion that article 31 should be deleted as it is redundant and confusing in light of article 3's comprehensive coverage.

The writings of the Chairperson of the Working Group are informative as to the correct interpretation.[52] In her explanatory note on the Draft Declaration, the Chairperson states that autonomy and self-government are the preferred means of exercising indigenous peoples' right to self-determination, but not the exclusive means of doing so.[53] She concludes that indigenous peoples must exercise their right to self-determination through the state's political and legal systems (i.e. constitutional reform that respects the rights of indigenous peoples to, amongst others, autonomy, self-government and participation) *unless* these systems are "so exclusive and non-democratic that [they] can no longer can be said to be representing the whole people."[54]

In light of the preceding, it would be accurate to state that indigenous peoples do have an unqualified right to self-determination in the Draft Declaration. Nevertheless, in exercising that right, indigenous peoples must work within the democratic and constitutional framework of the state, through the establishment of effective partnerships based upon good faith and mutual respect. The state has a corresponding duty to accommodate the exercise of indigenous peoples' right to self-determination through power sharing and legal, constitutional and democratic reform. This process has been termed "belated state building" in that it belatedly recognizes the right of indigenous peoples, in full partnership with the state, to define the democratic and political systems under which they will live.[55] Finally, the option of secession may only be exercised as an exceptional measure should the state fail to accommodate the rights of indigenous peoples and be so abusive and unrepresentative "that the situation is tantamount to classic colonialism... ."[56]

Whether the right to self-determination, as presently defined in the Draft Declaration and elaborated upon by the Chairperson, will survive what will undoubtedly be a contentious and highly political process in the CHRWG, remains to be seen. As noted above, a number of states have expressed hostility to any mention of the right to self-determination in an instrument on the rights of indigenous peoples. These states will use the CHRWG as a forum for reiterating their objections with the ultimate goal of deleting the language, limiting its scope or in some way qualifying it so as to deprive it of substance. This is further compounded by the fact that CHRWG will adopt its decisions by consensus, which will provide those states with objections, a means to force compromise or to confound the process. Nonetheless, indigenous peoples will continue to demand that their right to self-determination be respected and that the Draft Declaration be approved intact, if not improved upon.

The International Labour Organization

The recent work of the International Labour Organization ("ILO") on the rights of indigenous peoples is second in importance only to that of the Working Group, in particular as the ILO has developed the only binding treaties on the rights of indigenous peoples presently in existence - the 1957 *Convention on Indigenous and Tribal Populations* (Convention No. 107) ("ILO 107")[57] and the 1989 *Convention on Indigenous and Tribal Peoples* (Convention No. 169) ("ILO 169").[58]

The stated aim of ILO 107 was, and is, the integration and assimilation of indigenous peoples into the states within which they live.[59] Due to this lack of respect for indigenous culture and identity, ILO 107 became an embarrassment to the ILO,[60] and, in 1986, a decision was made to revise it according to the principle that indigenous peoples should "enjoy as much control as possible over their own economic, social and cultural development."[61] Consequently, in 1989, after a two year revision process, ILO 169 was adopted by the International Labour Conference in Geneva.[62]

ILO 169 is to date, the most important contribution of the ILO to the recognition of indigenous peoples' rights.[63] However, it should be noted at the outset that ILO 169 has its problems and has been severely criticized by many indigenous peoples, particularly with regard to its lack of self-determination language, provisions on lands and resources, consent standard[64] and the absence of indigenous participation in the revision process.[65] Nevertheless, a number of indigenous organizations are promoting the ratification of ILO 169 in those countries wherein indigenous peoples have expressed a desire to do so.[66] The primary reason for this is that for many indigenous peoples the ratification of ILO 169 will be a major step forward, for the protection of their rights as national laws are presently insufficient, unenforced or even hostile. Also, at a minimum, ratification of ILO 169 provides international oversight and a measure of transparency to indigenous-state relations, consultations and negotiations that were previously entirely within the jurisdiction of the state.

ILO 169 does not explicitly recognize a right to self-determination, autonomy or self-government. In fact, the ILO declared itself incompetent to recognize the right to self-determination for indigenous peoples, which it felt should be left to a UN body with the requisite authority.[67] Therefore, while the Convention does use the term 'peoples', it also includes qualifying language stating that the use of that term "shall not be construed as having any implications as regards the rights which may attach to the term under international law."[68] Obviously, this issue was very contentious and cause for disappointment and disillusionment among indigenous peoples, both during and after the revision process.

Although there is not an explicit recognition of the rights to autonomy and self-government, ILO 169 does recognize some measure of these rights by implication. For instance, one of the most important statements from, and a guiding principle of ILO 169 is as follows:

> The people concerned shall have the right to decide their own priorities for the process of development as it affects their lives, beliefs, institutions and spiritual well-being and the lands they occupy or otherwise use, and to exercise control, to the extent possible, over their own economic, social and cultural development.[69]

This provision recognizes that indigenous peoples have the right to some measure of internal autonomy with regard to their institutions of governance and in determining the direction and nature of their economic, social and cultural development. The precise scope of that internal autonomy is to be determined by reference to, amongst others: the participation provisions;[70] the provisions on health services;[71] education;[72] vocational training; [73] lands and territories[74] and; those concerning indigenous institutions.[75]

The quality of the relationship between indigenous peoples and governments, as expressed by the provisions on consultation and participation, is also a determining factor in how the autonomy provisions of the Convention will be applied in practice. This is true because a working, cooperative relationship based upon mutual respect and good faith can only enhance the quality and scope of the rights enjoyed. However, a major flaw in ILO 169 is that the indigenous peoples' consent is not required or even the objective of consultations. The goal of consultations is, rather, nothing more than to attempt to achieve a good faith agreement between the parties.[76]

ILO 169's provisions on lands, territories and resources have justifiably been criticized by indigenous peoples as being inadequate. Nevertheless, these provisions do contain a number of important protections over and above those found in many domestic legal systems. These provisions are framed by article 13(1) which requires that governments recognize and respect the special spiritual, cultural and economic relationship that indigenous peoples have with their lands and territories and especially "the collective aspects of this relationship."[77]

Art. 14 recognizes indigenous peoples' "rights of ownership and possession . . . over the lands which they traditionally occupy" and requires that states "shall take steps as necessary to identify" these lands and to "guarantee effective protection of [indigenous peoples'] rights of ownership and possession."[78]

Article 13(2), incorporates "the concept of territories, which covers the total environment of the areas which the peoples concerned occupy or otherwise use," into the definition 'lands' used in the Convention. This definition is stated in the present tense - "occupy" and "use" - and therefore, does not include historical claims to lands and territories. ILO 169 does, however, require that the state establish "adequate procedures . . . within the national legal system to resolve land claims."[79] Additionally, the state is required to protect, "in appropriate cases" the right of access to lands "not occupied by [indigenous peoples], but to which they have traditionally had access for their subsistence and traditional activities."[80] Exactly what is meant by "in appropriate cases" is unclear, although, the protection of, and requirement that subsistence practices be strengthened,[81] and, the recognition of indigenous control over lands that they "use" are informative.[82]

Indigenous peoples also have the right to "participate in the use, management and conservation" of natural resources pertaining to their lands and the right to have these resources "specially safeguarded."[83] Furthermore, in cases where the state owns mineral or other sub-surface rights pertaining to indigenous lands and wishes to exploit these resources, it must "establish or maintain procedures through which [it] shall consult [indigenous] peoples" to determine the extent to which "their interests would be prejudiced" prior to engaging in, or allowing these activities.[84] The peoples concerned, "wherever possible", must share in any benefits derived from these activities and receive compensation for any damages incurred.

In conclusion, although ILO 169 has some significant deficiencies and is not an ideal instrument from the perspective of all indigenous peoples, a reading of its provisions supports the conclusion that for many indigenous peoples it is a useful instrument. At worst, it provides some protection for rights not previously recognized or respected and some transparency to indigenous-state relations. At best, it provides for a functional, semi- autonomous, self-governing regime in which indigenous peoples can enjoy some of the attributes of the right to self-determination: self-control over social, economic and cultural development, some measure of control over lands, territories and natural resources and respect for indigenous customs and institutions, to name a few.

Those states that have ratified ILO 169 have adopted legislation and/or amended their constitutions in order to implement the rights contained therein, as have a number of non-ratifying states.[85] Colombia, for instance, revised its Constitution in 1991, after ratifying ILO 169 in that same year.[86] Although the Constitutional revision was not based entirely on ILO 169, which was enacted through legislation,[87] many of its principles are incorporated in the new Constitution.[88]

With regard to lands, territories and self-government, articles 246, 287 and 330, provide that indigenous territories are self-governing, autonomous entities, authorized to devise, implement and administer internal, social, economic and political policies, that exercise jurisdiction in accordance with indigenous customary law and procedures. Indigenous territories, which are considered of equal legal status to districts, municipalities and departments, are communally held, inalienable and not subject to seizure.[89] Indigenous peoples are also authorized to participate in the management and conservation of natural resources within their territories and to participate in any resource exploitation programs initiated by the state. Additionally, these programs must account for any negative environmental, cultural and economic impacts that may be experienced by the people(s) concerned and include contingency and remediation plans.[90]

The 1991 Constitution also recognizes a number of social and cultural rights, in addition to those provided for under the autonomy provisions. It specifically provides that indigenous languages are the official languages within indigenous territories;[91] for culturally-appropriate, bilingual education;[92] for special rights to cultural heritage, including joint management of archaeological sites[93] and; for rights to maintain contact with other indigenous peoples separated by international borders.[94]

The provisions noted above are relatively progressive and are certainly an improvement over previous rights and guarantees recognized in Colombia, despite its reputation for having a benign indigenous policy. However, many of the provisions are subject to national legislation which may be modified to limit the rights defined therein.[95] Also, these measures are far below the aspirations of indigenous peoples, as expressed in the Draft Declaration and in various declarations and policy statements issued by them.[96] Furthermore, once the law is enacted and implemented it must be enforced, in the case of indigenous peoples, often in the face of widespread intolerance, racism and discrimination.[97] Consequently, positive steps must also be taken by the state to ameliorate negative societal and official attitudes about indigenous peoples, particularly in the media, educational systems and elsewhere, if the law is to be truly effective.

Cases Before Intergovernmental Human Rights Bodies

Intergovernmental human rights organs, such as the UN Human Rights Committee ("HRC") and the Inter-American Commission on Human Rights ("IACHR"), have examined a number of complaints filed by indigenous peoples under both the First Optional Protocol to the International Covenant on Civil and Political Rights ("ICCPR"),[98] and the American Convention on Human Rights ("American Convention") and the American Declaration on the Rights and Duties of Man.[99]

The results to date have been mixed and fall far short of providing effective guarantees for indigenous peoples. This is for the most part a reflection of the individualistic bias of the rights defined in the relevant instruments and the reluctance of the organs themselves, presumably motivated by concerns about institutional integrity and respect, to address the right to self-determination, effective land rights and rights to autonomy and self-government. For instance, the HRC has, in response to a case instituted by indigenous peoples, declared that the right to self-determination is not justiciable under the Optional Protocol's individual complaints procedure as it is a right that attaches to peoples rather than individuals.[100] One case of particular interest that did look at what rights indigenous peoples have to autonomy and self-determination is a petition filed with the IACHR on behalf of the Miskito, Sumo and Rama peoples ("Miskito") against the government of Nicaragua.

Report on the Situation of Human Rights of a Segment of the Nicaraguan Population of Miskito Origin[101]

The complaint that initiated the Report on the Situation of Human Rights of a Segment of the Nicaraguan Population of Miskito Origin ("Miskito Report") was submitted in early 1982. Additional complaints were filed in the following months and heard by the IACHR in special sessions devoted to the situation of the Miskito.[102] The complaints alleged violations of rights under the American Convention[103] and violations of the rights of indigenous peoples (or, as stated by the IACHR, the "special rights of ethnic groups"), not specified in the Convention, to self-determination and autonomy, to lands and territories and to cultural integrity.[104]

The events that gave rise to the Miskito Report primarily occurred in 1980-83, following the Sandinista revolution that overthrew the Somosa regime. Basically stated, after taking power, the government attempted to implement a program of territorial and cultural integration. The Miskito resisted and asserted their rights to cultural, political and territorial autonomy. Nicaragua responded by defining the Miskito as a counterrevolutionary and separatist movement and initiated a number of extensive and brutal, military operations in Miskito territory that involved widespread and systematic human rights abuses.[105]

The IACHR action began with an on-site, fact finding mission to Nicaragua, followed by a failed attempt to reach a friendly settlement and concluded with a Final Report on the situation published in 1984.[106] This Final Report contains a detailed analysis of violations of the Miskito's rights and an analysis of the rights that the Miskito may enjoy under international law based on their status as a distinct, cultural and ethnic group.

While recognizing that the Convention guarantees only the rights of individuals, as opposed to groups or peoples, the IACHR found that:

[t]he present status of international law does recognize the observance of the principle of self-determination of peoples, which it considers to be the right of a people to independently choose their form of political organization and to freely establish the means it deems appropriate to bring about their economic, social and cultural development. This does not mean, however, that it recognizes the right to self-determination of any ethnic group as such.[107]

However, with regard to Nicaragua's policy of cultural assimilation and integration, the IACHR stated that:

the absence of a right to political autonomy or self-determination on the part of the Miskitos, Sumos and Ramas of the Atlantic coast [does not] grant the government the unrestricted right to impose complete assimilation on those Indians.[108]

In conclusion, the IACHR added that:

[a]lthough the current status of international law does not allow the view that the ethnic groups of the Atlantic zone of Nicaragua have a right to political autonomy and self-determination, special legal protection is recognized for the use of their language, the observance of their religion, and in general, all those aspects related to the preservation of their cultural identity. To this should be added the aspects linked to productive organization, which includes, among other things, the issue of ancestral and communal lands. Non-observance of those rights and cultural values leads to a forced assimilation with results that can be disastrous. For that reason, the Commission considers that it is fundamental to establish new conditions for coexistence between the ethnic minorities and the Government of Nicaragua, in order to settle historic antagonisms and the serious difficulties present today. In the opinion of the IACHR, the need to preserve and guarantee the observance of these principles in practice, entails the need to establish an adequate institutional order as part of the structure of the Nicaraguan state. Such an institutional organization can only effectively carry out its assigned purposes to the extent that it is designed in the context of broad consultation and carried out with the

direct participation of the ethnic minorities of Nicaragua, through their freely chosen representatives.[109]

As can be seen from the above, the IACHR does recognize that the Miskito do have some inherent rights as a distinct culture. In particular, the protection of "all those aspects related to cultural integrity" including language, religion, subsistence and economic activities and "the issue of ancestral and communal lands." While the recognition of the need to protect subsistence practices and issues pertaining to lands is important, it is clear that the IACHR has looked to article 27 of the ICCPR for guidance here, but has failed to exceed the rights protected under that article.[110] Furthermore, precisely what is meant by "the issue of ancestral and communal lands" is unclear, except by reference to the statement that "a study [should be undertaken to find] a solution to the problem of the Indians' ancestral lands that would take into account both the aspirations of the Indians and the economic interests and territorial unity of [Nicaragua]" contained in the final report's conclusions and recommendations.[111]

The IACHR's examination of the human rights situation of the Miskito concluded in 1984 with the publication of its Final Report and a resolution containing the IACHR's conclusions and recommendations.[112] However, in that same year, the Nicaraguan government, in an attempt to halt hostilities, initiated a dialogue with indigenous leaders about the structure and parameters of an autonomous region for the Miskito. The final result was the 1987 *Autonomy Statute*.[113]

The *Autonomy Statute* essentially established two, semi-autonomous regions on the Atlantic coast of Nicaragua, one for the North and one for the South. Each region has an elected Regional Council of limited authority. Each Council is authorized to participate in the national development program for the Atlantic region and to administer local functions including health, education, cultural, transportation and community services programs. Additionally, each Council is authorized to submit legislation for consideration to the national legislature, develop policies in coordination with the state for the rational use of natural resources and develop a regional taxation policy.[114]

The *Autonomy Statute* also provides for the inalienable, collective and individual ownership of communal lands, free from taxation by the state and, subject to the state's national development plan, the right to use natural resources.[115] Furthermore, rights pertaining to cultural integrity including bilingual education, religious and cultural freedoms and culturally-appropriate, social programs are recognized.

Although, many of the autonomy rights recognized by the *Autonomy Statute* are ultimately subject to state law and regulation and are certainly substantially lower than those rights demanded by the Miskito, Nicaragua has arguably complied with the conclusions and recommendations set forth by the IACHR. Whether the *Autonomy Statute* and the decision to enter into a dialogue with the Miskito are directly attributable to the IACHR action is uncertain. However, if it is not directly attributable, the correspondence between the measures adopted by Nicaragua and the IACHR's recommendations more than suggest that the two are substantially related.

This case illustrates both the utility and shortcomings of intergovernmental oversight procedures to indigenous peoples. On the positive side, these procedures do put pressure on states to bring their behaviour into compliance with international norms and do facilitate the establishment of a dialogue between the parties. However, to be effective, the state must cooperate in the proceedings and accept and implement any recommended measures or proposals. This is particularly troublesome for indigenous peoples as many of the issues raised - rights to lands, territories and resources and to political and cultural autonomy - are politically sensitive and divisive. Furthermore, indigenous peoples are forced to rely upon the goodwill of states to give effect to their rights, when in most cases the state is the very entity from which they seek protection.

Conclusion

As should be readily apparent even from the limited discussion above, indigenous peoples are making headway in the international arena. The significance of the Draft Declaration cannot be overstated, but even if approved intact, a tremendous amount of work will need to be done in order to ensure its implementation and respect, particularly given the negative reaction of many states and the fact that it is a non-binding instrument. The Draft Declaration may also be used by human rights organs such as the IACHR to answer affirmatively the question of whether indigenous peoples have rights to self-determination, autonomy and self-government.[116] The establishment of a permanent forum, with the direct participation of indigenous peoples will also be an important step forward, in that indigenous peoples will for the first time be able to speak for themselves to the international community. However, there is still a long way to go and there is some danger that with the increased attention to and institutionalization of indigenous issues, what has been a vigorous and effective campaign will be co-opted and diffused among a variety of bureaucratic and administrative channels leading indigenous peoples the way of gender and disarmament in the UN: the subject of obligatory references and well-intentioned platitudes, but little concrete action.

Notes

1. William A. Means, International Indian Treaty Council, addressing the UN General Assembly at the inauguration of the International Year of the World's Indigenous People, 12 December 1992 (statement on file with author).

2. Convention (NO.169) Concerning Indigenous and Tribal Peoples in Independent Countries, International Labour Office, Official Bulletin, vol. 72, series A, number 2 (1989), pages 59-70 (hereinafter "ILO 169").

3. *The UN draft Declaration on the Rights of Indigenous Peoples* (hereinafter "Draft Declaration"). The authoritative text of the Draft Declaration is annexed to the *Report of the Working Group on Indigenous Populations on its eleventh session*, UN Doc. E/CN.4/Sub.2/1993/29 (1993). The UN Conference on Environment and Development also produced a number of instruments that include indigenous peoples among their provisions. See, the *Convention on Biological Diversity*, entered into force 29 December 1993, reprinted in 31 I.L.M. 818; the Rio Declaration on Environment and Development, United Nations Conference on Environment and Development ("UNCED"), UN Doc, A/CONF.151/5 (1992) and; Chapter 26 of *Agenda 21*, UNCED, UN Doc. A/CONF.151/4 (PART III) (1992).

4. The Inter-American Commission on Human Rights of the OAS is currently developing a Declaration on the Rights of Indigenous Peoples. For the background to this instrument, see, *Report on the First Round of Consultations on the Future Inter-American Instrument on the Rights of Indigenous Populations*. Approved by the IACHR at its 83rd. Period of Meetings, March 1993; in Section V., Chapter V of its Annual Report 1992-1993. OEA/Ser.L/V/II.83 doc. 14, corr. 1, March 12, 1993.

5. World Bank Operation Directive 4.20 on Indigenous Peoples, 1991.

6. Asian Development Bank, Guidelines for Social Analysis of Development Projects, Manila, June, 1991.

7. UNDP draft Guidelines for Support to Indigenous Peoples, draft version, January 1995 (on file with author). These draft Guidelines will be reviewed by a UNDP Senior Management Committee, some time before August 1995, which will decide if the Guidelines should be approved. Phone interview with Marcel

Viergever, UNDP Focal Point for Indigenous Peoples.

8. See, for instance, *Report of the United Nations Technical Conference on Practical Experience in the Realization of Sustainable and Environmentally Sound Self-Development of Indigenous Peoples*, UN Doc. E/CN.4/Sub.2/1992/31 (1992) and; *Note by the Secretariat: Report of the Consultation between Representatives of Indigenous Peoples and International Development, Human Rights and Other Agencies*, UN Doc. E/CN.4/1993/AC.4/TM.3/1 (1993).

9. A permanent UN forum for indigenous peoples was proposed by the *Vienna Declaration and Programme of Action*, adopted by the World Conference on Human Rights UN Doc. A/CONF.157/23 (1993) and; UN General Assembly Res. 48/193 (1993).

10. GA Res. 164, UN GAOR, 45th Sess., Supp. No. 49, at 277, UN Doc. A/Res/45/164 (1990) (proclaiming the International Year of the World's Indigenous People); GA Res. 163, UN GAOR, 48th Sess., Agenda Item 114(b), pmbl. para. 8, at 2, UN Doc. A/C.3/48/163 (1993) (proclaiming the International Decade of the World's Indigenous People) and; Comm'n on Human Rights Res. 1994/26 of 4 March 1994, suggesting that a date be determined for an International Day of the World's Indigenous People to be celebrated every year of the International Decade. August 9, in commemoration of the first day of the Working Group on Indigenous populations in 1982, has been designated as the International Day.

11. R.J. Vincent, *Human Rights and International Relations* 129 (1986). The full quote reads: "The society of humankind stands opposed to the club of states, and one of the primary rules of the latter has been to deny membership to the former."

12. *Discrimination Against Indigenous Peoples, Report of the Working Group on Indigenous Populations on its sixth session.* UN Doc. E/CN.4/Sub.2/1988/25, at para. 68, (1988).

13. D. Sanders, Collective Rights, 13 *H.R.Q.* 368 (1991). Professor Sanders defines 'collectivities' as: "Groups that have goals that transcend the ending of discrimination against their members ... for their members are joined together not simply by external discrimination but by an internal cohesiveness. Collectivities seek to protect and develop their own particular cultural characteristics." Sanders

at 369.

14. The language "persons belonging to ... minorities" is taken from article 27 of the *International Covenant on Civil and Political Rights*, that protects the rights of individual members of minority groups as opposed to the group itself. Article 27 states that "In those states in which ethnic, religious or linguistic minorities exist, persons belonging to such minorities shall not be denied the right, in community with the other members of the group, to enjoy their own culture, to profess and practice their own religion, or to use their own language." International Covenant on Civil and Political Rights, adopted 16 Dec. 1966, entered into force, 23 March 1976, 999 U.N.T.S. 171, art. 27 [hereinafter "ICCPR"].

15. For an excellent overview of recent international developments involving indigenous peoples, see, R.L. Barsh, Indigenous Peoples in the 1990's: From Object to Subject of International Law, 7 Harv. Human Rights J. 33 (1994). See, also, D. Sambo, Indigenous Peoples and International Standard Setting Processes: Are State Governments Listening, 3 Transnat'l. and Contemp. Problems 13 (1993); S. James Anaya, Indigenous Rights Norms in Contemporary International Law, 8 Ariz. J. Int'l & Comp. L. 1 (1991); R.A. Williams, Encounters on the Frontiers of International Human Rights Law: Redefining the Terms of Indigenous Peoples Survival, 1990 Duke L.J. 660 (1990) and; E-I. Daes, On the Relations Between Indigenous Peoples and States, 2 *Without Prejudice* 41 (1989).

16. Economic and Social Council Resolution 1982/34 of 7 May 1982.

17. The UN Study on the *Problem of Discrimination Against Indigenous Populations*, in its Conclusions, Proposals and Recommendations, for instance, suggests that a Declaration on the rights of indigenous peoples be drafted, with a view to the development of a Convention, open to ratification by UN member-states. J. Cobo, *Study on the Problem of Discrimination Against Indigenous Populations, Conclusions, Proposals, and Recommendations.* UN Doc. E/CN.4/Sub.2/1986/7/ Adds. 1-3, at para. 31 (1986). This multi-volume report, initiated in 1971 and completed in 1983, can be obtained as UN SALES NO. E.86.XIV.3 (1987).

18. See, Miguel Alfonso Martinez, *Study on Treaties, Agreements and Other Constructive Arrangements Between States and Indigenous Populations*, UN Doc. E/CN.4/Sub.2/1992/32 (1992). A final report on this subject is expected

within the next two years.

19. See, *Study on the protection of the cultural and intellectual property of indigenous peoples*, E-I Daes, Special Rapporteur of the Sub-Commission on the Prevention of Discrimination and the Protection of Minorities and the Chairperson of the Working Group on Indigenous Populations. UN Doc. E/CN.4/Sub.2/1993/28 (1993) and; *Protection of the heritage of indigenous peoples. Preliminary report of the Special Rapporteur*, Mrs. E-I Daes, submitted in conformity with the Sub-Commission resolution 1993/44 and decision 1994/105 of the Commission on Human Rights. UN Doc. E/CN.4/Sub.2/1994/31 (1994). See, also, The Mataatua Declaration on Cultural and Intellectual Property Rights of Indigenous Peoples, in, *Other Matters Including Meetings and Seminars and The Voluntary Fund for Indigenous Populations*. E/CN.4/Sub.2/AC.4/1994/12 (1994).

20. See, *A Permanent forum in the United Nations for indigenous peoples*. Technical note by the Secretariat. E/CN.4/Sub.2/AC.4/1994/11 and Adds. 1 & 2 (1994); *The Report of the Working Group on Indigenous Populations on its twelfth session*. UN Doc. E/CN.4/Sub.2/1994/30 (1994); *The future role of the Working Group on Indigenous Populations*. Working paper submitted by Miguel Alfonso Martinez, member of the Working Group.; UN Doc. E/CN.4/Sub.2/AC.4/1994/10 (1994) and; *Future role of the Working Group*. Note by the Chairperson Rapporteur of the Working Group on Indigenous Populations. E/CN.4/Sub.2/AC.4/1993/8 (1993).

21. For instance, the Working Group included an article in the Draft Declaration providing for the establishment of a UN forum for Indigenous Peoples "at the highest level . . . with the direct participation of Indigenous Peoples." *Draft Declaration*, supra note 3, art. 41. The need to consider the establishment of a permanent forum was also recognized by the Vienna *Declaration and Programme of Action*. World Conference on Human Rights, UN Doc. A/CONF.157/23 (1993) and the General Assembly in its resolution proclaiming the International Decade, G.A. Res. 48/163 of 21 December 1993. (1993).

22. Indigenous proposals for a UN forum have included a UN High Commissioner for Indigenous Peoples, a Commission on Indigenous Peoples, an office of Indigenous affairs and observer status at the General Assembly.

23. See, *Consideration of a Permanent Forum for Indigenous People. Information received from Governments and indigenous organizations*. UN

Doc. E/CN.4/Sub.2/AC.4/1994/11/Add.1 (1994).

24. *Discrimination Against Indigenous Peoples. Report of the Working Group on its twelfth session*, UN Doc. E/CN.4/Sub.2/1994/30, at Annex I (1994).

25. With regards to development related activities, the Working Group noted in the report on its twelfth session, that ECOSOC and Agenda 21 have both called for system-wide coordination of development activities relating to indigenous peoples and stated that the proposed forum would be the "most appropriate mechanism for assuming those important responsibilities." *Id.* at 32, paras. 149 - 150.

26. The International Year was widely regarded by indigenous peoples as a UN public relations exercise, concerned more with the publication of posters and commemorative stamps than substantive issues.

27. For information on the Draft Declaration, see, inter alia, R. Coulter, The Draft UN Declaration on the Rights of Indigenous Peoples: What is it? What does it mean?, 13 *NQHR* 123 (1995); E-I. Daes, Equality of Indigenous Peoples Under the Auspices of the United Nations: The Draft Declaration on the Rights of Indigenous Peoples, 7 *St. Thomas L.R.* 493 (1995); J. Burger & P. Hunt, Towards the International Protection of Indigenous Peoples' Rights, 12 *NQHR* 405 (1994); D. Sambo, supra note 15.

28. *Draft Declaration*, supra note 3.

29. Id. at art. 3. Article 3 states that "Indigenous peoples have the right to self-determination. By virtue of that right they freely determine their political status and freely pursue their economic, social and cultural development." Compare this with article 1 of the ICCPR, supra note 14, which states that "All peoples have the right to self-determination. By virtue of that right they freely determine their political status and freely pursue their economic, social and cultural development." See, also, infra, notes 52-56 and accompanying text, for a discussion of the right to self-determination as defined in the *Draft Declaration*.

30. Id. at, inter alia, arts. 4, 31, 32 and 33.

31. Id. at PART VI.

32. Id. at art. 28.

33. Id. at arts. 4, 19, and 20.

34. Id. at arts. 6 and 7.

35. Id. at art. 36.

36. Id. at, inter alia, PARTS III, IV & V.

37. Commission on Human Rights Res. 1995/32 of 3 March 1995. *Establishment of a working group of the Commission on Human Rights to elaborate a draft declaration in accordance with operative paragraph 5 of General Assembly resolution 49/214 of 23 December 1994.* The CHRWG held its first session in Geneva, 20 November - 1 December 1995. The second session will be held most likely at the same time in 1996. The second session will commence with an article-by-article review and re-drafting of the Draft Declaration.

38. Id. at para. 1.

39. For an excellent article on the right to self-determination, see, S. James Anaya, A Contemporary Definition of the International Norm of Self-Determination, 3 *Transnat'l L. & Contemp. Probs.* 132 (1993). See, also, A. Cassese, *Self-Determination of Peoples: A Legal Appraisal* (Cambridge, Cambridge University Press: 1995); C. Brolmann, R. Lefeber, M. Zieck (eds.), *Peoples and Minorities in International Law* (Boston, Kluwer Academic Publishers: 1993) and; C. Tomuschat (ed.), *Modern Law of Self-Determination* (Boston, Martinus Nijhoff Publishers: 1993).

40. Mr. Tomkinson, the Australian representative to the General Assembly's 3rd Committee, for instance, states that "Self-determination should encompass the right of distinct peoples within a state, particularly indigenous peoples and national minorities to make decisions on their own affairs," provided that this is "compatible with the continued existence, unchanged, of the state [and] so long as the latter give effect to the right of those peoples to take effective control of their own affairs." UN GAOR 49th Session, Third Committee, *Summary Record of the 6th Meeting*, Agenda Item 94, Right of Peoples to Self-determination. UN Doc. A/C.3/49/SR.6, at 6, (1994).

41. H. Hannum, *Autonomy, Sovereignty & Self-Determination: The Accommodation of Conflicting Rights.* (Philadelphia, U. Penn. Press: 1990).

The right of states to sovereignty and territorial integrity, for instance, conflicts with the right of peoples to self-determination, particularly as incidences of pure nation-states are extremely rare.

42. E-I. Daes, Some Considerations on the Right of Indigenous Peoples to Self-Determination, 3 *Transnat'l L. & Contemp. Probs.* 1, 4 (1993). However, recent events in Eastern Europe, the Balkans and the former Soviet Union illustrate that the international community is willing to recognize that the exercise of the right to self-determination may result in the formation of new, independent states outside of the classic, colonial context.

43. In particular, the World Conference on Human Rights, Vienna 1993, has been called the "Battle of the 's'" by one commentator due to the prolonged and heated debate over people vs. peoples. The same debate also occurred at the Cairo International Conference on Population and Development 1994. In both cases, "people" was the terminology that was ultimately included in the texts of the final documents. S. Tullberg, Indigenous Peoples, Self-Determination and the Unfounded Fear of Secession, Indian Law Resource Center, August 1994 (on file with author).

44. For an example of how the use of the term 'peoples' has been qualified, see, ILO 169, art. 1(3), supra note 2, at infra note 68 and accompanying text.

45. *Explanatory note concerning the draft declaration on the rights of indigenous peoples, by Erica-Irene Daes, Chairperson of the Working Group on Indigenous Populations*, para. 7, at 2. UN Doc. E/CN.4/Sub.2/1993/26/Add.1 (1993) [hereinafter "Explanatory Note"]. Prof. Daes, defines a people according "to the extent to which the group making the claim shares ethnic, linguistic, religious or cultural bonds, although the absence or weakness of one of these bonds or elements need not invalidate a claim, [and by] the extent to which members within the group perceive the group's identity as distinct from the identities of other groups." E-I. Daes, supra note 42, at 5.

46. Id., Explanatory Note, at para. 8, at 2.

47. *Declaration on Granting Independence to Colonial Countries and Peoples.* G.A. Res. 1514, UN GAOR, 15th Session, Supp. No.16, at 66, UN Doc. A/4684 (1960), at art. 6.

48. *The Right to Self-Determination, Implementation of United Nations Resolutions.* H. Gros Espiell, Special Rapporteur. UN Doc. E/CN.4/Sub.2/405/Rev.1, at para. 90 (1980).

49. Explanatory Note, supra note 45, at para. 21, at 4. See, also, infra notes 52-56 and accompanying text.

50. *Declaration on Principles of International Law Concerning Friendly Relations and Cooperation Among States in Accordance with the Charter of the United Nations.* G.A. Res. 2625, Annex, UN GAOR, 25th Session, Supp. No. 28, at 121, UN Doc. A/8028 (1970) ["Declaration on Friendly Relations"].

51. Id. at 123.

52. See, E-I. Daes, supra note 42, E-I. Daes, supra note 27 and; E-I. Daes, Native Peoples Rights, 27 *Cahiers de Droit* 123 (1986).

53. Explanatory Note, supra note 45, at 5.

54. Id. at 4, para. 21. This is in accord with the 1970 Declaration on Friendly Relations which states that "Nothing in the foregoing paragraphs shall be construed as authorizing or encouraging any action which would dismember or impair, totally or in part, the territorial integrity or political unity of sovereign and independent states conducting themselves in compliance with the principles of equal rights and self-determination of peoples as described above and thus possessed of a government representing the whole people belonging to the territory without distinction as to race, creed or colour." Declaration on Friendly Relations, supra note 49.

55. See, Daes, supra note 42, at 8-9; Daes, Explanatory Note, supra note 45, at 26 and; Barsh, supra note 15, at 39.

56. Supra note 45, at 5, para. 23.

57. Convention Concerning the Protection and Integration of Indigenous and Other Tribal and Semi-Tribal Populations in Independent Countries (ILO No. 107), entered into force 2 June 1959, 328 U.N.T.S. 247.

58. Supra note 2.

59. ILO 107 remains in effect for those states that have ratified it, but have not ratified ILO 169.

60. H.R. Berman, "The ILO and Indigenous Peoples: Revision of ILO Convention No. 107 at the 75th Session of the International Labour Conference, 1988", 41 *Int'l Comm'n of Jurists* Rev. 48, 48-9 (1988).

61. *Partial revision of the Indigenous and Tribal Populations Convention, 1957* (No. 107), Report VI(1), at 117, International Labour Conference, 75th Session (Geneva 1988).

62. As of July 1995, the following states have ratified ILO 169: Mexico, Norway, Costa Rica, Colombia, Peru, Bolivia, Honduras and Paraguay. Fiji, Austria and Argentina have ratified in their respective legislatures but have yet to transmit their instruments of ratification to the ILO. The following states have submitted it to their national legislatures for ratification or are discussing ratification: Brazil, Chile, Ecuador, Guatemala, Venezuela, Denmark, Philippines, Finland, El Salvador, Panama, and Sri Lanka.

63. For a detailed analysis of ILO 169, see, R.L. Barsh, "An Advocates Guide to the Convention on Indigenous and Tribal Peoples", 15 *Okla. City L.R.* 209 (1990). Also, see, L. Swepston, "A New Step in the International Law on Indigenous and Tribal Peoples: ILO Convention No. 169 of 1989", 15 *Okla. City L.R.* 677 (1990).

64. For an indigenous critique of ILO 169, see, S. Venne, "The New Language of Assimilation: A Brief Analysis of ILO Convention No. 169", 2 *Without Prejudice* 59 (1989).

65. For discussion of the revision process, see, H.R. Berman, supra note 60.

66. The following international indigenous organizations are actively promoting the ratification of ILO 169: the Inuit Circumpolar Conference, the National Indian Youth Council, the Saami Council and the World Council of Indigenous Peoples. Additionally, many national indigenous organizations are promoting ratification, especially in Latin America and Asia.

67. *Partial revision of the Indigenous and Tribal Populations Convention, 1957* (No.107), Report IV(2A), at 12, International Labour Conference. 76th Session (Geneva 1989).

68. Supra note 2, at art. 1(3).

69. Id. at art. 7(1).

70. Id. at art. 6.

71. Id. at art. 25(1), "adequate health services ... under their own responsibility and control."

72. Id. at art. 27(2)(3), "[t]he competent authority shall ensure the training of members ... with a view to the progressive transfer of responsibility for conduct of [educational programmes]" and "the right of these peoples to establish their own educational institutions."

73. Id. at art. 22(3), "these peoples shall progressively assume responsibility for the organization and operation of such special training programs."

74. Id. at PART II.

75. Id. at arts. 7(1), 8(2) and 9. Article 8(2), for instance states that "these peoples shall have the right to retain their customs and institutions, where these are not incompatible with fundamental rights defined by the national legal system and internationally recognized human rights."

76. R.L. Barsh, supra note 63, at 219.

77. Supra note 2, at art. 13(1).

78. Id. at art. 14. Compare this with Draft Declaration, supra note 3, article 26, which states that " Indigenous peoples have the right to own, develop, control and use the lands and territories ... and other resources which they have traditionally owned or otherwise occupied or used. This includes the right to the full recognition of their laws and customs, land-tenure systems and institutions for the development and management of resources, and the right to effective measures by states to prevent any interference with, alienation or encroachment upon these rights."

79. Id. at art. 14(3). Compare with Draft Declaration, supra note 3, article 27, which states that "Indigenous peoples have the right to the restitution of the lands and territories which they have traditionally owned or otherwise occupied or used, and which have been confiscated, occupied, used or damaged without their

free and informed consent. Where this is not possible, they have the right to just and fair compensation. Unless otherwise freely agreed upon by the peoples concerned, compensation shall take the form of lands, territories and resources equal in quality, size and legal status.

80. Id. at art. 14(1).

81. Id. at art. 23.

82. Id. at art. 7.

83. Id. at art. 15(1).

84. Id. at art. 15(2). Compare with Draft Declaration, supra note 3, article 30, which states that "Indigenous peoples have the right ... to require that states obtain their free and informed consent prior to approval of any project affecting their lands, territories and other resources, particularly in connection with the development, utilisation or exploitation of mineral, water or other resources, compensation shall be provided for any such activities and measures taken to mitigate adverse environmental, economic, social, cultural or spiritual impact" (emphasis added).

85. Colombia, Bolivia, Norway and Mexico are prominent examples of constitutional reform processes prompted by ILO 169. Chile and Brazil which have not ratified the Convention, have both adopted legislation that reflect some of its principles. Argentina, for instance, which has ratified the Convention but has not notified the ILO of the ratification, revised its Constitution in 1994 to reflect some of the principles defined in ILO 169. Article 67 reads: "[The state] recognizes concurrently with the provinces, the preexistence of the Indigenous peoples that make up the Argentine nation, guaranteeing respect for their ethnic and cultural identity, the legal status of their communities, the possession and communal ownership of lands that they traditionally occupy; making available sufficient and suitable lands for their human development, which will be inalienable and not subject to seizure; assure their access to bilingual and intercultural education; and their participation in decisions regarding the rational use, administration and conservation of natural resources; in the development of their interests, and in national life." Argentina CONST., Art. 67, 1994. *El Acuerdo Sobre Identida y Derechos de los Pueblos Indigenas* (Agreement on Ethnicity and Indigenous Rights) (on file with author) signed by the Guatemalan Government and the Guatemalan National Revolutionary Unity (URNG) is also

heavily influenced by ILO 169, as are the policy guidelines and directives of the World Bank, Asian Development Bank, Inter-American Development Bank and ' the UNDP. The Duma of the Russian Federation is also examining legislation based upon the Convention.

86. Colombia CONST. 1991, *Editora Juridica de Colombia* (Rafael Ballén M. Ed.).

87. Law 21 of 4 March 1991.

88. For a general discussion of the revision process and information on indigenous rights in the 1991 Constitution, see, S. Ramirez, "Los Indígenas Colombianos en la Nueva Constitución", 32 *Boletin Americanista* 93 (1991) and; C. Gros, "Attention! un Indien peut en cacher un autre: droits indigènes et nouvelle constitution en Colombie", 59 *Caravelle* 139 (1992). For an extensive discussion of legislative, judicial and executive action concerning indigenous peoples in Colombia, see, R. Rodan, Fuero Indigena Colombiano. (Bogota, Ministero de Gobierno. Direcciòn General de Asuntos Indígena: 1994).

89. Supra note 86, arts. 63, 286 and 329.

90. Id. art. 330. See, also, arts. 79 and 80, which define a right to a healthy environment and the environmentally sustainable use of natural resources. Art. 79 also requires that communities participate in all decisions that may affect the environment. Compare this with arts. 4 (1)(2) and 15, ILO 169, supra note 2.

91. Colombia CONST., Id. art. 10.

92. Id. art. 68.

93. Id. art. 72.

94. Id. art. 96.

95. See, for instance, art. 246, which provides for the exercise of jurisdiction by indigenous authorities, "provided that [it is] not contrary to the Constitution and the national laws" (author's translation).

96. See, for instance, World Council of Indigenous Peoples, *Declaration of Indigenous Rights, Panama, 1984*, UN Doc. E/CN.4/Sub.2/1985/ 22, Annex I (1985) and; *Draft Declaration of Principles for the Defense of Indigenous*

Nations and Peoples of the Western Hemisphere. UN Doc. E/CN.4/Sub.2/1985/22, Annex IV (1985).

97. For a brief discussion of the observance of indigenous peoples' human rights in Colombia, see, *The Second Report on the Situation of Human Rights in Colombia*, OEA/Ser.l/V/II.84 doc. 39 rev., p. 234 et seq. (1993).

98. ICCPR supra note 14 and First Optional to the International Covenant on Civil and Political Rights, adopted 16 Dec. 1966, entered into force, 23 March 1976, 21 UN GAOR Supp. (No. 16) 59, UN Doc. A/6316 (1967). In particular, see, *Mikmaq Tribal Society vs. Canada* (No. 205/1985), UN Doc. CCPR/C/39/D/205/1986 (1990); *Lovelace vs. Canada* (No. 24/1977), *Report of the Human Rights Committee*, 36 UN GAOR Supp.(No. 40) at 166, UN Doc. A/36/40 (1981); *Bernard Ominayak and the Lake Lubicon Band vs. Canada* Communication No. 167/1984, *Report of the Human Rights Committee*, 45 UN GAOR Supp. (No.43) at 1, UN Doc. A/45/40 (vol. 2, 1990) and; *Kitok vs. Sweden, Report of the Human Rights Committee*, 43 UN GAOR Supp.(No. 40) at 221, UN Doc. A/43/40 (1988).

99. American Convention on Human Rights, adopted San José, Costa Rica, 22 Nov. 1969, entered into force, 18 July 1978, OAS Treaty Ser. No. 36, OAS Off. Rec. OEA/Ser.L/V/II.23 doc. 21 rev. 6 (1979) and American Declaration of the Rights and Duties of Man, OAS Res. XXX, adopted by the Ninth International Conference of American States (March 30-May 2, 1948), Bogota, OAS Off. Rec. OEA/Ser.L/V/I.4 Rev. (1965). In particular, see, *Yanomami Decision*, Res. No. 12/85, Case No. 7615, Inter-American Commission of Human Rights 1984-85, OEA/Ser.L/V/II.62, doc.10 rev.1 (1985) and; *Report on the Situation of Human Rights of a Segment of the Nicaraguan Population of Miskito Origin*, Case No. 7964, OEA/Ser.L/V/II.62, doc.26 (1984) [hereinafter "Miskito Report"].

100. *Ominayak and Lake Lubicon Band vs. Canada*, supra note 98.

101. Miskito Report, supra note 99. See, also, *Special Report on the Situation of Human Rights of the Miskito Indians of Nicaragua.* OEA/Ser.L/V/II.56, doc. 11, rev. 1 (1983).

102. Formal allegations against Nicaragua were made by a number of parties including: MISURASATA (an indigenous organization representing the Miskito, Sumo and Rama peoples), the Indian Law Resource Center, the Moravian

Church and a various leaders of the Indigenous nations of the Atlantic coast of Nicaragua.

103. The allegations included violations of the rights to life, to personal liberty, to personal security, to due process, to residence and movement, and to property.

104. Miskito Report, supra note 99, at 75, para. 3.

105. Human rights violations attributed to the military during this period include murder, torture, illegal detention, rape, disappearances, harassment of political leaders and destruction of property . One result of these abuses, was that many thousands of Miskito fled Nicaragua for refugee camps inside Honduras.

106. Miskito Report, supra note 99.

107. Id. at 78, para. 9.

108. Id. at 81, para. 11.

109. Id. at 81, para. 15.

110. Article 27 of the ICCPR, supra note 14. See, especially, *Ominayak and Lake Lubicon Band vs. Canada*, supra note 98 and *Kitok vs. Sweden*, supra note 98.

111. Miskito Report, supra note 99, at 133, para 3(j).

112. Id. at 135. Resolution on the Friendly Settlement Procedure Regarding the Human Rights Situation of a Segment of the Nicaraguan Population of Miskito Origin.

113. Autonomy Statute of the Atlantic Coast Regions of Nicaragua, Law No. 28 of 7 Sept. 1987.

114. Supra note 41, at 216.

115. Id.

116. See, Miskito case, supra note 99.

Analysis of How International Organizations and International Human Rights Law are Instrumental in Protecting and Promoting the Rights of National Minorities

RYSZARD D. KOMENDA

Introduction

The primary objective of this work is to examine ways in which international mechanisms for the protection of minorities and international institutions can be effective in resolving ethnic conflicts. These often violent conflicts present a dangerous threat to the territorial integrity and stability of the states, yet in a majority of cases, states oppose implementation of measures to protect minorities. The denial of minority rights is probably the single most important factor in the escalation of ethnic conflicts.

This essay attempts to answer the following questions: Why has the United Nations system failed to deliver effective protection of minorities? Why is the international community unable to enforce the currently limited provisions for international protection of minorities? Why do states object to any positive measures to protect minorities?

The essay proposes new means for dealing with the complex problems of majority/minority relations. It explores changing attitudes towards minorities in light of the theories of international human rights law. Special attention is paid to the emerging international phenomenon of non-governmental organizations.

The international protection of minorities is analyzed in its historical perspective. The tension between individual and collective rights, and the principle of equality is examined as one of the main elements in the social and legal development of humanity throughout history. The concept of ethnic and national minority is described, and issues touching on the difficulty of defining a minority are discussed.

The problem of international protection of minorities has become very important to the European and global communities after the collapse of the Soviet Union, especially after the fall of the Yugoslavian Communist Empire under the command of Marshal Tito. In 1992, ethnic conflicts rapidly developed all over the Balkans, central Europe and the former Soviet Union. It is important to point out that one of the countries which had been most active with respect to the protection and recognition of minorities in the forums of the United Nations and the Organization for Security and Cooperation in Europe (OSCE), was the former Yugoslavia. In 1978, Yugoslavia, with its complex minority situation, produced the first original draft of the United Nations *Declaration On the Status of People Belonging to Ethnic, Racial, Religious, and Linguistic Minorities*. On the CSCE scene, France, the United States of America and the Soviet Union strongly opposed the Yugoslavian proposal to include the issue of minorities as proceedings of the conference. It must be noted here that Yugoslavia had the most complicated ethnic situation in the world.

The definition of a minority

Before answering the question 'What are the rights of minorities?', one must first define what constitutes a minority.

Numerous attempts by scholars and politicians have failed to produce a universal definition of a minority, which shows how difficult it is to define "a minority". The absence of a commonly acceptable definition of a minority has forced international law experts to try to justify this absence, and to find arguments to ignore it. The most popular explanation for the absence of a universal definition of a minority is the complexity of the subject and the political need for urgent action to resolve a "minority problem".[1]

One possible explanation for the lack of a universal definition of what constitutes a minority might be that absence of a definition is a tactical measure used by states that wish to avoid consideration of substantive rights. Another explanation could be that a "minority problem" usually consists of a complicated mixture of historical, political, territorial and legal issues. Thus, the lack of a definition becomes an excuse for states to remain inactive regarding the protection of minorities.

In 1977, after several years of researching the issue, Francesco Capotorti, a Special Rapporteur appointed by the United Nations Sub-Commission on the Prevention of Discrimination and Protection of Minorities, submitted a final report entitled "Study on the Rights of Persons belonging to Ethnic, Religious and Linguistic Minorities."[2] This report contained a comprehensive study of the rights of persons belonging to ethnic, religious and linguistic minorities. In this report, the Special Rapporteur formulated a definition of the term "minority", limited in relation to Article 27 of the *International Covenant on Civil and Political Rights* (ICCPR). In this context, the term "minority" means:

A group numerically inferior to the rest of the population of a State, in a non-dominant position, whose members—being nationals of the State-

–possess ethnic, religious or linguistic characteristics differing from those of the rest of the population and show, if only implicitly, a sense of solidarity, directed towards preserving their culture, traditions, religion or language.[3]

The reoccurrence of "minority problems" in various states warranted further studies of the definition. The United Nations Sub-Commission on the Prevention of Discrimination and Protection of Minorities transmitted to the Human Rights Commission a text prepared by J. Deschénes. His definition of a minority was as follows:

A group of citizens of a State, constituting a numerical minority and in a non-dominant position in that State, endowed with ethnic, religious or linguistic characteristics which differ from those of the majority of the population, having a sense of solidarity with one another, motivated, if only implicitly, by a collective will to survive and whose aim is to achieve equality with the majority in fact and in law.[4]

The requirement of citizenship is mentioned at the very beginning of this definition. Other elements are listed after this requirement: numerical minority, requirement of non-dominance, ethnic, religious and linguistic characteristic, and the subjective requirement for the aim of the group to achieve equality with the rest of society.[5]

The Historical Background of the Protection of Minorities

In order to fully understand the contemporary challenges presented by the international protection of minorities, a historical perspective is essential. A number of current inter-ethnic conflicts are deeply rooted in negative relations of the past.

Some of the first texts which provide for favorable treatment of minorities can be found in international treaties dating back to the sixteenth and seventeenth centuries.[6] At that time, protection was limited to the European legal and political arena. The cornerstone of modern international law, the 1648 Treaty of Westphalia, contained certain guarantees for religious minorities.[7] Other international agreements, notably the Treaty of Osnabrück and the Treaty of Oliva (1660)[8] between Poland and Sweden, guaranteed the protection of religious rights of the different sects and separate schools. However, this early protection of religious rights should be not interpreted in the same way as contemporary minority rights.[9]

For the next two centuries, fragmented protection was offered mainly to religious minorities. Not until the end of World War I did the international community put in place a system for the protection of minorities. Some consideration for minority rights could be found in decisions of the Congress of Vienna in 1815, in the Treaty of Berlin in 1876, and in some domestic legislation in Europe (e.g. the Bulgarian Constitution of 1879).[10]

The first comprehensive and institutionalized system of protection for minorities was created by a series of international instruments, the so-called minority treaties.[11]

The main goal of establishing the minority treaties was to ensure the enjoyment of basic human rights for minorities, both in law and in practice.[12] The system of the minority treaties could be divided into three main categories:[13] The first category contained treaties between the Great Powers and states defeated in the First World War (Austria, Hungary, Bulgaria and Turkey). The second contained treaties imposed on newly created states or states with redrawn boundaries (Czechoslovakia, Greece, Poland, Romania, and Yugoslavia). The last category included regulated special territories under the supervision of the League of Nations (Åland Islands, the Free City of Danzig, the Memel Territory, and Upper Silesia).[14]

The most innovative element of the minority treaties was that rights were guaranteed by the League of Nations, rather than the customary guarantee by the great powers. Articles 86 and 93 of the Treaty of Versailles included this new method for enforcing the protection of minority rights.

The Advisory Opinions of the Permanent Court of International Justice (PCIJ) contained statements to the effect that real equality demands positive action and special measures for minorities, but this was rarely given effect. The fact of judicial supervision itself has been considered one of the important new elements in the post-World War I minority protection system.[15] Another innovative element of the League of Nations System was the guarantee of positive rights with respect to language, education, religious and cultural activities. These were collective rights and, as such, tended to conflict with the liberal, western tradition of individual rights. Individual rights for persons belonging to minorities were also included. Individuals were entitled to equal treatment, but not special treatment (i.e. different from other citizens of their state).

The additional element to the jurisdictional supervision was an advisory function of the Permanent Court.[16] In a number of advisory opinions, the PCIJ defined the main principles relating to the protection of minorities. Many of these remain valid in the contemporary context.[17]

The collapse of the League of Nations minorities system came after Germany left the organization in 1933, claiming that its minorities were mistreated in other member states. The following year, Poland announced that it would not abide by the Minority Treaties. Further developments included the dismemberment of Czechoslovakia in 1938 and, finally, in December 1939, after the eruption of World War II, the minority section of the League of Nations was disbanded.

Generally, the League of Nations system for the protection of minority rights did not work well. The system functioned for a period of twenty years during which only four individual cases were deemed admissible. Instead of the League bringing adequate and sufficient protection for all minorities, its fall, as well as the rise of the Nazis in the 1930s, brought about the opposite result--racism as an official policy of the Nazi State.

In the opinion of many scholars, the system of "minority treaties" was a failure.[18] This system had two standards: one for colonial empires, and a second for defeated states and newly created states.[19] Further shortcomings of this system included a lack of broad political or economic autonomy, limited application of the right to "self-determination," and a slow, bureaucratic approach.[20] The failure of the League of Nations minorities protection system, however, was not an indication that the **concept** of minority rights had failed. The system failed because of inadequate mechanisms for the protection of minorities.

Despite its shortcomings, the League of Nations system served as a basis for future systems for the protection of minority rights, and its failure should be viewed in the broader context of the general ineffectiveness of international relations at the time.[21]

Protection of Minority Rights under the United Nations System

World War II marked a turning point in attitudes towards the rights of minorities. Demands for international protection of minorities were countered by opposition from some states.[22] Despite attempts by famous international law scholars, such as Hersch Lauterpacht or Hans Kelsen, to promote protection of minorities, the new system for the protection of human rights, created after the Second World War, omitted minority rights and focused on guarantees for individual rights.

In the international arena, human rights standards have been established to cover all individual human beings, including members of minority groups. But only slow progress has been made in the development of standards for creating additional rights and making special arrangements for persons belonging to minorities and for minorities as groups, despite it being a stated goal of the United Nations.[23]

Existing international standards for the protection of minorities

Prohibition of discrimination and equal enjoyment of universal human rights are generally recognized rules of international law.[24] The cornerstone for universal application of these principles is found in the provisions of the United Nations *Charter* (1945) and the *Universal Declaration of Human Rights* (1948, article 2). Other more detailed UN instruments regulate issues of non-discrimination and equality. These instruments include the two International Covenants, on *Economic, Social and Cultural Rights* (ICESCR) and on *Civil and Political Rights* (ICCPR), both adopted by the United Nations in 1966. Non-discrimination is also included in a number of specialized international agreements and declarations. These include: the *International Convention on the Elimination of All Forms of Racial Discrimination* (United Nations, 1965); the *Convention on the Elimination of All Forms of Discrimination against Women* (United Nations, 1979); the *Declaration on the Elimination of All Forms of Intolerance and of Discrimination based on Religion or Belief* (United Nations, 1981); the *Convention on the Rights of the Child* (United Nations, 1989); the *Convention concerning Discrimination in Respect of Employment and Occupation* (ILO Convention No.111, 1958); the *Convention against Discrimination in Education* (UNESCO, 1978); and the *Declaration on Race and Racial Prejudice* (UNESCO, 1978).

These instruments include guarantees for the rights of individual members of a minority as well as for some group rights. Rights guaranteed with regard to persons belonging to minorities include, in particular, recognition before the law, equality before the courts, equality before the law and equal protection of the law. These rights are guaranteed by the provisions of Articles 6 and 7 of the *Universal Declaration* and Articles 14, 16 and 26 of the *International Covenant on Civil and Political Rights*.[25]

Non-discrimination is also established as a general rule in regional human rights instruments.[26] These include the *European Convention* (1950, Article 14), the *European Social Charter* (1961), the *Declaration regarding Intolerance -- A Threat to Democracy* (1981), the *Framework Convention for the Protection of National Minorities* (1994), the *American Convention on Human Rights*

(Organization of American States, 1969, article 1), the *African Charter* (OAU 1981, article 1). In the European arena, the body which has recently been most active in establishing new non-discrimination and equality standards, is the Organization for Security and Cooperation in Europe (OSCE). This organization adopted a number of important documents, such as the *Final Act* (Helsinki, 1975), the *Charter of Paris for New Europe* (Paris, 1990), the *Document of the Copenhagen Meeting of the Conference on the Human Dimension of the CSCE* (Copenhagen, 1990), the *Concluding Document of the Moscow Meeting of the Conference on the Human Dimension of the CSCE* (Moscow, 1991), *Report of the CSCE meeting of Experts on National Minorities* (Geneva, 1991), and the *Budapest Document: Towards a Genuine Partnership in A New Era* (Budapest, 1994).

Throughout the post-war history of the United Nations, the protection of minorities was related to the rule of non-discrimination. During the period of drafting of the United Nations *Charter* in San Francisco, Latin American states and the United States of America replaced the concept of "protection of minorities" with the concept of "prevention of discrimination".[27]

The omission of the direct reference to minorities in the United Nations *Charter* resulted in weakening the real possibilities for the international protection of minorities. The concept of non-discrimination included in the United Nations *Charter* was on its own insufficient to make the international community focus on the needs and interests of minorities.[28]

The *Universal Declaration of Human Rights*, adopted by the UN General Assembly on December 10, 1948, does not, as the UN *Charter*, contain any reference to the rights of persons belonging to ethnic, linguistic or religious minorities.[29] The General Assembly expressed its concern about the protection of minorities in resolution 217 C (III) of December 10, 1948. It was stated that the United Nations could not remain indifferent to the fate of minorities and, at the same time, that the "minorities problem" was complex and delicate.[30]

The positive protection of minorities was not included in United Nations treaties. Article 27 of the *Covenant on Civil and Political Rights* offers only negative rights to minorities. At the same time, however, the United Nations decided to commission numerous studies and reports to signal that, despite its absence in UN documents, minority protection remained an important issue. The main study on the rights of persons belonging to minorities was carried out by Francesco Capotorti,[31] a member of the Sub-Commission on the Prevention of Discrimination and Protection of Minorities.

In his final report in 1977, Mr. Capotorti recommended that full use be made of the procedures available under the *International Covenant on Civil and Political Rights* to implement its provisions on minorities (Article 27), and that there should be procedures at the national level to deal with violations of the rights of minorities established under this Article. He also proposed the drafting of an international declaration on the rights of members of minorities. The study has become a benchmark for the development of contemporary minority protection.

Another member of the Sub-Commission, Asbiørn Eide, was entrusted in 1989 with the preparation of a report on national experiences with regard to peaceful and constructive solutions to problems involving minorities. He submitted a preliminary report on the issue in 1989, and progress reports in 1991 and 1992.[32] His final report was presented in August 1993.[33] According to Mr. Eide's report:

> The framework for the solution of minority situation problems consists in a combination of several elements: (a) Respect for territorial integrity; (b) Ensuring equality and non-discrimination in the common domain; (c) Arrangements for pluralism in togetherness; (d) Where appropriate, pluralism by territorial subdivision.[34]

The Eide report was one of the most comprehensive reports prepared by the UN rapporteur, but unfortunately, the international community is very reluctant and slow to follow the recommendations of the report.

Existing provisions on special measures and special rights

As mentioned at the beginning of this chapter, when the United Nations was founded after the Second World War, the prevailing view was that if individual rights were properly protected, special provisions for the rights of minorities were not needed. As a result, the United Nations failed to properly understand and provide protection for minorities.[35]

The need for differential treatment of minorities, in order to preserve their distinct characteristics, was recognized in the pre-United Nations era.[36] An exposition of the need for positive actions and special measures can be found in the Permanent Court of International Justice Advisory Opinion on Minority Schools in Albania.[37]

It is regrettable that the United Nations stopped short of recognizing already established rules of international law. One of possible explanations may be that the post-World War II political agenda did not include minorities. Another reason may be that most states involved in the drafting of the United Nations instruments had no minority problems at all within their own borders.[38] The adoption of provisions incorporating special rights and measures for the protection of minorities might have prevented many serious violations of human rights throughout the United Nations' history. The United Nations was very slow in addressing these issues seriously, until recent eruptions of inter-ethnic violence. The adoption of the *United Nations Declaration on Persons Belonging to National Minorities* is a good example of its conservative approach. So far, the organization has only managed to offer weak solutions and ineffective programs of actions to deal with current problems of the protection of minority rights.

International law has established principles of special minority rights based on various elements.[39] The provision for the special rights can be found in Article 27 of the *Covenant on Civil and Political Rights*, which reads:

> In those States in which ethnic, religious or linguistic minorities exist, persons belonging to such minorities shall not be denied the right, in community with the other members of their group, to enjoy their own culture, to profess and practice their own religion, or to use their own language.[40]

This article is drafted in negative terms. It is not placing any obligation of positive action on states, a fact which is understood by a majority of states.[41]

The United Nations Human Rights Committee (UN-HRC), in a recent General Comment on Article 27[42], reversed its long history of negative interpretation. In this Comment, the Committee expressed the opinion that:

> 6.1. Although article 27 is expressed in negative terms, that article, nevertheless, does recognize the existence of a "right" and requires that it shall not be denied. Consequently, a State party is under an obligation to ensure that the existence and the exercise of this right are protected against their denial or violation. Positive measures of protection are, therefore, required not only against the acts of the State party itself, whether through its legislative, judicial or administrative authorities, but also against the act of other persons within the State party.[43]

Thus, the UN Human Rights Committee not only offered a new interpretation of Article 27 in favour of positive measures towards minorities, but also extended the responsibility of the State for actions of non-state parties within its jurisdiction. This is a significant change in the United Nations' attitude towards minorities.

United Nations minority protection machinery

The human rights machinery created by the United Nations is based on the UN *Charter*. The Economic and Social Council, with its subsidiary bodies, plays a leading role in the international control of human rights. The Council has established the Commission on Human Rights and the Commission on the Status of Women. The Commission on Human Rights, in turn, has established a Sub-Commission on the Prevention of Discrimination and Protection of Minorities.

The mandate of the Sub-Commission on the Prevention of Discrimination and Protection of Minorities is: (a) to undertake studies, particularly in the light of the *Universal Declaration of Human Rights*, and make recommendations to the Commission concerning the prevention of discrimination of any kind relating to human rights and fundamental freedoms and the protection of racial, religious and linguistic minorities; and (b) to perform any other functions entrusted to it by the Economic and Social Council or by the Commission.

From 1955 to 1971, the Sub-Commission almost entirely concentrated its activities on questions of discrimination.[44] There was no significant result of the work of the Sub-Commission on the definition of minority between 1947 and 1954. F. Capotorti stated in his report: "The only positive result of the work accomplished between 1947 and 1954 was therefore the preparation of the draft text of the article 27 of the Covenant."[45]

The second part of the machinery used to protect minorities by the United Nations is a system of control and implementation established in accordance with the United Nations human rights instruments. This part of the system includes the Committee on the Elimination of Racial Discrimination, the Human Rights Committee, the Committee on Economic, Social and Cultural Rights, the Committee on the Elimination of Discrimination against Women, the Committee against Torture, and the Group of Three established under the *International Convention on the Suppression and Punishment of the Crime of Apartheid*. In regards to the protection of minority rights, the position and function of the Human Rights Committee is particularly important.

For persons belonging to minority groups who consider that their human rights and fundamental freedoms have been violated, the United Nations offers the following confidential procedures:

Procedure "1503", established by Resolution No. 1503 of the United Nations Economic and Social Council. Communications which reveal situations affecting a large number of people over a long period of time are received by the Sub-Commission on the Prevention of Discrimination and Protection of Minorities. This procedure is highly criticized by non-governmental organizations (NGOs) because it is used frequently by governments accused of gross violations of human rights, as a tool to cover up and move the issue into a confidential, non-public procedure.

Under the Optional Protocol to the ICCPR, individuals who claim that any of their rights enumerated in the Covenant have been violated and who have exhausted all available domestic remedies, may submit written communications to the Human Rights Committee for consideration. No communication can be received by the Committee if it concerns a state party to the Covenant which is not also a party to the Optional Protocol. The Committee considers communications in light of all written information made available to it by the individual and by the state party concerned, and then forwards its views to both. This procedure is a general standard-setting process for international human rights law.

There are other United Nations procedures for individuals or groups who claim that their rights, for example as they are set out in the *International Convention on the Elimination of All Forms of Racial Discrimination*, have been violated. Under this mechanism, they may submit a written communication to the United Nations Committee on the Elimination of Racial Discrimination. Individuals and groups can also use procedures designed to bring complaints concerning human rights violations to the United Nations Educational, Scientific and Cultural Organization (UNESCO), and the International Labour Organization (ILO).

Proposals for the improvement of the United Nations system

The United Nations system for the protection of minorities would be more effective if its mechanisms could be changed. There is wide agreement that much more attention to minority issues is needed. Specific steps for improving the system could, for example include: 1) The creation of a working group of the UN Commission on Human Rights (or the UN Sub-Commission); 2) A more generous allocation of time to discuss minority issues at the Sub-Commission; 3) The creation of a specific agenda item and debate on minority issues at the UN Commission on Human Rights; 4) The High Commissioner on Human Rights should assume more coordination and reporting on minority issues within the United Nations.

All these measures could significantly impact on the current level of protection of minorities by the United Nations.

In addition to the structural changes in the United Nations system for the protection of minorities, several implementation measures should be adopted by governments, the United Nations and NGOs.

The following key measures should be adopted. First, a creation of an effective system of communication and dialogue between minorities and governments, both locally and at international levels. Second, governments and minorities should ensure that models of good examples of implementation of international standards on the protection of minorities are included in domestic legal systems. Third, emphasis should be placed on the quality, not on the quantity, of international mechanisms related to minorities, and such mechanisms should be afforded sufficient priority and resources.

The Council of Europe Activities Related to the Protection of Minorities

The three main goals of the Council of Europe are closely related to the full enjoyment of rights by ethnic minorities. Those goals are: to protect and strengthen pluralist democracy and human rights; to seek solutions to the problems facing society; to promote the emergence of a genuine European cultural identity.[46] Minorities can live in harmony with the majority in a state which is a member of the Council of Europe, if this state commits itself to fulfil the above goals.

The European Convention on Human Rights, a landmark achievement of the Council of Europe, is an international treaty which includes provisions for non-discrimination and protection of minorities. It sets out the inalienable rights and freedoms of each individual and obliges states to guarantee enjoyment of these rights and freedoms by everyone within the state's jurisdiction. In addition, it has established an international enforcement mechanism, whereby states and, under certain conditions, individuals, may refer alleged violations of the Convention to the Convention institutions in Strasbourg.

Despite extensive activities of the Council of Europe in the area of international protection of minorities, problems of violations of rights and discrimination have recently flared up in some states. The Council of Europe has responded relatively fast. The reform of the protection mechanisms included in Protocol No. 11. to the Convention, as well as the adoption of the *Framework Convention for the Protection of National Minorities*, may serve as examples of the Council of Europe's increasing concern about the development of effective instruments to protect minorities.

Non-territorial minorities and protection under the framework of the Council of Europe

The Council of Europe has long been active in matters relating to travellers and Roma (Gypsies). The Committee of Ministers, the executive body of the Council of Europe, has recommended several positive measures related to the social situation of nomads in Europe.

In Resolution (75) 13,[47] on May 22, 1975, the Committee of Ministers invited governments to take all necessary measures to stop any form of discrimination against nomads and to adopt national legislative safeguards to protect the cultural heritage and the identity of nomads.[48] The respective governments should promote policies to protect camping and housing, education, vocational guidance and vocational training. The resolution addresses issues of health and social welfare, as well as social security and guarantees of rights.

In May 1992, recommendation no. R(92)10 on the implementation of rights of persons belonging to national minorities was adopted.[49] In this instrument, the Committee of Ministers recommended that member states should, as a matter of urgency, ensure that they carry out all their obligations and commitments, as prescribed by various international instruments, to persons belonging to national minorities and that they use existing mechanisms to alleviate current problems.[50]

In addition, the Committee of Ministers has decided to open the *European Charter for Regional Minority Languages* for signature.[51] Most of the provisions of Part III of the *European Charter for Regional or Minority Languages* ("Measures to promote the use of regional or minority languages in public life") do not apply to languages which lack a territorial base, such as the Romany language. "Non-territorial languages" means languages which cannot be associated with a particular area of a state (article 1.c). On the other hand, Part II ("Objectives and Principles") can more easily be applied to "non-territorial languages."[52]

The Parliamentary Assembly of the Council of Europe adopted Recommendation 563 (1969) on the situation of Gypsies and other travellers in Europe, dealing with discrimination, construction of caravan sites, children's education, consultative bodies, social security provisions and medical care.[53]

Recommendation 1203 (1993), on Gypsies in Europe,[54] was also adopted. This recommendation notes that the number of Gypsies living in the Council of Europe area has increased significantly with the admission of new member states from Central and Eastern Europe. Although the Council of Europe has adopted a number of resolutions and recommendations concerning minorities, Gypsies require special protection because of their unusual status in Europe as a non-territorial minority.[55] The Assembly also considered that "the provisions of any additional protocol or convention relating to minorities should apply to non-territorial minorities".[56]

The Assembly recommended that the Committee of Ministers initiate, where appropriate, through proposals to governments or the local and regional authorities of member states, measures dealing with culture, education, information, equal rights and everyday life. Among the more general measures, the Assembly recommended that the Council of Europe grant consultative status to representative international Roma organizations and appoint a mediator for Roma.[57]

The material provisions of the *Framework Convention for the Protection of National Minorities*

The *Framework Convention* was a product of a political compromise of states members of the Council of Europe. In order to achieve this compromise, many of the provisions of earlier proposals were omitted, thereby weakening this instrument. For example, the definition proposed in the draft additional *Protocol on Minority Rights* to the ECHR[58] was not included in the final text of the *Convention*. The *Framework Convention* (CPNM) contains no definition of the notion of "national minority." The drafters decided to adopt a pragmatic approach, based on the recognition that, at this stage, it was impossible to arrive at a definition capable of attracting the general support of all Council of Europe member states. Moreover, an elaborate system of supervisory bodies, included in the three above mentioned proposals,[59] was substantially reduced.

The *Framework Convention* contains mostly programme-type provisions, setting out objectives which Parties undertake to pursue. These provisions, which are not directly applicable, leave a measure of discretion to the states concerned in the implementation of the objectives which they have undertaken to achieve, thus enabling them to take particular circumstances into account.

Implementation of the principles set out in this *Framework Convention* must be done through national legislation and appropriate governmental policies. The *Convention* does not imply recognition of collective rights. The emphasis is placed on the protection of persons belonging to national minorities who may exercise their rights individually and in community with others.[60] In this respect, the *Framework Convention* follows the approach of the texts adopted by other international organizations.

The structure of the *Convention* is divided into five sections.[61] The preamble expresses the concern of the Council of Europe and its member states about the vulnerability of national minorities and is inspired by Article 1, paragraph 1, of the *United Nations Declaration on the Rights of Persons belonging to National or Ethnic, Religious and Linguistic Minorities.*[62]

The reference to the United Nations Conventions and declarations is a reminder of the work done at the universal level, e.g. Article 27 of the *Covenant on Civil and Political Rights* (CCPR), and the *Declaration on the Rights of Persons belonging to National or Ethnic, Religious and Linguistic Minorities.* However, this does not imply that the Council of Europe accepts the definition of a national minority contained in any of those texts.

In the Preamble of the *Convention*, one may find references to the statutory aim of the Council of Europe, namely the maintenance and further realization of human rights and freedoms.[63] The Preamble is greatly influenced by the *Vienna Declaration of Heads of State and Government* of the member states of the Council of Europe.[64] The Preamble makes reference also to other sources of inspiration: the *Convention for the Protection of Human Rights and Fundamental Freedoms* (ECHR), United Nations instruments relating to minorities, and the OSCE commitments.[65] The main aim of the *Convention* is set out in the Preamble as follows:

...the effective protection of national minorities and of the rights and freedoms of persons belonging to those minorities, within rule of law, respecting the territorial integrity and national sovereignty of states.[66]

Article 1 of the *Convention* specifies that the protection of national minorities, which forms an integral part of the protection of human rights, does not fall within the reserved domain of states. Article 1 states:

The protection of national minorities and the rights and freedoms of persons belonging to those minorities forms an integral part of the international protection of human rights, and as such falls within the scope of international cooperation.[67]

Article 1 of the *Convention* refers to the protection of national minorities as such, and to the rights and freedoms of persons belonging to minorities.[68] This distinction and the difference in the wording make it clear that no collective rights of national minorities are envisaged.[69]

The Parties do, however, recognize that protection of a national minority can be achieved through protection of the rights of individuals belonging to a minority. Furthermore, paragraph 2 of Article 3 provides that the rights and freedoms flowing from the principles of the *Framework Convention* may be exercised individually or in community with others. It thus recognizes the possibility of joint exercise of those rights and freedoms, a notion distinct from that of collective rights.[70] The term "others" is to be understood in the widest possible sense and includes persons belonging to the same national minority, to another national minority, or to the majority.[71]

Article 4 contains a classic declaration regarding principles of equality and non-discrimination.[72] The text of the convention, in this respect, follows the general approach of international law in this matter and promotes special measures to achieve effective equality between persons belonging to a national minority and those belonging to the majority.[73]

The main purpose of Article 5 is to guarantee preservation of the culture and identity of members of a minority.[74] The reference to "traditions" in paragraph 1 of this article is not an endorsement or acceptance of practices which are contrary to national law or international standards.[75]

Article 6 of the *Convention* expresses the concerns related to racism, xenophobia, anti-Semitism and intolerance. This article placed an obligation on participating states to promote tolerance and inter-cultural dialogue.[76]

The purpose of Article 7 of the *Convention* is to guarantee respect for the rights and fundamental freedoms of every person belonging to a national minority. Article 7 states:

> The Parties shall ensure respect for the rights of every person belonging to a national minority to freedom of peaceful assembly, freedom of association, freedom of expression, and freedom of thought, conscience and religion.[77]

This Article may imply certain positive obligations of the Parties to the *Convention* to protect the freedoms mentioned against violations which do not emanate from the state. This is a step in a new direction from the traditional resistance of state leaders to accept the responsibility for non-state human rights violators.[78]

Section III of the *Convention* includes provisions related to minorities' obligation to respect the national constitutions and other relevant legislation. Article 20 states:

> In the exercise of the rights and freedoms flowing from the principles enshrined in the present framework Convention, any person belonging to a national minority shall respect the national legislation and rights of others, in particular those of persons belonging to the majority or to other national minorities.[79]

Section IV of the *Convention* contains a description of the supervisory mechanisms. The Committee of Ministers is responsible for monitoring the implementation by the Contracting Parties.[80] In comparison with other proposals for the protection of minorities[81], provisions of the *Convention* have a more political nature.

The importance of the new *Convention* cannot be underestimated. The vital interest in the protection of minorities in Europe could be illustrated by the fact that 22 states signed this instrument within less than half a year of its adoption by the Council of Europe.

An additional legal international instrument, solely dedicated to minorities, could be very helpful in providing practical protection of minorities. At the same time, the effectiveness of the existing instrument can only be measured by its application in specific cases. It is still too early to fully asses the impact of this instrument on problems related to minorities.

The Role of the Organization for Security and Cooperation in Europe (OSCE)[82] in the Protection of Minorities

The OSCE recently increased its role in the international protection of minorities. One of its important institutions, devoted solely to protecting minority rights, is the Office of the High Commissioner on National Minorities. A second important element for protecting minorities is the Human Dimension Mechanism. Other OSCE procedures include: the Valletta Mechanism (peaceful settlement of disputes); the Berlin Mechanism (consultations and cooperation in emergency situations); the OSCE Court of Conciliation and Arbitration, and the OSCE Conciliation Commission.

The Conference on Security and Cooperation in Europe (CSCE) originated in the mid-1970s. It underwent constant changes to accommodate changing political, social and economic challenges. At the end of the Cold War, the "Helsinki Process" was transformed into practice with the creation of CSCE institutions: the Secretariat in Prague, the Conflict Prevention Center in Vienna, and the Office for Free Elections in Warsaw.

The Human Dimension Mechanism (Vienna and Moscow mechanisms)

The single most important mechanism for the protection of minorities is the OSCE Human Dimension Mechanism. The OSCE Human Dimension commitments originated in 1975 in the Principles section of Basket I (questions relating to security in Europe) and Basket III (cooperation in humanitarian and other fields) of the Helsinki process. The Human Dimension was redefined and expanded in a series of meetings--Paris 1989, Copenhagen 1990 and Moscow 1991--as well as at the Paris Summit of 1990 and the second Helsinki Summit of 1992. By adopting the *Charter of Paris for a New Europe*,[83] the OSCE States committed themselves to ensuring full respect for human rights and fundamental freedoms, abiding by the rule of law and promoting principles of democracy and democratic institutions, including free elections and the protection of minorities and religious freedoms.

The original mechanism, negotiated at CSCE Conferences on the Human Dimension in 1990-91, mandates an effective exchange of information and extensive bilateral meetings on cases of a potential human dimension conflict.

A mission drawn from an official list of experts appointed by CSCE participating states may be sent to investigate human rights cases, following activation of the Mechanism by the concerned state or other participating states. If a "good offices" mission is regarded as unsatisfactory or if a state refuses a mission on its territory, a mandatory mission may be dispatched, if it has the support required from nine other CSCE states. In emergency cases, ten states may dispatch a compulsory mission without first traversing the "good offices" phase. In addition, individual states may request the services of these experts to assist in establishing human rights standards in their countries.

The Human Dimension Mechanism has been activated five times: 1) In Croatia, by twelve states of the European Community and the United States. 2) In Bosnia-Hercegovina, following reports of atrocities and attacks on unarmed civilians. 3) By Estonia, to study Estonian legislation and compare it with universally accepted human rights norms. 4) By Moldova, to investigate current legislation and minorities' rights and inter-ethnic relations in Moldova. 5) By the 22nd meeting of the CSCE Committee of Senior Officials to investigate reports of human rights violations in Serbia-Montenegro, in particular the beating and imprisonment of human rights activists Vuk and Danica Draskovic and the reported banning of the Serbian Renewal Movement.

At this time, the Human Dimension mechanism appears more flexible than the United Nations system with regards to addressing issues of violations of rights of minorities. For example, the appointment of an expert mission to the Chechnya Republic was possible, and accepted by the state in question. During the Chechnya crisis, the OSCE organized three expert trips to the region. The government of the Russian Federation agreed to a permanent OSCE presence in Chechnya, as well as to OSCE involvement in the short- and long-term political negotiating processes.[84]

At the forum of the 51st session of the United Nations Commission on Human Rights in February-March 1995, the participating states paid little attention to gross violations of human rights in the Chechnya Republic. Moreover, positions taken by the Russian Federation in the international arena prevented any significant attempt to focus attention on the human rights situation in Chechnya. A statement by the Chairman of the UN Commission on Human Rights was adopted to address this situation. This statement has less importance than resolutions of the Commission. The Russian delegation, through diplomatic and procedural maneuvers, was able to prevent serious and comprehensive examination of the violent war in Chechnya.

The advantage of the OSCE procedures over the formalized United Nations system may be their non-confrontational character. There is, however, a possible negative side of the Human Dimension mechanism: participating states may use it to evade questioning by the UN Commission on Human Rights (or by another UN human rights body or procedure). The state in question could manipulate the confidential nature of the Human Dimension mechanism to present itself in a positive light in the international arena.

In general terms, OSCE standards regarding the human dimension are higher than those of the United Nations.[85] This is mainly because the OSCE standards are of a political nature, while the UN standards are of a legal nature.

Another important point is that the OSCE's "intervention threshold" in response to possible violations of its standards, is lower than the United Nations. No OSCE state can reject intervention by another OSCE state by arguing that the problem is an "internal affair". The application of this principle was shown in the case of Chechnya[86] in two ways.

First, the principle laid down for the OSCE by the 1992 Helsinki Summit[87] stated that observance of commitments in the area of the human dimension is a matter of "direct and legitimate concern to all participating States and does not belong exclusively to the internal affairs of the State concerned."[88] Second, the principles of the Code of Conduct[89], included in the Budapest Summit[90] decisions, limit the use of armed forces within the State.[91]

Alternative minorities dispute settlement under provisions of the CSCE; The High Commissioner on National Minorities; Collective protection

The new institution of the High Commissioner on National Minorities has proven a challenge to all established ways of dealing with national minorities. This institution is more flexible and more political in its approach, and its main task is to provide advance warning to states participating in the Helsinki Process (OSCE) of potential eruptions of ethnic violence.

The Office of the High Commissioner functions as a protective body. Facing tremendous changes in Eastern and Central Europe, the Conference on Security and Cooperation in Europe decided to approach growing national minority tensions and possible violent conflicts by creating a new system for the protection of national minorities. The institution of the High Commissioner on National Minorities has a supplementary role to that of other existing systems of international protection of minority rights (described above).

The High Commissioner's Office has two main instruments at its disposal for conflict settlement. Under Chapter One, paragraph 23 of the Helsinki Decisions (July 10, 1992), the CSCE[92] High Commissioner can provide "early warning" and "early action" regarding tensions involving a national minority that have the potential to develop into a conflict within the CSCE area, thereby affecting peace, stability, or relations between participating states. The organizational base of the High Commissioner is the Office for Democratic Institutions and Human Rights (ODIHR), which is located in Warsaw.

Detailed functions of the High Commissioner on National Minorities are set out in Chapter II of the Helsinki Document (1992). The position of High Commissioner is established by the participating states.[93] The Mandate of the High Commissioner is to act under the aegis of the Committee of Senior Officials, and his/her role is to prevent conflict at the earliest possible stage.[94]

The activities of the High Commissioner are limited by two elements: 1) the High Commissioner may not consider national minority issues in situations involving organized acts of terrorism.[95] 2) the High Commissioner may not consider violations of CSCE guarantees of rights with regard to an individual person belonging to a national minority.[96] The main objective of the Office is to deal with the protection of collective rights in the OSCE system. This makes the High Commissioner a unique international institution, because most international protection mechanisms are devoted solely to the protection of individual rights.

The "early warning" is an action based on an exchange of communications and contacts with the relevant parties, in reaction to tensions and dangerous developments with respect to minorities. If the High Commissioner concludes that there is a *prima facie* risk of potential conflict (a conflict within the OSCE area affecting peace, stability or relations between participating states) s/he may issue an "early warning", which will be communicated promptly by the Chairman-in-Office.[97] The "early action" is an activity of the High Commissioner with regard to possible solutions by the participating states, following the information included in the "early warning."[98]

The High Commissioner's first recommendations (on April 6, 1993)[99] were directed to the Baltic States where the ethnic tension between the large Russian minority and the majority populations threatened to transform itself into open ethnic conflict. The OSCE High Commissioner on National Minorities, Max van der Stoel,[100] presented recommendations during his visits to Estonia, Latvia and Lithuania (on January 12-13, and March 30-31, 1993). In his communication to Trivimi Veliste, Foreign Affairs Minister of the Republic of Estonia, he recommended that the Estonian Government "implement a visible policy of dialogue and integration towards the non-Estonian population."[101]

In the past two years, the High Commissioner has become engaged in more than ten countries in the OSCE region: Albania, Estonia, Hungary, Kazakhstan, Kyrgyzstan, Latvia, (former Yugoslav Republic of) Macedonia, Romania, Slovakia and Ukraine. In addition, the High Commissioner prepared a study on the situation of Roma (Gypsies).

The High Commissioner does not function as a national minorities ombudsman, nor as an investigator of individual human rights violations; instead, the High Commissioner functions as an instrument to identify ethnic tensions that might erupt into a larger conflict.

The work of the High Commissioner on National Minorities is not highly visible. The main goal of the office is to achieve positive results and to forestall the possibility of an eruption of inter-ethnic hostilities. The diplomatic nature of the work of the High Commissioner on National Minorities requires that s/he maintain a low profile and controlled relations with the media.

NGOs representing national minorities have criticized the office of the High Commissioner on National Minorities. They argue that there is a lack of transparency in the proceedings of the office, and that the High Commissioner has not acted rapidly and decisively in situations of violent inter-ethnic conflict. The first argument is difficult to dispute because the Commissioner operates on a firm principle of confidentiality and does not provide any information to third parties. The second argument results from a misunderstanding of the mandate of the High Commissioner's Office. The main task of the Office is to prevent possible conflicts, not extinguish them.

The High Commissioner has said, in support of confidentiality:

> ... early involvement might actually escalate the dispute if parties are encouraged to exploit outside attention. This risk can be considerably reduced if a low profile is adopted. Indeed, the aspect of confidentiality which is characteristic of my mandate serves precisely this purpose....[102]

The High Commissioner strongly encourages parties involved in conflicts to lay grievances before outside, third-party conciliators. He stated:

... Specifically for the High Commissioner's involvement, they [the parties] should feel that his role is non-coercive, exploratory and low-key. The goal is to start and enhance a process of exchanges, views and cooperation between the parties, leading to concrete steps which would de-escalate tensions and, if possible, address underlying issues...[103]

It should be stressed that the new OSCE institution of the High Commissioner for the Protection of Minorities is a development in a fresh direction, i.e. towards the institutional protection of collective minority rights. The protection of minorities has political dimensions that strike at the heart of state sovereignty. For example, when a minority claims greater autonomy, it raises a political problem rather than one which can readily be addressed by a tribunal. Hence, a non-judicial body may be in a better position to find a compromise.

However, it is still too early to completely assess the functioning of the office of the High Commissioner for National Minorities. It has only existed for two years, under one incumbent. In addition, almost all the documentation on specific cases dealt with by the High Commissioner is still confidential and inaccessible, as the Office maintains a high level of confidentiality and is not willing to provide any material on past cases to parties not involved in negotiations.[104] The High Commissioner is accountable only to the OSCE institutions and OSCE governments, hence the lack of transparency of the Office may invite accusations of political manipulation, by governments and NGOs.

Finally, the High Commissioner's activities have been regarded by some governments as one of the "success stories" of the post-Cold War CSCE process.[105] This attitude may impede a serious attempt to evaluate the impact of the Office on the protection of minorities.

The Coordination of Instruments and Mechanisms between Inter-governmental Organizations in the Area of Protection of Minorities (Council of Europe, Organization for Security and Cooperation in Europe, and the United Nations)

A direct consequence of the rapid development of various international instruments related to the protection of minorities in Europe[106] is an increased need for inter-governmental cooperation to avoid duplication of resources and mechanisms, and to facilitate effectiveness of all existing protection machinery.

Due to new developments in Eastern and Central Europe, and as a result of the geographical and political enlargement of the Council of Europe, the

European Convention on Human Rights supervisory mechanism is faced with new challenges. In addition, the OSCE Human Dimension process is faced with the challenging task of regulating and stabilizing minority relations in Europe.[107]

The two systems of protection of minorities, i.e. the European Convention and the Human Dimension of the OSCE, have established certain standards of human rights.[108] In many respects, however, with regards to both their nature and their content, they differ from each other.[109]

The main difference is that the European Convention system for the protection of minorities is an instrument of international law, and has binding force. In contrast, the Human Dimension system laid down by the OSCE is a political one.[110] As it has been observed, the OSCE system operates with greater speed and is more flexible, whereas consideration of an application by a state under the European Convention is generally a long and difficult process.[111]

There is no competition between the two systems, on the contrary, they complement each other.[112] The future developments of those systems should follow the present direction. The OSCE system should maintain its politically flexible character, whereas the European Convention should provide legal and judicial standards.[113]

In addition to the OSCE and the European Convention systems, there is cooperation between other human rights institutional systems on the European arena. Such systems include the United Nations system, the systems of protection under specific treaty instruments, and the Council of the Baltic Sea States system. The United Nations system is universal and, naturally, covers all states. Therefore, its international instruments and mechanisms are applicable where needed.

Another regional system for the protection of minorities has been created by the Council of the Baltic Sea States (CBSS). The CBSS consists of the Foreign Ministers from the ten member states and representatives of the European Union,[114] and has been operating since March of 1992. The manadate of the CBSS Commissioner on Democratic Institutions and Human Rights, is to promote and consolidate democratic development and protection of human rights, including the rights of persons belonging to minorities in the member states.[115] The office of the CBSS Commissioner would cooperate with national institutions for the protection of human rights, NGOs, the Council of Europe, the OSCE, the UN Centre for Human Rights, and other international institutions.[116]

The CBSS Commissioner will seek to avoid duplication with other international institutions, such as the UN High Commissioner on Human Rights, the OSCE High Commissioner on National Minorities, and the Council of Europe institutions.[117] One of the goals of the CBSS Commissioner is to monitor the situation of minorities outside the mandate of the OSCE High Commissioner, and to deal with issues concerning the rights of indigenous peoples in the member-states (Saami, Greenlanders, Faeroese, Karelians, and Inuit).[118]

The Role of Non-Governmental Organizations (NGOs) in the Protection of Minorities

This section examines the role of NGOs in the international protection of minorities. Historically, NGOs have played a very important role in focusing international attention on the problems of minorities. Many minorities have used the structure and position of NGOs to advance their cause in the international arena after having exhausted domestic remedies. At the present time, however, the United Nations and other international bodies are not readily accessible to many national NGOs due to a variety of reasons, including economic, structural and procedural barriers.

The threat of publicly exposing human rights abuses is still a strong weapon of NGOs, and it has served as a deterrent to stop human rights abuses in states with a record of violations.[119] Most governments try to present themselves as respecting human rights. Public exposure of the maltreatment of minorities has, in many cases, helped achieve positive results.

NGO activists have developed a large number of specific tactics: fact finding missions and reports, urgent action networks, human rights awards to activists at risk, accompaniment, and use of international procedures and arenas.[120] These methods have, in many cases, had more practical impact on minority rights than the traditional approaches of using formal international procedures.

As discussed later in this section, the present role of NGOs in the consultative process is undergoing major changes. The United Nations Economic and Social Council has created the Open Ended Working Group on the Review of Arrangements for consultations with non-governmental organizations.[121]

One of the main difficulties for international human rights activists is finding a way to utilize the important role of national and regional NGOs representing racial and ethnic minorities. Despite the existence of NGOs that focus on minority rights (i.e. the Minority Rights Group, Human Rights Watch, Amnesty International), there is a lack of coordination of efforts between locally focused NGOs and such relatively influential NGOs (mainly based in New York or Geneva). This communication problem may be the main reason for the underrepresentation of problems specific to minorities in the formal international consultative process.

Conclusion

The "ethnic revival" is one of the surprises of the last thirty years. Canada did not anticipate the reassertion of French-Canadian nationalism, neither were the violent ethnic disturbances in the former Yugoslavia and the Soviet Union expected. Nevertheless, the reappearance of well-defined, strong ethnic conflicts is a fact of life and probably will remain so until the end of this century.

An analysis of international mechanisms for the protection of minorities clearly shows that the application of the principle of non-discrimination set forth in the United Nations treaties is a complicated matter. There is no uniform solution to the specific inter-ethnic conflicts.

Contemporary governments are still strongly opposed to positive measures to protect minorities, as they fear that awarding minorities a strong political representation and legal recognition may threaten state security and stability.

At the same time, a majority of states strongly oppose any recognition of the collective rights of minorities out of fear that the granting of collective rights to minorities will cause an increase in dangerous state-minority confrontations.

The post-Cold War international political situation of the present day is far from positive towards minorities. Intolerance, xenophobia, anti-semitism, attacks on foreigners, difficult economical times, and revival of neo-Nazism are not ideal situations for promoting the rights of minorities.

The main United Nations body entrusted with the task of protecting minorities, i.e. the Sub-Commission on the Prevention of Discrimination and Protection of Minorities has, throughout its existence, completed and submitted to the Commission on Human Rights various draft definitions of a minority, but unfortunately none of these have been finally approved. It is unrealistic to think that a universal definition of a minority will be accepted by a majority of states in the near future.

Positive solutions to the enrichment of the rights of minorities would require a multi-instrumental, custom-made approach to each individual conflict situation. The fifty years of standard setting by the United Nations organs have produced some guidance for resolving ethnic conflicts, but the main work of the prevention of conflicts has yet to be completed.

The universal system of protection has failed to prevent many injustices done to minorities. The United Nations System for the Protection of Minorities is legalistic, formal and not flexible enough to accommodate many of the problems of minority protection. Despite recent cosmetic changes to the UN system (see, *UN Declaration on National Minorities*), the system remains unable to address ethnic conflicts in a timely and just manner.

The recent proposals for new international instruments for the protection of minority rights in Europe are based on the idea of equal treatment of minorities. At the same time, the rapid development in international law in the area of international protection of minorities is a result of a reoccurance of conflicts in the same geographical areas in Europe.

Notes

1. See John Packer and Kristian Myntti (eds.), *The Protection of Ethnic and Linguistic Minorities in Europe*, Åbo Akademi University, 1993, pp. 23-65.

2. F. Capotorti, Special Rapporteur, *The Study on the Rights of Persons Belonging to Ethnic, Religious, and Linguistic Minorities*, U.N. Sub-Commission on the Prevention of Discrimination and Protection of Minorities (1979), U.N. Doc. E/CN.4/Sub.2/238/Rev.1.

3. Ibid.

4. Jules Deschénes, *Proposal concerning a Definition of the Term "Minority"*, U.N. Doc. No. E/CN.4/Sub.2/1985/31 and Corr.1.

5. Supra, note 1.

6. See, H. Hannum, "Contemporary Developments in the International Protection of the Rights of Minorities", in *Notre Dame Law Review*, Vol. 66, No. 5, 1991, p. 1431.

7. Ibid.

8. See, Treaty of Osnabrück or Treaty of Oliva (1660) between Poland and Sweden.

9. Supra, note 6.

10. Supra, note 6, at p. 1432.

11. Supra, note 6, at p. 1432.

12. See, E-I, A. Daes, in, *Freedom of the Individual under Law: A study on the Individuals Duties to the Community and the Limitations on Human Rights and Freedoms under Article 29 of the Universal Declaration of Human Rights*, United Nations Publication, Sales No. E.89.XIV.5. p. 2.

13. Supra, note 6.

14. Supra, note 6.

15. Supra, note 2.

16. Ibid., p. 24, para. 124.

17. Supra, note 2, at p. 24, para. 125.

18. Supra, note 6.

19. Supra, note 6.

20. Supra, note 6.

21. Supra, note 2, at p. 24, para. 134.

22. For example by Latin American States and the United States of America.

23. See, G. Alfredsson and A. de Zayas, "Minority Rights: Protection by the United Nations", *Human Rights Law Journal*, Vol. 14, No. 1-2, p. 1-2.

24. Ibid.

25. Supra, note 23, at p. 2.

26. Supra, note 23, at p. 2.

27. See, P. Thornberry, *International Law and the Rights of Minorities*, Oxford: Clarendon Press, 1991, p. 123.

28. Ibid.

29. Supra, note 2, at p. 27.

30. Supra, note 2, at p. 27.

31. Supra, note 2, at p. 27.

32. The first progress report, UN Doc. E/CN.4/Sub.2/1991/43, the second progress report, UN Doc. E/CN.4/Sub.2/1992/37.

33. The final report entitled: "Possible ways and means of facilitating the peaceful and constructive solution of problems involving minorities" submitted by Mr. Asbiørn Eide to the Commission on Human Rights Sub-Commission on the Prevention of Discrimination and Protection of Minorities at the forty-fifth session on August 10, 1993, UN Doc. E/CN.4/Sub.2/1993/34 and add.1, 2, 3, 4.

34. UN Doc. E/CN.4/Sub.2/1993/34, p. 27, para. 124.

35. Supra, note 27.

36. Supra, note 23.

37. The Permanent Court of International Justice, the Advisory Opinion on Minority Schools in Albania 1935, Ser. A/B, No. 64.

38. See, J. Helgesen, "Protecting Minorities in the CSCE Process", in A. Rosas and J. Helgesen, eds., *The Strength of Diversity: Human Rights and Pluralist Democracy* (Dordrecht: Martinus Nijhoff Publishers, 1992) p. 161.

39. Supra, note 23.

40. Article 27, International Covenant of Civil and Political Rights (New York, 1966), *Human rights in International Law, Basic Texts*, Council of Europe, (Strassbourg, 1985) at p. 38.

41. Supra, note 23.

42. See, United Nations Human Rights Committee (UN-HRCee), General Comment No. 23(50) on Article 27/Minority rights, adopted by the Committee at its 1314 meeting (fiftieth session) on April 6, 1994, UN Doc. CCPR/C/21/Rev.1/Add.5, adopted under Article 40, paragraph 4 of the International Covenant on Civil and Political Rights.

43. Ibid.

44. Supra, note 2, at p. 28.

45. Supra, note 2, at p. 28.

46. See, *Council of Europe: Achievements and Activities*, published by the Directorate of Information of the Council of Europe, August 1992, p. 1.

47. Resolution (75) 13, Containing Recommendations on the Social Situation of Nomads in Europe, adopted by the Committee of Ministers on May 22, 1975 at the 245th meeting of the Ministers' Deputies of the Council of Europe.

48. See, Council of Europe Information Document No. CDMG(94) 15, *Council of Europe Activities Concerning Roma, Gypsies and Travelers*, Strasbourg, August 19, 1994, p. 7.

49. Recommendation No. R (92) 10 on The Implementation of Persons belonging to National Minorities, adopted By the Committee of Ministers on May 21, 1992, at the 476th meeting of the Ministers' Deputies.

50. Supra, note 48, at p. 7.

51. The European Charter for regional or Minority Languages, The Committee of Ministers decision on 91st Session on November 5, 1992.

52. Supra, note 48, at p. 7-8.

53. Supra, note 48, at p. 7-8.

54. Recommendation 1203 (1993) on Gypsies in Europe, adopted by the Parliamentary Assembly on February, 2 1993, (44th Ordinary Session - 4th part, 1-5 February 1993).

55. Supra, note 48, at p. 7-8.

56. Supra, note 54.

57. Supra, note 48, at p. 8.

58. See, H. Klebes, "Introduction to the Draft Protocol on Minority Rights to the ECHR, adopted by the Parliamentary Assembly of the Council of Europe in Recommendation No. 1201 (1993)", in *Human Rights Law Journal*, Vol. 14, No. 3-4, 1993, p. 142.

59. S. Breitenmoser and D. Richter, *Proposal for an Additional Protocol to the European Convention on Human Rights Concerning the Protection of Minorities in the Participating States of the CSCE, Draft Protocol on Minority Rights to the ECHR*, adopted by the Parliamentary Assembly; a draft of a European Convention for the Protection of Minorities presented on Februar 8, 1991, by the Commission for Democracy through Law (Venice Commission).

60. See, Article 3, para. 2 of the framework Convention (CPNM).

61. Section I contains provisions which, in a general fashion, stipulate certain fundamental principles which may serve to elucidate the other substantive provisions of the framework Convention; Section II contains a catalogue of specific principles; Section III contains various provisions concerning the interpretation and application of the framework Convention. Section IV contains provisions on the monitoring of the implementation of the framework Convention. Section V contains the final clauses which are based on the model final clauses for conventions and agreements concluded within the Council of Europe.

62. UN Declaration on Minority Rights, UN Doc./G.A. Res. 47/135, Dec. 1992, Annex, adopted by the General Assembly on December 18, 1992.

63. See, *Framework Convention for the Protection of National Minorities and Explanatory Report*, Council of Europe Press, 1995, p. 23.

64. Ibid., at p. 24.

65. Supra, note 63, at p. 24.

66. See, text of the Preamble of the CPNM, para. 12.

67. Supra, note 63, at p. 6.

68. Supra, note 63, at p. 25.

69. See, Article 1 of the CPNM.

70. Supra, note 63, at p. 24.

71. See, art. 3, para. 2, of the framework Convention (CPNM).

72. Supra, note 63, at p. 25.

73. Supra, note 63, at p. 27.

74. Supra, note 63, at p. 27.

75. Supra, note 63, at p. 39.

76. Supra, note 63, at p. 28.

77. Supra, note 63, at p. 8.

78. Supra, note 63, at p. 29.

79. Supra, note 63, at p. 28.

80. Supra, note 63, at p. 12.

81. Supra, note 59.

82. From the last CSCE Summit Meeting in December 1994, in Budapest, the Conference has changed name to the Organization for Security and Cooperation in Europe (OSCE), effective on January 1, 1995.

83. See, CSCE, the Charter of Paris for A New Europe, Paris 1990.

84. See, the OSCE Secretariat, Department for Chairman-In-Office Support, Press Release, No. 19/95, March 20, 1995.

85. See, speech of the Secretary General of the OSCE Dr. W. Hoynck to the German Society for Foreign Policy and the German Atlantic Society, entitled: "Contributions of the OSCE to the New Stability", Bonn, January 26, 1995, p. 5.

86. Ibid.

87. Documentation, Conference on Security and Cooperation in Europe (CSCE), Helsinki Document 1992, "The Challenges of Change", in *Human Rights Law Journal*, Vol. 13, No. 7-8, at p. 288.

88. Supra, note 85, at p. 13.

89. See, the Code of Conduct on Politico-Military Aspects of Security in CSCE Budapest Document 1994, *Towards a Genuine Partnership in a New Era*, part V.

90. See, CSCE Budapest Document 1994, *Towards a Genuine Partnership in a New Era*.

91. Supra note 89, part V, para. 36.

92. Supra, note 87, at p. 288.

93. Ibid., at p. 289.

94. Chapter 2, supra, note 87, at p. 289.

95. Chapter 2, papa. 5(b), supra, note 87, at p. 290.

96. Chapter 2, para. 5(c), supra, note 87, at p. 290.

97. Chapter 2, paras. 11, 12, 13, 14, 15, supra, note 87, at p. 290.

98. Chapter 2, para. 16, supra, note 87, at p. 290.

99. See, Recommendations by the CSCE High Commissioner on National Minorities, Mr. Max van der Stoel, upon his visits to Estonia, Latvia and Lithuania, HCNM Doc. No. 206/93/L/Rev., in *Human Rights Law Journal*, Vol. 14, No. 5-6, pp. 216-221.

100. Mr. Max van der Stoel, formerly the Netherlands' Foreign Minister and Permanent Representative to the UN, was appointed CSCE High Commissioner effective January 1, 1993.

101. Supra, note 99, at p. 217.

102. See, Key-Note Address of Mr. Max van der Stoel, CSCE High Commissioner on National Minorities, to the Human Dimension Seminar Case Studies on National Minorities Issues: Positive Results, Warsaw, 24-28 May, 1993, in *ODIHR Bulletin CSCE*, Vol. 1, No. 3.

103. Ibid.

104. The author of this work enquired at the Office of the OSCE High Commissioner on National Minorities (HCNM) on the issue of access to information on work of the HCNM, and received the following response from the Office of the HCNM: "It is not possible to send documentation which NGOs provided to the High Commissioner. Confidentiality is a fundamental principle underlying the mandate of the HCNM, and we wish to apply that principle in the strictest possible terms." Dated March 28, 1995.

105. See, A. Bloed, "The CSCE Conflict Prevention Mechanisms and Procedures", in *ODIHR Bulletin CSCE*, p. 32.

106. Namely, the *Framework Convention for the Protection of National Minorities*; the *Helsinki Summit Declaration*, CSCE Helsinki Document 1992, "The Challenges of Change"; the Convention for the Protection of Human Rights and Fundamental Freedoms (ECHR).

107. See, Report of the Advisory Committee on Human Rights and Foreign Policy, *Democracy and Human Rights in Eastern Europe*, (1990), No. 11, p. 24.

108. Ibid.

109. Supra, note 107, at p. 25.

110. Supra, note 107, at p. 25.

111. Supra, note 107, at p. 26.

112. Supra, note 107, at p. 27.

113. Supra, note 107, at p. 27.

114. See, un-published speech by N. Mikkelsen, assistant to the Commissioner of the CBSS, Role of the Commissioner of the CBSS, presented in Postdam at

December 1994, p. 1.

115. Member states are: Denmark, Estonia, Germany, Latvia, Lithuania, Norway, Poland, Russia, Sweden, and the European Commission.

116. Supra, note 114, at p. 2.

117. Supra, note 114, at p. 3.

118. Supra, note 114, at p. 4.

119. See, Laurie S. Wiseberg, "Protecting Human Rights Activists and NGOs", *Human Rights Quarterly*, Vol. 13, 1991, p. 531.

120. Ibid., at p. 534.

121. See, M.H. Prosner and C. Whittome, "Status of Human Rights NGOs", *Columbia Human Rights Law Review*, Vol. 25, No. 2, Spring 1994, p. 275.

Select Bibliography

Buergenthal, T., R. Norris, and D. Shelton. 1986. *Protecting Human Rights in the Americas, Selected problems.* Kehl, Strasbourg, Arlington: N.P. Engel Publisher.

Cassese, Antonio. 1986. *International Law in a Divided World*, Oxford: Clarendon Press.)

Cassese, Antonio, ed. 1979. *UN Law/Fundamental Rights. Two Topics in International Law.* Sijthoff & Noordhoff International Publishers BV.

Cotler, Irwin & Pearl F. Eliadis, eds. 1992. *International Human Rights Law, Theory and Practice.* Montreal: The Canadian Human Rights Foundation.

Dinstein, Y. 1981. *Models of Autonomy.* Faculty of Law, Tel Aviv University, Transaction Books.

Drzemczewski, Andrew Z. 1983. *European Human Rights Convention in Domestic Law.* Oxford: Clarendon Press.

Fawcett, J.E.S. 1969. *Application of the European Convention on Human Rights*. Oxford: Clarendon Press.

Hannum, Hurst. 1993. *Documents on Autonomy and Minority Rights*. Dordrecht: Martinus Nijhoff Publishers.

Hannum, Hurst. 1990. *Autonomy, Sovereignty, and Self-Determination: The Accommodation of Conflicting Rights*. Philadelphia: University of Pennsylvania Press.

Ignatieff, M.. 1993. *Blood and Belonging: Journeys into The New Nationalism*. New York: Farrar, Strauss and Giroux.

Lauterpacht, H. 1973. *International Law and Human Rights*. New York and London: Garland Publishing Inc.

Lerner, N. 1991. *Group Rights and Discrimination in International Law*. Dordrecht: Martinus Nijhoff.

Lutz, Ellen L., H. Hannum, K.J. Burke. 1989. *New Directions in Human Rights*. Philadelphia: University of Pennsylvania Press.

McKean, W. 1983. *Equality and Discrimination under International Law*. Oxford: Clarendon Press.

Newman, Frank and David Weissbrodt. 1990. *International Human Rights: Law, Policy, and Process*. Cincinatti: Anderson Publishing Co.

Packer, John and Kristian Myntti, eds. 1993. *The Protection of Ethnic and Linguistic Minorities in Europe*. Institute for Human Rights. Åbo: Åbo Akademi University.

Petzold, Herbert. 1984. *The European Convention on Human Rights: Cases and Materials*. Köln, Berlin, Bonn, München: Carl Heymanns Verlag KG.

Pomerance, Michla. 1982. *Self-Determination in Law and Practice: The New Doctrine in the United Nations*. The Hague, Boston, London: Martinus Nijhoff Publishers.

Robertson, A.H. 1972. *Human Rights in the World*. Manchester: Manchester University Press.

Rosas A. and J. Helgesen, eds. 1992. *The Strength of Diversity: Human Rights and Pluralist Democracy*. Dordrecht: Martinus Nijhoff Publishers.

Sigler, J.A. 1983. *Minority Rights, A Comparative Analysis*, Westport, Connecticut: Greenwood Press.

Sohn, Louis B. and Thomas Buergenthal. 1973. *International Protection of Human Rights*. New York: Bobbs-Merrill Co.

Thornberry, Patrick. 1991. *International Law and the Rights of Minorities*. Oxford: Clarendon Press.

Wirsing, Robert G. 1981. *Protection of Ethnic Minorities: Comparative Perspectives*. Oxford: Pergamon Press.

Withaker, Ben. 1984. *Minorities: A Question of Human Rights?* Oxford: Pergamon Press.

Vierdag, E.W. 1973. *The Concept of Discrimination in International Law*. The Hague: Martinus Nijhoff.

CSCE (OSCE) Documents:

CSCE, Conference on Security and Co-operation in Europe, Final Act, Helsinki, 1975.

CSCE, Concluding Document of the Belgrade Meeting, 1977.

CSCE, Concluding Document of the Madrid Meeting, 1983.

CSCE, the Charter of Paris for A New Europe, Paris 1990.

CSCE, Document of The Copenhagen Meeting of The Conference on The Human Dimension of The CSCE, Copenhagen, 1990.

CSCE, the Document of the Moscow Meeting of the Conference on the Human Dimension of the CSCE, Moscow, 1991.

CSCE, the Report of the CSCE Meeting of Experts on National Minorities, Geneva, July 19, 1991.

CSCE, the Copenhagen Document, Challenged of Change, 1992.

CSCE, the Budapest Document, 1994, Towards a Genuine Partnership in a New Era.

Council of Europe Documents:

Council of Europe Information Document No. CDMG(94) 15, *Council of Europe Activities Concerning Roma, Gypsies and Travelers*, Strasbourg, August 19, 1994.

United Nations Documents:

Capotorti, F., Special Rapporteur, U.N. Sub-Commission on Prevention of Discrimination and Protection of Minorities (1979), *The Study on the Rights of Persons Belonging to Ethnic, Religious, and Linguistic Minorities*, U.N. Doc. E/CN.4/Sub.2/238/Rev.1

Daes, E-I. A., in, *Freedom of the Individual under Law: A study on the Individual's Duties to the Community and the Limitations on Human Rights and Freedoms under Article 29 of the Universal Declaration of Human Rights*, United Nations Publication, Sales No. E.89.XIV.5.

Deschenes, J., *Proposal concerning a Definition of the Term "Minority"*, U.N. Doc. E/Cn.4/Sub.2/1985/31 and Corr.1.

Eide, A., United Nations, Sub-Commission on Prevention of Discrimination and Protection of Minorities Report: *Possible Ways and Means of Facilitating the Peaceful and Constructive Solution of Problems Involving Minorities*, U.N. Doc. E/CN.4 /Sub.2/1990/46, of July 20, 1990.

United Nations, *United Nations Action in the Field of Human Rights*, (New York, 1983.)

United Nations Human Rights Committee, *General Comment No. 23(50) on Article 27/ Minority rights*, adopted by the Committee at its 1314 meeting (fiftieth session) on April 6, 1994, UN Doc. CCPR/C/21/Rev.1/Add.5

United Nations Declaration On the Rights of Persons Belonging to National or Ethnic, Religious or Linguistic Minorities, U.N. Doc. E/CN.4/Sub.2/1991/40 Rev.1:, December 12, 1991.

Articles and Reports:

Alfredsson, G. and A. de Zayas. "Minority Rights: Protection by the United Nations". *Human Rights Law Journal* Vol. 14, No. 1-2.

Barsh, Russel L. 1993. "Indigenous Peoples & Minorities: Present Status and Future Directions". *Human Rights Tribune*, Vol. 2, No. 1.

Bruegel, J.W. 1971. "A Neglected Field: The Protection of Minorities". *Human Rights Journal*, Vol. 4.

Capotorti, F. "Are Minorities Entitled to Collective International Rights?" in Yoram Dinstein and Mala Tabory, eds., *The Protection of Minorities and Human Rights*. Dordrecht: M. Nijhoff, 1992.

Comeau, Pauline. 1994. "Mood is Positive as the UN Begins Review of NGO Status." *Human Rights Tribune*, Vol. 2, No. 4, pp. 24-26.

Drzemczewski, Andrew. 1987. "The Role of NGOs in Human Rights Matters in the Council of Europe". *Human Rights Law Journal*, Vol. 8, No. 2-4.

Drzemczewski, A., and Jens Mejer-Ladewig. 1994. "Principal Characteristics of the New ECHR Control Mechanism, as Established by Protocol No. 11, Signed on 11 May 1994". *Human Rights Law Journal*, Vol. 15, No. 3.

Dinstein, Y. 1976. "Collective Human Rights of Peoples and Minorities". *The International and Comparative Law Quarterly*, Vol. 25.

Eide, A. 1987. "Internal Conflict under International Law: Focus on Ethnic Conflict, Minority Rights and Human Rights". *Bulletin of Peace Proposals*, vol. 18.

Helgesen, J. 1992. "Protecting Minorities in the Conference on Security and Co-operation in Europe (CSCE) Process", in A. Rosas and J. Helgesen, eds., *The Strength of Diversity: Human Rights and Pluralist Democracy.* Dordrecht: Martinus Nijhoff Publishers.

Lerner, N. 1988. "From Protection of of Minorities to Group Rights". *Israel Yearbook of Human Rights*, vol. 18.

Nowak, M. 1993. "The Right of Self-Determination and Protection of Minorities in Central and Eastern Europe in Light of the Case-law of the Human Rights Committee". *International Journal on Group Rights*, Vol. 1.

Pestieau, J. 1991. "Minority Rights: Caught Between Individual Rights and Peoples' Rights", *The Canadian Journal of Law and Jurisprudence*, Vol. IV, No. 2.

Prosner, Michael H. and Candy Whittome. 1994. "The Status of Human Rights NGOs". *Columbia Human Rights Law Reviev*, Vol. 25, No. 2.

Rodley, N.S. 1995. "Conceptual Problems in the Protection of Minorities: International Legal Developments". *Human Rights Quarterly*, Vol. 17, No. 1.

Thornberry, P. 1989. "Self-determination, Minorities, Human Rights: A Review of International Instruments". *International & Comparative Law Quarterly*, Vol. 38.

Wiseberg, Laurie S.1991. "Protecting Human Rights Activists and NGOs", *Human Rights Quarterly*, Vol. 13.

Human Rights Research from an East & Southeast Asian Perspective

LUO YANHUA

I.

With the end of the Cold War, international politics entered a new era. In trying to sketch out a rational blue-print for the post-Cold War international political structure, scholars from many countries have come up with various theories. Among them, the theory of a "clash of civilizations", put forward by Professor Huntington of Harvard University, has provoked much discussion. Professor Huntington points out in his theory that "[t]he great divisions among humankind and the dominating source of conflict will be cultural."[1] His theory has caused much controversy. Many scholars think that Huntington is putting undue emphasis on the impact of cultural conflict. Nevertheless, although there are many different opinions about the impact of cultural conflict, people have to admit that the point about cultural conflict raised by Huntington "...has its own reason, it is not totally groundless."[2] After the Cold War, many nations are attempting to strengthen national unity by emphasizing their own traditional culture and resisting the influx of foreign cultures. In addition, the influence of traditional cultures on international relations is becoming stronger. Sometimes, conflicts between cultures might even develop into the central issue of an international political conflict. A good example is the post-Cold War disagreement about human rights issues between Western countries and Third World countries, especially Asian countries. Huntington also addressed this point in his article:

> Basically speaking, the Western point of view is fundamentally different from that of other civilizations. Western ideas of individualism, liberalism, constitutionalism, human rights, equality, liberty, the rule of law, democracy, free markets, the separation of church and state, often have little resonance in Islamic, Confucian, Japanese, Hindu, Buddhist or Orthodox cultures.[3]

Thus, the deeper issues of civilization or cultural background have already become important and influential factors in contemporary international relations.

In the escalating conflict concerning human rights issues between Third World countries and Western countries, the manifestations of East and Southeast

Asian countries are drawing worldwide attention. Unlike in the past, East and Southeast Asian countries are now expressing themselves actively on the international stage. By using different international theories they boldly expound their own standpoints on the human rights issue. The confidence expressed by these countries in their sense of culture and worth is obviously closely connected to their great success in the area of economic development. After the 1960s, when the economic miracle of Japan took the world by surprise, the economies of the "four small Asian dragons" (Singapore, Taiwan, South Korea and Hong Kong) soared. In the 1980s, not only did Thailand, Malaysia and Indonesia rouse themselves to catch up and become new "dragons", but the economy of China also entered a period of rapid growth after the implementation of the reform and open-door policies. Particularly noteworthy are the 1990s because as the world economy entered into a recession, the economies of East Asia continued to thrive at a growth rate of 6-8%. All of this has caused the world to view the region with new eyes. The success of the East Asian development model has forced the West to offer a certain degree of affirmation to the culture, values and social mechanisms that formed the model. Thus, the countries of the region have become even more confident in their own cultures. As one Singaporean diplomat pointed out:

> Economic success has engendered a greater cultural self-confidence. Whatever their differences, East and Southeast Asian countries are increasingly conscious of their own civilizations and have (like some Western scholars) tended to locate the sources of their success in what is regarded as distinctive about their own traditions and institutions.[4]

Such confidence in one's own culture can influence a country's, a nation's or a whole region's opinion about many things. The world has always been a pluralistic mixture of cultures, and now, with the awakening of all kinds of cultures, the situation of an extremely conceited Western culture is slowly changing.

As a concept which explains the relationship between the individual and the state, the individual and the group, rights and obligations, and various other social relations, human rights "...touch upon extraordinarily delicate matters of culture and values."[5] Because of people's different cultural backgrounds, it is natural that their opinions on human rights are different, as well. So what exactly is East and Southeast Asia's perception of human rights? How does the unique cultural background, historical tradition and other social conditions of this region influence the formation of perceptions on human rights? These are the questions that will be discussed in this essay.

II.

Everyone knows that, within the large area of East and South East Asia, from Japan to Burma, the specific conditions of each country differ greatly. Because of the different cultural traditions, political structures and development levels, it is unrealistic to think that a single human rights perception exists which encompasses Confucianism, Buddhism, Islam, Indian religions, and other cultural traditions and which is accepted in all countries, regardless of their level of development. No wonder that in the vast region of East and Southeast Asia, people still argue over whether or not a common perception of human rights exists, despite the fact that they usually share a consensus within the Association of South East Asian Nations (ASEAN). While noticing these differences, however, we should also realize that it is only natural for countries of this region to stick together when debating human rights in the international arena. They hold many of the same or similar opinions, especially when it comes to issues about which they disagree with the West. As one Singaporean diplomat pointed out: "What is clear is that there is general discontent throughout the region with a purely Western interpretation of human rights."[6] Therefore, in discussing human rights from an East and Southeast Asian perspective, this essay will only address views on human rights issues which are representative and which are commonly accepted within the governments of the region. The main views of the countries in this region include:

1. Recognizing that human rights is a shared ideal for which people all over the world are fighting, and that every country has an obligation to promote and protect human rights.

The 1991 White Book on human rights, entitled "Human Rights in China", states: "Full enjoyment of human rights is an ideal which humanity has been pursuing for a long time."[7] South Korea believes: "Human rights is the ultimate goal which humanity will come to treasure and pursue."[8] The *Kuala Lumpur Declaration on Human Rights*, adopted by the semi-official ASEAN Inter-Parliamentary Organization in September 1993, points out that, "[i]t is the task and responsibility of every member state and every citizen to ensure the promotion, implementation and protection of human rights."[9] All the countries in this region are signatory states to the *United Nations Charter* and the *Universal Declaration of Human Rights*. Countries from the Asian region have played an important role and made undeniable contributions, such as the 1948 *Universal Declaration of Human Rights*, the 1968 Teheran World Human Rights conference and the *Teheran Proclamation*, the March 1993 Asian

Regional Preparatory Meeting, the World Conference on human rights and the *Bangkok Declaration*, the June 1993 Vienna World Conference on Human Rights and the *Vienna Declaration and Programme of Action*. All these Declarations further emphasize the above opinions.

2. Emphasizing that although human rights are in essence universal, in realizing them one must still pay due attention to the complexity and diversity of every country's specific culture, history and level of economic development. It is exactly such complexity and diversity that causes different countries and regions to understand human rights in different ways.

    In this respect, China believes that

    ...in emphasizing the universal principle of human rights one must integrate the specific situation of every country. ... Because of the difference in historical background, cultural tradition and social and economic development, each country's approach to realizing the universal principle of human rights may vary, from content to form, from method to move. It is impossible to ask different countries to use the same model and the same measure.[10]

    Malaysia comments: "As the world has numerous communities and the state of their development differs widely, it is only natural to expect that their concepts of human rights, of justice, and of obligation to the community differ and differ widely."[11] The ASEAN countries, being rather active in the human rights field, clearly state in the June 1991 "Joint Communiqué of the 24th ASEAN Ministerial Meeting" that, "...while human rights are universal in character, implementation in the national context should remain within the competence and responsibility of each country, having regard for the complex variety of economic, social and cultural realities."[12] The Communiqués of the 25th and 26th ASEAN Ministerial Meetings further emphasized this point. In June 1992, the ASEAN Institute for Strategic and International Studies (ISIS), composed by several brain trusts from ASEAN member countries, forwarded a report to the 25th ASEAN Ministerial Meeting. In this report, the ASEAN outlines eight principles on human rights policy, the second principle being the "Principle of Situational Uniqueness". This principle reads:

    In pursuing human rights in their comprehensive entirety, the ASEAN countries--as indeed all countries of the world--will be guided by the consideration of the unique blend of factors that condition and constitute each country's total environment, namely its history, demography, culture, economic condition, social situation and political evolution.[13]

Other East Asian countries such as North Korea also believe: "When dealing with human rights issues, it is important to integrate the history, cultural characteristic and stage of development of that region or country."[14] South Korea states: "In the process of promoting and protecting human rights, one must pay attention to the various regional and national factors."[15]

3. Believing that a country's right to independence and a nationality's right to self-determination are the necessary requirements and basic prerequisites to the full realization of human rights. The full realization of individual human rights and basic human rights can only be guaranteed by respecting each nation's right to self-determination in choosing their political system, economic model and path of development.

In this regard, China asserts:

According to the *United Nations Charter* and the principles of international law, every country has the right to choose its own political system, path of development and value system, and no other country has the right to interfere. ... A country's right to sovereignty is the foundation on which to realize the human rights of its citizens.[16]

The third chapter of the ASEAN *Kuala Lumpur Declaration on Human Rights* reads: "Every one has the right to self-determination. According to this right, people are free to choose their political status and to pursue economic, social, political and cultural progress." Burma also believes that "the best way that the international society can help us is by abstaining from any kind of interference or pressure, and by letting the Burmese people move forward along their own path to realize the goal of freely choosing a free and democratic society."[17]

At the same time, these countries also oppose using a nationality's right to self-determination to destroy a state's right to sovereignty, an intact territory and political independence.

4. Believing that interpreting and realizing human rights is within each country's jurisdiction and responsibility. No country may use human rights problems to interfere in other countries' internal affairs.

China consistently maintains that human rights issues come under the domestic jurisdiction and are the responsibility of the individual country. Respecting a country's right to sovereignty and not interfering with its internal affairs are commonly recognized principles of international law. They apply to all other areas of international relations, and should naturally also apply to the issues of human rights.[18]

Vietnam also believes: "...the human rights of a given nation is the work of that nation and the responsibility for the promotion of human rights in a state rests primarily with that state." Vietnam supports respect for human rights but is against any country interfering in other countries' internal affairs.[19]

The communiqué of the 24th and 25th ASEAN Ministerial Meeting also emphasizes that interpretation and realization of human rights come under the individual country's jurisdiction and responsibility, and realization of human rights should not violate a nation's right to sovereignty. Chapter 5 of the ASEAN *Kuala Lumpur Declaration on Human Rights* further points out that "universal promotion and protection of human rights should be carried out through international cooperation based on the principle of respecting national sovereignty, territorial integrity and non-interference into other countries' internal affairs."

5.   These countries believe that the people's right to subsistence and the right to development are the most basic and important human rights for developing countries.

China is of the opinion that "[t]he principal human rights for a nation are the right to subsistence and the right to development."[20] North Korea believes that "...according to the present reality, a developing country should first consider realization of the right to subsistence and the right to development..."[21]

Meanwhile, lack of economic development and resulting poverty and starvation are the main obstacles for many developing countries to realize human rights. Thus, only through development and elimination of poverty can basic human rights be guaranteed. And, "...guaranteeing development of a nation, peaceful and comfortable lives and enjoyment of basic human rights for all its citizens, is only possible by maintaining justice, order and stability in the state and in society."[22]

Besides creating a favourable domestic environment for development, these countries also believe that an unequitable international economic order is the main obstacle for developing countries to realize their right to development. Therefore, in order to promote human rights, it is necessary to establish a new international economic order. China calls for "...the international community to work hard at establishing a new, fair and equitable international economic order, and create a favourable international economic environment for developing countries to develop their economies."[23]

North Korea maintains:

At the present, the problems of poverty, disease, a heavy debt burden and unfair international economic and trade relations which threaten developing countries, not only prove a major obstacle for the people of these countries to enjoyment of the right to subsistence and the right to development, but also prevent them from achieving political rights. ... Without delay, the international community should create a new international environment and take action to realize developing countries' right to subsistence and right to development.[24]

Indonesia believes: "Efforts to establish a universal standard of international human rights should go hand in hand with efforts to establish a just and a fair international economic order."[25]

6. On the issue about the relationship between human rights and development, believing that economic development is a prerequisite for the realization of human rights.

China asserts that "[t]he fundamental path to realizing democracy, freedom and human rights in a country goes through progress and stability in society, and economic development."[26] South Korea believes: "Without security and economic development, human rights cannot be genuine. Without attaining a certain level of economic prosperity, democracy and human rights also cannot be perfected. So it cannot be denied that there is a close linkage between human rights and development."[27]

Indonesia points out: "The preservation and promotion of human rights cannot be separated from economic and social development as it is meaningless to talk about political freedom under the extremely heavy burden of poverty, backwardness and disease."[28]

And in Singapore's experience, "...economic development is a necessary foundation for any system which claims that it can raise the dignity of human beings, and order and stability are the basis for development."[29]

7. As the countries in this region agree about the relationship between human rights and development, they are beginning to advocate the idea of "a good government" (hao zhengfu). They believe that, only a good government can guarantee economic development, raising of the living standard and full realization of human rights.

Singapore's Cabinet Advisor Lee Kuan-Yew (Li Guanghui) is the main proponent of the idea of a "good government." He points out that "...although democracy and human rights are admirable concepts, we should nevertheless understand that the real goal is a good government. People in every country need a good government. A country must first develop its economy, then democracy may follow." His definition of a "good government" is

...a government which is honest, effective and efficient in protecting its people and allowing opportunities for all to advance themselves in a stable and orderly society where they can live a good life and raise their children to do better than themselves.[30]

The idea of a "good government" is very popular in Malaysia. The slogan for the present government is "honest and upright, efficient and trustworthy."[31] The idea of a "good government" has received positive feed-back in this region.

Although each country has its own definition of a "good government" because of each country's unique situation, almost all countries in the region emphasize a government's authority, and a government's role in developing society and promoting human rights, and they see society's development and prosperity as the goal for a government's efforts. In Indonesia, for example, President Suharto emphasizes that "[t]he ultimate responsibility for upholding human rights in a nation state rests with the government of the country concerned." With respect to the government of Indonesia, four tasks have been clearly outlined: "Protection of all the people of Indonesia and the entire Indonesian territory, progress in overall welfare, enlightenment of the people and participation in the establishment of an orderly world based on independence and eternal peace."[32]

Malaysia further emphasizes a strong government. Mahathir thinks:

Developed countries can do with weak governments or no governments. But developing countries cannot function without authoritarian governments. Unstable and weak governments will result in chaos, and chaos cannot contribute to the development and well-being of developing countries.[33]

These countries further advocate that allocation of economic aid from Western countries should be based on whether or not the recipient country's government is a "good government" and whether or not it is engaging in social development. Allocation of economic aid should not be based on a country's human rights situation. Lee Kuan-Yew (Li Guanghui) points out that countries should be measured against the characteristics of a good government, not against democratic form. A good government "...should be the criteria for official development aid."[34] China also believes:

> The key standard against which to measure and inspect the human rights situation of a developing country should be whether or not its policies and actions are favourable to economic and social development, and whether or not they are favourable to solving the problem of feeding and clothing its people and raising their welfare and standard of living.[35]

8. Believing that the development and perfection of human rights in every country is a historical process, and that it evolves through internal forces only.

In this regard, China indicates that:

> [h]uman rights are manifested in a historical process. All countries without exception are part of this process. A country's human rights situation will inevitably be conditioned by the degree of social development in that country and, at the same time, it will continuously improve in the wake of social development and a deeper understanding of human rights...[36]

Lee Kuan-Yew advocates: "Greater respect for human rights is a worthwhile objective. The only practical way forward is to proceed step by step."[37] Thailand's Prime Minister Chuan Leekpai points out: "Human rights should evolve at their own pace if they are to be peaceful and sustainable" and "[c]hanges to human rights must emerge primarily from within and not be imposed from the outside."[38] The ASEAN *Kuala Lumpur Declaration on Human Rights* also notes that

> ...people in ASEAN countries accept the notion that human rights exist within a process of development and evolution, and that all countries have their own inherent historical experience and transforming

economies, societies, political and cultural realities and value systems, and all of these should be taken into consideration.

9. While emphasizing the right of the individual, these countries also emphasize the individual's obligation to society.

Western countries generally emphasize the rights of the individual. The individual's obligation to society tends to be overlooked. East Asian and South East Asian countries believe that rights and obligations are closely connected. The constitutions of these countries all have specific regulations concerning the basic rights and obligations of citizens. The Third Chapter of the ASEAN *Kuala Lumpur Declaration on Human Rights* specifically addresses the basic rights and obligations of member countries and their citizens. The *Declaration* also states that "[p]eople of the ASEAN countries recognize that there are two equally important aspects to human rights: the individual's rights and freedom, and the individual's obligations to society and to the state."

Meanwhile, with regards to the relationship between individual rights and interests and collective rights and interests, these countries believe that there should be a balance between the two, that is, exercise of the former should not interfere with the latter. Article 51 of the Chinese Constitution stipulates: "When citizens exercise their freedoms and rights, they should not violate the interests of the state, society and the collective, nor should they violate the rights and freedom of other citizens."[39] China also contends that "[i]t is very important that the interests of the individual should correspond with the interests of the public. Only through advancement of the whole society can true democracy, freedom and human rights be realized for the individual."[40]

Indonesia believes:

The realization of human rights includes the demand to keep a balanced relationship between the human rights of individuals and their obligation to society. Without such a balanced relationship, the rights and interests of society as a whole could be denied... In Indonesia, like in other developing countries, there is a balanced relationship between the rights and interests of the individual and the rights and interests of society. In other words, individual rights and interests are balanced in relation to respect for other people's rights and interests and in relation to the individual's obligations to society and state. Indonesia's culture and its ancient, relatively well-developed customary law have traditionally always emphasized the rights and interests of society and state but, at the same time, they do not neglect the rights and interests of individuals or groups. ... In Indonesia, and perhaps also in other developing countries, we could not possibly approach the human rights issue from a purely individualistic point of view because we could not neglect the interests of our society and state.[41]

And Mahathir points out: "ASEAN countries put special emphasis on trying to preserve a balance between individual rights and the needs of society as a whole in order to maintain political stability."[42] In this regard, the First Chapter of the ASEAN *Kuala Lumpur Declaration on Human Rights* provides that "...freedom, progress and a nation's stability can be achieved through balancing the rights of the individual with the interests of society."

10. Economic, social and cultural rights and civil and political rights are inter-dependent and should not be separated but be paid the same amount of attention.

China believes: "Human rights is a complete concept which includes individual rights and collective rights. Under individual rights are included civil and political rights as well as economic, social and cultural rights. All aspects of human rights are inter-related and cannot be separated or neglected."[43] The Joint Communiqué of the 26th ASEAN Ministerial Meeting noted that "[h]uman rights are inter-connected and cannot be separated, they include civil, political, economic, social and cultural rights. These rights are equally important. They should be demonstrated in a balanced and inter-connected way..." Among the eight principles drawn up by the ASEAN ISIS, this one is referred to as "the principle of comprehensiveness", and it reads that the ASEAN countries believe that all dimensions of human rights--economic, social, cultural, civil and political--should be improved and promoted. Equal importance should be afforded to the pursuit of economic, social and cultural rights as to the pursuit of civil and political rights.[44] These countries strongly oppose the tendency of some countries to select certain aspects of human rights based on political motives, and to neglect economic, social and cultural rights which relate directly to guaranteeing the basics of life for humanity. They believe that this practice of dividing the concept of human rights should be relinquished. In this regard, South Korea's former Foreign Minister Jeong Woo Kil (Han Shengzhou) states: "Human rights are universal, indivisible and interdependent. They cannot be altered according to circumstances. It is neither justifiable nor appropriate to deny some human rights in order to guarantee others..."[45] Indonesia is also of the opinion that "[a] unified and balanced way should be found to promote and protect these rights, and it is entirely wrong to emphasize only one kind of rights and neglect other kinds of rights."[46]

11. These countries oppose the practice of linking human rights to economic assistance, they oppose politicising human rights issues and they oppose adopting a double standard in realizing human rights.

The ASEAN is very firm on these issues. In 1991, the ASEAN firmly opposed the attempt by the European Union (EU) to include human rights issues in the new ASEAN-EU cooperative agreement. In 1992, the Joint Communiqué of the 25th ASEAN Ministerial Meeting clearly asserted: "Concern about environmental and human rights issues should not become a condition for economic and development cooperation." China was also of the opinion that, "...to make human rights a condition for providing international economic aid and engaging in international economic and development cooperation is not only unrealistic but basically impossible."[47]

On one occasion, Indonesia persistently refused the request of the Dutch Minister of Development Aid to exchange human rights for economic aid. Indonesia would rather have given up economic aid than yielded to the pressure from the Netherlands on the issue of democracy and human rights:

> Indonesia cannot accept the practice of linking human rights issues with economic and development cooperation, thereby turning the realization of human rights into a political condition for such cooperation. Such a link between human rights and economic cooperation can only damage both issues.[48] Unfortunately, human rights issues are often mistakenly used to rationalize various politically motivated activities which do not at all stem from a true concern for human rights.[49]

North Korea believes: "The phenomenon of neglecting the critical situation of developing countries' right to subsistence and development, and of setting up political conditions for economic assistance under the excuse of internationalization of human rights, should be stopped."[50]

The Communiqué of the 26th ASEAN Ministerial Meeting emphasized: "Promoting and protecting human rights should not be politicised." "The politicisation of human rights will inevitably lead to differential treatment and application of double standards when examining violations of human rights."[51]

Malaysia stated:

On the one hand, other governments are threatened because of some minor breach of human rights; on the other hand, when western interest is not at stake they are prepared to allow the most brutal violation of human rights to take place before their very eyes." ... "It is rather difficult for us to agree to and accept this double standard." [52]

12. With respect to disagreements in the human rights field, these countries suggest solving their problems in a non-confrontational manner, through dialogue and cooperation.

The Chinese government is willing to take part in the international dialogue on human rights. It is normal to have disagreements on human rights issues in the international community, thus countries should engage in dialogue and exchange ideas, they should not apply pressure and impose sanctions. Dialogue is much better than confrontation. There are many real examples to prove that countries can increase understanding, gain deeper insight, eliminate misunderstandings and reach agreement through dialogue. [53]

The fourth principle of the ASEAN ISIS's eight principles is called "the principle of cooperation, not confrontation." It provides:

ASEAN members welcome cooperation, incentives and assistance for the promotion of human rights in their respective countries from other countries and the international community and multilateral institutions. Such cooperation, incentives and assistance are best formulated through mutual consultation and dialogue. Cooperation, not confrontation, should be the guiding principle. [54]

The *ASEAN Human Rights Declaration* further accentuates this point.

In the large area of East Asia and South East Asia, Japan, as the only developed country in the region, holds a very different point of view on human rights than the many developing countries in the region. Japan regards the violation of human rights as an international issue which should never take second place to economic progress and development.

Human rights should never be sacrificed to development. Rather... respect for human rights will facilitate development." ... "To express concern over any grave violation of human rights, be it arbitrary detention, enforced disappearance or torture... should not be regarded as internal affairs.[55]

As the world's biggest provider of economic aid, Japan's overseas aid is conditional on human rights. Therefore, at the 1993 Vienna World Conference on Human Rights, Japan was regarded as part of the "Western Camp" lead by the United States. At the Asian Regional Conference on Human Rights, Japan, although declaring some reservations, signed the *Bangkok Declaration* which reflects most Asian developing countries' view on human rights. Later, a Japanese official stated that several aspects of the declaration were indeed not "fully compatible"[56] with Tokyo's policy on human rights.

It should be pointed out, however, that Japan's interpretation of human rights and its approach to implementing a human rights policy still differs significantly from those of Western countries. Japan is of the opinion that

...it is precisely the group, however--the family, the school, the firm or the government--which offers fulfilment to the individual. ... [T]o the Japanese, it is the right to belong to a group and to become involved in a demanding but protective world of duties that is the core of human rights. ... Public welfare in Japan, as compared with individualism in the United States, is the key concept.[57]

This is very evident in the standard conduct of Japanese people. Although the Japanese suggest linking economic aid to human rights, they carry out this policy in a different way than the Western countries. In 1988 and 1989, Japan cut development assistance to Burma and China because of human rights violations. Within a year, however, assistance to Burma and China was reinstated. Japan did not even cut aid to Thailand after the 1991 military coup. Japan also has not taken any action with respect to the issue of East Timor. Japan's conduct stems from both its cultural tradition and its economic interests, but of course also from its strategic deliberations of "returning to Asia".

III.

East Asian and South East Asian countries' main viewpoints on human rights have been briefly outlined above. Why do these countries, whose concrete situation and level of democratic development are so different[58], hold such identical or similar views on human rights? In fact, the answer has already been mentioned above. It is the result of a combination of the region's specific historical background, cultural tradition, level of economic development and other factors which has made countries in the region form a shared approach to human rights. (This article will not discuss this issue further.)

Historical background

As mentioned before, these countries wholeheartedly support promoting and protecting human rights. They not only take part in relevant activities of the international community such as the United Nations, but they have also established special human rights commissions in some countries, including Indonesia, the Philippines and Thailand. This might confuse Western countries because, if Asian countries are not against protecting human rights, why would they then consistently stress the point that human rights belong under a country's domestic jurisdiction, and thereby ignore other countries concerns? In fact, the reason lies in historical conditions created by Western countries.

Countries in this region, except for Japan and Thailand, were, over a long period of time, reduced to the status of colony or semi-colony of Western imperialist countries. During that time, these countries were subjected to invasion, pillage and exploitation. They did not have sovereignty, and their people's most basic right to life could not be guaranteed. As is pointed out in China's White Paper on human rights:

It was mainly imperialist invasion that threatened the Chinese people's lives. During the 110 years from 1840 to 1949, Britain, America, France, Japan, Russia and other imperialist forces invaded China hundreds of times and caused unmeasurable harm to the lives and property of the Chinese people. ... Sovereignty was lost, society's wealth was looted, and the Chinese people lost the necessities of life.[59]

It is not only China that has gone through such a painful experience. Malaysia's Prime Minister Mahathir points out that prior to World War II,

...the Europeans who had nicely divided the world into empires, where they were free to do what they liked with their colonial inhabitants, did not believe in the universality of human rights. ... The non-white colonial people had to accept white rule totally. ... For them human rights practically did not exist. For the imperial nations of Europe, human rights were only for their own people. ...[60]

Therefore, those countries that had once been colonized by Western colonial powers and deprived of their human rights became rather suspicious of the sincerity of the Western countries when they began to advocate human rights after the end of the Cold War. The Western countries' practice of using double standards on human rights issues for those countries that fell within their strategic interest during the Cold War, further intensified the scepticism of the former colonial countries. Meanwhile, because of the painful experience of colonial times when countries had no sovereignty and people had no human rights, these former colonial countries wholeheartedly support the protection and promotion of human rights.

Although these countries, through long and bitter struggles, achieved national independence and embarked on the road to steady development, they will not easily forget their painful history. While the former colonized countries cherish their hard-won independence, the former colonial powers of the West cannot fully accept the fact that they are now independent. Thus, they still try to exert their influence over them. As Mahathir states: "When we achieved independence we thought we would be free. But the North is still subjecting us to imperial pressures."[61] Therefore, although these countries have been liberated politically, "...the process of mental emancipation, both on the part of the colonised and the colonisers, is taking much longer."[62]

In recent years, Western countries have continuously been preaching to Third World countries on issues of democracy and human rights, and this has created widespread hostility from Third World countries. In this regard, some Western scholars also believe that "in part their rejection of the democratic ideal is a response to the perceived 'reactionary imperialism' of the West".[63]

In the human rights sphere, such a reaction is demonstrated by these countries' insistence on state independence and national self-determination; persistence in keeping the human rights issue within a country's domestic jurisdiction; opposition to using human rights issues to interfere with other countries' internal affairs; opposition to any country forcing its own democratic and human rights standards on others; opposition to any country acting as judge of another country; and, opposition to making human rights a condition for economic aid.

Economic development

When these countries achieved independence, they were faced with a stern reality. After such a long period of colonial plunder and wars, full-scale reconstruction was needed. Eliminating poverty and backwardness, and helping their citizens escape starvation and disease became their top priority. Therefore, economic development has become the common goal for these countries. Only through development will their people be able to enjoy the basic necessities of life, and these countries will be able to consolidate their hard-earned political independence. Therefore, "[e]conomic development is the only force that can liberate the Third World."[64] This is why these countries stress that the right to subsistence and the right to development are the most basic and most important human rights.

After a few decades of independence, these countries have already made some progress in the area of economic development, and the living standard of their people has been raised considerably. Some Western countries, however, continue to criticize the fact that political freedom cannot be guaranteed in these countries, while at the same time, they neglect to mention these countries' substantial progress in realizing economic, social and cultural rights. It is obviously very unfair. Therefore, these countries emphasize that economic, social and cultural rights should be given the same amount of attention as civil and political rights, and that these rights cannot be separated. People in developing countries are in much more urgent need of economic, social and cultural rights. Therefore, these countries are proud of any progress in these areas. For example, China believes that feeding and clothing its people, "...is a historical achievement for the Chinese people and the Chinese government in their struggle for and protection of human rights."[65]

These countries also believe that, with economic development, people may attain even greater civil and political freedom. But this is a slow process. In this regard, Lee Kuan-Yew states:

Indeed, the history of democracy in developed countries shows it to be a slow, almost glacial process. They reached full universal suffrage only after they had achieved a high level of economic growth with an educated population."..."What the UK, US and France took 200 years to evolve, these new countries, without the economic, educational and social pre-conditions, were expected to work upon independence, when during all the years of colonial tutelage, there were no elections and no democratic system.[66]

This is unrealistic. Therefore, these countries conclude that developing their economies is the precondition for realizing democracy and human rights, and that it should be done through a step by step process.

In order to guarantee a smooth process of development, these countries believe that it is necessary to establish an environment suitable for development. On the one hand, it is necessary to maintain domestic social order and political stability; on the other hand, it is necessary to establish a new international economic order conducive to economic development in the developing countries.

In order to maintain domestic political stability and economic development, there must be a strong government. As Mahbubani points out: "What Asia needs at its present stage of development are governments who are committed to rapid economic development."[67] And such governments must be strong. "In Asia the public will not tolerate a weak government. It is destined to fail." "You could say that those that govern best are those that govern most."[68]

Being able to keep stability and development also becomes the symbol for "good government." The success of economic development in this region further illustrates the importance of this kind of government. As one scholar from the United States Honolulu's East-West Centre wrote: "The experience of East and Southeast Asian countries, in their view, clearly suggests that economic growth and law and order were achievements of enlightened authoritarian governments-- and that democratization, as in Taiwan, South Korea, and Thailand, followed economic success and not vice versa."[69]

It should also be pointed out that the level of economic development is uneven in the developing countries of East and Southeast Asia. The "newly industrialized countries" are advancing rapidly towards becoming developed countries, but there are also Indo-Chinese countries that are just beginning to reconstruct their countries after years of war. The majority of countries in the region belong to the group of countries advancing towards becoming developed countries. In the West, "the modernization approach" is a popular theory which argues that economic development will create a wealthy and well-educated middle class. This middle class will, in turn, demand a more democratic government and a political environment more favourable to participation, and this will push the country towards democracy. Does this theory apply to the situation in East and Southeast Asia? Along with economic growth, a "pragmatic, upwardly mobile and highly urbanized middle class" is already emerging in some of the faster-growing countries of the region. But, "[a]s the major beneficiary of thirty years of economic growth, the new middle class is highly dependent on state largesse." "...we discover instead governments that are ideologically, economically, and sometimes ethnically homogeneous with the new Asian middle class.""[70] This middle class is opposed to "increasingly pluralistic liberalism" and emphasises "stability", "order" and "true reliability". This characteristic of the East and Southeast Asian middle class is an important reason why the logic of "growth--stability--strong government" continues to be meaningful.

Cultural tradition

Respecting authority

The idea of a "strong government" stems from the influence of cultural traditions. The influence of the Confucian theory of respecting authority is widespread throughout East and Southeast Asia. Confucius' "ruler/subject and father/son" concept is the primary standard for Confucian behaviour. The "ruler/subject" concept protects the authority of the ruler and demands that the people obey the ruler, while the "father/son" concept protects the authority of the father and demands that people obey their elders. The idea of respecting authority has reached far beyond the boundaries of Confucian culture and has become a special characteristic of the even vaster Eastern or Asian culture. This is demonstrated mainly through its popularity in countries of South East Asia where religions and beliefs differ. As one Malaysian scholar writes: "Razak lists respect for authority as one Asian trait his country should keep."[71]

Historically, these countries were all authoritarian kingdoms. After they achieved independence, each country had its own system of government, but power was usually in the hands of one ruling group for a long time. Some countries have even gone through long periods of military rule.

As imported Western democratic ideas and democratic mechanisms mix with traditional Asian culture, a special Asian-style political system has formed, called the "dominant party system." It refers to when a party or a political alliance monopolizes power for a long period of time. With the exception of the Philippines, there has never been a situation in this region where power rotated between political parties.

This type of political system represents an adaptation of Western democratic practices to serve Asian or Confucian political values. Democratic institutions work not to promote Western values of competition and change but Confucian values of consensus and stability.[72]

This is because these countries emphasize authority in order to maintain harmony and order in society. For this reason, "[c]onflict between ideas, groups, and parties tends to be viewed as dangerous. Political competition, as Lee Kuan-Yew said, is 'not the way the Japanese, the Chinese or the Asian cultures do it. That leads to contentiousness and confusion.'"[73]

The individual in the group

In traditional East and Southeast Asian culture, Confucianism and Islam clearly regulate the relationship between the individual and society, rights and obligations.

According to Confucianism, the family is the centre of activity in society. "The root of a country is the family." Loyalty and filial piety are the two goals that people pursue throughout their lives. Loyalty means loyalty towards the state. It refers to the relationship between the individual and the state. Filial piety refers to the individual's obligations to the family. According to Confucianism, the individual only exists within a group. The individual is one of either a family or of the world, and if the group is harmed, protection of the individual's life cannot be guaranteed. Confucianism places the interests of the family, the state or the nationality before the interests of the individual and requires the individual to follow the interests of the group and of society.[74]

Apart from this, there is no clear-cut conception of rights in traditional Confucianism. People only pay attention to moral obligations. The "Book of Rites" instructs that the father should be affectionate, the son should be filial, the older brother should be good, the younger brother should be respectful, the husband should be righteous, the wife should listen, the elder should be kind, the child should be obedient, the ruler should be benevolent, and the subject should be loyal. These are called the "ten righteous rules" which strictly regulate the obligations of everybody from the ruler to the average citizen.

The Islamic point of view concerning the relationship between the individual and society, rights and obligations, has many similarities with Confucianism. "In the Islamic society, [...] the individual's role and society's role are complementary and inter-dependent. Between the two there is unity in society as well as collective responsibilities and obligations. Every one is responsible for the happiness and prosperity of society." As the individual is

...a part of society or of the state, he/she must try to accommodate his/her interests and rights to the interest and rights of others through mutually beneficial ways. Should an individual hold an opinion about an issue which relates to public affairs, and should this person find that the majority of the people held a different opinion which was not against the law of Allah, then the individual must yield to the majority in order to protect the benefits of unity and cooperation.

According to Islamic law, human rights are a "result of people's obligations, not a prerequisite for obligations."

We have obligations to God, to nature and all creatures and to other people. [...] As the result of fulfilling these obligations, we have gained certain rights and freedoms as indicated repeatedly in the law of God ... Obligations can be seen as the other side of rights, it is as if rights and obligations have formed two wings with which society soars into the promising horizon.[75]

From the above Confucian and Islamic ideas about the relationship between the individual and society, and rights and obligations, we can easily find a theoretical foundation for relevant aspects of the East and South East Asian human rights concept.

IV.

Based on the main contents of the East and Southeast Asian conception of human rights and its historical, economic and cultural background, we can understand that the existence of an East and Southeast Asian conception of human rights is not a coincidence, it is the product of specific historical, cultural and economic conditions. It should be said that the East and South East Asian conception of human rights is of a definite representative nature and that it has many similarities with the conception of human rights of South American and African developing countries. This is due to the fact that they all have similar historical experiences and that they are at a similar level of development and, therefore, they are facing the same kinds of problems. There is no doubt that every country displays its attitude towards international issues based on its own interests.

Realization of human rights is a shared ideal of all human beings. Promotion of human rights is the common cause of all the people in the world. The world, however, is made of distinct countries. There are not only developed countries but also developing countries. As the concrete circumstances of each country differ, human rights protection in each country differs as well. The effort and experience of each country should, however, become part of this great cause. In the struggle for this cause, everyone is equal, and every country is equal. The experience of each country and each region is equally precious. Developed countries hold certain human rights views and have certain experiences in realizing human rights. Developing countries hold their own particular human rights views and experiences. This is not contradictory, however. It only illustrates that each country has chosen a different path in pursuit of the same goal. Therefore, they should learn from each other, borrow from each other and respect each other. Only then will they be able to move forward. When one side acts superior and tries to force its model on the other or criticizes the other's methods without reason, it is of no benefit to the development of the world human rights cause.

Every society progresses at its own pace and the motivation for progress ultimately comes from within a society. Every country should form its policies and measures of implementation according to its own specific situation, and as long as it makes an honest effort, the international community should offer encouragement. At the same time, every country or region should respect the choices of other countries and regions, and no country should try to influence others to speed up certain areas of development, because this kind of behaviour could backfire. As time passes, and as economies develop, the substance of the East and South East Asian conception of human rights will change as well, but only with respect to becoming more complete and more systematic.

During the first decades after the adoption of the *Universal Declaration of Human Rights*, only the voice of the West was heard in the international human rights arena. But nowadays, the voices of the West and the East can both be heard, and the voices of developed and developing countries can all be heard. Every country and every region in the world is expressing its own opinion about human rights. This is a positive phenomenon, as it means that the whole world is paying attention to human rights issues and working hard towards a full realization of human rights.

East Asian civilization forms an important part of world civilization. The East and Southeast Asian concept of human rights also forms an important part of world human rights thinking. Just as this region's economic development model is worth studying, this region's human rights concept is also worth paying attention to and researching.

Translated by Shengtao Jiang and Anne-Marie Traeholt

Notes

1.-3. Samuel P. Huntington, "The Clash of Civilizations?", *Foreign Affairs*, Summer 1993, Vol. 72, No. 3, p. 22 and p. 40.

2. Jin Canrong, "Wenming chongtulun de qishi yiyi" (The insightful significance of the theory of the clash of civilizations), *Shijie Zhishi* (World Knowledge), 1995, Vol. 9, p. 11.

3. *Supra*, note 1.

4. Bilahari Kausikan, "East and South Asia and the Post-Cold War International Politics of Human Rights," *Studies in Conflict and Terrorism*, Vol. 16, 1993, pp. 248-249.

5. Bilahari Kausikan, "Asia's Different Standard", *Foreign Policy*, No. 92, Fall 1993, p. 26.

6. *Ibid.*

7. Guowuyuan xinwen bangongshi (State Council Information Office): "Zhongguode renquan zhuangkuang" (China's human rights situation), Zhongyang wenxian chubanshe, 1991, p. 1.

8. Speech by the South Korean Foreign Affairs Minister at the Vienna World Conference on Human Rights, in *Fazhanzhong guojia yu renquan* (Developing countries and human rights), edited by Liu Nanlai. People's Publishing House of Sichuan, 1994, p. 10.

9. "Kuala Lumpur Declaration of Human Rights", adopted by the ASEAN Inter-Parliamentary Association (AIPO), September 20-25, 1993.

10. Speech by Li Ruihuan at the [huangjia] Research Centre for International Relations in Belgium, "China's foreign policy and modernization", in *Renmin ribao* (People's Daily), May 19, 1994.

11. Mahathir, "Human rights not the sole privilege of the West", *The Star*, December 7, 1994.

12. "Joint Communiqué of the Twenty-Fourth ASEAN Ministerial Meeting", Kuala Lumpur, 19-20 July, 1991.

13. Jusuf Wanandi, "Human Rights and Democracy in the ASEAN Nations: The Next 25 Years", *ASEAN-ISIS Monitor*, Issue No. 5, Oct.-Dec. 1992, p.9.

14. From *Fazhanzhong guojia yu renquan* (Developing countries and human rights), edited by Liu Nanlai, p. 4.

15. Ibid.

16. Speech by Liu Huaqiu, the head of the Chinese delegation to the Vienna World Conference on Human Rights, in *Guangming Ribao* (Guangming Daily), June 17, 1993.

17. Speech by the Burmese representative to the 45th Session of the United Nations General Assembly, in *Fazhanzhong guojia yu renquan* (Developing countries and human rights), edited by Liu Nanlai, p. 8.

18. State Council Information Office, *China's Human Rights Situation*, 1991, p. 68.

19. Quoted in "Asian countries stands firm in opposing outside interference". *The Straits Times*, June 18, 1993.

20. Li Peng's response to a question by a Xinhua News Agency reporter on the eve of the 40th anniversary of the peaceful liberation of Tibet, May 19, 1991.

21. Speech by the head of the North Korean delegation to the Vienna World Conference on Human Rights, in *Fazhanzhong guojia yu renquan* (Developing countries and human rights), edited by Liu Nanlai, p. 9.

22. Supra, note 16.

23. Supra, note 16.

24. Speech by the head of the North Korean delegation to the Vienna World Conference on Human Rights, in *Fazhanzhong guojia yu renquan* (Developing countries and human rights), edited by Liu Nanlai, p. 36.

25. Speech by the Indonesian Foreign Minister at the Vienna World Conference on Human Rights, in *Fazhanzhong guojia yu renquan*, edited by Liu Nanlai, p. 295.

26. Conversation between Jiang Zemin and an American reporter, in *Guangming Daily*, November 2, 1991.

27. Speech by the South Korean Foreign Affairs Minister at the Vienna World Conference on Human Rights, in *Fazhanzhong guojia yu renquan* (Developing countries and human rights), edited by Liu Nanlai. People's Publishing House of Sichuan, 1994, p. 11.

28. Dong Yunhu, "Yazhou guojia dui shijie renquan shiye de xin gongxian" (Asian countries' new contribution to the world human rights cause), in *Guangming Daily*, June 28, 1993.

29. Speech by Huang Gencheng, the Foreign Minister of Singapore, at the Vienna World Conference on Human Rights, in *Fazhanzhong guojia yu renquan* (Developing countries and human rights), edited by Liu Nanlai, p. 29.

30. Lee Kuan-yew, "Be prepared to intervene directly or don't force pace of change, West told", *The Straits Times*, November 21, 1992.

31. Mohamed Jawhar, *Malaysia: Cultural Traditions, Good governance and the Universality of Human Rights?* p. 19.

32. Suharto, "Towards a More Human, Just, Peaceful and Prosperous Society", *Telstra*, No. 20, Jan.-Feb. 1993, p. 7.

33. Mahathir, "Human rights not the sole privilege of the West", *The Star*, December 7, 1994.

34. Supra, note 30.

35. Speech by Liu Huaqiu, the head of the Chinese delegation to the Vienna World Conference on Human Rights, in *Guangming Ribao* (Guangming Daily), June 17, 1993.

36. Speech by Li Ruihuan at a Research Centre for International Relations in Belgium, "China's foreign policy and modernization", in *Renmin ribao* (People's Daily), May 19, 1994.

37. Supra, note 30.

38. Chuan Leekpai, Opening address at the Asian Regional Meeting on Human Rights, March 29, 1993, Bangkok *Thailand Foreign Affairs Newsletter*, 1-3/93.

39. *Zhonghua renmin gongheguo xianfa* (The Constitution of the People's Republic of China), 1984.

40. Conversation between Jiang Zemin and an American reporter, in *Guangming Daily*, November 2, 1991.

41. Speech by the Indonesian Foreign Minister at the Vienna World Conference on Human Rights, in *Fazhanzhong guojia yu renquan*, edited by Liu Nanlai, p. 23.

42. Dong Yunhu, "Yazhou guojia dui shijie renquan shiye de xin gongxian" (Asian countries' new contribution to the world human rights cause), in *Guangming Daily*, June 28, 1993.

43. Speech by Liu Huaqiu, the head of the Chinese delegation to the Vienna World Conference on Human Rights, in *Guangming Ribao* (Guangming Daily), June 17, 1993.

44. Jusuf Wanandi, "Human Rights and Democracy in the ASEAN Nations: The Next 25 Years", *ASEAN-ISIS Monitor*, Issue No. 5, Oct.-Dec. 1992, pp. 8-9.

45. Jeong Woo Kil, "South Korea's Human Rights Concerns in the Context of Inter-Korean Relations", *Korea and World Affairs*, Winter 1993, p. 724.

46. Speech by the Indonesian Foreign Minister at the Vienna World Conference on Human Rights, in *Fazhanzhong guojia yu renquan*, edited by Liu Nanlai, p. 291.

47. Speech by Liu Huaqiu, the head of the Chinese delegation to the Vienna World Conference on Human Rights, in *Guangming Ribao* (Guangming Daily), June 17, 1993.

48. Speech by the Indonesian Foreign Minister at the Vienna World Conference on Human Rights, in *Fazhanzhong guojia yu renquan*, edited by Liu Nanlai, p. 55.

49. Speech by an Indonesian delegate at the third committee of the 46th Session of the UN General Assembly, in *Fazhanzhong guojia yu renquan* (Developing countries and human rights), edited by Liu Nanlai, p. 51.

50. Speech by the head of the North Korean delegation to the Vienna World Conference on Human Rights, in *Fazhanzhong guojia yu renquan* (Developing countries and human rights), edited by Liu Nanlai, p. 36.

51. Speech by an Indonesian delegate to the Asian regional preparatory meeting before the World Conference on Human Rights, in *Fazhanzhong guojia yu renquan* (Developing countries and human rights), edited by Liu Nanlai, p. 52.

52. Supra, note 11.

53. Speech by Li Ruihuan at the [huangjia] Research Centre for International Relations in Belgium, "China's foreign policy and modernization", in *Renmin ribao* (People's Daily), May 19, 1994.

54. Jusuf Wanandi, "Human rights and Democracy in the ASEAN Nations: the Next 25 Years", *ASEAN-ISIS Monitor*, Issue No. 5, Oct.-Dec. 1992, pp. 9-10.

55. Quoted in "Japan joins us in tough stand on human rights abuse," *The Sunday Times*, June 20, 1993.

56. Tan Lian Choo, "Stop tying aid to human rights, Asian countries tell the West", *The Straits Times*, April 3, 1993.

57. Ardath W. Burks, "Japan: The Bellwether of East Asian Human Rights?", in *Human Rights in East Asia: A Cultural Perspective*, edited by James C. Hsiung, (New York: Paragon House Publishers, 1985), pp. 45-47.

58. Peter H. Merkl says in *Contemporary Democratic Countries* that Japan is an old democratic country, and the Philippines and South Korea are new democratic countries. *Guoji shehui kexue zazhi* (Journal of International Social Sciences), 1994, Vol. 2, p. 12.

59. Guowuyuan xinwen bangongshi (State Council Information Office): *Zhongguode renquan zhuangkuang* (China's human rights situation), Zhongyang wenxian chubanshe, 1991, pp. 1-3.

60. Supra, note 11.

61. Mahathir, in his address to representatives of 55 developing countries in Kuala Lumpur to set the third World agenda for the Earth Summit held in Rio in June 1992. See *Far Eastern Economic Review*, March 14, 1992, p. 22.

62. Kishore Mahbubani, "An Asian View of Human Rights and Press Freedom", *The Straits Times*, March 14, 1993.

63. Muthian Alagappa, "Democracy's Future -- The Asian Spectrum", *Journal of Democracy*, Vol. 6, No. 1, January 1995.

64. Kishore Mahbubani, "Live and let live -- allow Asians to choose their own course", *Far Eastern Economic Review*, June 17, 1993, p. 26.

65. Guowuyuan xinwen bangongshi (State Council Information Office), *Zhongguode renquan zhuangkuang* (China's human rights situation), Zhongyang wenxian chubanshe, 1991, p. 6.

66. Supra, note 30.

67. Supra, note 62.

68. Zakaria Haji, quoted in "Asia's Different Drum", *Time*, June 14, 1993, p. 17.

69. Muthian Alagappa, "Democratic Transition in Asia: The Role of the International Community", *East-West Center Special Reports*, No. 3, October 1994, p. 9.

70. David Martin Jones, "Asia's Rising Middle Class--Not a Force for Change", *The National Interests*, No. 38, Winter 1994/95, pp. 46-48.

71. Razak Baginda, quoted in "The Asian Way", *Asiaweek*, March 2, 1994, p. 23.

72. Samuel P. Huntington, "American Democracy in Relation to Asia", see *Democracy and Capitalism: Asian and American Perspectives*, eds. Robert Bartley, Chan Heng Chee, Samuel P. Huntington and Shijuro Ogata. (Singapore: ISEAS, 1993), p. 41, p. 39.

73. Ibid.

74. Hammudah Abdalati, *The Essence of Islam* (Yiselanjiao de jingyi), Chinese translation by Ma Kainan, International Islamic Federation of Student Organization, Al Faisal Press, 1989.

75. Luobote Teleiye , "Human Rights in Islam", in *Fazhanzhong guojia yu renquan* (Developing countries and human rights), edited by Liu Nanlai, pp. 335-336, and p. 333.

3 Economic and Sociological Foundations of Human Rights, Collective Rights and the Right to Development

Human Rights and Development: the Chinese Experience in an International Context

JIANG WENRAN

Ever since the Enlightenment Movement, liberty, equality and fraternity have been the highest human ideals that have rallied people all over the world in their struggles against oppression, colonialism, racism, injustice, discrimination and other forms of human abuses. While the world is marching toward the new millennium, human rights issues are being debated more than ever before on a global scale, in the various United Nations fora and in the rapidly expanding world press. Countries that violate human rights are often exposed and criticized beyond nation-state borders. Yet, human rights are defined differently in different parts of the world and the human rights debate takes on many dimensions.

The primary concern of this paper is the impact of economic and political development models on human rights and human development in general. Many works on development related issues do not explore this relationship in depth.[1] In recent years, considerable contributions have been made to the discussion of human rights in China, but the focus seems to have been mostly on political and civil rights.[2] In this paper, I first examine the broader research agenda of the relationship between development and human rights. Then, I analyze and assess the development strategies of the People's Republic of China (PRC) and their influence on human rights and human development. Finally, I expand the discussion by looking at China in an international context, and by examining development experiences in other parts of the world with more empirical data.

Introduction

The 1991 "Human Development Report" published by the United Nations Development Program (UNDP) contains two indicators on human rights and human development: the human development index (HDI) and the human freedom index (HFI).[3] The HDI measures 160 countries by three major indicators: national income (living standards), adult literacy (knowledge) and life expectancy (longevity). The HFI ranks 88 UN members by their scores on 40 concrete indicators.[4] Do these indicators accurately reflect the reality of human rights and human development in these countries? Is this data scientific? Is it acceptable to the member countries involved? The fact that the UNDP no longer publishes the human freedom index in its annual human development report offers a partial answer to these questions.[5] In addition, the two indices raise a number of questions regarding the relationship between economic development and human rights: is there a positive correlation between human rights and economic development, as is clearly indicated by the HFI in the UNDP Report? What is the general trend regarding the improvement of human rights when a country is experiencing rapid economic growth? Do particular types of economic development models promote or hinder the improvement of human rights?[6]

As we bring China into the picture, things become more complicated. According to the UNDP Report, China ranked 82 among 160 countries in the HDI, but scored only 2 points (together with Ethiopia) out of 40 in the HFI, just ahead of countries such as Iraq (0) and Romania (1). South Africa, with its apartheid system, scored higher than China with 3 points.[7] The Report positively states that "there seems to be a high correlation between human development and human freedom."[8] However, China, with its medium HDI score and its low HFI score, does not fit into the overall picture. Then, what is unique about China's development path as it relates to human rights and human development? I approach this question from different angles: First, I discuss some recent theoretical trends among Western political scientists in the field of development studies. Second, I examine the differences between Western countries and Third World countries (including China) in their definitions of human rights. Finally, I look at the various models of development that China has implemented, and the impact of these development models on human rights and human development.

Paths of Development and Human Rights

The collapse of the Soviet Union and certain east European regimes was regarded as a failure of a particular economic and political development model.[9] The emergence of several theoretical trends in the West intensified the human rights debate in a number of ways.

First, there is the theory of the end of history and the end of ideology. "The Birth and Death of Communism in the Twentieth Century" (the subtitle of Zbigniew Brzezinski's popular book) was an important chapter in the worldwide socialist/communist movement, at least for the Soviet type.[10] One of the main causes of the downfall of the Soviet regimes in East European countries was that the Soviet model not only had a poor economic development record, but also a poor human rights record. Some have taken the historical change of the late 1980s and early 1990s to a telescopic level in arguing that the end of communist rule in the Soviet bloc signalled the end of ideological struggles of the past several hundred years, and that our search for a better ideology to serve us has come to an end. In that sense, we have also come to the end of history, as far as our experiments with different social-economical-political systems are concerned. This is the exact point of Francis Fukuyama's well-known article "The End of History?".[11]

Second, it has become conventional orthodoxy in the West that the promotion of democracy and human rights is either a precondition for economic growth or an indispensable process of it. A group of American political scientists, headed by Gabriel Almond, conducted a series of studies on political development models, linking political development with economic growth and social progress. Their works were undermined by both the reality of Third World development and the emergence of the Dependency approach. In the past several years, the political developmentalists of the 1960s have vigorously argued, citing the fall of the former Soviet Union and other East European regimes, that they should be vindicated for advocating that economic development does foster democratic changes.[12] Here the emphasis is not on who has won the Cold War, but rather on which political and economic development models are better for promoting human rights and human development. In this case, China presents a unique challenge. Although market reforms were introduced over fifteen years ago in China, the Chinese Communist Party retains its power and there has been no change toward other forms of government. Any discussion of development models must take this reality into account.

Third, in relation to these developments, socialism as an economic, social and political development alternative has been largely discounted in recent theorizing of development. Not long ago, in 1982, Chalmers Johnson published his "MITI and the Japanese Miracle", in which he credited the Japanese and certain other East Asian economies as the work of a "developmental state", while acknowledging the existence of the two dominant development models, the market economy and the command economy.[13] Recently, in a widely publicized article entitled "Capitalism and Democracy", veteran American political scientist and former president of the American Political Science Association, Gabriel Almond, presented an interesting lecture on the relationship between capitalism and democracy.[14] Citing the classic work of Joseph Schumpeter's "Capitalism, Socialism and Democracy" in the current context, Almond cautions that "[u]nlike Schumpeter I do not include Socialism in my title, since its future as a distinct ideology and program is unclear at best."[15] From Johnson to Almond, we can see that the most widely discussed development models have become two: countries that primarily depend on market mechanisms and others that have more state intervention in their economic activities. China is often regarded as moving toward the latter group of countries, becoming more and more like a developmental state similar to that of other East Asian countries.

All this points to the ultimate positive linkage between capitalism and Western style liberal democracy.[16] It is not surprising that the human rights record of China and other developing countries are increasingly judged by these standards.[17] Before rushing to the universality of grand theories, it is necessary to look at how often used concepts, such as development and human rights, are defined in different parts of the world.

Defining Human Rights in a World Longing for Development

A thorough review of the definitions of human rights and development is beyond the scope of this study. It is important to recognize the existence of different interpretations of human rights and to place these differences in a historical context. There is no commonly accepted agenda for the totality of human rights and there is a lack of clarity in the in-depth examination of the content of particular rights. Bilder aptly notes that:

> The issue of definition is not trivial. For what we think human rights really are will inevitably influence not only our judgement as to the types of claims to recognize as human rights, but also our expectations and programs for implementation and compliance with these standards.[18]

Historically speaking, Western countries tend to emphasize individual rights in terms of freedom of the press, freedom of speech, freedom of association and freedom of participation in the political process. This could be interpreted in light of the evolution of capitalist development in western Europe and the United States. Several hundred years ago, the newly emerged industrial and commercial classes in Europe had to fight with powerful monarchies and religious forces for power. The growth of capitalism as an economic system required a free market, free competition and free movement of labour. Thus, the guarantee of individual rights was indispensable for the protection of bourgeois interests at the beginning of capitalist development. In contrast, social and economic rights took a secondary place in the early stages of capitalism in the West, as the state was less involved in economic and social programs. Later, all social classes, especially the working class, contributed to the achievement of universal suffrage and many of the welfare measures of today's Western societies. This particular evolution of political economy is partially responsible for Western countries' emphasis on civil and political rights in the human rights debate. In this sense, it would be problematic to ignore history and talk about human rights exclusively in terms of cultural traditions.

In other parts of the world, history developed in different ways.
There is the legacy of colonialism. The development of capitalism in the West led to colonialism and imperialism in what is today's Third World countries. The worldwide national independence movement of the early twentieth century, especially after World War II, placed unity and dignity of a nation as a whole, above the consideration of individuals' rights. To the Chinese, this goal meant getting rid of foreign powers, unequal treaties and extra-territorialities, as well as the signboards in China that read "Chinese and dogs are not allowed to enter." Most people would agree that without ending national humiliation and achieving national independence, human rights are empty words. South Africa's apartheid system was an isolated regional phenomenon in recent history, but this system used to exist across national borders.[19] The Chinese experience was very typical in this respect. Along with the establishment of the People's Republic of China came the challenge of both consolidating the power base of the Chinese Communist Party and defending the newly independent state. With the invasion of Russia by Western powers after the 1917 October Revolution in mind, the Chinese leadership was determined to do everything to defend the new People's Republic. The fear of being humiliated again prompted many developing countries, socialist or not, to put a very high priority on collective national interests.[20]

There is also the increased role of the state in the economic development of Third World countries in the second half of the twentieth century. Due to the fact that late industrializers and newly independent states must function in an environment set by early industrializers, state intervention in economic development has become a regular phenomenon, from Germany and Japan to the former Soviet Union and China to South Korea and Singapore. To leave the legacies of the past behind and proceed with modernization has become the goal of most Third World countries. In stressing social and economic development, the main emphasis has been on the interests of the collective, vis-à-vis political rights which pay more attention to the interests of the individual. This clear emphasis by Third World countries on social and economic rights has produced a statist approach to development. The argument that collective rights are more important to a country's survival and security has made it possible for the state in developing countries to carry out state-centred development programs. Some argue that a society must satisfy the basic needs of its people before one can begin to talk about political rights.[21] Although this statist view has been dominant in many Third World countries' development strategies, a more society-oriented view contends that the contents of collective rights should primarily be economic, social and cultural. This, however, does not mean that individuals should be subordinate to state control, thus having their political and civil rights undermined.

The fact that more countries have begun to pay attention to the economic, social and cultural aspects of human rights has contributed to the dynamic and evolutionary nature of human right ideals. This is reflected in the UN perception of human rights and human development. A brief look at the UN resolutions on these issues reflect, not only increased concerns for human rights by the world community, but also some changes in understanding the contents of human rights. In the *Universal Declaration of Human Rights*, adopted by the UN in 1948, only about five (Articles 22 to 27) out of thirty articles are devoted to what we may define as economic, social and cultural rights.[22] The crimes of fascism, Nazism and militarism against humanity and the terror of war contributed greatly to the elaboration of the contents of the *Universal Declaration*. Thus, the United States and other Western countries in the UN placed their mark of dominance on the document.

In the decades following World War II, the world witnessed a decolonization process. Many newly independent countries joined the UN and have subsequently moved the UN toward making the difficulties in Third World development a part of the human rights agenda. The two documents, the *International Covenant on Economic, Social and Cultural Rights* and the *International Covenant on Civil and Political Rights* were created by the UN in 1966 after many years of work. These Covenants were commonly seen as a detailed extension of the *Universal Declaration*, with one difference being the fact that by separating the two covenants, economic and social rights were given the same weight as civil and political rights. In the 1970s, both Covenants entered into force, accompanied by increased pressure from Third World countries for a new international economic order. This momentum reached another height in 1986, when the UN adopted the *Declaration on the Right to Development* by a vote of 146 to 1 (the United States), with 6 abstentions.[23]

The *Declaration on the Right to Development* is, in various ways, significant to the study of the relationship between development and human rights. First, by passing a declaration exclusively on the right to development, the global discourse on the content of human rights has moved in the direction of favouring Third World countries. This shift, from defining human rights on the basis of the Western conceptualization of natural law to incorporating economic and social development as human rights, has intensified the global human rights debate.[24] Second, there is not only a clear statement on development as part of the human rights idea, but also an implication that economic and social rights, such as the right to development, are more fundamental and important than political and civil rights.[25] The right to development, as Article 1 of the Declaration states,

> is an inalienable human right by virtue of which every human person and all peoples are entitled to participate in, contribute to and enjoy economic, social, cultural and political development, in which all human rights and fundamental freedoms can be fully realized.[26]

Finally, despite Article 2 briefly mentioning that "[t]he human person is the central subject of development and should be the active participant and beneficiary of the right to development,"[27] almost all the subsequent articles are devoted to the right and the duty of states.[28] This reveals a strong preference by UN members for the importance of the state's role in implementing economic development goals.[29] The question remains: What development models can best serve the right to development, while promoting political, civil, economic and social rights?

The Chinese leadership's answer to such a question is the so-called "socialism with Chinese characteristics." Beijing has made it very clear that the Chinese understanding of human rights is different from that of the West.[30] As Deng Xiaoping stated:

> What are human rights? They are the rights of how many people, of a majority, a minority, or of all the people? What the West calls human rights and what we call human rights are two different things, with different standpoints.[31]

The first Chinese "White Paper on Human Rights", a fifty thousand word document published in 1991 by the State Council, can be seen as an official effort to introduce these "different standpoints" to the world.[32] To elaborate on the White Paper, several Chinese writers summarize the different conceptualizations of human rights between China and the West as follows:

> 1. While the West emphasizes individual rights, China stresses collective rights (including anti-colonialism and the right to development) which are the precondition and guarantee of individual rights;

2. While the West emphasizes political rights and neglects economic rights, China does not separate the two and puts more effort into improving living standards;

3. While the West contends that the protection of human rights should go beyond national borders, China views the state as the main actor in the protection and improvement of human rights;

4. While the West regards human rights as universal, China (following Marxist theory) analyzes human rights through the lense of the class struggle.[33]

These viewpoints and the White Paper do not seem to place the Chinese government's perception of human rights far from the majority of Third World countries.[34] Rather, the above discussion seems to show that it is the political economy of the Third World countries, rather than any particular type of culture, that is more responsible for these countries' conceptualization of human rights.[35] To measure the validity of these changing perceptions of human rights, we need empirical data to see how different development models may affect human rights.[36] Let us look at the Chinese experience since 1949.

Chinese Development Models and Human Rights

At the risk of over-simplifying the issue, one could say that the study of China's human rights situation can be roughly divided into two groups, an idealist group and a realist group. The former is radical in its assessment of human rights in China, focusing more on abuses of political and individual rights. Yan Yiaqi and Fang Lizhi are among the main representatives of this group.[37] The realist group tends to observe China's development and human rights record along two major categories: political and civil rights on the one hand, and economic, social and cultural rights on the other.[38]

The following is a look at the various Chinese development models and their effects on human rights and human development in light of a framework employed by some people to analyze the relationship between human rights and development in the Third World: the "trade-off" theories.[39]

As Jack Donnelly critically observes, the relationship between development and human rights is being conceptualized as various "trade-offs."[40] First, there is the "needs trade-off" which contends that high levels of poverty need to be tolerated for rapid industrialization. Such a trade-off ranges from the exclusion of consumption-oriented human rights from development planning to the reduction of consumption for increased investment. Second, there is the "equality trade-off" which utilizes the inverted U-hypothesis presented by Simon Kuznets: in the early stages of a country's industrialization, income inequality increases, and the gap closes when the country is industrialized.[41] This hypothesis also accepts the coexistence of traditional and modern economic sectors, with the former lagging behind. Certain economic regions and/or sectors may be allowed to develop first in order for prosperity to "trickle down" later. Third, according to the "liberty trade-off", certain political and civil rights have to be temporarily suspended for other development objectives.

In the following discussion, I use this trade-off analysis in a modified way. First, the range of issues and factors used to examine these trade-offs should be broader. When we talk about basic needs or income levels, it is problematic to use nation-states as the unit of analysis. Regional differences, urban-rural disparities, minority groups and gender, are some of the indicators that must be taken into consideration. Second, I am not focussing on whether or not there should be such trade-offs between development and human rights in China's modernization process. My primary concern is whether these types of trade-offs have taken place in China, and if so, how they differ in different development models that have been implemented by the Chinese leadership.

The PRC has so far experimented with three development models: the Soviet model in the 1950s, the self-reliance model in the 1960s and for most of the 1970s, and a "socialist market" model since the late 1970s.

The Soviet model (1949-1958)

China adopted a comprehensive package in the Soviet model. Chinese society was completely restructured through the establishment of state ownership, people's communes and other socialist measures. Although the economy became highly centralized, controlled and planned in this period, the people's economic, social and cultural welfare improved dramatically. Land reform and other social programs made the distribution of wealth more equal than before. Therefore, the Chinese experience in this period tends to negate the equality trade-off analysis.

At the same time, a Soviet style investment pattern was established: moving capital from the agricultural sector to the industrial sector for the purpose of rapid industrialization. By investing heavily in industry, especially heavy industry, the Chinese government used the agricultural sector to serve the industrial sector. The living standard of 80 percent of the Chinese population was affected negatively by this process. It was an obvious "needs trade-off".

In the political sphere, the Chinese Communist Party (CPP) firmly established its one-party dictatorship through the Thought Reform Movement and the Anti-Rightist Movement, in spite of the existence of other small parties. Guided by Mao's theories of the class struggle and the two types of contradictions in socialist societies (antagonistic and non-antagonistic), the Chinese government continuously introduced more measures to limit political freedom and civil rights. As a result, a significant portion of the Chinese population, including intellectuals, often became the "subjects of the class struggle." This liberty trade-off was not simply a matter of development priorities. The CCP was pursuing a particular type of social system with a very strong ideological commitment. The Korean War and the subsequent confrontation with the United States convinced Beijing that China's sovereignty and national security were constantly being threatened. To Mao and his colleagues, these concerns were probably far more important than others. In summation, in this period, there was a needs trade-off, a complex liberty trade-off, but no equality trade-off.

The self-reliance model (1960-1978)

In this period, although the Soviet development model was firmly established, it was also being challenged and modified to fit the visions of the Chinese leadership. I use the word "visions" in a plural form because within the CCP, two development strategies were conceptualized and they competed for dominance. One of these strategies was Mao's radical approach to creating an egalitarian society, an approach which was centred on the idea of "red". The other, represented by Liu Shaoqi and Deng Xiaoping, was more pragmatic, with a technocratic orientation around "expert". In spite of this "red" versus "expert" conflict, China's development strategies could be characterized as strategies of self-reliance. The 1960s saw the PRC go through its most isolated period, after the break up with the Soviet Union.

There were great similiarities between the self-reliance model and the Soviet model with respect to the development trade-offs. Although Liu and Deng managed to implement some pragmatic measures in the countryside (the family plot, for example) in the early 1960s, the needs trade-off deepened during this period, as agriculture continued to be sacrificed for the development of heavy industry. Through compulsory state planning, China achieved the highest savings and investment rate--"compulsory capital accumulation"--in the world. A substantial portion of the population lived in poverty, although there was a relative but slow improvement of living standards. Despite the impressive growth rate in both agriculture and industry, "[s]ectors closely associated with living conditions, such as light industry, commerce, services, education, sanitation and housing, were neglected."[42] There was also a tremendous amount of waste being generated by a central planning system that simply did not work well, and this cancelled out some of the high growth figures.

China, however, continued the policy of equal distribution in these years. This meant a compulsory implementation of national price control, a fairly equal allocation of resources among different regions, an improvement in living standards in remote minority areas, etc. It is worth mentioning that under both the Soviet and the self-reliance models, gender equality was perceived as an indispensable part of socialism and many measures were taken by the Chinese government to improve the status of women. Thus, it seems that there was no equality trade-off.

The liberty trade-off intensified during this period, especially during the Cultural Revolution. During the peak of the Cultural Revolution, a twisted form of freedom (*Daminzhu*) was given to the Chinese people, but many were still persecuted simply for being in a leadership position, for being intellectuals, or for joining the "wrong" group. The goals of the Cultural Revolution were very ideological. Thus, in a sense, the liberty trade-off can only be seen as serving a larger socialist project, as opposed to serving short-term development targets. It is important to note that this negative lesson became a positive incentive for establishing a comprehensive legal system in China after 1978.

The socialist market model (1978 -)

In comparison with the two earlier periods, since China began its domestic reforms and open-door policy, some significant changes have occurred to all three major rights vs. development trade-offs. Economic reforms at different stages have reorganized China's investment patterns. Rural reforms were very successful ,and both income and living standards in the countryside improved rapidly in the early 1980s. The needs trade-off has given way to emphasis on consumption and the quality of life. The equality trade-off became a part of government policy almost overnight following Deng Xiaoping's well-known speech in which he said that a part of the population should be allowed to "get rich" first, and that to get rich is glorious.

The policy implication of this approach and its consequences are twofold. First, a part of the population in any given region is allowed to get financially ahead of others, making income inequality a policy option. Second, development priorities were assigned to selected regions, allowing the emergence of a traditional/modern division in China. As a result, we have seen an increase in the income gap between urban and rural areas since the mid-1980s, a classical phenomenon of industrialization. We have also seen the largest regional growth disparities in the PRC's history. The impact on social and economic rights is obvious. There are also indications that the status of women and children have suffered as a result of introducing market forces. It is common to see women and children working long hours in poorly protected working environments. Hence, the reform process has both intended and unintended consequences. The equality trade-off finally became a part of the PRC's drive for modernization. Some people simply call this "primitive accumulation, Chinese style."

Again, it is difficult to measure the liberty trade-off. One important change felt by many inside China, but comprehended by few outside China, has been the "de-ideology" process of Chinese society. At the top, Deng and his associates have been committed to ending the Mao-style mass political movement, and trying to regulate society by setting up a legal system. At the bottom, compared to the time of the Cultural Revolution, people now have much more freedom to express their political views. Nevertheless, the Chinese government retains tight control over society based on the liberty trade-off argument. New Authoritarianism might be a better term.[43]

Overall, the Chinese development models seem to demonstrate a high level of achievement in the area of economic and social rights, while there are severe limitations on political and civil rights.[44] The Chinese experience also tends to refute the claims by the trade-off theorists that the trade-offs are both temporary and self-correcting.[45]

International Comparisons

If, as shown in the Chinese case, certain trade-offs do exist between development and human rights and that the paths of economic, social and political development are often unbalanced, how then do we compare China's experience with those of other countries? We can look at the development situations in three major areas: East Asia, Latin America and Eastern Europe.

First, a number of China's neighbours in East Asia have undergone rapid economic growth. South Korea, Taiwan, Hong Kong and Singapore, the four dragons, achieved a very high growth rate without having a Western style democratic system. In fact, Hong Kong is a British colony (until June 1997), and the political systems of the other three states are still labelled as authoritarian.[46] Only recently have Korea and Taiwan begun a "democratization" process that allows multiparty elections to take place. Despite the limited scope of these countries' experiences, many conclude that under a controlled political environment, rapid economic development, with a certain level of equal distribution, is possible.

Today, countries such as Malaysia, Indonesia and Thailand all appear to be following such a path. Joined by China, these countries argue that a certain amount of political control is required in order to maintain a stable environment which, in turn, is necessary for a country to compete internationally. These countries also contend that they have done well in improving the living conditions of their people. Any western criticism of the human rights records of these countries is met with strong resistance.[47] As Malaysian Prime Minister Mahathir Bin Mohamad put it:

> While we and our neighbours try to make socio-economic progress, we cannot but lament the external impediments which threaten to derail us. We are concerned about pressures and other means by some in the North to erode our limited comparative advantages, particular labour and natural resources. The North had exploited fully these very same assets in their own countries and in ours when they ruled us. Now they seek to stifle our growth by involving human rights, the social clause and environmental conditionalities. Did they care for these things when they were at our stage of development?[48]

These views are shared by many Third World countries.[49] We might call it the East Asia development model, and it seems to be the model which the Chinese leadership has chosen to follow.

In Latin America, democracy and development do not have a fixed evolutionary pattern. Many countries have experienced economic development, political instability, coups d'état and democratization. A very common problem, however, is the extreme inequality which is a result of high level economic growth. It is well-known that tens of thousands of children live in the streets of Sao Paulo and that half of Peru's population lives below the poverty line. The lack of fundamental changes in social conditions has also resulted in human rights violations in many countries. The status of women has not improved, it has in fact worsened in some cases.[50] In the period prior to 1978, the PRC did better in the distribution and equality aspects. Since 1978, market forces and decentralization have eroded some of the progress that was achieved earlier. There are now serious problems with child labour and with the status of women in China. China could learn many a lesson from the Latin American experience with regards to human rights protection.

Finally, let us examine the situation in Eastern Europe. The countries of Eastern Europe carried out democratic reforms first, making their respective political systems open to the challenges of different societal forces. This is in sharp contrast to China's experience since 1978. The former Soviet Union and other Eastern European countries, however, are suffering in terms of economic development. There are many signs in these societies that the newly established political systems are very volatile. Hence, these countries may experience "the decline of democracy", to borrow a phrase from Zehra Arat who argues that unbalanced human rights policies may lead to the failure of democratic institutions.[51] Malak Poppovic and Paulo Sergio Pinheiro summarize Arat as follows:

> In the first phase of the process of democratization, civil and political rights follow an upward trend, whereas social and economic rights do not follow suit. In spite of the growing gap between the two groups of rights, the newly acquired political equality and liberties constitute the source of legitimacy. In the second phase, the country has stable civil and political democratic practices, while social and economic rights still lag behind. Enthusiasm about political participation starts to wane and the legitimacy of the system is questioned. In the third phase, as the gap between the two groups of rights increases, discontent among the disadvantaged groups takes the form of social unrest, which in turn provokes a chain reaction of coercive policies on the part of the authorities, that are likely to jeopardize democratic efforts and apparently consolidated political rights.[52]

We have yet to see if the former Soviet states and other European countries will take such a path.[53]

It is difficult to make generalizations regarding the relationship between human rights and development models, but we need comparisons to make sense of this important relationship.

Conclusions

In studying the relationship between development models and human rights, China presents a unique case due to its history, culture, population, geographic size, etc. On the other hand, China's paths of development and their impacts on human rights are indicative in many ways.

First, as a Third World developing country, China deserves credit for its remarkable achievements in enriching the economic and social rights of its people. China's success in these aspects have made it a strong voice among Third World countries for broadening the content and redefining the meaning of human rights.

Second, as a socialist country, China is the only one that has managed its economic transformation without a political transformation. We may loose our sense of history if we refuse to acknowledge that Chinese socialism, together with Democratic socialism and the now defunct Soviet form of socialism, has had a direct impact on the development of capitalism and the evolution of democracy. In the process of the historical evolution of different social systems, capitalist and socialist ideas and institutions penetrated each other. The state in capitalist countries has moved away from the classical Marxist definition, and now protects a wide range of rights for different social classes. Socialist countries have introduced market mechanisms for reforming the economy (China has made it so far, while the former Soviet Union failed). As a result, neither system remains pure in its original "ideal form", but has transformed itself and become more complex.

Third, as part of the rapidly industrializing East Asia, China could become an entity that is classified neither as a Third World model nor as a socialist model, but a model of Confucian capitalism. There is a large body of literature in Asia (especially in Japanese), which turns Max Weber's theory of capitalist development upside down, arguing (or justifying) that the so-called East Asian miracle has a cultural base: Confucianism can produce not only benign authoritarianism but also sustainable economic development.

Finally, all the development models experimented with in China feature the central role of the state in either enhancing or hindering human rights. The global dialogue on human rights in the past several decades seems to confirm this reality.

To return to the UNDP's efforts in measuring human development and human freedom, it appears that we have a long way to go. The fact that China scores well with the HDI but poorly with the HFI indicates that we have yet to find a better way of evaluating human rights and human development experiences in our complex world. The human development indicators that China has so far succeeded in improving, such as life expectancy, medical care and poverty relief, are much more stable than political indicators. The latter tends to be more volatile. The collapse of the Soviet Union and other East European regimes revealed that political conditions can change at an unpredictable pace but a nation's life expectancy cannot become longer over night. However, to use such an argument to further the trade-off theory between freedom and other development priorities would only prove short-sighted. Meeting basic human needs and promoting economic rights and the right to development are important but incomplete goals for any society. Animals can be satisfactorily fed in a zoo and prisoners can live a long life in a well-managed jail. The fundamental desire for freedom is unique to human beings, but its universality is often neglected by those who advocate political control. In the end, we must not forget that it was Karl Marx, the father of the world communist movement, who claimed that the ultimate goal of human development is to leap from the "realm of necessity" to the "realm of freedom."

Notes

1. For different approaches on development, see Lucian W. Pye, "Political Science and the Crisis of Authoritarianism." *American Political Science Review*, Vol.84, No. 1, 1990; Samuel Huntington, "The Goals of Development", in Myron Weiner & Samuel Huntington, eds. *Understanding Political Development*, Glenview: Little Brown, 1987; G. O'Donnell, P.C. Schmitter and L. Whitehead, eds. *Transition from Authoritarian Rule: Prospects for Democracy.* Baltimore: The Johns Hopkins University Press, 1986; Blomström, Magnus and Björn Hettne, *Development Theory in Transition.* London: Zed Books Ltd, 1984; Frank, Andre G., *Capitalism and Underdevelopment in Latin America.* New York: Monthly Review Press, 1967; W.W. Rostow, *The Stages of Economic Growth: A Non-Communist Manifesto.* Cambridge: Cambridge University Press, 1960.

2. See Susan Whitfield, ed., *After the Event: Human Rights and their Future in China*, London: Wellsweep Press, 1993; John Copper, Franz Michael and Yuan-li Wu, eds., *Human Rights in Post-Mao China*, Boulder: Westview Press, 1985; Yuan-li Wu, et. al. eds., *Human Rights in the People's Republic of China*, Boulder: Westview Press, 1988; Asia Watch, *Punishment Season: Human Rights in China after Martial Law*, New York: Asia Watch, 1990; Ann Kent, *Human Rights in the People's Republic of China: National and International Dimensions*, Canberra: Australian National University, 1990.

3. The United Nations Development Program, *Human Development Report*, New York: Oxford University Press, 1991.

4. Here Charles Humana's methods and 1985 ranking were adopted by the UNDP Report.

5. For a critical assessment of the HDI, see Paul Streeten, "Human Development: The Debate about the Index." *International Social Science Journal*, No. 143, March 1995.

6. Some have attempted to make detailed modifications to the HDI. See Sudhir Anand and Amartya Sen, "Human Development Index: Methodology and Measurement." *UNDP Occasional Papers No.8*, 1993; "Technical Note 2. Human development Index: A Survey of Recent Reviews." *Human Development Report*, New York: UNDP, 1993. See also, Donald McGranahan, "Measurement of Development: Research at the United Nations Research Institute for Social Development". *International Social Science Journal*, No. 143, March 1995.

7. The UNDP, *Human Development Report*, Chapter 1.

8. UNDP, *Report*, p. 21.

9. Many argue that even before the collapse of the Soviet system in these countries, the world had gone through a process of democratization. See for example, Tatu Vanhanen, *The Process of Democratization: A Comparative Study of 147 States*, 1980-88. New York: Crane Russak, 1990.

10. Zbigniew Brzezinski, *The Grand Failure: The Birth and Death of Communism in the Twentieth Century*, New York: Charles Scribner's Sons, 1989.

11. Francis Fukuyama, "The End of History?" *The National Interest* 16 (Summer 1989):3-18. Also, *The End of History and the Last Man*, New York: The Free Press, 1992.

12. For details, see Gabriel Almond, *A Discipline Divided: Schools and Sects in Political Science*. London: Sage Publications, 1990.

13. Chalmers Johnson, *MITI and the Japanese Miracle*, Stanford: Stanford University Press, 1982.

14. Gabriel Almond, "Capitalism and Democracy", *PS: Political Science and Politics*, September 1991, pp. 467-474. See also *Comparative Politics 94/95* (Annual Editions), Guilford, CT: The Dushkin Publishing Group Inc., 1994, pp. 253-259.

15. *PS: Political Science and Politics*, Ibid., p. 467.

16. Many people have articulated the fact that between 1974 and 1990, more than 30 countries in Latin America, Europe and East Asia shifted from

authoritarian to democratic political systems. This has created a large body of literature on the so-called third wave of democracy. See for example, Samuel Huntington, *The Third Wave*, Norman: Oklahoma University, 1991.

17. For an assessment of China's human rights situation based on Western standards, see Human Rights Watch, *Human Rights Watch World Report 1995*, New York: Human Rights Watch, 1995, pp. 142-149.

18. Bilder, *Rethinking International Human Rights: Some Basic Questions*, 1969.

19. It is also worth noting that with all the constitutional changes, such a system continued to exist even within the United States up to the mid-1960s, when African-Americans were not allowed to ride in the same part of a bus and schools were separated along racial lines.

20. For a treatment of the relationship between traditional Chinese culture and human rights, see Jeremy T. Paltiel, "Cultural and Political Determinants of the Chinese Approach to Human Rights." Paper presented at a workshop on Human Rights, International Organizations and the Right to Development, Ottawa, October 27-28, 1995.

21. For a good analysis on the basic needs approach in relations to human rights and human development, see Frances Stewart, "Basic Needs Strategies, Human Rights, and the Right to Development", *Human Rights Quarterly*, Vol. 11, 1988.

22. UN General Assembly Resolution 217A (III), December 10, 1948. According to the records of the commission, the rights named in the first twenty articles are called "political and civil rights" and the new rights are called "economic rights". See Maurice Cranston, *What are Human Rights?* London: the Bodley Head Ltd., 1973. p. 54.

23. United Nations General Assembly Resolution 41/128.

24. In fact, some Chinese writers regard the right to development as one of the two breakthroughs (the other one is self-determination as a collective right) achieved by the developing countries on the issue of human rights. See Zheng Hangsheng and Gu Chunde, eds., *Renquan Shihua* (A History of Human Rights), Beijing: Beijing Chubanshe, 1993, pp. 365-370.

25. For a good overview on the issue of the right to development, see Russel Lawrence Barsh, "The Right to Development as a Human Right: Results of the Global Consultation", *Human Rights Quarterly*, Vol. 13, No. 3, 1991.

26. Ibid.

27. Ibid.

28. This certainly raises a series of questions about the primary concerns of human rights. It is beyond the central theme of this paper to discuss these issues.

29. For more analysis on the different perceptions regarding human rights on the UN platform, see Errol P. Mendes, "The Legal and Constitutional Basis of Human Rights, the Right to Development and the Law of Proportionality: A Canadian Attempt to Bridge the Turbulent Waters between Chinese and Western Conceptions of Human Rights." Paper presented at a workshop on Human Rights, International Organizations and the Right to Development, Ottawa, October 27-28, 1995.

30. For a Chinese analysis of the Western human rights conceptualizations, see Shen Zongling, "Er'zhanhou Xifeng Renquan Xieshuo de Yanbian" (The Evolution of Western Human Rights Ideas in the Postwar Period), *Zhongguo Shehui Kexue*, No. 77, May 1992.

31. Quoted from Ann Kent, *Between Freedom and Subsistence: China and Human Rights*, Hong Kong: Oxford University Press, 1993. p. 51.

32. Guowuyuan Xinwen Bangongshi, *Zhongguo de Renquan Zhuangkuang* (Human Rights in China), Beijing: Zhongyang Wenxian Chubanshe, 1991.

33. Lai Pengcheng, Ni Shixiong and Yuan Zheng, *Guoji Renquanlun* (International Human Rights), Shanghai: Shanghai Renmin Chubanshe, 1993. Chapter 7. For additional elaborations on the White Paper, see Zheng Hangsheng and Gu Chunde, eds., *Renquan Shihua* (A History of Human Rights), op. cit.

34. For an account of the Marxist view on human rights as understood by the Chinese scholars, see Zhu Feng, "Makesi Renquan Lirun Runyao" (A Brief Review of Marxist Human Rights Theories), *Zhongguo Shehui Kexue*, No. 74, February 1992.

35. Recently, the number of human rights related publications in China have increased. See, Ibid. See also, Huang Dengsen, et. al. eds., *Dangdai Zhongguo Renquan Lun* (Human Rights in Contemporary China), Beijing: Dangdai Zhongguo Chubanshe, 1993; Zheng Hangsheng and Gu Chunde, eds., *Renquan Shihua* (A History of Human Rights), Beijing: Beijing Chubanshe, 1993.

36. To date, China has not ratified any of the major UN documents on human rights, including the *Universal Declaration*, the two Covenants on *Civil and Political Rights* and on *Economic, Social and Cultural Rights*. For a brief but critical review of the PRC's attitudes toward human rights definitions, see John F. Copper, "Defining Human Rights in the People's Republic of China", in Yuan-li Wu, et al, eds, *Human Rights in the People's Republic of China*, Boulder: Westview Press, 1988.

37. See Fang Lizhi, *Bringing Down the Great Wall*, New York: Alfred A. Knopf, 1991, and many publications after the 1989 Tiananmen crackdown on the student movement.

38. See, for example, Stephen C. Thomas, "Chinese Economic Development and Human Rights in the Post-Mao Era", in George Shepherd Jr. And Ved Nanda, eds., *Human Rights and Third World Development*, Westport: Greenwood Press, 1985; Ann Kent, *Between Freedom and Subsistence: China and Human Rights, 1993; Ann Kent, Human Rights in the People's Republic of China: National and International Dimensions*, Canberra: Peace Research Centre, The Australian National University, 1990; John Copper, Franz Michael and Yuan-li Wu, *Human Rights in Post-Mao China*, Boulder: Westview Press, 1985.

39. See Sylvia Ann Hewlett, "Human Rights and Economic Realities: Tradeoffs in Historical Perspective", *Political Science Quarterly*, Vol. 94, No. 3, Fall, 1979; Jack Donnelly, "Human Rights and Development: Complementary or Competing Concerns?" *World Politics*, No. 1, October 1983.

40. Jack Donnelly, *Universal Human Rights in Theory and Practice*, Ithaca: Cornell University Press, 1989. Part V. He characterized these trade-off theories as "conventional wisdom" that do not reflect reality.

41. Simon Kuznets, "Economic Growth and Income Inequality", *American Economic Review*, 45, March, 1955.

42. Ryoshin Minami, *The Economic Development of China: A Comparison with the Japanese Experience*, London: Macmillan, 1994. p. 163.

43. For a good analysis of Chinese new authoritarianism, see Mark P. Petracca & Mong Xiong, "The Concept of Chinese Neo-Authoritarianism", *Asian Survey*, Vol. XXX, No. 11, 1990. On authoritarianism and corporatism as development models, see Guillermo O'Donnell, *Bureaucratic Authoritarianism*. Berkeley: University of California Press, 1988; Philippe C. Schmitter, "Reflections on Where the Theory of Neo-Corporatism Has Gone and Where the Praxis of New-Corporatism May be Going", in G. Lehmbruch & P.C. Schmitter, eds., *Patterns of Corporatist Policy-Making*. London: Sage Publications, Ltd., 1982.

44. For more details regarding the Chinese government's accounts on China's human rights achievements, see *Human Rights in China*, Beijing, 1991.

45. See Jack Donnelly, "Human Rights and Development: Complementary or Competing Concerns?" Supra note 39, p. 257.

46. For an account on human rights and development in Singapore, see Keith Suter, "Singapore: Modernisation and Human Rights", *Contemporary Review*, Vol. 240, No. 1393, February 1982.

47. Even India, labelled as a Western style democracy, tends to stress the impact of its culture on its development. See Satish Kumar, "Human Rights and Economic Development: The Indian Tradition", *Human Rights Quarterly*, Vol. 3, No. 3, Summer 1981.

48. Statement by the Honourable Dato Seri Dr. Mahathir Bin Mohamad, Prime Minister of Malaysia, at the United Nations World Summit for Social Development in Copenhagen, Denmark, 11 March 1995.

49. See for example, Shri Justice Ranganath Misra, Chairman for the National Human Rights Commission of India, "National Interests and Human Rights", Address at the Conference on Human Rights and Changing Global Values: The Universal Declaration, the Vienna Conference and Beyond, Edmonton, November 4, 1995; Jeremy Williams, "Capitalist Development and Human Rights: Singapore Under Lee Kuan Yew", *Journal of Contemporary Asia*, Vol. 22, No. 3, 1992.

50. See E.A. Cebotarev, "Women, Human Rights and the Family in Development Theory and Practice (with reference to Latin America and the Caribbean)", *Canadian Journal of Development Studies*, Vol. 9, No. 2, 1988.

51. Zehra Arat, *Democracy and Human Rights in Developing Countries*, London: Lynne Rienner Publishers, 1991.

52. Malak Poppovic and Paulo Sergio Pinheiro, "How to Consolidate Democracy? A Human Right Approach", *International Social Science Journal*, No. 143, March 1995, pp. 76-77.

53. The African countries are not covered here. For a brief overview on the African experience on development and human rights, see Joseph R.A. Ayee, "The State, Development and Human Rights: Some Aspects of the African Experience", *Canadian Journal of African Studies*, Vol. 25, No. 1, 1991.

The Right to Development and China's Project to Help the Poor Through Development

RAO GEPING

Subsistence and development are topics of eternal importance to humanity. The right to subsistence and the right to development are the most basic rights for human beings, and they are of primary concern to developing countries. To confront and eliminate poverty is a pressing task for the international community and developing countries in promoting the right to development.

This essay attempts to demonstrate China's progress in the areas of eliminating poverty and promoting the universal right to development, through the example of the project to help the poor through development.

The Right to Development is the Most Basic Human Right and of Primary Concern to Developing Countries

The introduction of the right to development into the human rights field was an important and logical development in modern human rights thinking, which has already been universally recognized by the international community. The notion of human rights is very wide and complex. It covers every area of human life. The state of human rights differs greatly from country to country or between the various stages of development within one country, due to conditioning factors such as the unique historical background, social system, economic development and cultural tradition of each country. Therefore, different countries emphasize different points in the realization of human rights. In developing countries, where the majority of the world's population lives and where a third of the population still lives below the poverty line, the most urgent human rights problem is still subsistence/life and the right to improve living conditions, i.e. economic, social and cultural rights. Enjoyment of these rights is dependent on economic development in these countries. In the developing countries, therefore, it is not merely a theoretical issue to make the right to development a priority in the promotion of human rights, it is a very real need.

Faced with the urgent issue of how to promote economic and social development in the newly independent countries, the U.N. has, since the 1960s, been calling on every country to pay attention to the inter-dependent relationship between economic and social factors within the process of balanced and stable development, and to link this relationship together with the human rights issue. At its 24th session, on December 11, 1969, the U.N. General Assembly passed resolution no. 2542(XXIV) and issued the *Declaration on Social Progress and Development*. This Declaration pointed out that the goal of social progress and development should be to "continuously raise the material and spiritual standard of living of all members of society" while showing respect for and keeping in line with human rights and fundamental freedoms.

In the 1970s, developing countries put forward the idea of the right to development for the first time and demanded that it be listed as a basic human right. This elicited a strong reaction from the international community.[1] The U.N. Commission on Human Rights has held many meetings specifically to discuss the issue of the right to development and, in January 1978, the Commission passed Resolution no. 5(XXXV) which confirmed that the right to development is a human right and emphasized that "equality of opportunity for development is a prerogative both of nations and of individuals who make up nations". On December 4, 1986, on the basis of a draft provided by the Working Group of Experts of the Commission on Human Rights, the U.N. adopted the *Declaration on the Right to Development* through its Resolution no. 41/128. Thus, the U.N. officially recognized that the right to development is an inalienable human right, and that so called development refers to "...a comprehensive economic, social, cultural and political process, which aims at the constant improvement of the well-being of the entire population and of all individuals on the basis of their active, free and meaningful participation in development and in the fair distribution of benefits resulting therefrom."

The Declaration underscored the right of the people of a country to equality of opportunity for development, and it pointed out that "states should undertake, at the national level, all necessary measures for the realization of the right to development and shall ensure, *inter alia*, equality of opportunity for all in their access to basic resources, education, health services, food, housing, employment and the fair distribution of income." Governments of each country should see to it that "appropriate economic and social reforms should be carried out with a view to eradicating all social injustices".[2]

Of all examples of social injustice, the gap between rich and poor, as well as absolute poverty are the ones which most affect people. People have long been aware of the disparity between North and South and the gap between developed and developing countries. They call them "the most dangerous time-bombs of the future."[3] Absolute poverty on an international level is even more shocking. The standard that an annual income of less than 370 dollars equals poverty indicates that there are more than 1 billion people living in poverty in the world, and every year tens of thousands of people die from starvation. Poverty is a very real fact of life, and "absolute poverty and social rejection are insufferable violations of the dignity of human beings".[4]

The U.N. has selected October 17 of every year as the "International Day for Helping the Poor Regions Develop" and appeals to the international community to confront and eliminate poverty. One could say that, in the process of realizing human rights in the developing countries, no other task is more urgent than emphasizing the right to development and eliminating poverty.

China is Faced With the Serious Challenge of Reducing and Eliminating Poverty

At present, in the process of promoting universal respect for and observance of human rights, China, as the largest developing country in the world, is giving top priority to the right to development. The issue of the right to subsistence and the right to development in poverty-stricken areas is of even greater concern to the Chinese government which must give priority to solving these problems.

There are close to 1.2 billion people in China, 80% of them are living in the countryside. Arable land in China, however, only constitutes 7% of the world's arable land. The average amount of land per capita in China is 1.3 *mu*, which is much lower than the United States average of 12.16 *mu* and the world average of 4.52 *mu*, and yet, China has to shoulder the responsibility of feeding and clothing 22% of the world's population. For many centuries, the Chinese people have been living in poverty, and to have enough to eat and enough to clothe themselves has always been their minimum demand. Ever since the People's Republic of China was established in 1949, the government has devoted itself to the great task of helping its people escape poverty. As a result, the living conditions of the Chinese people have improved fundamentally, and the problem of food and clothing has now basically been solved. This has especially been true since 1978, as China, with a focus on economic reconstruction, began promoting reform and the open-door policy. The gross national product has increased 9% annually; overall development of the national economy has been promoted, the combined strength of the country increased greatly, people's living standard improved markedly, and a general trend of prosperity has prevailed in the entire nation.

However, when looking at the situation in its entirety, it becomes clear that the strength of China's economy is still rather limited and that China remains a low-income country. According to information provided by an authoritative source at the State Statistical Bureau in July 1993, the average GNP per capita in China was only 374 US dollars--calculated according to the rate of exchange at that time--and China remains a developing country, far behind most countries. In particular, it must be pointed out that economic development in China is very unbalanced, and regional disparities are great. In the coastal regions of eastern China the economy is developing rapidly, and some regions have already become relatively well-off. But the vast regions of the mid-west are only developing slowly, and many areas remain rather poor. For example, according to statistics from 1991, the highest average GDP per capita was 6,675 yuan in Shanghai and the lowest 890 yuan in Guizhou, i.e. the former was 7.5 times higher than the latter. The average level of consumption was 1,908 yuan in Shanghai and 445 yuan in Guizhou, i.e. consumption in Shanghai was 4.5 times higher than in Guizhou. The size of the population and the level of poverty in the poverty-stricken regions are rather alarming.

According to World Bank standards which put the measure of abject poverty at an average per capita consumption of 275 US dollars and poverty at an average per capita consumption of 370 US dollars, there were 210 million people living in poverty in China in 1985. This constituted 18.8% of the 1.2 billion people living in poverty in all the developing countries. Of the 210 million Chinese living in poverty, 80 million were living in abject poverty. This constituted 12.6% of the 640 million people living in abject poverty in all the developing countries.[5] According to the Chinese government's own statistics, by the end of 1985, there were 125 million people living in poverty in the countryside with an annual net income of less than 200 yuan. They made up 14.8% of the total population in the countryside. Of these 125 million, 40 million people had an average annual income of less than 150 yuan, and they were living in a situation of utter destitution.[6] This group of people is concentrated in eighteen mountainous regions in west and central China. Geographically, they are divided into six main, large areas, i.e., the south-west karst mountain regions (north-west Guangxi, south Yunnan and the Wumeng mountains); the Huang Tu highlands, the eastern and western plains and contiguous mountain regions; the arid regions of Inner-Mongolia and Xinjiang; the highlands of Qinghai and Tibet; and the hilly regions in the east. The natural conditions in these regions are typically very harsh. The methods of production are backward, the industrial structures are simple, and the market is very limited. Basic facilities are lacking, the peasants are unsophisticated, transportation is inconvenient, and communication is inefficient. The eco-system is out of balance, the disproportionality between population and resources is acute, exploitation of the region is extremely difficult, and producing and surviving is very hard for the people.[7] These regions are traditionally referred to as the "old, minorities, remote and poor" regions, because, during the war, the countryside revolution took place according to regions, i.e. areas with a high concentration of national minorities, remote areas and border areas. Within these regions, poverty is most prevalent in the western parts, where the poverty rate is 22%. The western provinces of Gansu and Tibet have the highest rates of poverty, i.e. more than 30%.[8] In these regions, a significant number of people still do not have enough food and clothing, and more than 7 million livestock have difficulty finding enough to drink. The rate of illiteracy and semi-illiteracy has reached an average high of 35%, and in the minority regions the rate of illiteracy is about 60%. In the impoverished mountain regions, over half of the villages cannot be reached by public road. Close to half of the farmers do not have electricity. In 97% of the poor counties endemic diseases prevail in varying degrees. Almost all the poor regions are in financial difficulties and 83% of the poor counties rely on the government for financial assistance.[9] According to the statistics, of the close to 2000 counties in China, at least 699 counties fall within the category of poor counties that receive varying degrees of financial support from the central and regional governments.[10] These counties make up more than a third of all counties in China.

As a result, a sharp contrast has emerged in the development of contemporary China: On the one hand, the Chinese social economy has undergone huge changes since the reform and open-door policy was implemented. This is especially true for the coastal regions in the east where astonishing progress has been achieved. The Yangtze River delta, the Pearl River delta, the triangular region of Fujian and south-eastern China and the regions surrounding the Bohai Bay are all thriving and prosperous, and they have become among the fastest growing, most vital regions in the global economy. On the other hand, in sharp contrast to this prosperity, there is the poverty and backwardness of the under-developed central and western regions. The economic and social development of these regions has already become an acute and glaring problem. Elimination of poverty, universal development and shared prosperity have become the most arduous tasks currently facing the Chinese government, and these tasks are also of great importance to achieving the goal of alleviating and eliminating poverty in the world.

Implementation of the Chinese Project to Help the Poor Through Development

With regards to the relationship between human rights and the right to development, the U.N. *Declaration on Social Progress and Development* emphasized that "...rapid expansion of national income and wealth and their equitable distribution among all members of society are fundamental to all social progress, and they should therefore be in the forefront of the preoccupations of every State and Government." The Declaration specifically raised the issue of "assurance to disadvantaged or marginal sectors of the population of equal opportunities for social and economic advancement in order to achieve an effectively integrated society." In planning social development measures, governments should take into account the "diversity of the needs of developing and developed areas, and of urban and rural areas, within each country,...". In order to emphasize the importance of balanced development and equality in society, the Declaration specifically set out, as some of the main goals for social progress and development, "the elimination of hunger and malnutrition", "the elimination of poverty", "the eradication of illiteracy", and "the achievement of the highest standards of health"[11]. The principles and goals set out by the U.N. to achieve social progress and development are of importance as overall guidance. In fact, these principles and goals have already been fully integrated into the Chinese government's policy and measures to combat poverty.

In Chinese culture, there has always been a solid tradition of "supporting the poor and helping those in trouble". The Chinese government has always viewed elimination of poverty and shared prosperity as its undeniable responsibility. During the process of reform and opening up to the outside world, the Chinese government, through an extensive survey on national conditions, paid the highest amount of attention to the huge gap between rich and poor and the extreme poverty in some regions. The Chinese government treated the issue of alleviating and eliminating poverty as being related to other serious issues and strategic goals, such as the success or failure of the reforms, political stability, national unity, social stability and balanced development of the national economy. Since the mid 1980s, the government has carried out a large-scale planned and organized project of eliminating poverty.[12] From a human rights perspective, this project can be seen as a sincere, down-to-earth effort by the Chinese government to respect and realize the right to development and to seek social justice.

In the past fifteen years, the Chinese government has adopted significant measures in the following 10 fields in order to support and promote economic and social development in the poor regions:[13]

1. In June 1986, the "State Council Leading Working Group for Helping the Poor through Development" was established

This group was composed of leaders from 25 ministries and committees, and has a mandate to draw up the guiding principle, policy and plan for economic development in the poor regions, and coordinate the efforts to develop the economies of all regions in the country.

Directly under the Leading Working Group was a standing administrative body--the "Office of Helping the Poor Regions through Development." In some provinces, regions and counties with rather large concentrations of poor areas, similar structures were established to form a relatively complete, top-down system which ensured that the responsibility of eliminating poverty was carried out at all levels.

2. The target areas of the project were designated in order to assist the development of the poor regions

On the basis of many surveys and findings, the State Council standardized the indicators of a poor region and designated 331 poor counties as target recipients of assistance from the central government. Similarly, each province and region designated 368 poor counties as target recipients of provincial and regional assistance. That adds up to a total of 699 counties, or a third of all counties in the country. Designating the target areas of the project to help the poor, by county, combines the fight against poverty with regional development, and it is the foundation upon which the Chinese government will carry out its plan of combatting poverty region by region.

3. The Chinese government has adjusted the guiding principle and policy of eliminating poverty

The project to assist the poor regions has been changed from an emergency relief project to a development project. This means, with the necessary support from the government, promoting the use of local natural resources to develop production and to encourage people to rely on themselves to eliminate poverty and become prosperous. At the same time, the government moved from allocating poverty relief funds according to a region's average number of poor people to allocating poverty relief funds according to projects and results. There was a change from simple reliance on systematic government support to reliance mainly on economic organization; and a change from a simple input of capital to a diversified input of capital, technology, materials, training and services. All of the above changes strengthened the function and efficiency of the project to help the poor through development.

4. The government increased investment in the project to help the poor regions and implemented preferential policies beneficial to their rehabilitation and growth

Since 1986, on the basis of the original poverty relief funds, the government has been increasing financial allocations, special no-interest loans for assisting the poor regions in general, special no-interest loans for assisting the poor regions specifically in pastoral areas, special loans to the poor counties for setting up enterprises, special funds for the "work to replace aid" progam, etc. By 1993, the government had already invested a total of 40 billion yuan in the project to assist the poor regions. In 1994 alone, the government invested 9.7 billion yuan in the project to assist the poor regions, half of which were low-interest or no-interest loans. These funds were to be spent mainly on ventures which would benefit the public--such as the construction of basic facilities, culture, education and health care--and on projects to develop production. At the same time, each year the government provided large amounts of production materials to the poor regions at favourable prices, and drew up various tax reduction and exemption policies and other favourable policies in order to ease the financial burden of the poor regions.

5. The government has controlled the rapidly increasing population in the poor regions, and raised the quality of the population

In order to lessen the imbalance between population and resources in the poor regions, the government upheld the principle of combining the fight against poverty with family planning, thereby controlling the excessive increase of the population in these regions. At the same time, in a well-planned and organized fashion, the government started to relocate people from over-populated and resource-depleted regions to new areas where they could escape poverty.

6. Large-scale training of cadres and farmers in the poor regions has been instituted

Over many years, the Office to Assist the Poor Regions Develop, of the State Council, has been directly responsible for training more than 18,000 cadres and professionals in poor regions, counties and townships. In addition, the regional governments have trained 40 million farmers and technical personnel, thus enhancing the qualifications of the officials in the poor regions and contributing to a significant growth of the pool of technical personnel.

7. Every government department and every group in society has been mobilized to help develop the poor regions

Since 1987, 113 departments, committees and bureaus of the State Council have dispatched working groups to 320 poor counties, or established contact points to assist in the development of a certain impoverished region or several impoverished counties. They have set up long-term, stable relationships with these impoverished regions and provided assistance in the form of capital, technology, human resources information, etc. They would not sever these relationships until they had eliminated poverty.

Provincial, regional and county governments also mobilized and organized those departments suitable to the task to target certain impoverished regions in need of assistance.

In addition, the army, the democratic parties, social organizations, factories and mines, research institutions, universities and colleges all did their best to help in the development of the poor regions.

8. Economic and technical cooperation between the flourishing coastal areas and medium to large size cities and the poor regions have been strengthened in an effort to spread out the benefits and let all regions develop together

Such cooperation was mainly carried out through the exchange of cadres from both sides, and to date, 27 provinces, regions and counties and 11,000 cadres are involved in this exchange. Several thousand projects were implemented in the poor regions. The developed regions and medium to large size cities created more than 10 million employment opportunities in the poor regions. Many provinces and regions also initiated activities which involved rich counties, townships, villages and families helping designated poor counties, townships, villages and families.

9. Assisting the development of the poor regions through technology

For more than ten years, governments at all levels have tried to introduce various technical and educational projects into the poor regions, e.g. the "Meteor Project", the "Harvest Project", the "Prairie Fire Project", etc. Governments have also sent large groups of scientific and technical personnel and teachers from research institutions and universities to the poor regions to assume positions of county vice-mayor and village vice-chief. Many were organized to do contract work at the grass-roots level. In 1991, the State Council further suggested shifting the focus of the project to more of a dependence on scientific and technical development and to raising the inherent qualifications of the peasants and emphasizing promotion of economic development in the poor regions through science and technology.

10. Special projects were implemented to help the poor through development

Faced with the special problems and circumstances of some regions, the State Council carried out several special projects, including:

The special agricultural construction project in the "Three West" region

The "Three West" region refers to the dryland in central Gansu province which is represented by the county of Ding Xi, the He Xi regions, and the Xi Hai Tu region of Ningxia Autonomous Region. There are 47 counties and 12 million people in the "Three West" region. It is situated in the Huang Tu Highlands where the ecological balance is seriously damaged and where the annual amount of precipitation is 200-300 mm while evaporation is more than 1900 mm. The living conditions are harsh, there is a lack of water, grain, electricity and money and, for a long time, people have been depending on government aid.

In order to get to the root of the special difficulties of the "Three West" region, the State Council has, since 1983, allocated an annual amount of 0.2 billion yuan over ten years to be used specifically for agricultural reconstruction and water conservancy facilities in the region. In the past ten years, more than ten pumping and irrigation projects have been completed along the Yellow River and its tributaries. The annual pumping capacity is 0.7 billion cubic metres of water, 0.12 million hectares of land have been newly cultivated, and the amount of land covered by vegetation has increased from an original 5% to about 14% in the region. The number of electrical connections in the countryside has increased from 50% to more than 90%. Agricultural production has doubled. The average per capita net income has increased nearly 7 times, and the average portion of grain per capita has increased to 120 kilograms. Four hundred and fifty thousand people managed to escape poverty by relocating to new land. The percentage of impoverished people in the region has decreased from an original 75% to 10% of the total population.

The "work to replace aid" project

This is a public construction project which combines aid and development with the aim of improving the basic facilities in the poor regions. Since 1984, the

State Council has provided a total of six batches of grain, cotton, cloth, and medium to low grade industrial products, worth 12.8 billion yuan, to the poor regions. While providing aid, the government also helped the poor regions build 1,280,000 kilometres of public roads and 7,800 bridges, dredge 1800 miles of inland rivers, solve the drinking water problem for 27 million people and 18 million heads of livestock, make more than 1500 towns and 10,000 villages accessible by motor vehicle, improve and irrigate 33.49 million mu of new land, and increase small hydro-electric installations by 330 million watts. The implementation of this project has created the necessary conditions for further development of the poor regions, and it has also provided short-term employment opportunities and some income for the poor.

The project to provide food and clothing

The aim of this project is to increase grain production in the highlands, colder areas and in the drylands, and to solve the problem of grain shortages on farms in the poor regions. In accordance with the aim of the project, agricultural departments at all levels have, since 1989, provided capital, materials and technology to 471 poor counties in 16 provinces. They have introduced the production technologies of cross-breeding corn and covering the ground with transparent plastic over an area of 4,470,000 hectares of land which resulted in an increase in grain production of 11.2 billion kilograms. Each year, an average of 15 million farmers were able to overcome their grain shortage problems.

The project to solve the drinking water problem for people and livestock

Water resources in China are scarce. The average amount of water per capita equals 1/4 of the world average, and the average amount of water per capita in the poor regions is only 1/4 of the national average. In 1985, more than 70 million people and 40 million large domestic animals in the poor regions had difficulty finding enough drinking water.

In order to solve the problem, the government provided large amounts of capital, steel and cement to the poor regions and implemented a plan through "local labour, public funds". This plan made it the responsibility of water conservation departments at all levels to organize the local people to divert and store water, drill wells and build water reservoirs. The plan helped solving the drinking water problem for 55% of the people and 51% of the large domestic animals. In 1995, in order to solve the drinking water problem once and for all, the government increased the funds for "work to replace aid" by 0.3 billion yuan, to be used specifically on construction work for the drinking water project.

Other projects

Other projects include the "Project of Hope" and the "Project of Love" which mobilized social forces to support school attendance of children in the poor regions and make them part of the immunization program. The "Transportation Project" and the "Electricity Project" helped improve transportation and electrical facilities in the poor regions.

For nearly 15 years, The Chinese government, in the process of promoting overall social and economic development, has devoted much attention to and protected the right to development of the people in the poor regions. In order to relieve and eradicate poverty, the government has adopted down-to-earth and multi-faceted measures and expended much effort, and its achievements have drawn the attention of the international community.

The number of people living in poverty in the countryside has dropped sharply. In 1978, there were 0.25 billion people living in poverty in the countryside. In 1993, this figure dropped to 80 million. This means that each year, over a period of 15 years, there were, on average, 11,330,000 less people living in poverty in the countryside. The percentage of people living in poverty in the countryside dropped from 31% in 1978 to 8.8% in 1992. Apart from reforms of the economic system in the countryside and an increase in the price of agricultural products, as well as the success of the reform and open door policies in the entire country, such a significant drop can be attributed to the Chinese government's well-organized, well-planned and large-scale efforts to help the poor through development. In 1992, the average annual net income per capita in the 331 poor counties targeted for government support had increased from 208.6 yuan in 1985 to 450 yuan in 1992. This represents an increase of 65%. The average amount of grain production per capita had increased by 39.5 kilograms, and 93 counties exceeded the national average of grain per capita. In the entire country, 35 counties were able to rid themselves of the "poverty label". It could be said that for the majority of China's poor, the problem of food and clothing has basically been solved.[14] Compared to the 1980s, when the number of impoverished people in the world was high, the sharp decline in the number of impoverished people in China is indeed commendable. It is no wonder that the World Bank, in its 1990 issue of the «World Development Report» entitled "Overcoming Poverty", praised the Chinese government highly for its diligent efforts to help the most backward rural regions escape poverty. The World Bank estimated these efforts to be "much more successful than the efforts made by other developing countries." China has already become one of the developing countries in Asia, and even in the world, with the lowest incidence of poverty.[15] China's great success in relieving and eliminating poverty is a remarkable contribution to the world anti-poverty cause, and it is also an important step for China towards achieving universal and equal enjoyment of the right to development for all members of society.

Looking Ahead: Elimination of Poverty and Shared Progress are the Long-Term Tasks and Goals for Chinese Society

In the past 15 years, China has solved the problem of food and clothing for 0.17 billion people living in the countryside and greatly advanced towards the realization of the most basic human rights for people living in the poor regions. The results are obvious to all. However, this does not mean that the problem of extreme poverty in China has been entirely solved. Elimination of poverty and shared development are long-term tasks and goals for China in the process of modernizing Chinese society. In these regards, three points in particular should be raised:

First, the current standard of poverty in China is very low. The poverty standard for poor counties is actually a kind of working standard which the Chinese government uses to determine levels of assistance to the poor. This standard is much lower than the poverty standard set by the World Bank and many other countries. Calculated according to international standards, the actual number of people living in poverty is much higher than the current estimate of 80 million. The extent of poverty in China is evidence that China remains one of the least developed countries in the world. Because of various reasons, development is not consistent enough in the regions which have already escaped poverty, and some of these regions fall back into poverty.

Second, in the area of socio-economic development, the gap between the poor regions in western China and the coastal regions in the east is widening. From 1980 to 1990, the gap between the average annual net income of farmers in the 11 western provinces and regions and the 10 fast-developing coastal provinces and cities has grown from 70 yuan to 427 yuan. The annual net income of farmers in the more than 100 counties in the western regions is still less than 250 yuan.[16] In 1992, the average GDP per capita was 2800 yuan in the eastern coastal regions and 1517 yuan in the western regions. In 1992, the eastern coastal regions attracted 12.1 billion U.S. dollars in foreign investment, while only 1.1 billion U.S. dollars were invested in the western and central regions.[17] It can be predicted that the gap between east and west, the gap between the interior and the coastal regions will remain for a long time, and that it might widen even further in the future.

Third, it is very difficult to completely solve the problem of extreme poverty. In China, the majority of the 80 million people who still do not have enough food and clothing is concentrated in 592 poor counties. These counties are located deep in the mountain regions, the stone mountain regions, the desert, the highlands and cold mountain areas, the Huang Tu Highlands, and in regions where endemic diseases prevail. The living and working conditions in these regions are very harsh. In 1993, the average annual net income per capita among farmers in these counties was only 53% of the national average and, in 175 counties, the average net income per capita was less than 400 yuan. The average revenue per county was only about 30% of the national average, and the average amount of irrigated land and agricultural machinery capacity, respectively, were 20% and 18% less than the national average.[18] It is obviously much more difficult to eliminate the food and clothing problems of farmers in these regions than in more "normal" poor regions.

In order to eliminate the problems of extreme poverty for these 80 million people once and for all, the State Council drew up and promulgated the "8th National 7-year Plan to Combat Poverty" in March of 1994. The objective of this plan was to solve the food and clothing problems of these 80 million people within the last seven years of this century. The reason for calling this the "Combat Plan" was that the government was fully aware of the difficult nature of the task and thus resolved to attack it head on. This plan was the guiding principle for the Chinese government's work to help the poor through development and to eliminate poverty within the next seven years and it was an important component of the national plan for economic and social development. The success or failure of the plan will not only have an effect on the realization of the "Second Strategic Goal of the Modernization of China", it will also influence the historical progress in eliminating extreme poverty in the world.

In order to realize the above-mentioned goals, the plan put forward some concrete measures, including:

1.   Increasing the capital input for assisting the poor regions.

From 1995 to 2000, each year, the State Council will increase funds for the "work to replace aid" program by 1 billion yuan plus 1 billion yuan for special interest-free loans. The annual amount of government input in the project to assist the poor will thus reach 10 billion yuan. At the same time, regional governments at every level are also required to include, in their budgets, a special allowance for assisting the poor regions and to allocate annual amounts specifically to assist them.

2. Narrowing down the scope of the project to assist the poor regions in order to guarantee assistance to the targeted areas.

The government should gather together scattered funds to support the 592 poor counties recently targeted by the government for assistance. The population of these counties constitute more than 70% of the 80 million people living in poverty. These counties are mainly located in the central and western parts of the country. This plan emphasizes that the poorest townships, villages and families in the impoverished counties should always be the main targets of the work to help the poor through development.

3. Reforming the management and usage of funds for assisting the poor regions and optimizing the benefits.

The principle of combining social benefits with economic benefits must be upheld, and investment should focus on plant cultivation, propagation, processing, labour and service export and county enterprises. The project to assist the poor regions must be reformed to become a project based on a system of lending and repaying funds according to contracts.

4. hanging the format of the project to assist the poor from a format of isolating the impoverished regions to a format characterized by openness.

This means enhancing and developing organized and well-planned labour export and coordinating appropriate levels of migration to explore new land; linking together development of the impoverished mountain regions with reform and the opening up of the coastal regions, so as to merge development of the poor regions with development of the advanced regions.

5. Strengthening the project to assist the poor regions through technology and applied technological training for farmers.

This means shifting the emphasis of the project to assist and develop the poor regions to an emphasis on science and technology, and boosting the inherent qualities of the farmers.

6. Establishing a provincially managed provincial leaders' responsibility system, under the guidance of the central government, for the work to assist the poor regions.

7. Mobilizing even wider circles of society to participate in the work to assist the poor regions, while also rallying the international community and international organizations for support and cooperation.[19]

Conclusion

It is clear from the above-mentioned plan that the Chinese government, based on the sum of its experience over the past ten years, has developed even more practical and more efficient concrete measures to assist the poor regions. If these measures can be fully implemented, they will effectively guarantee the realization of the plan to combat poverty in China.

The implementation of China's project to help the poor through development clearly illustrates that, while China is undergoing rapid economic and social development, serious problems of poverty and unbalanced development still exist. In China, the real work to promote human rights lies in eliminating poverty and respecting the universal and equal right to development. The Chinese government has paid a great amount of attention to this work and has brought together the forces of society as a whole, adopted many highly efficient measures and achieved great success in its cause to combat poverty. Still faced with the long-term and arduous task of the complete elimination of poverty, China must uphold the policies of opening up and reform, uphold its emphasis on the universal and equal right to development and maintain the current direction of the plan to combat poverty. A just, equal and overall prosperous China will then emerge before the international community.

Translated by Shengtao Jiang and A-M Traeholt

Notes

1. The *African Declaration on Human and People's Rights*, passed by the Organization of African Unity in 1982, has become an important international document in which development has been clarified as a right.

2. The United Nations, *Human Rights: A Compilation of International Instruments* (Chinese edition), pp. 479-483, *Declaration on the Right to Development*, foreword and article 8.

3. See the speech by the Chairman of the 46th Session of the U.N. General Assembly, quoted in Li Xiaolin's book: *The Expectations of History--a Report on the Project to Help the Poor Regions Develop in China* (Lishi de qidai--zhongguo fupin kaifa jishi), People's Liberation Army Cultural Publishing House, 1994, pp. 11-12.

4. A telegram from U.N. Secretary-General Ghali, quoted in Li Xiaolin's book, ibid, p. 18.

5. Ibid, pp. 50-51.

6. Yang Zhong, "Zhongguo xiaochu pinkun de xingshi he duice" (China's situation and method of eliminating poverty), in the journal *Zhongguo pinkun diqu* (China's poverty-stricken regions), no. 1, 1995, p. 19.

7. Ibid, at p. 19.

8. Supra, note 3 at pp. 50-51.

9. The Chinese Foundation for Assisting the Poor, ed., *Dong xi huzhu, gongtong fazhan* (Mutual help between east and west, shared development). Renmin Chubanshe (The People's Publishing House) 1992, p. 18.

10. Supra, note 6 at p. 20.

11. United Nations, "Declaration on Social Progress and Development" in *Human Rights: A Compilation of International Instruments*, pp. 381-383.

12. In September 1984, the Central Committee of the Party and the State Council issued a joint circular, «On assisting impoverished regions in improving their situation as quickly as possible», in which Party committees and governments at all levels were required to adopt measures to focus their energy on assisting the clusters of impoverished regions in improving their living conditions, raising their production capacity and escaping poverty. In 1986, the National People's Congress made poverty alleviation an important issue to be included in the "7th five-year" development plan of the national economy (1986-1990).

13. For an outline of these measures, see Yang Zhong's article, supra, note 6 at pp. 20-22.

14. Ibid, pp. 18-19.

15. Quoted from a report by a State Council member, Chen Junsheng, March 3, 1991, supra, note 9 at p. 34.

16. Supra, note 9 at p. 77.

17. Quoted in a report by Xiang Nan, the Head of the Chinese Foundation to Assist the Poor Regions: "The Interior and the Coastal Regions Fly Together", 1994.

18. Supra, note 6 at p. 22.

19. See Yang Zhong's article, supra, note 6 at pp. 22-23.

Regional Disparities and Canada's Human Development

DOUGLAS M. BROWN & JAMES P. GROEN

Introduction

In 1994, Canada reclaimed its first place position among the 173 countries ranked by the United Nations (UN) Human Development Report, which examined trends in human development categories such as life expectancy, enrolment in school, income generated per person, and expenditures on education and health care.[1] Yet, among the countries classified by the United Nations as "industrialized market economies", Canada is one of the most highly regionalized, and its economy one of the most fragmented.[2] Every country in the world is plagued with regional disparities -- the tendency of some regions to lag far behind others in terms of economic and human development and prosperity. In the Canadian federation, this phenomenon is particularly notable as the forces producing regional diversity are great and the fabric binding the regions together is fragile. Referring to the many efforts to combat regional disparities, a recent analysis concluded:

> The attitude towards regional development lies deep in Canadian history: the settlement from east to west, and the resulting moving frontier; the rivalry between French and British; the feeling in the Maritimes that its people were cheated by Confederation and the federal policy of east-west, as opposed to north-south, development that came after it; the suspicion and mistrust of the dominant financial and industrial powers in the east among the farmers in the west. The whole story of Canadian development generates strong regional interests and rivalries....Regional development policy, in this context, has been and remains an attempt to keep the federation from falling apart.[3]

While the existence of large regional economic disparities has been documented for much of Canada's history, it is only since World War II, and more specifically the 1940 Report of the Royal Commission on Dominion-Provincial Relations (Rowell-Sirois Report) that intensive government initiatives have been implemented to redress regional disparities.[4] Yet despite these efforts, another Royal Commission in 1985 reported that the "general [economic] disparity has changed little over the last 60 years for which data are available, although individual rankings [of provinces] have occasionally altered." The Commission recognized that "in a federal system regional economic disparity is an inherently contentious issue." Regional communities in economic decline also tend to experience political decline, if for no other reason than the common adjustment of out-migration. The constituent communities' very role in a federal system can thus be slowly but permanently altered by increasing regional disparity.[5] In any case, international comparisons of regional inequality have confirmed that Canada displays one of the highest degrees of regional imbalance of six of the most highly developed countries (Canada, United States, Sweden, United Kingdom, New Zealand and Australia).[6]

General interest in the extent and causes of regional disparity in Canada stems, in part, from the value which Canadians place on equality. There are several views about what constitutes equality (or "equity") and how it might best be achieved, a full discussion of which is beyond the scope of this paper. Nonetheless, equality of opportunity has been the most widely accepted approach to equity in Canada. Another view of equity, equality of results, has also come to receive wide attention.[7] While the majority of Canadians are not greatly perturbed by fairly wide variations in personal economic well-being and opportunity, *regional* disparities, of the kind which will be identified below, are viewed by many Canadians to be unacceptable.[8] Political pressure for intervention by the federal government has centred upon reductions of gaps in levels of per capita incomes and unemployment among provinces. Many Canadians view the achievement of an appropriate balance in the country's economic development as an important tenet of national unity. Indeed, during his period in office, former Prime Minister Pierre Trudeau stressed that the problem of regional disparities was as threatening to national unity as the language issue.[9] And such is the importance attached to reducing regional disparities that the Canadian Constitution, amended in 1982, contains a section headed "Equalization and Regional Disparities" which commits the federal and provincial legislatures and governments to:

a) promoting equal opportunities for the well-being of Canadians;
b) furthering economic development to reduce disparity in opportunities; and
c) providing essential public services of reasonable quality to all Canadians.[10]

It is for this reason that Donald Savoie has observed that, "the sharing of prosperity among Canadians wherever they live has been part of the bargain of Confederation."[11]

There is nonetheless, a continuing tension in Canadian political life (and in policy trends) regarding equity. On the one hand, there has been an emphasis on reducing regional inequality through intergovernmental transfers and social programs designed to distribute income more assiduously to disparate regions (e.g. the unemployment insurance program). On the other hand, there has been an emphasis on reducing interpersonal inequality more generally through social programs which operate without regard to regional considerations (e.g. federal transfers for medical care and pensions). Canada's federal Constitution and its political institutions tend to have a bias towards regional equality/inequality, often to the detriment of national (i.e Canada-wide) community equality.[12]

This paper does not directly place the issue of regional development and disparities within the international context of the "right to development". In part, this is because the debate has not been commonly framed in these terms in Canada. There are many aspects of the international discourse that have relevance, however.[13] The concept of regions as collectivities with social rights is an important, if not always prevailing, idea in Canada. The state-centred norms that drive the right to development approach also have a long historical foundation in Canada, as too do alternative, non-market development practices. Throughout the Canadian discussion of regional development, the relationship between economic and social development is never far from the surface.

This paper does provide an overview of the issue of regional disparities in Canada's human development and examines the continuing ability of the Canadian federation to provide regional equity. The next section (II) begins with an examination of how regions are defined in the Canadian context -- largely but not exclusively by reference to the provinces. We proceed in Section III to briefly discuss the nature of regional disparities, and how they are most commonly measured in economic terms. A series of five tables[14] provide a statistical supplement to this section. The causes of regional disparities are the subject of section IV, followed by an overview of the attempts by Canadian governments to reduce regional disparities in section V. The final section provides an overall assessment of the issue.

Regionalism, Regional Disparities and Human Development

Most observers of Canadian politics agree that regionalism is a "profound and fundamental" feature of Canadian political life, and that the concept is deeply embedded in popular political culture.[15] Indeed, a majority of Canadians are said to think in regional terms.[16] Yet, a certain degree of confusion has accompanied the term because of a common failure to distinguish between three distinct variations of the concept: region, regionalism and regional disparities.[17] The term *region* simply implies a sameness within a geographic space that separates or differentiates it from some other geographic space. Thus, one analyst defines a region as "a territorial entity having some natural and organic unity or community of interests that is independent of political and administrative boundaries."[18] Regions can be defined in terms of topography, climate, demography, and economic output, all of which emphasize *regional differences*. Traditionally, students of Canadian history and politics have relied upon geographic and economic criteria for designating regions. The familiar division of Canadian territory into six regions -- the Atlantic provinces, Quebec, Ontario, the Prairies, British Columbia and the North -- is a product of this approach.[19] Sometimes, the number of regions is reduced to three: the Atlantic provinces, Central Canada (Ontario and Quebec) and the West -- or four if one includes the North. However, this tendency to divide Canada into a number of geographic regions ignores the differences in economic interests between the provinces and the explicitly political nature of regionalism in Canada. For example, Quebec's "distinct society" stems from its majority French language and culture. This makes it increasingly difficult to consider Ontario and Quebec as a single regional entity.

The term *regional disparities* explicitly acknowledges these political dimensions of the phenomenon because it refers directly to differences in the distribution of resources and development across geographic space. Dwelling upon indicators of these differences (such as income or unemployment rates) is nonetheless an expressly political process because it implies a value judgement about the effect of such differences, and about the units of analysis in the first place. As Mathews notes, when a region is declared to be "in disparity when compared to other regions," it is "not merely a declaration that certain differences exist among the regions but a judgment about the meaning and implications of such differences."[20] It emphasizes inequalities in power or resources between territorial units and seeks to determine why some territorial units gain or lose in relation to other territorial units.[21] It also places value on the territorial unit as the focus of analysis as compared to other foci, such as national communities, classes or individuals.

Flowing naturally from this investigation into the political dimension of regionalism, students of regionalism have tended to equate regions with provinces and the formal boundaries of federalism.[22] It is argued that to become fully mobilized, regional differences must have an institutional focus. The provinces provide this focus and, in turn, serve to mould and reinforce regionalism.[23] For purposes of drawing regional comparisons, the provinces are considered to fulfil the primary criteria of political and administrative coherence and homogeneity. Their status as important decision-making units and their role in the administration of regional policies makes them suitable for selection as criteria for delineation of regions.

Nonetheless, it must be recognized that this method of determining regional boundaries presents certain conceptual problems, for it implies that Canada has ten distinct economic regions whose boundaries perfectly overlap provincial ones. Yet Northwest Ontario, for example, has much more in common with Manitoba and the West than it does with Southern Ontario. Northern Ontario and Northern Quebec face many of the same problems as the Northwest Territories, as do Northern Manitoba, Northern Saskatchewan or the whole of Labrador. More specifically, within each province there are areas, often geographically large, which suffer from lesser economic prosperity, underdevelopment, unexploited resources, and unemployment and poverty. Thus, the problem of equating provinces with regions is that transprovincial patterns of inequality may be obscured by the institutional boundaries of federalism.[24] Nonetheless, despite this frequently noted caveat, in Canada regional inequalities have been generally examined on the basis of provincial boundaries. It is a practice which we will also follow in the presentation of data in this paper.

The tendency to resort to institutional and geographical determinism as the source of regional disparities -- a feature common to federal unions -- is to a certain extent, at odds with the consensus emerging in the human development literature that the primary objective of development should be to ensure that economic growth translates into the improved well-being of people, not the strengthening of political or economic power of regions with respect to one another.[25] Traditionally, the term "development" has been considered synonymous with growth in gross national product (GNP). While it is true that access to income may permit exercise of many other human options, there is no perfect correspondence between material enrichment and the enrichment of human lives as measured in life expectancy, infant mortality, literacy and educational enrollment rates, and so on.[26]

Nonetheless, in Canada, government intervention through public services has insured that in recent decades there is a relative equality in all of these areas -- except for income. Expansion of provincial per capita income and employment in the poorer regions has been seen therefore as the next logical step towards greater human development. The difficulty in understanding the causes of Canadian regional disparities stems, in part, from the fact that regional economic conditions alone do not explain the disparities. Social, ethnic, political, linguistic, educational, and geographic conditions also correlate with economic disparities in Canada, and it is highly likely that they interact in a causal way. Thus, general socio-economic conditions may be more fundamental indicators of regional disparities than purely economic conditions.[27]

While there are a number of potential measures of regional disparity, this article concentrates upon the most commonly used economic indicators, namely gross domestic product (GDP), income, and rates of employment or unemployment. The effects of uneven economic productivity and labour force participation and their concomitant role in determining per capita income have the greatest and most direct bearing upon measures of social and economic well-being in Canada. Although per capita income is, at best, a rough proxy of human development and material well-being, it is used as the basis for a variety of government programs and policies and other elements of social welfare. In turn, measures of employment are important in determining levels of human development because of the income it produces and because it is a major source of acceptance and self-esteem in Canadian society. Thus, our framework of analysis reflects a traditional view of regional development in Canada, namely a comparison of economic performance against the national average, using provinces as the basis of comparison. This having been stated, we shall return in the concluding section to the concept of human development in order to point out the limitations of the traditional economic development approaches and to assess Canadian experience in broader terms.

The Extent of Regional Disparities in Canada

The most obvious measure of inequality is disparity in family incomes.[28] Table 1 presents an average of family income by province derived from employment, farm income, business income and investment income, plus income received from government transfer payments. From 1980-94, family income disparities in Canada have continued unabated. Family incomes in the Atlantic provinces and Quebec are still at most 80 percent of the national average, a condition relatively unchanged from the early 1980s. Moreover, the position of the poorer provinces would be much worse if government transfer payments such as unemployment insurance, family allowance, old age pensions and assistance to the poor were removed. Indeed, to the extent that disparities have narrowed in the past 30 years, it is largely the result of government transfers to the less wealthy regions.

Table 1

Average Family Income by Province: Selected years, 1981-94

($CDN)

	1981	1986	1989	1990	1991	1994
Nfld	25,870	30,383	39,648	40,770	41,654	44,181
PEI	23,455	32,029	38,726	39,701	42,779	47,122
NS	24,862	35,352	43,123	44,385	45,130	48,121
NB	24,608	33,313	40,670	42,356	44,323	47,394
Que	28,568	38,110	44,860	47,158	48,634	47,394
Ont	32,322	45,778	57,330	57,027	58,634	63,628
Man	28,606	37,875	46,551	47,178	46,621	55,153
Sask	30,575	37,025	42,978	44,234	45,930	48,701
Alb	36,279	43,729	49,734	51,985	55,552	60,230
BC	33,687	40,590	49,442	54,448	54,895	60,809
Canada	30,973	41,240	50,083	51,633	53,131	57,696

While data on income constitute a good starting point in measuring regional disparities, it should be noted that this indicator overstates regional income disparities because it ignores several important elements. First, Canada's progressive income taxes take a larger share of the incomes in wealthy provinces, so that regional disparities in disposable income are not as large as differences in family income. Second, this indicator ignores the fact that the cost of living differs from region to region.

Table 2 presents a comparative overview of provincial gross domestic product (GDP) in relation to a national average. It serves to confirm the data on income, demonstrating that the Atlantic Provinces, for example, continue to lag behind the rest of the country in their capacity to generate wealth and, as a "region", remain consistently weaker in economic terms. Nonetheless, there is clear evidence that over the past decade, disparity has been reduced, though this may be due in large part to the decline in the economies of Ontario and Alberta in the late 1980s and early 1990s. If the economies of these two provinces rebound in the second half of the 1990s, extraordinary gains in income growth will be required in the "have not" regions if regional disparities are to be closed. In the extreme case of Newfoundland, for example, the provincial rate of growth of GDP will likely have to be four times the national average over the next decade for that province to approximate the national level. Quebec, Manitoba and Saskatchewan continue to represent a second tier above the Atlantic, though Quebec's relative position is clearly improving.

Table 2

Provincial Gross Domestic Product at Market Prices,
Per Capita Selected Years, 1966-1993,
Relationship to National Average (Canada = 100)

	1966	1971	1976	1981	1984	1987	1990	1992	1993
Nfld	52.1	56.2	53.6	52.0	59.5	63.3	63.1	65.1	65.3
PEI	48.4	52.3	52.2	50.5	56.5	63.8	63.7	68.9	71.8
NS	63.	67.9	66.	61.3	69.	76.3	76.3	79.7	78.6
NB	61.3	63.7	63.8`	63.1	65.1	75.	73.0	76.9	78.8
Que	89.9	88.9	88.1	86.0	85.7	90.8	90.5	93.1	90.
Ont	117.4	117.3	109.4	106.5	108.	112.4	111.3	109.2	107.8
Man	87.1	90.7	91.4	88.1	90.5	86.3	86.6	87.6	86.6
Sask	99.6	86.9	101.2	108.8	99.7	91.8	85.9	86.2	88.2
Alb	109.3	110.8	137.1	146.0	147.1	115.5	116.3	114.6	118.1
BC	109.2	106.8	108.6	109.4	100.1	97.8	98.9	100.1	104.8

There are a number of ways of disaggregating these gross indicators of income disparity. One frequently cited study concluded that roughly 60 percent of the regional differences in earned income per capita were due to regional variations in earnings per worker, while the remaining 40 percent were accounted for by differences in unemployment rates, labour force participation rates and population age-structures.[29] Regarding the issue of disparities in earned income, a number of factors have been used to explain regional variations including differences in industrial and occupational structures; hours worked per week; labour quality; technology; and capital investment per worker -- in other words, the productivity of labour and capital employed. These factors will be further explored in the next part of this paper.

Comparisons of unemployment rates have also been widely employed as indicators of regional disparities. The unemployment rate not only reflects differences in productive employment (which cause differences in incomes), but also partly explains income per capita differences. Over the past twenty years for example, income per employed individual in the Atlantic provinces has been 15 percent below the national average, whereas income per capita has been 30 per cent below.[30] With the exception of the prairie provinces, those provinces with lower levels of family income also experience higher rates of unemployment. Furthermore, when the average Canadian unemployment rate rises, it rises faster in the economically disadvantaged regions, particularly the Atlantic region and Quebec.

Though the unemployment rate is an imperfect indicator of the true nature and extent of unemployment in a region, the large regional variations shown in table 3 are disturbing. Though there have been some changes in the relative positions of various provinces over the years, particularly in Ontario and the western provinces, the overall stability in the pattern of regional disparities in unemployment rates is remarkable. Between 1970 and 1993, unemployment rates in Manitoba, Saskatchewan, Ontario and to a lesser extent, Alberta, were almost always below the Canadian average, while those in the Atlantic provinces of Newfoundland, Prince Edward Island, New Brunswick and Nova Scotia, as well as Quebec and British Columbia, were nearly always above. Furthermore, there is little evidence of a reduction in the degree of inequality in unemployment rates over recent periods. Also noteworthy is that during periods of change in unemployment rates, there were wider variations in some provinces than in others, particularly the Atlantic provinces and Quebec. This reflects the higher levels of seasonal unemployment experienced in these two regions, a condition which is exacerbated by their primary-based economies, limited degrees of diversification and industrial underdevelopment (discussed further below).

Table 3

Canadian Unemployment Rates: Selected Years, 1970-93

	1970	1975	1980	1985	1987	1988	1989	1990	1991	1992	1993
Nfld	7.3	14.0	13.3	20.8	17.9	16.4	15.8	17.1	18.4	20.2	20.2
PEI	n.a.	8.0	10.6	13.3	13.2	13.0	14.1	14.9	16.8	17.7	17.7
NS	5.3	7.7	9.7	13.6	12.3	10.2	9.9	10.5	12.0	13.1	14.6
NB	6.3	9.8	11.0	15.1	13.1	12.0	12.5	12.1	12.7	12.8	12.6
Que	7.0	8.1	9.8	11.8	10.3	9.4	9.3	10.1	11.9	12.8	12.6
Ont	4.4	6.3	6.8	8.0	6.1	5.0	5.1	6.3	9.6	10.8	10.6
Man	5.3	4.5	5.5	8.2	7.4	7.8	7.5	7.2	8.8	9.6	9.2
Sask	4.2	2.9	4.4	8.1	7.4	7.5	7.4	7.0	7.4	8.2	8.0
Alb	5.1	4.1	3.7	10.0	9.6	8.0	7.2	7.0	8.2	9.5	9.6
BC	7.7	8.5	6.8	14.1	11.9	10.3	9.1	8.3	9.9	10.4	9.7
Canada	5.7	6.9	7.5	10.5	8.8	7.8	7.5	8.1	10.3	11.3	11.2

Regional economic differences thus exist in Canada, not only in terms of economic rewards to the residents, but also in terms of their economic structure. Table 4 presents an overview of employment in Canada's industries by province for the year 1993. Some of the more striking features are: the lower levels of employment participation in the Atlantic provinces; the greater reliance in the Atlantic provinces, Alberta and British Columbia on agriculture and other primary industries (fishing, trapping, forestry and mining); Ontario and Quebec's greater proportion of employment in the capital intensive manufacturing sectors as well as the high income financial service sectors; and Alberta and B.C.'s increasing reliance on the service and trade sectors.

Table 4

Employment in Canada's Industries by Province, 1993
Expressed as a Percent (%)

	Canada	Nfld	PEI	NS	NB	Que	Ont	Man	Sask	Alta	BC
All Industries/	42.7	31.8	40	38.8	38.4	40.9	44.3	43.5	43.4	46.5	43.6
Services	15.7	11.6	15.7	14.9	13.8	14.9	16.2	15.9	15.0	17.0	16.5
Trade	7.3	6.1	6.7	7.2	7.2	6.8	7.4	7.1	6.9	8.3	8.3
Manufacturing	6.2	2.9	3.0	4.0	4.7	7.2	7.7	2.2	2.4	3.5	4.8
Utilities	3.1	2.7	3.0	2.8	3.3	3.0	2.9	2.9	3.2	3.3	3.5
Government	2.9	3.0	3.7	3.3	3.0	3.0	2.9	2.6	2.9	2.8	2.6
Finance	2.6	1.0	0.8	1.8	1.7	2.4	3.1	2.2	2.3	2.4	2.6
Construction	2.2	1.5	0.	1.9	2.1	1.8	2.3	1.9	1.6	3.0	3.0
Agriculture	1.5	0.	0.	0.6	0.5	1.0	1.1	3.8	7.7	3.2	0.8
Primary	0.8	2.7	0.	1.7	1.7	0.5	0.3	0.6	1.0	2.7	2.0

Interprovincial variations in the size of the manufacturing sector is also particularly important. Manufacturing employment is viewed as desirable for a number of reasons; traditionally, it commands higher wages than do the service or primary sectors, is less seasonal, and points to a more mature and stable urban economic structure than the non-industrialized rural or semi-rural areas of the country. The relative importance, performance, and viability of the manufacturing industries vary greatly from one province to another and within provinces. Table 5 summarizes the degree of employment and average salaries in the manufacturing sector in 1992. In addition to the huge variations in the numbers employed in this sector across the provinces, employees in Ontario and British Columbia earned significantly more than the national average while those in the Atlantic provinces, and to a lesser extent Quebec and the prairies, earned less.

Table 5

Manufacturing: Number of Employees and Average Salaries and Wages
by Province, 1992

	Number of Employees	Average Salaries
Canada	1,673,740	34,746
Nfld	12,323	28,093
PEI	3,910	21,713
N.S.	37,168	29,694
Que	454,767	32,945
Ont	828,384	35,975
Man	48,263	29,710
Sask	19,588	31,718
Alta	88,330	34,646
B.C.	148,979	38,189
Yukon & N.W.T.	478	29,288

While we concentrate here upon disparities in income and unemployment, there are of course other measures of disparities in Canada. If one uses as measures of social welfare the number of telephones, infant mortality, poverty, number of doctors per 100,000 inhabitants, education expenditures or other such indicators, these tend to follow the trend in income disparities. It is also important to consider regional disparities in social areas such as housing, health, environment, and education, which provide some alternative indicators of individual well-being. These may in fact reveal that there are non-monetary advantages to living in a region where incomes are lower that may adequately compensate for differences in income. Nonetheless, it would be misleading to suggest that high unemployment levels and lower incomes are compensated by lower living costs, by income in kind, by the joy of living in an unpolluted environment, or by the pleasures of maintaining traditional life-styles. Social indicators cloud the disparity issue somewhat, for who can say categorically that lower divorce and suicide rates in the Atlantic provinces do not outweigh lower incomes and poorer job opportunities? Nonetheless, it is economic well-being and the possibilities for human development in Canada which are sharply affected by the region in which one happens to reside. In short, the disparities are real.

In summary, of all the regions, the four Atlantic provinces are below the national average in urbanization and have less developed secondary and tertiary sectors. Their unemployment rates are always above the national level, their per capita and per family incomes are the lowest in the country, the fiscal capacity of their provincial governments is limited, and they remain dependent upon federal government transfers for up to 50 percent of provincial revenues. While the western provinces have experienced periods of economic difficulty, Alberta and British Columbia rank with Ontario as "have" provinces and Manitoba and Saskatchewan join Quebec as "middle-income" provinces. Western dependence upon resource extraction is not as disadvantageous as in the Atlantic region because the western resources are both more plentiful and more valuable. Ontario has generally exhibited the highest per capita income and, until recently, the lowest unemployment rates. Finally, based on its size, population and resources, Quebec is a more prosperous province than any in the Atlantic region, and its gross provincial product is second only to Ontario. Nevertheless, on a per capita basis Quebec can rank anywhere from fourth to sixth in the country in terms of income and unemployment and the provincial government is a recipient of federal equalization payments.

Causes of Disparity

Regional development economists agree that no single theory exists to explain regional disparities.[31] Regions have distinct geographic characteristics which, when combined with historic and contemporary settlement patterns, often make Canada understandable only through these characteristics. For example, Ontario's relative proximity to US markets, its rich agricultural and resource hinterland, and its relatively hospitable climate have all contributed to its position as the leading province in terms of population and manufacturing output. Newfoundland, by contrast, is far from urban markets, has few agricultural resources but significant marine resources, has a small manufacturing base and a harsher climate. Therefore, this province has a much smaller population and very different economic interests than Ontario. Such unique characteristics can be repeated for every province and every geographic region of Canada. Yet, Canadian analysis illustrates a sharp debate over the causes of disparity and interaction between geographic, economic and policy factors. Here we briefly examine four sets of explanations: resource staples theory; a theory of policy-induced disparities; market development theories; and sociological factors.

It is obvious that the economic prosperity of a region is enhanced if it has an abundance of marketable resources, and one of the most frequently cited explanations for Canada's regional economic disparities, Harold Innis' staples theory, contends that the varying economic fortunes of different areas of Canada are explained by the varying availability and marketability   of natural resources.[32] Simply put, Innis maintained that when a region experiences a decline in the marketability (prices) of its products, such as the Atlantic provinces have experienced at various times with respect to fish, lumber and coal, the result is a drop in production, growth, wages and employment respectively. There is no doubt that the Canadian economic union is characterized by regional specialization determined by proximity to markets and regional resource endowments. The down-side of this dependence upon a narrow range of geographically concentrated exports is a proneness to cyclical instability.

Yet, while the staples theory tells part of the story of disparities in some regions of Canada, there are significant limitations to "natural resource" explanations for disparities. First, resources represent only one factor determining the productivity of a region; others such as physical or human capital, the level of technology, scale economies and so on have been demonstrated to be of greater importance.[33] Second, some of the poorest provinces as well as the richest have larger resource endowments than the most industrialized provinces. For example, Newfoundland is ,by any measure, a resource-rich province, and has for several decades been the largest producer of iron ore in Canada. Third, the pattern of unemployment in Canada does not entirely conform to the staples theory. While agriculture has declined in the prairies as a source of unemployment, the prairies have long maintained low unemployment rates, and, furthermore, despite B.C.'s access to marketable resources, unemployment rates are persistently high. Thus, the staples theory cannot adequately explain one of the major aspects of regional disparities -- regional differences in unemployment -- thereby suggesting the importance of competing explanations.[34]

The historic circumstances of the initial founding and development of the Canadian federation have also been important in determining the present day disparities in economic development. The roots of Canadian regional alienation -- if you will, the politics of regional envy -- lie in Canada's initial development strategy, which was established in 1879 with the passage of a national economic development policy known as the "National Policy". In this respect, one may refer to "policy-induced" disparity in Canada.

The National Policy was an attempt to weld a collection of very different economic regions into a viable economic and political unit. It required linking the regions together both physically, in terms of transportation links, and economically, to prevent American commercial interests from capturing the profits of the trade and resources of Canada's western regions. This also required the settlement of the west to prevent American expansion into these otherwise sparsely settled regions. These were the goals of the National Policy, and they were accomplished by railways, tariffs and land settlement policies. The policy was successful in terms of securing the political union. However, over time, and likely unforeseen at the beginning, the National Policy contributed considerably to Canada's uneven pattern of economic development. As a consequence of intensifying waves of integration, manufacturing dwindled in the Atlantic provinces and became increasingly concentrated in Ontario and Quebec while, in the western provinces, resource production became dominant.[35] This Canadian project of economic and political integration both reinforced and contradicted the more "natural" linkages of economic geography. This can be illustrated by examining three regions. Prior to Confederation, the Maritime colonies had the fourth largest merchant marine in the world, supported by the timber, fishing, sugar import and shipping industries. These staples of Maritime trade found their prime markets in Britain and the West Indies, with most of the remainder shipped to the American seaboard. With the National Policy of 1879, the policy of protecting Canadian industries to let them sell unchallenged in the domestic market was fixed as a tenet of Canada's economic policy. However, the effect of the policy on the Maritimes was to force integration with central Canada. This, combined with the overexpansion of manufacturing capacity in central Canada, the merging and subsequent closure of smaller competitive firms in the maritimes during periods of economic contraction, and the integration of the financial services sector, marked a period of de-industrialization in the Atlantic provinces.

Similarly under the National Policy, the prairies were to provide a frontier for central Canadian investment, a market for the commercial trade of the St. Lawrence merchants. Though economic development through the exploitation of its resources was achieved more successfully in the prairies, the pattern of development led to long-standing grievances among the residents of the western Canadian provinces. These included the high cost of goods due to the federal tariffs, the monopoly powers of the railways, the operation of the banking system, the inadequacy of the grain marketing system, federal retention of control over Prairie natural resources until 1930, and federal intervention in the markets for Western petroleum and mineral resources, particularly before 1984.[36]

Even in Quebec, federal tariff, transportation and development policies have been criticized for operating to the benefit of neighbouring Ontario. Thus, Ontario's greater strength relative to Quebec in the production of capital and durable goods has often been explained by federal economic policies, including: federal automobile tariffs and the signing of the Autopact which encouraged the automobile industry to locate in Ontario; the canalization and federal subsidization of the St. Lawrence Seaway which redirected shipping from Montreal to Ontario ports; the centralization of Canada's nuclear industry in Ontario; and Canadian energy policy (more precisely the "Borden Line" policy) which encouraged the greater expansion of the petrochemical industry in Ontario as opposed to Quebec.[37]

The policy-induced disparities argument is, of course, an historic one with perhaps decreasing validity as the original circumstances change. Nonetheless, the integrated Canadian economic "space" remains a chief feature of the Canadian economy -- including the basic regional division of labour originally fostered by the National Policy. Even as transportation, tariff and immigration policies are radically altered in the 1990s, the cumulative effects of national development set in place in the past century have been retained.

Thus, it becomes more difficult over time to separate out the causation factors: when do policy-induced development patterns give way to market-determination? No theory of Canadian development could deny, for example, the natural advantages and the likely predominance of southern Ontario in any potential economic configuration of Canada (or, indeed, of North America). Such reinforcing factors may be illustrated by examining three related concepts of market development which further explain the existence of regional disparities since the 1940s: productivity, urbanization and capital accumulation.

While the key elements in the "resource" based explanations for disparities are apparent, development economists contend that factors such as education and human capital, degree of urbanization, capital accumulation, the level of technology and social structures and attitudes also determine productivity and wealth.[38] Productivity is usually regarded as the main determinant of prosperity and income differentials, and regional productivity disparities are viewed as being a result of the quality of the labour source, adoption of new technology, capital investment costs and so on. Income disparities in Canada are especially related to productivity differences. Productivity in turn is influenced by quality of labour, or more specifically, educational attainment. The educational levels of the labour force have important consequences for regional development in that people with higher education are more likely to be employed than those with less. Unemployment rates, for example, are consistently three times higher for persons with no higher education than for those with a university degree. There has been a steady upward trend in all regions in the proportions of the population having specified levels of formal education.

Urbanization is also seen as a factor influencing economic growth, earned per capita income and employment opportunities. This is because many of the service functions in a modern economy take place in cities. Such functions include financial administration, research and development, and headquarters activities. Urban size also appears to have a positive influence on income and productivity because of economies of scale in transportation and distribution and also because of agglomeration economies.[39] There are significant variations across Canada in terms of the rural-urban population distribution which appear to match the patterns of income disparity. Because both the Atlantic and Prairie provinces have experienced large net-outmigration and weak population growth, their disadvantages become magnified. Nonetheless, it is more difficult to determine the cause and effect in urbanization and regional disparities: are these regions poor because they are rural, or rural because they are poor?

A third category, capital accumulation, is thought to be particularly important in creating disparities. It is generally acknowledged that the amount of capital investment per worker is an important determinant of per capita earnings and a significant factor in the observed regional disparities in productivity. Studies have concluded that provincial variations in capital investment intensity explained one-half of the variations in output per worker and was responsible for the below-average productivity performance of Quebec and the Atlantic provinces.[40] In particular, technology-intensive industry has tended to be even more concentrated than manufacturing alone, with southern Ontario again exhibiting the highest intensity.

Finally, sociological factors within regions may play a role in reinforcing disparities. Studies have indicated the development of a distinctive political culture in the Atlantic region and portions of Quebec, to which labels such as underdeveloped, subject, alienated, traditional, conservative and marginal have been applied. Many of these elements can be understood in terms of the "marginal work world" in these regions, which is characterized by small, traditional, labour-intensive firms that pay low wages.[41] These social-cultural attitudes should not be considered in isolation for they are, in fact, shaped by an interplay of economic, social/cultural and political forces.

However, the application of sociological theory to development is a complex field and one which we will not attempt here. Yet it is worth noting that there arises, from decades of regional decline, types of social and political movements and attitudes which may more openly reject orthodox interpretations of market economics or of national economic development. Such aspects of political culture, if you will, are reinforced when combined with ethnic or linguistic factors, as especially is the case with Quebec.

Quebec illustrates the complex interplay of factors causing regional disparities. The province with its majority french-speaking population exhibits both economic disparity and cultural-linguistic minoritization in Canada.

Historically, the two factors have been reinforcing, as the francophone population of Canada was economically marginalized until recent decades.

Based on its size, population, and resources, Quebec is a more prosperous province than any in the Atlantic region, yet on a per capita basis, Quebec can rank anywhere from fourth to sixth in the country and is considered for federal equalization purposes as a "have-not" province. Apart from hydro-electric power, none of its resources is remarkable in quantity or value, and many of its operations, whether farming or manufacturing, are small scale.[42] Other obstacles to prosperity include the high birth rate and poorly trained labour force (until 1960), labour-intensive industries, seasonal jobs, reliance on imported technology, the vulnerability of its exported products to international market fluctuations, and foreign competition for imports. The social and political position of french-speaking Canadians in Quebec exacerbated the economic problems. For a variety of reasons, including neocolonial attitudes on behalf of English-speaking Canadians, francophones were disproportionately employees and rural labourers while anglophones were disproportionately employers and entrepreneurs. These latter trends have reversed dramatically in the past thirty years with the rise of a French-speaking business class and the reduction of income disparities among English and French-speaking residents. Nonetheless, Quebec remains a striking example of the intermixture of regional and sociological factors in explaining disparities.

In conclusion, the causes of regional disparity are complex and elusive. On a macro-economic level, it is apparent that areas relying on staple exports have seen their economic fortunes fluctuate with the demand for their staples. The most stable regions are those in which manufacturing became firmly established, and the industrialized areas have also been consistently among the most affluent parts of the country. A central fact of Canada's regionalized economy is the existence of a well-established heartland -- that is, a region in the form of central Canada whose population is large enough, dense enough, and rich enough to exceed the threshold necessary to sustain a wide range of secondary activities. In this sense, both capitalist development patterns and government policies have played a role in creating the dominance of this heartland and the resulting disparities with other regions. The reinforcing of market economics with policy-induced development makes it difficult to separate out specific causes to disparities; and as we shall discuss in the next section, this complication renders a consideration of the solutions more difficult and more contentious.

In any case, we emphasize again that economic integration was a chief objective of the political integration created by the federal union of Canada in 1867. The state (both federal as well as provincial) has had to respond to the social and political effects of intensifying economic integration, through the development of the "welfare state" -- and through various means of intervening in the private economy to induce regional growth or to redress the balance of certain forms of economic development. These efforts have had mixed results -- perhaps due to the continuing lack of consensus on just what has caused the disparities in the first place.

Perceptions of disparity, its causes and its solutions, differ fundamentally depending upon the prevailing views about the role of the market economy, and about the ability and desirability of state efforts to direct the economy. Perceptions also differ on where one sits: one region's just claims may be another region's just desserts.

Solutions to Disparities

The Canadian approach to narrowing regional disparities has taken three definable thrusts. The first, and that most typical of federal systems, is the set of intergovernmental provisions available through "fiscal federalism". The second main approach is the federal and provincial governments' direct efforts at regional development. Third is the special role of state enterprise in the mixed Canadian economy.

Fiscal federalism

The evolution of federal-provincial fiscal arrangements over the post-war years has been directly related to the principle that Canada, as a federal system, is committed to the pursuit of equity as a policy goal. This equity goal is in fact recognized in section 36 of *The Constitution Act, 1982*, entitled "Equalization and Regional Disparities". Part 1 commits both levels of government to: i.) [promote] equal opportunities for the well-being of Canadians; ii.) [further] economic development to reduce disparity in opportunities; and iii.) [provide] essential public services of reasonable quality to all Canadians. Part 2 commits the federal government to: "the principle of making equalization payments to ensure that provincial governments have sufficient revenues to provide reasonably comparable levels of public service at reasonably comparable levels of taxation."

Transfers from the federal government to provincial and local governments include the major programs of equalization, Established Program Financing (EPF), and the Canada Assistance Plan (CAP). Direct cash transfers in 1994 were the equivalent of as much as 42 percent of total provincial expenditures in Newfoundland and Prince Edward Island, to 12 percent in Ontario and Alberta.

Quebec, being a "have not" province, depends more than Ontario on federal transfers, with transfers financing about a fifth of Quebec's expenditures.

Canada has probably gone further than most federal systems in addressing the problem of the economic and fiscal balance among its regions. As noted above, the equalization program has been instituted on the principle that citizens in all provinces should be entitled to receive from their provincial governments reasonably comparable levels of public service at reasonably comparable levels of taxation. These unconditional payments from the federal treasury directly to the general provincial revenue funds are recognized as the federal government's chief instrument to fulfill its mandate to ensure equity in the public services available across the country. The federal payments allow the decentralization of responsibility for the provision of public services, without infringing on provincial autonomy in the process. Equalization has been described as "the glue that holds Canada together".[43] It is certainly an essential feature of the existence of Canada as a sharing community, given the great differences among the province's abilities to raise revenue.

The calculations for the equalization payments are based on 32 different provincial revenue sources including, among others, personal income tax, corporation income tax, sales tax and natural resource taxes. For each revenue source, the federal government applies a standard of the per-capita revenue generating potential in five average provinces -- Quebec, Ontario, Manitoba, Saskatchewan and British Columbia. The formula calculates a standardized tax yield from these five provinces (it does not equalize actual tax effort), paying out to the seven provinces whose fiscal capacity is below the national average. In fact there has been recent efforts to strengthen the federal commitment to making equalization payments.[44]

Federal transfers under EPF and CAP complement the functioning of the fiscal equalization program.[45] Under Established Program Financing (EPF), the federal government provides equal per capita transfers to the provinces for health care and post-secondary education expenditures. Relative consistency in national standards in health care has been achieved by the general conditions imposed upon the provinces by the *Canada Health Act* (since 1984). The EPF program has enjoyed strong political support because it is the transfer program that helps to maintain a universal, publicly-funded and administered hospital and medical care insurance plan in all provinces. While the range of health care services and fees can vary significantly across provinces, they still conform overall to the broad principles of the national system.

Under the Canada Assistance Plan (CAP), the federal government shares with the provinces the cost of eligible provincial expenditures for social assistance and social services. CAP has been in place since 1966 and has been the only remaining major federal program where payments are directly tied to matching provincial expenditures (i.e. cost-sharing). Although the federal government shares in the costs incurred by the provinces under the plan, the provinces have remained solely responsible for the administration of the programs including their design, the degree of comprehensiveness, eligibility requirements and method of delivery.

In February 1995, the federal government announced its intention to combine the EPF and CAP transfers into a single program called the Canada Social and Health Transfer (CSHT) to take effect April 1, 1996. While the provincial shares of this transfer are subject to intergovernmental negotiation, the federal intent is to provide the funds as a block (i.e. like EPF), untied to specific expenditures (i.e. unlike CAP). The other major federal objective is to reduce the overall payments in the first two years from cash entitlements of $16.3 billion in 1995-96 to $10.3 billion in 1997-98. This federal expenditure restraint policy is discussed further below.

Until these most recently-announced reductions, the redistributive effect of the three programs combined has been significant; in 1992-93, federal transfers amounted to $20.8 billion under EPF, $7.2 billion under CAP, $8.4 under equalization and $3.6 billion in other transfers. The federal Department of Finance estimates that 27.2 percent of total provincial gross revenues could be attributed to the major fiscal transfer programs. In dollar amounts, this represents $35.5 billion, of which $24.2 billion is in the form of cash transfers, representing almost 22 percent of total federal government program expenditures. However, the relative importance of these fiscal transfers as a percentage of revenues varies significantly across provinces, ranging from 44 percent in Newfoundland, to 30 percent in Quebec, and 20 percent in Alberta.

These intergovernmental grants smooth out large variations in the wealth and fiscal capacity of the provinces and contribute to competitive stability.[46] In a recent analysis, Peter Leslie concludes that there is a substantial redistributive effect of the major fiscal transfers from Ottawa to the provinces. Taking the fiscal year 1989-90 as a recent example, he concludes that the three major transfer programs reduced the initial provincial revenue disparity gap between the richest province (Alberta) and the poorest province (Newfoundland) from a ratio of 2.1/1 to 1.32/1.[47]

Other federal programs -- while not intergovernmental in nature -- also demonstrate evidence of the principle of a "sharing community". The unemployment insurance program, in particular, is almost as regionally redistributive in practice as is the equalization program. In 1990, individuals residing in Quebec received a net payout of $1.13 billion in U.I. benefits (or $167 per person), Newfoundland $651 million (or $1,137 per person), while

Ontario realized a negative U.I. payout of $-2.050 billion (or $-210 per person).[48]

In summary, a crucial aspect of the practice of fiscal federalism in Canada has been the dual concepts of equalization and regional autonomy over program implementation. This has been combined with the retention of sufficient federal control over the personal and corporate income tax fields to enable the central government to maintain fiscal transfer programs. Canada's commitment to the sharing of wealth on a regional basis is large by any measure.[49] It is apparent from these figures that federal attempts to implement a certain degree of regional equality have had very significant impacts in terms of regional distribution of GDP, population and employment. In a decentralized federation such as Canada, intergovernmental transfers also allow expenditures to be made in a more independent and sensitive manner, fashioned according to regional demands, while still allowing for a centralized method of revenue raising.[50] Finally, the stability such transfers provide to the federation is the primary reason that the "have" provinces have accepted them.[51] The population and governments of the richer provinces, in general, accept redistribution mainly because the cost of such transfers is far outweighed by the benefits received from their membership in a larger economic and political unit.[52]

The problem for the Canadian federal system is the current unsustainability of the specific fiscal federalism measures built up in recent decades. As a result of continuing federal budget deficits in every year since 1975, the federal government's debt servicing payments have, in recent years, inexorably crowded out the room for expenditure growth in other programs -- including intergovernmental transfers. As noted, 1995 represents a watershed year in which the federal government has signalled a substantial reduction in the level of transfers. The consequences of this fiscal restraint for the continued ability of fiscal federalism to contribute to disparity reduction are taken up in the next section.

Regional economic policy

During the period from Confederation to the mid-1950s, the federal government had no explicit policy of regional development, and economic policy was directed towards the development of the national economy. The prevailing belief was that a strong national economy, based on east-west trade, would benefit all regions. In short, growth rather than regional balance was the objective of national economic policy. However, by the mid 1950s, the federal government began to display greater concern for a regional balance in economic activity, perhaps because regional differences in wealth became much more apparent in these years.

The federal government's directed efforts towards regional development can be summarized in three phases: an initial phase of tentative efforts to 1969; an intensive, coordinated effort from 1969 to 1982; and a later, more diffuse and declining effort since 1982.

The first phase of efforts by federal agencies were aimed at the rural economy and agriculutural sector and at specific, hard-hit micro-regions (i.e. "regions" within provinces). These efforts were mainly concentrated in the Atlantic Provinces in general and on infrastructure improvements in particular.

The Trudeau government, elected in 1968, promised a much more comprehensive approach to regional development -- one which could respond to national unity concerns as well as to traditional regional grievances, an approach which came to dwell increasingly on Quebec. In 1969, Parliament created the Department of Regional Economic Expansion (DREE), and passed legislation to enable DREE to provide extensive incentives to the private sector in targetted regions and, after 1972, to enter into comprehensive agreements with the provincial governments. These ten-year General Development Agreements (GDAs) signed with every Canadian province in 1974, encompassed literally dozens of subsidary agreements. The GDAs involved differential cost-sharing for a wide variety of projects in various sectoral and micro-regions, often directed at very specific economic opportunities. The federal government funded up to 50 percent of costs for projects in Ontario, British Columbia and Alberta; 60 percent in Quebec, Manitoba and Saskatchewan; 80 percent in Nova Scotia and New Brunswick and 90 percent in Newfoundland. In total, DREE spending more than doubled over the period from $208 million in 1967-70 to $573 million in 1981-82.[53]

After 1982, the federal effort began to wane. Ottawa became disenchanted with the joint intergovernmental approach, and while it signed a series of successor 10-year agreements with the provinces (Economic and Regional Development Agreements -- ERDAs) in 1984, the funding levels dropped eventually, as did the number of cooperative projects.[54] By 1986, the entire federal effort became further diffused and decentralized with the establishment of specialized agencies for each region (e.g. the Atlantic Canada Opportunities Agency and the Western Diversification Office). The period since 1986 has also been one of more general fiscal retrenchment in the federal budget devoted to regional development overall, and to a much less interventionist approach in terms of industry targeting. By the mid-1990s, the federal government is essentially out of the business of incentive grants to industry, and is selecting its cooperative efforts with the provinces more carefully.

The federal government had thus, over a thirty-year period ending in the late 1980s, embarked on a long series of programs, policies and departmental and agency formats to deliver development assistance to the disparate regional economies. In so doing, there has been ample evidence, on the one hand, of bureaucratic over-organization, political meddling and "pork-barrel"; and on the other hand, of inconsistent and unsustained effort.[55] Despite these shortcomings, one must put this overall effort in context. While further comments are made in the next section, suffice to say here that the infusion of less than $1 billion per year in directed development programs pales in comparison to the economic impact of such regulatory measures as tariff and transportation policies. Also, the direct expenditures on regional development have not been nearly as important as the intergovernmental fiscal transfers discussed above, or as the regionally significant personal transfers such as unemployment insurance. However, the direct funding did enable hundreds of firms to be established (not without many high-profile failures) and facilitate long-term improvements in such important public infrastructure as highways, port facilities, industrial parks, forest nurseries, geological mapping, and university research facilities, among others.

Uneven development across Canada has also stimulated the provincial governments to make their own efforts to encourage and even control industrial development. Particularly since the 1960s, provincial governments have established industrial and economic development agencies to stimulate development, to introduce a multitude of "buy provincial" schemes, industrial assistance measures in the form of loan guarantees, subsidies, preferential regulation, and provide various forms of industrial infrastructure. Such provincial efforts have often only been partly successful and have often proved costly to provincial treasuries. Yet, in some high-profile "bail-outs" such as the purchase of the regional steel mills Sidbec and Sysco, the provinces were reacting to the divestment decisions of American or British foreign multinationals who would have otherwise liquidated the operations and caused high levels of regional unemployment.

State enterprise

The Canadian tradition has also been one in which governments have taken a strong lead in creating national transportation and communication structures and in developing resources. From the Canadian Pacific Railway in the 1880s, state involvement in the St. Lawrence canal system, to energy megaprojects in the 1980s, Canada has been developed by a marriage of public sector and private sector endeavours, with some of the most vital entrepreneurship residing in the state sector. Many of Canada's most famous public corporations --including Air

Canada, Canadian National Railways and Petro-Canada -- are creations of the federal government. Of the variety of reasons encouraging federal involvement in the private sector, uneven regional development has often been at or near the top of the list. These corporations have also arisen from the need to ensure that Canada is not pulled wholly into a north-south axis dominated by private American capital. Indeed, this was the motivating factor for the creation of Petro Canada (1975), which was designed to ensure secure energy supplies and reduce the level of foreign ownership in the oil and gas sector; Atomic Energy of Canada (1952) and Eldorado Nuclear (1944), which spearhead Canada's nuclear energy industry; and De Havilland Aircraft of Canada (1974) and Canadair (1976), which were nationalised in order to restore Canada's place in the world aircraft industry.

Over the years, a number of federal government "crown corporations" have been explicitly mandated to stimulate regional development. For example, the Cape Breton Development Corporation (DEVCO), established in 1967, was originally designed to fill the economic vacuum created by the decline of the coal and steel industries on Cape Breton Island. Though it encouraged diversification, in 1971 it returned government attention to the coal industry by refinancing new coal handling and preparation facilities operations. Other crown corporations have, to varying degrees, been given mandates to assist regional development. The Canada Development Corporation (CDC), created in 1971, was designed to take equity positions in high-technology and resource industries in order to enhance Canadian ownership. Exports have been encouraged through the Export Development Corporation (EDC) (which by 1975 was financing forty percent of Canada's capital goods exports outside North America) and the Canadian Wheat Board (1935), which was designed to assist the prairie provinces by acting as a single exporting agent for wheat and other grains.[56]

The Canadian provinces have also engaged in the purchase of public enterprises in order to spur economic development. Beginning at the turn of the century, provincial governments began establishing crown corporations to integrate their economies and facilitate staples extraction. Ontario was the first to establish a provincially owned utility in the form of Ontario Hydro in 1906, and the other provinces followed suit. Early development of communications capabilities was also given priority by several provinces, particularly in the sparsely populated west. The Manitoba Telephone System, Saskatchewan Communications and Alberta Government Telephones were all placed under public ownership in 1908. In their decisions to take control of hydro-generating capacity or telephone service, the provinces were responding to the pressures of local interests -- small manufacturers, merchants, and municipalities -- and their need for cheap, reliable sources of power for industries, and by farmers who wanted rural telephone services.

In the 1960s and 70s, provincial governments also moved directly into the highly profitable resource sectors through takeovers of subsidiaries of multinational enterprises (Potash Corporation of Saskatchewan, National Asbestos Corporation in Quebec) and in joint ventures with private enterprise as exemplified by Alberta's Soquip, the Saskatchewan Oil and Gas Corporation and the Manitoba Oil and Gas Corporation. In sum, 72 percent of the several hundred provincially owned corporations and 58 percent of federal government enterprises were created after 1960.[57]

Since the late 1980s, few new crown corporations or other forms of state enterprise have been established. Indeed, many have been privitized or wound-up. The crown corporation as the instrument of choice in economic policy has seemingly had its day, and governments increasingly require their state enterprises to operate "like a business" and to avoid losses, and are increasingly reluctant to provide them with developmental mandates. The reasons for this trend are both practical and ideological -- to which we turn in the next section.

Concluding Assessments

In drawing conclusions about the Canadian odyssey of regional development and the reduction of regional disparities, one must remember the Canadian context. Canada began and remains the northern extension of a North American economy, but with a political mission to be separate from the United States. Canadians share in American prosperity, but must take a much more active role to replicate what the market can take for granted in the huge and dynamic economy to the south. The geography here is more unforgiving, the task of national integration more onerous. Natural regionalism is reinforced by the institutional regionalism of the federation, which makes the politics of disparity indistinguishable from the politics of federalism. Yet the disparities are real: where one lives in Canada has historically and remains an important determinant of economic opportunities and human development potential.

Part of the "federal bargain" of Canada has been to ensure a measure of equity across the regions in return for participation in the nation-building enterprise of political and economic integration.[58] The task of promoting regional equity has been a difficult one, more especially as the Canadian economy is still small by some standards and increasingly open, and the Canadian territory is vast and relatively unpopulated. Within these parameters, however, the efforts to reduce disparity have been impressive. Reducing disparities has been one of the leading national objectives, enshrined in the Constitution and applied through conscientious institutions, policies and programs. Equality of opportunity among the regions (provinces) and even the equality of outcomes -- especially as applied to the benefits of the state to citizens -- have been perceived as important Canadian values.

At the practical level, the achievements of fiscal federalism in particular have gone a long way to eliminating the disparities of provincial governments to provide "reasonably comparable levels of public services at reasonably comparable levels of taxation" (as stated in the constitutional commitment). There is, of course, much room for debate about whether provincial programs meet putative national standards, but given the inevitable and indeed desirable variations among provinces, the overall fiscal disparities among provincial governments have been substantially narrowed. This has helped to preserve the integrity of the federal system by enabling all provinces to maintain their constitutional autonomy, and, at the end of the day, to retain a large measure of control over local development priorities.

The more direct efforts of the federal and provincial governments to intervene and to stimulate economic development in the poorer regions are more difficult to evaluate. Public infrastructure across the country has been improved by the thirty-year effort, even if now the funds to maintain the infrastructure are scarce. And while one can point to few entire industrial sectors which have emerged from government intervention in the regional economies, most of the provinces have more diverse and sophisticated economies than previously, and several individual enterprises -- such as Michelin Tire in Nova Scotia, which is now the largest single private sector employer in that province -- continue as a testament to the value of start-up incentives to the private sector when the overall industrial strategy is sound. It is difficult to believe that none of this economic progress would have happened without the regional development programs and the activities of state enterprises; indeed there is substantial if not always conclusive evidence that these efforts were crucial.

Nonetheless, recent Canadian efforts do point to a number of failures and unsustainable policies. First, the actual funds for proactive removal of development barriers have been dwarfed by the programs for unemployment insurance which gave only passive relief to the labour market in the poorer regions. Second, some of the policies of the federal and provincial governments alike have fragmented the national economy and have been judged by most observers to be counterproductive -- at the very least, by reducing the pool for redistribution. Third, the centrally controlled and coordinated bureaucratic programs for regional development have often stifled rather than stimulated local initiative and entrepreneurship.

There is also broader criticism that none of these measures have "worked" in that they have all been futile attempts by governments to spit in the wind of market forces. The extent to which development policies must bow to market realities is a very contentious debate in Canada, especially so in the past decade as so much of the old order of national development policy has disintegrated in the face of "globalization" and its more proximate phenomenon, free trade with the USA. Yet there has been a strong and influential body of thought, and not only confined to neoclassical economists, who have doubted the efficacy of much if not all of the regional development approach in particular. However, from the perspective of those in the poorer regions, there is perceived to be as much self-interest as there is sound advice in the calls from Ontario and other richer provinces for a more market-oriented approach.

There remain critics of Canada's economic and industrial policies, tied as they are to continental (and global) free trade. Do free trade agreements prevent a return to a more interventionist industrial policy, one that might also be more regionally balanced? This topic is beyond the scope of this paper, except to point out that an industrial policy with objectives and means akin to the National Policy that prevailed for most of the first century of the Canadian federation, appears increasingly unlikely if not undesirable.

From the perspective of human development in its broader terms one must indeed weigh the benefits of national economic integration and its wealth creating potential for the greater number of persons in the country, against the potential costs of wealth dissipating efforts to support regional balance in economic activity. In the final analysis, the sustaining rationale for reducing regional disparity may hinge on its role in the economic integration process, in which equity and efficiency go hand in hand. For economic integration depends crucially on labour mobility, not only as an adjustment mechanism for the poorer regions, but also as an assurance that there is an efficient distribution of labour across the country. Despite all of the direct efforts to support the regional economies, substantial outmigration does occur. And the relative ease of labour mobility -- Canadian labour mobility is among the highest in OECD countries -- is clearly enhanced by the programs of fiscal federalism which ensure comparable levels of education, health and other services in all provinces.[59] Programs to equalize the levels of public services play an important role in ensuring that people move for the "right" reasons (gainful employment, social fulfilment) not for the "wrong" reasons (better public services).

The reality then, is that alleviating poverty in peripheral economies is just as likely to increase outward migration as it is to improve the lives of those who remain. It certainly increases choice. Individuals and families are better able to make their own trade-offs between the quality of life and community attachment in the region of their birth and the greater economic or social opportunities of leaving. In this context, economic union in the federation brings with it the goals of regional equity, as well as the broader social goals of enhanced human freedom and individual social development. In this sense, the "right of development" and broader human rights are closely linked.

This leads, however, to a somewhat darker set of concluding comments. Enhancing human development potential requires at least a minimum effort to promote regional equity. As has been alluded to in this paper, the Canadian commitment to regional equity will be sorely tested in the years to come. There are both secular and ideological trends at play to reduce the commitment. The secular trend, which Canada shares with several other industrialized countries, but which is nonetheless very severe, has been a run up of deficit financing of government expenditures in the context of more slowly growing revenues. In Canada, this process has been ongoing since 1975 and is only now forcing major reductions in payments to individuals, intergovernmental transfers and other government programs. The other secular trend has been intensifying global competition for Canadian business, reducing the opportunities for successful government intervention and reinforcing existing market forces working against certain regions.

The more ideological trend has been to make a virtue of the necessity of the secular trends. Thus, "neo-conservative" (or more appropriately, perhaps, neo-liberal) parties and governments argue against state intervention in the economy, whether through regulation, subsidization or public ownership. The thirty-year effort of direct programming for regional development has become a conspicuous target for those in the federal government or the national business community who support a dramatically reduced role for the state. This sentiment is complicated by a fatigue in the richer provinces with the perceived "coddling" of the "have-not" provinces -- Quebec in particular. Moreover, the overall political commitment to sharing is clearly under attack from an overtaxed middle class. It may be that the commitment to regional equity is under less severe attack than is interpersonal equity, In that of the major transfer programs, equalization has been, thus far, relatively spared.[60] However, in the long run one cannot expect regional programs to be spared if the citizens of the richer provinces do not perceive themselves as receiving their dividends from national integration.

To the extent that some aspects of the political trend to de-regulation and liberalization undo the distortions of Canadian national development -- e.g. free trade as compared to protected trade -- the need for compensating equity measures to certain of the regions may be reduced. While it is too early to make confident assessments, there is in fact a renaissance of business activity in some of the poorer provinces, based in part on opening global markets. Such recovery may continue to feed on market forces to produce a private sector led rebalancing of the Canadian economy. On the other hand, further integration into the North American economy is likely to increase the peripheral predicament of many industries and communities in Canada, inducing new patterns of disparity.

In conclusion, it may be several more years before the full impact of recent trends towards secular globalization and public expenditure reduction on regional disparities in Canada is known, let alone the more ideological trend of eliminating many of the tools used in Canada to alleviate disparities. For now, it seems clear that the public commitment to regional equity is considerably weakened, if not in relation to the commitment to equity overall, certainly in relation to former levels of concern and expenditure of effort in absolute terms. What remains to be seen is whether the underlying regional disparities will widen as a result, or whether a more narrow range of disparities will rationalize the reduced government expenditures.

Notes

1. The rankings of the top ten countries were as follows: Canada, Switzerland, Japan, Sweden, Norway, France, Australia, U.S.A., Netherlands, United Kingdom.

2. The Economic Council of Canada, *Living Together: A Study of Regional Disparities* (Ottawa: Minister of Supply and Services, 1977).

3. Benjamin Higgins and Donald J. Savoie, "Comparing Australian and Canadian Regional Development Policy: Lessons for Canada," *Canadian Journal of Regional Science* Vol. 17, No. 1 (spring, 1994), pp. 1-22, p. 3.

4. Canada, *Report of the Royal Commission on Dominion-Provincial Relations* The Rowell-Sirois Commission Report (Ottawa: Queen's Printer, 1940). See also Clyde Weaver and Thomas Gunton, "From Drought Assistance to Mega Projects: Fifty Years of Regional Theory and Policy in Canada," *Canadian Journal of Regional Science* Vol. 5, pp. 5-37.

5. Royal Commission on the Economic Union and Development Prospects for Canada, *Report*, Volume 3 (Ottawa: Supply and Services, 1985), pp. 198-201.

6. Robert L. Mansell and Lawrence Copithorne, "Canadian Regional Economic Disparities," in Kenneth Norrie ed., *Disparities and Interregional Adjustment* Collected Research Studies of the Royal Commission on the Economic Union and Development Prospects for Canada, Volume 64 (Toronto: University of Toronto Press, 1986), pp. 1-45; J. G. Williamson,"Regional Inequality and the Process of National Development: A Description of Patterns," *Economic Development and Cultural Change* Vol. 13, 1965, pp. 3-45.

7. For a discussion see Economic Council of Canada, *Eleventh Annual Review: Economic Targets and Social Indicators* (Ottawa: Information Canada, 1974), pp. 8-9.

8. Lars Osberg, *Economic Inequality in Canada* (Toronto: Butterworth & Company, 1981), p. 1.

9. For a discussion see R.W. Phidd and G. Bruce Doern, *The Politics of Management of Canadian Economic Policy* (Toronto: Macmillan, 1978).

10. *The Constitution Act*, 1982 Part III, 36(1).

11. Donald J. Savoie, *Regional Economic Development: Canada's Search for Solutions* (Toronto: University of Toronto Press, 1986), p. 139.

12. For an analysis on the outcomes of the federal system with respect to the building of the Canadian welfare state, see Keith G. Banting, *The Welfare State and Canadian Federalism* (second edition), Kingston: McGill-Queen's University Press, 1987. See also Raymond Breton "Regionalism in Canada", in David Cameron (ed.), *Regionalism and Supranationalism* (Montreal: Institute for Research on Public Policy, 1981), pp. 57-79.

13. The author is indebted to the views of his colleagues in this project on the topic. See Pitman Potter "The Right to Development: Philosophical Difference and Political Implications", and Rao Geping "The Right to Development and China's Project to Help the Poor Through Development".

14. The Tables were created by the authors, the data obtained from Statistics Canada.

15. A classic study is David Elkins and Richard Simeon (eds.) *Small Worlds: Provinces and Parties in Canadian Political Life* (Toronto: Methuen, 1980),

p. vii.

16. Jon H. Pammett, "Public Orientation to Regions and Provinces," in David J. Bellamy, Jon H. Pammett, and Donald C. Rowat, (eds.) *The Provincial Political Systems: Comparative Essays*, Toronto: Methuen, 1976, pp. 86-101.

17. Ralph Mathews, *The Creation of Regional Dependency* (Toronto: University of Toronto Press, 1983), Ch. 1.

18. Garth Stevenson, "Canadian Regionalism in Continental Perspective," *Journal of Canadian Studies* (Summer 1980), p. 17.

19. W. Westfall, "On the Concept of Region in Canadian History and Literature," *Journal of Canadian Studies* (Summer 1980), p. 6.

20. Mathews, *The Creation of Regional Dependency*, p. 19.

21. Janine Brodie, *The Political Economy of Canadian Regionalism* (Toronto: Harcourt Brace Jovanovich, 1990), pp. 12-13.

22. The influential Task Force on Canadian Unity endorsed this view, arguing that provincial political institutions are the primary frameworks through which regional populations can organize and express themselves. Task Force on Canadian Unity, *A Future Together* (Hull: Supply and Services, 1979), p. 27.

23. Elkins and Simeon, *Small Worlds*, pp. xi-xii.

24. N. Harvey Lithwick, "Is Federalism Good For Regionalism?" *Journal of Canadian Studies* (Summer 1980)

25. See, for example United Nations Development Programme, *Human Development Report 1990* (New York: Oxford University Press, 1990), Chapter 1.

26. For more on this see Keith Griffin and Terry McKinley, *Implementing a Human Development Strategy* (London: MacMillan Press, 1994).

27. For a discussion, see B.N. Boots and A. Hecht, "Spatial Perspectives on Canadian Provincialism and Regionalism," *Canadian Journal of Regional*

Science Vol. 12, No. 2 (Summer, 1989), pp. 187-206.

28. Family income is selected rather than personal income as a more accurate measure of human development. Per capita income does not take into account the substantial scale economies associated with household size or the fact that the number of wage earners per household falls as household size increases.

29. S.E. Charnick, *Interregional Disparities in Income* Economic Council of Canada, Study 14 (Ottawa: Queen's Printer, 1966), p. 50.

30. Anthony Myatt,"Provincial Unemployment Rate Disparities: A Case of No Concern?" *Canadian Journal of Regional Science* Vol. 15, No. 1 (Spring, 1992), pp. 101-119.

31. For a discussion, see Donald J. Savoie, *Regional Economic Development: Canada's Search for Solutions* (Toronto: University of Toronto Press, 1986), pp. 3-11.

32. For the classic study see Harold Innis, *The Cod Fisheries* (Toronto: University of Toronto Press, 1954).

33. Lawrence Copithorne, "Natural Resources and Regional Disparities: A Sceptical view," *Canadian Public Policy* Vol. 2 pp. 181-194.

34. Economic Council of Canada, *Living Together*, p. 24.

35. For an overview see Douglas M. Brown and Peter M. Leslie, "Economic Integration and Equality in Federations: The Case of Canada," in Anne Mullins and Cheryl Saunders, *Economic Union in Federal systems* (Annandale: The Federation Press, 1994), p.93. For an overview of economic comment and analysis on the impact of the National Policy and related measures (in particular the tariff on manufactures) see Ronald A. Shearer, "Regionalism and International Trade Policy" in J. Whalley (ed.) *Canada-United States Free Trade* vol. 11 of the Collected Research Studies of the Royal Commission on the Economic Union and Development Prospects for Canada, (Toronto: University of Toronto Press, 1985).

36. F.J. Anderson and N.C. Bonsor, "Regional Economic Alienation: Atlantic Canada and the West," in Kenneth Norrie (ed.) *Disparities and Interregional Adjustment*, pp. 185-221.

37. Mireille Éthier, *Regional Grievances: The Quebec Case* in Kenneth Norrie (ed.), *Disparities and Interregional Adjustment*, pp. 159-182.

38. Economic Council of Canada, *Living Together*, p. 25.

39. Ingrid Bryan, *Economic Policies in Canada* (Toronto: Butterworth & Co., 1982), p. 205. It should be noted that some studies indicate that the degree of urbanization explains little, if any, of the regional differences in earnings per worker. Robert L. Mansell and Lawrence Copithorne, "Canadian Economic Disparities: A Survey, in Kenneth Norrie (ed.) *Disparities and Interregional Adjustment* Vol. 64 of the Royal Commission on the Economic Union and Development Prospects for Canada (Toronto: University of Toronto Press, 1986), p. 18. ; F.T. Denton, *An Analysis of Interregional Differences in Manpower Utilization and Earnings* Study prepared for the Economic Council of Canada (Ottawa: Queen's Printer, 1966), p. 13.

40. L. Auer, *Regional Disparities of Productivity and Growth in Canada* Study Prepared for the Economic Council of Canada (Ottawa: Minister of Supply and Services Canada, 1979); Economic Council of Canada, *Living Together: A Study in Regional Disparities*, p. 82.

41. For a discussion see Richard Apostle and Paul Pross, "Marginality and Political Culture: A New Approach to Political Culture in Atlantic Canada," Canadian Political Science Association, 1981, p. 22.

42. For example, some half of employment in manufacturing has traditionally been the light consumer non-durable sectors such as food and beverages, clothing, textiles, leather and furniture, though the province has successfully sought industries which use large quantities of electricity, such as aluminum, which have been powered by Hydro-Quebec's expansionism and low power rates.

43. Thomas J. Courchene, *Equalization Payments: Past, Present and Future* (Toronto: Ontario Economic Council, 1984), p. 406.

44. The "Charlottetown Accord" of constitutional reform proposals included such provisions, but was defeated in referenda in October, 1992, for reasons unrelated to the provisions on equalization. See Canada, *Consensus Report on the Constitution: Final Text* Charlottetown, August 28, 1992.

45. See Robin W. Boadway and Paul A. R. Hobson, *Intergovernmental Fiscal Relations in Canada* (Toronto: Canadian Tax Foundation, 1993).

46. Albert Breton,"Statement" in Canada, Royal Commission on the Economic Union and Development Prospects for Canada, *Report*, Vol.3 (Ottawa: Supply and Services Canada, 1985), pp. 508-516.

47. Peter M. Leslie "The Fiscal Crisis of Canadian Federalism" in P.M. Leslie, Kenneth Norrie and Irene Ip, *A Partnership in Trouble: Renegotiating Fiscal Federalism*, Policy Study 18, Toronto: C.D. Howe Institute, 1993; Table 4; p. 35.

48. Peter Leslie, "The Fiscal Crisis of Canadian Federalism,", p. 38.

49. A thirty year study by Robert Mansell and Ronald Schlenker of net federal fiscal balances, (ie. total federal revenues collected in the region minus total federal expenditures and transfers to the region) from 1961 to 1989 (measured in 1990 dollars) revealed that Quebec experienced a net financial inflow for the 1961-1989 period of $140 billion. By comparison, $78 billion in net inflow was achieved by Nova Scotia and $49 billion for New Brunswick, the second and third largest "recipient" provinces. Conversely, Alberta's net outflows during the entire period totalled $148 billion. Robert L. Mansell and Ronald C. Schlenker, "A Regional Analysis of Fiscal Balances under Existing and Alternative Constitutional Arrangements," in Paul Boothe ed. *Alberta and the Economics of Constitutional Change* Publication No. 3 (Edmonton: University of Alberta, Western Centre for Economic Research, 1992), pp. 211-259.

50. Robin Boadway and Frank Flatters,"Fiscal Federalism: Is the System in Crisis?" in Keith G. Banting, Douglas M. Brown and Thomas J. Courchene, *The Future of Fiscal Federalism* (Kingston: Queens University, School of Policy Studies, 1994), p. 34.

51. Albert Breton, "The Existence and Stability of Interjurisdictional Competition," in Daphne A. Kenyon and John Kincaid, eds. *Competition among States and Local Governments* (Washington, D.C.: The Urban Institute Press, 1991), pp. 50-51.

52. For an interesting discussion of this issue, including extensive references to Canada see Benjamin Higgins,"Economic Development and Regional

Disparities: A Comparative Study of Four Federations," in Russell Mathews ed. *Regional Disparities and Economic Development* (Canberra: Australia National University, Centre for Research on Federal Financial Relations, 1981).

53. McGee, *Getting It Right*, pp. 34-86.

54. Ibid., 170-17.

55. For two critical views of federal efforts see R. Harley McGee, *Getting It Right: Regional Development in Canada* (Kingston: McGill-Queen's University Press, 1992); and Senate of Canada, Standing Committee on National Finance, *Report on Government Policy and Regional Development* (Ottawa: Minister of Supply and Services, 1982).

56. Similarly the Canada Commercial Corporation (CCC) was reoriented in the 1970s to promote purchases of Canadian goods by foreign countries, and in 1982-83, secured $600 million in contracts for Canadian companies. See Jeanne Kirk Laux and Maureen Appel Molot, *State Capitalism: Public Enterprise in Canada* (Ithaca: Cornell University Press, 1988), p. 58.

57. Donald J. Savoie, *Regional Economic Development*, p. 101.

58. For a fuller discussion see Leslie and Brown, op. cit.

59. See for example Robin Boadway and Frank Flatters, *Equalization in a Federal State: An Economic Analysis* (Ottawa: Economic Council of Canada, 1982).

60. Such observations in light of the 1995 federal budget are made by Keith Banting in T.J. Courchene (ed.), *The 1995 Federal Budget: Retrospect and Prospect* (Kingston: J. Deutsch Institute, Queen's University, 1995).

Social Security and Human Rights in China

JIA JUNLING

The Research Range of Chinese Social Security

The concept of social security

Social security is a commonly used term in modern society. It no longer refers to the budding ideas of the early 19th century, but has already become one of the government's important socio-economic policies. The right to social security is not only a basic concept on the domestic human rights agenda but also a component of internationally recognized human rights.

The sociological definition of social security is as follows: When a member of society looses his/her ability to work or when he/she has met with difficulties in life because of old age, illness, disability, unemployment, child-birth, death, disaster, etc., that person is guaranteed support from the government and society in securing the basic necessities of life. As an important part of the legal system, social security law is the overall term for all the legal norms that deal with the regulation of social insurance, social welfare, social assistance and other such relations. Therefore, the scope of social relations covered by social security law is very wide. Social security law belongs within the scope of rights protection law. It is very comprehensive, and there is some overlap with labour law.

The Chinese social security legal system

The social security system is very comprehensive. Since the foundation of the People's Republic of China, the Chinese government has promulgated many special social security regulations and concrete policies. However, no uniform and integrated legal system has been set up for the areas of social security that deal with the basic content, scope of application, management structures, benefit standards, legal responsibility, supervisory procedures, and others. The system of a socialist market economy which China is currently establishing is a uniform, integrated, systematic and complicated new economic system. A social security legal system is essential to completing the process of regulating the socialist market economy. It is also an important notion in human rights protection.

Completion of a social security law is key to establishing market economy legislation in China.

The components of Chinese social security law are as follows:

Social insurance (worker's social insurance): maternity benefits; old-age pension; medical insurance; worker's compensation; unemployment insurance; pension for the relatives of the deceased.

Social assistance: disaster relief; assistance to the urban poor; the "five guarantees" (guaranteed food, clothing, medical care, housing and burial expenses) for the elderly and disadvantaged in rural areas; assistance to people with special needs in both urban and rural areas; assistance to the disabled; assistance to beggars and homeless people.

Social welfare: subsidies to urban residents; cultural and recreational facilities; health care and medical insurance facilities; childcare facilities; welfare facilities for seniors; community welfare facilities; etc.

Within this system, social insurance is the most important part -the part that holds up the system. Social insurance involves the basic rights of all Chinese workers. The focus of the social security reforms that China is currently undertaking is on old-age pension and unemployment insurance. Establishment of a social insurance system and social insurance legislation should generally be done concurrently. Therefore, social insurance legislation is also the prerequisite for regulating the socialist market economy. Completion of social insurance legislation provides advance and follow-up legal safeguards for the establishment of a market economy. It guarantees material compensation and assistance to workers who participate in market activities. This essay focusses mainly on the human rights aspect of social security.

Human Rights Issues in Chinese Social Security Law

General manifestations of human rights issues in social security

The universal demand for social security

Social security is a reflection of the right to material help. The right to material help (including material help to support oneself) ensures the basic conditions for a person's right to subsistence. Regardless of the kind of system or the particular country, there will always be people who need help because of circumstances related to child-bearing, old age, sickness, death, disability, unemployment, etc. The use of specific legal structures to solve these problems is a common socio-economic issue of every country. Based on its own distinct social systems, historical phase, national circumstances and characteristics, each country establishes a social security system and model to suit its own unique situation.

Human rights are the basic rights that human beings enjoy and should enjoy under specific socio-historical conditions. Such basic rights include political, economic, personal and cultural rights, etc. Social security reflects the right to subsistence which holds direct economic significance. Chinese research on social security systems is mainly concentrated on social systems, social justice, social benefits, social stability, and other such areas. Research in these areas, as well as each item of the country's social security policies, are consistent with the principle of human rights protection. Whether one speaks of universal human rights or of special human rights, each country, within its own system and based on the protection of a person's right to subsistence, is establishing systemic guarantees for those who need assistance.

Illustration of personal rights and economic rights

Social insurance refers to a kind of social security system, established by the state through legislation, which ensures citizens or workers a certain level of material assistance and social services from the state, society or relevant government department in cases where they are having difficulty coping because of old age, childbirth, sickness, injury in the work place, disability, unemployment, death, or other circumstances. This kind of security system does not reflect human rights in the political sense, but rather human rights in the humanitarian sense of the term. It reflects the material help given by the state and society to those who are in need. It also reflects mutual help between members of society.

The realization of the right to material help essentially involves people's economic interests. In order to safeguard this kind of economic interest, China, whose economy is still not fully developed, has established a social insurance system which suits the particular circumstances of the country. Take for example the unemployment insurance system: In 1986, the State Council issued the *Temporary Regulations Concerning Unemployment Insurance for Workers in State Operated Firms*. In 1993, the State Council re-issued the *Regulations Concerning Unemployment Insurance for Workers in State Operated Firms*. From 1986 to 1994, 3.54 million people received unemployment benefits which assured them the basic necessities of life. The State paid 1.8 billion yuan in re-employment funds to help two million unemployed find new jobs. During the past two years, the unemployment rate decreased by 0.4% and 0.6% respectively. The average length of an unemployment cycle is six months. Other forms of social insurance, such as old age pension, health insurance and disability pension, all involve economic interests--the right to material help.

Differences in human rights protection at various levels of socio-economic development

The scope and nature of human rights protection in every country differs with each country's different phase of historical development. As social security is a reflection of economic interests, a social security legal system needs to be established to suit China's special conditions at different stages of development in the country's economy. The *Social Insurance Law of the People's Republic of China*, which is currently being drafted, needs to pay attention to adjusting the level of social insurance to the stage of socio-economic development of the country. The level of development of social production forces should include the value of average domestic production, the income level of urban and rural residents, and the pay level of workers, etc. For example, when setting the basic compensation rate for old age pensions, due consideration should be given both to the stability of the Chinese economy and to the reality that old age pensions, too, should benefit from the fruits of socio-economic development. Because of changes in work habits and family structures, developed countries are re-examining their social insurance systems. Governments have begun to emphasize the individual's responsibility and decrease the level of state interference. Governments are only prepared to provide basic social insurance. It is then up to individuals or employers to provide additional social insurance. For example, there is a growing tendency, in the area of old age pensions, towards having developing enterprises supplement pensions, raise the retirement age and restrain spending. More industrialized countries are looking for ways to combine unemployment insurance with employment and career training programs in order to accelerate normalization of production forces. Some countries provide financial assistance for career training for the unemployed. Therefore, protection of human rights via measures of social security must be adjusted by every country to suit its own level of socio-economic development. Only then can a social security system be fully realized.

Human rights standards and the special characteristics of Chinese social insurance

The mandatory standard of social insurance

Inherent conflicts exist between social justice and economic gains in the protection of human rights via measures of social insurance: management restrains welfare spending in order to increase economic gains; workers, in order to further their own material interests, demand improvements and increases in social insurance benefits. In protecting human rights via measures of social insurance, consideration should be given to the interests and demands of both sides. The social insurance law reflects the country's determination in the area of social insurance, and its mandatory character is very clear. Implementation of the different elements, scope of application and payment standards of social insurance are all mandatory according to the laws of the country. Usually, it is not up to the discretion of those who insure and those who are insured. Therefore, there is a strict difference between social insurance and commercial insurance. The mandatory character of social insurance is consistent with the international spirit of human rights protection.

The preventive standard of social insurance

Human rights protection via measures of social insurance often involves a worker's long-term interests. For example, fundraising for Chinese old age pensions will be based on the principle of combining society's contributions with individual contributions. The funds raised will be spent by workers several decades later. In order to secure long-term interests, standards of prevention must be raised to deal with the issue of maintaining and increasing the real value of social insurance funds. For example, should part of the funds be invested? Should invested funds be guaranteed? Who makes the decisions whether or not to invest social insurance funds? These preventive standards reflect the reality of human rights protection via measures of social insurance.

The standard of mutual help

Human rights protection via measures of social insurance reflects the principle of humanitarianism. Chinese social insurance policy emphasizes society's characteristic of mutual help. It means that assistance to people in need is both part of the government's welfare policy and also a shared social responsibility of all members of society. At present, China is reforming its social insurance system and is raising funds for old age pensions, unemployment insurance and maternity benefits, through means of contributions from society as a whole, etc. This reflects the characteristic of mutual help between members of society.

The Trend in Chinese Social Insurance Legislation

Integration of the social insurance legal system

Human rights protection via measures of social insurance is mainly reflected in the domestic protection of human rights. Human rights are guaranteed through social insurance legislation which suits China's particular circumstances. China is currently undertaking a process of integrating social insurance legislation. It wants to develop the social insurance legal system towards becoming universally applicable in society, and specialized, standardized and uniform. In Chinese social insurance law, legislation is found mostly in the areas of scope of application, specific insurance programs, and benefit standards. No uniform legislation, however, has been implemented between different regions, different ownership systems and different professions. In order to adjust to the demands of a streamlined market economy, the requirements for integrating the social insurance legal system are mainly as follows:

Universal scope of application of social insurance

Since introducing the market economy system, there has been a significant change in the way the economy behaves. In its management of socio-economic development, the government is replacing administrative regulations and measures with legal regulations and measures. The behaviour of the economy is based on the relationship between the principal interest holders of the market. After the labour force reserve enters the competitive market system, workers become free to choose employment. This pluralization of the market creates a constant state of change. Because of the constant shifts in the labour force, there is a need for universally applicable regulations under the social insurance law, in order to secure workers or work units reasonable and just application of the law in times of changes and shifts in their situation.

Uniformity of the parties involved in social insurance relations

The eligibility and conditions of the parties involved in social insurance relations should be regulated by law. If the insurer is a social insurance management structure clearly regulated by the law, it is a specially established structure and thus should be distinguished from commercial insurance companies. The contributor is the individual or organization who contributes social insurance fees according to the law. The insured is the person who enjoy the benefits of social insurance according to the law. The eligibility and conditions of the insured are dictated by the differing capacity of the contributor. The beneficiary is the person who has the right to obtain the social insurance payments according to the law. If the insured person is injured or dies, his/her legal relatives have the right to receive subsidies based on varying standards.

The demand for integrated social insurance legislation is consistent with the three basic features reflected in human rights, namely urgency, eligibility and universality.

Establishing International Standards of Social Insurance

Having gone through brutal wars or other violent events, people all over the world have long recognized the importance of protecting human rights. The first time that protection of human rights was recognized in writing as one of the main principles of an international organization was in the 1945 *United Nations Charter*. In 1948, the General Assembly of the United Nations approved the *Universal Declaration of Human Rights* which was the first international document about human rights. The *Universal Declaration of Human Rights*, however, is not an international treaty, and it is not legally binding on the international community. Every country has a unique historical background as well as a distinct social system and level of economic development. Each country also differs in its realization of human rights. Therefore, the human rights issue still belongs within a country's domestic jurisdiction and is closely related to state sovereignty.

The main international treaties which affect Chinese social security legislation are the *International Labour Convention* and the *International Labour Recommendations* issued by the International Labour Organization (ILO), for example no. 102, *Social Security (Minimum Standards) Convention*; no. 118, *Equality of Treatment (Social Security) Convention*; no.157, *Convention on Protecting Social Security Rights*; no. 167, *Recommendation on Protecting Social Security Rights*; no. 130, *Medical and Sickness Benefits Convention*; no. 128, *Invalidity, Old-Age and Survivors' Benefit Convention*;

no. 121, *Employment Injury Benefits Convention*; no. 168, *Convention on Promoting Employment and Unemployment Protection*, etc.

China is a member of the International Labour Organization. None of the above mentioned conventions on social security issues are included among the 17 international labour conventions that China has already approved. However, the ILO's Conventions and Recommendations are of value to Chinese social security legislation for reference purposes. For example, in no. 102 *Convention on Social security (Minimum Standards)*, the nine social insurance components--medical allowance, sickness allowance, unemployment benefits, old-age pensions, workers compensation, maternity benefits, family allowance, disability pension, allowance for the relatives of deaceased--can all, except for family allowance, be used as references when developing China's social insurance legislation. With respect to family allowance, as China is implementing family-planning policies, it is impossible to give allowances to families with many children. Apart from that, the various standards of the *International Labour Convention*, such as fund-raising methods, management structures and scope of application, are all of important reference value to developing Chinese social security legislation. In developing the contents of the social security legislation, China will give ample consideration to international standards, while keeping in mind the unique circumstances of the country.

Translated by Shengtao Jiang and A-M Traeholt

The Practice and Legal Protection of the Rights and Interests of Minors in China

YANG YIWEN

Introduction

Today's children will be tomorrow's citizens of the world. Therefore, their survival, protection and development are prerequisites for the future development of human beings... Their individual development and social contribution will mould the future of the world.

"Action Plan for Implementing
the World Declaration on the Survival,
Protection and Development of Children in the 90s"

Today's children will be the masters of the 21st century. The survival, protection and development of the children will not only affect the future of a particular country, but also the future of the entire world. Based on this common realization, the UN approved the *Convention on the Rights of the Child* in 1989. To date, 80 countries have signed the convention. In September 1990, leaders from 159 countries convened for the first global, high level international conference with a specific focus on children's issues, and the *World Declaration on the Survival, Protection and Development of Children* and the *Action Plan for Implementing the World Declaration on the Survival, Protection and Development of Children in the 90s* were passed. A series of joint international actions to promote the development of the children's cause in every country in the world played an important motivational role. It gave expression to the international society's focus on the global cause of the survival, protection and development of children as well as to the wide-reaching cooperation initiated on a global level in order to fulfil the promise made to the children.

China is a developing country. The number of children in China is the highest in the world. Guaranteeing the survival and development of children will not only play an important role for the future of the world, it will also have a long-term impact on promoting the progress of humankind and the protection of world peace. During the past few decades, through sustained efforts by the Chinese government, the level of development of the children's cause has been raised considerably, and China is the leader among the developing countries with respect to reaching the main targets in this field. During the past few years, since China has implemented the open-door and reform policies, and following economic development and social progress, the development of the children's cause has achieved astonishing results. To create a better environment for the children to grow up in and to educate them to become qualified citizens with ideals, morals, culture and a sense of order, are not only the development targets established by the state for the children's cause, but they have also become conscious actions of the Chinese people and common knowledge in society as a whole. In September 1990, the Chinese government signed the United Nations *Convention on the Rights of the Child*. In March 1991, the Chinese government signed the *World Declaration on the Survival, Protection and Development of Children* and the *Action Plan for Implementing the World Declaration on the Survival, Protection and Development of Children in the 90s*. In September 1993, at the east Asian and Pacific region Ministerial Consultative Conference on the development targets for children in the 90s, China signed the *Manila Joint Declaration*. China participates actively in international and regional activities related to the protection of children, and thus expresses once again to the world community the Chinese government's basic principles and consistent stance on the human rights issue.

Today, in order to fulfil its promise to the children of China and to the international community, China is protecting children's extensive and equal rights in the political, economical, social and cultural fields and providing legal guarantees for the realization of these rights. This symbolizes the development of China's system to protect human rights, it signifies the maturation of the Chinese legal system and exemplifies the level of social development and cultural progress in China.

This essay sets out from the core of human rights protection--i.e. legal protection--and elaborates on the basic situation regarding the protection of children's rights in China during the past few years. In view of the fact that the concept of "children" in the United Nations *Convention on the Rights of the Child* is identical to the concept of "minors" in Chinese law, this essay will apply the concept of "minors" as it is more suitable to the Chinese legal tradition and reality.

Legal Protection of the Rights and Interests of Minors

Protecting the rights and interest of minors and guaranteeing a healthy upbringing for them are goals which the Chinese Communist Party and the Chinese government have focussed on and pursued over many years. As early as the first revolutionary civil war, when the Chinese Soviet Republic established the *Constitutional Outline*, the *Labour Law*, the *Marriage Law* and other laws, there were regulations to protect minors' rights to survival, to study and to work. All of the four Constitutions formulated after the establishment of the People's Republic of China provided various degrees of constitutional guarantees for minors' rights and freedoms. Since China implemented the open-door and reform policies more than ten years ago, great progress has been achieved in the area of socialist democracy and construction of the legal system. Protection of the rights and interests of minors has been acknowledged and reconciled under the law with respect to the contents, the structure and the system.

When looking at the legal guarantees of the rights and interests of minors in China, a few special characteristics can be summarized:

A relatively complete system of legal guarantees is forming in China

The Chinese legal system is composed of the Constitution, the basic laws, the special laws, administrative laws and regulations and regional laws and regulations. The comprehensive nature of the system of legal guarantees for minors is reflected at every level of the legal system.

Protection of the rights and interests of minors under the fundamental law

The *Constitution of the People's Republic of China* (which came into force on December 4, 1982) solemnly proclaims that children should receive protection from the state in the form of a fundamental law and with the effect of the supreme law. The state will foster the development of the children's moral character, their intellect, their physique and more. The regulations of the fundamental law establish the constitutional basis and confirm the guiding principle for the protection and development of minors.

Protection of the rights and interests of minors under the basic laws

Chinese basic law affirms the basic rights and interests of ordinary citizens, and provides special substantive and procedural protection of the rights and interests of minors. For example, the *Principles of Civil Law of the People's Republic of China* (which came into force on January 1, 1987) sets out a system of guardianship to guarantee minors' legal rights and interests with respect to person and property. The *Marriage Law of the People's Republic of China* (which came into force on January 1, 1981) provides that when the People's Court handles a divorce case, it must consider the rights and interests of minor children. This reflects the basic guarantee of a healthy upbringing for minors. The *Criminal Law of the People's Republic of China* (which came into force on January 1, 1980) not only stipulates that anyone who violates the legal rights of minors will be severely punished, it also establishes the legal age of an offender with respect to under age offenders. And by adhering to the principle of reducing punishment for under age offenders, it reflects the state's commitment to educate and rehabilitate under age offenders. The *Criminal Procedure Law of the People's Republic of China* (which came into force on January 1, 1980) and the *Civil Procedure Law of the People's Republic of China* establish special measures to guarantee the rights and interests of minors with respect to litigation procedures. For example, the legal representative may take part in the litigation process; the court will appoint a defence lawyer for the accused minor; and, cases involving minors will not be tried in public. These measures all help to effectively protect the special rights and interests of minors.

Protection of the rights and interests of minors through special laws

Since 1979, the National People's Congress and its standing committees have drafted more than 170 laws, most of which are special laws, i.e. for regulating and standardizing the affairs relating to certain fields or particular groups of people. There are close to 20 laws which relate directly to the protection of the rights and interests of minors. These are divided into the following main categories:

1) Provision of overall protection of the rights and interests of minors. This category is exemplified by the *Law to Protect Minors* (which came into force on January 1, 1992). It is the first comprehensive law to provide systematic and overall protection of the rights and interests of minors. It stipulates that the responsibility for guaranteeing a healthy upbringing for minors lies with families, the schools, society at large and the judicial system.

2) Provision of special protection in certain areas of the rights and interest of minors. For example, the *Law of Compulsory Education* (which came into force on July 1, 1986) guarantees the right of minors to receive compulsory education. The *Labour Law of the People's Republic of China* (which came into force on January 1, 1995) provides certain restrictions and special protection for minors who are working.

3) Provision of protection to special groups of minors. The *Law to Protect Disabled People of the People's Republic of China* (which came into force on

May 15, 1991) provides measures of protection in the areas of special education and rehabilitation for disabled minors.

Protection of the rights and interests of minors under administrative laws and regulations

These are legal norms of an administrative nature which the State Council and the various departments under the State Council have drawn up in order to guarantee the Constitution and the implementation of the law. For example, the *Regulations to Prohibit the Use of Child Workers* and the *Detailed Rules and Regulations on Implementing Compulsory Education* drafted by the State Council; the *Working Regulations regarding the National Immunization Plan* drafted by the Ministry of Health; the *Kindergarten Management Regulations* drafted by the State Education Commission, etc. Of special interest is the *Guiding Principle of the Plan for the Development of Chinese Children in the 1990s*, an important legal document drawn up by the State Council in 1992. This dcoument is based on the tasks and goals set up by the *Chinese National Ten-Year Plan for Economic and Social Development* and the *Eighth Five-Year Plan*, and on the spirit of the two documents approved by the World Summit on Children. This document puts forward, for the development of the Chinese children's cause in this century, ten main objectives to strive for as well as management measures to realize these objectives. It reflects the concrete actions taken by the Chinese government in an effort to fulfil its commitment to the international community.

Protection of the rights and interests of minors under regional laws and regulations

China has a vast territory and a huge population. Due to historical and geographical reasons, political, economic, cultural and social development is uneven from region to region. Therefore, Chinese law in general only establishes the main principles of the regulations and then authorizes the legislative bodies in each province, autonomous region and municipality directly under the central government to establish their own regional laws and regulations according to the concrete circumstances of each administrative district and presupposing that they are not contradictory to the principles of the national laws. At present, 28 provinces, autonomous regions and municipalities directly under the central government have established special regional laws and regulations for the protection of the rights and interests of minors, and thereby pushed forward the development of the national cause to protect minors.

Apart from the above, it is also necessary to introduce the judicial explanatory documents which are closely related to the Chinese system of laws and which play an important role in protecting the rights and interests of minors. In the process of executing the law, the highest legal authorities in China, namely the Supreme People's Court, the Supreme People's Procuratorate, the Ministry of Public Security and the Ministry of Justice, publish, individually or jointly, documents which are based on the basic principles and spirit of the law and their own practical legal experience. The objective is to guarantee that the law be carried out efficiently. For example, in June 1991, the Ministry of Public Security, the Ministry of Justice, the Supreme People's Court and the Supreme People's Procuratorate jointly published the "Circular on Establishing a Complementary System of Work in Handling Criminal Cases Involving Minors". This document stipulated that every government department should adopt legal guarantees in handling criminal cases involving minors. In June 1995, the Supreme People's Court published the circular "Clarification of Certain Problems Related to Applying the Law in Handling Criminal Cases Involving Minors" which set up standards and regulations for the courts at every level to apply the law correctly when trying cases involving minors. These judicial explanatory documents effectively promote the implementation of the law to protect minors.

Basic principles of protection have been established

It is the responsibility of the state organs as well as the joint responsibility of society at large to guarantee that the constitutional and legal rights of minors are not violated. To this end, affirmation of the law alone is not enough. Thorough protection during the actual process of implementation is also needed.

The principle of giving priority to the protection of the rights and interests of children

In keeping with the principle of "giving priority to children" put forth in the United Nations *Convention on the Rights of the Child*, China not only gives priority to providing welfare-type protection for the survival and development of children, the principle of priority protection for children also surfaces in legislation.

Example one: "No one is allowed to smoke in the classroom in high schools, in elementary schools, in kindergartens or in day-care centres." (Article 27 of the *Law to Protect Minors*). This is the first time that the Chinese government, in appealing to the public to protect their health, has established a clear regulation under the law, and the main targets of this measure of protection are minors. At present, concerned government departments are considering drafting a law to prohibit smoking altogether. This would mean a gradual expansion of the target groups of such protection to include all adults.

Example two: "No organization or individual may disclose the private matters of a minor." (Article 30 of the *Law to Protect Minors*). This regulation was made in accordance with the spirit of the Constitution. It is the first time in China that protection of "privacy" and "the right to privacy" has been put into law and it is also the first time that it is being applied to protect the rights of minors. This type of priority protection can be found in other laws as well. It reflects the important status that legislation to protect minors holds in the Chinese system of laws.

The principle of social responsibility

To guarantee a healthy upbringing for minors, there is another special characteristic of Chinese law, i.e. bringing social obligations up to the level of legal norms and requiring society as a whole to act in accordance with the law.

For example, the way that parents manage the education of their children must conform to legal norms. The law will intervene in cases where parents do not send their school-age children to school to receive compulsory education. Teachers who manage the students improperly will be responsible under the law. If a store manager peddles publications not suitable for minors or allows minors to enter unsuitable places, he/she will be subject to administrative or even criminal punishment. The purpose of these and many other regulations is to ensure that minors will grow up in a postive environment and develop healthy bodies and minds; to supervise and urge people with special responsibilities to carry out their duty even more efficiently; and to enforce some necessary restrictions on certain aspects of social life in order to ensure a proper social environment.

The principle of investigating and dealing with violations of the law

The law must be reliable, the law must be followed, enforcement of the law must be strict, and violations of the law must be investigated and dealt with properly. These are the basic principles of the Chinese socialist legal system which are also applied to the protection of the legal rights and interests of minors. All violations of the laws and regulations, and of the legal rights and interests of minors, is duly punishable according to the laws and regulations:

-If the circumstances surrounding mistreatment or abandonment of a minor are vile, responsibility for the crime will be investigated according to the law. (Articles 182 and 183 of the *Criminal Code*).

-If a guardian violates the legal rights or damages the property of the person under his/her care, the guardian is civilly responsible under the law. (Article 18 of the *Principles of Civil Law*).

-School and kindergarten teachers who punish their students corporeally will be subject to administrative disciplinary action. (Article 48 of the *Law to Protect Minors*).

-Employers who hire minors under the age of 16 will be fined and their business license will be revoked. (Article 94 of the *Labour Law*).

In conclusion, it is beneficial both to the implementation of the laws and regulations and to the realization of the rights and interests of minors that those who violate the law be duly punished.

Existence of basic material guarantees

An important side to the protection of the rights of minors is that realization of the rights must be possible and be guaranteed the necessary material foundation. Empty slogans are not enough. The protection of the rights and interests of minors under Chinese laws is built on a realistic material foundation. The guarantee of such a foundation is reflected mainly in three areas:

a) The contents of the laws and regulations are guaranteed by the material foundation originally in existence. For example, the *Law to Protect the Health of Mothers and Infants of the People's Republic of China* (which came into force on June 1, 1995) stipulates that medical and health institutions must provide services for the growth, nursing and care of the infant and prevent frequently-occurring and common diseases. This regulation provides legal acknowledgement of the work performed by medical and health institutions during the past decades. Therefore, the material foundation was originally in existence to guarantee the realization of rights.

b) The contents of the laws and regulations are guaranteed by a recently established material foundation. For example, the *Law of Compulsory Education* regulates that students who receive compulsory education do not need to pay tuition fees. This represents a possibility for the realization of rights which the government has provided after attaining a certain level of economic development. Currently, state investment in education is increasing annually, and the trend is towards a graduate increase of the number of years of compulsory education.

c) The contents of the law are built on the possibility of developing the material foundation. For example, the *Law to Protect Minors* stipulates that: "The state supports publications such as books, newspapers, audio and video tapes which are especially targeted to minors." At the moment, the state is unable to offer full support to the above-mentioned categories of publications due to limited financial capacity. But as the economy develops, realization of this goal will become a real possibility. Thus, through legislation, the implementation of this provision can be accelerated.

The Main Contents of the Protection of the Rights and Interests of Minors

During the past several years, due to the government's high degree of attention to the children's cause and the joint efforts of society at large, the living environment for Chinese children has been improved markedly and their level of development has been raised noticeably. This has attracted worldwide attention. This is apparent mainly in the following areas:

-The infant mortality rate dropped from 200 per thousand in 1949 to 31.42 per thousand in 1992.

-With regards to the immunization plan for children, in 1990, the national BCG inoculation rate was 99%, the pertussis, diphtheria and tetanus inoculation rate was 97%, the poliomyelitis inoculation rate was 98%, and the measles inoculation rate was 98%.

-In 1992, there were 172,506 kindergartens in China with 24,282,100 children attending these kindergartens.

-In 1992, there were 712,923 elementary schools in China with 122,013,000 students attending these schools. The enrollment rate for children between 7 and 11 years old was already at 97.2%.

China is at the forefront of the developing countries when it comes to the development of children. In this regard, a former United Nations Foundation representative in China spoke with praise:

> In the history of humankind, there has been no society like China which, at its current stage of economic development, has done so many things on such a large scale to improve the well-fare of its people. Although the average annual income in China is only about US$300, the average statistical figures on the mortality rate and the occurrence of disease of Chinese children and infants; the standard of nutrition of mothers and infants; the anti-illiteracy campaign; the population increase; and the rate of school enrollment of children, equal those of countries with an average annual income that is four times higher than that of China.

Indeed, the Chinese government has made a huge effort to promote the development of the children's cause. The following is an introduction to the basic contents of the scope of the legal protection of the rights and interests of minors.

Protection of the right to subsistence

The right to subsistence is the pre-condition and the foundation upon which all other rights of minors exist. Without the protection of the right to subsistence, the protection of other rights will loose their substance and reliability. Protection of the right to subsistence of minors under the law is demonstrated in the following areas:

Lowering the rate of mortality among children and improving the living environment for children

Both the *Law to Protect the Health of Mothers and Infants* and the *Guiding Principle of the Plan for the Development of Chinese Children in the 1990s* provide basic guarantees for the subsistence of children. In areas such as health care for those not yet married, family planning, pregnancy health care, child nutrition, immunization plans, clean drinking water, etc., concrete measures have been drawn up in order to ensure that the child survival rate and the living environment will reach the desired standards before the end of this century.

Strengthening parenting responsibilities to guarantee the foundation of the children's subsistence

The *Marriage Law* and the *Law to Protect Minors* provide that parents must carry out the responsibilities and obligations of caring for and raising their under-age children. When parents fail to carry out their obligations, under-age children have the right to request that they pay the cost of their upbringing. After a divorce, when one parent raises the children, the other parent must pay part of or the full amount of the children's living expenses and the cost of education. If parents mistreat or abandon minors and if the circumstances are particularly vile, they will be investigated and held responsible for their criminal behaviour according to articles 182 and 183 of the *Criminal Code*.

Measures of social protection

When a problem occurs with respect to the safeguarding of minors in their homes, society must assume the responsibility of protecting them. The *Law to Protect Minors* provides that in cases of child beggars and street kids whose parents cannot be located, the civil and administrative government departments must set up welfare institutions to care for and raise these minors. The *Adoption Law of the People's Republic of China* (which came into force on January 1, 1992) provides that institutions and citizens with the proper conditions to adopt a child may, according to the law, adopt minors who are orphans, abandoned or whose parents are unable to support them because of special difficulties. The *Inheritance Law* stipulates that under-age beneficiaries should be given special attention during the division of inherited property.

Protection of minors' right to health

Protecting the health of minors is an important basic step towards realizing minors' right to development. There are two aspects to guaranteeing the right to health:

Protecting the physical health of minors

The *Law to Protect Minors* provides that parents and teachers must employ proper methods to educate and discipline minors, and the use of corporeal or disguised corporeal punishment is forbidden. Foods, toys, articles for daily use, playground facilities, etc. which are made for children should not contain materials harmful to their safety and health. The *Labour Law* stipulates that employers are not allowed to hire minors under the age of 16. In addition, workers between 16 and 18 years old must not be made to work in underground mines, in places with toxic or harmful materials, or to undertake work which requires extreme physical strength. Under-age workers should undergo regular medical examinations.

Protecting the healthy minds, spirits and characters of minors

The *Law to Protect Minors* provides that parents should encourage minors to engage in activities which are beneficial to their mental and physical health and prevent and curb the incidents of minors smoking, drinking, and engaging in illegal activities such as gambling, taking drugs and prostitution. Schools should counsel their young students in the areas of morality, intellectual development, aesthetics, work, and puberty, and guide them in social life. It is not permitted to discriminate against students who are ill-behaved or have difficulties learning, and it is not permitted to injure a student's dignity and character. No organization or individual is allowed to disclose the private matters of a minor. No one is allowed to open the mail of a minor without legal permission. No one is allowed to peddle or rent obscene, violent, horrible or other unhealthy books, newspapers, video and audio products to minors.

Protection of the right to development

To protect minors' right to development is, in essence, to equip them with the basic tools for adapting to society and give them a real ability to contribute to society.

First of all, the Constitution and the *Law to Protect Minors* have formulated clear goals for the development of minors, i.e. to promote the general development of minors with respect to morality, intellectual capacity and physique, and to train them to become idealistic, righteous, cultured and disciplined heirs to the socialist cause.

The development of minors must be guaranteed under the law. For example, the *Law of Compulsory Education* guarantees minors' equal right to compulsory education. The *Law to Protect Disabled People* stipulates that the state must establish scholarships in order to help poor disabled students get an education. While educating disabled minors in the fields of ideology and culture, the state should also strive to make up for any mental or physical disadvantages experienced by this group, and provide occupational training so as to create the right conditions for the future development of disabled minors. The *Law to*

Protect Minors guarantees minors' right to intellectual achievement and encourages them, while they are still developing, to contribute to society.

Finally, protecting the development of minors is necessary for the development of society. In this regard, the objective for the development of minors and the obligations of society in general have been established under the law, and the basic material guarantees have been provided for the realization of the rights and interests of minors.

Legal Practice in the Protection of the Rights and Interests of Minors

Over the course of more than 10 years, Chinese legislation on minors has developed at an unprecedented pace. The Chinese government and society in general have also made constant efforts to carry out the law and to realize the rights and interests of minors. The cause for the protection of the rights and interests of minors has drawn much attention from society. Clear development objectives have been established and encouraging results have been achieved. This is a historical leap in the development of the work to protect the rights and interests of minors in China.

The following are three areas of legal practice where the rights and interests of minors are protected:

An authoritative and social network of protection

There are currently four kinds of organizations for the protection of minors in China:

a) Structures established within the national legislative organs to handle youth affairs, such as the Special Group on Youth of the Internal and Judicial Affairs Commission under the National People's Congress.

b) Protection structures established by the government, such as the Committee for Women's and Children's Work under the State Council. This Committee is authorized by the State Council to deal with women's and children's affairs.

c) Quasi-governmental structures, such as the Committees for the Protection of Minors and the Committees for Coordinating Work with Children and Youth, which have been established in the provinces, autonomous regions and municipalities directly under the central government and which operate with the support of key government leaders. The membership of these committees includes relevant government departments, judicial organs and affiliated social organizations.

d) Organizations of a social nature, such as the Work Committee on China's Concern for the Next Generation, the Chinese Communist Youth Organization, the Women's Federation, the labour unions, the youth federations, the student associations and the Young Pioneers, etc. These diverse organizations exist at all levels in most areas of China and together they form an intricate network for the protection of rights. According to their individual areas of responsibility and with a view to achieving a common goal, these organizations are playing an important role in the area of protecting the rights and interests of minors. In Beijing alone, according to preliminary statistics, there are close to one thousand organizations of this nature.

Wide-reaching and efficient protection measures

Spreading knowledge of the law through propaganda

This sums up the experience of Chinese legal practice over the last ten years. This is exemplified with respect to the propaganda for the *Law to Protect Minors*. For a few years now, large scale propaganda activities have been set in motion at the central government level all the way down to the provinces, autonomous regions and municipalities directly under the central government. Such activities have subsequently become routine in some areas, and others have even joined in the plan for the development of the children's cause. For example, the City of Beijing was the first to establish the goal to disseminate knowledge of the law to 90% of high school and elementary school students and to more than 60% of adults before 1995. By the end of 1994, Beijing had already distributed more than 5 million copies of propaganda material on the protection of the rights of minors. More than 6 million people were reached through this method of spreading knowledge of the law through propaganda. The level of legal understanding of the protection of minors was raised immensely among the people of Beijing. Minors were especially active in spreading propaganda about this law for the protection of their own rights and interests. They not only distributed propaganda in the streets and to people's houses, they also established organizations to protect their rights, such as the "Red Scarf Council for the Protection of Rights" and the "Red Scarf Cultural Market Supervisory Team". Through self-education and self-management, minors try to improve their understanding of how they can defend their rights and promote the implementation of the law.

Safeguarding the rights and interests of minors through strengthening society's responsibility to protect

The work to protect the rights and interests of minors is a complicated social project which requires the participation, support and cooperation of society as a whole. Organizations that take part in this project include those that protect the rights and interests of minors, administrative and legal organs which are responsible for carrying out the law, and relevant social organizations. Therefore, in protecting the rights and interests of minors it is very efficient to let every organization play a role by attending to its own duties while also cooperating closely with others. Since 1989, two large scale "anti-pornography" movements have been organized throughout the country. The ministries of communication, culture, radio, film and TV, public security, industry and commerce, and taxation, along with youth organizations, made an unprecedented concerted effort to clean up the cultural markets, and protect the physical and mental health of minors. In 1991, the public security, procuratorial, justice and judicial organs got together again in an effort to coordinate their work with the goal of implementing measures for the legal protection of minors. Many of the country's laws have very clear regulations concerning the guarantee of minors' right to education. Nevertheless, there are still students in some remote and impoverished regions who drop out of school because their families are poor. While the government is helping to alleviate poverty in these regions, social organizations launched the "Project of Hope" and the "Spring Blossom Plan" which received positive feedback from all levels of society. In the last five years or so, a total of 1,010,000 students have returned to school and more than 700 "elementary schools of hope" have been established. The concerted efforts of Chinese society as a whole have improved minors' chance of obtaining concrete and effective protection of their rights.

Guaranteeing the physical and mental health of minors through the development of social services

At present, China is moving quickly towards a market economy. Thus, the entire society must turn its attention and offer more direction to the upbringing and development of minors. For this reason, the development of social services is an effective method to guarantee the physical and mental health of minors. Social services include developing social assistance for orphans and disabled children, promoting children's medical insurance, carrying out anti-illiteracy campaigns and education, providing mental health guidance, etc. With respect to mental health guidance, for example, several youth psychology consulting hotlines have recently been established nationwide, and many psychology consulting structures have been set up in order to help minors solve their problems and to provide guidance for their development. Since the "Beijing Youth Law and Psychology Consulting Centre" was established two years ago, it has received letters, visits and telephone calls from approximately 10,000 people from 19 provinces, autonomous regions, municipalities directly under the central government, Hong Kong, Macao and other areas. Practice has proven that this is important work which is beneficial to the growth and development of youths and to maintaining social stability.

Protecting the rights and interests of minors who have violated the law; working to educate and rehabilitate them. This principle is mainly reflected in the following areas:

a) When handling cases involving minors who have violated the law, the principle of "education first, punishment second" must be demonstrated. During the process of pre-trial, prosecution, trial and reform through labour, the guiding principles of education, persuasion and rehabilitation must be upheld. At present, the public security, procuratorial, justice and judicial organs have all set up special pre-trial units, special prosecution units, youth courts or appointed special personnel in order to deal with criminal cases involving minors in a way that is suitable to their physical and mental development.

b) Adopting measures which are beneficial to reforming minors who have violated the law. For example, with respect to those minors who have violated the law only occasionally; whose level of animosity towards society is only superficial; who do not pose a threat to society; and who have expressed regret over their crime, every attempt should be made to give them a suspended sentence so as to ease their re-entrance into society. Through exemplary education, regular reporting and social guidance, the judicial organs urge minors to repent, make a fresh start and become useful to society.

c) Working actively to help minors who have violated the law settle down so as to maintain social stability. The Reform Through Labour Bureau of Beijing has co-signed an "instruction and help to settle down agreement" with 18 district and county governments, which requires the protection agencies of the districts or counties to which the youths belong to regularly visit the "reform through labour camp" to offer instruction to minors who have violated the law. This activity greatly encourages minors in the labour education and reform camps to take their re-education seriously and boosts their faith in re-entering society as upright persons. By instructing and educating minors who have violated the law, the instance of minors re-offending has been maintained at a relatively low rate in Beijing.

Results of this promising cause

The benefits of the cause to protect the rights and interests of minors can be seen today and the merits will be visible long into the future. The task of protecting the legal rights and interests and guaranteeing the health of minors is of important strategic significance, as well as of long-term historical significance to China as it is entering the 21st century. Practical legal work in protecting the rights and interests of minors is also political work in that it has injected new blood into the future development of China and thereby filled it with hope. Through the continued efforts by the Chinese government and people over many years, the work to protect the rights and interests of minors has already achieved great success. Awareness in society of the need to protect the rights and interests of minors has reached an unprecedented level, and each citizen's understanding of protection has greatly improved. Through the joint participation of people from every walk of life, the social mechanisms to protect the rights and interests of minors are gradually being perfected. This has provided enough leeway and material guarantees for the survival, protection and development of minors, and 0.4 billion Chinese minors are going to greet the arrival of the next century with a brand new attitude.

Conclusion

Since the establishment of the new China, especially since the implementation of the opening up and reform policies, legislation for the protection of the rights and interests of minors has progressed along with economic and social development, and a comparatively complete legal protection system has been established. The development plan and strategy for the protection of minors have already drawn widespread attention from society and received abundant recognition from the international community. However, China remains a developing country, and protection of the rights and interests of minors in China must be appropriate for the level of economic and social development. From now until the end of this century, in the wake of economic development and social progress, China will further strengthen and perfect legislation and enforcement mechanisms for the protection of the rights and interests of minors. China has the largest number of minors in the world, and the effect that the development of China's minors is going to have on the rest of the world should not be underestimated. Raising the calibre of China's minors is of great significance to the world as it is about to enter the 21st century. Therefore, in the process of developing, China also needs attention and support from the international community. Let us review the promise we made to the children of the world: Let us give every child an even brighter future.

Translation by Shengtao Jiang and A-M Traeholt

4 The Role of Women in Human Rights, Collective Rights and the Right to Development

Chinese Law and the Protection of Women's Human Rights

MA YINAN

General Theories About the Law and Women's Human Rights

Human rights are all the rights that human beings should enjoy according to the basic nature of human beings. In other words, they are the rights of human beings. The traditional human rights concept only includes the rights and freedoms of the individual. With the progress of history, the concept and connotation of human rights develops. Today's human rights concept has already developed from a concept comprising only political rights to a concept comprising political, economic, cultural and social rights. It has grown from a concept of individual rights to a concept which combines individual rights and group rights.

Human rights can be divided into individual rights, group rights and national rights. I believe that women's rights comprise both the rights of individual women and the rights of women as a group. The concept of women's rights includes the rights which should be enjoyed by society as a whole and all of humanity, such as the rights to life/subsistence, freedom, equality, peace, and environmental rights. It also includes some special rights which only women enjoy, such as the right to bear children and the right to special labour protection. Aside from women's rights, the rights of other special groups, such as children, seniors, disabled people, minorities, etc., can all be divided into both individual rights and group rights.

Looking at the concrete content of human rights, women's human rights include the right to subsistence/life, political rights, economic rights, the right to education, social rights and personal rights.

I support the argument put forward by some scholars which divides the existence of human rights into three categories: 1) the rights which people should enjoy; 2) legal rights; and 3) the rights which people enjoy in reality.[1] I believe such a division also applies to women's human rights.

"The rights which people should enjoy" is the initial and most complete category. According to the original meaning, women's human rights refer to the "rights which women should enjoy".

"Legal rights" are the result of applying legal tools to the "rights which women should enjoy" in an effort to legalize, systematize and achieve effective protection of those rights. The existence of "the rights which people should enjoy" is the prerequisite and the base which defines "legal rights", because the existence of "rights which people should enjoy" gives rise to questions of whether or not and how to apply the law in order to affirm and protect those rights. The existence of the "rights which people should enjoy" has provided a standard of evaluation and a development objective for improving and completing the human rights legislation.

The category of "rights which people enjoy in reality" refers to the rights which women are able to enjoy in reality. In any country, there is often a huge gap between "legal rights" and the actual human rights situation.

The category of "rights which people should enjoy" is always larger than the one of "legal rights", and the category of "legal rights" is always larger than the one of "rights which people enjoy in reality". It is precisely such contradictions which give impetus to the continuous realization of human rights.

One of the fundamental goals of a modern society ruled by law is to provide complete and effective legal protection of women's rights. This is also one of the signs of modern society. Today, law has already become the most effective means of regulating social relationships between women and men, women and society, women and the state, etc. Why is it that people emphasize the importance of using the law to guarantee women's rights, thereby turning the rights which people should enjoy into legal rights? It is because the law represents basic characteristics--the will of the state, standardization of behaviour, widespread efficiency, enforceability--and it is the most authoritative, direct and efficient method of guaranteeing women's rights. After the law recognizes the "rights which women should enjoy" and they become "legal rights", these kinds of rights become very clear and concrete. They become the will of the state and, as such, become universally and legally binding on all citizens of that state. And by its power to enforce the law, the state will be able to realize these rights. The law is capable of guaranteeing women's human rights to a greater extent then the regulations of societies, village rules, morals and ethics combined. As a result, women around the world have always regarded the law as the most important tool in fighting for their rights. The call for legal protection of women's rights and interests and the establishment of legislation have always accompanied the women's liberation movement. In these times where civilization has already reached a high level of development, we could say that where there is no law, there are no human rights for women; where the law is being trampled upon, women's human rights evaporate into thin air.

Women's Human Rights in Chinese Law

Protection of women's human rights takes on two forms in Chinese law:

a) Regulation of substantive rights, i.e. outlining in detail the implication of every single right and establishing the corresponding obligation; and, regulating the appropriate punishment for actions which are in violation of the law and women's human rights.

b) Regulation of procedural rights, i.e. the establishment of procedures and measures to protect these rights, so as to offer recourse to women whose rights have been violated.

Chinese legislation relating to women tends to focus on regulations of a protective, cooperative, punitive and alleviating nature, in order to ensure that women's concrete rights can be realized in real life.

Women's substantive rights and their protection under Chinese law

Political rights

According to the Constitution, political rights which Chinese citizens enjoy, include the rights to vote and to be elected, freedom of speech, freedom of publication, freedom of assembly and association, freedom to take part in protests and to demonstrate, the right to criticize and give suggestions to government organizations and officials, as well as the right to report on or make accusations about any illegal activities to the state.

In guaranteeing women's political rights, Chinese law specifically stresses women's right to vote and to be elected, and their right to take part in managing public affairs and to seek public employment. The *Law to Protect Women's Rights and Interests* emphasizes that women should enjoy the right to vote and to be elected on an equal basis with men and that they have the right to participate in the management of the affairs of state and society through various means. In addition, it states that there should be an appropriate number of women representatives in the National People's Congress, and that attention should be given to training and promoting women cadres to senior positions.

Cultural and educational rights

According to the *Law to Protect Women's Rights and Interests* and other legal regulations, women's cultural and educational rights mainly include: the equal right to enrol in and start school; the equal right to a job after graduation; the equal right to receive a degree and be sent overseas to study; the right to receive compulsory education, literacy classes, career training and technological training; and the right to engage in science, technology, literature, arts and other cultural activities.

In protecting women's cultural and educational rights, Chinese law stresses the importance of enrolling girls in school and wiping out illiteracy among women. *The Law to Protect Women's Rights and Interests* stipulates that parents or other guardians are obligated to ensure that girls enroll in school at the appropriate age; that the government, society and the schools adopt effective measures to guarantee that girls receive compulsory education; and that the people's governments at all levels adopt organizational structures and work patterns in accordance with women's special characteristics in order to organize, supervise and implement the task of eliminating illiteracy among women.

Employment rights and interests

According to the law, women's employment rights and interests include: the right to employment; the right to equal pay for equal work; the right to vacation; the right to safety and health protection; the right to special labour protection; and the right to social insurance.

In protecting women's employment rights and interests, Chinese law stresses women's right to employment and to labour protection. The *Law to Protect Women's Rights and Interests* and the *Labour Law* both provide that, when recruiting workers, no work unit is allowed to refuse to hire women on the basis of gender or to raise the recruitment standards for women. In addition, no work unit is allowed to dismiss women workers or unilaterally cancel a contract citing marriage, pregnancy, maternity leave or nursing as excuses for such actions; except in situations involving employment or positions which are unsuitable for women. *The Law to Protect Women's Rights and Interests*, the *Labour Law* and the *Regulations for the Protection of Women Workers* require that all work units protect women's safety and health in the work place and that they not arrange for women to work at positions which are unsuitable to them. These laws also provide women with special protection during menstruation, pregnancy, maternity and nursing.

Property rights and interests

There are three categories of regulations in the law to protect women's property rights and interests:

a) Proprietary rights produced by civil relations; property rights which are related to proprietary rights (such as contract management rights, mining rights, the right to use and profit from natural resources, etc.); creditor's rights and intellectual property rights.

b) The right to payment for work.

c) Joint property rights, the right to be provided for, and property inheritance rights between husband and wife in marriage and family relations; the right to be provided for and property inheritance rights between parents and children.

In protecting women's property rights and interests, Chinese law stresses, as important for women in the countryside, the right to contract management of land under the responsibility system and land for producing grain for personal consumption, as well as women's joint proprietary right and right to inherit family property. *The Law to Protect Women's Rights and Interests* stipulates that women and men should enjoy equal rights with respect to receiving land under the responsibility system and land for producing grain for personal consumption in the countryside. When women marry or divorce, their right to land should be protected. In marriage and family relations with joint property, women's legal rights and interests should not be violated. Women should not be discriminated against when establishing the order of legal heirs. Widows have the right to handle inherited property, and no one has the right to interfere.

Personal rights

According to the law, personal rights are divided into rights of the person and status rights.

The rights of the person enjoyed by women mainly include: the right to life and health; to personal freedom; the right to her name; the right to her own likeness; the right to protection of reputation; and the right to freedom of marriage.

The status rights include: kinship rights; guardianship rights; the right to dignity and honour; and manufacturer's rights.

In protecting women's personal rights, Chinese law stresses the importance of the right to health and personal freedom. *The Law to Protect Women's Rights and Interests* stipulates that it is forbidden to:

- drown, abandon or cruelly injure female infants;
- discriminate against or mistreat women who give birth to girls or women who are barren;
- use superstition and violence to cruelly injure women;
- mistreat or abandon elderly women;
- illegally detain women or, by other means, to deprive women of or limit women's personal freedom;
- illegally search a woman's body;
- kidnap and trade in women or to buy women who have been kidnapped or traded;
- organize, force, invite or introduce women to prostitution or hire and invite women or other people to engage in obscene activities.

Marriage and family rights and interests

According to the law, the marriage and family rights and interests which women enjoy mainly include: the right to marry freely; personal and property rights of husband and wife arising from marital and family relations; other family members' personal and property rights; and the right to bear children.

In protecting women's marriage and family rights and interests, Chinese law stresses the importance of the right to marry freely and the right to bear children. The law provides that no one is allowed to interfere with women's right to marry and divorce freely, and that those who interfere with women's freedom by selling women in marriage or arranging marriages should be punished; women have the right to bear children, and they also have the freedom not to bear children; the relevant government departments should provide safe and effective contraceptive drugs and technology and protect the health and safety of those women who are sterilized.

Those who do not comply with their legal obligations or who violate women's legal rights and interests should be investigated, according to the law, to establish their legal responsibility. According to the current law, legal responsibilities such as administrative, civil and criminal responsibilities can be applied to activities which constitute violations of women's human rights. Regulations with regards to this can be found in articles 50, 51 and 52 of the *Law to Protect Women's Rights and Interests* and in other relevant legislation.

Women's procedural rights in Chinese law

Substantive rights and procedural rights cannot be separated. Procedural rights are the prerequisite for and the basis upon which to realize substantive rights. If women have many legal rights but have no means of seeking redress when their rights are violated, then legal protection of their human rights exist only on paper. The procedural rights established under the law are there purposely to solve the problem of venues and means of redress for women whose rights have been violated.

With rights, they should also be remedies. Remedies for women's human rights in Chinese law are reflected in two areas: a) acknowledgement of the responsibility of certain organizations to protect women's human rights and; b) establishment of remedial procedures to protect women's human rights.

As women's rights and interests are reflected in all areas of society and life, the law acknowledges that governmental administrative organizations, the People's Courts and women's organizations, all have the responsibility to support women.

Administrative redress

The administrative organs which are authorized under the current Chinese law and regulations to handle cases of violations of women's rights and interests are: the public security organs, labour organs, civil administration organs, education organs, and the people's governments at the grassroots level, etc.

Violations of women's personal rights, such as bullying women, illegally restricting women's personal freedom, seducing, inviting or introducing women to prostitution, can all be referred to the public security authorities.

Violations of women's employment rights and interests, such as illegally refusing to recruit women workers or raising the employment standard for women, asking women to engage in work which is unsuitable, or hiring women who are under sixteen, can all be referred to the labour authorities.

Violations of women's right to marry freely can be referred to the civil administration authorities, while violations of women's educational rights can be referred to the education authorities.

Some disputes involving women's personal rights and property rights can be referred to the people's government at the grassroots level.

Women whose rights and interests have been violated and who are seeking a means of administrative redress should, on the basis of the nature of the violated rights and interests, request redress through the administrative organs with the appropriate jurisdiction. When handling a violation of women's rights and interests, administrative authorities must adhere strictly to the laws and regulations which pertain to the limitation of power, the procedures and the time frames. Cases which do not fall within their jurisdiction should be passed on to the administrative organs with the appropriate jurisdiction to handle the case.

Judicial redress

Legal redress refers to the way in which the People's Court uses litigation procedures to protect women's rights and interests.

The law states that when the actions of an administrative organ violate a woman's legal rights and interests, the woman can initiate an administrative lawsuit in the People's Court according to the regulations of the *Administrative Procedural Law*. If the actions of the administrative organ are in violation of a woman's rights and interests and have resulted in damage to the woman, she can initiate an administrative lawsuit to request compensation. When a woman's legal rights have been violated and have resulted in damage, the woman can initiate a civil lawsuit in the People's Court according to the regulations of the *Civil Procedural Law*. When violation of a woman's rights and interests contravene the criminal law, it is up to the state procuratorial organ or the victim herself to initiate a criminal lawsuit in the People's Court in accordance with the regulations of the *Criminal Procedural Law*. If the victim suffers material damage caused by criminal activity, she can initiate a civil suit for compensation simultaneously with a criminal suit.

Compared to administrative redress, the use of judicial redress to handle violations of women's rights and interests is much broader in scope and the procedures are stricter. Some cases involving the violation of women's rights and interests do not fall within the jurisdiction of the administrative organs, e.g. a case which is in violation of a woman's personal rights as well as the criminal law, so the victim has no choice but to seek redress via judicial channels.

Some cases fall within the jurisdiction of both the administrative and the judicial organs. If the victim chooses to seek help from the administrative organ first but then is not satisfied with the result, she can seek further help through the judicial organ. When the victim chooses judicial redress, she cannot seek any further administrative redress for the same case. If either side is dissatisfied with the judgment of the local court, the case can be appealed to a higher level court.

Other means of redress

The law provides that when a woman's legal rights have been violated, the victim can make a complaint to a women's organization which should then request the relevant government department or work unit to handle the case, and thereby protect the violated woman's legal rights and interests. Strictly speaking, complaining to a women's organization is not a sufficiently independent redress procedure, as the women's organization itself does not have the jurisdiction to handle cases of violation of women's rights and interests. It can only help the victim make a request to the relevant government department or work unit to handle the case, i.e. help a woman seek a means of redress.

After receiving a complaint, the women's organization can request and supervise the complaint and push the relevant authority or work unit to deal with the case, thereby helping to prevent and reduce incidents of dismissed or delayed cases in law enforcement work.

Apart from this, the *Law to Protect Women's Rights and Interests* also states that when a woman's rights and interests have been violated, the victim can ask the work unit to which the violator belongs, or a higher level authority, to handle the case. (The unit can order the violator to correct his/her activity and take administrative disciplinary action against him/her according to the circumstances). This can also be seen as an important means of redress, apart from the government redress mechanisms (including administrative redress and legal redress).

Further Steps Towards Perfecting Legislation Pertaining to the Human Rights of Women in China

Scholars generally think that legislation on women's human rights in China is comprehensive, systematic, focussed and well-directed. I believe such comments to be objective. And yet, one should not disregard the fact that although these few characteristics reflect the success of women's rights legislation in China, they also reflect its inadequacies. Legislation which is aimed at achieving lofty and comprehensive goals cannot avoid lacking content. Legislation which only criticizes the faults of society and cannot raise any effective solutions will give people an impression of weakness and impotence. Legislation which is overly wordy and principled with no emphasis on the real operational aspects of the law might be difficult to put into practice.

The white book, *The Chinese Human Rights Situation*, points out that, although China has achieved great success in protecting and promoting human rights, there are still many areas which need to be perfected. It remains a long-term, historical task for the Chinese people and the Chinese government to continuously promote the development of human rights and to achieve the lofty goal of fully realizing human rights, as required by Chinese socialism. Since the implementation of the *Law to Protect Women's Rights and Interests* in 1992, China has achieved some progress in the area of the protection of women's human rights, but major gaps remain in the legislation.

In this essay, I will be probing deeper into the issue of perfecting legislation to protect the human rights of women in China. It is an extremely difficult task to turn the existing human rights pattern of "rights which people should enjoy" into "legal rights". This is not only restrained by the pattern of development of legislation for women, but also by national politics, economics and the standard of the legal system in society as a whole.

My discussion mainly revolves around further enhancing women's substantive rights, substantiating and strengthening procedural human rights and realizing complete and comprehensive legislation for the protection of women's human rights.

Enhancing the content of women's substantive human rights

On the proportion of women representatives in the National People's Congress

Women's participation in government is a global trend of the women's movement. Some countries have already implemented legislation which clearly regulates the proportion of women representatives in Congress, e.g. Norway and Germany.

At some of the regional preparatory meetings held before the opening of the Fourth World Conference on Women, suggestions were put forward concerning the strengthening of women's participation in politics and creating a regulation which clearly sets out the exact number of women who will fill positions of power. I believe that Chinese women's participation in government is an important indication of the extent of women's political rights. An important guarantee for women's participation in government is a definite proportion of women representatives in the People's Congress. When the *Law to Protect Women's Rights and Interests* was drafted, the plan was to put a number on the proportion of women representatives in the People's Congress. But in the end, when taking into account the reality of the low representation of women at the time ,as well as the disparity in the level of women's participation in government throughout the country, it was only possible to establish regulations of a guiding nature which did not include a specific number: "Among the representatives in the National People's Congress and the regional People's Congresses should be an appropriate number of women, and the proportion of women representatives should be raised gradually."[2] During the past three years of the implementation of this law in the provinces, autonomous regions, and municipalities under the central government, the voice calling for a specific number of women representatives in the People's Congresses to guarantee the full realization of Article 10 Part 2, has become unusually strong. Some provinces, in implementing the law, have established rules which directly regulate the proportion of women representatives in every level of the People's Congress. Other provinces have established rules to regulate the proportion of women candidates for election to the People's Congress. I agree with the point of view of certain specialists[3] that the latter method is more appropriate, because to regulate the proportion of women representatives in the Congress would involve changing the electoral law. At the same time, should the number of women representatives not reach the proportion required by law, the election could become invalid. One could, however, apply the method of separately counting the ballots for female and male candidates in order to ensure that the number of women representatives would reach the proportion required by law, but this would also involve changing the electoral rules.

By regulating the proportion of women candidates in the election, one can avoid these problems. For example, one could require, by regulation, that the proportion of women candidates in elections to the People's Congresses at the provincial and city levels should not be less than 30% of the total number of candidates; and that the proportion of women candidates to the People's Congresses at the county and village levels should not be less than 25% of the total number of candidates. According to Article 27 of the *Election Law*, which deals with the election requirements, regulations such as the above, would to a certain extent, promote the goal of raising the proportion of women representatives.

On protecting women's labour rights and interests

The provisions in the *Law to Protect Women's Rights and Interests* pertaining to the protection of women's labour rights and interests, are rather sweeping and general, and the legal responsibilities are not clearly defined. With the development of the market economy, some regulations have already fallen behind the reforms in the labour system, and that has affected the implementation of the law. For example, there are no prohibitive or protective provisions in the *Law to Protect Women's Rights and Interests* with regards to the problem of women workers being forced to take prolonged vacations or early retirement as a result of reforms in the labour system. The *Labour Law*, promulgated in July 1994, only deals with this problem in a few rules of principle. I believe that when governments in all regions draw up measures to implement the *Law to Protect Women's Rights and Interests*, or when enterprises work out plans to arrange for surplus workers, they should take steps to restrict the practice of forcing women workers to take prolonged vacations or early retirement. It should be strictly forbidden to violate the laws of the country by forcing women workers to take prolonged vacations or disguised early retirement. Activities which violate the law and women's legal rights and interests should be dealt with through administrative disciplinary measures and punishment. Women workers who have suffered economically because of enforced prolonged vacations or early retirement should receive financial compensation.

Faced with the new circumstances and problems which have emerged in the area of protecting the rights and interests of women workers as a result of the reforms to the labour system, all regions, in implementing the *Law to Protect Women's Rights and Interests* or relevant regulations made by the State Council, should look closely at the principles of the legislation and work out some concrete solutions. I am pleased to note that some provinces, in drawing up measures for the implementation of the *Law to Protect Women's Rights and Interests*, have already incorporated the following types of directives: When an enterprise changes its management structures and reforms its system of hiring, it is not permitted to discriminate against or reject women workers on the basis of gender. No work unit is allowed to lower the salary, benefits or overall conditions of women workers or unilaterally cancel a contract because of pregnancy, maternity leave, nursing, or other such circumstances. All work units must adhere to the principle of equal rights between men and women when allocating or selling subsidized housing. It is forbidden to formulate regulations like "the man is the master" or other such regulations which discriminate against women.

Another important measure to strengthen the protection of women workers' rights and interests is to establish, under the law, a new system of maternity insurance for women workers, which is suitable to the market economy. Under the planned economy, a woman worker's maternity expenses were covered exclusively by the work unit to which she belonged, and this created a situation of uneven financial burdens between enterprises. In their effort to achieve the highest possible economic profits with the lowest possible investment in labour, enterprises generally do not like to hire women workers. In order to alleviate the conflict between a company's economic interests and the protection of women's right to work, some gradual steps have been taken to implement, on a trial basis, a new system by which maternity related expenses are covered by social/public funds. Under this system, a work unit contributes to the social funding organization according to the number of workers in the unit. When a woman worker has a child, the social funding organization will return the money to the work unit or give the money directly to the woman. This measure of reform has proven rather successful in that it evens out the burden of maternity expenses amongst enterprises and provides favourable conditions for companies with many women workers to participate in the market competition. In December 1994, on the basis of the conclusion of this trial project, the Ministry of Labour issued a set of "Trial Measures to Provide Maternity Insurance for Enterprise Workers", and on January 1, 1995, these trial measures were implemented. The trial measures contain concrete provisions regarding the scope of basic maternity insurance, collection criteria, management structures, and more. They are simple to apply and easy to carry out. These measures can be improved in the process of putting them into practice so as to form a rational system of maternity insurance which corresponds to the demands of the market economy.

In recent years, phenomena involving violations of women's labour rights and interests in county firms, private firms and joint ventures have become rather serious. Some companies use marriage, pregnancy, child-birth and nursing as excuses to arbitrarily fire women workers or unilaterally cancel their employment contracts. They arrange for women workers to engage in work which is unsuitable for women or to work in places with excessive levels of toxins.

Governments should not tolerate this kind of action. They should intervene forcefully with legal means. In view of the fact that the regulations in the *Law to Protect Women's Rights and Interests*, the *Labour Law* and the *Regulations to Protect Women Workers* have not been well implemented in the county firms, private firms and joint ventures, the state should take note of the special characteristics of these kinds of firms and promptly draw up suitable and realistic rules to protect women workers. Before legislation was established at the national level, local governments could draw up implementation guidelines or specific measures for county firms, private firms or joint ventures to implement the *Law to Protect Women's Rights and Interests*, the *Labour Law* and the *Regulations to Protect Women Workers* according to the actual local conditions. In 1991, Shanghai was the first in the country to establish the *Temporary Regulations for the Protection of Women Workers in Shanghai County (Township) and Village Collectively Owned Enterprises*. The contents of the regulations are in accordance with the principles of the national laws, and they also suit the real circumstances of the county and township enterprises. Thus, the work to protect local women's labour rights has been advanced both in scope and depth. With this kind of legislation, special attention should be paid to the issue of establishing supervisory structures to protect women workers' labour rights, and to clearly define responsibilities and methods of punishment or incentives.

*On guaranteeing land under the responsibility system and land to grow
grain for personal consumption for women in the countryside*

This is one of the difficult issues in the implementation of the *Law to Protect
Women's Rights and Interests*. The crux of the problem lies in the fact that the
different regions' land allocation policies have not been integrated with the *Law
to Protect Women's Rights and Interests*. The *Law to Protect Women's Rights
and Interests* is very general with respect to the issue of land allocation, and the
punishments for violating women's rights in this area are limited only to
administrative disciplinary action. Therefore, the methods used to implement this
law should be more concrete and the legal responsibilities should be
strengthened. For example, regulations could be made to guarantee that women
in the countryside who have reached the legal working age enjoy the same rights
as men with respect to obtaining land under the responsibility system. After
marrying, a woman should keep the land originally allocated to her in her home
village until new land is allocated to her in her husband's village. When
allocating land to a newly married woman, the village should abide by the local
standards. After the woman has been allocated new land, her old land allocation
goes back to the home village. Women who remarry after a divorce should be
able to keep their land allocation.

I am of the opinion that an administrative punishment should be given to
those who violate women's rights to land. Compared to disciplinary sanctions,
the method of administrative punishment is more applicable and effective.

*On the legal responsibilities of violating the law to protect women's rights
and interests*

Most of the laws and regulations on this topic are consolidated in the *Law
to Protect Women's Rights and Interests*, and some can be found in other
relevant laws and regulations. When looking at the current laws and regulations
pertaining to the legal responsibilities for violating the law to protect women's
rights and interests, I find at least two shortcomings:

a. There are no regulations dealing with the legal responsibilities of someone
who acts in violation of women's legal rights and interests. Many of the norms
in the *Law to Protect Women's Rights and Interests* only regulate the content of
rights and obligations.

There are no regulations dealing with the legal responsibilities of someone
who violates these rights and obligations. The composition of laws and

regulations should include presumption, handling and punishment, but many of the regulations in the *Law to Protect Women's Rights and Interests* do not include provisions for punishment. For example, Article 41 states: "The state protects women's right to freedom of marriage. Nobody is allowed to interfere with a woman's right to freedom of marriage and divorce." However, the current laws do not include concrete regulations with respect to punishment for actions which violate the right to freedom of marriage. Article 47 states: "In accordance with the relevant government regulations, women have the right to bear children, and they also have the right not to bear children." However, the current laws do not include any concrete regulations with respect to punishment for actions which violate women's right to bear children.

b. Some regulations on administrative and legal responsibilities do not correspond to the reality of the market economy system, and it is difficult to pin down the legal responsibilities of the violator.

To deal with violations of women's legal rights and interests, the *Law to Protect Women's Rights and Interests* and other relevant laws and regulations have established certain administrative legal responsibilities. However, most are in the form of administrative disciplinary action and not administrative punishment. In the market economy system, the scope of application and the effectiveness of administrative disciplinary action are rather limited in particular areas. For example, when enterprises refuse to recruit women in situations where they should; when enterprises raise the recruitment standards for women or; when enterprises dismiss women workers because of marriage, pregnancy, maternity leave, or nursing. When these violations of rights occur in state-operated firms or collective companies, administrative disciplinary action can still prove effective. When they occur in independent businesses, private companies or joint ventures, however, administrative disciplinary action is not only difficult to implement, if implemented it is also of little use in terms of punishment. In the countryside, it is even more difficult to enforce administrative disciplinary actions for activities which violate women's legal rights and interests with respect to allocation of land. As the reforms become ever more deep-rooted, the role of administrative disciplinary action will become less effective in cases such as the above-mentioned, and the role of administrative punishment will become stronger.

In order to perfect the legal responsibilities in the law to protect women's rights and interests, it is most important to try to make up for the two above-mentioned short-comings through further legislation. In this regard, I suggest:

a. Enlarging the scope of application of the legal responsibilities to an appropriate level so as to establish a complete set of legal responsibilities for all kinds of violations of women's legal rights and interests. For example, corresponding administrative legal responsibilities and civil legal responsibilities should be amended to deal with behaviour which violates women's right to freedom of marriage or women's right to bear children.

b. When an act which violates women's legal rights and interests is subject to administrative legal responsibilities, administrative punishment should be used more often as the form of punishment, and the scope of application of administrative punishment should be widened. For example, the six types of cases subject to administrative disciplinary action as outlined in Article 50 of the *Law to Protect Women's Rights and Interests*, could all be subject to administrative punishment.

Setting up organizational structures to protect women's rights and interests

A most important mechanism to guaranteeing women's human rights is organizational guarantees. In seeking effective legal strategies, most women in the world support the idea of establishing specialized structures to implement the laws relating to women.

How can this kind of structure be established in China? This question was at the centre of discussion during the drafting of the *Law to Protect Women's Rights and Interests*. Thus, the conditions were already in place for international comparison and dialogue in this field. However, the conditions at that time were not yet ripe for the establishment of a set of substantive, specialized structures. Thus, the *Law to Protect Women's Rights and Interests* only stipulated, in principle, that the "State Council and people's governments in every province, autonomous region and municipality directly under the central government should adopt organizational measures and coordinate the relevant departments in working to protect women's rights and interests." After the law was approved, every province, autonomous region and municipality directly under the central government set up its own committee to protect women's rights. These committees, under the leadership of the above-mentioned levels of government, were composed of persons from relevant government departments as well as from different mass organizations, and they became the functional organizations specially in charge of the work related to the protection of women's rights and interests. Committees to protect women's rights and interests were also established at the district and county levels. Many villages, townships and neighbourhood committees established their own women's rights protection groups that became responsible for guiding, coordinating, examining and supervising the work to protect women's rights and interests of the relevant government departments and work units.

In light of the requirements of Article 4 of the *Law to Protect Women's Rights and Interests* and the fact that governments at every level have established organizations to protect women's rights, it is necessary to turn the work of these organizations into law. When governments throughout the country draw up measures to implement the *Law to Protect Women's Rights and Interests*, they could first acknowledge the legal status and responsibility of such an organization. The concrete scope of the work, the procedures and the administrative structures of such organizations could be decided upon by the governments of each province, autonomous region and municipality directly under the central government.

Clarifying the means of redress, and widening the scope of redress

Although the the Chinese regulations on redress for actions in violation of women's legal rights and interests are fairly complete, it appears, after several years of practical experience, that there are many shortcomings to these regulations. For example, in Article 50 of the *Law to Protect Women's Rights and Interests*, one of the examples of violations of women's legal rights and interests listed in Article 50 calls for the victim's work unit or the higher level authorities to rectify the situation, or if circumstances warrant, to take administrative disciplinary action against the person directly responsible for the violation. In many cases, however, the actions which are in violation of women's legal rights and interests are carried out on the basis of decisions made by the head of the work unit to which the victim belongs. Furthermore, many violations of rights--such as firing women workers because of marriage, pregnancy, maternity leave or nursing; violating the principle of equal rights between men and women in allocating land--are perpetrated by the leader or person in charge of the work unit to which the victim belongs. Under such circumstances, it is very difficult to expect the heads of the unit to rectify the situation or take administrative disciplinary action against the person directly responsible for violating a woman's rights and interests. Similarly, it is not to be expected that the higher level authority would handle the case, because the concept of "higher level authority" is not clearly set out in the current laws and, in reality, it is often impossible to find out which "higher level authority" is the right one according to the law. This is especially true for private and township enterprises and joint ventures. Apart from this, if the head of the work unit to which the victim belongs or the higher level authority does not take any action against the violator, according to the *Administrative Procedural Law*, the victim cannot start an administrative suit in the People's Court.

Because of the above-mentioned problems, there are still no reliable guarantees for the protection of women's legal rights and interests.

In view of the above-mentioned situation, in order to protect women's legal rights and interests and to perfect the means of redress available to women, I suggest:

a. Changing the term "higher level authority" to "higher level authority or the department responsible for the work" in Article 50 Section 1 of the *Law to Protect Women's Rights and Interests*. In the same article after the line "take administrative disciplinary action against the violator", I suggest adding the words "or impose a fine on the violator by the department responsible for the work".

b. Through explanation of the legislation and the judicial system, governments should widen the scope of the *Administrative Procedural Law* in such a way that victims would be able to sue those administrative organizations who fail to carry out their duty to investigate a violator's administrative responsibilities, and thereby request the People's Court to order the administrative organization to carry out its legal duty.

Translated by Shengtao Jiang and A-M Traeholt

Notes

1. See Li Buyun, "A discussion of the three categories of human rights" in *Faxue yanjiu* (Research in Law), no. 4, 1991.

2. Article 10, Part 2 of the *Law to Protect Women's Rights and Interests of China*.

3. See Yang Dawen, "Some opinions on drafting a method to implement the *Law to Protect Women's Rights and Interests*", in *Faxue jia* (Jurist), no. 4, 1993.

Family Protection of the Rights and Interests of Girls, Adult Women, and Elderly Women

WANG DEYI

Chinese law has always emphasized the importance of protecting women's rights. Because women's rights span all areas of society such as politics, economics and culture, various categories of legal norms are needed to regulate women's rights. For example, the current *Constitution*, the *Criminal Code*, the *Procedural Law*, the *Labour Law* and the *Marriage Law* supplement one another and are jointly responsible for protecting women's rights. The *Law to Protect Women's Rights and Interests* of the People's Republic of China which was promulgated on October 1, 1992, is an important component of the Chinese system of laws and regulations to protect women's rights. It is a composite and specialized law which protects women's rights. The promulgation and implementation of this law symbolizes the perfection of the Chinese system of laws and regulations to protect women's rights.

The notion of women's rights is very comprehensive and the subjects of these rights are diverse. This essay mainly focusses on the rights and interests related to girls, adult women and elderly women.

Girls' Right to Life and Health

Both developed and developing countries are now paying more attention to children. Because the development of modern society not only depends on economics and technology, but even more on the quality of its people, one could say that the conditions for and the quality of children today will affect a nation's future and a country's destiny. In China, the protection of children is not only the responsibility of the whole nation but also the duty of every family.

In China, people under the age of 18 are referred to as children. There are close to 0.4 billion children in China, half of which are girls. The Chinese government has always emphasized the importance of protecting the rights and interests of girls. The *Constitution*, the *Marriage Law*, the *Inheritance Law*, the *Adoption Law*, the *Criminal Code*, the *General Principles of Civil Law*, the *Law of Compulsory Education*, the *Law to Protect the Health of Mothers and Infants*, the *Law to Protect the Rights and Interests of Women*, and the *Law to Protect Minors*, all contain articles and regulations on the protection of the rights and interests of girls. Apart from this, 23 provinces, autonomous regions and municipalities directly under the central government have established local regulations to protect minors, suitable to the current conditions of the region in question. These rules and regulations have provided ample legal foundation for protecting the healthy growth of China's girls.

The rights of girls include personal rights, property rights and the right to education, amongst others. But the right to life and health is the most basic right. The *Marriage Law* stipulates that parents are obligated to support their children. If the parents are incapable of supporting their children or if they die, the children's grandparents, if capable, are obligated to support them. If the grandparents have already died or if they are incapable of supporting the children, the elder brothers/sisters, if capable, are obligated to support the younger children. According to the *General Principles of Civil Law*, parents are the legal guardians of their daughters, and they are obligated to educate and protect their children. They are responsible for protecting girls' rights to personal safety, to property and other legal rights and interests.

Since 1980, the annual divorce rate in China has been constantly on the rise. According to statistics from relevant government departments, in 1980, 340,000 couples were divorced; and in 1994, 980,000 couples were divorced. The Chinese *Marriage Law* stipulates that the relationship between parents and children does not disappear after parents divorce. After a divorce, the children still belong to both parents, regardless of where the children end up living. Both the mother and the father are responsible for supporting their non-adult children. When a couple gets a divorce, they often disagree about the children: a) they both want the children; or b) neither want the children. Article 45 Section 2 of the *Law to Protect Minors* stipulates:

> When the People's Court hears a divorce case in which the parents cannot reach an agreement about who should raise the children, the Court shall make its decision based on the principle of protecting the rights and interests of the children and the concrete circumstances of the parties involved.

Children under the age of two would normally go to live with the mother. If the mother has an incurable infectious disease or another serious illness and it is inconvenient for the children to live with her, the father cannot refuse the responsibility of raising the children. In cases involving children over the age of two, when both parents want the children, the People's Court shall make its decision based on the rights and interests of the children. In certain cases, special consideration could be given to a parent who has been sterilized or lost the ability to have children because of other reasons, and who does not have any other children. In cases of children over the age of ten, their own opinion must be solicited as to which parent they should live with. The cost of raising the children should be shared by both parents, and the amount of child support should be based on the real need of the children. The amount of child support to be paid by the parent who is not directly raising the children should not exceed 30% of his/her total income. If the originally fixed amount of child support is insufficient to maintain the actual local standard of living, or if the children fall ill or if other valid reasons warrant more money, the amount of child support can be increased according to the circumstances. Article 8 of the *Law to Protect Minors* further stipulates that parents or other guardians should assume the task of guarding and raising the children. They must not mistreat or abandon minors, and it is prohibited to drown or abandon infants. In China, an infant regardless of its sex has a legal right to life and health from the moment it is born, and nobody can take away an infant's right to life or violate its right to health. It is a form of criminal behaviour to deprive a female infant of her life and it is also a crime to abandon a female infant. The Chinese *Adoption Law* stipulates that a person who abandons an infant will be fined a maximum of 1000 yuan by the Public Security Authorities. If the circumstances are vile enough to constitute a crime, the violator will be charged under the *Criminal Code*. Nevertheless, because of the influence of many thousands of years of traditional culture which valued men more highly than women, the phenomenon of drowning and abandoning female infants cannot be eliminated. According to the statistics, Chinese welfare institutions take in close to 20,000 abandoned infants each year, and the majority of abandoned infants are female or disabled. Female infants make up 90%, and disabled infants make up 80-90%. Apart from the disabled infants that are taken in by Chinese welfare homes, the majority of the healthy infants are female. They make up 90% of all the healthy infants. The Shanghai Child Welfare Home is a relatively large welfare home in China. At present, there are 711 orphans and abandoned children in the Shanghai Child Welfare Home, and out of these children, 443 (i.e. 62%) are girls; out of the 58 healthy children, 48 are female. Clearly, feudal ideas such as "to have no descendants is the worst form of disobedience", "the ancestral lineage will continue with the son" and "a son will take care of the elderly parents" are still very deeply rooted in some regions of China, especially in the countryside. Therefore, there is a need to strengthen propaganda, education and law enforcement mechanisms, and to raise every citizen's level of understanding of the law with respect to protecting children and adequately guaranteeing the legal rights and interests of girls.

Adult Women's Right to Work

The right to work is an extremely important right for adult women. To be working is not only a method of earning a living, it can also develop the individual's creative ability, enrich her social interaction and give her dignity. The Chinese government is putting much effort into developing social welfare and child-care institutions and is encouraging women to work and to seek economic independence. The country's laws protect employment for women, provide for equal pay for equal work, and give women special labour protection.

At present, the rate of employment for women in the cities is higher than 96%, which is only 2% less than the employment rate for men. The book entitled "The Situation of Chinese Women", published by the State Council Information Bureau, points out:

> In China, women employees make up 44% of society's total work force. This is higher than the world proportion of 34.5%. In 1992, 72.33% of all women over 15 years old were employed; in the countryside, women make up half of the entire work force, and in the cities, the number of female employees has increased from 600,000 in 1949 to 5,600,000 at present.

They make up 37.4% of the urban work force. This makes China one of the leading countries in the world where employment for women is concerned.

Since the 1980s, the shift towards a system of market economy has deeply affected the employment pattern of urban enterprises. In their constant pursuit of efficiency, enterprises have to fire surplus workers, and women workers are the first to be affected. According to a 1987 survey of 660 firms in 11 provinces conducted by the Department of Women Workers of the National Labour Union, 64% of 27,000 fired workers were women. In the large group of surplus workers, 62.5% were women. Since 1990, the phenomenon of women workers losing their jobs has changed slightly for the better. According to the findings of another National Labour Union survey of 1230 firms in 7 provinces, women made up 60% of the total number of workers who lost their jobs.

There are various reasons why women workers lose their jobs. From an objective point of view, the first reason is that the supply of labour is bigger than the demand, and both men and women are having difficulties finding employment. The second reason is that the traditional employment system is undergoing changes, and the old model of assigning jobs administratively is being replaced by a new model of choosing and selecting the best for the job. Thus, it is unavoidable that enterprises have to fire surplus workers.

From a subjective point of view, women carry the heavy responsibility of reproducing humankind, but their contribution in this area has not yet been recognized by society as a whole. At the same time, women workers are, in general, physically weaker than male workers and, as China's current standard of production is relatively low and the level of automation is limited, physical work still makes up for a large proportion of all production activities. Under these circumstances, not only is the scope of work available to women limited, many women are also bound to loose their jobs under the new employment system because they had been assigned unsuitable, heavy-duty work under the old system of a planned economy. The old employment model under the planned economy, on the one hand, did not pay enough attention to women and, on the other hand, was over protective of women. Thus, certain women workers lost their spirit of independence. As enterprises start to reform and to get rid of the "loss caused by gender", this group of women cannot avoid ending up in an awkward position.

With the reforms of the employment system, it is normal for companies to move from a system of permanent positions to improving the composition of workers. This is not to say that companies should not cut women workers, but that they should not only target women workers. However, in improving the composition of workers, some companies have simply cut all women workers and sent them home on a "prolonged vacation". According to the National Labour Union survey, 88% of company managers stated that their main reason for cutting women workers was that they worried that they might negatively affect the company's economic efficiency because of child-birth and nursing. Certain enterprises, especially those that are leased or contracted, fire women workers or unilaterally cancel their contracts, using pregnancy, child-birth and nursing as excuses. Other enterprises have established regulations for hiring unequal proportions of men and women. According to a survey of 77 commercial enterprises, the recruitment score for men was 115, but as high as 127 for women. Some companies openly refuse to recruit women university students. At present, most universities have to adopt the rather rigid measure of making companies recruit a woman student along with each male student in order to be able to place women students. According to Article 50 of the *Law to Protect Women's Rights and Interests* of the People's Republic of China, if a woman should be hired according to the laws and regulations, but is refused the job, or if the company raises the recruitment standard for women, or if the company fires a woman because of marriage, pregnancy, maternity leave or nursing etc., the person directly responsible for such action must be ordered by the work unit or the higher authorities to correct the situation and, if circumstances warrant, be subjected to disciplinary action.

At present, one important measure for strengthening the protection of women's right to work is to establish a new system of maternity insurance for women workers, which is suitable to the market economy. Under the system of a planned economy, women workers' maternity-related expenses were covered by the work unit to which the women belonged, thereby creating the "loss caused by gender". For this reason, enterprises generally do not want to recruit women workers and they dismiss them in large numbers. In order to alleviate the conflict between a company's economic interests and the protection of women's right to work, some places in China have already implemented, on a trial basis, a new system by which maternity-related expenses are covered by social/public funds. Under this system, a work unit contributes to the social funding organization according to the number of workers in the unit. When a woman worker has a child, the social funding organization will return the money to the work unit or give the money directly to the woman. This reform measure balances the burden of maternity expenses relatively well among enterprises and provides favourable conditions for participating in the market competition for companies with many women workers.

In order to further strengthen the protection of women's right to work, it is necessary to increase the rules concerning priority employment of women workers under the relevant legislation. Under the current law, there are many rather detailed regulations concerning special labour protection for women workers. And yet, under current circumstances, women still do not enjoy the equal right to work. It is necessary, while excluding women workers from certain types of work, to also establish rules under the relevant legislation which give priority to women workers in fields such as secretarial work and accounting in which men and women are equally qualified. In this way, the equal right of both men and women to work can be promoted.

Elderly Women's Right to Support

The older generation of women have contributed a lot of energy to the revolution. They have created wealth for the country and raised a new generation for the nation. When they grow old and weak, society as a whole and the family should respect and take care of them. Children should care for their parents, support them financially and comfort them spiritually, so that they may spend the rest of their lives in happiness. This is both a legal and a moral obligation.

China has the largest number of elderly people in the world. According to statistics from the State Statistical Bureau, at the end of 1993, there were 124,000,000 Chinese people who were over 60 years old, and of these

124,000,000, 64,050,000 were women, i.e. 51.7%. They live in 270,000,000 families, and are spread out over 1,070,000 village committees and 110,000 city neighbourhood committees at society's lowest level of community. As they age physically, mentally and spiritually, they not only need material safeguards and help in their daily life, but also spiritual sustenance.

In China, it is first and foremost the government's direct responsibility to care for the elderly women and to deal with their problems. The Chinese Constitution states:

Citizens of the People's Republic of China have the right to special assistance from the state and society when they are old, sick or have lost their ability to work. The government will develop the necessary social security, social relief, and medical and health care facilities for citizens to be able to enjoy these rights.

According to the current system, different measures are being applied to urban and rural areas. In the city, after retiring or stepping down, former government employees or employees of state-operated enterprises are all guaranteed financial support, medical care, or welfare housing. Society has established many retirement homes, nursing homes or welfare homes so that aged women without relatives can still receive proper care.

At the present, however, China cannot provide public support for all the elderly and meet all of their needs. The family has to assume a large part of the responsibility of caring for and supporting the elderly. This is especially true for the vast countryside. There are more than 80,000,000 people over the age of 60 in the Chinese countryside, and of these, 41,000,000 are women. After the implementation of the land contract responsibility system, depending on family support has become the only choice for elderly women in the countryside.

No matter whether in the city or in the countryside, there are three main aspects to family support: a) financial support, i.e., children provide their parents with a monthly allowance to cover their necessary living expenses; b) daily care, i.e., children provide their parents with clothing, food, housing and transportation, as well as medical care; c) spiritual sustenance, i.e., parents live happily together with their children.

In China, showing respect for and giving support to the elderly are not only requirements of socialist ethics, but also legal principles which control family relations. In the relationship between parents and children, Chinese law protects the rights and interests of the children, and of parents and the elderly. According to the regulations of the Chinese Constitution and the current *Marriage Law*, adult children have an obligation to support their parents. If the children do not carry out their responsibility, those parents who have lost the ability to work or who are having difficulties getting by have the right to request financial support from their children. Grandchildren on both sides of the family who are capable of supporting their grandparents have a responsibility to do so if their own parents have already died or are unable to do so. The law will punish those who mistreat or abandon elderly people.

In China, most elderly women are being comforted and cared for by their own families, and they enjoy a happy old age. However, there are still a few people who neglect their duty of caring for their elderly parents. Some even mistreat them or abandon them to a life of loneliness and misery. Faced with this kind of situation, it is necessary to continue propaganda and education in order to teach adult children and society as a whole about their obligation to care for the elderly. Through legislation and investigations, acts of crime such as neglecting to care for the elderly, mistreating or abandoning elderly people should be punished according to the law. Through exemplary education, the sections of the *Marriage Law* which deal with respect for the elderly will become common knowledge in all families and households, and people's awareness of their legal and moral responsibilities to provide for the elderly will be raised. Mediation organizations should help elderly women sue those adult children who purposefully neglect to provide for their elderly parents in order to get the Courts to order the adult children to pay parental support and to enforce this order, for example by asking the work unit to which the defendant belongs, to deduct parental support from his/her pay cheque.

Providing for elderly women is not only an economic issue. As mentioned above, there are many other real-life problems. In recognition of the real needs of the elderly, communities have established universities, clubs, activity centres, community service centres, residences, daycare centres, marriage introduction centres, rehabilitation centres, special beds in the hospital etc., for the elderly. According to incomplete statistics, there are 70435 service facilities for the elderly in China. Out of these, there are 5824 elder-care service centres, 40504 activity stations, 5212 rehabilitation centres, and 3940 schools. These facilities have created the right conditions for the elderly to be able to continue to study, be active, to enjoy themselves, and to receive medical care and support from society.

People often depict love and marriage between the elderly as love in the twilight years. Such love and marriages are very common in other countries. In China, however, the feudalist traditions are so strong and deeply-rooted that it is very difficult even for middle-aged people--let alone elderly people--whose spouses have died or who have divorced, to remarry. The good news is that, with the policies of reform and opening up to the outside world, it has become more common for elderly people to remarry.

In Beijing, many elderly people have already married happily. Several marriage introduction centres for the elderly have emerged in different parts of Beijing. These centres act as go-betweens for the elderly and provide marriage services. In Shanghai, the first major industrial city in China with a large aging population, more than 2500 elderly couples were married in 1987 alone. For example, the 64 year old retired cadre Mr. Zhang married the 58 year old retired worker Ms. Zhao with the help of the marriage introduction centre for the elderly. Every day, the couple take an early morning walk in the park and practice taijiquan. In their spare time, they often go on outings, and they are very content.

However, many people still harbour deep prejudices against elderly women who remarry. Some adult children are either influenced by feudalist thinking, or they fear that the family property may fall into someone else's hands, or that no one will take care of the domestic work, and so they flagrantly interfere with their elderly mother's wish to remarry. The following statistics clearly demonstrate how difficult it is for elderly women to remarry. According to statistics from the 4th national census in 1990, among the total number of people over 60 years old, 3,720,000 had lost their spouses. Of these, 2,630,000 were women. Furthermore, there were 18,000 elderly women who had divorced, and a relatively large group of elderly women who had never married. Of this large group of single elderly women, less than 1% re-marry. According to a national survey of 36,000 elderly people, 5.4% of the elderly remarry in the cities, in the townships less than 1% of those whose spouses have passed away remarry, and in the countryside this figure is even smaller. Among the few elderly people who do remarry in the countryside, very few are elderly women.

In order that elderly people who have lost their spouses may find some fulfilment in life, find a partner to share their worries with and lead a happy life, it is necessary to show ample support from society to those who remarry, to combine esteem and care for the elderly with respect for their freedom to remarry, and thereby to solve in an appropriate manner the issues of love and marriage. Organizations in society should advocate, propagate and support the elderly's wish to remarry and respect their right to choose freely. This may make people understand that marriage is not a special right reserved only for the young, but that the elderly also have the right to fall in love and get married. Whether an elderly person marries or not, the community should always offer its support. Communities at all levels should establish clubs for the elderly and arrange beneficial activities for them, so as to widen their social life and strengthen their physical and mental health.

Elderly women have contributed all their lives to society and to their families, and they have the right to share the material and spiritual achievements of social development. Their legal rights and interests must be respected and protected by all members of society. However, as the level of economic development in China remains rather low and as development in different parts of China remains unbalanced, community service facilities are still rather limited. The policies of the past of low wages to ensure employment have resulted in low pensions and low living standards for those who are retired. Although the state has made a considerable effort in dealing with the issue of welfare and social security for the elderly, social institutions which provide for the elderly still cannot catch up with the needs of a growing population of elderly. According to the statistics, there are currently 25,330 elder residences in China. These residences are only able to take in 370,000 elderly people. Most of these people belong to the group who enjoy the "five guarantees", and yet, they only make up 1/10 of all the elderly who are entitled to the "five guarantees". Generally speaking, except for a few well equipped residences for the elderly, most residences are poorly equipped and the standard of care is low.

Along with the decrease in the birth rate, and the development of production and improvement of medical and health care conditions, people's lives are being prolonged and the proportion of elderly people in the population will continue to increase. We appeal to people from all walks of life to pay even more attention to the real difficulties that elderly women are faced with, and to adopt efficient measures, increase economic input in social welfare facilities, raise the standard welfare allowance for those in need and develop elder residences, so as to help solve the problems and worries of elderly women and let them spend the rest of their lives in happiness.

The Women's Federation and its Role in Protecting Women's Rights and Interests

XU WEIHUA

General Description of the Women's Federation

The emergence and development of the Women's Federation

The Women's Federation consists of the All China Women's Federation as well as the regional Women's Federations and their local units.

From March 24 to April 3, 1949, Chinese women held the first Women's Congress in Beijing. Women workers, women farmers, women soldiers, women militia, women intellectuals, and women patriotic personages of every nationality came together. They discussed the principle of a liberation movement for Chinese women. The Congress approved the administrative organization of the All China Democratic Women's Federation. Since then, Chinese women have had a universal national women's organization.

From September 9 to 20, 1957, Chinese women held the Third National Congress in Beijing. The Congress approved the "People's Republic of China Women's Federation Charter." The Congress also changed the Federation's name from the "All-China Democratic Women's Federation" to the "People's Republic of China Women's Federation."

From September 8 to 17, 1978, Chinese women held the Fourth National Congress in Beijing. According to the "All-China Women's Federation Charter" which was passed by the Congress, the name of the Federation was changed from the "People's Republic of China Women's Federation" to the "All China Women's Federation".

The name of an organization is a special symbol of the organization. Each time the Women's Federation's name changed, its tasks and functions also changed and its work and its goals improved. While trying to adjust to the development of society, the Women's Federation tried to perfect and develop itself. The Federation tried to mould itself according to the real meaning of its name.

The nature and task of the Women's Federation

The "All China Women's Federation" is a social mass organization under the leadership of the Chinese Communist Party, made up of women from every nationality and all walks of life. Its task is to further the liberation of Chinese women. It is the Chinese Communist Party's bridge and link to the large masses of women, and the people's government's support in society. The Women's Federation is a massive, extensive and united organization and it is one of China's largest NGOs.

In the primary stages of socialism, the Women's Federation performs the task of uniting and educating numerous women, and implementing the basic line of the Party. It plays an active role in building "socialist material civilization and spiritual civilization." Its basic functions are to represent and protect the interests of all Chinese people, with an emphasis upon promoting equality between men and women, and realizing women's liberation.

In accordance with the Chinese Constitution and law, and the Chinese Communist Party's basic line and principle in the primary stages of socialism, and taking women's special needs into consideration, the Women's Federation has drawn up the following tasks for the years to come:

First, the Women's Federation will mobilize, call on, unite and lead the masses of women to commit themselves to building the socialist market economy, the reform and open door policy, the modernization of society and the promotion of social development and progress.

Second, the Women's Federation will organize women to energetically promote the construction of a socialist spiritual civilization, democracy and legal system. It will educate women, encourage the spirit of "having ideals, having morals, having culture, having discipline" and "self-respect, self-confidence, self-reliance, and self-improvement" among Chinese women, and encourage them to educate themselves, study technology, science, management and law to enhance their individual qualities.

Third, the Federation will represent and protect women's rights and interests. It will combat the phenomena of discriminating against, maltreating, cruelly injuring and killing women. It will raise the consciousness of society with respect to the issue of protecting women's rights and interests, and enhance women's ability to protect their own rights and interests.

Fourth, the Federation will train and educate youth and children, and help them grow up to be healthy.

Fifth, the Federation will contribute to the cause of uniting the nation. It will assist in enhancing world peace and development, maintain unity and cooperation among women of the world, and increase communication and understanding among women of different countries.

Sixth, special attention will be given to reforming and strengthening the Women's Federation. The Federation will work towards becoming an efficient and influential social mass organization with real power and appeal to women.

The establishment and structure of the Women's Federation

According to the regulation of the "All China Women's Federation Charter", the Federation has established a leading organization at the national level. It has, furthermore, set up regional and local organizations according to the administrative divisions of the whole nation. At the same time, the national organization and its regional offices have all set up administrative offices as needed.

The All China Women's Federation

The National Women's Congress is the decision-making body for the All-China Women's Federation. It holds one meeting every five years. The Congress selects several people to form the executive committee. When the Congress is not in session, the executive committee is the decision-making body. The executive committee selects one chairperson, one vice-chairperson, and several committee members to form the standing committee. The standing committee becomes the decision-making body when the executive committee is not in session. Since the Second National Congress, a Secretariat has been set up under the executive committee. The Secretariat is responsible for the day-to-day work of the All China Women's Federation. Seven National Congress meetings have been held from 1949 to 1993. Because of special historical reasons, there were no National Congress meetings between 1962 and 1978.

Regional Women's Federations at every level

Since the assembly of the first National Chinese Women's Congress, regional Women's Federations were established according to the national administrative divisions. The decision-making body for every regional Women's Federation is the Regional Women's Congress. Every regional Women's Congress above the county level conducts its meetings every five years. Women's Congresses at the township and neighbourhood levels hold their meetings every three years. Except under special circumstances, most of the regional Women's Congresses are able to hold their meetings according to this schedule. In 1992, Women's Federations were established in all 30 provinces, autonomous regions and municipalities directly under the central government, with the exception of Taiwan. Women's Federations were also established in 376 prefectures, 2,825 counties, 47,635 townships, and 6,012 neighbourhoods.

Women's Congresses at the grass-roots level

The grass-roots level Women's Congress is the basic unit of the Women's Federation. In the rural areas, village level units are also set up. In some townships and neighbourhoods where there are large numbers of women, Women's Congresses or Women's Working Committees are set up. In 1993, there were 746,814 local Women's Congresses at the village level, 89,090 Women's Congresses at the neighbourhood level, and 71,062 Women's Congresses at the township level.

Women's Committees are also established in state-operated organizations such as the Communist Party and the government, in many mass organizations, and in other state-operated organizations such as the Scientific, Educational, Cultural and Health ministries. In 1993, there were already 71,062 Women's Committees nationwide. The women's organizations at the grass-roots level have developed rather significantly in the process of getting fully established.

The Main Task for the Women's Federation is to Protect Women's Rights and Interests

The importance of protecting women's rights and interests

(1) Protecting women's lawful rights and interests is very important to the cause of giving full play to women's great role, improving socialist modernization and establishing socialism with Chinese characteristics.

China has 1.1 billion people. Women make up half of the national population. It is a great human resource. They are a main force in building the socialist economy and socialist modernization. Especially in recent years, Chinese women have actively devoted themselves to building a socialist market economy, to reform and to the open-door movement. They have made extraordinary contributions to developing economic, scientific, cultural and educational undertakings and building both a material and spiritual civilization. Their contributions have gained recognition and praise from society. At the same time, Chinese women have taken on a special responsibility and made a special contribution in the area of human reproduction, building the family and raising the younger generation. Chinese women play a vital role in advancing social progress and development, creating social wealth and child bearing. It is of the utmost importance to fully respect and protect women and their special interests in order to foster their enthusiasm, bring their "half of heaven" role into full play, and build socialism with Chinese characteristics.

(2) It is extremely important to protect women's rights and interests and to solve the problem of violating women's rights and interests, in order that social stability and development can be guaranteed.

Traditionally, China has stressed the importance of protecting women's rights and interests, and has implemented effective measures to fulfil them. However, China is still at the primary stage of socialism. It is restricted and influenced by economic, cultural and material conditions. It still falls short in achieving real equality between men and women and in protecting women's rights and interests. This is evident from the following facts: The percentage of women involved in politics is still low. Women's educational level and their scientific and cultural merits are not high. During the transformation of state-run companies, many women workers have become unemployed. Many privately owned, foreign owned and joint venture companies do not have sufficient legal knowledge, and the problem of violating women workers' rights is very serious there. In the cities, some units overtly regulate that they will only allocate houses to male workers. In the countryside, the problem of allocating land to women under the contract responsibility system, land to grow crops for personal consumption or residential land has not been resolved. Incidents of discrimination, mistreatment and cruelly injuring and killing women are still happening. Distressing social phenomena such as kidnapping and selling women and children, and prostitution are re-surfacing. All these problems demonstrate that although women, according to the law, enjoy equal status in the areas of politics, economics, culture, social and family matters, many of their rights are not being realized. In some regions, the problem of the violation of women's rights is very serious. The impact of this problem is not only limited to women, it is a social issue. It involves many people and has a strong social impact. Thus, the problem cannot be neglected. To effectively protect women's rights and to solve the problem of the violation of women's rights is important for the stability and development of society, and for the establishment of a good social environment, social customs and steady economic growth.

The Women's Federation has a special advantage in representing and protecting women's rights and interests

The Women's Federation is both the bridge which links the Party and the government to the masses of women, and the organization which represents and protects women's rights and interests. The Federation has close connections with women and its roots are among women. The Federation understands women's situation and needs, listens to their requests and promptly relays their problems and requests to the Party and the government. It calls on people from all walks of life to focus their concern and attention on women's issues, and helps women solve their problems and concerns through various means. Thus, the Federation is regarded by women as their refuge whenever they have problems. The Women's Federation has gained women's understanding, trust, support and help through its hard work. Because the Women's Federation is established on the foundation of trust and support from women, it has a special advantage over other organizations in representing and protecting women's rights and interests. This is demonstrated in many ways:

(1) Wide representation. The fundamental and most important characteristic of the Women's Federation is that it is massive, far-reaching and united.

Massiveness is one of the most basic characteristics of the Women's Federation. In uniting people, the Federation does not distinguish by age, nationality, occupation, clique, belief, or whether they are advanced, less advanced or backward. As it only distinguishes people by their sex, it embraces patriotic women from every nationality, occupation and walk of life. Compared to other organizations, the Women's Federation consists of the largest number of people and its branches are the most far-reaching.

Another basic characteristic of the Women's Federation is that it is far-reaching. The Federation not only represents Chinese women who make up half of the national population, it also takes on the responsibility of raising and educating teenagers and children who constitute one-third of the population.

The Women's Federation is also united. It unites women from every nationality and every occupation. It also unites and keeps in touch with women in Taiwan, Hong Kong and Macao.

(2) The scope of the Federation's work is wide.

The Women's Federation is a social mass organization. It has a very strong character of social magnanimity. The Federation mainly works for women, and women are working in every occupation. Therefore, the Federation's work touches every segment of society.

(3) It has a strong appeal to women.

Through many different activities which are accepted and well-liked by women, the Women's Federation unites and links women from every nationality and all walks of life. Thus, it successfully represents and protects women's rights and interests. Women understand and actively take part in the work and activities of the Federation. They easily embrace and actively respond to the appeal of the Federation. The Federation's strong appeal stems from its whole-hearted and practical work for women, and at the same time, from its working style which is suitable to the special characteristics of women.

(4) The Federation is trying to perfect itself.

The Federation is divided into central and regional women's federations and nationwide women's grass-roots units according to the country's administrative divisions, as well as women's organizations in all segments of society and different democratic parties. The Federation also includes women's friendship organizations and research institutes. Through these various avenues the Federation ensures the successful linkage of women.

(5) The Federation has many qualified cadres.

The Federation has almost 90,000 cadres at all levels. What is so special about them is that they love to work with women's issues and they are good at it. These cadres play important roles in bringing women together, solving their problems in a timely manner, and representing and protecting their rights and interests.

The 12th Chinese Communist Party Congress required the Women's Federation to "become the mass organization with authority which can represent women's interest, as well as protect and educate women and children." In 1983, following the request from the central government, the 5th National Women's Congress in Beijing approved the following working principle: "To firmly protect women's and children's legal rights and interests, to raise and educate juveniles and children and help them grow up healthy, to fulfil women's important role in building a socialist material and spiritual civilization." This principle corresponds to the real situation and demands of women's work. It reflects women's aspirations and is widely supported by women.

In September 1988, the Federation held its 6th National Women's Congress in Beijing. According to the demand for further opening up and reform, the Congress approved the following principles: "To unite and educate women, to carry out the basic principle of the Party, to support women's legal rights and interests, to play a more important role in furthering a rich, strong, democratic and civilized socialist modernization, and to advance women's liberation." This Congress re-emphasized the basic principle of representing and protecting women's rights and interests.

In September 1993, the 7th National Women's Congress was held in Beijing. It was clearly stated that the Women's Federation's basic function is to represent and protect women's rights and interests and to achieve equality between men and women. Since the 5th National Women's Congress, the Women's Federation's status as the organization which represents and protects women's rights and interests has been solidified.

The Women's Federation must focus on current problems that concern women's rights and interests. The Federation must increase its efforts to protect women's rights and interests

Reform and the open-door policy has brought rapid economic growth to our society. At the same time, it has changed people's way of thinking and living. There is no doubt that it is an opportunity and also a challenge to women. On the one hand, many women have taken advantage of this opportunity and applied their knowledge and skills in all kinds of occupations. They have become "strong women", entrepreneurs, scientists, and model workers. They have become the pioneers of the open-door and reform policies. They have made important contributions and have attracted society's attention.

On the other hand, the open-door and reform policy is also a challenge to women. Under the new historical conditions of opening up and reform, women's rights and interests are facing many serious challenges and problems:

(1) There is still only a limited number of women cadres at the top leadership level and at the grass-roots level. The number of women cadres make up only 30% of the number of men cadres in state-operated organizations. Women cadres only account for 10% of all cadres above the county level. A phenomena of "three more and three less" exists among women cadres: "more assistant positions and less chief positions; more empty positions and less executive positions; more lower level positions and less higher level positions". This situation does not correspond to the percentage of women in the entire national population and their important role in building the economy.

(2) Women's level of education is not high. Their scientific and technological knowledge is limited. It has already been 40 years since the liberation and, although the percentage of illiteracy among women has dropped from 90% in 1949 to 32% in 1993 and 110,000,000 women have become literate, serious problems still exist. In some remote and minority areas, the incidence of illiteracy is still very high. In some impoverished and underdeveloped areas there are still many girls who quit school or who do not have the opportunity to go to school. The state of education for women and girls is still an important factor in women's development.

(3) In recent years, along with opening up and reform, there has been a lot of changes in the employment system. These changes have posed a challenge to the old employment philosophy and practice of "high employment, low efficiency" which most women had already got used to, and many working women were thrust into the competitive world. During the transformation of state corporations' management mechanisms and reform of the employment system, many people lost their jobs. In some state firms, many women workers also lost their jobs. Many of them found it very difficult to find new jobs. Inequality still exists between women and men in the areas of hiring, admittance to school and distribution of housing. In some organizations, problems of "equal work, unequal payment" between men and women continue to exist. In some privately owned, foreign owned, county and township owned firms and joint ventures, women workers are not being protected properly and their safety is not guaranteed.

(4) The very serious problems of the violation of women's personal rights and interests still exist. In some regions, the criminal offence of kidnapping and selling women and children persist. The occurrence of distressing social phenomena such as prostitution and pornographic services have escalated. Problems of producing and selling pornographic and illegal publications are still very serious. Some reading materials contain vulgar descriptions of women. Those who are seriously influenced by the feudalistic point of view that men are more important than women even abandon their girl infants. There are many incidents of women becoming victims of family violence and many incidents where women have been mistreated, hurt and killed.

(5) The phenomenon of arranged marriages still exists in some remote areas. Divorced women have trouble finding housing and some women have no place to go. In the countryside, some married women are having problems obtaining their allotment of land under the contract responsibility system, land to grow crops for personal consumption or residential land.

Although the government and women have fought against the above-mentioned problems and achieved great success, we must point out that the problem of the violation of women's rights and interests still exists. Some problems are very serious, and the Women's Federation, as the representative and protector of women's rights and interests, understands this very clearly. With a positive attitude and through implementation of effective measures, the Federation has demanded that all Party and government departments and all segments of society place emphasis on solving the problem. At the same time, the Federation leads women in their fight against the problem of the violation of women's rights and interests, and supports them in protecting their own rights and interests.

The Function of the Women's Federation is to Protect Women's Rights and Interests

Representing and protecting women's rights and interests are the basic functions and responsibilities of the Women's Federation. In order to do this job well, the Federation not only needs noble aspirations and enthusiasm, but also a good grasp of the practical work involved. What kind of work has the Federation done to represent and protect women's rights and interests and what kind of role does it play?

1.   The Women's Federation takes an active part in activities related to the legal protection of women's rights and interests. In order to promote and improve the part of the legal system which concerns women's rights and interests, and strengthen the system of rights protection, the Federation has embarked on the path of legal system reform and standardization.

Since its establishment in 1949, the Women's Federation has pushed for the establishment of various laws concerning women's rights and interests. For example:

In 1949, the All-China Women's Federation was present at the Chinese People's Political Consultative Congress and took part in drawing up a "Common Programme." It called for the abolishment of the feudal system which restrains women's rights, achieving equality between men and women, and including the law to protect the rights of mother and child in the "Common Programme".

In 1950, in cooperation with the Legal Committee of the State Council, the All China Women's Federation participated in drafting and establishing the first law in the new China--*The Marriage Law*. In 1980, the Federation also participated in discussing and amending *The Marriage Law*.

In 1988, in cooperation with the Department of Health, the National Union and the Department of Labour, the All China Women's Federation drafted "The Rule Concerning the Protection of Women Workers."

The Women's Federation also participated actively in and cooperated with other organizations in drafting, discussing and amending important laws or regulations concerning women's rights and interests.

In 1983, the Central Committee of the Chinese Communist Party decided that the protection of women's and children's lawful rights and interests would be the main task for the women's organizations. From then on, the Women's Federation took full responsibility for the protection of women's rights. From 1983 to 1985, under the promotion, advocacy and participation of all the regional Women's Federation organizations, 28 provinces, autonomous regions and municipalities directly under the central government established regional regulations to "Protect Women and Children's Lawful Rights and Interests".

With the development and strengthening of our country's democracy and legal system, the establishment of a special legal system to protect women's rights and interests is also under way. Through fervent appeals from women, the demands for the establishment of a law to protect women's rights and interests have caught the government's attention. In May 1989, the All China Women's Federation, the Department of Civil Administration and the China National Union accepted the task assigned to them by the Legal Committee of the State Council. They were asked to form a "drafting committee" to deal with the establishment of a law to protect women's rights and interests. On April 3rd, 1992, the law to protect women's rights and interests was approved by the 5th All-Member Meeting of the 7th Chinese National People's Congress. Since then, Chinese women have had a law for the overall protection of their rights and interests.

Since 1992, every region has established its own regulations to fulfil the *Law to Protect Women's Rights and Interests*, while also taking the particular local circumstances into consideration. With help from all levels of the Women's Federation, every province, autonomous region and municipality directly under the central government has established regulations to implement the law to protect women.

At the same time, in order to incorporate the protection of women's rights and interests into the every-day work situation, governments at every level are required to establish a goal and to draw up measures to reach that goal. They are required to draw up a general principle and plan of action for furthering the cause of women's development. In August 1993, the Working Committee for Women's and Children's Affairs of the State Council decided to complete the "Programme for Women's Planning and Development." In December 1993, the

Working Committee for Women's and Children's Affairs of the State Council began to organize the Drafting Committee which included the State Planning Commission, the State Education Commission, the Public Security Ministry, the Labour Ministry, the Public Health Ministry, the State Family Planning Commission, the State Bureau of Statistics and the All China Women's Federation. The Drafting Committee began drafting the "Programme for Women's Planning and Development." Now the Drafting Committee has completed the draft for consulting and is waiting for approval from the State Council.

In order to carry out the "Programme", every province, autonomous region and municipality directly under the control of the central government must establish its own "women's development plan." Through implementation of the "Programme for Women's Planning and Development", governments at every level should take measures to carry out the protection of women's rights and interests.

Our country has already established a legal system to protect women's rights and interests and to promote equality between men and women. Such a legal system is based on the Constitution, on laws which pertain to women's rights, and on various laws and regulations and administrative by-laws. Such a legal system provides a well-organized mechanism and a good legal environment for protecting women's rights and interests. It makes it possible to protect women's rights effectively on the basis of law, regulation and order.

2.   The Women's Federation actively takes part in the investigation of serious cases involving the violation of women's rights, kidnapping and selling of women, and prostitution. It provides useful evidence to policy-making departments to crack down on the illegal activities of violating women's rights and interests.

Recent years have seen the reemergence of some distressing social phenomena which was thought to have died out a long time ago, such as kidnapping and selling of women, and prostitution. Such illegal and criminal activities destroy social stability and public order, damage the overall social climate, and lead to the break-up of many families. They cause great pain to the victims and bring disaster to the whole nation and to the younger generation. Such activities also interfere with the smooth development of opening up and reform.

To deal with the situation, in 1980 and 1982, in cooperation with the Public Security Ministry and the Justice Ministry, the All China Women's Federation conducted an investigation into the activities of the kidnapping and selling of women and children, and prostitution. It submitted a report to the central government and aroused its attention. The Central Committee of the Party called for a "firm crack down on the criminal activities of kidnapping and selling women and children." At the same time, the Standing Committee of the National People's Congress also approved the "Decision to severely punish criminals who threaten social order and stability." In the "Decision", criminals who are involved in the selling and buying of women become targets of severe punishment. These punishment measures had a definite effect on the criminal activities of kidnapping and selling women and children.

Since 1985, the kidnapping and selling of women and children, and prostitution have spread again. In cooperation with the Public Security Ministry and other ministries, the All China Women's Federation has conducted a special investigation into the problem. The Women's Federation analyzed and studied the causes and special nature of kidnapping and selling women and children and prostitution, and it recommended cracking down on such activities. This caught people's attention and prompted law-enforcement organizations to carry out several severe punishment movements to combat the criminal activities of kidnapping and selling women and children and prostitution. Since then, these activities have been curbed. At the same time, in cooperation with the Public Security Ministry and the Justice Ministry, the Women's Federation takes an active part in rescuing women and children who have been kidnapped and sold. The Federation teaches them to settle down and to get involved in developing their hometown. It guides them in the challenging activities of "studying culture and technology, and comparing results and contribution", and it helps them escape poverty and embark on the road to wealth. The Women's Federation also helps women who have broken the law to understand the concept of self-respect, to re-establish their ideals and hopes for a better life, and to re-enter and contribute to society.

3. Through improved mail-in and walk-in grievance services and through legal consulting, the Women's Federation has learned to grasp and understand the issues related to the violation of women's rights and interests. It establishes contacts with, coordinates, and cooperates with other related departments and pays special attention to the serious and difficult cases. The Federation urges the other related departments to diligently work out the problems of women.

The mail-in and walk-in grievance services and the legal consulting which the Women's Federation offers have become a means through which the Federation acquaints itself with women's problems. They are also the important bridge which links women to the Women's Federation and an effective way for the Federation to provide legal help to women. The Federation regularly summarizes and analyzes the contents of the letters, the visits, the legal consulting and various complaints from women, and a report is sent to the higher level leaders to draw their attention to the problems. At the same time, according to the nature of the problem, the Federation usually establishes contact with the leader of the relevant department and, after necessary coordination, the Federation will ask the department in question to handle the problem appropriately according to the law and regulations and the principle of protecting women's rights and interests.

In cases of a major, rather prominent and representative problem, where ordinary cooperation will not solve the problem, the Federation will ask the central government and the State Council for help. In some cases, support from the public is needed, and the Federation will make a public appeal through the media to call on society to recognize the importance of protecting women's rights and interests.

Should the Federation, through letters and visits or through legal counselling, discover cases involving serious violations of women's rights and interests, it will cooperate with other organizations to investigate the problem. After uncovering the facts of the case, the Federation will ask the relevant authority to find an appropriate solution to the problem. The Federation also uses many cases to educate women about their legal rights, in order that women should concern themselves with resolving these serious cases and learn to protect their rights.

In some representative cases, the Federation will hire its own legal advisor or lawyer to act as the attorney for the victim. These attorneys will be involved in the entire legal process. They will provide suggestions to the legal authority based on the facts and the law.

4.   In cooperation with the Justice Ministry, the Women's Federation has initiated legal education and propaganda in society as a whole and amongst women.

The Women's Federation realizes that, as the protection of women's rights and interests is the shared responsibility of society as a whole, women's rights and interest can only be guaranteed and take root among the masses after a healthy social climate of respecting and protecting women has been established. Therefore, it is necessary to further legal education and propaganda amongst all citizens and women in particular.

From the end of 1983 to the Spring of 1984, 13 government bodies including the Propaganda Department, the Commission for Inspecting Discipline, the Justice Ministry and the All-China Women's Federation launched a month-long activity to promote legal education for the public. Because of the attention given by the leaders at every level coupled with the strong support and cooperation from all segments of society and all government departments, the adopted method of education was accepted by the people, and the month-long activity was very successful.

At the end of 1985, the All China Women's Federation together with the Justice Ministry and other departments, launched a five-year legal education project for women. It was called the "first five" legal education project. Recently, a "second five" project has been launched. On April 3rd, 1992, the *Law to Protect Women's Rights and Interests* was approved. The task of implementing that law has been incorporated into the "second five" legal education project. At the same time, the Federation decided to organize a month-long, nation-wide legal education exercise. The results of the exercise have been surprisingly good.

Through the legal education projects for women, the Federation has effectively protected women's rights and interests, inspired women's enthusiasm in building modernization, encouraged them and raised their self-respect. It has also strengthened women's ability to fight against the violation of their rights and interests. At the same time, all citizens have received legal education concerning the protection of women's rights and interests and have come to understand that "protecting women's rights and interests is the shared responsibility of society as a whole." Citizens have, furthermore, become conscious of protecting women's rights and interests.

Because our country has been influenced by feudal ideas for such a long time, ideas like "men are more important than women, look up to men but look down on women" still exist in some people's minds. Furthermore, economic and cultural development is not balanced between regions. Therefore, in some regions and among some people, violation of women's rights and interests still occurs. Problems such as discrimination, mistreatment, and injuring and killing women will continue to exist for a long time. Thus, the protection of women's rights and interests is going to be a long-term job for the Women's Federation. In order to achieve equality between men and women and to realize women's liberation, the Women's Federation will continue to work hard to represent and protect women's rights and interests, to play a real role, and to live up to the expectations of the women of China.

Translation by Shengtao Jiang and by A-M Traeholt

The Praxis of Women's Rights as Human Rights With a Special Emphasis on the Right to Development: An Analysis of MATCH International Centre and the Comité Québécois Femmes et Développement

LINDA CARDINAL[*]

Introduction

A concern exists with feminist human rights activists that the human rights approach in relation to women's rights will become gradually more successful as it moves out of the hands of big states and international bodies, and into the day to day activities of grassroots organisations (Kerr, 1993). Such an assumption leads to rather simple questions: who are those grassroots organisations or women's groups promoting a praxis of women's rights as human rights? Why or how did they become active? What are their politics and perspectives on women's issues? How can grassroot groups make the approach of women's rights as human rights more successful?

This paper is concerned with the praxis of women's rights as human rights with a special emphasis on the right to development as it has been developed within two non-governmental organisations (NGOs) in Canada (and Québec): MATCH International Centre (MATCH) and the Comité Québécois Femmes et Développement (CQFD). Other organisations in Canada, such as the International Centre for Human Rights and Democratic Development and the Canadian Council for International Cooperation have been promoting women's rights as human rights, especially since the 1993 conference on human rights in Vienna. MATCH and the CQFD are the two first NGOs in Canada explicitly addressing women's issues from such a framework. The CQFD represents an

---

[*] An important part of the research for this paper has been done by Martine Perrault, a candidate in the master's programme in the sociology department at the University of Ottawa. I would like to thank her for her excellent work as well as Edith Smith and Caroline Andrew for reading and commenting a first version of this text.

important number of groups[1] and individuals from Québec, linking feminism and development locally, nationally and globally. MATCH is based in English-Canada, acting mainly as a funding agency for Third World women's groups.

While feminist human rights activists have been more active on the front line of women's struggles for empowerment in the past years, the issue has been on the United Nations' agenda since the seventies, whether dealing with the elimination of discrimination against women (1979)[2], rights of refugee women (1980)[3], or genital mutilation (1990)[4], to give a few examples. It is also worth mentioning that in 1979, Georgina Ashworth founded one of the first organisations for the rights of women as human rights. CHANGE was established "to advance the recognition of the inalienable human rights and dignity of women and to publicize their abuse, whether by state, commercial or individual interest" (Ashworth 1993: 150).

Despite these accomplishments, it is really only since the beginning of the nineties that we are witnessing a globalisation of the issue of women's rights as human rights to the whole of the women's movement, or as Elisabeth Friedman writes, that we are witnessing the emergence of a movement for women's human rights (Friedman 1995: 18). Feminist human rights activists now constitute an important lobby group capable, partly because of the position of privilege that legal activists have in this community, of pressuring governments to take women's issues more seriously. For feminist activists, the growing interest in the question of women's rights as human rights is the result of the recognition by many of the power of the human rights framework (Friedman 1995: 19). I would suggest that it is also important to look at the general context in which the emergence of a movement promoting women's rights as human rights is taking place. Such context, I would argue, is macro-political. It is situated in the dynamics of global politics.

More specifically, according to Choukri, we are witnessing the consolidation of what he calls "a modern, global historic bloc" (Choukri 1995: 13). In this bloc, societies are now composed of disenchanted and free individuals, not communities, based on economic rationality, a complex system of state relations and social forces such as the global feminist movement. In this new configuration, all strategies have to be global and therefore, if social forces want to have a place in such an order, they must think globally.

The language of human rights is a part of this broader picture, the global scene and the politics of modernization. Feminists play a role in this scene even though it is not always clear where they fit in the actual process of globalization. Is the feminist movement reinforcing the individualization process which contributes to the disembededness of social relations or is it a force which can alter such process while keeping its most progressive elements? Politics has become an abstract system which excludes people. According to Choukri (1995: 28)[5] "civil society organisations are part and parcel of actors' attempts to re-embed abstract politics in social life". Thus, the idea of a politics of women's rights as human rights also seems to be a good case study for a broader discussion about the direction of global politics today.

First, this paper will look at the specific context from which to understand the work of MATCH and the CQFD involving women's rights as human rights. Second, it will present the work of MATCH and of the CQFD. I will not provide a detailed history of both organisations[6], but rather concentrate on a review of their policy work and projects dealing with women's rights as human rights and assess, more generally, the potential but also the problems emerging from a praxis of women's rights as human rights. To conclude, I will discuss briefly the general context that links women's rights, human rights and development, that is, the dynamics of global politics.

The Context

The development of a global feminist movement

Experiences of past international meetings, including the United Nations conferences on women in Mexico (1975), Copenhagen (1980) or Nairobi (1985), have led feminists such as Charlotte Bunch to believe that feminism had to go beyond a naive and classist view of sisterhood.[7] Global feminism had to incorporate issues such as absolute poverty, structural adjustment, international capitalism and racism into its analyses and strategies for change. Feminism had to deal with the challenge posed at the United Nations conference for women in Copenhagen in 1980: "to talk feminism to a woman who has no water, no food and no home is to talk nonsense".[8]

Since then, the emergence of a movement raising questions about the androcentric approaches to development based on economic rationality and efficiency, also led to criticism which forced international organisations to start taking women's needs into consideration within their programmes and projects. Groups like DAWN (Development Alternatives for Women in a New Era) have shown that it is not enough to add women and to stir them into development projects, but that they need alternative frameworks of development in order to improve the situation of women from the South.[9]

Gradually, the need to address women's issues from a global perspective became very important in order to understand the ways in which the multiple aspects of women's lives were connected and, in particular, the aspects of their struggles. The emergence of a global feminist approach, mainly formulated by North American feminists, also stressed the necessity to address or explore issues that were not seen as development ones, i.e. those related to sexuality, violence against women and sexual slavery. But how could women be integrated into development projects and programmes if they were being beaten, raped, exploited, thus not even recognized as human beings to begin with? These kinds of fundamental questions contributed to linking global feminism to development. By focussing on violence against women globally, feminists were then led to address an element common in all women - their need to be treated as human beings.

However, the link between global feminism and the development community has not always been so clear. A gender and development framework which has evolved from the latter community has helped address questions about economic and political structures. It also allowed for a re-examination of social structures, a possible transformation of the sexual division of labour, and the promotion of the rights for women to own land and have access to credit. According to Carolyn Hansen-Anderson, while work is being done to incorporate gender in socio-economic rights, less is being done for civil and political rights (Hansen-Anderson 1993:119). But it does seem that gender justice is now recognized as "an essential component of the linkage between human rights and democratic development" (Gillis & Dias 1993:4), especially since the 1993 conference on human rights in Vienna.

One of the main actors promoting women's rights as human rights internationally, has been the Centre for Women's Global Leadership, founded in 1991 by Charlotte Bunch. She also created the Women's Global Leadership Institute, the goal of which is to develop strategies that will link women's rights to human rights (Bunch 1993: 146). Every year the Centre holds the "16 Days of Activism Against Gender Violence", which starts November 25, the International Day Against Violence Against Women, and continues until December 10, International Human Rights Day (Bunch 1993: 146-7). In 1992, the Institute also launched a petition campaign which asked the General Assembly of the United Nations during the 1993 Vienna Conference on Human Rights to recognize women's human rights, and that gender-based discrimination as a violation of women's human rights required immediate attention. More than 150,000 signatures were brought to the UN by Bunch and her colleagues (Bunch 1993: 147; Tomasevski 1993: 135).

It is worth mentioning that the final text of the conference does mention the rights of women as a priority for governments and for the UN. It condemns violence against women in the public and in the private sphere as well as recognizing that sexual harassment, exploitation and sexual slavery, access to proper health services and family planning are human rights issues. (Centre international des droits de la personne et du développement démocratique 1993b: 1). In its plan of action, the conference also adopted an International Declaration on the Elimination of Violence Against Women as it had been proposed by the Canadian delegation, as a demand coming from the NGO community and written in consultation with the latter (Canada. Affaires extérieures et Commerce extérieur 1993: 4; Centre international MATCH 1993b: 6; Connors 1994: 198; Pypops 1993b: 26; Wade 1993: 2). The Conference also created the position of Special Rapporteur on Violence Against Women. Thus, the Vienna Conference seems to have been a culminating point for feminist human rights and development activists.

Some theoretical issues arising from a politics of women's rights as human rights

While the context we have just described provides a more specific understanding of the praxis of women's rights as human rights globally, a certain number of theoretical debates which have arisen from the global feminist approach are also worth mentioning. They structure the way in which activists address women's rights as human rights and how they are dealt with in practice by NGOs.

These issues are first, the fact that a White qua essentialist Western feminist point of view within the global feminist movement undermines the understanding of the way in which all women are constructed within social systems of class, race, language, ethnicity, nationality, and culture.

As noted by most White Western feminists in the human rights community, Third World feminists have often criticized the fact that White women take for granted that their concerns are shared worldwide. However, for Hilary Charlesworth, among others, "while no monolithic 'women's point of view' can be assumed, it is [also] important to acknowledge commonalities across cultures." (Charlesworth 1994:63). While no one seems to dispute that there are commonalities amongst women, it seems obvious that White Western feminists have great difficulty accepting that all women are constructed through social systems defined in terms of class, race, ethnicity, language, nationality and culture, including the white anglo-saxon culture. In fact, the debate here is about theorizing women's experience, while White Western feminists may have a tendency to reduce theory to strategy. Should feminists take an essentialist or a contextualist point of view? This question is not answered in any satisfactory way when emphasizing women's commonalities or differences. Clearly, more theory is needed if there is going to be a better understanding of the use of the human rights framework to address issues universal to women, such as violence.

Second, most Western feminists also use the private/public distinction which they universalize to all societies while others, such as Maila Stivens, consider that such categories are of a particular Western point of view (quoted by Charlesworth, 1992:198)[10]. Stivens proposes instead that we expand our notion of politics in order to address women's subordination. Here, feminists universalize even more the already universal while others seem to promote, once again, a more contextualized approach to the issue. This has an impact on the praxis of women's groups and whether they will act at the international and/or the national levels. The legal approach will privilege the universal basis of the private/public distinction in order to call for action, while the more anthropological look will propose to analyse how politics work. The latter reveal again the importance of the context, while feminist legal activists seem to emphasize the universality of patriarchy, which may unconsciously lead to a non-critical attitude on the part of feminists toward the actual process of global modernization.

A last concern within the feminist human rights community, which has more to do with theories of human rights per se, is that until now the different generations of rights have been based on a male "human rights" principle (Charlesworth 1995: 106; Wright 1992: 241). According to Charlesworth, "the three generations have in common the exclusion of the experiences of women" (Charlesworth 1992: 106). As Wright also points out, "the division between civil and political, or economic and social rights, is a false division. Both categories of rights privilege individuals who are constructed as male" (Wright 1992: 264). According to some, none of these generations of rights then address the public/private division and how it affects the capacity of women to be full citizens (Charlesworth 1992; Sullivan 1995). This may be an exaggerated and even biased criticism given the fact that some women's issues have been debated within the language of human rights. For Andrew Byrnes, "it is clear that attention is given to women who are victims of classical human rights violations (...). For example, issues of discrimination on the basis of sex, torture or arbitrary imprisonment of women, and practices of particular importance for women (such as trafficking women, forced prostitution and female genital mutilation) have a place on the agenda of "mainstream" bodies" (Byrnes 1992: 229). However, according to Charlesworth, "the most pervasive harm against women tends to occur with the inner sanctum of the private realm, within the family" (Charlesworth 1995: 106). It is generally a space, as she comments, "outside the scope of both national laws and international human rights laws" (Ibid.). It is not surprising then, that a politics of women's rights as human rights proposes to challenge the private/public distinction, particularly using the issue of violence against women. For Charlotte Bunch, there is a need for a feminist transformation of human rights by "looking first at the violations of women's lives and then asking how the human rights concept can change to be more responsive to women" (Bunch 1990: 496). Bunch calls for a woman-centered stance and refuses "to wait for permission from some authority to determine what is or is not a human rights issue" (Bunch 1990: 497).

Bunch calls for a feminist transformation of the human rights concept, while there is an ambiguity she does not address in her criticism with regards to the use of the terms 'women's rights as human rights' or 'women's human rights'. These expressions, according to Andrew Byrnes, are used extensively but they are never defined properly (Byrnes 1992: 215). Byrnes suggests that women's rights violations, for example, would refer to "gender-specific" violations, while the term women's human rights in the context of violence would recognize that "the violations are not gender-specific and men are, or could, equally well be victims of essentially similar violations" (ibid.). Again, the terms need to be more fully clarified in order to broaden our understanding of human rights and to ask how this concept can be more responsive to women.

This last comment ends our extremely broad overview of how feminism, development and human rights issues came to meet. It is worth recalling that for feminists, the possibility of a politics of women's rights as human rights is grounded in the women's movement and its attempt to address women's issues by focussing on what unites women while recognizing, sometimes not without some difficulty, their differences and diversities. The emphasis on the right to development in this context becomes problematic to feminists insofar as it appears to put states and national needs before women's needs. But for others, the concern is the context in which women's rights are promoted. For a more global understanding of women's issues, I would also argue that feminists have to investigate more fully the relationship between global feminism, national contexts and the global politics of modernization. Such an exercise may provide important insights for a better understanding of the context and of the way in which it also contributes to the formation of women's issues.

Like Bunch, feminists in Canada and Québec did not wait until the 1993 conference in Vienna to start addressing women's issues as human rights issues. Organisations such as MATCH International Centre and the Comité Québécois Femmes et Développement have been active in defining a politics of women's rights as human rights in the context of the right to development, since the late eighties. It is the story of such a praxis at MATCH and at the CQFD that we will now turn to, in light of the above discussion and the debates that it raises.

Women's Rights as Human Rights at MATCH

A brief analysis of the organisation's mandate

MATCH was established in 1976-1977 in the aftermath of the United Nations International Women's Year conference in Mexico. It was founded by two Canadians, Norma Walmsley and Suzanne Johnson, in their effort to give support through funding or services to Third World women (Cardinal *et.al*, 1993: 410). MATCH was one of the first organisations that attempted to match "the needs and resources of Canadian women with the needs and resources of women in the South. It is an international development agency run 'by and for women' in the belief that only through global solidarity will women's lives truly improve" (MATCH's Brochure 1994). Before MATCH became explicitly feminist, it committed itself to fund women's projects from a development point of view. It meant solidarity more than economic rationality but without escaping the pitfalls of neo-patrimonialism, i.e. clientelism and hierarchical forms of management, even though MATCH was concentrating on the needs of women.

In 1987, MATCH underwent an important review by its main funder, the Canadian International Development Agency (CIDA), and was asked to re-evaluate its *raison d'être* (Cardinal *et al.* 1993: 412). According to CIDA, other development agencies were integrating women into their programmes and working more and more with Third World women. Why would MATCH continue as it did, since it was no longer needed as a leader linking women and development. Feminists within the organisation took this opportunity to promote an explicitly feminist vision of development. MATCH had witnessed the emergence of feminist groups in the Third World and after a process of consultation with their overseas partners, the organisation decided that its new role would be to work towards the building of a global women's movement, linking women's groups globally. As of 1988, then, MATCH decided to define itself as "a Canadian-based women's organization committed with our Third World sisters, to a feminist vision of development ... the eradication of all forms of injustice, particularly the exploitation and marginalization of women" (MATCH, Philosophy and Mission Statement, 1988).

In 1994, six years later, MATCH's philosophy and mission statement are still consistent with their original reformulation while perhaps being less radical and anticipatory. They now read as follows: "MATCH International Centre is a women's organization guided by a feminist vision of sustainable development which recognizes the diverse realities of women and respects their efforts at self-determination" (MATCH's Brochure, 1994).

MATCH focusses its work on three major themes built into three programmes: violence against women, women and development and words of women. These programmes provide conditions for more long-term development and for the funding of projects from a feminist perspective. More specifically, through programme work planned and executed by Third World and Canadian women's groups, MATCH attempts to contribute to the development of networks, linking women's groups in Canada and in the Third World, providing gender training where needed, and addressing issues not debated by the Canadian international development community (Cardinal *et.al* 1993: 419; King et Parikh 1990: 1, 3).

Linking violence against women, development and human   rights

Violence against women is one of the programmes at MATCH from which a praxis of women's rights as human rights has evolved in collaboration with other women's groups, such as the Centre for Women's Global Leadership (USA), and the Association de lutte contre les violences faites aux femmes (ALVF-Cameroun), to name a few. The programme, designed for English-speaking groups at first, was initiated by Tracy Heffernan in 1988, then programme officer at MATCH. A French component was added in 1989-90 under the supervision and leadership of Annette Pypops, also a programme officer at MATCH until 1995. Pypops worked, at the beginning of the programme, in collaboration with Marie-Louise Etéki, a feminist leader from Cameroon.

The programme on violence against women, established in 1988, grew out of a consultation with MATCH's partners both in the Third World and Canada. At first, when organized for an English speaking community including Spanish-speaking groups, it involved three components: "the funding of small projects related to violence, a series of workshops examining the global dimension of violence, and a resource kit based on submissions from both Canadian and Third World groups working on th[e] issue" (Cardinal *et.al* 1993: 422). When the French component was added to the programme, linking groups working on the issue of violence against women across Francophone Africa also became a priority. To date, the violence against women programme at MATCH gives its financial support to projects in Francophone and Anglophone Africa, Asia, the Caribbean and Latin America. They range from "implementing sensitization campaigns, awareness-raising activities, assertiveness and para-legal training, popular theatre, and action-research" (MATCH's brochure).

At the time of its inception, the underlying understanding behind the violence against women programme was that violence against women is a development issue; that women need to fight violence through coalition building and networking, that they have to build a global feminist movement. By linking violence to development, feminists at MATCH were showing the need to transform the development process into one which is more aware of women's vulnerability to specific forms of violence. The focus was also on supporting the ways in which women were organising and fighting back. Women's right to security became important to feminists at MATCH, even though development agencies, such as CIDA, did not quite understand the importance of linking violence and development. Meanwhile, Third World women's groups were insisting that it was the most devastating problem for them and that, globally, it was the major obstacle to their full participation in the economic, social and political life of their countries (King & Parikh 1990: 4).

Feminists at MATCH were inspired by the work of Charlotte Bunch and her ideas about the necessity of working globally. In 1990, she gave a presentation to the members of the organization at its thirteenth general assembly. It was clear then that for Bunch, violence against women had to be addressed as a human rights issue. Two years later, in 1992, women at MATCH argued that "only when women are free to enjoy the full measure of their human rights, free from threat of violence, will they be able to become fully active and equal participants in the process of development" (MATCH, Human rights and violence against women, May 3, 1992). As a result, the Board of Directors of MATCH adopted a resolution that,

> reaffirm[ed] the mandate and commitment of MATCH International Centre to the recognition of all forms of violence against women as a violation of fundamental rights. MATCH International Centre is pledged to working with its partners to create an awareness of the global violence against women, to work toward its elimination, and to secure the practical enjoyment of human rights and fundamental freedoms for women everywhere. (MATCH, Human rights and violence against women, May 3, 1992).

Since 1992, MATCH has been working on the issue of violence against women from a perspective of linking women's rights, development and human rights. Among its activities, MATCH, in collaboration with the Centre for Global Women's Leadership and other groups, has been involved in promoting women's rights in anticipation of the Vienna Conference on Human Rights in 1993. MATCH became committed to increase its effort in order to see the principle implemented (Ramkhalawansingh 1993: 3). For example, the organisation joined the campaign lauched by the Women's Global Leadership

Institute for 16 days of activism to sensitize the public against violence against women (Centre international MATCH 1993a: 5). Annette Pypops represented MATCH at the Vienna Conference where she also participated in the organisation of an International Tribunal on the violations of women's rights. MATCH was also involved in lobbying the Canadian government to get the United Nations General Assembly to adopt a declaration against violence against women, as mentioned in the introduction.   Since Vienna, MATCH has worked to define more specifically its perspective on human rights and development. Its latest draft statement on the subject takes its principles directly from Charlotte Bunch's work and calls for a feminist transformation of human rights while recognizing that a holistic perspective on human rights is needed, "one that includes the realities of women as well as men" (MATCH's Perspective on Human Rights and Development 1995, draft). According to the women at MATCH, such a perspective must include an understanding of women's rights as political and civil rights; of women's rights as socio-economic rights; of women's rights and the Law; and of a feminist transformation of human rights. This last statement summarizes the evolution of MATCH's approach to women's rights as human rights since 1987.

MATCH and global feminism

MATCH's politics has evolved from an understanding that something was fundamentally wrong with the fact that development agencies were not linking violence as a development issue to a praxis of women's rights as human rights. In its latest declaration, MATCH recognizes that the expansion of the concept of human rights to be more responsive to women can be applied to any issue, but the organisation has chosen to focus on violence and family crimes, such as forced marriage and female genital mutilation (MATCH's Perspective on Human Rights and Development 1995, draft).

Clearly, MATCH wants to be considered a leader in forging a political programme for struggling globally against violence in all its forms. Its programme is clearly drawn up from a global feminist perspective. However, it is not clear how the organisation applies this holistic human rights approach to its other programmes. More analysis is needed here.

MATCH had also committed itself to promoting a different kind of relationship with its Third World partners, one that went beyond the funder/recipient approach (King & Parikh 1990: 4). It is also not clear whether, and, if so, in what ways the organization's way of functioning avoided the problems of clientelism or neopatrimonial forms of relationship between women's groups. It would be important to look more carefully at the importance this debate took on within MATCH and the NGO community. Most organisations are structured within the confines of the development community and of the dependent relationship with CIDA.

I would suggest that the dependency of MATCH on CIDA probably limits its capacity to go beyond the funder/recipient relationship, despite its global feminist framework. Ultimately, the way development agencies inform the structures of women's groups may limit the promotion of a global feminist politics. Since women's groups are very much concerned with the objective of building a global women's movement but perhaps not concerned enough with examining the means left to obtain such a goal, their insistence on women's commonalities may be, unconsciously, a way of avoiding such important issues as clientelism, democratic process and organisational politics.

The Comité Québécois Femmes et Développement (CQFD)

A brief history of the CQFD

The CQFD was created in 1984 as a committee of the Association Québécoise des organismes de coopération internationale (AQOCI) by five women active within the organisation. Two years after its establishment, more than forty groups and individuals were members of the group. The CQFD had also became a well-known group in the Québec women's movement for providing leadership in its fora on women and development.

The committee is the result of criticisms by feminists involved in the Québec development community about the lack of women from the South and the North in the decision-making processes. The existence of the CQFD also symbolizes the growing consciousness that women were trying to develop alternative visions of development.

The CQFD defined itself as a "forum for exchanges, of information and of expertise on questions addressing the theme of "women and development" here and in the Third world"[11]. It is also a group which "promote[s] concertation, distribution of information and consultation on activities dealing with women and development here and in the Third world"[12]. The CQFD wants to "create fora for women from the North and the South to connect and to exchange about their realities in order to promote in such a way a concrete solidarity between women from here and the Third world"[13]; "develop alternative visions of development"[14], and "make sure that NGOs will give women an important place, particularly women from the grassroots, in their programming and in their decision-making structure"[15]. Unlike MATCH, the CQFD does not fund projects or programmes.

It is a policy oriented group, concerned with addressing the exclusion of women from structures of power. The CQFD has chosen to promote means of action such as organizing discussions and exchanges, promoting strategies to define means to make sure development projects take women's experiences and women's research into account; promoting research and analysis of women's real participation in development projects as well as practices of autonomous development by women; organising consciousness-raising and educational activities; making sure that decision-making positions available within the NGO community are open to members of the CQFD.[16] The CQFD's programme may seem less ambitious than MATCH when it says it wants to build a global women's movement, but it is still nevertheless a real challenge to confront the development community as directly as the group has been doing over the past ten years.

The CQFD provides gender and development analysis to the development community,[17] emphasizing the fact that women are not involved enough in the decision-making process, as well as insisting on the necessary transformation of the relations of inequality among men and women (Comité québécois femmes et développement 1990: 4). The CQFD has also become well known for its organization of meetings with women from the South[18] and for its capacity to act as a forum for debate on the subject of women and development.

Since its inception, the CQFD has provided consistent criticism of the way in which the development process excludes women. The group has taken its message to different organisations, including the popular sector, the universities, the unions, and the Québec's women's movement, not forgetting its "parent-body", the AQOCI. As a result, in its Charter on Development, the AQOCI has recognized explicitly the important role played by women in the development of their people, and that their participation at all levels of the decision-making process is needed. The AQOCI also acknowledges that such treatment is important within the development community as well. (AQOCI 1987: 4) The CQFD has provided leadership in addressing governmental policies and their inadequacies in responding to women's strategic needs for change. The group has systematically criticized CIDA's approach to the integration of women in the development process as being too influenced by economic imperatives, whether it be structural adjustment programmes or the needs of the Canadian economy over the needs of Third World women. For Louise Chicoine, these policies force women to integrate into a development process in which they have no power (Chicoine 1993: 17). Perhaps this on-going discussion of CIDA's policies explains, in part, why the group is no longer receiving any funding from the governmental agency.

Clearly, the CQFD is playing an important role in addressing issues of power at all levels of the development community. It stresses the need for a real integration of women into the development process while also concentrating its efforts in ensuring that women from the South and the North meet in order to exchange and promote alternative visions of development.

The CQFD and its praxis of women's rights as human rights

In keeping with its mandate of promoting alternative visions of development, in 1990, the CQFD organised a first meeting on the theme "Women and the defense of human rights"(CQFD 1991: 3). In 1991, the committee was led to define explicitly women's rights as human rights. From then on, the group adopted a human rights framework as a means of promoting women's issues as an objective for justice and development.[19] The CQFD, "believe[s], that fundamental human rights include the right to pure air, water, the right for food, housing, health, and welfare for everybody. Those rights are denied to millions of people across the world, of which an important majority are women (Lagacé 1991: 22-23).[20] The CQFD also proposed an approach to women's rights as human rights which stresses the right to reproduction and free choice as a fundamental right for every person[21]. The group links human rights, reproductive issues and women's poverty.[22] The CQFD stresses the importance of social rights in relation to women's rights.

In 1992, the CQFD also took part in the formulation of the AQOCI's new Charter of Principles on Human Rights and Development (Charte de principes sur les droits humains et le développement) which aims at promoting an inclusive definition of human rights, addressing rights of women and men, individual and collective rights as well as the rights of peoples (AQOCI 1987,1992: 12). The document defines those rights in keeping with the existing international Charters and Declarations. However, the AQOCI's Charter does specify that women's rights mean explicitly their right to reproduction, thus confirming the CQFD's focus on socio-economic rights. Article 11 of the new Charter takes into consideration women's rights as human rights by stating that "the specific rights of women as well as systematic forms of discrimination against them calls for particular attention and promotion and defense".[23]

For the AQOCI, there is no doubt that development and human rights go together. As the preamble of the organisation's Charter states: "Relationships of inequality existing between the North and the South are an obstacle to the exercice of the fundamental rights of persons, collectivities, peoples across the world. The struggle for the full recognition of those rights and their full exercise for all human beings goes hand in hand with the instauration of a just and equitable international order" (AQOCI 1992: 11). By stressing the link between development and human rights, the AQOCI and the CQFD propose an inclusive approach to women's rights. Its framework is not essentialist in comparison with global feminism's insistence on commonalities. It leaves room for debates on inequality of power among and between men and women, and between the North and the South.

In 1992, the CQFD also defined violence against women as a violation of their human rights by keeping them from a free use of public space, and as a development issue (Chicoine 1994: 3; Mantha 1992: 6,8). As a result, the group organised an exploratory meeting on violence against women, an issue rarely discussed at the time in the development community (Lagacé 1992: 4). A year later, the group was still active and organising meetings and discussions on the theme of violence against women. Such meetings allowed the group to decide on the kind of work it would promote on the issue of violence against women within the NGO community and in collaboration with women's groups already working in Québec.

The work of the CQFD around violence against women prepared them well for attendance at the Vienna Conference on Human Rights in 1993. They did not hesitate to criticize, with the AQOCI, the Canadian government's subordination of human rights to utilitarian principles of security, stability, and competion. They insisted on the proposition according to which a global approach to human rights must include the rights of women, and the recognition that violence against women is a development and a human rights issue (AQOCI 1993: 10).

Following the Vienna Conference, the CQFD was busy with the preparation of its position for the Cairo Conference on Populations. Once again, the group demanded that the Canadian government assure the respect of fundamental rights, and that it protect women against all forms of discrimination and against all politics involving the forced control of the population (Mantha 1994: 4). Following the representation of the CQFD in the two international events mentioned above, the group participated in the process which led to the revision of Canada's foreign policy, as well as kept the debates going on violence against women by organising meetings on the topic. Among its ongoing consciousness-raising activities, the CQFD also prepared an important meeting to examine the relationship between cultural contexts and violence as well as strategies to end violence (Chicoine 1994: 4; Lagacé 1994).

The group initiated, in collaboration with the AQOCI and the Canadian Council for International Cooperation, a study of the way in which NGOs integrate women and development into their work. The study revealed that the NGO community had a limited application of the principles of equity. Policies for better access to equality and equity for women were not implemented in the development community and the latter had no strategies to end systemic discrimination. NGO's did not seem to give priority to women's issues (Cloutier 1994: 38). The study also noted that since 1986, CIDA was imposing on NGO's its own approach to the integration of women in the development process. Institutional and financial constraints from CIDA, as it is an important source of money for NGOs, left them with hardly any room to promote other visions of development (Cloutier 1994: 39-41).

The CQFD and Global feminism

This general review of the activities of the CQFD and its consistent attempts to provide an alternative vision of development reveals a group active on many fronts: local, national, international. It is involved with women's groups in Québec and in the Third World. The CQFD has also worked with MATCH in promoting gender and development approaches within the development community. It does policy work directed to the development community and the government. The CQFD does not do field work *per se* since it is done by the members of the AQOCI.

Politically, the CQFD does not seem to be informed by a global feminist approach in the same way MATCH is. For example, it does not stress the issue of commonalities amongst women the way global feminists do. The CQFD does insist on women's reproductive rights as an important component of the human rights framework, but it seems more concerned with cultural and economic contexts. However, by stimulating exchanges and solidarity amongst women without entering into the politics of clientelism and neopatrimonialism, the CQFD can be considered as working towards the building of a global women's movement, concerned with the promotion of alternative visions to development. It addresses issues of power directly, by focussing on the structures in which development takes place and excludes women.

Although the CQFD has been successful in articulating women's rights as human rights, which perhaps it did in a broader way than MATCH, its insistence on rights is no substitute for its political activism. The group seems to be more effective than MATCH in evaluating the policies of other NGOs or of the government in dealing with women. It does not limit itself to a strict "rightist" framework which global feminism can lead to by insisting on the human rights approach. In this way, the CQFD is not as pragmatic as North American feminists can be. It is more confrontational, and this may be the result of the political culture from which it emerged, i.e. the Québec context. Again, the question of context may inform different attitudes towards politics and rights which global feminist should address more comprehensively. I think that the examination of the experience of the CQFD leads to such questions, among others.

It is quite clear that the committee has become an important leader in Québec in defining a praxis of women's rights as human rights with a special emphasis on the right to development. However, given that the Canadian government has, since the spring of 1995, cut all funding to groups such as the AQOCI and the CQFD, the latter will probably be going through important revisions to its mandate and activities. MATCH seems to have survived this round of cuts, perhaps as result of the fact that it is considerably less criticial of governmental policies. MATCH also promotes small projects overseas which appear to have been spared in the last round of cuts.

Conclusion

Both MATCH and the CQFD have a praxis of women's rights as human rights. In my view, the CQFD is more concerned with the right to development, even though MATCH has linked violence against women with development. Our analysis has revealed the growing importance of such a praxis in the activities of the two groups over the years. Women's rights as human rights has been informed at MATCH by a global feminist approach, while the CQFD came to the issue through its ongoing criticism of the development process. In both cases, the human rights framework has become an important lever for more action.

However, both organisations have not yet provided examples of ways to solve problems such as clientelism, neopatrimonialism, cultural rights and relativism. The CQFD confronts these issues perhaps more directly than MATCH by insisting on a more comprehensive approach to women's issues and one focussed around the socio-economic questions. To be sure, more in-depth analysis and case studies are needed in order to address more fully the possibilities of alternative visions and praxis of development and of the expansion of the human rights concept.

I would suggest that such work also needs to be accompanied by a broader discussion of the dynamics of global politics. It structures the context in which NGOs attempt to re-embed abstract politics in social life. The global context imposes a pattern of modernization which groups like the CQFD seem to be aware of. Yet, it is not clear that NGOs succeed in reversing such logic which is based on economic rationality, not women and peoples. How do they escape the pitfalls of a vision in which women are also becoming free and disenchanted individuals, more autonomous, but depoliticized, as they are no longer able to identify with a community? Is this the only pattern to development and modernity? I think that much of the confrontation between feminists from the North and the South reside in their difficulty in answering this question, which is also connected to their understanding of women's experiences globally. I would suggest that it is also by an ongoing analysis of the relationship between the politics of modernization and the capacity of the feminist movement to contribute to re-embed abstract politics, that is, the abstract individual in social life, that the human rights approach in relation to women's rights will also gradually become more successful. It is an important challenge since its notion of the individual stems from an individualistic vision of "society".

Notes

1. Amongst which we find Le Cinquième Monde, Développement et Paix, Entraide missionnaire, SUCO, CIDMAA.

2. In 1979, the United Nations adopted the *Convention on the elimination of all forms of discrimination against women* (Kerr 1993a: 5; Tomasevski 1993: 46). In 1992, the latest recommendation to be added to the *Convention* by the United Nations Committee responsible for its promotion is recommendation number 19 which states explicitly that there is a link between violence against women and systematic forms of discrimination based on gender (Connors 1994: 197). According to Hilary Charlesworth (1994: 64), recommendation 19 apparently recognizes the importance of the private sphere as one in which women are oppressed.

3. In 1980, the United Nations General Assembly recognized the particular vulnerability of women refugees and called upon the States to protect their right to security. According to Tomasevski, such mention of women's right to security contributes to the possibility of addressing the rights of women refugees as human rights (Tomasevski 1993: 78).

4. Recommendation 14 formulated by the United Nations committee responsable for the promotion of CEDAW requires the full eradication of genital mutilation done to women and the elimination of all forms of cultural, economic or other pressures allowing the perpetuation of such traditional practices (Connors 1994: 197).

5. See also Anthony Giddens (1990).

6. For such details see Linda Cardinal, Annette Costigan and Tracy Heffernan (1994) as well as Geadah, Yolande (1988).

7. See Charlotte Bunch (1985).

8. See Cardinal *et al.,* op cit., p.416.

9. See Peggy Antrobus (1991); Sen & Grown (1987); Anita Anand (1984); Development Dialogue (1982).

10. See Maila Stivens (1989).

11. "Un lieu d'échange, d'information et d'expertise sur les questions touchant au thème de "femmes et développement" ici et dans le Tiers Monde" (CQFD/AQOCI 1984: 3).

12. "de favoriser la concertation et la diffusion de l'information et la concertation sur les activités concernant les femmes et le développement ici et dans le Tiers Monde" (Ibid.).

13. "de créer des lieux de contact entre les femmes du Nord et celles du Sud afin d'échanger sur nos réalités respectives et ainsi favoriser une solidarité concrète entre femmes d'ici et dans le Tiers Monde" (Ibid.).

14. Ibid.

15. "de s'assurer que nos organismes de développement accordent une place plus importante aux femmes, particulièrement les femmes à la base, dans leur programmation et dans leur structure décisionnelle" (Ibid.).

16. Ibid.

17. For an extensive description and analysis of such approach see *Un autre genre de développement. Un guide pratique sur les rapports femmes-hommes dans le développement*, prepared by the Conseil canadien pour la coopération internationale, MATCH and the Association québécoise des organismes de coopération internationale, Ottawa, août 1991; see also Chicoine, Louise (1993).

18. According to some analysts and members of the CQFD, "elles ont permis de tisser des liens concrets entre femmes d'ici et d'ailleurs, et plusieurs initiatives se sont engagées dans la foulée de ces rencontres" (Paiement 1993b: 7).

19. "Les droits des femmes, ce sont aussi des droits humains! Voilà l'approche de travail que nous avons choisie de privilégier au Comité Québécois Femmes et Développement (CQFD) pour les prochaines années. Peut-être qu'ainsi la promotion des femmes n'apparaîtra plus comme une liste de `revendications' mais comme un objectif de justice et de développement" (in Lafleur 1991: 32).

20. "Nous croyons que les droits humains fondamentaux incluent le droit à l'air et à l'eau pure, le droit à la nourriture, au logement, à la santé et au bien-être pour tout être humain. Ces droits sont niés à des millions de personnes à travers le monde dont la majorité écrasante sont des femmes" (Lagacé 1991: 22-23).

21. Dans sa *Déclaration Femmes, populations et environnement- Version commentée*, le CQFD stipule, au point 4, que: "Le droit à la santé reproductive et au libre choix est un droit fondamental pour toute personne. Les femmes sont constamment lésées dans ce droit par les politiques de contrôle des populations. La capacité des femmes de déterminer si et quand elles auront des enfants est un pré-requis pour leur santé reproductive, leur auto-détermination et leur pouvoir sur leur propre vie. Toute tentative de priver les femmes de leur choix reproductif et de l'information nécessaire pour exercer ce choix en toute connaissance de cause est condamnable" (CQFD 1992: 5).

22. "Au Nord comme au Sud, les femmes sont aliénées de leur droit fondamental à l'égalité, non seulement par des conditions structurelles qui les discriminent mais par la maternité même. Les sociétés, même celles que l'on dit modernes, sont ainsi faites qu'elles ne permettent pas à celles qui produisent la vie d'être citoyennes à part entière. Cet acte d'engendrer, loin d'être reconnu socialement et pris en compte dans les priorités politiques, implique des responsabilités qui accentuent la pauvreté des femmes"(Lagacé et Mantha 1992: 6).

23. "Les droits spécifiques des femmes ainsi que la discrimination systématique exercée à leur égard exigent un travail particulier de promotion et de défense" (AQOCI 1992: 16).

Bibliography

Agence canadienne de développement international (ACDI). 1993. *Les femmes, les droits de la personne et la démocratie: des liens cruciaux.* Ottawa: ACDI.

Agence canadienne de développement international (ACDI). 1984. "Les femmes et le développpement ", *Éléments de la stratégie canadienne d'aide publique au développement.* Ottawa: Approvisionnement et services, pp. 32-33.

Anand, Anita. 1984. "Rethinking women and development: The case for feminism". 1984 *CUSO Journal*, pp. 18-23.

Antrobus, Peggy. 1991. "Development alternatives with women", in *The future for women in development: Voices from the South.* Proceedings of the Association for Women in Development Colloquium. Ottawa: The North-South Institute, pp. 74-86.

Ashworth, Georgina. 1993. "Preparing for the millennium: challenge and change", in Joanna Kerr, ed., *Ours by right. Women's Rights As Human Rights.* London: Zed Books/Ottawa: North-South Institute, pp. 150-152.

Association québécoise des organismes de coopération internationale (AQOCI). 1995. *Les droits sociaux, économiques et culturels et le droit au développement.* Présentation aux Consultations annuelles du Ministère des Affaires étrangères et du commerce international en vue de la 51e session de la Commission des droits de l'homme des Nations Unies, Ottawa (18 janvier, 1995).

Association québécoise des organismes de coopération internationale (AQOCI). 1993. *Les droits humains et la démocratie.* Révision de la politique étrangère canadienne (Montréal, décembre). Montréal: AQOCI.

Association québécoise des organismes de coopération internationale (AQOCI). 1992. *Charte de principes sur les droits humains et le développement.* Montréal: AQOCI.

Bauer, Jan. 1994. *Rapport de la réunion d'experts des ONG consacrée au*

Mandat du Rapporteur spécial sur la violence à l'égard des femmes, ses causes et ses conséquences. Montréal: CIDPDD.

Bunch, Charlotte et Niamh Reilly, eds. 1994. *Demanding Accountability. The Global Campaign and the Vienna Tribunal for Women's Human Rights.* New York: United Nations Developement Fund for Women (UNIFEM)/New Jersey: Centre for Women's Global Leadership.

Bunch, Charlotte. 1995. "Transforming Human Rights from a Feminist Perspective" in Julie Peters and Andrea Wolper, eds., *Women's Rights, Human Rights.* New York: Routledge, pp. 11-18.

Bunch, Charlotte. 1993. "Organizing for women's human rights globally", in Joanna Kerr, ed., *Ours by Right. Women's Rights As Human Rights.* London: Zed Books/Ottawa: North-South Institute, pp. 141-149.

Bunch, Charlotte. 1991a. "Communication", *Violence faite aux femmes: une question de développement et des droits de la personne.* (Ottawa, 9 mars 1991). Ottawa: Centre International MATCH et la Division de l'intégration de la femme dans le développement de l'ACDI, pp. 29-37.

Bunch, Charlotte. 1991b. "Violence against women: global perspectives", in Laura Lederer, ed., *A Wind of Change: Funders Working to End Violence Against Women: Conference Highlights of the National Network of Women's Funders (NNWF) Seventh Annual Conference.* Chicago (April 18-21). Minnesota: NNWF, pp. 6-8.

Bunch, Charlotte. 1991c. "Women's rights as human rights", in Centre for Women's Global Leadership, ed., *Women, Violence and Human Rights.* New Jersey: Centre for Women's Global Leadership, pp. 14-21.

Bunch, Charlotte. 1990a. "Women's rights as human rights: toward a re-vision of human rights". 1990 *Human Rights Quarterly* 12(4), pp. 486-498.

Bunch, Charlotte. 1990b. "La violence contre les femmes s'inscrit dans un contexte mondial de violation des droits de la personne". 1990 *Bulletin MATCH* hiver, p. 5.

Bunch, Charlotte. 1987. *Passionate Politics: Feminist Theory in Action.* New York: St. Martin's Press.

Bunch, Charlotte. 1985. *Feminism in the '80s: Bringing the Global Home.* Book III, Colorado: Antelope Publications.

Byrnes, Andrew. 1992. "Women, feminism and international human rights law-- methodological myopia, fundamental flaws or meaningful marginalisation? Some current issues". 1992 *Australian Year Book of International Law* 12, pp. 205-240.

Canada. Affaires extérieures et Commerce extérieur, *Rapport concernant la Conférence sur les droits de l'Homme des Nations Unies.* Vienne, 14-25 juin 1993.

Cardinal, Linda, Annette Costigan and Tracy Heffernan. 1994. "Working Towards a Feminist Vision of Development", in Huguette Dagenais and Micheline Piché, eds., *Women and Development/Femmes et Développement.* Montréal, McGill-Queen's, pp. 408-426.

Centre for Women's Global Leadership. 1992. *1991 Women's Leadership Institute Report: Women, Violence and Human Rights.* Douglas College: Rutgers University.

Centre international MATCH. 1995. *MATCH's Perspective On Human Rights and Development: Draft.* Ottawa: MATCH.

Centre international MATCH. 1994a. *Programme 1994-95.* Ottawa: MATCH.

Centre international MATCH. 1994b. "Conférence internationale sur la population et le développement". 1994 *Bulletin MATCH* automne, p. 6.

Centre international MATCH. 1993a. "Programme pour 1993-1994", *Bulletin MATCH* été, pp. 4-7.

Centre international MATCH. 1993b. "Le pouvoir des milliers de voix (Vienne, Autriche)", *Bulletin MATCH* automne, p. 6.

Centre international MATCH. 1992. *Human Rights and Violence Against Women: MATCH's Mandate.* Ottawa: MATCH.

Centre international MATCH. 1991. *Consultation internationale et rencontre de planification sur la violence faite aux femmes: Rapport Final.* (Ottawa,

18-22 mars 1991). Ottawa: MATCH.

Charlesworth, Hilary. 1995. "Human Rights as Men's Rights", in Julie Peters and Andrea Wolper, eds., *Women Rights, Human Rights*. New York: Routledge, pp. 103-114.

Charlesworth, Hilary. 1994. "What are Women's International Human Rights?", in Rebecca J. Cook, ed., *Human Rights of Women. National and International Perspectives*. Philadelphia: University of Pennsylvania Press, pp. 58-84.

Charlesworth, Hilary. 1992. "The public/private distinction and the right to development in international law". 1992 *Australian Year Book of International Law* 12, pp. 190-204.

Chicoine, Louise. 1994. *La violence faite aux femmes au delà des cultures au delà des frontières*. Compte-rendu de la rencontre du CQFD (Montréal, 19 avril 1994). Montreal: CQFD.

Chicoine, Louise. 1993. *Programme de formation sur mesure. Genre et développement*. Bilan et perspectives (Montréal, jeudi 11 novembre). Montréal: CQFD.

Choukri, Ezzedine. 1995. "Encounters of Civilizations or Global Restructuring? The Concept of World Hegemony Revisited". (forthcoming in *Millenium*, 1995), 33 pages.

Cloutier, Luce. 1994. *Les politiques femmes et développement dans quelques organisations de coopération internationale (OCI)*. Montréal: CQFD et CCCI.

Comité québécois femmes et développement (CQFD). 1994. *Rapport d'activités 1993-1994*. Montréal: CQFD, AQOCI.

Comité québécois femmes et développement (CQFD). 1993. *Rapport d'activités 1992-1993*. Montréal: CQFD, AQOCI.

Comité québécois femmes et développement (CQFD). 1992. *Déclaration: Femmes, populations et environnement*. Version Commentée. Montréal: CQFD, AQOCI, juin 1992.

Comité québécois femmes et développement (CQFD). 1991. *Rapport d'activités 1990-1991*. Montréal: CQFD, AQOCI.

Comité québécois femmes et développement (CQFD). 1990. "Une question de genre...", Inter-Mondes. 1990 *Journal de l'Association québécoise des organismes de coopération internationale (AQOCI)* 6(2), p. 4.

Connors, Jane. 1994. "Gouvernement measures to confront violence Against Women", in Miranda Davies, ed., *Women and Violence. Realities and Responses Worldwide*. London et New Jersey: Zed Books, pp. 182-199.

Cook, Rebecca J., ed. 1994a. *Human Rights of Women. National and International Perspectives*. Philadelphia: University of Pennsylvania Press.

Cook, Rebecca J. 1994b. "State responsibility for violations of women's human rights". *Harvard Human Rights Journal* 7 (spring), pp. 125-175.

Davies, Miranda. 1994. *Women and Violence. Realities and Responses Worldwide*. London: Zed Books.

Development Dialogue, "Another Development with Women", 1982, no. 1/2.

Eisler, R. 1987. "Human rights: towards an integrated theory for action", 1987 *Human Rights Quarterly* 9, pp. 287-308.

Friedman, Elisabeth. 1995. "Women's Human Rights: The Emergence of a Movement", in Julie Peters and Andrea Wolper, eds., *Women's Rights, Human Rights*. New York: Routledge, pp. 18-36.

Geadah, Yolande (Coordonnatrice du CQFD). 1988. *Bilan des réalisations du Comité québécois femmes et développement (CQFD) depuis sa formation en 1984*. Montréal: AQOCI.

Giddens, Anthony. 1990. *The Consequences of Modernity*. Berkeley: Stanford University Press.

Goldberg, Pamela et Nancy Kelly. 1993. "International human rights and violence against women". 1993 *Harvard Human Rights Journal* 6 (spring), pp. 195-209.

King, Cynthia et Rita Parikh. 1990. "Avec ses nouveaux programmes, MATCH hisse les étendards du féminisme mondial". 1990 *Bulletin MATCH* hiver, pp. 1, 3-4.

Lafleur, Guy. 1991. "Les droits des femmes sont aussi des droits humains", Inter-Mondes. 1991 *Journal de l'Association des organismes de coopération internationale (AQOCI)* 6(4), pp. 32-33.

Lagacé, Hélène. 1994. *Lettre d'invitation à une journée de réflexion organisée par le CQFD: «La violence faite aux femmes, au delà des cultures, au delà des frontières»* (Montréal, 19 avril 1994). Montréal: CQFD, AQOCI.

Lagacé, Hélène. 1992. *Mettre fin à la violence envers les femmes. Actes de la rencontre exploratoire du CQFD* (Montréal, 20 mars). Montréal: CQFD, AQOCI.

Lagacé, Hélène. 1991. "Femmes, environnement et développement: compte-rendu de Miami", *Notes sur l'éducation au développement (AQOCI)* décembre 1991, pp. 22-23.

Lagacé, Hélène. 1990. "Un programme de formation sur l'analyse des rôles homme-femme dans le développement", 1990 *Inter-Mondes. Journal de l'Association québécoise des organismes de coopération internationale (AQOCI)* 5(4), p. 5.

Lagacé, Hélène et Chantal Mantha. 1995. "Quelle place la politique étrangère canadienne réserve-t-elle aux droits de la personne?", 1995 *Inter-Mondes. Journal de l'Association québécoise des organismes de coopération internationale (AQOCI)* 10(3), pp. 6-7.

Lagacé, Hélène et Chantal Mantha. 1992. "La pauvreté au féminin pluriel", 1992 *Inter-Mondes. Journal de l'Association québécoise des organismes de coopération internationale (AQOCI)* 7(3), pp. 6-8.

Larbi, Madonna. 1992. "Quelques mots sur MATCH", *Genre, développement et droits humains. Atelier conjoint MATCH-KARMIKA* (New Delhi, 25-30 novembre). Ottawa: Centre international MATCH.

Mantha, Chantal. 1994. "Les droits des femmes. De Rio à Beijing en passant par Copenhague", 1994 *Inter-Mondes. Journal de l'Association québécoise des organismes de coopération internationale (AQOCI)* 10(1), p. 4-5.

Mantha, Chantal. 1992. "Dans la rue comme à la maison, la répression contre les femmes", 1992 *Inter-Mondes. Journal de l'Association québécoise des organismes de coopération internationale (AQOCI)* avril, pp. 6-8.

Mantha, Chantal. 1991. "Le contrôle des naissances dans les pays du sud: promotion des droits des femmes ou intérêts du Nord", Inter-Mondes. 1991 *Journal de l'Association québécoise des organismes de coopération internationale (AQOCI)* 7(1), pp. 6-8.

Mantha, Chantal. 1990. "L'ajustement structurel: à l'origine d'une inégalité croissante entre les sexes", 1990 *Notes sur l'éducation au développement de l'AQOCI* 5(5), pp. 22-23.

Mantha, Chantal. 1989. "Pas de développement dans la peur", Inter-Mondes. 1989 *Journal de l'Association québécoise des organismes de coopération internationale (AQOCI)* 5(1), p. 7.

Organisation des Nations Unies (ONU). 1982. *Convention sur l'élimination de toutes les formes de discrimination à l'égard des femmes.* Ottawa: La Division des droits de la personne, Secrétariat d'État, 1982[80].

Organisation des Nations Unies (ONU). 1993. *Quatrième Conférence mondiale sur les femmes.* Beijing (Chine) 4-15 septembre 1995: "La conférence doit fixer l'ordre du jour des femmes pour le siècle prochain". New York: ONU.

Paiement, Marc-André. 1993a. "Femmes et violence en Haïti", Inter-Mondes. *Journal de l'Association québécoise des organismes de coopération internationale (AQOCI)* 9(1), p. 4.

Paiement, Marc-André. 1993b. "Les 'millieux alliés' (III): Le mouvement des femmes et la solidarité internationale", Inter-Mondes. *Journal de l'Association québécoise des organismes de coopération internationale (AQOCI)* 8(3), pp. 6-8.

Peters, Julie et Andrea Wolper, eds. 1995. *Women's Rights, Human Rights.* New York: Routledge.

Pypops, Annette. 1993a. "Le centre international MATCH", *Mettre fin à la violence faite aux femmes: Les initiatives des africaines* (Harare, Zimbabwe, 22-26 février). Ottawa: MATCH.

Pypops, Annette. 1993b. "Vienne : Une étape importante pour les femmes...", *Option Paix* 11(3-4), pp. 24-28.

Ramkhalawansingh, Ceta. 1993. "Message de la présidente", *Bulletin MATCH* été 1993, p. 3.

Raymond, Valérie. 1993. *Intervention de la Délégation du Canada sur l'égalité de condition et les droits fondamentaux de la femme devant la Grande Commission de la Conférence mondiale sur les droits de l'homme* (Vienne, le 23 juin 1993). Ottawa: Délégation du Canada.

Romany, Celina. 1993. "Women as aliens: A feminist critique of the public/private distinction in International human rights law", 1993 *Harvard Human Rights Journal* 6 (spring), pp. 87-125.

Sen, Gita & Carent Grown. 1987. *Development Crises and Alternative Visions: Third World Women's Perspectives.* New York: Monthly Review Press.

Stamatopoulou, Elissavet. 1995. "Women's Rights and the United Nations", in Julie Peters and Andrea Wolper, eds., *Women's Rights, Human Rights.* New York: Routledge, pp. 36-51.

Stivens, Maila. 1989. "Why Gender Matters in Southeast Asian Politics", 1989 *Asian Studies Review* 4, 5.

Sullivan, Donna. 1995. "The Public/Private Distinction in International Human Rights Law", in Julie Peters and Andrea Wolper, eds., *Women's Rights, Human Rights.* New York: Routledge, pp. 126-135.

Tomasevski, Katarina. 1993. *Women and Human Rights.* London: Zed Books.

Wade, M. Scott. 1993. (Directeur des politiques de bon gouvernement et de droits de la personne-ACDI), *Intervention de la Délégation du Canada sur les droits de la personne et la démocratie devant le Comité principal de la Conférence mondiale sur les droits de l'Homme.* Vienne, le 17 juin, 1993.

Waring, Marilyn. 1992. "Gender and international law: women and the right to development", 1992 *Australian Year Book of International Law* 12, pp. 177-189.

Working Group on Women's Rights. 1993. *Final Recommendations of the Working Group on Women's Rights of the NGO Forum at the World Conference on Human Rights*. Vienna, June 10-12, 1993.

Wright, Shelly. 1992. "Economic rights and social justice: a feminist analysis of some international human rights conventions". 1992 *Australian Year Book of International Law* 12, pp. 241-264.

Analysis of Various Theoretical Perspectives on Women's Rights as Human Rights and Strategies for Implementation

KATHLEEN MAHONEY[*]

Introduction

"No country in the world treats its women as well as its men."[1] Systemic and widespread inequality and discrimination, often embedded in the national laws of countries, creates double jeopardy and double standards for women from all social classes, cultures, and races, in all societies.[2]

What constitutes equality for women and how they can achieve it, are questions at the heart of the feminist legal project. Any attempt to use the legal system to combat inequality must begin with an evaluation and understanding of the relationship between equality and the sexual and social differences between women and men. But the voices of mainstream legal theory, for most of history, have been exclusively male voices.[3] The voices of women have been absent. For those familiar with the law, this fact is not surprising. All of the institutions of the law, whether they be law schools, legislatures, the judiciary, law enforcement agencies, or the bar, have been almost exclusively male up until the most recent times. As a result, laws have been made, interpreted, and enforced by men, and their explanations are creations of the male imagination.

The absence of female perceptions has left foundational reflections on the purpose, nature, and concept of law biased, incomplete, and sometimes even inept in dealing with, explaining or comprehending the reality of life for most people. But the dominant male view has been so complete and unremitting that it has become accepted as neutral and objective. Theories of human development are never more limited or limiting when their biases are invisible and feminist legal theory performs the vital service of illuminating some of the deepest biases of all.

For the past several decades, feminist legal theorists have been attempting to address theoretical bias in the midst of the massive social, economic, and

---

[*] This article was previously published in the *Brooklyn Journal of International Law*, Vol. XXI, No. 3, 1996.

cultural changes of the twentieth century. Not surprisingly, there are a variety of explanations because feminist approaches to jurisprudence and legal theory are diverse.[4] When basic societal structures previously taken for granted are themselves undergoing fundamental change, not only does rethinking the role of law in a gendered society often defy conventional legal categorization, it is surprising there is any consistency at all.

Feminist theories often overlap, and many are not yet fully formed or complete. Some are difficult to define, others tend to affect or alter one another. While they may differ in their analyses of power and in their suggested strategies of action, divisions are seldom exclusive. All seem cumulatively to grow and evolve as feminine awareness grows and develops.

The continuous ideological thread of feminist theory through time and across continents is the common understanding that male power is linked to the subjugation and servitude of women in the home. As a result, feminist theories share a much different definition of what is political than theories developed from the male perspective. Male theorists from Aristotle to Locke have always understood "political" to mean matters in the public domain. To them, the private domain, namely the home, is beyond politics.[5]

Feminist theorists, on the other hand, see the private realm as the heart of politics.[6] The most distinctive slogan of the post-1968 women's movement, "The personal is political," derives from this view.[7] To feminists of all stripes, there is little difference between the relationship of the citizen to government in exercising judgment and making laws, and the father and husband who govern from "natural" authority. One is every bit as political as the other. In this way, feminism has implicitly and explicitly constituted a new definition of what is political.

In Part II of this paper, four feminist theories of equality--liberal feminism, cultural feminism, radical feminism and post-modern feminism--are explained.[8] Their origins, development, and relevance to women's rights as human rights are discussed. Each theory has significant value for women's fight against oppression, but some are more effective and relevant than others. It is also apparent, however, that none of the theories are the whole answer or are completely discreet from one another. There appears to be a process of evolution occurring in which the remedies and applications blend.

Decisions of the Supreme Court of Canada, which since 1982 has used feminist theory more than any other court in the world, are used to explain or exemplify how some feminist arguments and theories have been translated into law.[9] These decisions provide the reader with an appreciation of how feminist theories can succeed or fail in practice, how legal arguments can be made, and the strengths and weaknesses of the different approaches.

Part III of the paper deals with women's rights as human rights in international law. It explains the international instruments designed to protect women's rights, problems associated with them, and recent attempts at reform. Part III demonstrates that strategies at the international level are theoretically grounded in the four theories discussed in Part II and evaluates and explains them.

Feminist Theories

Liberal feminism

The classic formulation of liberal feminism is found in Mary Wollstonecraft's *A Vindication of the Rights of Women*[10] and in John Stuart Mill's *The Subjection of Women*.[11] The starting point of liberal feminist theory is the understanding that women are in fact the same as men, and therefore equal to men. Women are autonomous individuals who should be as free as men to choose their own life plans and have their freedom equally respected by the state. Liberal feminists say the relationship of the state to the individual must be the same for both women and men and that the root of female subordination is in customary and legal constraints that block women's entrance into and/or success in the public world. To be equal, women must have more choices.[12]

The meaning of equality

In the legal realm, a dominant doctrinal issue discussed by early liberal feminists was how broad the scope of the equality concept should be. The legal exclusion of women from participation in public life, including in the academy, politics, and the marketplace, led liberal feminists to adopt a sex-blind posture. They believed if legislatures understood women to be similarly situated to men, they would not be able to treat women differently. As a result, they concentrated on dismantling legal barriers which prevented women from being treated like men in the public sphere. To accomplish this goal, they thought gender-neutral rules, providing equal opportunity to participate in the legal system and equal benefit of the law, would suffice. Known as the formal equality approach, early liberal feminists used it successfully to attain legislation granting women the right to vote, to hold public office, to participate in the professions, to hold, use, and enjoy property on the same basis as men during and outside of marriage, and to equal custody and guardianship of their children.[13]

One of the most important victories for formal equality was the legal challenge Canadian feminists made to their exclusion from the Senate of Canada. The case, *Edwards* v. *Attorney General of Canada*,[14] was the last in a series of cases in Great Britain, the United States, Canada,[15] and Australia[16] which challenged the fact that women were denied the right to vote, hold office, or take part in the legal profession because such activities statutorily required participants to be "persons"[17]. Women were excluded because the judicial interpretation of "persons" excluded women. On an appeal from Canada's highest court to the Privy Council in England, the British Court held that women could be appointed to the Senate because they were "persons" as much as men.[18]

Although *Edwards* was a landmark case for women's equality, equal treatment for women within existing law has its drawbacks.[19] Often the sex-blind postures women are required to adopt in order to demonstrate they are the same as men are contorted and unconvincing. In addition, the vocabulary, epistemology, and political theory of the status quo does not comprehend the kind of equality women really need.

Like other liberal ideologies, liberal feminism emphasizes individual rights (constitutional and property-owning) as the measure of well-being. Aspects of life which cannot be ordered into these categories, such as the domain of equal opportunity, are seen as beyond the reach of the liberal philosophy of law. This means that no consideration can be given to the fact that a right to hold and use property is irrelevant if women have no economic opportunities to acquire it in the first place.[20] Although liberal feminism stresses that the individual woman must realize her "true self" by rejecting rigid sexual roles, the intrinsic differences between women and men are discounted. This concept has led some critics to say liberalism's preference for "abstract rights" and individual rights is really a veiled protection of male privilege.[21]

The emphasis on individual rights leads to the further misunderstanding that discrimination is individualized and isolated behavior. Structural injustices are not examined because the concepts supporting formal equality start from the fundamental assumption that basic institutions of society are fair. However, formal equality cannot address systematic issues such as the fact that women continue to be underrepresented in the professions, in politics, and in the judiciary, that women rather than men will perform unpaid work in the home, and that child care facilities and economic opportunities outside the home are often unavailable. Similarly, the organizational structure of the labor market designed to employ women in low paying and low status occupational job ghettos while reserving better paying jobs and professional occupations for workers who do not have family responsibilities, cannot be challenged as a form of discrimination. Remedies such as rearrangements of the work week, part-time employment, affirmative programs to encourage occupational desegregation, and child rearing support that is affordable, are beyond formal equality's ability to deliver.[22] Blindness to institutionally structured male privilege and female disadvantage limits the usefulness and effectiveness of formal equality.

The male normative standard

Within a male-defined jurisprudence, the principles and goals of formal equality can be thwarted. The Aristotelian principle which underlies formal equality asserts that everyone must be treated the same if they are the same. But then the question is, the same as who? This question is important because the normative standard adopted usually determines whether a claim for equal rights will be successful. In practice, the equality norm used is the dominant group. In every society existing in the world today, the dominant group, regardless of race, religion or ethnicity, is a male group.

When women are compared to men, their opportunity to be treated as equal is limited to the extent that they are the same as men. This standard of comparison severely limits and circumscribes women's equality claims. Issues such as pregnancy discrimination, rape, sexual harassment, wife abuse, prostitution, and pornography fall outside equality considerations because men have no comparable need. The similarly situated test is not met and thus, there is no legal basis for complaint. In other words, "[i]f men don't need it, women don't get it."[23] Many legally sanctioned abuses women suffer are not considered equality issues at all. In this way, the formal equality theory effectively works to obscure the systemic, historically embedded, disadvantaged status of women.

Judicial treatment of liberal feminism

The problems with using sameness and difference as the test for discrimination in a male dominated legal system are exemplified in the Canadian Supreme Court's decision in *Attorney General of Canada v. Lavell*.[24] In this case, two aboriginal women challenged the Indian Act[25] for disqualifying them from their statutory Indian status when they married outside their race.[26] Some of the consequences of losing their status included having to leave their reserve, not being allowed to own property on the reserve, being required to dispose of any property held up to the time of their marriage, being prevented from inheriting property, and taking no further part in band business.[27] Because their children were not recognized as Indian, they too were denied all of the cultural and social amenities of the native community. The women could also be prevented from returning to live with their families on the reserve notwithstanding dire need, illness, widowhood, divorce, or separation.[28] The effects even reached beyond life since they could not be buried on the reserve with their ancestors.[29]

The challenge of sex discrimination was made because the legislation exempted from similar disqualification Indian males who married non-Indian women. Upon marrying non-Indian women, males not only retained their Indian status, the legislation automatically conferred full Indian rights and status on their non-Indian wives and children.[30] When the claim was put before the Supreme Court of Canada, the Court found there was no sex discrimination in the legislation.[31] The Court held that Indian women were not the same as Indian men and could not be compared to them.[32] As long as all Indian women were treated in the same way, there was no violation of "equality before the law" as guaranteed in the Canadian Bill of Rights.[33] The judges interpreted equality to guarantee only procedural, not substantive, equality, and the sameness test was considered procedural.[34]

The arbitrary use of the male standard of comparison to establish sameness and difference in the *Lavell* case demonstrates how formal equality fails as an effective tool. Its fundamental flaw is its unprincipled approach to deciding what constitutes sameness or difference. In the *Lavell* case, the mere difference of gender excluded women from the same treatment as men. No defensible rationale was provided for choosing the male standard.

A similar result occurred in a case involving sex discrimination on the basis of pregnancy. In *Bliss* v. *Attorney General of Canada*,[35] the Court was asked to consider the validity of a legislated benefit provision, the Unemployment Insurance Act.[36] This Act required that before an unemployed pregnant woman could qualify for maternity benefits, she must have been employed for ten weeks.[37] At the same time, qualifications for unemployment benefits were less demanding for men and non-pregnant women. The differential treatment of pregnant women was particularly disadvantageous because women in the fifteen weeks immediately surrounding the birth were barred from receiving ordinary benefits,[38] even if they were able and willing to work.

When this inequality was challenged, the Supreme Court refused to strike down the discriminatory benefits provision because it could find no breach of the equality guarantee.[39] Instead, the Court came to the bizarre conclusion that discriminatory treatment of pregnant women was not discrimination on the basis of sex.[40] A comparable application in the disability and race context would prohibit discrimination against the blind or against Sikhs, but would not prohibit discrimination against guide dogs or the wearing of turbans.[41] The exact words in the judgment are as follows:

Assuming the respondent to have been "discriminated against," it would not have been by reason of her sex. Section 46 applies to women, it has no application to women who are not pregnant, and it has no application, of course, to men. If s[ection] 46 treats unemployed pregnant women differently from other unemployed persons, be they male or female, it is, it seems to me, because they are pregnant and not because they are women.[42]

The *Bliss* decision demonstrates that the male normative standard cannot take into account the specificity and differences of women's lives. Excluding pregnancy as a component of sex limits equality rights for women to the ways they are the same as men. Moreover, use of the male standard further influenced the Court's decision when it said that any benefits or positive rights conferred by statute were not subject to the equality protections because the legislation[43] conferred a special benefit for a "voluntary" condition.[44]

In summary, both the *Lavell* and *Bliss* decisions are good illustrations of how the liberal feminist's formal equality solution can actually perpetuate inequality. Refusal to examine the substantive effects of the law, use of the male normative standard, and the view that equality is a mere negative right--the right to be free from something--ensures that the historically, economically, and culturally disadvantaged groups can never legally claim an equal share of society's benefits.

Cultural Feminism

The limits of liberal feminism in the face of persistent inequality led feminists toward a fundamental rethinking of rights. Today, women around the world are seeking to undermine the current distribution of power in the economic, social, and political spheres.[45] They are demanding extensive transformations not only of existing human rights frameworks, but of other forces obstructing their rights, including national governments, religion, culture, legal systems, international institutions, and families.[46] One of the theories that emerged from dissatisfaction with the sameness of treatment model of equality was cultural feminism--a theory which started from difference.

Cultural feminists describe sexual differences in oppositional terms. They believe that women have been prevented from developing their unique female identities because of social constraints, so they challenge anything which devalues or suppresses femininity. They stress the positive aspects of female characteristics in sterotypically feminine terms. Passivity, emotion, and connectedness are affirmed as being as important and valuable as aggression, abstractness, and individuality.[47]

The value of cultural feminism lies in both its ability to highlight the almost total exclusion of women's experiences from the development of the law and to challenge the law's claim to neutrality and objectivity. According to cultural feminists, "reconstructive jurisprudence" should originate in a woman's distinctive existential and material state of being.[48] The case for women-specific rights associated with reproduction and childbirth, work in the home, literacy, and sex-based violence, for example, is made by demonstrating that current regimes lack any comprehension of women's experience.[49] The substantive value of cultural feminism is that it moves the discussion of women's rights beyond the non-discrimination principle,[50] and breaks down the public/private barrier which has kept women's needs beyond the reach of the law for so long.

The gendered nature of justice and morality

The work of child psychologist Carol Gilligan has been influential in the formation of cultural feminism. Gilligan's important contribution to legal theory lies in her challenge to the Freudian notion that men have a well-developed sense of justice and morality whereas women do not.[51] She argues that while men and women have different conceptions of morality, each is equally coherent and equally valid. While pointing out the important differences in male and female modes of thinking about moral issues, Gilligan's main point is that the universal standards developed using the male model are seriously and fundamentally underinclusive and gender-biased because they do not reflect the important divergencies in women's style of moral reasoning.[52]

Through her empirical work, Gilligan discovered that regardless of age, social class, marital status or ethnic background, females have a conception of the self that is different from that of typical males. Whereas men tend to see themselves as autonomous, separate beings, women see themselves as interdependent beings whose identity depends on others.[53] These differences in self-awareness, Gilligan says, account for at least four different ways in which men and women make moral decisions.[54]

First, women tend to stress their connection and responsibility to others, whereas men tend to stress their formal, abstract rights.[55] One of the results of this difference is that unlike men, women will forsake some of their rights if they can improve relationships. Second, when making moral decisions, women tend to think of the consequences for those who will be touched by such decisions.[56] Men, on the other hand, espouse a non-consequentialist point of view, focusing on the principles that must be upheld. If some people get hurt in the process, that is a necessary price to pay for the good of the principle involved.Third, women will more readily accept excuses for bad moral behavior whereas men generally look to moral unjustifiability as a complete reason to condemn the wrongdoer.[57] Finally, women will usually interpret a moral choice within the historical context of the circumstances that produced it, whereas men usually abstract choices from their particularities, analyzing them as universal, moral choices.[58]

Many cultural feminists point out that the law predominantly reflects the male model of moral reasoning. Its hierarchical organization, adversarial format, language, imagery, and abstract methodology of resolving competing rights claims make the law an intensely male institution.[59] Cultural feminists assert that a woman's as well as a man's mode of expression must find its place in the legal system. The limited and biased representations of human experience in models of justice and moral development are unacceptable in any system of law that purports to respect equality as one of its fundamental principles.

But critics of cultural feminism see it as a potential "Uncle Tom's Cabin" for feminism.[60] They point out that it is difficult to determine what authentic "women's voices" are, since women have never been allowed to speak outside the structure of patriarchal societies.[61] To affirm qualities of caring, conciliation, and responsibility for others as essentially feminine characteristics is to accept a male vision of womanhood which has been foisted upon women. Cultural feminists respond that women's oppression and its consequences ought not to be celebrated because caregiving, cooperation, and an interpersonal responsibility ethic are worthy values in and of themselves. Such values can help restructure laws for a good society.[62]

Cultural feminism in law

Recent case law in Canada shows the influence of cultural feminism. This influence is particularly evident in *Brooks* v. *Canada Safeway Ltd.*,[63] a constitutional case decided by the Supreme Court of Canada under the *Canadian Charter of Rights and Freedoms*[64] (Charter). In *Brooks*, the issue of pregnancy discrimination was revisited, ten years after the *Bliss* case.[65] The issue, whether discrimination on the basis of pregnancy was discrimination on the basis of sex, was identical to that argued in the *Bliss* case, but the result was utterly different.[66]

In *Brooks*, as in *Bliss*, pregnant women workers had received disfavored treatment. On this occasion, however, the Court held that the disfavored treatment constituted sex discrimination.[67] The Court not only avoided the male normative standard, but also specifically looked to the disadvantages pregnant women suffer because of their condition, namely, their difference from men.[68] In order to determine whether or not discrimination on the basis of sex occurred, the Chief Justice situated pregnant women in their own context.[69] Once this step was taken, the invidious nature of the disparate treatment, as well as its social costs, were obvious.

The influence of cultural feminism and its "women's voice" is evident in the words of the Chief Justice as he speaks for a unanimous Court:

> Combining paid work with motherhood and accommodating the child-bearing needs of working women are ever-increasing imperatives. That those who bear children and benefit society thereby should not be economically or socially disadvantaged, seems to bespeak the obvious. It is only women who bear children; no man can become pregnant. As I argued earlier, it is unfair to impose all the costs of pregnancy upon one half of the population. It is difficult to conceive that distinctions or discriminations based upon pregnancy could ever be regarded as other than discrimination based upon sex, or that restrictive statutory conditions applicable only to pregnant women did not discriminate against them as women.[70]

It is clear from this example that cultural feminism expands the scope of equality guarantees and exposes underlying facts and issues that were previously hidden. The case demonstrates that when women's real life experiences are put before the courts, equality rights can powerfully redress past wrongs and remove barriers impeding progress and justice for the historically disadvantaged. By going beyond the abstract principles of formal equality in favor of a context-based analysis, the Court in *Brooks* was able to reach the deeply embedded discrimination women suffer based on their unique difference from men.

Another decision seemingly influenced by principles of cultural feminism was *R. v. Lavallee*,[71] which raised the issue of self-defense where a woman killed her common law spouse by shooting him in the back of the head. The shooting occurred after an argument in which the accused had been physically abused and was fearful for her life as well as having been taunted with the threat that if she did not kill him first, he would kill her. She had frequently been a victim of his physical abuse.[72]

In assessing the accused woman's defense, the Court recognized the inequities perpetuated by the sameness-of-treatment model of equality in the common law. Using a contextual approach,[73] the Court found that the traditional common law self-defense was gender-biased.[74]

In deciding the case, the Court took into account the gender specificity of battering and the different life experiences women have in battering relationships.[75] In reasoning similar to that in *Brooks*[76], Justice Wilson, writing for a unanimous court, questioned the male-defined concept of "reasonableness" when it is women who are attempting to use the defense:

> If it strains credulity to imagine what the "ordinary man" would do in the position of a battered spouse, it is probably because men do not typically find themselves in that situation. Some women do, however. The definition of what is reasonable must be adapted to circumstances which are, by and large, foreign to the world inhabited by the hypothetical "reasonable man."[77]

In its conclusion, the court determined that the law's traditional concept of self-defense evolved out of a "bar-room brawl" model that comprehends only a male concept of reasonableness.[78] In order to be fair to women and (presumably) to recognize their right to equal protection and equal benefit of the law, the Court reconstructed the defense to allow women to fight back in a way different from men.[79]

Radical feminism

Where cultural feminism focuses on difference, radical feminism focuses on power. Its central premise is that women's oppression is caused by social and cultural arrangements which require women to submit to men because of their sex.[80] As such, gender inequality is the most fundamental form of oppression. It is deeper, more widespread, and the most difficult form of human oppression to eradicate, even in a gender neutral or classless state.[81] Radical feminists believe reforming the legal and political structures of societies is not enough to achieve social equality for women. Gendered power, dominance, hierarchy, and competition imbued in social and cultural systems, especially the family, the church, and the academy must be changed as well.

The meaning of discrimination and equality

Radical feminists agree with cultural feminists that legal thinking must connect with women's concrete reality but argue that neither liberal feminism nor cultural feminism can achieve sex equality because both use the male yardstick as the reference point from which all discrimination is measured.[82] Using the male norm reinforces and perpetuates the hierarchical, gender-based social system keeping women "out and down,"[83] whether the remedy sought is sameness of treatment (liberal feminism) or different treatment (cultural feminism).

Radical feminists criticize the central concepts of liberal thinking in particular for not speaking to women's experience.

Catharine MacKinnon, the most consistent and influential exponent of radical feminism, proposes that instead of using the male norm to decide the discrimination question, the inquiry should be, whether the policy or practice in question integrally contributes to the maintenance of an underclass or a deprived position because of gender status.[84] The use of this test would require the law to take systematic sex subordination into account, and support freedom from it, making it a qualitatively different approach from formal equality which does not even acknowledge that sex-based subordination exists.

The closest any court in the world has come to expressly adopting the radical feminist approach to discrimination is the Supreme Court of Canada. The leading case on equality, *Andrews v. Law Society of British Columbia*,[85] required an interpretation of the meaning, scope, and purpose of the constitutional equality guarantee in the Charter of Rights and Freedoms. Rather than following the traditional liberal approach of the U.S. Supreme Court and earlier Canadian jurisprudence,[86] the court took a whole new approach. Most importantly, it threw out the Aristotelian "similarly situated" test of discrimination in no uncertain terms, saying it was so unprincipled it could justify Hitler's Nuremberg laws.[87] The Court created a new test which focuses on the impact of laws rather than on intention, and on the context of the plaintiff rather than sameness to a male norm.

Similar to the test proposed by MacKinnon, the court's test provides that if a person is a member of a persistently disadvantaged group, and can show that a distinction based on personal characteristics of the individual or group continues or worsens that disadvantage, it is discriminatory treatment regardless of intention.[88] Under this analysis, disadvantage is determined by examining the plaintiff's social, political, and legal reality.[89]

The difference between the test of "disadvantage" and the liberal "similarly situated" test is that the former requires judges to look at women and other claimants in their place in the real world and to confront the reality that the systemic abuse and deprivation of power women experience is because of their place in the sexual hierarchy. Under the new test, women can challenge male-defined structures and institutions and demonstrate that equality will only be achieved through norms based on their own needs and characteristics. In some cases, identical treatment with men will be appropriate. In other situations however, the male comparator will be irrelevant. The Supreme Court's result-oriented, contextual view of equality permits both facially neutral and gender specific laws or policies to be questioned for a disparate impact on individual women or on women as a group.

The social construction of gender

Like cultural feminists, radical feminists are concerned with the general question of how legal doctrine works in conjunction with other systemic factors to keep women oppressed. But radical feminists look more at how female sexuality is constructed and controlled by complex social practices, including the law. When the meaning of gender in terms of power allocation between the sexes is analyzed, the primary conceptual framework is the woman's body. By politicizing the female body, sexuality, child rearing, and childbearing practices, radical feminism turns abstract western political theory and western political practice on its head. Radical feminists assert that to ignore the politics of sex is to ignore that women are deprived of power over their own bodies and sexuality, and thus are deprived of their humanity.

Attention is focused in two directions. First, it is focused on the ways in which women's bodies are controlled, either through violence, restrictive contraception, abortion or sterilization. Second, attention is focused on the ways men have constructed and defined female sexuality to serve male interests. Radical feminists believe overcoming the negative effects biology has had on women (and perhaps also on men),[90] requires social and legal strategies capable of deconstructing the way women's sexuality has been socialized and commodified.

An early idea was to promote the practice of androgyny. Adherents thought if men and women could freely explore both their feminine and masculine characteristics through practising androgyny, they would develop a much greater and healthier sense of human wholeness and the social construction of male and female roles would be broken down.[91] Eventually, however, androgyny was rejected as a liberation strategy for the reason that it required women to moderate their femininity.[92] Women came to realize that just as biology is not the problem for them, neither is femininity. The real problem is the low value the masculinist society assigns to female qualities of nurturance, emotion, connectedness, and responsibility to others. Some feel if the "feminine" was valued as much as the "masculine," women's oppression would disappear. Others disagree, insisting that femininity as we know it has been constructed by males for patriarchal purposes and is not authentic. They say true femininity is a concept of the future which eventually will be understood as a state of being without the need for an external male reference point. But until women are self-determining and freed from the yoke of male oppression, the content of the term "feminine," will remain unknown.[93]

Another strategy crucial to radical feminist theory is the empowerment of women to control and determine their own reproduction. Where at one time radical feminists understood female biology to enslave women,[94] most radical feminists now view women's biology, especially their reproductive capacity and the nurturing role that flows from it, as a potential source of liberating power.[95] Unlike non-feminist opponents, radical feminists reject the premise that there is a "natural order" of things which subordinates women to men because of their biological natures. They do see women's biology as oppressive, but only because men have used child rearing and childbearing as ways of controlling women. To achieve an equal status with men, women must be able to decide for themselves when or whether to use reproduction-controlling technologies such as contraception, abortion, and sterilization or any reproduction-aiding techniques such as artificial insemination, in-vitro fertilization, and surrogacy.[96]

The understanding that women must maintain reproductive control as a central criterion of their human rights and human dignity underlies the decision of Madam Justice Bertha Wilson in the case of *R. v. Morgentaler*.[97] In *Morgentaler*, the Canadian legislation regulating abortion was struck down by the Supreme Court as a violation of the constitutional guarantee of "the right to life, liberty and security of the person and the right not to be deprived thereof except in accordance with the principles of fundamental justice."[98]

Justice Wilson, in a concurring opinion, linked the reality of being a woman with the reality of being human, leaving no doubt that women's rights are human rights even though they are different from men's rights. She rejected male-centered norms that influence the concept of liberty for the reason that the experiences of pregnancy, birth, and abortion are ones men do not and cannot experience. In explaining the dilemma women face with an unwanted pregnancy, she said the following:

It is probably impossible for a man to respond, even imaginatively, to such a dilemma not just because it is outside the realm of his personal experience (although this is, of course, the case) but because he can relate to it only by objectifying it, thereby eliminating the subjective elements of the female psyche which are at the heart of the dilemma. As Noreen Burrows, lecturer in European Law at the University of Glasgow, has pointed out . . ., the history of the struggle for human rights from the eighteenth century on has been the history of men struggling to assert their dignity and common humanity against an overbearing state apparatus. The more recent struggle for women's rights has been a struggle to eliminate discrimination, to achieve a place for women in a man's world, to develop a set of legislative reforms in order to place women in the same position as men. It has not been a struggle to define the rights of women in relation to their special place in the societal structure and in relation to the biological distinction between the two sexes. Thus, women's needs and aspirations are only now being translated into protected rights. The right to reproduce or not to reproduce which is in issue in this case is one such right and is properly perceived as an integral part of modern woman's struggle to assert her dignity and worth as a human being.[99]

For radical feminists, Wilson's opinion was historic and crucially important because it struck down the abortion laws, thereby restoring power to women to control their own bodies. It also interpreted the dispute from the perspective of the experiences and aspirations of women, making visible the problems that unwanted pregnancies present for them. Moreover, it incorporated women's reality into the supreme law of Canada and it expressly rejected the male norm as relevant to the development of women's rights. Once the law begins to respond to women's needs in this way, radical feminists believe the challenge of transforming the culture is not so impossible.

Violence against women

Violence against women is a major preoccupation of all contemporary feminist theory, especially radical feminism. But because of its hidden nature, this has not always been the case. Before Catharine MacKinnon's pioneering work on identifying and classifying sexual harassment as a legal wrong,[100] it was "just life." Most forms of sexual oppression, including pornography and prostitution, are so deeply ingrained and accepted, they appear either natural or inevitable.[101] Radical feminism requires feminist analysts to look "for that which we have been trained not to see . . . [to identify] the invisible."[102]

Even when violence was recognized as a problem, major investigations into the status of women did not see violence against women as a feminist issue.[103] Physical, sexual, and psychological violence and coercion were regarded more as social problems than equality issues. It was not until the 1980's that its characterization changed.[104]

The first step in radical feminist law reform efforts is to make the violent abuse of women visible. By collecting evidence and experiences of violence against women from women, radical feminists provide a base of authentic information on the extent, interconnectedness, and conventions of violent male behavior.[105] The next step is to analyze how laws can be reformed to support freedom from the subordination caused by violence. This approach requires that the real injuries and harm women suffer from male violence be acknowledged and become a central part of the law reform process.

One of the most important areas for radical feminist analysis is the crime of rape. All feminist theorists agree that reform of rape laws is required, but they have different views as to why the current law is inadequate and what directions reform should take.[106] Liberal feminists have been responsible for much of the rape law reforms to date. Consistent with their central premise that women and men are the same, they think rape should be characterized as a gender neutral crime of violence rather than as a gender specific sex crime.[107] The Aristotelian approach leads them to argue that victims of rape are victims of violence, just like other victims of violent crime. It follows that sameness of treatment argues against laws that treat rape as a "special" or "different" crime. For example, wives of men who rape them should not be exempted from the protection of the law accorded to other women.[108]

The liberal feminist analysis and activism successfully resulted in changes to the rape laws in most western countries. The scope of the crime was expanded to include a wider range of sex-based assaults[109] and the requirement for penetration was eliminated, as was the marriage exemption.[110] The emphasis on violence and same treatment led to evidentiary changes including making a victim's past sexual history irrelevant to consent.[111] The corroboration requirement was also dropped because of the insistence on equal treatment.[112] Moreover, as Katharine Bartlett notes, reforms stimulated by the liberal feminist critique in the 1970's "included further refinements in the grading system for sexual offenses, language changes to make the nomenclature gender-neutral, and alterations to the requirements of force and non-consent to facilitate convictions."[113]

But radical feminists look at rape law in terms of its impact on women as a class, and ask, have liberal-inspired reforms actually protected more women from male violence? They say that in spite of the reforms, the incidence of sexual assaults has increased and the rate of conviction has increased only slightly,[114] leading them to conclude that addressing rape as a gender-neutral crime misses the point.

Catharine MacKinnon argues that feminists should revisit the liberal feminist's theory of rape.[115] She fundamentally disagrees with the theoretical distinction made between sex and violence, saying it does not exist.[116] The simple fact that women do not rape men takes rape out of the category of a gender-neutral violent crime. Moreover, the violent part of the sexual assault must be experienced as a part of the sex, otherwise violent men would just beat women up.[117] When sexual assault is properly understood as sexual sadism, it follows that sexual assault eroticizes and sexualizes women's subordination to men, making sex into violence and violence into sex.[118] In the broader context of women's inequality in the society, sexual assault is part of, and connected to, the dominance and subordination of women generally. Until reforms are rooted in the understanding that rape is an institution of inequality, changes in the law will do little to benefit women.

It follows that for radical feminists, any law reform must start with a redefinition of the crime of rape. At present, the law in most jurisdictions defines sexual assault as intercourse or sexual activity perpetrated by force without the consent of the victim. By requiring proof of non-consent, the law places women in the position of having to disprove consent even where there is violence.[119] Rather than protecting women from violence and condemning it, the law perpetuates the idea that women consent to violent sex.

MacKinnon and other radical feminists suggest that a better way of dealing with sexual assault would be to remove the requirement of non-consent from the victim entirely.[120] They would redefine rape as "sex forced by physical aggression, threat, or authority, and thus a crime of sexual inequality."[121] The mens rea would go to force, which would take into account dimensions of social life which heighten vulnerability to sexual assault such as age, race, ethnicity, and disability.[122] The defendant would have the onus to show that the woman consented.[123]

Another dimension of violence against women which concerns radical feminists is the production, distribution, and possession of pornography. Distinguishing between erotic, consensual depictions, and violent, degrading ones, radical feminists take the position that pornography is not so much about sex per se as it is about male power exerted over females.

The Canadian case of *R. v. Butler* applies the radical feminist theory of violence to pornography.[124] The decision marked the first time in 500 years of common law that a Supreme Court examined pornography in its social context and from the perspective of women. In so doing, it found that pornography exists in a context of social inequality and sexual violence against women and girls. As a result, the Court held that when pornography presents sexual representations that degrade and dehumanize the participants, subjects them to violence, or uses children, it presents a serious risk of harm to women and children and can be constitutionally limited without violating freedom of expression guarantees.[125] Equality-promoting legislation, such as the criminal obscenity laws, took on constitutional significance in these circumstances because of the constitutional value of equality.

The Canadian Supreme Court's characterization of pornography as an injury to women[126] was an important victory for radical feminists. The Court's conclusion that pornography discriminates against women by attempting to control and define female sexuality in a harmful way[127] is consistent with radical feminism's analysis of male power and female subordination. In constitutionally upholding the obscenity laws for the reasons it did, the court affirms the radical feminist analysis that equality can only be achieved by removing those policies or practices which contribute to the maintenance of the underclass of women.

Similar understanding is apparent in sexual harassment jurisprudence where the Supreme Court of Canada understood the relationship between sexual harassment and the social construction of gender which subordinates women in the workplace.[128] Chief Justice Dixon, writing for the Court, first discussed how sexual harassment has a different impact on women in terms of the gender hierarchy of the labor force and the inherent "abuse of both economic and sexual power" that harassment entails.[129] These factors, when combined with the social and economic realities of women, led him to conclude that sexual harassment is a form of sex discrimination.[130] As in *Butler,* the judgment confronted the social context behind sexual harassment and found it to be a deeply sexist one that objectifies women's bodies and perpetuates a male-defined image of sexual attractiveness. Consistent with the radical feminist argument, it found that the practice of sexual harassment cannot be separated from the unequal relations of sexual interaction that disadvantage women.[131]

Largely due to the efforts of radical feminists, violence against women now dominates legal agendas in many countries and in the international arena. Pornography, prostitution, sexual harassment, rape, and women battering as well as suttee, purdah, genital mutilation, and sexual abuse of children are being uncovered and analyzed through principles of radical feminism.[132]

Post modern feminism

The roots of postmodern feminism are found in the work of Simone de Beauvoir. Her question, "why is woman the second sex?"[133] showed that Beauvoir understood that woman is oppressed by virtue of "otherness." Woman is the "Other" because she does not have power.[134] Man is the free being who defines the meaning of his existence, whereas woman has her meaning and existence defined for her. Beauvoir said woman must transcend the definitions and labels that limit her existence if she is to become self-determining.[135]

The concept of otherness

While contemporary postmodern feminists accept that women are the "Other," they do not accept De Beauvoir's view that "otherness" is a status to be transcended. To the contrary, they say that from the position of "otherness," women can stand back and criticize the norms, values, and practices that the patriarchy seeks to impose on everyone.[136] Consistent with their principal insight that objectivity is a fiction, the postmodern approach is to criticize everything, including particular ideas or social injustices and the structures upon which they are based, the language in which they are thought, and the systems in which they are safeguarded.[137]

Postmodern feminists' rejection of traditional assumptions about truth and reality also leads postmodernists to refuse to accept universal feminist definitions or any one overarching theory providing an explanation and solution for women's oppression.[138] They argue that attempts to find integration and agreement within feminist theory or to establish one specifically feminist standpoint, is yet another instance of a "phallocentric" way of thinking. They claim that it is typical male thinking to seek "one true, feminist story of reality."[139] Such a synthesis is neither feasible nor useful because of the differences in women's lives across race, class, and cultural lines. It is to be expected that feminism is multifaceted because women are not all the same. Post-- modernists believe the more feminist thoughts we have, the better. Some even resist the label "feminism" in the spirit of non-essentialism.[140]

Critics of postmodernism say, however, that overemphasizing differences may lead to a weakening and even disintegration of intellectual and political progress. If feminism has no common stand, it will become difficult to make claims based upon the general well-being of women.[141] They point out that societies systematically accord different power on the basis of religion, ethnicity, sexual preference, and many other grounds in addition to sex. If we are to abandon the category "women," replacing it with all the other "categories," there will be an infinite fragmentation of the feminist project which could result in maintaining the status quo.[142] While inevitable tensions will arise between universal theories and local experience, critics caution postmodernists not "to become paralyzed to the point of total relativism . . . to insist that feminism disintegrate into a series of local or regional struggles."[143] The focus should rather be on areas common to all women's experience.[144]

The meaning of equality

In postmodern theory, equality is not dependant upon a single doctrinal standard. Rather, equality is sought through questioning, recontextualizing, and attempting to unsettle existing laws in a wide range of areas.[145] Unlike the other theories of equality, differences among women are explicitly acknowledged.[146] For example, differences are understood through the relationships or contexts in which they are asserted.[147] This method allows an exploration of specific rules or doctrines that are of importance to particular groups of women and allows for an analysis of complex social practices in which laws are used.[148] By invoking diverse, multiple images of women, and by taking an anti-essentialist view of women's nature and equality, postmodernists feel they have the potential to break through more rigid doctrines proposed by other theorists, and allow for shifting and evolving points of view.[149]

An example of the application of postmodern theory in the Canadian context is the Supreme Court of Canada's decision in the case of *Moge v. Moge*.[150] The case dealt with the question of spousal support where the dependent spouse was a middle-aged immigrant woman with limited English language skills, who had been married for several years and assumed the homemaker role in the marriage.[151] Until the *Moge* case was decided, courts favored a "gender neutral" approach to marriage based on the liberal feminist assumption that sexual equality as sameness of treatment should be applied to marriage and its breakdown. In awarding spousal support, the "sameness" approach translated into a "self-sufficiency" or "clean break" model, which assumed that a dependant wife, regardless of age, education, or experience, could find a job and support herself in a limited time period following the divorce. In the *Moge* decision, the Supreme Court recognized that this "equality" posture masked real differences between the lives of men and women, such as unequal opportunities for education, career options and advancement, unequal remuneration for paid work, inadequate valuation for unpaid domestic work, a double work day, and the threat of sexual, physical, and emotional violence.[152] The court recognized that if the "clean break" model was applied to all women without accounting for women's social and economic disadvantage, awards would increase women's inequality and perpetuate the feminization of poverty.[153] The Court also made it clear that not all women's needs are the same and that decisions on spousal support must be made by identifying, understanding, and alleviating inequalities that exist for individual women in their own marriage contexts, rather than on the basis of sameness of treatment with either men or women.[154] The *Moge* decision affirms postmodern principles because it favors individualized decision-making and recognizes that just as women are not the same as men, neither are they the same as other women.

Gender and race

An issue of particular concern to postmodern feminists is the relationship between gender and race, class, ethnicity, religion and other situated experiences.[155] In some instances they see the sex equality project interfering with competing claims of cultural identity and survival.[156] The universal oppression of women is accepted, but with the qualification that "not all women are equally oppressed, or oppressed equally."[157] For feminists of all races and ethnicities, it is increasingly intolerable to separate the many forms of oppression that harm them.[158]

Where nineteenth century women consistently used the singular word "woman" to demonstrate their conception of the unity of the female sex, the language of the 1960's and 1970's linguistically comprehended more plural forms by speaking of the "women's movement."[159] Critics nevertheless say many white feminists have appropriated the category "women" to speak only about middle-class white, heterosexual, Christian, and able-bodied women's experiences of sexism.[160] They say the use of these norms hides a preferred position and shields it from other possible alternatives[161] just as does the use of the male norm. For example, postmodernists ask why is sexism considered worse than racism? To suggest that it is, as radical feminists do, denies the experience of women who see race as the paradigm of their disadvantage.

The opinion of many minority women and their postmodern supporters is that focusing solely on theories of sex inequality generated by Anglo-American and French feminists is imperialist, racist, Eurocentric, and exclusionary.[162] Much of the criticism starts with universities and the production of knowledge. For example, in her book, *Ain't I a Woman*, bell hooks criticizes the content of women's studies programs in the United States. She says:

> the hierarchial pattern of race and sex relationships already established in American society merely took a different form under "feminism": . . . the form of women's studies programs being established with all-white faculty teaching literature almost exclusively by white women about white women and frequently from racist perspectives; the form of white women writing books that purport to be about the experience of American women when in fact they concentrate solely on the experience of white women; and finally the form of endless argument and debate as to whether or not racism was a feminist issue.[163]

Similar criticisms are directed at Canadian programs by black women, women of color, and aboriginal women.[164]

Women of color further criticize white feminists for excluding them from decision-making positions or at least, doing little to help advance their careers in the academy.[165] They demonstrate how institutionalized discrimination embedded in hiring practices of universities, funding procedures, and the composition of editorial boards of important journals marginalizes working-class women and women of color.[166] Their findings suggest that the current organization of the academy perpetuates the production and distribution of knowledge that is both Anglo- and middle-class centered.[167]

Postmodern feminists say women in positions of power should develop strategies to ensure that minorities are hired to teach in women's studies programs, that bibliographies, course offerings, and curricula are inclusionary and diversified, and that anti-racist guidelines are developed for feminist journals.[168] Work which examines and theorizes about racist and classist assumptions underlying the academy should be encouraged.[169] Unless such strategies are pursued, there is a real risk of further dissociation between white women, third world women, and women of color.[170]

North American postmodernists say in order to understand the interrelatedness of gender, race, and class, feminist theory must come to grips with the historical roots of racism in the slave societies.[171] Alliances between white women and white men on the common ground of racism as well as the privileges gained by white women over black women within patriarchal and capitalistic societies through slavery, raise a multitude of unresolved issues which create conflict between black and white women.[172]

A contemporary example of devaluation of black women as compared to white women was the media and public reaction to the Central Park Jogger case, where a middle class white woman was brutally raped by a group of young black men. Postmodern feminist critics compare the massive publicity of the case with 28 other cases of rape, mostly of women of color which occurred in New York City during the same week.[173] No media attention was directed to them at all, not even to the gang rape of a black woman who suffered multiple fractures and internal injuries when she was sexually assaulted, sodomized, and thrown fifty feet off the top story of a building.[174] Black women say this incident typifies the sexual hierarchy existing between white women and black women that pervades western culture and is visible at all levels, including at the level of law reform.[175] They say law reformers, including feminists, tend to concentrate on protecting white women from sexism and view racism primarily in terms of inequality between men.[176] By erroneously assuming racism is the same for black women as it is for black men and sexism for black women is the same as it is for white women, black women's concerns under both the gender and race categorizations are often not met.[177]

An example is the recent sentencing studies of rape prosecutions in the United States, the purpose of which was to look into the question of racism in the courts. The studies showed that average prison sentences given to both white and black males convicted of raping black women are much more lenient than sentences given to black men convicted of raping white women.[178] The studies resulted in changes to sentencing practices towards black men because of their racially discriminatory nature.[179] The equally discriminatory treatment of black women disclosed by the studies, however, was not mentioned.

The theme that black men are victims of laws relating to rape and racism goes back to the white culture's stereotypical casting of all black men as potential threats to the sanctity of white womanhood.[180] While racism may explain why black men have been targeted for both legal and extralegal violence for sexually violating white women,[181] postmodernists say feminist theory must look to racism and sexism to explain why black women are marginalized within the prevailing political and social science agenda.[182] They warn that unless racial stratification among women is understood and eliminated, efforts to politicize violence and other forms of discrimination against women will further isolate and marginalize black women, and the Women's Movement will be seriously weakened.

Angela Harris criticizes the radical feminist analysis of rape, saying it cannot be generalized to all women. She says, while it may tell us what rape means to white women, it has nothing to do with the experience of black women.[183] The experience of rape for black women is as deeply rooted in color as it is in gender and is a far more complex experience than radical feminists describe. During the times of slavery, the rape of black women by any man, white or black, was not considered to be a crime at all.[184] While rape laws may have operated to deny protection to white women based on what they did or failed to do, black women were denied protection based on who they were.[185] Harris also points out that the experience of rape for black women was often linked to racism and servitude to whites.[186] As domestic servants, even after emancipation, black women's vulnerability and experience of sexual abuse and rape were inextricably linked to their relationship to dominant sexist and racist whites.[187] Postmodernists say that the failure of feminist theories to consider the unique vulnerability of black women to rape and the lack of legal protection from it, imposes a kind of "gender essentialism."

Catharine MacKinnon disagrees that the radical feminist analysis of rape applies only to white women.[188] She says a distinction must be made between essentialism that says "all women are alike," and the understanding that all women experience subordination.[189] In other words, gender "is not a common essence but a common predicament."[190] The group "women," in all its variations, has a collective social history of disempowerment, exploitation, and subordination.[191] She says to speak of the social treatment women experience "as women" in this sense does not invoke any homogenous, generic, or ideal type, but rather, refers to the material reality of social meanings and practices.[192]

Race-based, postmodern critiques of white feminist scholarship also apply to basic concepts and principles underlying civil law. For example, a postmodern critique of feminist analysis of child custody suggests that generalized ideologies of motherhood offensive to white feminists do not necessarily apply to black women.[193] The stereotype that mothers should stay at home with their young children is neither black women's experience nor a black woman's stereotype. They say ideologies of black female domesticity and motherhood are constructed around the expectation that black women do work outside their own homes (more often than not as domestics and surrogate mothers to white families).[194] As a result, the stereotype that women's role is in the private sphere is a white woman's stereotype. Ideologies of motherhood, domesticity, and work in child custody cases would therefore operate quite differently for black women than for white women and require a more complex consideration of factors than the white feminist analysis allows.[195]

Another feminist "orthodoxy" that postmodernists challenge are the conclusions about reproduction and reproductive control. Whether inadequate discussion with respect to race and class issues has contributed to the conditions which make pregnancy and motherhood such unattractive alternatives for large numbers of women is raised to question the deadlock between pro-life and pro-choice women.[196] Increasingly, attention is focused on the right to reproduce as well as the right not to reproduce.[197] At its most obvious, feminists say the right to reproduce includes the right not to be interfered with in such ways as forced sterilization, forced abortion or coercive birth control programs.[198] Abuses are compounded by discriminatory sterilization and birth control practices visited upon minority women in both first world and developing countries.[199]

Reproductive technology also has created new scholarship and analyses in recent decades. A host of scientific techniques such as in vitro fertilization, embryo freezing, surrogate motherhood, and other mechanisms have been developed to "assist" infertile women or men to reproduce.[200] Although the feminist theorists have been reluctant to advocate the end of infertility research and experimentation, sexist, racist, eugenicist, and homophobic ideologies and stereotypes identified in the monopolized, male-dominated medical profession have caused concern.[201] In addition, increasing commercialization of reproductive technologies has created fears that some women's access to reproductive technology may require violations of other women's rights. This concern has led many postmodern and other feminists to the view that reproductive technology has minimal potential to contribute to feminist goals.[202]

Finally, postmodern feminists question whether drawing boundaries between the various feminist perspectives is useful. Although describing feminist thought in a number of categories may have some analytical usefulness, postmodernists say these descriptions can be both limiting and distorting.[203] Others disagree, saying labels can be of value because they locate different ideas about feminism on a spectrum of feminist thought and provide a framework within which to understand the different stages of evolution and growth of feminist theory.[204]

In summary, the challenge of reconciling pressures for diversity and difference on the one hand, with those of integration and solidarity on the other, makes feminist analysis difficult and evolutionary. Although each of the feminist theories discussed above has been criticized by other feminists, I would argue that all the theories are important and have a place in the early unfolding of the massive feminist project ahead. Although they are not all equally correct or effective in specific areas, the challenge is to understand which is best for the particular issue at hand. There is considerable room for growth, improvement, reconsideration, and expansion as time goes on. As Ngaire Naffine describes it, the feminist project in law is less a series of discrete interpretations than "a sort of archaeological dig"[205] because different techniques are appropriate at different levels of the excavation.[206]

In the section that follows, important issues facing the women's movement internationally are discussed in light of the different feminist perspectives discussed above. This discussion should enable the reader to appreciate how some of the theories work separately and together and to evaluate their effectiveness in the international context.

Women's Rights in International Law

International human rights instruments

Since 1948, the United Nations has recognized the centrality of human rights to peace and harmony in the world,[207] and has continued for the past forty-seven years to create more detailed and comprehensive rights instruments. There are three large categories of rights in the international regime. The "first generation" of rights are civil and political rights. These are rights which Western countries consider the most important to the maintenance of democracy and individualism.[208] "Second generation" rights are economic, social, and cultural rights, a category of rights preferred in socialist and communist regimes. The "third generation" group or peoples' rights are of greatest interest to developing countries.

For the vast majority of women in the world, the rights created are hollow. Notwithstanding the proliferation of newer and more complete legal instruments, international human rights law is largely meaningless to women because the definitions and development of the rights are built on the male experience and have not responded to women's needs or realities. Feminists from all countries agree that the same androcentricity privileging the male world view in national legal systems is imbued in international human rights law. This inequality is also true in the composition of international human rights institutions.[209]

There are a number of international instruments in existence which purport to protect women's rights. These include The United Nations Convention on the Political Rights of Women,[210] the United Nations Convention on the Nationality of Married Women,[211] the UNESCO Convention on Discrimination in Education,[212] and the non-discrimination norms contained in both the International Covenant on Economic, Social and Cultural Rights (Economic Covenant) and the International Covenant on Civil and Political Rights.[213] All these instruments are premised on the view that to achieve equality, women should be treated the same as men.[214] As in domestic law, this kind of formal equality has some value, but it has been inadequate to address the deeper, more structural subordination of women world-wide for the same reasons that it does not improve the status of women in their own countries.[215]

In addition to the call for formal sex equality in the specific instruments listed above, the Convention on the Elimination of all Forms of Discrimination Against Women (Women's Convention), was drafted to deal with sex discrimination of all forms.[216] The product of thirty years of work by the United Nations Commission on the Status of Women, it is a blend of feminist theories. Although the majority of provisions require women to be treated the same as men in similar situations, read as a whole, the concept of equality in the Women's Convention clearly extends beyond formal equality.[217]

The Women's Convention deals with civil rights, the legal status of women, reproduction, and the impact of cultural norms on gender relations. It emphasizes rights of political participation, nationality, and non-discrimination in education, employment, and economic and social activities.[218] It asserts equal rights and obligations of women and men with regard to choice of spouse, parenthood, personal rights, and command over property.[219] It states that rules intentionally or unintentionally treating women differently from men cannot be tolerated, particularly when they are based on prejudice and inaccurate generalizations about women.[220]

In the area of reproduction, it recognizes that equality requires legal norms to go beyond gender neutrality. The Women's Convention comes to grips with the realities of gender differences and the social and economic consequences of pregnancy by recognizing that women's equality requires states parties to guarantee a woman's right to decide on the number and spacing of pregnancies and to have access to information and the means to exercise these rights.[221] By demanding fully shared responsibility for child rearing on the part of both sexes, it acknowledges that gender discrimination is often caused by stereotyped sex roles. Moreover, cultural radical feminist norms are evident in the provision that says States Parties have the responsibility to provide services that enable individuals to combine family responsibilities with work and participation in public life.[222] The Women's Convention thus acknowledges that maternity protection and child care are essential positive rights.

The Women's Convention identifies the generic, structural sources of inequality when it identifies culture and the use of stereotypes, customs, and norms as potential barriers to women's enjoyment of equality.[223] States are exhorted to modify such customs and practices when they encourage the domination of women by men.[224] In other words, it obliges them to change not only negative laws, but also negative culture. In sum, it recognizes that in order to achieve gender equality, a multi-faceted approach, similar to that advocated by postmodernists, is required. In some instances, equality requires that women not be denied opportunities and benefits enjoyed by men. In others, women must be empowered to determine their own priorities and needs. Unlike the non-interference role required for the protection of civil liberties, the Women's Convention says states have a crucial, pro-active role to play if gender equality is to be achieved. It is worth noting that the Women's Convention makes no distinction between the public and the private in its guarantees and requirements.

While considered a good idea at the time it was created, and still considered to be an accurate description of much of what causes women's subordination, the Women's Convention is now considered by many feminists to be largely responsible for the marginalization of women's human rights in international law.[225] Institutions created to draft and monitor women's rights continue to be notoriously underfunded. "Mainstream" human rights bodies ignore or downplay the human rights of women by referring "women's issues" to the Women's Convention. In addition, the implementation procedures and obligations in the Women's Convention are much weaker than those in other human rights instruments.[226]

All of these factors, combined with the widespread practice of states opting out of fundamental provisions of the Women's Convention, have rendered it ineffective where its provisions are needed the most.[227] Women around the world agree that inequality is too deeply embedded to be removed by a mere comprehensive catalogue of women's rights which has very weak, if not non-existent, enforcement capabilities. They say reforms must move away from setting norms and toward the implementation of rights, the equal representation of women in national and international decision-making bodies,[228] and in structured, political change.

Feminist theory in international law

In recent times, mutual vulnerability and resistance to human rights violations have mobilized women to become a potent political force in the world community. Their efforts have made women's issues a priority on the international human rights agenda, such that the Vienna Declaration and Program of Action,[229] which stated "the human rights of women and of the girl child are an inalienable, integral and indivisible part of universal human rights,"[230] is now recognized as a watershed event that transformed the international human rights agenda in a fundamental way. The Fourth U.N. World Conference on Women's Rights in Beijing and its Platform of Action passed by a significant majority of the 189 countries attending,[231] indicate continuing momentum and progress.

The theoretical premises underlying the concept that women's rights are human rights are rooted in the theories discussed in the first section of this paper. Feminist analyses of the public/private distinction, in particular, are central to feminist theories of international law and have driven much of the substantive reform and other progessive developments of recent times.

The public/private analysis takes two directions. The first is that international law and human rights theories, in their present form, exclude the private domain from their scope and thus are fundamentally flawed because they shut out most of the world's women. In order for human rights to be universal and include women in their scope, international law has to be reconceptualized to incorporate the private sphere.

The second and more hopeful argument has a less radical solution. Proponents of this view say that doctrinal tools are presently available to accommodate women's rights in human rights,[232] but international law incorrectly uses the public/ private divide as a convenient tool to avoid addressing women's problems. Feminist analyses show how the public/private dichotomy in international law is irrational and inconsistently applied,[233] and how a double standard is applied to the rights of women.

Some even say the public/private distinction is a "myth" because international law enters the private realm all the time in other areas.[234] They cite examples of international law regulating the rights of the family, preventing slavery, or holding states responsible for the acts of non-state actors in disappearance cases. They conclude that a state's failure to protect its members from human rights violations in the private sphere is indistinguishable from direct state action.[235]

The case of *Velasquez-Rodriguez v. Honduras*,[236] decided by the Inter-American Court of Human Rights (Inter-American Court), supports this position.

In that case, a man was violently detained, tortured, and accused of committing political crimes by an unofficial death squad.[237] He disappeared and was never found. The Inter-American Court ignored the public/private distinction and legally imputed the crimes to the state of Honduras for the reason that the abuse committed by "private" actors was systematically tolerated by the government.[238]

The irrationality and unprincipled nature of the public/private distinction when it is applied inconsistently, has led to the wide acceptance of the strategy to link women's rights with human rights.[239] Women see some hope in the pursuit of such a strategy because at the present time, all governments are legally obliged under the United Nation's Universal Declaration of Human Rights[240] not to violate the human rights of their citizens.[241] Women argue that existing protections which protect men from violations of equality, security, liberty, integrity, and dignity, when applied to women, will strengthen the whole body of human rights because both halves of the human race will be represented in the scope of human rights. Rather than "ghettoizing" women's human rights as the Women's Convention does, the "women's rights are human rights" strategy emphasizes the ways in which women are specifically affected by any human rights issue,[242] and can be applied to all three "generations" of human rights.

To make the argument that women's rights are human rights involves at least three analytical steps. First, human rights must be defined from women's perceptions of what is central to their basic integrity as human beings.[243] Second, the violations of women's human rights must be made visible. Third, the breaches of women's rights must be analyzed through the existing human rights regimes, but in a way that takes account of women's lives.[244] In other words, the strategy is to use, where applicable, all of the feminist theories discussed in the first section to both undermine the public/private distinction and maximize the possibilities for women in all areas of life. Analyzing the distinctions between the public and private spheres in this way reveals the existing pervasive gender bias in international law which, once exposed, is difficult to defend.

In the following sections, I will examine each of the three "generations" of rights to demonstrate how the women's rights as human rights strategy can be argued.

The first generation: civil and political rights

Civil and political rights essentially create the public/private dichotomy. By definition, civil and political rights exist to prevent the public world from intruding into particular areas of private life.[245] By their very content, they require an examination of what "private" means. In international law, definitions of "private" include life in the home. For women, this definition is problematic for their enjoyment of rights, including the rights of citizenship and the right to bodily security.

The rights of citizenship

Understanding citizenship from a woman's perspective requires an examination of women's experience, or lack of it, in public life. Although most women today are entitled to vote, in many countries cultural or family constraints deny them effective political participation. Women, who are forbidden the right to travel without the permission of their male relatives,[246] who are denied free speech rights, and whose freedom of association is curtailed by family members obstructing their ability to attend public events or political activities,[247] would probably define the citizenship right quite differently than men. They would likely make linkages between effective democracy in the public sphere and the need for democracy in the private sphere,[248] thereby demonstrating that recognition of women's human rights requires movement into the so-called "private sphere."

The second step, making violations visible, is accomplished by documenting facts through empirical studies, NGO reports, and personal accounts which explain the lack of women's participation in public life. This step is a strategy unto itself. "[P]romoting change by reporting facts,"[249] is a human rights methodology based on the belief that violations are rampant partly because they remain hidden.[250] Known as the "human rights method,"[251] the reporting of abuses is effective because it has a universal language, moral authority, and a measure of accountability which can invigorate local struggles and put pressure on governments to end state-sponsored or tolerated abuse of women.[252] Moreover, it educates men about how human rights violations are committed against women in ways they do not experience and how all women, regardless of culture, experience this gender gap.[253]

The third step, analyzing the claim through existing, but expanded human rights mechanisms, requires an examination of the elements of the right to citizenship as enshrined in international law and the meaning of effective democracy. The questions that should be asked at this stage are: Has the law been used to exclude women from the public sphere? What activities are considered to be the business of law and what are left unregulated? Why is lack of regulation of particular areas of social life significant for women? How can the law be interpreted so that gender status is not used to deprive women from exercising their citizenship rights?

The response to these questions will make it obvious that if women are to enjoy the citizenship right, they must have access to political participation and the ability to enter the public realm where human rights are defined and defended, and where they can help to change and shape the policies which affect women in their daily lives.[254] Democracy in the home would be an essential part of what enables women to have the social, economic, and political capability to exercise democracy in the public sphere. One goes hand in hand with the other.

The right to bodily security

A similar analysis can be applied to the issue of violence against women. The right, designed to protect people from violence and set out in Article 6 of the International Covenant on Civil and Political Rights,[255] is often labeled as the "most important of all human rights."[256] However, the traditional interpretation of this right limits protection to individual victims of violence perpetrated by the state. The "private" sphere, where much of the risk of violence or death exists for women, is not reached by this interpretation. At the same time, empirical evidence of "private" forms of violence against women is overwhelming and undisputed.[257] Millions of women are victims of forced abortion and infanticide from pressure to have sons, malnutrition from preference for males in times of food shortages, beatings by husbands, and less access to health care. However, because of the narrow, gender-biased interpretation of human rights laws, they are not included within the "right" to bodily security.

The right to be free from torture, another centrally important civil and political right, is similarly interpreted.[258] The definition of torture requires that it take place in the public realm, "inflicted by or at the instigation of or with the consent or acquiescence of a public official or other person acting in an official capacity."[259] Feminists argue that government inaction to prevent the torture of women committed by non-state actors is government "action" as much as if the state were committing the violence.[260] In particular, failure by states to act against sexual torture and violence represented by massive rates of rape, battering, and trafficking women, effectively condones such behavior.[261]

Read with even minimal formal equality rights, which most states guarantee, it is clear that women are discriminated against by the state through the ways in which laws are enforced. Brazilian feminist activists, collaborating with Americas Watch on the First Women's Rights Project, have used this analysis to attack systematic acceptance of violence against women in the everyday administration of justice in Brazil.[262] The "legitimate defense of honor," used by judges in a routine manner to acquit men who killed their wives,[263] was contrasted with husband-murder, which was treated far more seriously.[264] By documenting a structure of discriminatory non-prosecution and sometimes overt acceptance of wife-murder, battery, and rape, they were able to demonstrate that the state denied women equal protection under the law and was in breach of its international human rights obligations. The project demonstrated that state legalized sex inequality is as serious and harmful as the state using rape as an instrumentality.[265]

Amnesty International and other NGO's have found that in many areas of the world, rape is used by government agents to elicit information or confessions from women held as political prisoners, to humiliate and intimidate women, and to punish them for political activity. Indeed, as Amnesty International discovered, "[s]ometimes women are raped because police officers or soldiers think they have a right to do so."[266] In India, hundreds of cases of police rape of women in custody have been reported, but convictions are rare.[267] India, however, is by no means unique in this respect.[268] Many other countries, such as Chile, Honduras, and the United States for example, have failed to investigate reports of widespread sexual abuse of women in prisons.[269] These cases are less about breaking down the public/private distinction than they are about blatant failure to provide equal protection of the law.

Other than the right to life and the right to be free from torture, the interpretations of other civil and political rights such as freedom of expression and privacy rights, also work against, rather than for, women's human right to be free from violence. In many countries, the distribution, manufacture, and use of pornography, which directly contributes to violence against women and girls, is protected by the freedom of expression right.[270] The right to free expression is considered to be a "public" realm issue, whereas the use of pornography to hurt women falls within the private sphere.[271]

Similar arguments are used to protect trafficking and prostitution of women and children. Governments and businesses which profit from the international sex trade in women and children argue for continued and expanded exploitation of women and children in the name of women's rights.[272] They say that prostitution is "commercial sex work" done by women exercising their freedom of choice and labor rights.[273] At the same time, they lobby for and decrease the age of consent for minors to engage in sexual activity.[274] They say prostitution must be destigmatized and regulated so that the prostitutes will become more "professional" and more "dignity" will accrue to their "work."[275] Feminists argue the more likely result will be the dignifying of the sex trade industry and the men who buy the bodies of the women and children trapped in prostitution.[276]

The "regulationist" approach protects men at the expense of women by making "prostitution a [legitimate] and necessary social service performed by a separate class of women. It integrates that work into the social structure through taxation, health checks, and other administrative measures."[277] Not only does this characterization of "rights" serve the needs of the exploiters of women, it masks the harm of prostitution, such that its human rights dimensions are invisible.[278] Moreover, if countries, international banks, monetary agencies, and labor organizations are permitted to incorporate prostitution and trafficking in women into global economies, as some are proposing, then governments are much less accountable for making dignified and sustainable employment available to women.[279]

Civil and political rights are also used to prevent government scrutiny of cultural and religious practices which oppress women.[280] Alliances formed between fundamentalist religious groups and conservative political groups, which seek to destroy women's rights to sexual autonomy, sexual orientation, bodily security, and other citizenship freedoms under the guise of religious freedom, demonstrate the importance of scrutinizing the effects of "civil rights" claims on the rights of women.[281] Religious freedom to submit oneself to God is often interpreted by male religious leaders to mean submission to men.[282] A "women's rights are human rights" analysis uncovers such discrimination in the rights balancing process.

The second generation: socio-economic rights

At first glance, socio-economic rights appear to be more accessible to women than civil and political rights. Rights to development, health care, food, shelter, and employment protected in the Economic Covenant,[283] do not invoke the "individual versus state" paradigm, and are thus less tied to the public/private distinction. Yet, the "public sphere" distinction is still used to deny women access to these rights. In reality, gender distinctions and gender bias prevail in definitions of the socio-economic rights just as they do for civil and political rights.

The Economic Covenant creates a "public sphere" by relying on the assumption that all power resides in the state.[284] Feminists say that in order to respect women's socio-economic rights, international law must recognize that there are many other instrumentalities of power, all male-dominated.[285] Defining power exclusively in terms of what the state does renders the socio-economic rights seriously underinclusive for women. When one half of the human race is subject to unjust abuses of power by the other half, it is gender biased to limit protection only to state action.[286]

The consequences of creating a "public sphere" defined by the exercise of state power can be seen in the Article 7 definition of the right to "just and favourable conditions of work" and "conditions of work not inferior to those enjoyed by men, with equal pay for equal work."[287] The Economic Covenant defines these rights as applicable only to work in the "public" sphere.[288]

However, economic activity in the home, the fields, and the marketplace, performed without pay, is considered the private sphere.[289] When the majority of the world's women work in the "private" sphere, the protections in Article 7 are meaningless.[290] The definition makes the extent and tremendous economic value of women's work invisible.[291]

An analysis based on the principle that "women's rights are human rights" would find the definition of "work" in Article 7 discriminatory. Moreover, national accounting systems, as well as international rights that operate on the assumption that women's work is of a lesser order than that of men, could be attacked for violating equality guarantees in international law.[292]

Third generation rights

Third generation rights are rights of groups or collective rights. Their underlying premise is that the welfare of the community is more important than the welfare of the individual. Group-based rights are usually thought to be more sensitive to the needs and priorities of women than civil and political rights because they are more centered on the family and community rather than on individuals. In practice, however, the exercise of third generation rights, such as the right to development, supports male economic dominance.[293] Similarly, the exercise of the right to self-determination, which allows "[a]ll peoples . . . [to] freely determine their political status and freely pursue their economic, social, and cultural development,"[294] oppresses women.

Often cited examples are structural adjustment programs imposed by international actors subject to international law, such as the International Monetary Fund and the World Bank. They have caused disproportionate disadvantage to women because their theories, strategies, and solutions for development, growth, and underdevelopment tend to ignore women and the role they fulfill in their societies. When development policies are interpreted and implemented in a gender-blind way,[295] women's work burden in developing countries increases while social expenditures decrease concomitantly, employment creation for women is weakened, and institutional gender inequality in the formal and informal sectors of national economics goes unnoticed.[296] Moreover, the financing conditions of international lending institutions compromise women's economic and social progress by suppressing wages, undermining the contributions and livelihoods of small producers, undermining trade unions, and placing social services, particularly health care and education, out of their reach.[297]

If development and self-determination rights were understood to include women in their scope, the World Bank and the International Monetary Fund would be legally obligated to avoid structural development policies which discriminate against women.[298] As international actors in breach of international law, they would be confronted by NGO's and state governments to ensure women share equally in the benefits of their loans.

The challenge of cultural relativism

One of the difficulties the "women's rights are human rights" strategy presents is the accusation that women's rights will result in cultural destruction. Many governments breach human rights treaties with impunity, using the argument that human rights must be subject to the interests of national security, economic strategy, and local traditions.[299] While feminists accept the view that diversity and difference must be respected, they also agree that rejection of the universality principle endangers not just women's rights, but also rights of men and children. Once individual governments begin to define what fundamental human rights are, or who may enjoy those rights, the whole international and domestic system of human rights is jeopardized.

Amnesty International, which recently took up the cause for women's human rights, asks, "Would the woman who is raped and murdered in Indonesia for standing up for workers' rights consider this a justifiable price to pay for a nation's "right" to interpret human rights according to local economic conditions?"[300] Others argue that harmful customs such as child marriage, genital mutilation, and inferior education and nutrition for girl children cannot be legitimately passed off as "cultural."[301] Such practices are more accurately characterized as discriminatory and harmful human rights abuses.

Not all cases, however, are so easily analyzed. Muslim women, for example, argue that modernization, urbanization, and other 20th century developments have motivated women to look for security in tradition.[302] They say if they accept Western ways and products, they will be forced to give up their traditions. The delicate task is to avoid homogenizing universalism on the one hand and the paralysis of cultural relativism on the other.[303] An inevitable tension within feminist theory comes from the understanding that diversity is the norm and there are no monolithic categories, and the recognition of the need to work in solidarity with common causes, commitments, and approaches.

Respecting culture while promoting the universality and indivisibility of human rights requires sensitivity to both the process and substance of strategies employed. Feminist analyses of law in one type of society cannot be imported wholesale into other types of societies or into the international human rights system. The means chosen to combat discrimination or inequality need to be varied according to their particular contexts but the ultimate result can be the same.

For example, the public/private analysis used above could potentially create a problem when applied to some social and legal systems. In Western culture, the distinction is drawn between matters outside the home, of a public nature, with which the law is concerned, and matters in the home, of a private nature, which generally fall outside the scope of the law. The analysis is intended to show that women are more vulnerable to abuses in the private sphere because their rights are unprotected there.

In other cultures, however, the public/private distinction may be used to achieve positive results.[304] What is private in one society may well be public in another. Sometimes the public distinction may be used to illuminate areas of oppression otherwise unobserved. These problems can be resolved without abandoning the public/private analysis and its exposure of women's human rights violations. Perhaps better language could be used in the international context to examine "the women's domain," which is consistently devalued in most cultures, whether it is in the "public" or "private" sectors.

Another trap to be avoided is dividing the world into bipolar categories.[305] For example, western feminists cannot assume that the West is always progressive on women's rights or that the East is backward.[306] Feminists in the East must be equally cautious not to subscribe to the reverse notion that the East is superior to the West.[307] The reality is that in both areas of the world, both traditions exist. There are instances where traditional laws have been more progressive than modern legislation and the colonial encounter actually robbed women of pre-existing rights.[308]

In summary, the accusation that human rights activists are out to destroy the culture can be a powerful tool in the hands of those who wish to maintain the status quo of female subordination. Yet, in any society, unless women's rights have sufficient legitimacy within the culture they will not be respected. It must be recognized that the foundation for a civil society must be laid according to its particular context so that it will strike a responsive chord in the general public consciousness.[309] But the competing idea that there has to be standards by which one can hold individuals and states accountable, must also play a role in any complete analysis.

Notes

1. Amnesty International, <u>Human Rights Are Women's Rights</u> 85 (1995).

2. For an analysis of the history of women's political, cultural, physical, and economic repression in the global society, see Marilyn French, The War Against Women (1992). See generally, Amnesty International, supra note 1; Charlotte Bunch, Bringing the Global Home: Feminism in the '80s (1985); Empowerment and the Law: Strategies of Third World Women (Margaret Schuler ed., 1986); Marilyn French, Beyond Power: On Women, Men, and Morals (1985); Latin American Committee for the Defence of Women's Rights, Women: Watched and Punished (1993); Maria Mies, Patriarchy and Accumulation on a World Scale: Women in the International Division of Labour (1986); Sisterhood is Global (Robin Morgan ed., 1984); United Nations, The World's Women 1970-1990: Trends and Statistics (1991); Marilyn Waring, If Women Counted: A New Feminist Economics (1988).

3. For example, the list of "great law-givers" who over the centuries contributed to the growth of law in many nations include: Hammurabi (1950 B.C., Babylon); Moses (13th Century B.C., Egypt); Confucius (551-479 B.C., China); Justinian (483-565 A.D., Roman Empire); Mohammed (570-632 A.D., Arabia); Grotius (1583-1645 A.D., Holland); Napoleon (1769-1821 A.D., France); Menes (3100 B.C., Egypt); Solomon (973-933 B.C., Israel); Lycurgus (9th Century B.C., Greece); Draco (7th Century B.C., Greece); Solon (600 B.C., Greece); Augustus (63 B.C.-14 A.D., Roman Empire); St. Louis (1214-1270 A.D., France); Blackstone (1723-1780 A.D., England); John Marshall (1755-1835 A.D., U.S.A.). Gerald Gall, The Canadian Legal System 32-33 (3d ed. 1990).

4. For a thorough discussion of feminist theories and the history of their development, see Rosemarie Tong, Feminist Thought (Routledge 1992) (1989).

5. Sarah Benton, "Feminism", in Ideas That Shape Politics 78, 81 (Michael Foley ed., 1994).

6. Id.

7. Carol Hanish was one of the first to use the term in her 1971 essay, "The Personal, is Political." Id., at 81.

8. These theories were chosen because until now they appear to have had the most influence on the law. Many other theories of feminism exist which could be discussed, including Marxist feminism, Psychoanalytic feminism, Socialist feminism, Eco Feminism, and Existentialist feminism. The limits of this paper, however, do not permit their coverage.

9. See infra, notes 63, 71, 85, 97, 124, 150 and accompanying text.

10. Mary Wollstonecraft, A Vindication of the Rights of Women (Prometheus 1989) (1792).

11. John Stuart Mill, "The Subjection of Women", in John Stuart Mill & Harriet Taylor Mill, Essays on Sex Equality 125, 184-85 (Alice S. Rossi ed., 1970).

12. See, e.g., Mary Eberts, "Sex-Based Discrimnation and the Charter", in Equality Rights and the Canadian Charter of Rights and Freedoms 183 (Anne Bayefsky & Mary Eberts eds., 1985).

13. Id., at 184-87.

14. [1930] 1 D.L.R. 98 (P.C.) (Can.).

15. Eberts, supra, note 12, at 185 n.4 (citing cases from Great Britain, United States, and Canada).

16. Re Kitson, [1920] S.A.S.R. 230, 231-232, 236-37 (Austl.); Re Edith Hayes, 6 W.A.L.R. 209, 213-14 (1904) (Austl.); Ex Parte Ogden, 16 N.W.S.L.R. 86, 88 (1893) (Austl.).

17. Edwards v. Attorney General of Canada, [1930] 1 D.L.R. 98 (P.C.) (Can).

18. Id., at 99.

19. Hilary Charlesworth, "What are Women's International Human Rights"?, in Human Rights of Women: National and International Perspectives 58 (Rebecca Cook ed., 1994).

20. Eberts, supra, note 12, at 186.

21. Catharine A. MacKinnon, "Toward Feminist Jurisprudence", in Feminist Jurisprudence 610, 610-19 (Patricia Smith ed., 1993).

22. Mary Joe Frug, "Securing Job Equality for Women: Labor Market Hostility to Working Women", 59 B.U.L. Rev. 55, 94-103 (1979).

23. Catharine A. MacKinnon, "Reflections on Sex Equality Under Law", 100 Yale L.J. 1281 (1987).

24. 1974 S.C.R. 1349 (Can.).

25. Indian Act, R.S.C., ch. I-6 (1970) (Can.).

26. The Indian Act provides: "The following persons are not entitled to be registered [as Indians], namely . . . (b) a woman who married a person who is not an Indian . . . ." Id., § 12(1)(b).

27. Kathleen Jamieson, Indian Women and the Law in Canada: Citizens Minus 1 (1978).

28. Id.

29. Id.

30. Id.

31. Attorney General of Canada v. Lavell, 1974 S.C.R. 1349, 1350 (Can.). For a detailed discussion of the Lavell case, see Jamieson, supra note 28, at 79-88.

32. Lavell, 1974 S.C.R. at 1372.

33. Id. at 1366; see, Canadian Bill of Rights, 8 & 9 Eliz. 2, ch. 44 (1960), R.S.C., App. III (1970).

34. Lavell, 1974 S.C.R. at 1373.

35. Bliss v. Attorney General of Canada, [1979] 1 S.C.R. 183 (Can.).

36. Unemployment Insurance Act, ch. 48, 1970-1972 S.C. 981 (Can.).

37. Id. § 30(1).

38. Id. § 46.

39. Bliss, [1979] 1 S.C.R. at 184.

40. Id.

41. Dale Gibson, The Law of the Charter: Equality Rights 31 (1990).

42. Bliss, [1979] 1 S.C.R. at 190-91 (quoting the opinion of Pratte, J., in a lower court's decision in Re Attorney-General of Canada and Bliss, [1977] 77 D.L.R.3d 609, 613 (Fed. Ct.)) (emphasis added).

43. In this case, the legislation was the Canadian Bill of Rights, 8 & 9 Eliz. 2, ch. 44 (1960), R.S.C. App. III (1970).

44. This "voluntarism" rationale is still propounded by some as a justifiable limit on the right to equal treatment. See, e.g., Thomas Flanagan, "Manufacture of Minorities", in Minorities and the Canadian State 107, 109 (Neil Nevitte & Allan Kornberg eds., 1985). For a reply to Professor Flanagan's rationale, see Dale Gibson, "Stereotypes, Statistics and Slippery Slopes: A Reply to Professor Flanagan & Knopff and Other Critics of Human Rights Legislation", in Minorities and the Canadian State, supra, at 125, 125-37.

45. For a collection of essays on the topic by an international group of feminist scholars, see Ours By Right: Women's Rights as Human Rights (Joanna Kerr ed., 1993) [hereinafter Ours By Right].

46. Joanna Kerr, "The Context and the Goal", in Ours By Right, supra note 45, at 1, 6.

47. See generally Leslie Bender, "From Gender Difference to Feminist Solidarity: Using Carol Gilligan and an Ethic of Care in Law", 15 Vt. L. Rev. 1, 36 (1990).

48. Robin West, "Jurisprudence and Gender", 55 U. Chi. L. Rev. 1, 61 (1988).

49. Noreen Burrows, "International Law and Human Rights: The Case of Women's Rights", in Human Rights: From Rhetoric to Reality 80, 97 (Tom Campbell et al. eds., 1986).

50. Id.

51. Carol Gilligan, In a Different Voice: Psychological Theory and Women's Development (1982).

52. Id. at 1-22.

53. Id. at 99.

54. See generally, id. at 64-105.

55. Id. at 25-38.

56. Id. at 27-28.

57. Id. at 65, 97-104.

58. Id. at 31-37.

59. See, e.g., Cynthia Fuchs Epstein, Women in Law (1981); Carrie Menkel-Meadow, "Portia in a Different Voice: Speculations on a Women's Lawyering Process", 1 Berkeley Women's L.J. 39 (1985); Mary Jane Mossman, "Feminism and Legal Method: The Difference it Makes", 3 Austl. J.L. & Soc. 30 (1986).

60. Ann Scales, "The Emergence of Feminist Jurisprudence: An Essay", 95 Yale L.J. 1373, 1381 (1986). See also Frances Olsen, "Feminism and Critical Legal Theory: An American Perspective", 18 Int'l J. Soc. L. 199, 204 (1990).

61. To quote Catharine MacKinnon, "For women to affirm difference, when difference means dominance, as it does with gender, means to affirm the qualities and characteristics of powerlessness. . . . [W]hen you are powerless, you don't just speak differently. A lot, you don't speak." Catharine MacKinnon, Feminism Unmodified: Discourses on Life and Law 39 (1987). She concludes: "Take your foot off our necks, then we will hear in what tongue women speak." Id. at 45.

62. Bender, supra note 48, at 7-8.

63. Brooks v. Canada Safeway Ltd., [1989] 1 S.C.R. 1219 (Can.).

64. The Canadian Charter of Rights and Freedoms is Part I of the Constitution Act, 1982, enacted as Schedule B of the Canada Act, 1982, ch. 11 (U.K.) [hereinafter Charter].

65. Bliss v. Attorney General of Canada, [1979] 1 S.C.R. 183 (Can.).

66. The Court based its decision on the arguments put forward by an Intervener in the case, the Women's Legal Education and Action Fund, (LEAF), a feminist litigation strategy group whose purpose is to create legal principles in the jurisprudence which reflect women's reality and respect their rights as human rights.

67. Brooks, [1989] 1 S.C.R. at 1250-51.

68. Id. at 1243-44.

69. Id.

70. Brooks, [1989] 1 S.C.R. 1219, at 1243-44.

71. [1990] 1 S.C.R. 852 (Can.).

72. Id. at 857.

73. The Court used the same analysis adopted in the leading Supreme Court decision on the meaning and scope of constitutional equality guarantees. See, Andrews v. Law Soc'y of British Columbia, [1989] 1 S.C.R. 143 (Can.).

74. See, Lavellee, [1990] 1 S.C.R. at 876.

75. Id. at 874.

76. Brooks v. Cananda Safeway Ltd, [1989] 1 S.C.R. 1219 (Can.).

77. Lavallee, [1990] 1 S.C.R. at 874.

78. Id. at 876-77.

79. Id. at 875.

80. MacKinnon, supra note 61, at 3.

81. Other fundamental premises of radical feminists include the following: 1) women were the first oppressed group; 2) women's oppression is the most widespread, existing in virtually every known society; 3) women's oppression causes the most suffering to its victims, qualitatively as well as quantitatively, although the suffering may often go unrecognized because of the sexist prejudices of both the oppressors and the victims; and 3) women's oppression provides a conceptual model for understanding all other forms of oppression. Alison M. Jaggar & Paula S. Rothenberg, Feminist Frameworks: Alternative Theoretical Accounts of the Relations Between Men and Women 120-22 (3d ed. 1993).

82. MacKinnon, supra note 61, at 33-34.

83. Id. at 205.

84. MacKinnon, supra note 61, at 40-45.

85. Andrews v. Law Soc'y of British Columbia, [1989] 1 S.C.R. 143 (Can.). See also two subsequent decisions which further clarified the principles articulated in Andrews, namely, Reference Re Workers' Compensation Act, 1983 (NFLD.), [1989] 1 S.C.R. 922 (Can.) and R. v. Turpin, [1989] 1 S.C.R. 1296 (Can.).

86. The British Columbia Court of Appeal, whose decision was appealed to the Supreme Court of Canada, adopted the Aristotelian approach using the similarly situated test of equality. Andrews v. Law Soc'y of British Columbia, 2 B.C.L.R.2d 305, 311 (B.C. Ct. App. 1986).

87. Andrews, [1989] 1 S.C.R. at 166 (McIntyre, J., concurring in part and dissenting in part).

88. Id. at 174 (McIntyre, J., concurring in part and dissenting in part).

89. Id. at 152. Although many third parties intervened in the appeal, the court adopted the arguments put forward by the intervener, described supra note 67.

90. See, Mary O'Brien, The Politics of Reproduction (1981).

91. See Kate Millett, Sexual Politics (1970) and French, Beyond Power, supra note 2, for two different perspectives on androgyny.

92. See, e.g., Janice Raymond, The Transsexual Empire (1979).

93. See supra note 32 and accompanying text. See also Carol Smart, Feminism and the Power of Law 75-76 (1989) (questioning whether women "can ever avoid the omnipotent grip of the patriarch who is in our hearts, bodies, and minds").

94. See, e.g., Shulamith Firestone, The Dialectic of Sex 72-104 (1970).

95. See, e.g., O'Brien, supra note 91.

96. For a discussion of reproduction-aiding technologies, see Gena Corea, The Mother Machine: Reproductive Technologies from Artificial Insemination to Artificial Wombs (1985). See also Margrit Eichler, "Human Rights and the New

Reproductive Technologies--Individual or Collective Choices?", in Human Rights in the Twenty-First Century: A Global Challenge 875 (Kathleen E. Mahoney & Paul Mahoney eds., 1993) [hereinafter A Global Challenge]; Renate Klein, "The Impact of Reproductive and Genetic Engineering on Women's Bodily Integrity and Human Dignity", in A Global Challenge, supra, at 889.

97. [1988] 1 S.C.R. 30 (Can.).

98. Charter, supra note 65, § 7.

99. Morgentaler, [1988] 1 S.C.R. at 171-72 (Wilson, J., concurring) (citations omitted).

100. See Catharine MacKinnon, The Sexual Harassment of Working Women (1979).

101. In Canada, very little discussion of the harm of pornography and prostitution occured prior to the 1980's. Until that time, it was generally regarded as a moral issue. See Kathleen E. Mahoney, "Obscenity, Morals and the Law: A Feminist Critique", 17 Ottawa L.J. 33 (1985); Communications and Public Affairs, Department of Justice Canada, Report of the Committee on Sexual Offences Against Children and Youths and The Report of the Special Committee on Pornography and Prostitution, Can. Doc. J2-58/1985, at 9-12 (1985) [hereinafter Pornography Report].

102. Scales, supra note 61, at 1393.

103. See generally Report of the Royal Commission on the Status of Women in Canada (1970).

104. An important turning point in Canada with respect to understanding rape occurred with the publication of Lorene M.G. Clarks' and Debra J. Lewis' Rape: The Price of Coercive Sexuality (1977). The thesis of the book is that the law of rape is not conceptualized as a violation of women, indeed even as a form of gender specific violence, but rather as a property crime against the capitalistic ownership rights of men. Quickly following this book was a proliferation of feminist analyses of laws dealing with different forms of violence against women.

105. See, e.g., Final Report of The Canadian Panel on Violence Against Women: Changing the Landscape: Ending Violence V Achieving Equality, Can. Doc.

SW45-1/1993E (1993). See also Pornography Report, supra note 102, at 18-22, which is less woman-centered, but at least acknowledges a woman's perspective on prostitution and pornography. Id. at 18-22.

106. Some women disagree with most feminists whose emphasis is on individual issues of consent. First Nations women, for example, see the larger, still unresolved issue of consent to an imposed legal system as more important. See Patricia A. Monture-Okanee, "The Violence We Women Do: A First Nations View", in Challenging Times: The Women's Movement in Canada and the United States 193 (Constance Blackhouse & David H. Flaherty eds., 1992) [hereinafter Challenging Times].

107. Catharine MacKinnon, "Feminism, Marxism, Method, and the State: Towards Feminist Jurisprudence", 8 Signs 635, 642-43, 646-53 (1983).

108. Susan Brownmiller, Against Our Will: Men, Women and Rape 15 (1975).

109. For a summary of the changes in Canadian law, see Christine L.M. Boyle, Sexual Assault (1984). For changes in the United States, see Patricia Searles & Ronald Berger, "The Current Status of Rape Reform Legislation: An Examination of State Statutes", 10 Women's Rts. L. Rep. 25 (1987).

110. See Searles & Berger, supra note 110, at 28.

111. See R. v. Seaboyer, [1991] 2 S.C.R. 577, 634-36 (Can.).

112. Seaboyer is the leading case in Canada on this point. [1991] 2 S.C.R. 577. For a postmodern analysis of the law of rape and consent, see the dissenting opinion of L'Hereux-Dubé, J. Id. at 643.

113. Katharine T. Bartlett, Gender and Law: Theory, Doctrine, Commentary 700 (1993) (citing Stephen J. Schulhofer, "Taking Sexual Autonomy Seriously", 11 L. & Phil. 35, 38-39 (1992)).

114. Catharine MacKinnon, "Feminist Approaches to Sexual Assault in Canada and the United States", in Challenging Times, supra note 107, at 186, 190.

115. See generally id.

116. Id. at 190.

117. Id.

118. Id. at 190-91.

119. An example of this thinking is the decision of Justice Bollen of the Supreme Court of South Australia in the unreported case of *R. v. Johns*, where in a spousal rape case, the judge said:
[t]here is, of course, nothing wrong with a husband, faced with his wife's initial refusal to engage in intercourse, in attempting, in an acceptable way, to persuade her to change her mind, and that may involve a measure of rougher than usual handling. It may be, in the end, that handling and persuasion will persuade the wife to agree. Sometimes it is a fine line between not agreeing, then changing the mind and consenting. You will bear that in mind when considering the totality of the evidence about each act of intercourse.
Question of Law Reserved on Acquital Pursuant to Section 350(1A) Criminal Law Consolidation Act, No. 93/1-3896, 1993 AUST SASC LEXIS 1450, at *14 (S. Ct. S. Austl., Ct. Crim. App. 1993) (quoting Justice Bollen in R. v. Johns).
    On appeal, the ruling was found to be wrong in law, partly because of the suggestion to the jury that any agreement produced by "rougher than usual handling" might nevertheless constitute valid consent. Id.

120. In Canada, this approach is followed in part where the newly amended rape law requires that consent be meaningful. It does this by requiring voluntary agreement and by stipulating what is not consent, including where another person purports to consent for the woman, where she is rendered incapable of consenting, where a position of trust or authority has been abused, or where she has indicated that she has not consented. Criminal Code of Canada, R.S.C., ch. 38, § 273.1 (1992) (Can.).

121. MacKinnon, supra note 115, at 192.

122. Id.

123. Id.

124. See R. v. Butler, [1992] 1 S.C.R. 432 (Can.).

125. Id. at 454-55.

126. Id. at 454.

127. See id. at 479.

128. See Janzen v. Platy Enterprises, [1989] 1 S.C.R. 1252 (Can.).

129. Id. at 1284.

130. Id. at 1253.

131. A further indication that the Court was applying Radical feminist theory was the fact that Catharine MacKinnon's book, Sexual Harassment of Working Women: A case of Sex Discrimination, was affirmatively cited in the decision. Id. at 1279-80.

132. For example, in December, 1993, the United Nations General Assembly adopted the Declaration on the Elimination of Violence Against Women. G.A. Res. 104, U.N. GAOR, 48th Sess., Supp. No. 49, at 217, U.N. Doc. A/46/49 (1993). It defined violence as "any act of gender-based violence that results in, or is likely to result in, physical, sexual, or psychological harm or suffering to women, including threat of such acts, coercion or arbitrary deprivations of liberty, whether occurring in public or private life." Id. art. 1. The Declaration lists abuses that fall into the category of violence against women as: 1) physical, sexual, and psychological violence occurring in the family and in the community, including battering, sexual abuse of female children, dowry related violence, marital rape, female genital mutilation and other traditional practices harmful to women; 2) non-spousal violence; 3) violence related to exploitation; 4) sexual harassment and intimidation at work, in educational institutions and elsewhere; 5) trafficking in women; 6) forced prostitution; and 7) violence perpetrated or condoned by the state. Id. art. 2.

133. Simone de Beauvoir, The Second Sex 41 (H.M. Parshley ed. & trans., First Vintage Books 1974) (1949). Her analysis of how women became separate from and inferior to men is developed in the first three chapters of the book.

134. Id. at xix.

135. Id. at 795; see also Simone de Beauvoir, The Prime of Life 291-92 (Peter Green trans., 1965).

136. See e.g., Mary Joe Frug, Postmodern Legal Feminism 125-53 (1992).

137. Id.

138. See, e.g., Sandra Harding, The Science Question in Feminism (1986).

139. Id. at 28.

140. For different perspectives within postmodern feminism, see generally Judith C. Greenberg, "Introduction to Postmodern Legal Feminism", in Postmodern Legal Feminism, supra note 137; Sherene Razack, Canadian Feminism and the Law (1991); Jennifer Wicke, "Postmodern Identity and the Legal Subject", 62 U. Colo. L. Rev. 455 (1991).

141. See Jennifer Nedelsky, "The Challenges of Multiplicity", 89 Mich. L. Rev. 1591, 1601-09 (1991) (reviewing Elizabeth V. Spelman, Inessential Woman: Problems of Exclusion in Feminist Thought (1988)).

142. See id. at 1600.

143. Hillary Charlesworth, "Alienating Oscar? Feminist Analysis of International Law", in Reconceiving Reality: Women and International Law 1, 4 (Dorinda G. Dallmeyer ed., ASIL Studies in Transnational Legal Policy No. 25, 1993).

144. Id.

145. Mary Joe Frug, "Sexual Equality and Sexual Difference in American Law", 26 New Eng. L. Rev 665, 674 (1992).

146. Id.

147. Id.

148. Id.

149. Id. at 674-75.

150. Moge v. Moge, [1992] 3 S.C.R. 813 (Can.).

151. Id. at 813.

152. See generally id.

153. Id.

154. Id. at 875.

155. See Martha Minow, "Feminist Reason: Getting It and Losing It", J. of Legal Educ., Mar.-June 1988, at 47.

156. Id. at 51.

157. Glenda Simms, "Beyond the White Veil", in Challenging Times, supra, note 107, at 175, 179; see also Angela P. Harris, "Race and Essentialism in Feminist Legal Theory", 42 Stan. L. Rev. 581 (1990); Marlee Kline, "Race, Racism and Feminist Legal Theory", 12 Harv. Women's L.J. 115 (1989).

158. Mari Matsuda, "Crime and Punishment", Ms. Magazine, Nov.-Dec. 1994, at 86.

159. Nancy F. Cott, The Grounding of Modern Feminism 283 (1987).

160. Minow, supra note 156, at 48; see, e.g., bell hooks, Ain't I a Woman: Black Women and Feminism (1981); Angela Y. Davis, Women, Race, and Class chs. 11-12 (1981); Brenda Eichelberger, "Voices on Black Feminism", Quest, Spring 1977, at 16.

161. Minow, supra note 156, at 48.

162. Arun Mukherjee, "A House Divided: Women of Colour and American Feminist Theory", in Challenging Times, supra note 107, at 165.

163. hooks, supra note 161, at 121-22.

164. See generally Patricia A. Monture-Okanee, "The Violence We Women Do: A First Nations View", in Challenging Times, supra note 107, at 193; Mukherjee, supra note 163; Shelina Neallani, "Women of Colour in the Legal Profession: Facing the Familiar Barriers of Race and Sex", 5 Can. J. Women L. 148 (1992); Tarel Quandt, "Learning Exclusion: A Feminist Critique of the Law School Experience", 4 Educ. L.J. 279 (1993); Simms, supra note 158; Mary Ellen Turpel, "Aboriginal Peoples and the Canadian Charter: Interpretive Monopolies, Cultural Differences", 6 Can. Hum. Rts. Y.B. 3 (1990).

165. See Maxine B. Zinn et al., "The Cost of Exclusionary Practices in Women's Studies", in Reconstructing the Academy: Women's Education and Women's Studies 125, 127-29 (Elizabeth Minnich et al. eds., 1988).

166. Id.

167. Id.

168. See generally Marinna Valverde, "Racism and Anti-Racism in Feminist Teaching and Research", in Challenging Times, supra note 107, at 160.

169. Id.

170. Id.

171. Simms, supra note 158, at 178-79; bell hooks, Talking Back: Thinking Feminist, Thinking Black (1979).

172. See Hazel V. Carby, "On the Threshold of Women's Era: Lynching Empire and Sexuality in Black Feminist Theory", in Race, Writing, and Difference 301 (Henry L. Gates, Jr. ed., 1986).

173. Kimberly Crenshaw, "The Intersection of Race and Gender in Rape Law", in Mary Joe Frug, Women and the Law 800, 801 (1992).

174. Id.

175. Id.

176. See id. at 800.

177. Id. at 803-04.

178. Id. at 803.

179. This is not true with respect to capital punishment, however. In the United States, the racism evident in the proportion of people of color sentenced to death for killing whites and the overall percentage of executed criminals since 1976 (38%) has led feminists to suggest that the death penalty is an issue feminists must confront. See Matsuda, supra note 159, at 88.

180. See Crenshaw, supra note 174, at 800. Susan Estrich, "Rape", 95 <u>Yale L.J.</u> 1087 (1986), refers to a study which reveals that between 1930 and 1967, 89% of the men executed for rape in the United States were black. Only 2% of the defendants convicted of rape involving any other racial combination were executed. Id. at 1089-95.

181. See id.

182. Id. at 802.

183. Harris, supra note 158, at 598.

184. Id. at 599.

185. Crenshaw, supra note 174, at 801.

186. See Harris, supra note 158, at 598-99.

187. Id. at 599.

188. Catharine A. MacKinnon, "From Practice to Theory or What is a White Womon Anyway?" 4 <u>Yale L.J. & Feminism</u> 13 (1991).

189. Id.

190. Beatrice A Cameron, "Nametaking: A Model for Feminist Identity", 6 <u>Wis. Women's L.J.</u> 141, 146 (1991).

191. MacKinnon, supra note 189, at 15. For a similar response, see Cameron, supra note 191, at 145-46.

192. MacKinnon, supra note 189, at 16.

193. See Kline, supra note 158, at 132-34, where she critiques Susan Boyd's work on child custody law.

194. See id. at 130.

195. Id.

570   HUMAN RIGHTS: CHINESE & CANADIAN PERSPECTIVES

196. See, for example, M. Patricia Fernandez Kelly, "A Chill Wind Blows: Class, Ideology, and the Reproductive Dilemma", in Challenging Times, supra note 107, at 252.

197. See generally Christine Overall, "Feminist Philosophical Reflections on Reproductive Rights in Canada", in Challenging Times supra note 107, at 240.

198. Id.

199. Id.

200. See generally Corea, supra note 97; Infertility: Women Speak Out About Their Experiences of Reproductive Medicine (Renate Klein ed., 1989); Renate Klein, The Exploitation of a Desire: Women's Experiences with In Vitro Fertilization (1989); Royal Commission on New Reproductive Technologies, Proceed with Care: Final Report of the Royal Commission on New Reproductive Technologies (1993); Marie Ashe, "Law-Language of Maternity: Discourse Holding Nature in Contempt", 22 New Eng. L. Rev. 521 (1988); Bartha M. Knoppers, "Reproductive Technology and International Mechanisms of Protection of the Human Person", 32 McGill L.J. 336 (1987).

201. See generally Klein supra note 97, at 889. Much of the knowledge and many of the procedures used today in modern gene and reproductive technology were developed by Nazi scientists and doctors. Heidrun Kaupen-Haas, "Experimental Obstetrics and National Socialism: The Conceptual Basis of Reproductive Technology Today", 1 J. Reprod. & Genetic Engineering 127 (1988).

202. See generally Klein, supra note 97, at 901-03.

203. Tong, supra note 4; Kathryn Abrams, "Ideology and Women's Choices", 20 Ga. L. Rev. 761 (1990).

204. See Judith Butler, Gender Trouble: Feminism and the Subversion of Identity 3-4 (1990); see also Nedelsky, supra note 142, at 1607-09.

205. Ngaire Naffine, Law and the Sexes: Explorations in Feminist Jurisprudence 2 (1990).

206. Id.

207. U.N. Charter arts. 1, 55-56.

208. For example, see generally Marc Bossuyt, "International Human Rights Systems: Strengths and Weaknesses", in A Global Challenge, supra note 97, at 47.

209. The Vienna Declaration and Programme of Action of 1993 recognized the paucity of women in decision-making posts in the U.N. Secretariat and urged the United Nations to appoint and promote women in accordance with the mandate for equality in the Charter of the United Nations. Vienna Declaration and Programme of Action, U.N. GAOR, World Conf. on Hum. Rts., 48th Sess., pt. II, U.N. Doc. A/CONF.157/24 (1993). In 1993, women represented only 11.3% of the decision-making positions at the United Nations. In 1991, there were two women among the eighteen members of the Economic Social and Cultural Rights Committee. Hillary Charlesworth et al., "Feminist Approaches to International Law", 85 Am. J. Int'l. L. 613, 624 n.67 (1991). There was only one woman among eighteen on the committee on the Elimination of Racial Discrimination, two among the eighteen on the Human Rights Committee, and two among the ten on the Committee Against Torture. Id. Moroever, there has never been a women judge on the International Court of Justice or the International Law Commission. Id. at 623-24. The same pattern exists in specialized agencies. In 1989, of the twenty-nine senior officials of the United Nations Children's Fund, only four were women; the Food and Agriculture Organization had none out of fifty-one; the World Health Organization had four women out of forty-two senior employees; no senior woman was employed at the International Monetary Fund; and only one woman held a senior position in the office of the United Nations High Commission for Refugees. Id. at 623 n.60.

210. Convention on the Political Rights of Women, opened for signature Mar. 31, 1953, 27 U.S.T. 1909, 193 U.N.T.S. 136.

211. Convention on the Nationality of Married Women, done Feb. 20, 1957, 309 U.N.T.S. 65.

212. Convention Against Discrimination in Education, adopted Dec. 14, 1960, 429 U.N.T.S. 93.

213. International Covenant on Economic, Social and Cultural Rights, adopted Dec. 16, 1966, 993 U.N.T.S. 3 [hereinafter Economic Covenant]; International Covenant on Civil and Political Rights, adopted Dec. 19, 1966, 999 U.N.T.S.

171.

214. For an overview of the instruments addressing formal equality, see Malvina Halberstam & Elizabeth F. Defeis, Women's Legal Rights: International Covenants as an Alternative to ERA? 18-33 (1987).

215. Exceptions would be the International Labour Organization conventions designed to protect women workers in ways that men were not protected. See, e.g., Convention (No. 89) Concerning Night Work of Women Employed in Industry (Revised 1948), adopted July 9, 1948, 81 U.N.T.S. 147.

216. Convention on the Elimination of All Forms of Discrimination Agianst Women, opened for signature Mar. 1, 1980, 1249 U.N.T.S. 13 (entered into force Sept. 3, 1980) [hereinafter Women's Convention]. The Convention was adopted by the U.N. General Assembly in 1979 and ratified or acceded to by 104 countries as of January 1990. The Convention was preceded by a Declaration on the Elimination of Discrimination Against Women which was adopted unanimously by the General Assembly on November 7, 1967. G.A. Res. 2263, U.N. GAOR, 22d Sess., Supp. No. 16, at 35, U.N. Doc. A/6716 (1967).

217. One glaring omission, however, was the recognition of the role violence against women plays in their inequality with men.

218. Women's Convention, supra note 218, arts. 2-5, 7-11, 13, 1249 U.N.T.S. at 16-19.

219. Id. art. 16, 1249 U.N.T.S. at 20.

220. Id. art. 5(a), 1249 U.N.T.S. at 17.

221. Id. art. 16(e), 1249 U.N.T.S. at 20.

222. Id. art. 11(2)(c), 1249 U.N.T.S. at 19.

223. Id. art. 5(a), 1249 U.N.T.S. at 17.

224. Id.

225. Shelly Wright, "Human Right and Women's Rights: An Analysis of the United Nations Convention on the Elimination of All Forms of Discrimination Against Women", in A Global Challenge, supra note 97, at 75, 87.

226. See Kathleen Mahoney, "Human Rights and Canada's Foreign Policy", 47 Int'l J. 555, 567-72 (1992).

227. Article 28(2) of the Women's Convention permits ratification subject to reservations, provided that the reservations are not "incompatible with the object." Women's Convention, supra note 217, art. 28(2), 1249 U.N.T.S. at 23. However, the Convention does not set out any criteria of incompatibility. As a result of this loose arrangement, over 40 of the 105 parties to the Convention have made a total of almost one hundred reservations to its terms, significantly undermining the Convention's integrity if not making a mockery of it altogether. Belinda Clark, "The Vienna Convention Reservations Regime and the Convention on Discrimination Against Women", 85 Am. J. In'tl L. 281 (1991); Rebecca Cook, "Reservations to the Convention on the Elimination of All Forms of Discrimination Against Women", 3 Va. J. Int'l L. 643 (1990). For general principles governing reservations and objections to reservations to Conventions in international law, see Vienna Convention on the Law of Treaties, May 23, 1969, arts. 19-23, 1155 U.N.T.S. 331, 336-38; Reservations to the Convention on the Prevention of and Punishment of the Crime of Genocide Case, 1951 I.C.J. 15 (May 28).

228. Rebecca Cook, "International Human Rights Law Concerning Women: Case Notes and Comments", 23 Vand. J. & Transnat'l L. 779 (1990).

229. Vienna Declaration and Programme of Action, supra note 210.

230. Id. ¶ 18.

231. "The Fourth UN World Conference on Women Action for Equality, Development and Peace", Beijing Update, Fall 1995, at 1 (Canadian update on the Fourth United Nations World Conference on Women, Beijing, China, Sept. 1995).

232. See, e.g., Riane Eisler, "Human Rights: Toward an Integrated Theory for Action", 9 Hum. Rts. Q. 287 (1987); Wright, supra note 228, at 78-79; Charlesworth et al., supra note 210, at 627-29.

233. Karen Engle, "After the Collapse of the Public/Private Distinction: Strategizing Women's Rights", in Reconceiving Reality: Women and International Law, supra note 144, at 143, 144.

234. Eisler, supra note 235, at 293.

235. See Catharine A. MacKinnon, "On Torture: A Feminist Perspective on Human Rights", in A Global Challenge, supra note 97, at 21, 31.

236. Case 7920, Inter-Am. C.H.R. 40, OEA/ser. L/V/II.68, doc. 8 rev. 1 (1986).

237. MacKinnon, supra note 239, at 29.

238. Id.

239. See Vienna Declaration and Programme of Action, supra note 210.

240. Universal Declaration of Human Rights, G.A. Res. 217, U.N. GAOR, 3d Sess., at 71, U.N. Doc. A/180 (1948).

241. Charlotte Bunch, "Organizing for Women's Human Rights Globally", in Ours by Right, supra note 45, at 141; Amnesty International, supra note 1, at 5.

242. Bunch, supra note 245, at 143.

243. Id. at 141.

244. See id. at 144-45.

245. Dorothy Q. Thomas, "Holding Governments Accountable by Public Pressure", in Ours by Right, supra note 45, at 82.

246. Bunch, supra note 245, at 142.

247. Id.

248. Id.

249. Diane F. Orentlicher, "Bearing Witness: The Art and Science of Human Rights", 3 Harv. Hum. Rts. J. 83, 84 (1990).

250. Amnesty International, supra note 1, at 3.

251. The basic steps of the method are: (a) careful documentation of alleged abuses; (b) a clear demonstration of state accountability for those abuses under international law; and (c) the development of a mechanism for effectively exposing the abuse nationally and internationally. Thomas, supra note 249, at 83 (citing Orentlicher, supra note 253).

252. Thomas, supra note 249, at 84.

253. Id.

254. Bunch, supra note 245, at 142-43.

255. International Covenant on Civil and Political Rights, supra note 214, art. 6, 999 U.N.T.S. at 174-75; see also Universal Declaration on Human Rights, supra note 244, art. 3; European Convention for the Protection of Human Rights and Fundamental Freedoms, Nov. 4, 1950, art. 3, 213 U.N.T.S. 222, 224.

256. Yoram Dinstein, "The Right to Life, Physical Integrity, and Liberty", in The International Bill of Rights: The Covenant on Civil and Political Rights 114 (Louis Henkin ed., 1981).

257. See generally U.N. Centre for Social Developement & Humanitarian Affairs, Violence Against Women in the Family, U.N. Doc. ST/CSDHA/2, U.N. Sales No. E.89.IV.5 (1989).

258. See generally Convention Against Torture and Other Cruel, Inhuman or Degrading Treatment or Punishment, G.A. Res. 46, U.N. GAOR, 39th Sess., Supp. No. 51, at 197, U.N. Doc. A/39/51 (1984).

259. Id. art. 1.

260. MacKinnon, supra note 239, at 27.

261. See id. at 29.

262. For a description of this project, see Thomas, supra note 246, at 85.

263. Id.

264. See Americas Watch, Criminal Injustice: Violence Against Women in Brazil 35 (1991).

265. MacKinnon, supra note 239, at 27.

266. Amnesty International, supra note 1, at 87. It has further been reported that one of two factory workers in East Java, Indonesia in January, 1993 said that the soldier who raped her had boasted: "Go ahead and report us to the commander. He's not going to do a thing. This is our right!" Id.

267. Id.

268. Id.

269. Id. at 87-88.

270. See R. v. Butler, [1992] 1 S.C.R. 432 (Can.); **MacKinnon**, supra note 61; Kathleen Mahoney, "Pornography and Violence Towards Women - Comparisons Between Europe, the United States and Canada", in International Human Rights Law: Theory and Practice 333, 333-58 (Irwin Cotler & F. Pearl Eliadis eds., 1992).

271. Catharine A. MacKinnon, "Not a Moral Issue", in Feminism Unmodified: Discourses on the Law, supra note 25, 146, 155.

272. For a discussion of prostitution, trafficking, and violence against women, see Janice G. Raymond, Report to the Special Rapporteur on Violence Against Women: Coalition Against Trafficking in Women (1995).

273. Id. at 10-13.

274. In August 1995, immediately preceding the Beijing Conference, the Netherlands lowered the age of consent to 12 years. At the same time, their government delegates deplored "forced prostitution" and child pornography at the conference. See Laura Lederer, International Legal Responses to Pornography (1995) (unpublished, available from the Center on Speech, Equality and Harm at the University of Minnesota Law School).

275. Raymond, supra note 276, at 11.

276. Id.

277. Id. at 3.

278. Id. at 4, 13, 15.

279. Id. at 12. For a discussion of the complicity of governments in the trafficking of women, see Rehana Hakim, "Governments Part of Global Mafia on Trafficking of Women", **Forum '95**, Sept. 3, 1995, at 5.

280. Arvind Sharman, Women in World Religions (1987).

281. Nadia Hijab, "Countering Conservatism", Forum '95, Sept. 3, 1995, at 2.

282. Abdullahi Ahmed An-Na'im, "State Responsibility Under International Human Rights Law to Change Religious and Customary Laws", in Human Rights of Woman 167, 177 (Rebecca Cook ed., 1994); Radhika Coomaraswamy, "To Bellow like a Cow: Women, Ethnicity, and the Discourse of Rights in Women's Human Rights", in Human Rights of Woman, supra, at 39.

283. Economic Covenant, supra note 214.

284. Shelley Wright, "Economic Rights and Social Justice: A Feminist Analysis of Some International Human Rights Conventions", 12 Austl. Y.B. Int'l L. 241, 248-49 (1992).

285. Id. at 249.

286. MacKinnon, supra, note 239, at 27.

287. Economic Covenant, supra note 214, art. 7, 993 U.N.T.S. at 6.

288. Marilyn Waring, "The Exclusion of Women From "Work" and Opportunity", in A Global Challenge, supra note 97, at 109, 113, 116; see also Charlesworth, supra note 20, at 74.

289. Waring, supra note 292, at 116; see also Waring, supra, note 1.

290. Charlesworth, supra note 20, at 74.

291. Id.; see also Waring, supra note 1.

292. See generally Waring, supra, note 1.

293. Hilary Charlesworth, "The Public/Private Distinction and the Right to Development in International Law", 12 Austl. Y.B. Int'l L. 190, 194 (1992).

294. Economic Covenant, supra note 214, art. 1(1), 993 U.N.T.S. at 5.

295. Sény Daigne, "Defending Women's Rights: Facts and Challenges in Francophone Africa", in Ours by Right, supra note 45, at 43.

296. See generally Report of the Special Rapporteur to the Sub-Commission on Prevention of Discrimination and Protection of Minorities in the Realization of Economic, Social and Cultural Rights, U.N. ESCOR, 44th Sess., Agenda Item 11, ¶¶ 139-69, U.N. Doc E/CN.4/Sub.2/1992/16 (1992).

297. The Copenhagen Alternative Declaration, "Living Differently", Copenhagen 95, Concluding Issue 1995, at 4.

298. See, e.g., Akua Kuenyehia, "The Impact of Structural Adjustment Programs on Women's International Human Rights: The Example of Ghana", in Human Rights of Women, supra note 19, at 422.

299. Amnesty International, supra note 1, at 5-6.

300. Id. at 6.

301. Veronika Sarkany, "Child Marriage: An Evil Custom", Forum '95, Sept. 5, 1995, at 14; Bernadette Cole, "Thomas Speaks on Female Circumcision in Africa", Forum '95, Sept. 3, 1995, at 10; Veronika Sarkany, "Girl Child in S. Asia, Victims of Abuse", Forum '95, Sept. 3, 1993, at 14.

302. Rashida Patel, "Challenging Tracing Women in Pakistan", in Ours by Right, supra note 45, at 32, 36; Marie Aimée Hélie-Lucas, "Women Living Under Muslim Laws", in Ours by Right, supra note 45, at 52, 53.

303. Coomaraswamy, supra note 283, at 39.

304. Charlesworth, supra note 20, at 58.

305. Coomaraswamy, supra note 307, at 40.

306. Id.

307. Id.

308. Id.

309. Ashis Nandy, <u>At the Edge of Psychology</u> 40 (1980).

International Human Rights Law and the Elimination of Violence Against Women: China's Theory and Practice

BAI GUIMEI

Violence against women has already become a common world-wide phenomenon. Whether countries are developed or not, whether their level of civilization is relatively high or low, problems of different forms of violence against women exist in all countries.[1] Because violence against women constitutes a direct violation of women's human rights and hinders the advancement of the status of women, it has attracted widespread attention in the international community. As a result, the question of how to eliminate or reduce violence against women has already become a United Nations (UN) agenda item. The "Declaration on the Elimination of Violence against Women" (hereafter referred to as "The Declaration") passed by the UN General Assembly on December 20, 1993, is an important international document which focusses specifically on solving this problem. The Declaration ties violence against women closely with protecting women's human rights, and reaffirms the various human rights and fundamental freedoms regulated by other important international instruments, such as the "Universal Declaration on Human Rights", the "International Covenant on Civil and Political Rights", the "International Covenant on Economic, Social and Cultural Rights", and the "Convention on the Elimination of All Kinds of Discrimination Against Women".

This essay integrates China's theory and practice in this area and discusses the role of international human rights law in the areas of protecting women's human rights and eliminating violence against women. It also elaborates upon the existing problems and basic measures needed to solve these problems, with a focus on the regulations of the Declaration.

A Brief Introduction To and Evaluation of the Declaration

Even though the Declaration was passed as a resolution by the General Assembly without putting it to a vote,[2] it has nevertheless taken on the form of an international convention and includes a preface and six articles:

- Articles 1 and 2 of the Declaration are definitions of concrete forms of "violence against women";
- article 3 reiterates eight human rights that women should enjoy equally;
- article 4 stipulates that states should pursue, by all appropriate means and without delay, a policy of eliminating violence against women;
- article 5 requires all UN organizations and special agencies to promote the affirmation and realization of the rights and principles stated in the Declaration; and
- article 6 defines the relationship between the Declaration and similar international conventions, treaties, other documents and domestic laws. Any regulation which is even more conducive to eliminating violence against women is not to be influenced by the Declaration.

Even though, strictly speaking, the Declaration is not a legally binding document, it has at least had an influence in the following areas, and this kind of influence, whether big or small, is conducive to eliminating or reducing violence against women:

Defining "violence against women"

The definition of "violence against women" in the Declaration includes not only violence against women in the public realm but also in the private realm. This is a result of the recent years' struggle against violence against women. In this regard, the Declaration is in sharp contrast to other international human rights documents. As Professor Chinkin points out, international law assumes and even reinforces the division between public and private behaviour. International law first distinguishes between problems of international concern and issues which belong under a country's domestic jurisdiction. The problems of international concern are then divided into public (i.e. the state) behaviour and private (i.e. the individual's) behaviour. The lives of women often get placed outside the scope of international law.[3] In reality, even though they fall within the scope of domestic law, certain actions against women are often seen as private behaviour. This constitutes an obstruction of the efforts to combat violence against women, because elimination of violence against women in the private realm is key to solving the problem at large. And yet, as violence against women in the private realm is mainly a case of husbands beating their wives, the offender often escapes due punishment under the excuse of "not...interfer[ing] in people's private lives". It is significant that the Declaration includes violence against women in the private realm, in the overall definition of violence against women.

Linking the elimination of violence against women closely with respect for women's human rights and fundamental freedoms

Even though the Declaration only lists eight human rights and it does not offer any explanation or clarification of the relationship between these rights and violence against women, it is apparent that the objective for listing these rights is to emphasize the close link between these two issues. In the preface to the Declaration, it is stated that "violence against women constitutes a violation of the rights and fundamental freedoms of women and impairs or nullifies their enjoyment of those rights and freedoms". Article 3 of the Declaration rules that "women are entitled to the equal enjoyment and protection of all human rights and fundamental freedoms in the political, economic, social, cultural, civil, or any other field." These rights include the following, in particular:

(a) the right to life;
(b) the right to equality;
(c) the right to freedom and security of person;
(d) the right to equal protection under the law;
(e) the right to be free from all forms of discrimination;
(f) the right to the highest standard attainable of physical and mental health;
(g) the right to just and favourable conditions of work; and,
(h) the right not to be subjected to torture, or other cruel, inhuman or degrading treatment or punishment.

Most of the eight rights listed in the Declaration are basic human rights and freedoms, and women's enjoyment of these rights can only become a reality when violence against women has been eliminated, because any type of violence against women constitutes a violation of these rights. In practice, however, whether in the international community or in the domestic sphere, women's right not to be violated is not always treated as a human right. For example, in the 1980 "Convention on the Elimination of All Kinds of Discrimination Against Women", currently the most important international convention relating to the protection of women's human rights, violence against women is not explicitly included in the definition of "discrimination against women". Therefore, it is immensely important that the Declaration emphasizes that women should enjoy the above human rights on an equal basis with men.

Requiring that "states pursue by all appropriate means and without delay a policy of eliminating violence against women"

The Declaration requires that states, in order to eliminate violence against women, make an effort in at least 17 areas, including:

• ratifying the 'Convention on the Elimination of All Forms of Discrimination against Women' or withdrawing reservations to that Convention;
• preventing, investigating and, in accordance with national legislation, punishing acts of violence against women;
• providing access to the mechanisms of justice to women who are subjected to violence;
• ensuring that women subjected to violence receive specialized assistance;
• promoting all kinds of investigations and research into violence against women and publicizing the results;
• promoting and strengthening the women's movement and the work of non-governmental organizations, and more.

These are the main practical sections of the Declaration, and the requirements are very concrete and comprehensive. For example, states are required to: develop, in a comprehensive way, preventive approaches and measures of a legal, political, administrative and cultural nature that promote the protection of women against any form of violence or harm (item (f)); allocate sufficient resources of the government's budget to activities related to the elimination of violence against women (item (h)); implement specialized training for law enforcement officers and government officials (item (i)); adopt measures to change the social and cultural patterns of conduct of men and women, and eliminate prejudices, customary practices and all other practices based on ideas of the inferiority or superiority of either of the sexes (item (j)); etc.

One cannot deny that these concrete requirements of the Declaration are important to the elimination or reduction of violence against women.

If all states were willing to act according to the above requirements, it would not be difficult to achieve the goal of eliminating violence against women. In reality, however, there will be many difficulties in converting these requirements into real actions, especially the requirements of item (j), which are hard to achieve in the short term. The prejudices, customary practices and all other practices based on ideas of the superiority of men and inferiority of women as outlined in item (j) are exactly the hard-to-regulate root cause of violence against women.

Requiring all UN organizations and special agencies to take concerted action

The Declaration requires all UN organizations and specialized agencies, within their respective fields of competence, to take concerted action to promote the recognition and realization of the rights and the principles set forth in the Declaration, including the promotion of international and regional cooperation, the promotion of all kinds of meetings and seminars, and cooperation with non-governmental organizations, in order to solve the problem of violence against women. In the 50 years since the establishment of the UN, several specialized structures have been put in place to protect human rights and to safeguard the rights of women. Examples include the "Commission on Human Rights"; the "Human Rights Committee" based on the human rights covenant of 1966; the "Commission on the Status of Women"; the "Committee on the Elimination of Discrimination against Women", etc. These commissions and committees have played a definitive role in protecting and promoting the human rights of women. Nevertheless, in the male-dominated UN system, the protection of women's rights has met with two kinds of resistence: on the one hand, the UN human rights mechanisms are likely to run into all sorts of problems because of political, economical and social reasons; on the other hand, in addition to the standard problems, the mechanisms to protect women's human rights are also likely to encounter problems caused by ideas of male superiority or traditional ideas which discriminate against women. Therefore, it is of immense significance that the Declaration stresses enhancing the role of non-governmental organizations. Time has proven that non-governmental organizations involved in the protection of women's rights and interests have made a large impact. They have accomplished a lot of real work in the area of eliminating violence against women.[4]

The Forms of Violence Against Women and Their Violation of Women's Human Rights

According to article 1 of the Declaration, the definition of "violence against women" is

> ...any act of gender-based violence that results in, or is likely to result in, physical, sexual or psychological harm or suffering to women, including threats of such acts, coercion or arbitrary deprivation of liberty, whether occurring in public or in private life.

There are many different forms of violence against women. Article 2 of the Declaration stipulates that "violence against women shall be understood to encompass, but not be limited to, the following:

(a) Physical, sexual and psychological violence occurring in the family, including battering, sexual abuse of female children in the household, dowry-related violence, marital rape, female genital mutilation and other traditional practices harmful to women, non-spousal violence and violence related to exploitation;

(b) Physical, sexual and psychological violence occurring within the general community, including rape, sexual abuse, sexual harassment and intimidation at work, in educational institutions and elsewhere, trafficking in women and forced prostitution;

(c) Physical, sexual and psychological violence perpetrated or condoned by the State, wherever it occurs.

No matter whether it is battering, abuse of female children, marital rape, female genital mutilation or other acts of violence, such as non-spousal violence which occurs in private life, or whether it is rape, sexual abuse, sexual harassment, trafficking in women, forced prostitution or other acts of violence which occurs in public life, all of the above constitute violations of women's human rights. Of course, violation of women's human rights and fundamental freedoms is far from limited to violence against women. For example, sexual discrimination, as in illegal deprivation of women's rights to education and work, is not considered an act of violence against women, but it is a violation of women's human rights. What is certain, however, is that any form of violence against women constitutes a serious violation of women's human rights.

Women's right to life, liberty and security of person

Serious forms of violence against women are violations of women's rights to life, liberty and security of person. Article 3 of the "Universal Declaration on Human Rights" and articles 6 and 9 of the "International Covenant on Civil and Political Rights" all state that everybody has an inherent right to life, liberty and security. These rights should be protected by law and not be arbitrarily taken away. Women should enjoy these rights on an equal basis with men. And yet, unfortunately, a woman's right to life, liberty and safety is at risk from the very moment she is born, and throughout her entire life[5]. In a society or family where the attitude that men are better than women still prevails, a female life might be taken before it is born. This is because people use advanced medical technology to determine the sex of the foetus, with the result that the majority of terminated pregnancies involve female foetuses. After her birth, a female child's right to life might very soon be taken away by drowning or might be seriously threatened. After becoming an adult (or before adulthood) a woman's right to life, liberty and security might again be violated or seriously threatened by abduction and selling, rape, beatings and other violent actions.[6]

Women's right to equality, dignity and respect

The occurrence of sexual harassment and domestic violence in society constitutes violations of women's right to equality, dignity and respect. The 26th article of the "International Covenant on Civil and Political Rights" states that "all persons are equal before the law and are entitled without any discrimination to the equal protection of the law." The principle of equality between men and women is also an important principle recognized in the "Convention on the Elimination of All Kinds of Discrimination Against Women". Article 2 of this Convention requires state parties to ensure that "the principle of equality of rights shall be embodied in the constitution or otherwise guaranteed by law". The right to equality is an extremely important and basic human right. The principle of equality between men and women is important to ensure that women do not meet with discrimination in society or in the family. Any kind of violent behaviour against women is a serious form of discrimination. For example, rape, beatings resulting in injury or death, drowning/neglect of infant girls, kidnapping and selling of women, and forcing women into prostitution, is considered a crime in the criminal codes of most countries. It not only violates a woman's right to life, liberty and security, it also violates her right to equality, dignity and respect. Those who commit acts of sexual harassment, whether in the theatre, on a bus or in other public places, whether in the school, in the office or other places of study or work, do not place women's equality, dignity and respect on the same level as men's. To them, women have become a tool for their pleasure. Thus, women's rights have been seriously violated.

Sexual harassment is also a common phenomenon in China. Yet, according to a survey, the cause and background of sexual harassment in China has been shown to be rather complicated.[7] China still does not have any specialized legislation to deal with sexual harassment. In the Chinese criminal code, there are regulations on indecent behaviour[8] which are somewhat related to sexual harassment. However, these regulations are only applied to serious cases of sexual harassment. The regulations that are related to sexual harassment in "The

Law to Protect Women's Rights and Interests of the People's Republic of China" also only apply in extreme circumstances or to cases of insult and harm to women where there are specific consequences. With regards to those acts of sexual harassment which do not qualify as criminal acts but which, nevertheless, constitute serious assaults to women's physical and mental health, China still has not developed a social atmosphere of reproach against acts and behaviour which discriminate against women and violate women's human rights.[9]

Domestic violence is also quite a serious problem in China. According to the results of a 1994 random sample of married people (total of 2118 people) in Beijing, conducted by the Beijing City Marriage and Family Research Association, incidents of husbands beating their wives had occurred in 21.3% of the households. This is a relatively high percentage. Data from a random sampling of 3,300 cases of divorce in Beijing between 1991 to 1992, revealed that 25% were initiated as a result of domestic violence. The results of an investigation into the status of women, conducted by the All China Women's Federation in 1990, revealed that in cases of conflict between husband and wife, the one subjected to beating was, in most cases, the woman.[10] Some scholars divide domestic violence into three categories according to the different stages of the marital relationship in which it occurs and the causes:

(1) violence which occurs in the process of establishing a marriage/family;
(2) violence in an established marriage/family; and,
(3) violence in the process of dissolving a marriage/family.

The first category refers to acts of violence against women related to obstruction of a woman's right to marry freely, enforced marriage or bride-kidnapping. Even though article 4 of the 1980 "Marriage Law" of the People's Republic of China stipulates that both the man and the woman must be willing to enter into a marriage, that neither party must coerce the other party and that no third party must interfere, this still happens from time to time in certain remote villages and mountain areas. The use of force against women in order to attain a certain goal is quite a common occurrence.[11]

The second category refers to the kind of violence against women, mostly husbands beating their wives, which takes place while the marriage is in existence.[12] There are two root causes as to why husbands beat their wives: Firstly, there is the influence of feudal ideas about men's superiority and the trammels of old theories on ethics. Secondly, there is the fact that the economic status of battered women is usually lower than that of their husbands.[13]

The third category refers to violence against a woman committed by either her husband or another family member for the purpose of interfering with her right to divorce. Some husbands who will not allow their wives to file for divorce might lock them up, go to the courthouse to forcibly bring them home, or sometimes beat them to the point of disabling them.[14]

Domestic violence exists in many more forms and categories than the three described above, and the causes of domestic violence are various. Faced with these complicated forms and causes, there are two main paths to eliminating violence against women in the home: The first is legal protection while the second is education and influencing public opinion in society as a whole.

Chinese legislation to protect women's personal rights and interests is relatively comprehensive and systematic. Apart from the principles of the Constitution, the "Civil Law General Rules", the "Criminal Code", the "Marriage Law", the "Law to Protect the Rights and Interests of Women", the "Public Order Management Regulations" as well as the measures adopted by some provinces, cities and autonomous regions to implement the "Law to Protect the Rights and Interests of Women", all have specific regulations concerning this matter.[15] The key issue is enforcement of the law. Like the rest of the world, China also distinguishes between public life and private life. Hence, the old sayings, "even the Qing official finds it hard to settle a family matter" and "domestic shame should not be made public". The battered woman is unwilling to "publicize" her situation, or the law enforcement officers are unwilling to meddle in the "hard to settle family matters". This becomes a great obstacle to ensuring legal protection of the rights and interests of the battered woman.

With respect to education and public opinion, the political, economical and social status of women has improved considerably since 1949. Chinese women are now working outside of the home and actively participating in building up the country, and they enjoy the same political rights as men do. However, fighting between husbands and wives has, in China, always been regarded as a minor matter not worth mentioning, and many people still hold that opinion. "Domestic violence" is a novel, rarely heard term to ordinary Chinese people. Until 1994, the international year of the family, Chinese academics had only just begun to touch upon the issue of "domestic violence", a topic which had already been widely debated abroad.[16] China, as well as the international community, still has a long way to go to influence public opinion on domestic violence, to eliminate prejudice through education, and to make it clear that any kind of violence against women is a violation of women's human rights.

International Human Rights Law and Fighting Against and Eliminating Violence Against Women

Under pressure from women's liberation and women's rights movements in countries all over the world and from regional and global women's movements, the UN has finally begun to pay attention to the issue of fighting against and eliminating violence against women. In the "Nairobi Forward-Looking Strategies" (Nairobi Strategies), which was approved by the 3rd World Conference on Women's Rights in 1985 and which was recognized by the international community as a guiding document on women's rights, various problems relating to violence against women were raised under the headings "Young women" (paragraph 287), "Abused women" (paragraph 288), "Women victims of trafficking and involuntary prostitution", etc. Paragraph 288 gravely points out that "gender-specific violence is increasing and Governments must affirm the dignity of women, as a priority action." The "Nairobi Strategies" states, in this paragraph, that governments of all countries should, apart from providing immediate assistance to victims, set about raising the public's awareness about violence against women, develop policies and legal measures to eliminate this behaviour and, finally, push for the development of methods to educate and re-educate abusers. Ten years after the "Nairobi Strategies" were passed, under the pressure and influence of various women's organizations and groups, the international community has made some encouraging progress in the area of fighting against and eliminating violence against women. One of the most significant achievements is the "Declaration on the Elimination of Violence Against Women", approved by the UN in 1993. But there are still many problems within this area in international law.

Firstly, to date, there is no universal international agreement which relates to the issue of eliminating or reducing violence against women. In a strict sense, according to the "UN Charter" regulations, the 1993 "Declaration" is a General Assembly Resolution and, as such, is not legally binding on member countries, and even less binding on non-member countries. Currently, there is only one relevant international agreement, the "Inter-American Convention on the Prevention, Punishment and Elimination of Violence Against Women", passed on June 9, 1994, and this is only a regional international agreement.

Secondly, under the current circumstances of having only a limited number of international agreements on women's rights, there are very few regulations on the prevention, punishment and elimination of violence against women. Even though the most important international convention on women's rights, the "Convention on the Elimination of All Kinds of Discrimination Against Women",[17] includes various articles that touch on some forms of violence against women,[18] the Convention's definition of "discrimination against women" nevertheless, does not mention violence against women. In 1992, the Committee on the Elimination of Discrimination Against Women (The Committee), while going through the regular recommendations at its 11th session, raised the point that the "definition of discrimination includes gender-based violence, and that gender-based violence is a form of discrimination which seriously affects women's ability to enjoy rights and freedoms on an equal basis with men". Howver, when looking at the regulations of the Convention, we can see that the Committee did not clarify the power of the Convention. With this kind of interpretation of the Convention, it is difficult to say exactly how much influence it might have on each country party.

Finally, existing international agreements on women's rights lack enforceability. Except for the "Convention on the Elimination of All Kinds of Discrimination Against Women" (CEDAW), only a few countries are parties to other international agreements on women's rights. Consequently they lack universality. Concerning the CEDAW, if the definition of discrimination includes gender-based violence, it tends to lack enforcement power due to numerous factors. The main factors are that:

• The reservations to the Convention made by party countries are too numerous and too general. The reservations made by some countries are in direct conflict with the purpose and the goal of the Convention, while some are directly opposed to the entire Convention;

• even though the Convention follows the example of other human rights conventions and the Committee on the Elimination of Discrimination Against Women was established to facilitate monitoring of the Convention, the Committee, nevertheless, does not have the authority to receive communications of complaints from countries parties to the Convention against another country, and no authority to receive complaints from individuals. Yet, the two parallel committees established to monitor the "International Convention on the Elimination of All Kinds of Racial Discrimination" and the "Convention against Torture and other Cruel, Inhuman or Degrading Treatment or Punishment", are both authorized to receive complaints from countries and individuals. Some NGOs have recommended and drafted a suitable document in an effort to authorize the Committee to receive country and individual complaints, but it is uncertain whether or not this recommendation will be accepted by each country party. How long it will take for the Committee to obtain this kind of authority still depends on the energetic efforts of all concerned parties, including the government of all countries, all the relevant UN bodies and organizations, as well as NGOs, experts and scholars.

Conclusion

In the ten years since the passing of the "Nairobi Strategies", the international community has made some progress, albeit at a rather slow pace, in the area of eliminating or reducing violence against women. It should be noted, however, that although international human rights legislation still has problems in this area, there has been some developments in recent years. The Americas have already passed a specialized international agreement and the UN General Assembly has passed a resolution specifically with the aim of resolving this problem. Although this resolution is not legally binding, it could significantly affect development in this area of international law, and could even form the basis for formulating a UN international agreement in this area. Hopefully, in the not too distant future, we will have an official international instrument which is legally binding. Yet, even so, to realize the goal of eliminating violence against women, we must still rely on each country to implement measures in all areas of domestic law, politics, economics and society. Therefore, this author is of the opinion that the best way to achieve this goal would be to combine the efforts of the international community with the concrete measures adopted by each country. In order to promote the development of international human rights law in the area of eliminating violence against women, and to speed up each country's domestic activities in this area, this author suggests the following steps:

On the international arena:

• Urge the relevant UN bodies to draft a feasible international convention on the "elimination or reduction of violence against women" as soon as possible.
• Urge the Committee on the Elimination of Discrimination Against Women to recommend revising the "Convention on the Elimination of All Kinds of Discrimination Against Women" so as to include violence against women in the definition of discrimination against women, and to make this revision as soon as possible.
• Urge the governments of all countries not presently party to the "Convention on the Elimination of all Kinds of Discrimination Against

Women" to become parties. Urge countries with inappropriate reservations to the Convention to revoke these reservations.

On the domestic front:

• Strengthen the construction of the legal system, enforce the law strictly, so as to ensure due punishment for all kinds of violence against women. In order to accomplish this, it is necessary to revise or formulate the legislation, so as to give the judiciary reliable laws with which to combat domestic violence, sexual harassment, etc. It is also necessary to conduct appropriate training for law enforcement officers in order to raise their awareness of violence against women.

• Strengthen education, cultivate the acceptance of equality between men and women, eliminate the belief in the superiority of men and other traditional attitudes. This education should begin with the children in order to cultivate an acceptance of the equality between men and women early on in life.

• Establish effective social assistance structures or advisory services so as to give abused women a place to go to for help. Continue to promote the role of the All China Women's Federation and its organizations at all levels, and demand that the government allocate funds for establishing shelters or similar refuges for abused women.

Translated by A-M Traeholt

Notes

1. For general information on this issue, see Hilary Charlesworth and Christine Chinkin, "The Gender of Jus Cogens", *Human Rights Quarterly*, vol. 15, no. 1, February 1993, pp. 71-72.

2. Passed by the General Assembly without voting on December 20, 1993. (GA Res. 48/108)

3. Supra, note 1 at p. 69.

4. For more information on the role of women's non-governmental organizations, see Charlotte Bunch and Namh Reilly, *The Global Campaign and Vienna Tribunal for Women's Human Rights*, Chapter 9: "NGO Activity and the Media in Vienna", pp. 94-99, New York: United Nations Development Fund for

Women (UNIFEM)/New Jersey: Centre for Women's Global Leadership.

5. Supra, note 1 at pp. 70, 63 (1993).

6. Ibid., p. 71.

7. Tang Can, "Cong xingsaorao wenti kanzhong xifang funude xingquanli zhuangkuang yu baozhang" (Looking at the situation and protection of women's sexual rights in the West through focussing on sexual harassment), a paper presented to the International NGO Forum on Women and Human Rights, May 16-18, 1995, Beijing, at p.2.

8. "Zhonghua renmin gongheguo xingfa" (The Criminal Code of the People's Republic of China), article 160 states: Those who offend women or commit other kinds of indecent acts, will be sentenced to a maximum of 7 years imprisonment... .

9. Supra, note 7, p. 4.

10. Tong Xin, Qu Wen, "Xue ren re tan: jiating baoli" (Intellectuals debate: domestic violence), *Funu yanjiu luncong*, 1994, no. 3, p. 38.

11. Fan Tuo, «Lun fandui he xiaochu zai jiatingzhong dui funu de baoli» (Discussion on fighting against and eliminating violence against women in the home), a paper presented to the NGO Forum on the Elimination of Violence Against Women held in Shanghai, Nov. 26-28, 1994, pp. 2-3.

12. This kind of domestic violence also includes gender-based violence against girls committed by the parents or other family members. In more serious cases, the phenomenon of drowning baby girls.

13. Supra, note 10, p. 39.

14. Supra, note 11, p. 4.

15. See «Baohu funu quanyi fagui huibian» (A compilation of regulations on the protection of the rights and interests of women), edited by the Legal Advice Bureau of the All China Women's Federation, 1990, Legal Publishing Society.

16. Supra, note 10, p. 37. Actually, in 1993 there were discussion meetings of relatively small scope, e.g. the "Shanghai discussion meeting on the protection

of women's rights and interests and on the prevention of violence against women", organized by the Women's Federation Group in the City of Shanghai.

17. Currently, this is the international convention on women's rights which has the largest number of participating countries. China is one of them.

18. Article 6 stipulates that countries parties should implement all appropriate measures, including drafting laws, to stop all trafficking in women with the intent of profiting from selling the women into prostitution.